Charles W. Chesnutt

Essays and Speeches

Charles W. Chesnutt

ESSAYS AND SPEECHES

Edited by
Joseph R. McElrath, Jr.
Robert C. Leitz, III
Jesse S. Crisler

Stanford University Press
Stanford, California

1999

Stanford University Press
Stanford, California
© 1999 by the Board of Trustees of the
Leland Stanford Junior University
Printed in the United States of America
CIP data appear at the end of the book

Frontispiece: Charles W. Chesnutt in 1928,
photograph courtesy of the Western Reserve
Historical Society, Cleveland, Ohio

In loving memory of
Gregory Mark McElrath
"Gator"
1969–1996

Acknowledgments

We are indebted to John C. Slade, executor of the Chesnutt estate, for permission to make available to the public the nonfiction writings of Charles W. Chesnutt. We also thank Ann Allen Shockley, Associate Librarian for Special Collections, for granting us the privilege of using the Fisk University Library's Charles W. Chesnutt Collection, the manuscript and printed materials of which have served as the foundation for this edition. Beth Howse, too, has earned our gratitude on innumerable occasions by assisting us as we performed our research in that unparalleled collection. We thank Anne Sindelar of the Western Reserve Historical Society Library for the help she kindly extended as we examined its various collections related to Chesnutt and his contemporaries and for permission to reproduce both the texts of manuscripts in its possession and the photograph of Chesnutt serving as the frontispiece portrait.

Special thanks go to Gregory Martinson, Esq., for researching the many references to legal decisions that Chesnutt makes in his essays and speeches; to former Congressional Historian Raymond Smock for demystifying many oblique allusions made by Chesnutt to political events occurring at the turn of the century; to Anthony Phelps for providing access to the records of the Rowfant Club; to Dean H. Keller, Jeanee Somers, and Cara Gilgenbach for assistance in locating Chesnutt's speeches to the Ohio Stenographers' Association; to Bernice M. Boilesen for identification of clerical figures mentioned by Chesnutt; and to Joel Myerson for helping us locate articles in South Carolina newspapers referred to in the essays and speeches.

Numerous others made it plain that research of the kind we conducted is inevitably a collaborative enterprise. This edition would not have been possible without the kind assistance of Lil Crisler, Jack Morrison, Mary Morrison, Vincent Marsala, Laurene Zaporozhetz, David Koraleski, Richard Downey, Kathy Homer, Geraldine Duclow, Tammy L. Martin, Mark Grandstaff, Robert Means, Jennifer Pollei, Kristen Anderson, Kate Faeber, Douglas B. Durbin, Kristine Gerdy, Giancarlo Pesci, Craig Anderson, Gary Hill, Isaac Paxman,

David Johnson, Darryl Dickson-Carr, William T. Lhamon, Jr., Donald Foss, Fred L. Standley, Jay Fox, Randall Jones, and Van Gessell.

Funding for the extensive travel necessary for this project was made available by Florida State University, Louisiana State University in Shreveport, and Brigham Young University.

J.R.McE., Jr.
R.C.L., III
J.S.C.

Contents

Preface

> It is perhaps well for all of us, sometimes, to get out of our own narrow rut, so far as we can, and to look out upon the world about us, even if we must look through prison bars, and view the world and mankind in their broader aspects— as something not merely for to-day or tomorrow, but for all time.
>
> —"Literature in Its Relation to Life," 1899

Over the past three decades Charles Waddell Chesnutt (1858–1932) has emerged from the obscurity that was soon his after his sixth book and third novel, *The Colonel's Dream*, appeared in 1905. He had been drawing national notice since 1887, when the *Atlantic Monthly* first published one of his short stories. In the summer of 1898 his reputation as a contributor to periodicals peaked as "The Wife of His Youth" drew applause from across the country; and in 1899 he earned considerable attention when he became known as the author of not only two books of short stories but a biography of Frederick Douglass. The next year his first novel was published, and 1901 saw the appearance of another. Further, he had assumed visibility on the national stage in a special way. In 1898 his racial status had become the common knowledge of literary essayists and book reviewers. Close on the heels of Paul Laurence Dunbar, Chesnutt was making history as one of the very first African-American authors to cross the "color line" into the Anglo-American publishing world of his time. But the interest of book buyers never quite corresponded to that shown by reviewers and commentators on the state of American letters at the turn of the century, and disappointing sales figures led Houghton, Mifflin & Co. and then Doubleday, Page & Co. to lose interest in a writer whose promise as a commercially viable author had not been realized. Over a half-century would pass before his works would again receive the kind of attention they enjoyed around 1900.

Through the early decades of the twentieth century, Chesnutt was not wholly forgotten. Those puzzling over the question of the relative merits of particular racial and national groups focused on him as an exemplary individual whose intellectual achievements challenged the concept of the innate inferiority of American blacks. On the other hand, because he was of mixed racial ancestry, he—like Booker T. Washington and W. E. B. Du Bois—was also cited in support of a contrary point of view: since this particularly fair-skinned man represented a variant type, he did not provide a true measure of blacks' capabilities or lack thereof. Commentators with more straightforwardly cultural interests portrayed him in a less inflammatory way that did not involve demeaning others as his unique contribution to American life was recalled: he was lauded by black and white historians as a pioneer in the African-American literary tradition. But, then again, relatively little attention was given to that tradition through the mid-1960's, and Chesnutt was a marginal figure at most in descriptions of the whole of American literary history. It was not until the end of that decade, when the widespread effects of the Civil Rights Movement were registering, that Chesnutt was "rediscovered" by literary and social historians and, consequently, their students.

His two "tragic mulatto" novels, *The House Behind the Cedars* (1900) and especially *The Marrow of Tradition* (1901), are now recognized as milestones in the history of U.S. protest literature. In both, Chesnutt-as-narrator not only pictures African Americans cruelly victimized by Southern whites but holds forth in his own voice, with some regularity explaining to his reader exactly what it means to find oneself in the outrageously unfair predicaments known by his heroines and heroes who are "tainted" by color. The second novel is also an exposé of the chicanery of the white North Carolina Democrats who precipitated the November 1898 race riot in Wilmington. The two 1899 collections of short stories—*The Conjure Woman* and *The Wife of His Youth and Other Stories of the Color Line*—are also seen as major steps forward in the African-American literary tradition, by virtue of the fact that both artfully took, and still take, their readers beyond stereotypes to more empathetic perceptions of the fin-de-siècle experience of blackness. At last the largely indifferent mass readership of Chesnutt's time has been succeeded by a generation that appreciates both the aesthetic qualities of Chesnutt's fictions and the "messages" they were designed to deliver.

Much less familiar is Chesnutt's nonfiction. There is no prior collection of these writings. The vast majority of the previously published pieces appeared in contemporaneous magazines and newspapers; and few have since been reprinted in other periodicals. They are gathered here for the first time. Before now, only a single essay was included in a book; one speech only was given separate publication in pamphlet form. No fewer than 38 of the 77 works in this edition make their debuts as printed works. Even those who have sedulously studied the collections of Chesnutt's papers at Fisk University and the Western Reserve Historical Society will now have their first encounters with texts only recently discovered by the editors both in manuscript and in published forms not previously noted by scholars. One cannot be certain, but it is very likely that Chesnutt's 1952 biographer, his daughter Helen, was not aware of all that her father had wrought as an essayist and a public speaker.

What one finds in over two-thirds of these works is that this nonfiction writer and orator was as energetic an advocate of the African American as he was in his novels and many of the short stories. In the earliest surviving speeches addressed to his fellow blacks in Fayetteville, N.C., he is a Southern educator of the 1880's who brings Booker T. Washington to mind as he exhorts his listeners to acquire the skills necessary for African Americans to find a place in mainstream American life. Both Washington and W. E. B. Du Bois are echoed in later works as Chesnutt reflects upon the remarkable post-bellum accomplishments of African Americans and the increasing likelihood of their realizing their full potential as the long-term effects of living conditions in the ante-bellum period are gradually effaced. In other speeches and essays, an outraged Chesnutt keenly sensitive to reversals of the intended effects of the Thirteenth, Fourteenth, and Fifteenth Amendments to the U.S. Constitution proves considerably more militant than Washington and seems of a like mind with the anti-Bookerite William Monroe Trotter.

It will be seen that Chesnutt is a dedicated integrationist and a foe to incipient Black Nationalism. It will also be seen, to the dismay of some today, that Chesnutt was a particularly aggressive, radical integrationist in that he advanced "racial amalgamation" as the ultimate solution for "The Negro Problem." Ironically, white racist politicians whom Chesnutt loathed, such as Benjamin R. Tillman and James K. Vardaman, were proven not far off the mark so far as Chesnutt was concerned when, in their demagoguery, they excited their constituencies with the specter of miscegenation. Chesnutt did, indeed, see multi-generational "race mixing" as the panacea par excellence. But what the writings focusing on race, politics, and social amelioration in fact document is a wide variety of experiments in devising a way to motivate both blacks and whites to mold a nation in which all may find equality in gaining access to economic opportunity, in exercising full civil rights, and in experiencing Americanness at its finest.

This collection features a Charles W. Chesnutt who may be viewed by some as one of the successors to Frederick Douglass and as an essayist and speaker who anticipated numerous other blacks who have established themselves as forceful protestants against the status quo. One would make a mistake, however, in pigeonholing him solely as a black civil rights activist, and thus unwittingly assigning him the kind of delimiting, race-related identity that he viewed as the bane of his age. Yes, he was black and a dynamic advocate of the African American. But, as his minimally politicized and wholly apolitical works in this edition illustrate clearly, he had—to put it simply—other interests not related to color. For example, "Methods of Teaching" is the product of a professional educator called upon to address his peers. The papers delivered before his fellow bibliophiles in Cleveland's Rowfant Club gauge a cultivated man of Victorian tastes whose identity is not defined by race but by the humanistic orientation that led him to the study of the lives and works of Samuel Johnson, George Meredith, and François Villon. Even essays such as "Superstitions and Folk-Lore of the South" and "The Free Colored People of North Carolina"— while they deal with things African-American—are relevant in this respect, for the perspective and voice of their author is more transracial than black. In both he is simply reporting on matters that are innately interesting and would, in the editors' opinion, appeal to any reader with a modicum of curiosity about North Carolina folkways and history.

In this edition are assembled in chronological order all of the known non-fiction works of Charles W. Chesnutt. The editors' intent is to make available the means of taking the full measure of the man—not just the social activist calling for recognition of the full citizenship constitutionally bestowed upon blacks, but the sophisticate who knew that he was at least equal to the whites of his time and that both his fictional and nonfiction writings were the palpable proof.

Editorial Note

This chronologically arranged collection of Charles W. Chesnutt's essays and speeches is the most comprehensive gathering of his nonfiction works now possible. Chesnutt is known to have given more public addresses and fashioned other introductions to public readings from his fiction, but their texts do not appear to have survived. Also, it is likely that he wrote additional, still undiscovered essays published in periodicals, which historians may chance upon at some time in the future. The 77 works in this edition, however, constitute the entirety of the known canon of his creative endeavors as a speaker and expository prose writer from 1881 to the early 1930's.

Once these discrete works were identified by the editors, the next goal was to determine the most authoritative form in which each was extant. That is, which could be said to represent most accurately Chesnutt's intended or final text for each? The candidates for this status fell into three categories.

First, the works that were published during Chesnutt's lifetime, and for which no manuscripts (handwritten or typed) survived, presented little problem with respect to the selection of an editorially emendable source text: each was available in only one printed form; and each was, by default, the only possible means of establishing the text of the work.

Second, other writings were represented in print and in both complete and incomplete manuscripts of four kinds: typed transcriptions, or copies, of already published works; final holograph and typed versions; highly "finished" but not necessarily final forms; and early, clearly superseded drafts. Each form required analysis for the sake of determining (a) which best reflected Chesnutt's final intentions and thus (b) which would serve as the source text.

The third category was never-published manuscripts. These documents were the most problematic for several reasons. While some were complete and quite polished, others were made up of leaves gathered together by Chesnutt from multiple drafts and were not consecutively paginated throughout. Some of the speeches were still in relatively "rough" shape, rather than brought by a typist to a "fair copy" state, when Chesnutt read them. Also, while the final form of a handwritten and/or typed text may have been complete at one time, what has been preserved for posterity was not necessarily that final form, and some leaves were either used by Chesnutt for a final version no longer available or were, in one way or another, lost. In short, to have an emendable source text the editors had to reconstruct so far as was possible such gap-ridden essays and speeches in the light of available evidence indicating the *probable* final form Chesnutt either gave them or intended them to have. As will be seen, unbridgeable gaps within a work are identified by a row of three asterisks, while ellipses mark the absence of a beginning or a conclusion.

The source text is identified immediately following each essay or speech, as are other relevant states of a text that the editors located, analyzed, and occasionally employed for emendation.

Once the source texts were identified, the editors produced verbatim transcriptions of them, the accuracy of which they verified by at least two collations against the originals. That is, they entered on disk even obvious slips of the pen and typographical errors, refraining from editorial emendation until the next stage of processing. A noteworthy problem encountered during the transcription of Chesnutt's manuscripts had to do with how to interpret Chesnutt's use of handwritten parentheses and hand-drawn circles enclosing sentences, groups of sentences, and paragraphs. In some cases he indicates with a deletion sign that such word groups are canceled; in others he signals retention with "stet" or stet-marks. When he does not do either, it is unclear what his intention was. All such sections, possibly canceled or instead highlighted thus either for emphasis during oral delivery or reconsideration during a subsequent stage of composition, were examined in the context of the whole document. If a rationale for cancellation was not inferable, the word group was retained.

The editorial treatment of the transcribed source texts was guided principally by the desire to preserve what the evidence indicated Chesnutt intended to write and the need to correct readings that clearly violated his discernible intentions. Spelling errors, including misspellings of proper names, were emended, while now archaic or merely variant spellings popular in Chesnutt's time were not. Respected in most instances was Chesnutt's punctuation, which is typical of contemporaries who did not always employ a grammar-based system and instead frequently used punctuation "oratorically," for pauses and emphases commonplace in oral discourse and even printed texts of the nineteenth century. Chesnutt's commas, for example, do not necessarily set off phrases and clauses but often function as breath marks do in a musical score. The editors emended punctuation of this kind only when they agreed that reproducing exactly what Chesnutt wrote would ineluctably result in confusion for the reader proceeding through his sometimes complexly qualified, serpentine sentences.

There are seven exceptions to the rule regarding conservative treatment of

Chesnutt's formal usages. First, when quoting prose at length, Chesnutt or his typist typically does not indent the passage. Rather, the quotation appears within quotation marks and, no matter how long, the text is flush with both the left and the right margins. In this edition, Chesnutt's opening and closing quotation marks are excised and the whole passage reproduced is indented from the left. Second, Chesnutt is more conventional when quoting lines of poetry, centering the quotation on the page; but he uniformly employs opening and closing quotation marks as well, when neither monologue nor dialogue is being reproduced. The editors have eliminated the redundancy. Third, most of the source-text readings conform to modern practice with regard to the spatial arrangement of the closing parenthesis and the period. That is, in discrete statements appearing wholly within parentheses, the period appears to the left of the sign; when the parenthetical statement is positioned at the end of a sentence to which it is added, the period appears to the right of the sign. But Chesnutt is inconsistent, and the editors have regularized his usage. Fourth, regularization to the dominant practice also occurs when Chesnutt or his typist occasionally positions a comma or a period to the right of a close-quotation mark. In each instance in the edited source texts, the comma and period now appear at the left. Fifth, the source texts are again inconsistent with regard to the italicization of foreign-language phrases, words, and abbreviations. If judged to have become commonplace English usages before 1930, they are allowed to stand in roman, e.g., "fiancée" and "e.g." itself. Those not in this category—e.g., "*dura mater*" and "*viz.*"—have been italicized. Sixth, when Chesnutt is quoting someone and interjects a comment on what has been stated, he does so within parentheses rather than brackets—this possibly raising the question of who made the parenthetical statement, Chesnutt or the author quoted. For the sake of clarity, all such comments by Chesnutt appearing in the midst of quotations are bracketed. Seventh, the first paragraphs of the essays and speeches are unindented; this is solely a styling feature of this volume.

Emendations resulting in a more substantive effect are made when it is apparent that what Chesnutt intended to state was garbled because of an obvious omission of a word or words, a replication of a word or phrase, or a patent typographical error. With such cruxes, the editors emend according to what the context suggests was the intended reading. A more complex situation was encountered, however, when Chesnutt originated an error of fact. On the one hand, he certainly did not intend to err; on the other, it is clear that he deliberately did state as fact what appears in the source text. For example, in "The Disfranchisement of the Negro," he misnamed a court decision, and when he marked the proof he did not correct the erroneous citation. Less significant but as incorrect are the dates of publication and the wording of the titles of publications he cites in several essays and speeches. The editorial response to such factual errors was determined ad hoc, in the light of two considerations: the se-

riousness of the immediate effect produced for the typical readers of this volume when Chesnutt erred, and the editors' desire to preserve the biographically
significant indications of how pressed for time Chesnutt was as he fashioned
the majority of these works.

That Chesnutt was predisposed to burn candles at both ends—even during
his 1899–1902 "retirement" from business when he finished two published
novels, worked on other literary manuscripts, gave public presentations in the
North and South, and wrote several essays—is the consensus among all who
have studied his life. While meeting the exacting demands of his 1899–1902
belletristic schedule and those of a highly successful stenographic career before
and after, he continued his self-education regimen, systematically surveyed the
evidence in periodicals of the state of race relations in the United States, participated in local civic affairs and national organizations advancing the African-American cause, and in what time remained frequented the Cleveland Public Library to perform the research requisite for writing and speaking on subjects ranging from the life and works of François Villon to the social status of
former slaves in the Caribbean. That a fully occupied businessman could accomplish so much as he did in his hours away from the office is more than remarkable. That he erred so infrequently as he did, relative to how often he was
accurate, is what surprises—given the frenetic pace he maintained. The editors
of this volume, at least, found enviable his performance in the face of a dearth
of time and research resources. At the same time, they concluded that the documented consequences of his identity as a part-time author, a man with an avocation rather than a professional writer and speaker, should not be effaced. To
correct editorially every error in his texts and not to note his inaccuracies in the
annotations of those texts would be tantamount to assuming a role of coauthorship and thus distorting the reality of who and what Charles W. Chesnutt was.

Substantive emendations of authorial errors, then, are made according to a
practical consideration. Not every reader of this edition, and perhaps only a
minority, will consult the annotations. They will, instead, read the texts and
assume that the factual content is not open to question in the way that Chesnutt's interpretations of course are. This being the "real-world" situation,
when a "fact" stated by Chesnutt has been judged as of high importance for
the reader, the editors have emended to correct the error when doing so does
not involve what would be termed extensive revision. In "The Disfranchisement of the Negro," for example, they saw it as essential that the judicial decision in the case of Giles v. Harris be referred to in the text rather than the erroneous "Jackson vs. Giles"; further, why an emendation was necessary was recorded in an annotation signaled by a superscript number. On the other hand,
in "The Right to Jury Service," Chesnutt's reference to the holding in Strauder
v. West Virginia and his quotation of it are not so amenable to such minimally
intrusive emendation. Chesnutt does not actually quote that decision but, in-

stead, the holding in Plessy v. Ferguson. To emend appropriately would have meant nothing less than rewriting the introduction to the Plessy v. Ferguson quotation, and so the clarification of what was quoted was necessarily relegated to an annotation. Unemended also are errors that the editors viewed as of much less importance for the envisioned readers. When the correct publication date of a book, for example, is judged not truly essential to the observation or argument Chesnutt is developing, the minor inaccuracy of a misdating is merely noted in an annotation.

Neither emended nor noted in the annotations, however, is one kind of irregularity: Chesnutt's misquotations. When quoting, not only is Chesnutt prone to modify the initial phrasing to make the quotation fit the context of his own prose but, much more frequently, he deliberately elides sentences and even whole paragraphs without indicating that he is doing so. The actual language of the originals is not restored for the obvious reason: Chesnutt wanted the quotations to read the way he had refashioned them to read in order to emphasize what he viewed as essential. This occurs so often that such alterations are not commented upon in the annotations. Generally speaking, the reader should simply take it for granted that Chesnutt wrote and spoke with a different conception of the function of quotation than is now current and that, like many another author who came to maturity in the nineteenth century, he saw nothing inappropriate in modulating the voices of others to make them resemble his own.

While the annotations explain editorial emendations and clarify other textual particulars, the main functions they perform are: to recreate the historical context in which Chesnutt is writing and speaking; to make accessible to late-twentieth-century readers both the knowledge and the perspective that Chesnutt could take for granted in his contemporaries; and to complement when appropriate the information Chesnutt provides. Annotated upon their first appearances in the essays and speeches are Chesnutt's references and allusions to individuals, organizations, events, and publications (including court decisions and laws enacted), as are quotations and paraphrases.

Introduction

On 21 November 1899, at the age of 41, Charles Waddell Chesnutt delivered the first of several lectures he would give before one of the preeminent black organizations of the day, the Bethel Literary and Historical Association. Like the similarly named group in Boston to which he spoke almost six years later about "Race Prejudice: Its Causes and Cures," this society in the District of Columbia comprised cultivated, middle-class Americans of African descent whose interests included, but were not myopically limited to, what might have been termed "The White Question" but was then known as "The Negro Problem." As was not the case in 1905 with the Boston Literary and Historical Association,[1] however, Chesnutt had come to the nation's capital to offer a diversion. He was intent on ensuring that his 1899 audience had the pleasure of rising above vexatious, mundane concerns to reflect upon cultural matters not tied to race. After some preliminary remarks facilitating a transition to a "larger view" of life, Chesnutt addressed his listeners as thoughtful citizens of the world who shared a cultural history as fin-de-siècle Americans that was delimited in only one way: he treated them as fellow participants in a western humanistic tradition going back to the Renaissance. The Bethel Association was, while Chesnutt was speaking, almost indistinguishable from white America's Chautauqua Assembly.

Like the whites and blacks in Cleveland, Ohio, with whom Chesnutt had associated since departing the less socially congenial and more racially restrictive town of Fayetteville, North Carolina, in 1883, the Bethel members appreciated Chesnutt as one who, in several of his published short stories, had risen above the nagging, seemingly inescapable, "eternal question" of how race relations could be improved and equality achieved. Biologically and self-professedly a man of color, although not visibly so, this fair-skinned gentleman sym-

[1]This association has been referred to in the literature on Chesnutt and in Chesnutt's correspondence as the Boston Historical and Literary Association, the Boston Historical and Literary Society, and the Boston Literary Society. The correct nomenclature is given here.

bolized to them what it meant not only to live literally on the color line but to be able to cross freely between the two camps as though that line did not exist, exercising his talents as both a businessman and a literary artist to the applause of whites and blacks alike. In short, Chesnutt represented an ideal; or, he came as close to embodying the ideal condition for an African American as anyone was likely to at the time. One was given by Chesnutt the vicarious experience of feeling free to venture upon life without the double consciousness W. E. B. Du Bois described in *The Souls of Black Folk* in 1903.

At the turn of the century, however, such transcendence could be only temporary. One 1889 short story included in Chesnutt's soon-to-be-published *The Wife of His Youth and Other Stories of the Color Line,* "The Sheriff's Children," sensationally indicated that he was not always so unflappable but could sometimes be very much engaged in an animus-driven assault on white racists. In the present collection of his essays and speeches, the two nonfiction pieces "An Inside View of the Negro Question" and "What Is a White Man?"—also written in 1889—show Chesnutt again brooding over the slings and arrows of outrageous fortune, that is, the consequences of blackness in America. Later, in 1901, he was far from a detached observer of the 1898 race riot in Wilmington, N.C., when he wrote *The Marrow of Tradition.* In its main plot he pilloried the whites he viewed as wholly responsible for the riot, and in the novel's subplots he wielded the tar brush in as vigorous a manner—whereupon he alienated one of the most distinguished white advocates of the African American of the Progressive Era: the novelist, literary critic, and power-broker within the American publishing establishment William Dean Howells. Previously Howells had known Chesnutt as a sanguine man who remained above the fray, a "sweet," unresentful literary fellow whose talent made it clear that there was no color line in literature. When he read *Marrow* and encountered the angry obverse of Chesnutt's personality, Howells's disillusionment was as complete as it was dramatic. He wrote to Henry Blake Fuller, "Good Lord! How such a negro must hate us."[2] In his review of *Marrow,* he praised its author as a stalwart champion of his people—that is, Howells's sympathy for African Americans was unabated—but he had to lament the "bitter, bitter" tone of the novel.[3]

This was in the future, however, as were the commercial failure of *Marrow,* the appearance of several positively insulting reviews, and the psychological consequences accounting in part for the volcanic tonality of a long piece he published in a volume of essays entitled *The Negro Problem* (1903). Chesnutt

[2]Howells to Fuller, 10 November 1901, in *Selected Letters of W. D. Howells, Volume 4: 1892–1901,* ed. Thomas Wortham *et al.,* volume 24 of *A Selected Edition of W. D. Howells* (Boston: Twayne Publishers, 1981), 274.

[3]"A Psychological Counter-Current in Recent Fiction," *North American Review,* 173 (December 1901), 872–88.

would recover his equanimity; but there was no sweetness and light in the stern preachments he delivered in "The Disfranchisement of the Negro."

As of November 1899, however, the Chesnutt the Bethel audience knew was the one Howells once thought he understood thoroughly: the witty, charmingly droll creator of seven delightful short stories given book publication by Houghton, Mifflin & Co. of Boston a few months earlier. The author of *The Conjure Woman* was adept at providing seductive, "feel-good" experiences not only to white Clevelanders—who knew him as the very successful, well-mannered, and intellectually acute head of a stenography firm—but to readers across the nation who did not want to deal with complications related to color every time they encountered, in person or in Chesnutt's short stories, the African American. Bethel Association blacks too did not need constant reminders of their problematic identity, and thus the hiatus that was his speech on "Literature in Its Relation to Life"—a topic that would, he believed, interest *all* thoughtful, tasteful contemporaries.

The sprightly middle-aged speaker of diminutive physical stature was still trim, even wiry. It would be several years before his girth would correspond to the substance and weight of what he had to say in his essays and in public addresses. As dignified and amiable as Booker T. Washington, who had also appeared before this group, he soon made it clear that he was a good deal more sophisticated. W. E. B. Du Bois might also have offered the quotation of German philosopher Arthur Schopenhauer and the commentary on his pessimism that Chesnutt did; the measure of the remarkable Ohio businessman was that, without the Ph.D. Du Bois had earned from Harvard, he had elevated himself to the same intellectual plane. How many prose fiction writers, white or black, could do what he had done in the recently published short story "The Gray Wolf's Ha'nt," that is, incorporate without ostentation a quotation of Herbert Spencer's intellectually turbid *First Principles*?[4] (Indeed, how many actually read far enough into that internationally famous but roily tome as Chesnutt did to encounter the passage he reproduced?) In 1882, he had given a lecture on "Self-Made Men" to a literary society in Fayetteville; by 1899 he had joined company with and intellectually outstripped the two role-model figures he had focused upon, Horace Greeley and Frederick Douglass. He was living proof of the potential and real equality claimed for African Americans during the post–Civil War decades, as well as the warrant that Horatio Alger could be a transracial icon.

Listening to this capable, seemingly insouciant fellow, many of the other intellectuals present and those desirous of a culturally uplifting experience may not have been able to imagine just how hard Chesnutt had worked to refine himself the way he had, largely through a strenuous self-education regimen. They could not read his 1874–82 journals as we can now to plumb the depth of

---

[4]Chesnutt's short story first appeared in *The Conjure Woman*, published about 24 March 1899; the initial version of *First Principles* saw print in 1862.

his dedication to the self-cultivation ideal. Although he could neither refer to his alma mater nor even point to a high-school diploma, this 1870's prodigy at the Howard School for blacks in Fayetteville began teaching at the age of sixteen and became the principal of the Colored Normal School there in his early twenties. By the 1890's, the still ambitious ex-teacher had developed an extensive national network with middle-class African Americans, and those in the audience who knew him more intimately may have been wondering how this dynamo could so stylishly hold in check the bristling energy that accounted for his being able to afford to retire from business in October 1899 in order to give all his time to *belles lettres*.

Born in 1858 in Cleveland, Ohio, to free parents of modest accomplishments who did not enjoy a noteworthy economic rise when they moved back to Fayetteville after the Civil War, Chesnutt had not found his ultimate benchmark in becoming one of the preeminent African-American educators in his state; determined to continue his ascent and having mastered stenography, he moved in 1883 to New York City and then Cleveland to become one of the wealthier members of that city's black community as, by 1887, a member of the Ohio Bar Association whose savvy as an attorney ensured that he would be a fully occupied court reporter also able to process legal documents for corporate clients. His rise had been meteoric, propelled by the tremendous force of an achievement-oriented personality that would settle for nothing less than excellence, and the rightful monetary rewards thereof.

He cut a heroic figure before the Bethel Association in another way as well. As then-admiring Howells would soon point out for a national readership in an early 1900 essay on Chesnutt's writings, here was an ostensibly white man who had volunteered identification with the African American when, seemingly, there was no necessity for thus exposing himself to bigotry.[5] To Howells, this was magnanimity writ large. The Bethel audience did not, perhaps, think in terms of Chesnutt's magnanimity in acknowledging to the world his racial make-up and, years earlier, having decided not to "pass" into the white world. But that he had volunteered to serve as one of their champions was manifest, as was a dedication to their cause that might cost him dearly. It was conceivable that the sales of his books and future prospects might be affected because he had in no way disguised his relationship to a minority group as scorned as eastern-European Jews then migrating to America.

Earlier in 1899 the Anglo-American novelist Frank Norris had featured in *McTeague: A Story of San Francisco* a classic caricature of the avaricious Jew, and no reviewer had protested. Treating African Americans in the media as stereotypical "niggers" had, on the other hand, long been protested; and yet they had been disfranchised in state after state while Jews, and even the "shanty Irish," enjoyed full civil rights. Chesnutt had donned the mantle of responsi-

---

[5]"Mr. Charles W. Chesnutt's Stories," *Atlantic Monthly*, 85 (May 1900), 699–701.

bility as a nationally visible spokesman for the victimized. And already he had struck a major blow for a new kind of emancipation. Who would not benefit in some degree from his having shown that the hand which, allegedly, was hereditarily best suited for the plough could become the graceful wielder of the pen? Already he had changed things by being one of the very first African-American authors to integrate the de facto segregated world of commercial publishing in the United States. Like Paul Laurence Dunbar, he had proved what the African American might achieve on the basis of demonstrated merit; as Booker T. Washington would do in 1901 with the publication of *Up from Slavery*, Chesnutt had become a name in the mainstream publishing industry.

Exactly how Chesnutt was introduced by the Bethel Association's president, attorney and lecturer on Law at Howard University William H. Richards, is not known. But one note had to have been loudly and clearly sounded. Chesnutt, like Howells, was an *Atlantic Monthly* author; his serio-comical Uncle Julius short stories had been appearing in that most prestigious of American magazines since 1887. He was the creative artist who had drawn national praise a little over a year earlier when "The Wife of His Youth" not only brought a tear to the eye of a white novelist then at the acme of his career, James Lane Allen,[6] but gladdened the heart of many sympathetic white readers as it sentimentally pictured the upper-middle-class African American exactly as principled as they assumed they themselves were. What Booker T. Washington continued to demonstrate by way of his own upright character—the potential for achievement among African Americans—Chesnutt had rendered in art that powerfully plucked the heartstrings. Further, Richards introduced an author whose second and third of three books published in one year, 1899, would both appear later that month.

The American publisher Houghton, Mifflin & Co. had been selling copies of *The Conjure Woman* since March. An advertisement brochure printed by this firm was distributed among the Bethel audience, touting *The Wife of His Youth and Other Stories of the Color Line*. Chesnutt, who was markedly aggressive with regard to the marketing of his books, undoubtedly prompted Richards to note as well the impending publication of his *Frederick Douglass* volume in the "Beacon Biographies of Eminent Americans" series of another Boston firm, Small, Maynard & Co. Whereupon Chesnutt, bedecked in laurel, finally stepped to the podium.

In this collection of essays and speeches spanning the years 1881 through 1931, the 1899 address "Literature in Its Relation to Life" occupies a unique

---

[6]While "Wife" appeared in *Atlantic Monthly*, 82 (July 1898), 55–61, copies of the issue were mailed to subscribers in June. Allen expressed his enthusiasm in a 27 June letter to *Atlantic* editor Walter Hines Page; see *"To Be An Author": Letters of Charles W. Chesnutt, 1889–1905*, ed. Joseph R. McElrath, Jr., and Robert C. Leitz, III (Princeton: Princeton University Press, 1997), 109.

position—hence the attention given to this special moment in Chesnutt's career when the future seemed bright with promise and his confidence in himself and how he would give shape to the years ahead was virtually unbounded. As has been recently documented in *"To Be An Author": Letters of Charles W. Chesnutt, 1889–1905*, the brilliant literary career he envisioned in his journals through 1882 and formally initiated in 1885 with the publication of the short story "Uncle Peter's House" had undeniably become incarnate by late 1899.

And thus the tragedy that the letters record. The following year appeared *The House Behind the Cedars*, which he would in a subsequent decade refer to as his best-selling novel. But though it received many positive reviews, it was not actually a best-seller. The two collections of short stories did not generate strong demand either; and though the volume on Frederick Douglass went through three printings by 1912 and another at some time thereafter, royalties on all four books were far less substantial than he had expected. Despite an unprecedentedly energetic advertising campaign on behalf of *The Marrow of Tradition* in 1901 and Chesnutt's conviction that it would be recognized as the successor to *Uncle Tom's Cabin* (a claim repeatedly made in advertisements for the novel), it too failed to meet Chesnutt's or Houghton, Mifflin's heady expectations; and it proved to be Houghton, Mifflin's last act of faith in Chesnutt's salability. By 1902, Chesnutt could no longer afford to remain retired from business; it was necessary to go back into harness, advertising himself in the Cleveland city directory as attorney, stenographer, and notary public. *The Colonel's Dream* (1905) saw two printings, but this third novel failed to catch fire. He would thereafter publish other short stories; over the years he fashioned manuscripts of novels that his contemporaries would never see; and the N.A.A.C.P. would appreciate his achievement in 1928 by awarding him the Spingarn Medal. But it was as an essayist, speaker, social activist, and businessman that he would be principally known by the public between 1906 and 1932.

When he appeared before the Bethel Literary and Historical Association in November 1899, all of this was unpredictable, even unthinkable. The promising author then stood on Mount Pisgah as one who was about to enter a land of milk and honey—perhaps leading his people into an America where a race that was elevating itself in the manner prescribed by Booker T. Washington would finally be accepted as citizens with full civil rights and equal economic opportunity. Neither development materialized in his lifetime. Chesnutt's was more the experience of Moses than of Joshua. His visit to the literary Canaan he had for decades longed to occupy was of brief duration. As will be seen in the present collection, Chesnutt would continue at various times to display the benign equipoise that was his when measuring "Literature in Its Relation to Life." But, to his credit as a scourge of white supremacists, he also persisted in playing Joshua, striving mightily to bring under humane control the too-alien land that was segregated America. Again, he did not succeed; but neither did other contemporary black activists determined to bring their foes to heel.

Yet one should not exaggerate the figure Chesnutt cut as reformer. He was a true scion of the New England abolitionists whose fervor he admired and whose indignant perspective he preserved through the Jim Crow era. But, compared with Du Bois or Marcus Garvey, he was a decidedly minor player in the history of social protest. He spent much more energy maintaining and, until the Great Depression, improving his hard-won position in the upper middle class as he worked long, long hours at his office in downtown Cleveland. Du Bois lightly chided him for that.[7] To be fair to Chesnutt, however, one must contextualize his situation and empathize so far as is possible when noting that he did not sell all that he had and give the proceeds to the good cause to which he was, in his own way, devoted.

Chesnutt, unlike Du Bois at the turn of the century, did not enjoy an academic appointment allowing him to dovetail scholarly research with social activism. Later in the twentieth century, he was a member of the local branch of the N.A.A.C.P., but he did not draw a salary from the national office as did Du Bois, James Weldon Johnson, and William Pickens. Unlike Harry C. Smith, the editor of a black weekly newspaper, the *Cleveland Gazette*, he was not positioned to turn an avocation into a paying vocation, having discovered that his writings could only be contributions to progress rather than a way of making a living. Likewise, he did not have access to the coffers of Garvey's Universal Negro Improvement Association. His active commitment to the cause was necessarily a part-time commitment—though one may hasten to add, as Chesnutt undoubtedly did when reflecting upon the rigors of his schedule, that his socio-economic success as an African American was not without significance and propagandistic value. As Booker T. Washington pragmatically observed on many occasions, the most promising argument for an end to disfranchisement and like indignities was to be found in the accomplishments and behavior of representatives such as Chesnutt. And the man who gave "Advice for Businessmen" in a 1930 speech spoke with earned authority.

Another pertinent consideration is the duration of Chesnutt's commitment. The first speech in this volume finds Chesnutt not merely practicing oratory but *doing* something in 1881 to improve in a long-term manner the condition of blacks living in Fayetteville. As the principal of the Colored Normal School there and as a lifelong integrationist who would come to despise Garvey's black nationalism as a counter-productive strategy (see "Race Prejudice"), he was already by the early 1880's as keenly aware as Washington of the need for the children of former slaves and antebellum freemen to adopt white middle-class values and manners. The idea was to fit in rather than maintain the status of victim—hence both the 1881 speech "Etiquette" and, many years later, the digression on appropriate behavior in his 1913 address to the students and

---

[7]Du Bois described a "peculiar temptation" when focusing on Chesnutt in "Possibilities of the Negro," *Booklovers Magazine*, 2 (July 1903), 2–15: that of "money making—why leave some thousands of dollars a year for scribbling about black folk?"

graduating seniors at Wilberforce University, "Race Ideals and Examples." He knew how the system worked, as was initially obvious in his rise to eminence in Fayetteville and, later, in Cleveland; rather than theorize about how things should be in these speeches and in the 1882 "Self-Made Men," he explained how one might qualify for competition in what he termed Darwinistically in 1913 "the struggle of life." "Advantages of a Well-Conducted Literary Society" (1881) was another speech of this kind, also addressed to rural Southern blacks and designed to inculcate a sense of how, in order to be taken seriously, one must think clearly and speak both coherently and convincingly among the educated men and women who controlled the means to a better life.

In 1889, with his career as an educator in the past, Chesnutt began addressing a different kind of audience when he seized an opportunity made available by the prose fiction writer and social reformer George Washington Cable. Cable, well connected in the world of periodical and book publishing, promised access to another group that needed to be "elevated": American whites. Cable, as it turned out, failed to place the essay he then encouraged Chesnutt to write, "An Inside View of the Negro Question"; it is published for the first time in this volume. But Chesnutt, though exasperated to find that Cable could not deliver, was undaunted. On his own he wrote "What Is a White Man?" and successfully submitted it to a politically liberal weekly, the *Independent*. It appeared later that year, and the rest is history. Thereafter, he never ceased producing essays and speeches on "The Negro Problem" for white readerships and audiences and, in a different manner, for blacks.

The themes or points of view encountered in these more polemical and decidedly moralistic works are consistently made manifest again and again, elaborated rather than significantly qualified as decade followed decade. Indeed, "An Inside View" encapsulates in 1889 much of what Chesnutt had to say for the next forty years. The major themes are easily identified, given how frequently they recur and how frequently they *had to be repeated* since conditions did not improve during his lifetime.

One theme relates directly to his personal perspective as a fair mulatto. It is more apparent in his fictional works, but it also reveals itself explicitly, or will be seen to create a sub-text, in nonfictional writings whose topics range from the desirability of racial amalgamation (the three "Future American" essays) to the admirability of less racist societies in Central and South America ("A Solution for the Race Problem") to the creative genius displayed by individuals with sub-Saharan racial antecedents ("Race Ideals and Examples"). Chesnutt, as the son of multi-racial parents whose appearance was as "white" as his, is outraged by the legal, political, and social consequences of the "taint" of "black blood."[8] That a

[8]The two photographic portraits of Chesnutt's parents, preserved at the Fisk University Library, are reproduced in Michael Flusche, "On the Color Line: Charles Waddell Chesnutt," *North Carolina Historical Review*, 53 (January 1976), 3.

soupçon of the same differentiates one from the mass of Americans, that state laws define the black-white genetic ratio so that the ignominious differentiation can be maintained, that the legal formula for racial identification determines who can marry whom and other relationships in society, and that political consequences for the individual follow—these are repugnant to both reason and humanity. More particularly, they are especially offensive to Chesnutt, who displays the characteristics of "the better class" of whites but is viewed as a Negro because of the white/black ratio of between 7/8 and 15/16 that is his and renders him "inferior." He advocates full civil rights for all African Americans but is particularly sensitive to the fact that even the typical members of Du Bois' "talented tenth" are the victims of discrimination.

Second, it is in the unspeakable South that African Americans are most victimized, to the degree that one can come to only one conclusion regarding the intentions of the vast majority of whites in that region: that their leaders reflect the will of their constituents in their determination to revive so far as is possible and then perpetuate the socioeconomic and political status quo of the antebellum era. Chesnutt's point of view is that the Civil War was fought for a single purpose: to put an end to slavery and the inhumane system of which it was a part. He never mentions any other cause for "the suppression of the rebellion," such as the Lincolnian fixation on the preservation of the Union or the incompatibilities of the North's and South's economic interests. Following the Civil War, conditions for blacks were improved dramatically as legislation, generated by former abolitionists and—as they were then known—Radical Republicans, effected enfranchisement and provided for the full exercise of citizenship by blacks. Despite the chicanery admittedly present during the "carpet bag" era, real progress was being made as the South was being reconstructed by the federal government. When that process was terminated in the mid-1870's, restoration of the old order immediately commenced as the Southern Bourbons acted to ensure that the former slave, while technically free, enjoy nothing more than the status of a retainer or serf. Chesnutt's anti-Southern perspective is consistently and energetically articulated from the late 1880's through the rest of his life.

Third, while racial discrimination and discriminatory attitudes are also present in the North, it is to Northerners that the African American must turn not only for the funding necessary for education but for the means of ameliorating their holistic condition as citizens. Federal intervention was a necessity leading to the Civil War; it continues to be necessary; and it is upon Northern voters and their representatives, whether Democrats or Republicans, that the mantle of moral responsibility falls. The Republicans, however, have a special responsibility: they were in the past the great black hope, and it is incumbent upon them to complete their mission. The whites in the party of Lincoln are obliged to ensure that true emancipation is a reality, and blacks should continue to exert what political power they have by voting Republican: only a black "fool" would vote for the Democrats controlled by the South, barks Chesnutt in "For Roosevelt."

Fourth, the Jim Crow era is an abomination in the eyes of God and man. The progressive disfranchisement of the African American and legally sanctioned segregation in education, public transport and lodging, and other aspects of American life must be checked and reversed. The Thirteenth, Fourteenth, and Fifteenth Amendments of the U.S. Constitution are being violated at the state level by the segregationists in power; Congress refuses to react appropriately by adjusting representation in the House of Representatives when a state reduces the number of voters by disfranchisement; and, when Chesnutt looks to the U.S. Supreme Court as the only source of relief, he is dismayed to find that it claims to be unable to provide it. From the late 1880's through 1930, Chesnutt's hope for change is repeatedly dashed by the legislative, judicial, and executive branches of the government. Even Republican President Theodore Roosevelt, who began well, eventually proved a nemesis.

Fifth, what Chesnutt consistently and reductively terms "color" is the sole reason for "The Negro Problem." While he may irritate some readers in the way Booker T. Washington does, by sometimes conceding other particulars— or alleged shortcomings of African Americans—focused upon by white racists, his rhetorical strategy is to charge "color" with primary significance and to root hostility to it in the South. This positions him as a commentator able to take the moral high ground when castigating his antagonists as unable to look beyond a superficial characteristic and see the shared humanity of the African American. His occasional concessions with regard to other specific differences between blacks and whites buttress his authority in that they pragmatically establish his clarity and comprehensiveness of vision as an observer intimately familiar with both black and white foibles. But since the vast majority of his concessions are lighthearted admissions of the kind seen in "The Negro in Cleveland" (addressed primarily to whites) and "Race Ideals and Examples" (addressed to blacks), they actually count for little in view of the heinous wrongs that they cannot possibly justify. As he says in "Race Ideals," "we are men, created of the same clay, by the same God"; and no shortcomings can obviate that metaphysical principle or the moral imperative it implies. Further, the rights guaranteed by the constitutional amendments were not given with qualifications that could legitimately be exploited by individual states seeking to deny the vote to black males on the basis of certain shortcomings; if they had been, identical inadequacies would also deny white males the exercise of full civil rights.

The last major theme is a positive one. While Chesnutt does not call for social equality, accepting as he does the idea that "a man's home is his castle" and in his private life he should be free to associate with whom he chooses, he sees no permanent obstacle to the formation of a social structure in which amicable and mutually profitable relationships between the races will be established. If that should eventually lead to "race-mixing," so much the better since, after multiple generations and decades, this is the one guarantee that "The Negro Problem" will necessarily cease to exist. In the meantime, the humane and just individual, if he will simply note and acknowledge the unfairness of contemporary abuses of the African American that Chesnutt cites, must admit that, were he or she in a similar predicament, amelioration or even revolutionary change would be in order. One finds in these essays and speeches a good many spirited demands being made; one should not, however, overlook Chesnutt's performance as the master of the soft-sell, fully exercising his considerable seductive powers when calling for a square deal for all.

The degree to which Chesnutt was a successful soft-sell artist will be seen in *The Conjure Woman* and *The Wife of His Youth and Other Stories of the Color Line* (excepting "The Sheriff's Children" and "The Web of Circumstance"). In such short stories, and in the introductions to public readings of his fiction that are included in this volume, Chesnutt is far from choleric; he seems incapable of truculence or even petulance. He is clearly on the high road, treating his white auditors and readers to what he hopes are delectable fruits of his labors. Blacks too can relax and enjoy his almost languid explorations of topics that are simply interesting, for their own sake. Said Chesnutt, when rejecting "The Negro Problem" as a topic for his 1899 Bethel speech,

> It is perhaps well for all of us, sometimes, to get out of our own narrow rut, so far as we can, and to look out upon the world about us, even if we must look through prison bars, and view the world and mankind in their broader aspects—as something not merely for to-day or tomorrow, but for all time. When we turn back, as we can through the medium of books, to the dawn of history, and follow its course down to our own time, the troubles of any one individual or any one race dwindle into comparative insignificance; and when we look around us and see the forces of progress in operation on every hand, imagination pictures for us a future for which the troubles of to-day are but a brief apprenticeship.
>
> And therefore, as one of these broader views, which include all mankind, and make no distinctions of time or place or caste or creed, I am going to speak to you of the relation of Literature to Life.

The editors of this volume assume that those turning to it will, in the main, be interested in what Chesnutt *qua* advocate of the African American of the Jim Crow era wrote. But to take a full measure of this unique man, it is important that this other voice of his be heard. Or, rather, there are several other voices meriting attention.

There is, first, that of citizen Chesnutt who, like other literate Americans, took pleasure in displays of wit and insight into human nature per se—a Clevelander who enjoyed Mark Twain and recognized the value of sometimes being waggish, even silly, as in his "Advice to Young Men" and "Things to Be Thankful For." This is the Chesnutt who, when reviewing *Pussy Meow*, a book written by a cat lover and for others similarly enamored, had the temerity to

observe, tongue-in-cheek, that it "will appeal to all lovers of dumb animals"—
he himself apparently not being among their number. This voice contrasts with
that of the professional educator of North Carolina whose earnestness and
high seriousness are encountered not only in his Fayetteville speeches on etiquette, self-made men as role models, and the well-conducted literary society
but in his ponderous paper "Methods of Teaching." Lest we forget, Chesnutt
was as much an eminent Victorian as Twain was when he wrote the atypical
and thus, today, largely unread *Personal Recollections of Joan of Arc*; what is
pomposity now was once emblematic of good breeding and a liberal education
including large doses of Thomas Babington Macaulay, John Stuart Mill, Ralph
Waldo Emerson, and Matthew Arnold.

Less stuffy is a third voice heard, for example, in "Lincoln's Courtships."
Chesnutt gravitated toward biography, writing the lively volume on Frederick
Douglass already noted and being so interested in his subject that a series of
letters addressed to editor and publisher Walter Hines Page led to the offer of a
contract for a full-scale biography—which he declined at the turn of the century only for the sake of giving his time to novel-writing. This was not his only
piece on Lincoln, one of the several secular saints he viewed in the most reverent terms; and the Reverend Joseph C. Price was another to whom he devoted a
considerable number of words as he fashioned a monument to the honor of
this great man still overlooked by historians. The essay on Price finds Chesnutt
at his animated best as a biographer, outside of the group of speeches on historically significant figures that he delivered to Cleveland's Rowfant Club. But
"Victorian" is again the qualification with a negative connotation that comes
to mind when he waxes idealistic about his figures. Chesnutt came to maturity
in a hero-worshipping age whose orientation toward "great men" was shaped
and encouraged by Thomas Carlyle and Ralph Waldo Emerson. And his idealism often knew no bounds when he turned from a personage to a concept inviting moralistic revery, for example, "The Ideal Nurse."

One wonders if any of the black nursing students who heard this speech
had not previously encountered the conventional exhortations to selfless dedication that Chesnutt reiterated and, contrarily, whether any of the listeners
understood the literary allusions with which he peppered his discourse. Would
any early-twentieth-century nursing students in the United States have understood his bit of Latin wordplay, that "*alma mater*" often proves a "*dura mater*"? One discovers how sophisticated Chesnutt was as a man of letters who
could bandy with Latin, German, and French; but, as was even more evidently
the case in another graduation speech, "Race Ideals and Examples," one also
notes that Chesnutt did not always successfully plan to avoid being taken for a
stuffed-shirt. One thus wonders how he will be perceived by present-day students, whose rejection of the signs of a snobbishness perceived as endemic to
pre-Modernist culture is encouraged by many high-school teachers and professors in the humanities. One also wonders if the lesson implied will be taken to

heart: that it is a mistake to assume modernity on the part of this thinker and writer. Chesnutt's fictional creations never smacked of the avant-garde; his novels look backward to mid-nineteenth-century models rather than to innovative developments emerging in the 1890's and reaching their apex by 1930. And even when he is writing with verve polemically, the majority of his essays and speeches can at any moment wax fustian.

This is not the case, though, in two pieces of reportage. "The Free Colored People of North Carolina" and "Superstitions and Folk-lore of the South" vie for honors with two of the best essays touching upon "The Negro Problem." Like "A Visit to Tuskegee" and "The White and the Black," both offer an intrinsically interesting narrative, anecdotal and yet straightforward, substantive and yet succinct, and exuding the wholly approachable personality of a likeable observer with a compelling tale to tell. Indeed, the four more than make up for the debt to the reader Chesnutt incurs when going on in so protracted a way in "A Solution for the Race Problem" and "Race Ideals and Examples." The casual reader will want to turn to them first in order to receive the impression of Chesnutt at his best as a nonfiction writer.

There is yet one other Chesnutt who elicits a separate description, the member of Cleveland's bibliophile society, the Rowfant Club. Blackballed because of race upon his first nomination for membership to this exclusive body, Chesnutt was inducted upon a second trial in 1910. Once a member, he had the opportunity to do again and again what he did when he spoke before the Bethel Literary and Historical Association in 1899. On nine occasions between 1911 and 1925, he escaped from race for the evening to revel in his identity as a bookman and as the "scholar" recognized by the Spingarn Medal Committee of the N.A.A.C.P. What is truly of importance here is the range of interests that characterized Chesnutt as a most uncommon stenographer and a social reformer who found more in life than the need to protest. He appears to have fit very nicely into the select group of fine-printing and artful-bookbinding connoisseurs that he had, in 1904, satirized in a short story entitled "Baxter's Procrustes"; once admitted to their august circle, he found nothing laughable about their eccentricities. Presumably, they saw nothing unusual in the presentations he made (the asterisks in the following list indicate texts that appear to have been lost to posterity):

11 November 1911	"Who and Why Was Samuel Johnson?"
22 February 1913	Story identified by the Club's *Year Book* statement that "Charles Waddell Chesnutt read a new Conjure Story, written by himself, and at that time unpublished"; Chesnutt's title and the nature of his introductory remarks are not known.*
11 April 1914	"Life and Works of Alexander Dumas"
20 March 1915	"Francis Villon"*
11 March 1916	"George Meredith"
13 January 1917	"Will of John Randolph of Roanoke"

14 February 1920   "The Diary of Philip Hone"*
12 March 1922   "The Autobiography of Edward Baron Herbert of
                          Cherbury"
16 February 1925   "Valentines"*

These works complete the composite portrait of Chesnutt the civil rights activist, literary artist, student of social history, educator, businessman, and cultural *savant* available in this volume. That is, in his "spare time" after 1910, when researching his essays and speeches at the Public Library in downtown Cleveland (never more than a few blocks away from his various business office locations), or reading and taking notes in his home study, Chesnutt practiced cultural scholarship. True, the surviving texts in this class prove quite derivative, rather than wholly original products. They will be found to be heavily dependent upon the books and periodical articles Chesnutt sedulously combed in that library; like the more political pieces requiring research, they embody numerous and extensive quotations from various information sources, as well as unacknowledged paraphrases of what the authorities consulted had discovered during their primary-data research—research of the sort Chesnutt himself hardly had time to perform because of the numerous demands made upon him. These speeches are the work of a talented amateur—which is not to gainsay their importance or to disparage the quality of Chesnutt's work. That he was at all able to do the reading he did and fashion these speeches in such a competent manner is startling testimony to the indomitable will and ever-vital curiosity of a man whose self-education regimen was never, and could never be, abandoned. Even the "Valentines" address written when he was in his mid-sixties was, we know from the notes he took when doing historical research on the subject, something of a tour-de-force.

What one finds in this edition of the essays and speeches of Charles W. Chesnutt, then, is a rather full enhancement of the image he has projected since the late 1960's when the "rediscovery" of this long-eclipsed but important figure in western cultural history began. How his short stories and novels fit into the matrix of American literary expression in his time, and particularly the protest tradition in prose fiction, has become increasingly clear. His daughter Helen's 1952 biography, and subsequent books and essays by others that focus upon the life that gave rise to such art, have referred to many of the published and previously unpublished essays and speeches, quoting and interpreting them to flesh out the personality suggested by his better-known works. But the published essays appearing in contemporaneous issues of periodicals, speeches given periodical publication, and one speech made available in a pamphlet that can be found in only a few research libraries—these have been relatively inaccessible, and few readers have directly consulted them. The unpublished essays and speeches preserved at the Fisk University Library in Nashville, Tennessee, and the Library of the Western Reserve Historical Society in Cleveland, Ohio, are yet more remote from the typical scholar, not to mention the student and general reader. Only one essay, "The Disfranchisement of the Negro," appeared in a book in Chesnutt's lifetime; until now, a volume offering a representative sampling of his nonfiction has been lacking.

The availability of Chesnutt's reflections, pleas, polemics, philippics, and near-jeremiads concerning "The Negro Problem" now makes possible a finer definition of his place as a spokesman for the African American in what he termed the "Post-Bellum, Pre-Harlem" period in American social history as he modulated his voice in such a way as to bring to mind, at different times, Booker T. Washington, Kelly Miller, W. E. B. Du Bois, Ida Wells Barnett, and William Monroe Trotter. On the other hand, one finds in other works signs of a far-from-monomaniacal, multi-faceted personality well adapted to the "struggle of life." One sees him often in opposition to the status quo, but one also finds him in the midst of white America, fully if not completely integrated into "the better class" of Euro-Americans, and demonstrating two unshakable facts: first, that he in person gave the lie to the myth of innate inferiority that had galled him since his youth in Fayetteville; and, second, that *their* culture was patently *his*. He thought, wrote, and spoke as did his early role-model figures—ranging from white Horace Greeley, William Makepeace Thackeray, and Albion W. Tourgée to others of sub-Saharan descent such as Alexandre Dumas, Frederick Douglass, and Joseph C. Price. He was the transracial product of a culture he admired and, like other Eurocentric thinkers of his time, saw as superior to all others despite its shortcomings. Afrocentrists will find no ally in Chesnutt. Even multiculturalists may be alarmed by Chesnutt's single-minded allegiance to the hegemonic worldview and values of a capitalist culture that required only improvement.

The immediate value of these writings for most, perhaps, is that they comprise a species of autobiography and thus position one to return to Chesnutt's major claim to fame, his short stories and novels, with the wherewithal to develop a new appreciation of his artistic achievement. They provide a nonfictional context in which to test one's hypotheses about what the prose fictions mean, making available empirical data that will serve the literary critic as well as the biographer and cultural historian. Their ultimate value, however, is that they allow us to spend more time in the presence of one of the most distinctive individuals to plumb the multifarious American character and to give a full measure of what it once meant to participate in and, at the same time, be excluded from the experience of the majority. Addressing both blacks and whites, serving as an emissary between the two groups on the opposite sides of the color line, Chesnutt wrote and spoke from both within and without the establishment, offering late-nineteenth- and early-twentieth-century readers and listeners a bi-focal as well as bi-vocal account of who and what they were. Few others of his age could do the same for his contemporaries—and for us.

Charles W. Chesnutt

Essays and Speeches

Etiquette (Good Manners)

Speech to the Normal Literary Society, Fayetteville, N.C., 1881

I have a very high ideal of those qualities, which, apart from his literary attainments and skill in teaching, should make up the character of an instructor of youth; and my ideal of a teacher can be tersely but clearly expressed in two words—*a Christian gentleman.* By the word Christian, I mean not merely a church-member or outward professor of religion; but one who is imbued with the true spirit of Christ; one who goes out, as did He, the Great Teacher, to instruct the world in the ways of truth. The Christian teacher considers his work, not in the light of mere toil for daily bread; but as a sacred trust committed to him, for the proper discharge of which he is responsible, not only to school-committees and parents, but to God, who gave him the talent to teach. A Christian teacher has only to know how to teach, and to have a right appreciation of his work, and he is sure to perform it properly.

A Teacher should be a Gentleman. And here I use not the word in its conventional sense. I do not mean that he should be of high birth or great wealth; that he should clothe his person in fine raiment,[1] or his speech in fine words: I use the word in its broadest signification—one who has a proper respect for himself, and a proper regard for the rights and opinions of others, and at the same time knows how to act in order that other people may know that he respects himself and them.

I have told you that a teacher should be a *Christian* gentleman. It is not my intention to attempt on this occasion to lay down any rules for the attainment of the Christian character. One who wishes to attain it can get instruction from both earthly and divine sources. It is my object in this paper, to state the principles, and a few of the rules, which if faithfully observed will enable a man to conduct himself properly in the society of well-bred people.

Some one has compared learning manners from a book to learning to swim on land. A certain individual who wished to learn to swim procured a frog, and put it in a basin of water. Carefully watching the motions of the swimming frog, he stretched himself out on the floor and imitated them till he thought he had mastered the art of swimming. He then marched proudly down to a pond to display his newly acquired skill, plunged into the water—and in a few minutes began to cry for help, for he was in imminent danger of drowning. He discovered that swimming on a carpet and swimming in the water were two entirely different operations. As it is better to learn to swim in the water, so it is much better to learn good manners from association with cultivated people. But as our ancestors had no opportunity for association with well-bred people, except in a menial capacity; and as our opportunities are almost as limited: we ought to try to learn, either by reading or such observation as we can have, those simple forms and customs which are common to well-bred people throughout the civilized world. It is only by knowing and observing them that we can feel at ease in society, or properly enjoy the intercourse of people of refinement.

The laws of etiquette are founded upon two great principles: *viz.*, a proper respect for one's self, and a proper regard for the feelings of others. It is not necessary to dwell upon the first further than to say that a man should never do or say anything that would lower him, or make him look small in the estimation of others. An ill-mannered boor, who violates every principle of decency and every rule of etiquette, is despised by everybody who knows better.

But the main principle which underlies every social system is a proper regard for the tastes and feelings of others. The civil law protects us against certain evils; but there are other evils which the civil law does not and cannot reach. A man knocks me down; I make him pay for it: he steals my property, and the law sends him to jail. But he may steal from me my good name;[2] he may stare me in the face, he may push against me in the street, and do a thousand other unmannerly things, and I have no legal redress. But society has laid down certain laws which men and women must observe in their intercourse with one another, or they will not be considered as gentlemen and ladies, or received in good society. I have no right, according to the laws of etiquette, to offend a man's sense of smell by coming into his presence with my clothes saturated with the odor of tobacco, or reeking with the fumes of the gin-shop; I have no right to offend his taste for the beautiful by coming into his presence dirty and unkempt; I have no right to offend his sense of hearing by talking too loud or too long, or by indulging in language which is offensive to him. We have no *right* to be ill-mannered. We should try in our intercourse with others, to remember the Golden Rule, "Do unto others as you would have them do unto you."

It is good policy to be well behaved. You know the old proverb, "Manners will carry you where money will not." The power of money is very great; but however much wealth you may have, there are others as rich as you, and all your money will not bring you into their society unless you can render yourself agreeable to them.

Many, many years ago, when the famous Sir Walter Raleigh was a young man, he went up to London to seek his fortune. One day he was standing in the streets of London when Her Majesty, Queen Elizabeth passed by on foot. As the dainty lady hesitated to place her foot on a muddy place in the path, the gallant young cavalier sprang forward, threw his rich cloak across the wet place, and stood by with a polite obeisance while the Queen stepped safely across. Of course Elizabeth, then a young and romantic maiden, inquired after the gallant youth, and finding him to be of good birth and breeding, invited him to court, took him under her special favor, and opened up for him his subsequent brilliant career as navigator, statesman and courtier.[3]

This is but one of many instances. Nothing in a young man or woman produces so favorable an impression upon others as a neat appearance and a graceful bearing. It is the outcropping of the metal on the surface, by which we detect the rich vein of ore beneath.

Having thus briefly stated the principles which underlie the Act of Correct Behavior, I shall now lay down a few of the rules for attaining it in use among polite people at the present day. I have selected as the order in which I shall arrange my subject the ordinary routine of daily life. My rules shall be given to you in the order in which you will need them. I shall consider

1. The Etiquette of the Toilet;
2. The Etiquette of the Table;
3. The Etiquette of the Street;
4. The Etiquette of Social Entertainment;
5. The Etiquette of Special Occasions.[4]

I. *The Etiquette of the Toilet.* —There is nothing like a good beginning. A man should not wait till he goes in company before he assumes the character of a gentleman. A celebrated actress was once complimented on the success with which she had protected herself from the temptations which always assail women of her profession, and maintained a reputation untouched by the tongue of scandal. "The secret is this," said she, "I have to sustain on the stage the characters of noble and virtuous women. I find it impossible to be a lady for two or three hours before the footlights, and not to carry out the character in private life. By making the character natural, I am saved the effort of assuming it." So the true lady or gentleman should begin the day as such, and the character can easily and naturally be sustained.

The first requisite of the toilet is cleanliness. The whole body should be bathed thoroughly in cold water, if the health is sufficiently robust to permit it. This is of special importance to students, as the cold bath will partly supply the place of exercise, of which students seldom take enough. "Cleanliness is next to godliness,"[5] and I can hardly see how a clean heart can exist in a dirty body for any great length of time. It wouldn't feel comfortable. The Mohammedan religion requires all true believers to wash four times a day; and I wish the same principle, at least a modified form of it, could be engrafted on our own faith, and *enforced*.

The teeth should be rubbed every morning and night with a brush, which can be bought for a few cents. It should be kept on the toilet-table, and used as regularly as the sun rises and sets. No man has a right to go into the company of others with a mouth like a slaughter-pen, dealing his pestilent breath around him to the disgust of everybody's nostrils. Sometimes bad breath proceeds from other causes; but it can generally be avoided by keeping the teeth scrupulously clean.

The hair should be neatly brushed, and occasionally washed with soap, or a little borax or soda in the water, to cleanse the scalp. A little oil may be used occasionally, if the hair is very dry and stiff. A man should have his hair trimmed as often as his means will allow, as there are few men to whom long hair is becoming. With the ladies, who have plenty of time to comb it, long hair is much better. "The glory of the woman," said St. Paul,[6] and the world is of the same opinion still.

The nails should be kept neatly trimmed and cleaned. Long dirty nails always remind me forcibly of the claws of a wild beast; a gentleman will keep his nails clean.

After a clean person, the next requisite is clean clothes. These should be changed as often as your means will allow. Above all things wear clean linen. I was reading a facetious paragraph in a newspaper not long since, in which the writer solemnly declared it to be his opinion that half the crime committed could be traced indirectly to dirty clothes. According to his theory, the man who wears a dirty shirt for any length of time loses all the finer feelings of humanity, gives way to his baser passions, and is then in a condition to commit almost any sort of crime. This is an extreme view of the matter, but there is a grain of truth in it.

A gentleman should always wear a collar. I emphasize this, because I observe that a great many of the students forget their collars quite often. Linen collars last a long time, and paper collars cost but a trifle. A cravat too, however worn or faded, is a badge of gentility. I wish the students of this school to be models for other young men in whatever constitutes a true gentleman. I do not wish to make you extravagant, or to lead you to do what you cannot afford. The things which I mentioned have cost but a trifle, and most of you can afford them.

With regard to the quality of a gentleman's clothing, I can say nothing more than that he should wear as good as he can afford. I think none the less of a man for wearing a faded coat or patched trousers; I honor him for it, if I know he is making sacrifices for the sake of an education. But however coarse the texture or bad the fit, a gentleman's clothes should be clean. A whisk-broom or a clothes-brush used every morning will remove the dust and add to the appearance of your clothing. There is one thing a gentleman generally does, and an ill-bred man hardly ever—he buttons up his vest.

The next thing to be considered is the feet. Blacking is very cheap, and it is as easy to brush the shoes every morning as to brush them once a week. Clean, polished shoes are a mark of the lady or gentleman, which should not be neglected.

A man who has made his toilet in the manner I have described above is prepared to begin the day feeling like a gentleman. "Well begun is half done"; and he can work better and enjoy life more than the dirty fellow who crawls out of bed, throws on his dirty clothes, wets his face and hands, makes a rake at his hair, and slouches off to his business feeling worse than when he went to bed.

My remarks in the course of this lecture are addressed chiefly to the male portion of my audience, but the *principles* apply equally to the ladies, and where the *rules* do not apply they must change them to suit the circumstances. They generally pay so much attention to their toilets, that they do not need a great deal of instruction on that head.

II. *The Etiquette of the Table.* —Men must eat, in common with all other animals; and the table is one place where man has an opportunity of showing his superiority over the lower animals. The lion, the tiger, the dog, snatch and tear their food, and lose every other feeling in the gratification of an animal instinct. The savage devours his food in a similar manner; but a gentleman shows at the table the same delicacy, the same regard for the rights and feelings of others as he does on other occasions. He does not pick out all the best bits of food, and choke himself in seeing how fast and how much he can eat. He does not spill his food on the table, his clothes, or the floor. He sees that the ladies and his elders are served; he takes only his fair share of the food, and eats like he were accustomed to eating—not as though he were half-starved.

The following are a few of the rules which should be observed at table:

Never spread your elbows on the table: it was intended to hold the plates.

Never put your knife to your mouth; you might cut yourself. If there is anything you cannot eat with a fork, use a spoon. No person of refinement puts his knife to his mouth; it was intended to cut the food with. Some people are under the impression that the fork should be kept in the left hand: this is not necessary, and would be very inconvenient, since we are required to use the fork so constantly. It should only be held in the left hand while cutting.

If there is a napkin by your plate, spread it over your knees to protect your clothing from any food which may drop while you are eating; or else keep it by your plate, and use it to wipe your mouth or your fingers. Never commit the vulgarism of wiping your forehead or nose with a table napkin as I have seen men do. If there is a napkin ring, fold up your napkin at the close of the meal and place it in the ring. When there is no napkin, you may use your handkerchief, but never put it on the table; keep it on your lap.

Never drink your tea or coffee from the saucer, but from the cup. If your hostess is so thoughtless as to give you scalding coffee, you must either wait till it cools, cool it with milk or water, drink it and burn your throat, or leave it. Never blow your food or drink to cool it; it is the height of ill-breeding. It is as bad as licking your fingers.

At a dinner or tea-party, never begin to eat till all the company have been served. You need not sit like a stone and eye the victuals with a fierce and hungry look, but keep up the conversation till all are ready to begin; then do justice to the fare, but do not be selfish, for it might make people think less of you; do not eat too much, for it might make you sick. Keep your mouth shut while chewing. Never make a noise while eating or drinking. It reminds one forcibly of the noise made by a dog or pig in similar circumstances. Conversation, wit, and anecdote will serve as sauce to your meal and make you enjoy it the more. Nowhere can you detect a man's ignorance of good manners so easily as at the table.

III. *Etiquette of the Street.* —After you have eaten your breakfast or dinner, you will probably then go to school, or, if you are not a student, to your usual place of business. The same principles should regulate your conduct on the street as elsewhere: *viz.*, a proper self-respect, and a proper deference for others. Your walk should be manly and dignified—or lady like. You should not wander from one side of the pavement to the other—someone might think you drunk. A straight-forward walk, as though you had somewhere to go and something to do, is much better.

If you meet a lady of your acquaintance on the street, lift your hat to her, always with the hand on the opposite side from the one the lady is on. For instance if she is on your right, use the left hand, and *vice versa*. It is not enough merely to touch your hat—*take it off*; it will come a little awkward at first, but you will soon become accustomed to it. A lady should bow in return to a gentleman's salute.

If you meet a male friend, you should lift your hat, bow, shake hands, speak a pleasant word, make a gesture with your hand, as the degree of your intimacy will allow. Take off your hat to one who is very much your superior, shake hands with a preacher or an old friend whom you have not met for some time. Never be so absent-minded as to neglect to recognize your friends.

If a gentleman meets a lady on the street, he should not presume to join her walk unless he is certain that his company will be agreeable. If it is not, the lady should frankly but politely say so. A married lady usually leans on her husband's arm; single ladies do not take a gentleman's arm in the daytime unless they are engaged.

If you have anything to say to a lady whom you meet in the street, *never* stop her, but turn and walk with her; you can leave at the next corner.

When you meet a lady or an elderly person on the street you should offer them the wall; i.e., the side next the houses. Ordinarily, you should keep to the right; an observance of this rule would prevent those collisions which are so frequent on crowded streets.

In walking with a lady it is customary to give her the right arm; but sometimes it is convenient to offer the left. You should offer your arm whenever her safety or comfort seems to require it—as when walking over a narrow bridge or ascending the steps of a public building.

In entering a room or a yard, always open the door or gate, and hold it open until the lady has entered. Never pass before a lady if you can help it, or without an apology.

There is an exception to this rule in ascending a staircase which is too narrow to permit the passage of both at the same time: In this case, delicacy requires that the gentleman should go up or down first—the lady following.

Never smoke or chew tobacco in the presence of a lady. Avoid the disgusting habit of spitting.

No one but a loafer will stare at a lady in the street.

After twilight it is not becoming for a lady to be on the street alone. A small boy is better than no company at all. A lady should so arrange her affairs that she will always have male company, or else not be out after dark.

If a friend meets you on your way to fulfill an engagement, and stops you for a talk, you may tell him of your appointment—politely, of course—and that you will see him again at the earliest convenient opportunity.

Do not think that because you have met a friend once during the day you should not notice him again. A nod, a smile, a gesture with the hand—some slight sign of recognition should be exchanged every time you meet.

A very common fault with students, especially girls, is that of walking four or five abreast, and blocking up the sidewalk. Never walk more than three abreast, and if you meet anyone, break ranks and give them plenty of room to pass. Loud talking or halloing on the street is also very unladylike, and should not be indulged in.

By a proper observance of the above rules, you will always conduct yourselves properly on the street, and your society will be agreeable to those who are with you.

IV. *Etiquette of the Social Entertainment.* —Under the term social entertainment I include balls, evening parties, and any occasion on which people are gathered together for conversation or amusement. The same rules will apply also to the family circle. A gentleman or lady will be as polite—not so formal and ceremonious perhaps—but essentially as polite at home as in any company, however distinguished. There are special rules for the ballroom and other public gatherings, but what I have to say has a general application; for special rules the books on etiquette may be read to advantage.

In making visits, always call at a reasonable hour, when the lady of the house is likely to be at leisure to receive you; the custom of the community will be the best guide as to the particular hour.

On entering the room where the guests are assembled, always bow first to the company. They may not be paying attention; nevertheless, good manners require that you should do your part, whether it appears to be noticed or not. You should then pay your respects to the lady of the house—the hostess—if she is near the door. It is not necessary, however, to walk the whole length of the room without noticing any one else, to find the hostess. It is her duty to be at or near the door to receive her guests. If she is not in the room, the gentleman of the house may receive in her place. It is very embarrassing to enter a company, to whom you may be an utter stranger, and have no one to introduce you or make you welcome.

Introductions

In a recently published book on etiquette, I find the following rules with regard to introductions, which are so concise and at the same time so complete, that I shall transcribe the whole section, in the language of the writer.

> The custom which prevails in country places of introducing everybody you meet to each other, is both an annoying and improper one. As a general rule, introductions should not be made, except where there is undoubted evidence that the acquaintance would be mutually agreeable and proper.
>
> But if you should find an agreeable person in private society, who seems desirous of making your acquaintance, there cannot be any objection to your meeting his advances half way, although the ceremony of an "introduction" may not have taken place; his presence in your friend's house being a sufficient guarantee for his respectability, as of course if he were an improper person he would not be there.
>
> It is customary in introducing people, to present the youngest to the oldest, or the humblest to the highest in position, if there is any distinction.
>
> In introducing a lady to a gentleman, address her first, thus: "Miss Mason, permit me to present you to Mr. Kent," or "Mrs. Trevor, I have the pleasure of presenting you to Mr. Marlow."[7] When one lady is married, and the other single, present the single lady to the matron—"Miss Harris, allow me to introduce you to Mrs. Martin."
>
> When you introduce parties whom you are quite sure will be pleased with each other, it is well to add, after the introduction, that you take great pleasure in making them acquainted, which will be an assurance to each that you think they are well matched, and thus they are prepared to be friends from the start.
>
> In introducing parties, be careful to pronounce each name distinctly, as there is nothing more awkward than to have one's name miscalled.
>
> In introducing a foreigner, it is proper to present him as "Mr. Leslie, from England"; "Mr. Samuels from Scotland" etc.
>
> When introducing any of the members of your own family, mention the name in an audible tone. It is not considered sufficient to say "My father," "My sister," or "My Brother"; but say, "My Father, Mr. Stanley" or "My Brother Mr. Weston." It is best to be explicit in all these things, for there may be more than one surname in the family. The eldest daughter should be introduced by her surname only, as "Miss Sherwood"; her younger sisters as "Miss Maud Sherwood," "Miss Mary Sherwood."
>
> In presenting a clergyman, do not neglect to put "Reverend" before his name. If you use only his surname, use Mr. also, as the "*Reverend Mr. Brown*"; if you use his Christian name, omit the "Mr."; as, the "Rev. John Smith." If he is a D.D. say, "The Reverend Doctor." If he is a bishop, then the word bishop is sufficient.
>
> When you are introduced to a person, be careful not to appear as though you had never heard of him before. If he happens to be a person of any distinction, such a mistake would be unpardonable, and no person is complimented by being reminded that his name is unknown.

If by any misfortune you have been introduced to a person whose acquaintance you do not desire, you can merely make the formal bow of etiquette when you meet him, which, of itself, encourages no familiarity; but the *bow is indispensable*, for *he* cannot be thought a gentleman who would pass another with a vacant stare, after having been formally presented to him.

What is called "cutting" another is never practiced by ladies and gentlemen except in some extraordinary cases of bad conduct on the part of the individual thus sacrificed. An increased degree of ceremony and formal politeness is the most delicate way of withdrawing from an unpleasant acquaintance. Indeed "cutting" is rarely ever practiced by well-bred ladies and gentlemen.

On introduction in a room, a married lady generally offers her hand, a young lady not; in a ball-room, where the introduction is to dancing, not to friendship, you never shake hands; and as a general rule, an introduction is not followed by shaking hands—only by a bow. It may perhaps be laid down, that the more public the place of introduction, the less hand-shaking takes place; but if the introduction be particular, if it be accompanied by personal recommendation, such as "I want you to know my friend Jones," then you give Jones your hand, and warmly too.

It is understood in society, that a person who has been properly introduced to you, has some claim on your good offices in future; you cannot therefore slight him without good reason, and the chance of being called to an account for it.

Conversation

But it is in conversation that a man most clearly shows what he is. I once met a young man at an evening party, who appeared to be a gentleman.[8] His dress was faultless, he could bow with consummate grace—but when he opened his mouth—puff!—it all vanished—he betrayed his utter lack of taste and education. A man who talks well may be presumed to be a man of intelligence.

Lord Chesterfield was an English nobleman who lived during the last century.[9] He was considered the most polite man of his time. He made politeness a science, and set the fashions for the whole English people. In one of his works on etiquette he says:

> Civility is particularly due to all women; and, remember that no provocation can justify any man in not being civil to every woman; and the greatest man would justly be reckoned a brute if he were not civil to the meanest woman. It is due to their sex, and is the only protection they have against the superior strength of ours.[10]

Do not press before a lady in a crowd. Do not sit when she is standing without offering her your place. Gentlemen should not get together in groups to the neglect of the ladies.

In conversing, do not speak in a loud and boisterous tone, as though you wished to attract attention. Do not indulge in loud laughter—horse-laughs, we say. Do not whisper in company. Writing on slates, making signs, talking in a foreign language—are all in the highest degree impolite. In a large company, a conversation can be carried on in a low tone without attracting any attention, but there should not seem to be any attempt at concealment. If you have any private information to communicate, take the person out of the room.

Do not talk slightingly of the absent. You do not know who will carry your remarks to their ears. Do as you would be done by.[11]

If you are bashful or unaccustomed to society, do not plant yourself in a corner and vegetate, like any other green thing; but enter into conversation with some one, and try to appear at ease. Notice the conduct of those whom you know have good manners and conform your own to theirs.

If the lady of the house asks you to sing or play, you can do so if you feel disposed, but not at the request of any one else. The reason of this is plain: the hostess studies the comfort and pleasure of her guests, and if she thinks that these will be promoted by music, she will probably ask you to sing or play. If you intend to do so, do not hesitate and begin to make excuses and keep the company waiting, but comply at once—not in a great hurry as though you were anxious to display your accomplishments, but in a leisurely way. When you have played or sung one or two pieces—stop. The company will get enough, after a while of even a good thing. While others are playing it is the height of ill-breeding to laugh and talk as though you did not hear the music; it is very embarrassing to the performer and very annoying to those who wish to enjoy the music.

Never ask a lady her age, unless you are on very intimate terms with her. Never ask the price of things—in company at any rate. This is a vulgar habit, and very common. I have been seated in a company composed partly of ladies, and have heard a coarse fellow inquire in a loud voice during a lull in the conversation, "Mr. Chesnutt, what did you pay for them shoes?" It was none of his business at best, but the question under the existing circumstances was a solecism utterly unpardonable. A very nice man may from motives of economy be wearing a second hand coat or hat, and in that case such a question would be rather embarrassing.

Don't talk shop: i.e., don't talk about yourself or your own affairs. It may be very interesting to you, but very stupid to other people. A preacher should not preach, nor a lawyer plead in the parlor. Talk about things that will interest the whole company.

Don't talk too much. There are generally others who wish to talk, and they should all have an opportunity.

Dr. Johnson was a great talker.[12] His fame as author and lexicographer is secondary to his fame as a conversationalist. On one occasion his audience sat during an entire evening and listened to Dr. Johnson talk, merely asking a question or putting in a word now and then. At the close of the evening when the company rose to depart, Dr. Johnson looked around with a pleased expression of countenance and remarked, "Well gentlemen, we have enjoyed a very pleasant and instructive conversation." It was a greater pleasure to hear Dr. Johnson than it was to talk, you must not imagine yourself a second Johnson.

Don't tell old stories. If you have anything new, let the company have the benefit of it. It is hard work to laugh at an anecdote that you have heard fifty times.

There are many other things which should not be done in good society, but they are too numerous to specify. There is one thing more, however, which I implore you not to do—*Don't*, for heaven's sake *don't* put on airs. Nothing is more disgusting than affectation. Be natural. We can put up with bashfulness, ignorance and some other things, but affectation is offensive to every one who has sense enough to perceive it. *Don't, please don't put on airs.*

V. *Etiquette at Church.* It is a very common thing, and a disgusting thing too, to see young people misbehave in church. No one who respects himself or who has any regard whatever for the divine character of the place will behave very badly in church; but the best-disposed people may from ignorance do things that are very reprehensible. A few of those errors which arise from lack of knowledge will be mentioned here.

A gentleman who accompanies a lady to church should, as a rule, sit by her, unless he is ashamed of her, and in that case he should not accompany her. Of course this would not apply in those cases where there are separate seats for male and female.

Always wait for the lady to enter the pew first; if the pew has a door, hold it open for her.

It is a very common habit on entering a pew to take a seat at the end next the entrance. Then every one who comes in must crowd by—the ladies must crush their dresses, and you must draw yourself up in to a knot to let them pass, or have them rub up against your knees, which is very disagreeable. Go to the other end of the pew; or if you take the first seat, move back when any one else enters the pew.

Another reprehensible habit is that of running out of church. A well-bred *man* will not disturb a congregation by going out during the service, unless some very urgent business demands his attention; but a woman who is in the habit of jumping up and going out time after time is very ill bred indeed. If she must go out it is better to stay than to come back unless it can be very quietly done. I have very little respect for a woman who is guilty of such very unbecoming conduct. When the Doxology is sung and the benediction pronounced, then well-bred people will go out. Only when necessity demands it, or when the services are very long and tiresome should this rule be violated. I hope I shall not notice any more instances of such conduct among the students of this school.

Whispering, talking, laughing, etc. it is not necessary for me to mention. No one who wishes to be considered decent will indulge in these things at church; and it would be throwing pearls before swine[13] to attempt to instruct those who do not wish to learn.

The rules for conduct on such special occasions as balls, weddings, funerals, etc., must be learned from the books, and from those who are acquainted with them. This is neither the time nor the place to discuss anything except the general principles of good behavior, and a few of those rules which apply to our daily lives.

Finally, dear students, remember that it is only by being a gentleman or a lady that you can act like one. Otherwise, like the ass in the lion's skin, you will betray yourself as soon as you begin to bray.[14] You cannot put on politeness with your Sunday clothes, for it will not keep like they. The *less* you wear them the better they look; the *more* you use your manners, the better they will fit. It is only by being a lady or a gentleman at all times that you can be a lady or a gentleman at any time. And remember the golden rule—"Do unto others as you" etc., and you will render yourself agreeable to all with whom you associate; your company will be sought after, your influence enlarged, and your success in life materially promoted. Ay, and if you will take this Golden Rule, and carry it beyond the mere surface to the heart, and make it and all the words of Him who first uttered it the law of your life it will lead you beyond mere material success.

↜

SOURCE: Holograph text at the Fisk University Library. Below the title Chesnutt wrote parenthetically, "A Lecture delivered before the Normal Literary Society, Fayetteville, N.C. 1881." Throughout this speech Chesnutt relies upon Samuel Roberts Wells's *Hand-book for Home Improvement* (1857). (See his 1874 transcriptions from this work in *The Journals of Charles W. Chesnutt*, ed. Richard Brodhead [Durham, N.C.: Duke University Press, 1993], 40–41.) Chesnutt does not identify here or elsewhere the "recently published book on etiquette" from which he quotes at length.

[1]*Ezekiel* 16:13.

[2]*Othello*, 3.3.159.

[3]Sir Walter Raleigh (c. 1552–1618); Elizabeth I (1533–1603).

[4]In the manuscript, Chesnutt used ditto marks for "The Etiquette of the" (items 2–4) and "The Etiquette of" (item 5).

[5]Paraphrase of John Wesley (1703–91), "Sermon XCII," *Sermons on Several Occasions* (1794–1801).

[6]1 Corinthians 11:15.

[7]In the holograph Chesnutt apparently transcribed parts of this paragraph dealing with the introduction "of a lady to a gentleman" inaccurately. He wrote "Mrs. Kent" and "Mr. Trevor" for "Mr. Kent" and "Mrs. Trevor."

[8]How Chesnutt completed this sentence is not known; the emendation "a gentleman" was determined by the context.

[9]Philip Dormer Stanhope, Fourth Earl of Chesterfield (1694–1773).

[10]The first two of these three sentences appear in the *Hand-book for Home Improvement* (see the "Source" note above). The original source for the whole quotation has not been identified.

[11]Stanhope, *Letters to His Son* (1775).

[12]Samuel Johnson (1709–84); see "Who and Why Was Samuel Johnson?"

[13]Matthew 7:6.

[14]Aesop (620?–560 B.C.), "The Ass in the Lion's Skin," *Fables*.

The Advantages of a
Well-Conducted Literary Society

Speech to the Normal Literary Society, Fayetteville, N.C., October 1881

I have thought it fitting on this occasion, the second meeting of our society for the session, to give you my views as to the real object of a Literary Society—the real ends to be attained by it, and the best means of attaining them. Some members of the society attend the meetings week after week, without any adequate conception of its object or its advantages. They join because it is the custom; they come because the crowd comes. Others have a general idea that the society is designed for improvement, but have no clear idea just exactly in what respect they are to be improved. It is in an attempt to make clear to the thoughtful student the distinct advantages which are to be derived from a well-conducted debating society, that I shall ask your attention for a short time.

Every human institution is established with some definite end in view. The human mind is so constituted that every act of the will is preceded by a feeling of desire. We are displeased with something; we feel a desire to get rid of it in some way; and this gives rise to an act of the will by which we attempt to remove the cause of our displeasure. Or, we perceive something good, and we feel a desire to possess it; this gives rise to an act of the will by which we try to obtain it. That a Literary Society is productive of something that would give pleasure its founders must first have conceived; and they must have felt a desire to obtain that good before they associated themselves together in such a society.

When this school was first opened[1] the teachers, believing that a society of this character would be a valuable auxiliary means of education, and in accordance with a custom in schools of high grade, established this society for the benefit of the older students. In the words of the preamble of the Constitution, the society was designed "for mutual improvement in the arts of composition and debate, and in other literary exercises."

While this is a general statement of what we expect to gain by means of our society, it can nevertheless be divided into several heads which will more fully express the manner in which we are profited.

I shall arrange these heads in what I consider the order of their importance— beginning with the least valuable result obtained and ending with the most important.

A good Literary Society is a means of improvement because it furnishes

1. Recreation;
2. Instruction in practical business knowledge;
3. Discipline for the mental faculties.

This last division I shall further subdivide as follows:

A good Literary Society furnishes mental discipline by teaching

1. Self-possession;
2. Self-control;
3. Respect for constituted authority;
4. The rules of argument.

I shall now consider each division of the subject in the above order and give some definite instructions how to obtain the benefit which is named in each.

1. *A Good Literary Society is a means of improvement because it furnishes recreation.* —The love of amusement is common to all animated nature. The little birds chirp, and sing, and play; the dog chases his own tail around in a circle, and barks at an imaginary foe; every one has noticed the frolicsome habits of the kitten; the horse turned loose in his pasture gallops madly around in conscious strength and freedom. In mankind the period of infancy and childhood is principally devoted to amusement; and in after life men are always seeking some means of diversion.

This universal desire for amusement rests upon a principle of our nature. The body and the mind both require rest; and rest is found to be most beneficial when combined with amusement. It is the combination of rest and amusement that we denominate *recreation*—a *re*-creation—a building up of our tired energies of body and mind. When the lower animals have wearied themselves in the search for food, or in supplying their other wants, their instincts prompt them to seek recreation and they amuse themselves according to their different natures. Man not only exhausts the body in supplying his natural and artificial wants, but also the mind. Sleep recuperates both body and mind by giving them absolute rest. But sometimes the mind is in need of recreation, which sleep cannot supply. In the schoolroom the mind is wearied in grappling with the elements of knowledge and comprehending the truths of science. It then needs recreation; and this recreation or mental amusement, is one of the ends sought and obtained by a well-conducted Literary Society.

Proceeding then upon the proposition, that recreation is necessary to mental growth, let us see in what manner a Literary Society can be made to furnish it.

In the first place, the mere change of employment furnishes recreation. A different set of faculties are brought into play, and act while the others rest; as the right hand of the driver rests while he holds the reins in his left.

Secondly, humorous or interesting readings are a means of recreation. The fancy may be pleased and the feelings excited, by the thoughts of other minds when these thoughts are properly presented to us. It is the love of literature, common to all cultivated minds, that furnishes a market for the works of the great army of poets and historians, novelists and journalists. I know of no purer intellectual pleasure than that derived from reading the great masterpieces of literature.

Good singing is another means of recreation. No instrument was ever invented that could reach the soul like the human voice. It is the voice of the soul. Its exquisitely modulated tones can express every variety of emotion. Soft, melting strains can woo to love; and bold martial lays will fire the soldier's breast. Who has not felt his heart saddened by those minor tones which seem to be the natural vehicle of grief? It is the love of music, common to all men, with few exceptions, that leads to the enthusiastic reception of those favored mortals who are gifted with voices of extraordinary power. Jenny Lind, Patti, Mary Anderson, Selika, the Hyers sisters,[2] and the other famous vocalists possess in their voices the power to draw tears from men's eyes; and what is more difficult still, money from their pockets. I have read of a man who paid $700.00 for a ticket to one of Jenny Lind's concerts.

A good debate is a source of pleasure to participants and listeners. It is a source of much satisfaction to the winning man, and frequently of much amusement to the audience. It furnishes ample opportunity for the display of the debaters' wit and wisdom, the one of which makes us laugh, either at the wit or at the debater, and the other of which may instruct us. Again, man is a pugnacious animal; he likes to fight. The early history of nations shows that they were continually at war. Man in his primitive state was constantly exposed to danger from wild beasts, and the Creator implanted in his nature the principle of self-defense. His food was obtained mainly by the chase, and there was given to him a natural love for sport. And though civilization has modified our blood-thirsty tendencies, we still love controversy. The best of men dispute, sometimes for the love of truth, and the triumph of the right; but too often for the mere love of disputation.

So we have seen that the change of employment, good singing, interesting and humorous readings, lively debates, and a "little nonsense now and then" are all means of recreation, which should be plentifully furnished by a good Literary Society.

II. *A Literary Society is a means of improvement because it gives its members instruction in practical business knowledge.*

We have seen that amusement or recreation is useful and even necessary. But only a short portion of our time can be devoted to it. Man was made to work. The dictum went forth from Deity, "In the sweat of thy face shalt thou eat bread,"[3] and labor has since been the lot of mankind. It is true there are some drones in the hive; but of the great mass of mankind it is true, that "he who will not work shall not eat."[4]

God did not make man to be idle;[5] nor did he make him with mere instincts of self-preservation like the beasts of the field. He gave him a destiny to work out. He placed him in the midst of the universe, and gave him a mind in the image of his Creator, to search out its laws, to discover its hidden mysteries, to appreciate its beauties. Mankind was first compelled to labor to supply the wants of the body. But when men became more civilized, provision was made for the needs of our mental natures. As men gathered in communities and thus gave birth to society new needs were created, and these had to be supplied by labor.

Since men are thus compelled to work, how important is it that this work should be properly done! A carpenter does not attempt to build a house without first learning how; a blacksmith must serve a tedious apprenticeship before he can shoe a horse or iron a buggy; a physician spends years in study before he is considered competent to practice the healing art. It is so in all arts, trades, and professions.

But the special art in which a Literary Society can instruct us is the art of conducting a public meeting, or a legislative assembly. Experience has laid down certain rules which will enable a body of men to act together in harmony, and decide in the shortest time those questions which they have met to discuss. Under our system of government, the democratic form, every intelligent citizen is likely, almost *certain* to be called upon at some time to take part in a public meeting, or to fill some public office. Hence it is perfectly clear that every intelligent citizen should acquaint himself with the rules of parliamentary procedure. A properly conducted literary society will furnish an opportunity for learning them and putting them into practice.

But this can only be done by paying proper attention to the rules themselves. Do not think that by merely gathering here, parliamentary knowledge will be poured down from heaven upon you; nor that you will soak it in like a sponge absorbs water. No such thing. In order to learn them, the rules of order and debate must be strictly observed. You should study the manuals, familiarize yourselves with the Constitution.[6] You can only become a good parliamentarian by paying a strict observance to the rules laid down by the best writers. Cushing & Jefferson are the standard works—the former for the British Parliament; the latter for the American Congress.[7] The book that we use[8] is compiled from these authors, those parts being omitted which are unnecessary for the use of a debating society. Every member should study these books, should govern his actions in the society by their rules, and should see that the members observe them. Thus and only thus will you acquire a practical knowledge of parliamentary usage.

III (and most important). *A Literary Society is a means of improvement because it furnishes discipline for the mind.* Knowledge is one thing; discipline is another. Study and observation will give us knowledge; Discipline will teach us how to make a wise use of it. *Remember what Cowper says.*

> Knowledge and Wisdom, far from being one,
> Have ofttimes no connection; Knowledge dwells,
> In heads replete with thoughts of others;
> Wisdom in minds attentive to their own.[9]

What I include under the term Discipline in this case are those special habits of the mind which are cultivated in a good Debating Society. They are all embraced, I think in the following classification: *viz.*,

1. Self-Possession
2. Self-Control
3. Respect for constituted authority.
4. An acquaintance with the laws of argument.

The practice of speaking in a Literary Society cultivates *self-possession.* Every one that has ever spoken in public knows what it is to stand before an audience for the first time. It is a terrible ordeal for a young person. Even in school exercises the student is frequently embarrassed, when he has no other audience than his daily associates.

A speaker frequently has a great many ideas as he sits in his seat and it seems to him that he has only to open his mouth for a torrent of burning eloquence to burst forth. But, alas! As soon as he stands up, his flow of thoughts ceases, he stammers, blushes, and breaks down.

It is related of Demosthenes, the greatest of ancient orators,[10] that on his first appearance before the Athenian people as an orator, his uncouth gestures, his stammering speech, so excited the ridicule of his audience that he was compelled to retire from the stand amid laughter and hisses. But he did not despair. He felt the fire of genius within him, and his failure only nerved him to greater effort. He had an ungraceful habit of shrugging his shoulders while speaking. To remedy this defect, he was accustomed to practice his speeches at home, with a naked sword hanging over his shoulder; so that, if he should forget and shrug his shoulders, the sharp edge of the sword would remind him of it. He had an impediment in his speech, to correct which he practiced speaking with a mouthful of pebbles. (Ex.)[11] His voice was weak; and to accustom himself to the noise of tumultuous assemblies, he would go down to the sea-shore and declaim amid the noise of the waves, and with only seabirds and fishes for an auditory. He shut himself up in a cave for days at a time, that he might study with less distraction. The results of these efforts ere long became apparent; he rose to be the first of the Grecian orators, and his speeches have been models of oratory down to the present time.

The youthful bashfulness and awkwardness of Daniel Webster, and his subsequent glorious career as orator and statesman; the early efforts of Henry Clay and his success—these are matters of history.[12] And they go to show clearly, that the greatest talent, the most god-like genius must be trained to speaking before it can succeed on the rostrum. A speaker must be able to think on-his-legs, and this he can do only after long practice. If Demosthenes or Henry Clay had had a good Literary Society to practice in, and on, they would not have been compelled to resort to the seashore and the barnyard to practice oratory. In the Literary Society a young man can begin gradually. He can commence by making a motion; he can speak to a motion; he can make a declamation; and he can chop logic and spout eloquence freely before a good natured audience which will not criticize him too severely. He thus gradually acquires self-confidence, and before long can stand without trepidation before a real audience, and discuss questions of public moment.

But in order to derive these advantages from a literary society, this practice must be founded upon certain principles and guided by certain rules. There is nothing which cannot be better done in a regular than in an irregular manner. The following are a few rules which will assist the youthful orator in acquiring self-possession:

1. *Be in earnest.* *"Ernst ist das Leben"*—Life is a serious thing.[13]

> Life is real, life is earnest,
> And the grave is not its goal;
> Dust thou art to dust returnest,
> Was not spoken of the soul.[14]

If you come to the meetings merely for fun, you will profit little by them. You can get amusement without sacrificing the main object—improvement.

2. *Prepare yourselves.* —Demosthenes was accustomed to write his speeches over several times, and commit them to memory before delivering them. Lord Macaulay, the brilliant British orator and historian,[15] polished off his speeches with the skill of an artist before he gave them to the public. A story is now going the rounds of the press about M. Thiers, late president of France.[16] A gentleman was expressing surprise that M. Thiers could deliver such brilliant speeches without preparation. (M. Thiers uses no notes.) "Sir," responded the ex-president, "it is no compliment to me to have it thought that I speak without preparation. I hold it criminal in a man to discuss great public measures without careful thought and study. *My* speeches are the result of long and painful preparation." This man has a proper idea of the vocation of an orator. "If the blind lead the blind, shall they not both fall into the ditch?"[17] There is a difference between an off-hand speech and an off-hand delivery. Almost any well-informed man is able to "make a few remarks" on any subject of general interest, and these are really off-hand speeches. A subject may be sprung suddenly in the course of a discussion, and a brilliant speech made on it. These are real extemporaneous speeches. But if a man has a subject assigned beforehand, and has time to prepare, he is not doing himself or his audience justice if he does not do so. You may let the words, the delivery, be off-hand, but the plan of the speech should be carefully arranged in the mind. The illustrations should be selected. Your stories should have some point to them. If you have thus arranged the argument in your mind, you can trust to the inspiration of the moment for the words. The life and fire of the extemporaneous language is often more effective than the polished elegance of the written speech. Dr. Blair, in his lectures on Rhetoric,[18] advises young men to write their first speeches, and commit them to memory; in this manner they can combine the advantages of good language and freedom of gesture. I shall have something more to say about this before I close.

By observing carefully the above rules you can acquire that graceful self-possession, that absence of fear or awkwardness on the floor, which is necessary to enable a man to do his best.

The second means of mental discipline which is offered by a properly conducted Literary Society, is *the opportunity for learning self-control*. Self possession as we have learned, is the ability to control the intellect before an audience; but *self-control* is the ability to govern the temper under like circumstances. "He that ruleth his own spirit is stronger than him that taketh a city."[19] Some men are so sensitive that the least word that can possibly receive a bad construction—the least expression which can apply to them, stirs up their anger. Their first impulse is to spring up and contradict the speaker; to threaten to knock him down if he doesn't retract; to make a display of passion, which, while it does no good, only serves to make the angry man ridiculous. This sometimes occurs in our own meetings.

Others are so proud and conceited that any action which seems to them like a slight is resented with great indignation. Sometimes they will sit and swell, and sulk in sullen silence during a whole meeting, and refuse to take part in the exercises.

These things, we all know are very disagreeable. The ability to control the temper is one of the highest marks of a gentleman. Notice the rude and ignorant. Like a woman from the lower class—most of you have met such a one somewhere. Her tongue runs from morning till night. She scolds her children; she lectures her husband; she quarrels with the neighbors; she makes her house a hell, simply because she has either never learned that it is coarse and unladylike to scold, or else does not care to learn it.

A gentleman is not easily insulted. And when he is, he does not spring up and curse, and rage like a wild bull. If he can get reasonable redress, he does so; if not, he ignores the insult—does not seem to notice it.

There are one or two directions which will assist young people in acquiring the habit of self-control.

1. *Do not think too highly of yourself.* Do not imagine that you are the most important man in the society. Do not labor under the delusion that the whole machinery of the organization would stop if *you* should withdraw from its membership. My friend, if you think so you make a great mistake. There is nothing so disgusting as conceit. There is no fool like a conceited fool. The greatest man in the world might die to-day, and tomorrow his place would be filled, and the world would jog on as usual, and forget him in a year. Our late lamented President was lying on his couch of pain when this lecture was written.[20] He filled a high position. He has passed to "That undiscovered country from whose bourne no traveler returns."[21] But another occupies the Presidential office and the government still lives and flourishes—"Seest thou a man wise in his own conceit? There is more hope of a fool than of him."[22]

2. *Be charitable.* "Charity suffereth long and is kind."[23] —When anything is said at which you could take offence, always consider carefully whether it was

meant for you or not. *Never* impute motives. Give your opponent credit for gentlemanly feelings, and before you answer a slight, be sure, perfectly sure, that it was intended for you. If a speaker says "No gentleman would whisper in church," don't rise up in sudden indignation and exclaim, "If the gentleman means *me*," etc, etc. The gentleman may not have meant you; and if he did, perhaps nobody knows it but you and himself. But by displaying temper you inform the whole audience that you were the man.

3. *Think twice before you speak.* —I hardly know which is worse, a bad temper or a long tongue. The man who talks too much will sometimes, perhaps unintentionally, tell what is not true. Men in the heat of debate frequently say things which upon reflection they would not utter. If you are offended, adopt the Scripture plan, go to your brother and ask an explanation.[24] If he has done you a wrong, and is any man at all, he will be willing to apologize; and if he has misrepresented you publicly, he will publicly retract his statements.

4. The fourth way in which a good Literary Society disciplines the mind is by *teaching a respect for constituted authority.* —Every good citizen will obey the laws. If a law displeases him, he should try to have it changed in a legal manner. But while it is law, and no great moral principle is involved he should submit to it. In a government like ours, "of the people, by the people, and for the people," submission to the laws is of special importance. The people make the laws, and they are treating themselves with disrespect if they refuse to obey them. The people recognize this, and while in no country the people have so much liberty as in ours, in no country are the laws better enforced, as a general thing. The first duty of a good citizen, is to obey the laws. It is not only a duty, but a necessity. Necessary, to the whole to protect society, and necessary to the individual if he would avoid the penalty imposed. So we have two motives to obey the laws—a sense of duty, and a fear of the consequences of disobedience.

The following rules will assist the young in learning to respect authority.

1. *Respect your officers.* —You should not put a man in office whom you cannot respect; but in case you should do so, respect the office. A man may be a thief, a liar, a villain of the deepest dye, and yet be fully competent to preside over a public body. If you don't like the man, put him out in a lawful manner, if you can; if you cannot, respect the authority of his office.

2. *Obey your own laws.* —It is a common thing for members, when fined, for instance, to declare that they will not pay the fine. A man is ordered to take his seat, and refuses to do so. *This should not be permitted.* If a man misbehaves, and refuses to stop, fine him. If he is obstinate, and refuses to pay the fine or obey the laws *expel him.* Don't permit a sickly sentimentality to prompt you to sustain a man in rebellion against the laws. When he refuses obedience to them, he insults the society, for the society made the laws, and its lawful officers have enforced them, as they are bound to do. I hope that such scenes will never again be permitted in this society.

The last, and most important respect in which a well conducted Literary Society affords discipline for the mind is in furnishing *an opportunity to acquire a knowledge of the laws of argument.* —A man may be self-possessed, have his temper under perfect control, have the highest respect for the laws; and yet, with all this may take the floor and say nothing. His words may flow like water; but it is all sound and fury signifying nothing[25] and no sense. All these things will be of small value to an orator, unless he has something to say, and knows how to say it. Language, gesture, wit, humor, are only the seasoning—the pepper and mustard—of the real feast, the argument. The pepper and mustard may render the feast more palatable, but they make a very unsatisfactory meal by themselves. The shallow and undiscerning may be pleased by a speech which is all wit and sophistry; but the men who lead, the thinking men, whom the orator wishes to convince are not deceived by such weak devices. Such men want character in a speech,—sound logic, clear reasoning.

But these cannot be attained without effort. The ability to argue well can only be acquired by study and practice. Logic—the laws of reasoning—should be studied. The written speeches of great orators should be studied. Demosthenes is said to have copied the *History* of Thucydides[26] eight times with his own hand, in order to become master of his style. The student should embrace every opportunity to hear good, logical speakers, and observe how they arrange their thoughts, and elaborate their arguments. The same rule that was given for acquiring self-possession will apply in this case: —*Always prepare yourself.* Think out your subject; get your speech divided into heads, and your arguments arranged under them. Only old and experienced debaters can argue well without preparation, and *they* always do better with it.

One fault which is very, *very* common among young debaters, I wish to warn you against: *Don't say anything that you can't prove.* I do not mean that you are to demonstrate everything with mathematical exactness; but make no statement unless you have argument to support it. Any other course is mere dogmatism. It convinces no one for you to declare your side is correct, and every sensible man ought to see it. There are two sides to every question, and you have to *prove* not merely assert, that your side is correct.

The following paragraphs, on the value of argument, and the rules which should govern it, I have taken *verbatim* from the excellent little work on Logic by Mr. Hedge.[27] They will form a fitting conclusion to what I have already said:

209. From the limited extent of human knowledge, and the different points of view in which the same subjects may be contemplated by different minds, it follows of necessity, that a diversity of opinions must be entertained on many subjects of speculation. In whatever manner people are first led to form their opinions, they are usually disposed to defend them afterwards with zeal and pertinacity. Hence arise controversies and disputes, which are oftentimes conducted with such intemperate and misguided zeal, as to inflame animosities, by which the comfort and harmony of society are impaired.

210. These are the worst fruits of controversy. They are, however, merely incidental effects; and are counterbalanced by others of an opposite character, and of

high importance to the interests of truth and virtue. The advantages of controversy consist in having questions of difficulty and moment settled in a satisfactory manner. The principles of government and law have been immovably fixed by the debates which have passed in deliberative assemblies and in courts of justice.

211. All questions, not susceptible of rigorous demonstration, can be correctly settled only by a full and impartial comparison of the reason on both sides. This is seldom done, with sufficient exactness by the solitary investigations of an individual. Men rarely enter on the examination of a question wholly free from the bias of a previous opinion respecting it, which makes them more solicitous to find arguments for one side than for the other. It is only when the talents of different persons are enlisted, and different opinions are contended for, that questions are traced in all their bearings, and the grounds of an equitable decision are fully exhibited.

212. The importance of controversy may be inferred from the use which has been made of it in every period of the world. It has been adopted as the principal mode of transacting business, in the halls of legislation and in courts of justice, where questions of the deepest concern to individuals and communities are decided. The minds of youth have been trained to it in seminaries of education, where the practice of disputation, in various forms, has been preserved as a salutary.

213. As controversy, especially when carried on from motives of victory or reputation, is liable to be productive of evil rather than of good, it is incumbent on all who engage in it, from whatever motives, to observe rigorously those laws and principles, by which the former may be avoided, and the latter secured. The following rules, sometimes called canons of controversy, have been highly approved by writers of learning and discernment.

214. Rule 1st. *The terms in which the question in debate is expressed and the precise point at issue, should be so clearly defined, that there could be no misunderstanding respecting them.* If this be not done, the dispute is liable to be in a great degree verbal. Arguments will be misapplied, and the controversy protracted, because the parties engaged in it have different apprehensions of the question.

215. Rule 2d. *The parties should mutually consider each other as standing on a footing of equality* in respect to the subject in debate. Each should regard the other as possessing equal talents, knowledge, and desire for truth with himself; and that it is possible, therefore, that he may be in the wrong, and his adversary in the right. In the heat of controversy, men are apt to forget the numberless sources of error, which exist in every controverted subject, especially of theology and metaphysics. Hence arise presumption, confidence and arrogant language; all which obstruct the discovery of truth.

216. Rule 3d. *All expressions which are unmeaning, or without effect in regard to the subject in debate, should be strictly avoided.* —All expressions may be considered as unmeaning which contribute nothing to the proof of the question; such as desultory remarks or declamatory expressions. To these may be added all technical, ambiguous, and equivocal expressions. These have a tendency to dazzle and bewilder the mind, and to hinder its clear perception of the truth.

217. Rule 4th. *Personal reflections on an adversary should in no instance be indulged.* —Whatever be his private character, his foibles are not to be named in a controversy. Personal reflections are not only destitute of effect in respect to the question in discussion, but they are productive of real evil. They obstruct mental improvement, and are prejudicial to public morals. They indicate in him who uses them a mind hostile to the truth; for they prevent even solid arguments from receiving the attention to which they are justly entitled.

218. Rule 5th. *No one has a right to accuse his adversary of indirect motives.*

Arguments are to be answered, whether he who offers them be sincere or not, especially as his want of sincerity, if real, could not be ascertained. To inquire into his motives, then, is useless. To ascribe improper motives to him is worse than useless; it is hurtful.

219. Rule 6th. *The consequences of any doctrine are not to be changed on him who maintains it, unless he expressly avows them.* If an absurd consequence be fairly deducible from any doctrine, it is rightly concluded that the doctrine itself is false; but it is not rightly concluded that he who advances it supports the absurd consequence. The charitable presumption, in such case would be, that he had never made the deduction; and that, if he had made it, he would have abandoned the original doctrine.

220. Rule 7th. —A truth, and not victory, is the professed object of controversy, whatever proofs may be advanced, on either side, should be examined with fairness and candor; and any attempt to ensnare an adversary by the arts of sophistry, or to lessen the force of his reasoning, by wit, cavilling, or ridicule, is a violation of the rules of honourable controversy . . . .[28]

∽

SOURCE: Incomplete holograph text at the Fisk University Library. Chesnutt wrote in brackets below the title, "A lecture delivered by C. W. Chesnutt, Prin. St. Normal School at Fayetteville, before the Normal Literary Society, Oct. 1881."

[1]The State Colored Normal School was established in 1877.

[2]Jenny Lind (1820–87), the "Swedish Nightingale," and Adelina Patti (1843–1919) were coloratura sopranos who sang opera; Mary Anderson (1858–1940) was an American actress who gave occasional charity concerts; Marie Smith Williams (c. 1849–1937), whose stage name was "Selika," and the Hyers sisters, Anna Madah (c. 1856–1930's) and Emma Louise (c. 1858–1899), were popular African-American singers who toured Europe and America during the 1870's and 1880's.

[3]Genesis 3:19.

[4]The motto of Captain John Smith while Governor of the Jamestown Colony (1608), based on II Thessalonians 3:10.

[5]Proverbs 19:15.

[6]Chesnutt appears to refer to the U.S. Constitution rather than that of the Normal School in Fayetteville.

[7]Luther Stearns Cushing (1803–56), *Manual of Parliamentary Practice: Rules of Proceeding and Debate in Deliberative Assemblies* (1845); Thomas Jefferson (1743–1826), *A Manual of Parliamentary Practice for the Use of the Senate of the United States* (1801).

[8]Not identified by Chesnutt.

[9]William Cowper (1731–1800), *The Task* (1785). In the manuscript, Chesnutt misattributes these lines to Alexander Pope (1688–1744).

[10]Demosthenes (384?–322 B.C.).

[11]Chesnutt here prompts himself, it seems, to mimic Demosthenes.

[12]Daniel Webster (1782–1852) and Henry Clay (1777–1852), American political figures famous for their oratorical skills.

[13]Johann Christoph Friedrich von Schiller (1759–1805), *Wallenstein* (1799).

[14]Henry Wadsworth Longfellow (1807–82), "A Psalm of Life" (1838).

[15]Thomas Babington Macaulay (1800–1859).

[16]Louis Adolphe Thiers (1797–1877), a French statesman and historian, was the first President of France's Third Republic (1871–73).

[17]Luke 6:39.

[18]Hugh Blair (1718–1800), a Scottish divine and professor of rhetoric at the University of Edinburgh, published his *Lectures on Rhetoric and Belles Lettres* (1783). See Chesnutt's transcriptions in *The Journals of Charles W. Chesnutt*, ed. Brodhead, 93–99.

[19]Proverbs 16:32.

[20]James A. Garfield (1831–81) was shot by Charles J. Guiteau (1841–82) in a Washington train station on 2 July 1881; he died on 19 September 1881. He was succeeded by Vice-President Chester A. Arthur (1830–86).

[21]*Hamlet*, 3.1.79–80.   [22]Proverbs 26:12.

[23]1 Corinthians 13:4.   [24]Matthew 5:23–24.

[25]*Macbeth*, 5.5.31–32.

[26]Thucydides (c. 471–400 B.C.), an Athenian considered the greatest historian of antiquity, wrote a *History of the Peloponnesian War*.

[27]Levi Hedge (1766–1844), *Elements of Logick, or a Summary of the General Principles and Different Modes of Reasoning* (1816). Chesnutt quotes from chapter 16, the paragraphs of which are numbered.

[28]Paragraph 220 (italicized in Hedge's book) was the last in chapter 16; added editorially are the final seven words. Like the conclusion of this speech, they are not present in the incomplete source text.

The Future of the Negro

Speech delivered in Fayetteville, N.C., c. 1882

Friends and Fellow-Citizens:—

We have come together on this occasion to celebrate the emancipation of a people from bondage; to rejoice in the progress which this people have made in their freedom; and to forecast the future—to look forward and see with prophetic vision those future triumphs which the stern and resistless logic of events is slowly, but surely bringing to pass.

Nineteen years ago, the pen of Abraham Lincoln, in the immortal words which you have just heard from the mouth of our distinguished friend, proclaimed to bondmen, that henceforth they were free;[1] and proclaimed to the world that four millions of freemen—not citizens, for the gift of citizenship came later on[2]—that four millions of freemen were to be added to the people of the United States; proclaimed to the world that at last the foul blot which had so long dimmed the lustre of the Stars and Stripes had been wiped out, and that at last our country was to be in fact what it had long been only in name—"The Land of the Free."

It is not my intention to paint to you the horrors of slavery. More eloquent tongues have discoursed upon them; and better men in former years have spent their lives, aye, have even laid down their lives in the endeavor to show to the world this American Institution in its true colors. I represent a new element, another generation. I never saw a slave. Half of the faces that surround me are the faces of those who never felt the weight of the lash—who never bowed under the yoke of bondage. We know slavery only from the traditions of our ancestors. They came up through great tribulation, through the valley of the shadow of death.[3] They can paint to us a picture of horrors from which we turn away in shuddering, and thank and praise God that that age is forever gone by. And to these gray-haired veterans must we of a younger generation look for those lessons of patience and long-suffering which sustained them in their long probation of bondage and fitted them to enjoy the blessings of liberty. Let us honor them and rejoice with them in the Providence that rescued us from servitude!

Abraham Lincoln! Blessed Martyr, thy name shall go down to ages, as the Liberator, the Martyr; the wise statesman who saw the finger of God[4] amid the smoke of the battle and the roar of the cannon, and obeying its behest, broke off the fetters of the slave, and proclaimed him free.

And it is fitting, while we speak of these times, to think of that noble band of heroes, who bore obloquy and shame and death for our sakes. They were not always wise, nor always right; but their very errors sprang from love of us and excess of zeal in our service. Old John Brown, crazy, fanatical and visionary as he was, loved us and gave his life up for us. Charles Sumner suffered, almost died in our service. Garrison, Phillips, Lovejoy, our own Douglass,[5] and a host of others wrought faithfully for us. Their burning words kindled the flame which burst forth and burned away our bonds. And shall we not love them, shall we not honor the living and venerate the dead? Their veriest enemies would call us craven and ingrate did we not. Yes we honor them. Their names shall be our household words. We will hold them up to our children as the brightest examples of heroism, and teach them to emulate their virtues!

And then, fellow-citizens, after the fiat of Freedom had gone forth, after a short period of doubt, as to who and what we were, whether citizens or aliens; whether freemen in fact or only in name; then were we clad with the garb of citizenship; then was placed in our hands the ballot,[6] the bulwark of our liberties at home, and the bayonet, our defence from foreign foes. Even in the bloody conflict itself in its later days, our soldiers showed that slavery had not crushed out the manhood of our race; they showed that black soldiers could face the music and the cannon. Their deeds at Fort Wagner, Milliken's Bend, Port Hudson, Olustee, Helena, Mobile, and Fort Pillow, have been, and will forever be recorded in the pages of impartial history as among the most brilliant exploits of the war.[7]

When the first black regiment went into battle, the world looked on. The enemies of the Negro said he would not fight; and his friends were afraid he would not. But what was the result? Hear the testimony of those who knew.

> Dark as the clouds of even,
> Ranked in the western heaven,

So still and orderly,
Arm to arm, knee to knee,
Waiting the dread event,
Stands the black regiment.

Down the long dusky line,
Teeth gleam and eyeballs shine,
And the bright bayonet
Bristling and finally set,
Flashed with a purpose grand
Waiting till stern command,
Of the fierce rolling drum,
Told them the hour had come
Told them that work was sent,
For the black regiment.

Charge!—Trump and drum awoke
Onward the bondmen broke
Bayonet and sabre-stroke
Vainly opposed their rush
Through the red battle's crush.
On through the flickering brands,
Onward with hundred hands
Down they tear man and horse,
On, in their awful course
Trampling with bloody heel
Over the crushing steel
All their eyes forward bent,
Rushed the Black Regiment.

"Freedom!" their battle-cry
Freedom, or leave to die—
Not then a party shout,
They gave their *spirits* out—
Trusted the end to God,
And on the gory sod,
Rolled in triumphant blood;
Glad to strike one free blow,
Whether for weal or woe;
Glad to breathe one free breath
Though with the lips of death
Wishing alas! in vain
That they might fall again,
Only once more to see,
That burst to liberty.[8]

Fellow-citizens, with such a tribute to the valor of our soldiers, we can well afford to be proud of them. And if our liberties are again assailed, we can look to our own citizen-soldiery, whom we see around us, to march to the front, and show that our people can fight, not only to gain their liberties, but to maintain them. Fellow-citizens, I hope never to see another war—bloody, remorseless, devastating war—but if, in the course of events, our country should be compelled to fight against a foreign foe, there will be one good thing about it—it will give the black man a chance to show the stuff he is made of.

We received the ballot, we became citizens; more than that, we became rulers. With a large proportion of the white race disfranchised,[9] the bottom rail got to the top, and for a while had a fine time. But this was not a natural state of affairs, and it did not last. Our northern white leaders—carpet-baggers they were called—were in many cases men who had no interest in the soil, no interest in good government—except their own interest. Our carpet-bag governments were in many cases sad failures—in South Carolina notably.[10] We lost our power—no matter how—some say because we were not prepared[11] to hold it;—others say that it was wrested wrongly from us. I do not know; I rather suspect it was a combination of the two. The bottom rail found its place again, and is likely to stay at the bottom till it becomes fit to go on top. Fellow-citizens, whatever the politicians may say, you may believe what I say or not, but I believe it—but, in every country, the men who have the intelligence, the will, the education, the money—will rule—by fair means or foul. We may talk of our rights, but we can never enjoy them in full, till we are ready to maintain them.

And now fellow-citizens let us see what the past has done for us, or rather, what we have done in the past. First freedom, then citizenship; the musket, the ballot, the jury-box. The thirteenth, fourteenth and fifteenth amendments confirming us in the enjoyment of our rights. Free speech, free religion, and last but first in importance, free schools. Fellow Citizens, ignorance is the rock we shall always split on, until we have blasted the rock away. Did not the white people know it? Did they not know that the spelling-book would free the slave? Did they not know, " 'Tis better to be much oppressed / Than to but know't a little?"[12] Ay! they knew it, and the spelling-book was padlocked and chained to keep it away from the slave; and the slave was muzzled to keep him away from the spelling-book. We need many things, we need money, for we are poor, and poverty and independence are two horses that will not work well together. We need more religion—true religion; not mere animal excitement, but a better knowledge of God's will, and a better conception of his attributes. But the first thing we need to learn is our own ignorance. Education will open our eyes. Like the magic stone of the Arabian Nights, which revealed to its possessor all the treasures of the earth, it will broaden our views; it will take us out of Fayetteville, out of North Carolina, out of America. It will take us beyond this narrow earth, which to the simple appears so great; and carry us far away to the glittering worlds above us. It will lift us above the mere pleasures of sense, and show us the power and wisdom and majesty of the Creator. The scholar is never proud, for he sees his weakness when compared with infinite power.

We need money; for in common but suggestive language "Money makes the man go."[13] And education will teach us how to make money. It will teach us how to save and to invest money. A very prominent colored man in this country has often advised the colored people to get money. He loves money, and he tells them to get money—honestly if they can—*but* get money. Fellow citizens, follow his advice as far as it is right and then stop. Get money—honestly if you can. If you can't get it honestly, *do without it. Ill-gotten gains never prosper.*[14] I would rather live on a dunghill and die in a ditch, than to live in luxury on money that I had not honestly earned. Get money, for it is useful, but get it by fair means, by honest labor either of head or hand.

The blessings of freedom and education are within our reach, and we may well rejoice in their possession. There are none I think, who would deprive us of them. The wise men of all classes see that the safety of the Republic lies in popular education. The purity of the ballot cannot be maintained without it. Illiteracy is always accompanied by certain evils which are incompatible with liberty or a high state of civilization. Superstition, religious bigotry, tyranny, priest-craft go hand in hand with ignorance; but among an intelligent people they cannot flourish. We find that in those countries where these are national evils, those who profit by them are invariably opposed to popular education. Russia, for instance, with a population consisting largely of emancipated serfs, and no public school system at all, groans under a despotism more intolerable than that which Caesar or any of his imperial successors imposed upon Rome.[15] Turkey, with a false religion, and no pretense at popular education has gone steadily down hill, has grown beautifully less and less,[16] till it will soon be like Germany before the Franco-Prussian war, a "mere geographical expression."[17] Italy and France still suffer from the priest-craft and ignorance to which they have for centuries been condemned. In Mexico, the Central American and South American Republics good government is unknown, on account of the ignorance and worthlessness of the people—the results of priest-craft and the want of schools.[18] The people of America have studied these lessons of history, and they clearly see, that only by popular education, fostered by a system of well-supported, free, public schools can the state be saved from anarchy. Knowing this, all thinking men not only acknowledge our right to an education, but vote to grant us our right. We have in North Carolina our fair proportion of the school monies. We have our Normal Schools, which, I should say, if I were not an interested party are doing good service in the cause of education. The high schools and colleges open to our youth are filled with earnest seekers after knowledge.

Of the blessing of liberty none can deprive us, and we fondly believe none would deprive us. Slavery was the curse of the South. Not only four millions of blacks but the whole population of the South were emancipated by this proclamation which you have heard read. It was a rude awakening. The diseased member was not amputated without pain. Even yet the South has not recovered from her loss of blood and treasure. But as her strength returns, and her waste places are built up,[19] she sees her prosperity will rest upon a solid, a permanent basis. Freemen are less expensive to the State than slaves, and wise men see it.

And now fellow citizens, having dwelt at length upon the past, let us for a moment, cast our eyes toward the future, and see what prospects are opening before us. Let no one think that we have finished our work. We have scarce begun it, and the greater part is yet to do.

We have civil liberty, and political equality—that is to say, we are equal so far as the laws of the United States can make us so. But it is still within the power of the States individually to make many unjust discriminations. These are the laws which require the white and colored people to be kept apart, which forbid them to intermarry, etc.

The honorable Frederick Douglass remarked the other day at the Atheneum Club in Boston, that the greatest thing that the colored race had obtained in this country is the recognition of their manhood—not the recognition of their equality, for this is conceded by but few of the dominant race. When the question was asked before the war, why do you hold the Negroes in slavery, the answer was often made, God put them in slavery, we didn't, "the Lord's will be done." Well God made them free, but "God's will be done" was not so often heard. We ask now, why are we set aside, and marked as an inferior and unclean race? And the answer comes, "God made you so." God made us all. With Him there is no respect of persons,[20] and he will in his own good time compel the world to acknowledge our manhood and equality.

But we must do our part. And here let me say, fellow-citizens that social equality is something that cannot be forced. The law can give us our political and civil rights and protect us in the exercise of them. But no man can compel us to associate with those we do not like. I am no socialist, no social equality theorist. I can think of nothing more disagreeable than for all men to be equal, unless indeed all men could be equally good. When the Millennium comes we may hope for this, but not sooner. But what I long for, and hope and pray for is the time when a man's social position and success in life will not depend upon his race or complexion. We do not want equality, but we want an equal chance. We want a fair start. When one of our young men wants to enter College, we do not want the doors shut in his face with, "You are too black." When a colored man runs for an office we do not want him voted down because he is not white. No, fellow-citizens, we simply want to be treated like other men, no better, no worse.

And what shall we do in the future to bring about this golden age? For we must do our part. Much prejudice must be wiped out. Much knowledge must be gained. What can we do to bring it about?

I have said that the people who have the education, the intelligence, the money, the will, are bound to rule. Then in order for us to rule, or to be among the rulers, we must have intelligence, the education, the money and the *will*. The figures of the late census show that God has abundantly blessed the colored people in one respect; they have increased and multiplied far beyond the expectation of any one. It was predicted that the Negro would languish in freedom.

That he could not live without the kind care of the master, the invigorating lash of the overseer, and the annual excitement of auction-block. Could men believe such things? That a beneficent Creator would make a race of men so mean that they could not enjoy that liberty which even the fowls of the air and the fishes of the sea delight in?[21] Ay! Men believed this and many other things under the influence of slavery. But time has falsified their theories. The Negro flourishes, and increases so fast, that it has been predicted that a hundred years hence, the whole of the Gulf States will be under his control. That is to say he will have the numbers; all that remains for him to do is to get the education, the money, the character.

I have spoken of the importance of education. It is first in order, if not first in importance. In order to understand our rights we must know how to read and understand the laws. Suppose an election were held to vote for a railroad appropriation or something of the kind? How would a man know whether he should vote for or against unless he could read the arguments? It is true he could follow the politicians; but alas! experience has shown that these are not always safe leaders. A wise man will see and know and act for himself, and only follow the advice of others when he can make it accord with his own convictions.

We must not only be educated in books. We must be educated in character. Go out on the road there and watch the carts pass. You will see a colored man go by. Perhaps he will be ragged and dirty; his clothes tied up with strings; his head sticking through his hat. His shoes—well don't talk about them. Now, wait a minute—here comes a poor white man. He's just as poor perhaps poorer than the colored man. But his shirt is clean. His clothes are whole, or at least neatly mended. His hat, his shoes, though coarse and common are whole and clean.

Now the colored man is not always dirty nor the white man always clean. But it is frequently the case. Now why is it that the colored man is content with his rags and dirt? It is because he has never been taught that self respect requires him to be clean. He would be very angry if any one should call him a dirty fellow and no gentleman. But that would be true. The colored man must be educated in character. He must learn to respect himself, to keep clean. To be on time. To keep his engagements. Our people will set a meeting at ten o'clock and come at twelve. They will make an engagement for Monday and come on Wednesday. Do you want a job of work done? Go down the street, find a workman; button hole him; take him with you, sit down there by him till he gets through, and then pay him half what he charges you. Gentlemen, present company is always excepted, this is not intended to apply to the workmen here, to-day, but it has been my experience.

Now in order to succeed, to respect themselves and to inspire respect in others, our people must be educated out of these and many other similar faults. And this will be a work of time.

We must get money; and how are we to get it? Fellow-citizens, I see but one way—we must work for it. God has given us broad backs, strong arms, and by using them we can get money. God has given us good minds, and when they are cultivated we can use them to advantage. I believe that the main hope of the colored people at present lies in agriculture—the cotton and the corn. Who are the people who send their sons to college, and make them lawyers and doctors and merchants? The farmers. The colored man understands this work, and he can make more at it now than at any thing else.

I wish to call your attention to a peculiar people, a remarkable people. Two hundred years ago and less, the Jews were oppressed far worse than the colored people are anywhere. (Specify.)[22] Now they are the richest people on earth. How was it?

They bought and sold—they went into trade, and became a race of traders. Did you ever see a Jewish lawyer or doctor or farmer or carpenter or anything else except a merchant? Very seldom. And did you ever see a Jewish drunkard? One in a thousand. Did you ever know a Jew to be in jail? Did you ever see a ragged Jew? No; or at least not often. They are a steady, economical people. They work hard, after their way, and save what they make. They get money in their purse and they snap their fingers at prejudice.

And so it will be with the colored people. When the great newspapers are conducted by colored editors, when colored lawyers and doctors and authors and poets are of world-wide fame; when colored men have seats in the stock exchange; when colored men own steamboats and build railroads, and have a controlling voice in the money market, then men will not even want to deny their equality.

Friends and fellow citizens, I shall not longer weary your patience. These things will surely be. I believe that right here, where God permitted our degradation, he will exalt us; that this land which saw us slaves, shall see us honored of men. We must be patient and wait. And above all, we must work; not each for himself alone, but one for all, and all together. Let us fight for the right, and against the wrong.

> Fight against Ignorance,
> This is our greatest foe,
> She on the field of death,
> Hath laid her thousands low.
>
> Cut down the hydra *vice*,
> Crafty and bold is she,
> Always be vigilant,
> Faithful and valiant be.

↰

SOURCE: Undated holograph text at the Fisk University Library. Chesnutt's reference to the Emancipation Proclamation as having been made 19 years earlier suggests the delivery of this speech in Fayetteville, N.C., in 1881 or 1882.

[1]Abraham Lincoln (1809–65) issued his Emancipation Proclamation on 22 Septem-

ber 1862, after the Battle of Antietam; but it was not until 1 January 1863 that it was formally signed into law.

[2]Citizenship was extended to African Americans by the Fourteenth Amendment in 1868.

[3]Psalms 23:4.

[4]Exodus 31:18.

[5]That is, Frederick Douglass (1817–95). Abolitionist John Brown (1800–1859) was hanged on 2 December 1859 for seizing the government arsenal at Harper's Ferry, Va., in an effort to incite a slave insurrection. Charles Sumner (1811–74) was a U.S. Senator from Massachusetts who led the attack against slavery in the Congress. William Lloyd Garrison (1805–79) was the publisher of *The Liberator*, through which he vented his radical anti-slavery views from 1831 to the end of the Civil War. Wendell Phillips (1811–84) was a distinguished anti-slavery orator. Elijah Parish Lovejoy (1802–37), the "Martyr Abolitionist," was killed by a mob on 7 November 1837.

[6]The right to vote was extended by the Fifteenth Amendment in 1870.

[7]Chesnutt refers to the battles at Fort Wagner, S.C., Milliken's Bend, La., Port Hudson, La., Olustee, Fla., Helena, Ark., Mobile, Ala., and Fort Pillow, Tenn.

[8]Quoted are the first four stanzas, part of the fifth, and none of the sixth stanza of "The Black Regiment" in *Poems of the War* (1864) by George Henry Boker (1823–90). The poem commemorates the Battle of Port Hudson, 27 May 1863, in which two regiments—composed of free blacks of French extraction (the First Louisiana Native Guards) and former slaves (the Third Louisiana Native Guards)—participated.

[9]Numerous Southern whites associated with the Confederacy were deprived by the Congress of the franchise and could not hold office immediately after the Civil War.

[10]Though the South Carolina state legislature ratified the Thirteenth Amendment, which abolished slavery, on 13 November 1865, it reconvened later that month to establish a code which minutely regulated the activities of the freedmen.

[11]Chesnutt originally used the word "fit"; he then canceled it and wrote "prepared" above the line and "competent" below the line.

[12]*Othello*, 3.3.336–37, in which "abused," rather than "oppressed," is the reading.

[13]Chesnutt modifies the maxim "Money makes the mare go."

[14]Charles Lamb, "Popular Fallacies," *The Last Essays of Elia* (1833); "Ill-Gotten Gains Never Prosper" is the title of its second section.

[15]Though the Russian serfs had been emancipated by Tsar Alexander II (1818–81) in 1861, the 1881–94 reign of his successor and son, Alexander III (1845–94), was an autocratic and harsh one. Tsar, like Kaiser in German, is derived from the Latin "Caesar," the actual name or title of the series of Roman emperors who succeeded Gaius Julius Caesar (102?–44 B.C.).

[16]In 1877, Turkey, an Islamic nation, was invaded by Russian troops eager to seize land viewed as rightly belonging to Russia. By 1885 the Ottoman Empire had lost Serbia, Rumania, Bulgaria, Montenegro, eastern Rumelia, Egypt, Cyprus, Tunis, and Thessaly.

[17]Paraphrase of statement by Klemens Wenzel Nepomak, Prince von Metternich (1773–1859), in a 19 November 1849 letter: "Italy is a [mere] geographical expression." Prior to the Franco-Prussian War (1870–71), Germany was a similarly disparate entity comprised of twenty-six states held together under the leadership of an emperor.

[18]While, earlier in this paragraph, priest-craft refers generically to the manipulation of a society by any kind of religious authority-figures, here Chesnutt more specifically reflects the contemporaneous Protestant-American point of view regarding the negative influence of clerics in all Roman Catholic countries.

[19]Isaiah 61:4.

[20]Conflated here, and in later nonfiction writings by Chesnutt, are two verses from Acts: that God is no respecter of persons (10:34); and that He of one blood made all the nations of the earth (17:26).

[21]Genesis 1:26.

[22]Here Chesnutt apparently cited examples of the persecution of Jews, referred to as "a peculiar people" in Deuteronomy 14:2.

Self-Made Men

Speech to the Normal Literary Society, Fayetteville, N.C., 10 March 1882

Mind is superior to matter. On the sixth day of the Creation, when the land and water had been separated, when the fish of the sea, the fowls of the air, the grass, the herb, cattle and all creeping things had been created and pronounced good; when the whole material universe had been evolved from the Divine mind, and placed under the control of immutable laws of growth and development; then the Creator, in his allwise providence said: "Let us make man, in our own image, after our likeness, and let them have dominion over the fish of the sea, and over the fowl of the air, and over the cattle, and over *all the earth*. And God saw everything he had made and behold, it was very good."[1]

God made man in his own image—not in his corporeal likeness; for God is a spirit, and does not, that we know, take on any visible, certainly no material form: but in his spiritual image. God planted in the heart of man the germ of immortality—the thinking, reasoning mind, which distinguishes him from inanimate things and from the brute creation. It is the immortal mind working up through the flesh, with which the Creator saw fit to cumber it, to the absolute, the ideal of perfection, that has enabled man to subdue the world. Observing the phenomena of nature, man has generalized them, classified them, sought out their hidden laws, and learned to control and use them for his own purposes.

By means of his great inventions he has conquered space, and the phrase, "with the speed of thought" has become a reality. Men have subdued the ocean; their stout vessels weather the severest storm; divers, clad in impervious armor, descend to the caves of ocean, and bring up its treasures; the mountains are torn open to afford passage to our steam cars. Fire, air, water, lightning, sound, all are brought under the control of man and made to minister to his wants. Truly, the fiat of the Creator is accomplished, and man has dominion "over all the earth."[2]

What is true of mind in the abstract is true of mind in the concrete; what is true of mankind is true of nations and of individuals. Some nations have developed higher powers of mind, and have dominated, by intellectual force, the rest of the world. The influence of the minds of Athens will always be felt in Art and Literature; the mental energy of Rome will always live in civil law and military science; while the influence of the Hebrew intellect, as exhibited in the Bible, has furnished, by the inspiration of God, those principles of justice and mercy, and charity which form the basis of modern civilization.

As nations have displayed superior powers of mind, so in every nation there are individuals whose mental ability and energy distinguish them from the common herd. And there is no part of History more fascinating or instructive than the biographies of eminent men, who show in the highest degree the development of the divine power of intellect, and its dominion over matter. The lives of great men are the landmarks of History, and we can best understand and remember it by grouping the events of an age about the lives of its heroes.[3]

But the class of men in whose lives we feel the most intense interest, is that class who are commonly known as "self-made men," men who, with few opportunities, few adventitious advantages, have exhibited the development of mind under what seemed to be insurmountable difficulties. When we see a youth, the son of wealthy parents, surrounded by the refinements of art and taste; with every advantage for intellectual culture;—when we see such a youth rise to a high station in life, we feel no wonder,—we expect it of him. He has only used his opportunities; we should have been surprised had it happened otherwise. But when we see a youth, born in poverty, cradled in obscurity;— when we see such a youth rise superior to his coarse surroundings, and vulgar associations, and, overcoming all obstacles, by sheer force of intellect and will attaining to a high rank in life; then we instinctively pause to admire, and rejoice in the power of mind.

Every age has produced some such men, but our own has been most prolific of them. The general diffusion of knowledge through the medium of cheap books and free schools, has placed the world's accumulated stores of knowledge within reach of the humblest. The recognition of the doctrine of human equality has given opportunity and impulse to the lower orders for their upward strivings. It has broken down the walls of the old aristocracy, which once monopolized power and position, and gave no place to merit in a lower rank in life. The tendency of the present age is toward the aristocracy of merit—nature's aristocracy. Some of the greatest men of the century are those who have fought hardest for fame and fortune. Lord Beaconsfield, the late Prime Minister of England, and the great Tory leader, was a Jew—and during the last century a Jew in Europe was treated worse than a Negro in America. But he conquered the prejudice and rose to the head of the British nation. Gambetta, the leading, recently deceased statesman of France was a Jew. Von Moltke the German Minister of War is a Jew.[4]

Our own country is most prolific of self-made men. Its history may almost be called the history of self-made men. Our Franklin, great in philosophy and diplomacy; our Taylor and Burritt in literature; our Garrison and Douglass in the Anti-slavery cause;[5] our Lincoln in "the time that tried men's souls";[6] our Grant, who led the Union armies to victory; our Vanderbilt (the Commodore), Stewart, and many others are bright examples of the kind of men America can produce.[7]

The fact that our country has given birth to so many such men is due to several causes. First, our political system, which leaves the highest positions within reach of the lowest. With the goal of office, of satisfied ambition before him, the American youth will strain every nerve to attain it. Our doctrine of free speech gives men opportunity to discuss in the public press every question of law, of government, of politics; and in consequence there is a general dissemination of such knowledge which does much to quicken thought and inspire effort. Our free school system has made knowledge the common heritage of the masses. In the Middle Ages, books were the property of the few. The learning of the world was locked up in monasteries and palaces, while the common people were ignorant of all but the knowledge necessary to carry on their dull round of toil. The effect of free schools may be seen in the fact that those sections of the country where they are best supported have produced more in art, science and literature than other sections. New England has done most; the South, least.

The extent of our territory, and the variety of our productions have given every man opportunity to acquire wealth or a competence. In most countries of Europe the land is held in large estates by rigid laws of entail, and the agricultural population are compelled to a life of villainage. But such is the extent of our territory and the cheapness of land, that every man may own a home, and by industry and economy, become wealthy and independent.

Our mines have been the source of wealth to many. The two richest mine-owners in America—Flood and O'Brien, were common Irish miners, but they struck a rich vein of ore, and are now among the magnates of the land.[8]

It is the combination of all these elements—a free government, equality before the law, free speech, free schools, the extent of our territory, our agricultural and mineral resources,—that make up our peculiar social system. When wealth, office, fame are open to all, then the most worthy will grasp them. Emancipated from unequal laws and artificial social restrictions, *brain must predominate*; and the history of self-made men is the history of the triumph of intellect.

To illustrate the process by which such men rise to eminence, and to encourage those of our own youth who may feel the fire of genius, or the thirst for knowledge in their bosoms, I have selected two names from the long list of eminent Americans of this class, Frederick Douglass, and Horace Greeley.[9] Many names eminent in church, state, and commerce might be added, but these two men are among those who have done the most with the fewest advantages; men who were not the product of the schools, but who were in the strictest sense of the word self-made men. Another reason why I have selected these names is because I presume very few of you are acquainted with the facts in the life of either of them. In speaking of these men, I shall first give a short sketch of the life of each, and then try to discover what were the qualities which made these men more than others—what was the secret of their success.

Frederick Douglass, the distinguished orator and journalist was born in Tuckahoe, near Easton, Md. His father was a white man, his mother a Negro slave. He was reared upon the plantation of his brother, Edwin Lloyd, until ten years old, when he was transferred to a relative of his owner in Baltimore. Here he worked in a ship-yard, and taught himself to read and write. In his autobiography,[10] published a few year's since, Mr. Douglass gives an interesting account of his first learning to write. He had an insatiable thirst for knowledge, and an ardent desire for freedom, as soon as he was old enough to perceive the cruel wrong of slavery. At the age of twenty-one he escaped on a vessel to New York and thence to New Bedford, Mass. (a free state), where he married a free woman of color. Here he worked as a laborer until 1841, when he attended an Anti-slavery convention, and spoke so eloquently of the evils of slavery—at this time he was twenty-four years old—that the Anti-slavery society employed him to lecture throughout the free states. He lectured four years with great success, easily winning the reputation of a brilliant orator. According to a friend of mine who heard him speak in those early days, when his heart was overflowing with sympathy for his enslaved brethren and indignation toward those who held them, his power as an orator was unequalled. He understood the dictum of Demosthenes: "Action."[11] His voice was strong but exquisitely modulated. He could melt his audience to tears, as he pictured in glowing words the sufferings of the slave, and fire the Northern heart with holy zeal in the cause of freedom.

In 1845 Mr. Douglass published his autobiography, or story of his life. In 1846 he accepted an invitation to lecture in Great Britain. He did so with great success, and while there, besides his salary and expenses a sum of 150 pounds ($750) was made up for him to purchase his freedom. He had been practically but not legally free. Returning to America he established at Rochester, New York, *Frederick Douglass's Paper* which was for a number of years an exponent of Abolitionism and did valuable service in building up the growing anti-slavery sentiment of the North. In 1855 he republished his autobiography under the title *My Bondage and My Freedom*. Continuing his labors as orator and editor Mr. Douglass had at last the satisfaction of seeing the freedom of the slave accomplished, and of knowing that he had contributed his share toward it.

In common with other Abolition leaders, Mr. Douglass at the close of the war found, like Othello, "his occupation gone."[12] But his fame and talents could not permit him to remain in obscurity. He received invitations to lecture to college societies and lyceums, and the ball once set in motion, he soon had plenty to do. By the advice of his friends, he established a paper at Washington, *The New National Era*, which he edited for a number of years, and at last discontinued for want of sufficient support.

Mr. Douglass has held since that time a prominent place in the eyes of the country as a representative colored man. In 1871, during Grant's Administration, he was Secretary to the Santo Domingo Commission. In 1872 he was a Presidential Elector for the State of New York. Under the administration of President Hayes he was appointed to the honorable and lucrative office of U.S. Marshal for the District of Columbia.[13] Under President Garfield he was made Register of Deeds for the District, which office he now holds.

In person Mr. Douglass is tall and well-proportioned. He is of an olive complexion[14] and his hair and beard, both very full, a snowy white. He has a prominent nose, and very bright deep-set eyes. I had the pleasure of hearing him speak on two separate occasions, a year or two ago—once in an Agricultural, and once in a political speech. He held the audience spell-bound for several hours. He had lost none of his old-time power, and the audience were alternately moved to laughter by his wit, or tears by his pathos. My heart swelled with pride and happiness as I saw the veteran abolitionist stand before an audience, half of former slave-holders, in a State where he once would have been hunted by bloodhounds or sold on the auction block.[15] They felt his power, and I felt that God in his providence had indeed wrought a mighty change in this land of ours. The slave had become the master, and his eloquence was a mightier power than the lash, and the bloodhound, and all the machinery of unholy laws. They felt his power; and grim governors and sleek senators laughed or wept with the varying mood of the speaker. (Anecdote of the Irishman: "What would a whole naygur do?")[16]

In addition to his labors as orator and journalist, Mr. Douglass has been a frequent contributor to the periodical press of the country. His style is simple, nervous and replete with wit and wisdom, and his productions all well worth reading. He now resides in a handsome residence at Washington, adorned with choice paintings and statuary. He holds a lucrative public office, and has a fortune of one hundred thousand dollars—a fine example of a man who has spent a useful life, and enjoys the reward of a peaceful and honored old age.

Another Eminent American whose career was in some respects similar to that of Mr. Douglass, was Horace Greeley the famous journalist, and founder of the *New York Tribune*. In their thirst for knowledge, their steady perseverance, their uncompromising hostility to slavery, Mr. Greeley and Mr. Douglass were alike. But the genius of Mr. Greeley fitted him to mold public opinion through the press, while Mr. Douglass best reached men's hearts and minds from the platform. With the outline facts in the life of Horace Greeley most of you, I presume, are familiar, and I only repeat them here for the better illustration of my subject.

Horace Greeley was born at Amherst, N.H., February 3, 1811. At an early age, he developed a remarkable fondness for books. At two years of age he began to study the newspapers given him to play with, and at four years, it is said, could read anything that was placed before him. (It is not to be supposed that he could read everything correctly or understandingly, but he could pronounce the words, and get a general idea—could read, in fact, as children generally do. Reading is the culmination of all other sciences. To read well requires a very extensive education.) At six, it is said, he could spell any word in the English language, had read the entire Bible, and knew something of Geography and Arithmetic. As he grew older, his love for books grew stronger. His parents were very poor,—his father was an unprosperous farmer and could not afford to do more than send him to the country schools near his home—a poor chance for an education, as all who have attended or taught them well know. A few prominent men in the neighborhood offered to pay his expenses at college, but the offer was refused—some think because the boy or his parents were too proud to accept charity,—others, because the family needed his labor at home. At any rate he never had a college education,—which was a great pity, for such a mind as his ought to have had the best education the country could afford.

During this period of his life, while working on his father's farm, Mr. Greeley exhibited the same qualities which distinguished him in after life. He never shirked or slighted any task, but did properly and well whatever the family needs required, mindful of the Scripture injunction, "Whatsoever thy hand findeth to do, do it with thy might."[17]

At the age of fifteen his love of books induced him to learn the printer's trade. He entered the office of the *Northern Spectator* at East Poultney, Vt., where he soon became an expert workman. He learned the trade almost without effort, by intuition, as he had learned to read in his infancy. He received the magnificent salary of forty dollars a year, the greater part of which he sent to his father, who had moved to Pennsylvania, and was as poor as ever.

In 1831, the *Spectator* failed, and he determined to seek his fortune in New York.[18] His worldly goods were tied up in a handkerchief, and slung over his shoulder. His cash capital amounted to ten dollars. The struggle for life in large cities is intense. For every place that is empty there are a hundred applicants; and many a weary day passed, while his ten dollars grew "beautifully less and less," before our hero found employment. His appearance was not prepossessing. A long, gawky, stoop-shouldered country lad, with short trousers, and no stockings to cover the gap between them and the coarse brogans which adorned his extremities; a short linen jacket, and a slouch hat completed his costume. He was a diamond in the rough, and required a great deal of polishing before the world would recognize his value.

But "*Perseverantia vincit*,"[19] and his perseverance was at last rewarded—with employment. Diligence, honesty, and ability won him a ready rise. As soon as he had money enough, he set out as editor of the *Morning Post*, a short-lived penny paper; afterwards of the *New Yorker*, which was very successful; the *Log Cabin*, a very popular campaign sheet, advocating the election of General Harrison[20] to the Presidency,—and lastly, the *New York Tribune*, the great journal which brought him wealth and fame.

The most marked feature of the *Tribune*, was the individuality of Horace

Greeley, which was shown on every page. He was greatly interested in Agriculture, and in the course of his life, delivered many lectures on this subject, in different parts of the country. He published two agricultural works, one on farming, and one on turnip-culture.[21] He spent his leisure time on his farm at Chappaqua, N.Y., where he carried on his experiments in agriculture.

Mr. Greeley was devoted to the building up of home manufactures. He was always in favor of a high tariff, because it encouraged the diversification of our national industries. Canals, railroads, and all labor-saving inventions were advocated by Mr. Greeley in the columns of the *Tribune*.

Remembering his own struggles, he was the friend of aspiring youth. Bayard Taylor, Whitelaw Reid,[22] and many other literary men who have since attained to eminence, owed their first start to the friendship of Horace Greeley. It was a famous saying . . . .

↬

SOURCE: Incomplete holograph text at the Fisk University Library. Chesnutt wrote below the title, "A lecture, delivered before the Normal Literary Society, Fayetteville N.C. Friday night, March 10th, 1882, by *C. W. Chesnutt*."

[1]Genesis 1:6–31.

[2]Daniel 4:22.

[3]Chesnutt here participates in the Hegelian "hero-worship" mentality of the nineteenth century, making evident the direct or indirect influence of Scottish historian and philosopher Thomas Carlyle (1795–1881): "The history of the world is but the biography of great men" (*On Heroes, Hero-Worship, and the Heroic in History*, 1841). American poet and essayist Ralph Waldo Emerson (1803–82) was of a like mind. See his *Representative Men* (1850), particularly the essay "On the Uses of Great Men," for another influential example of belief in the notion that the superior individual, rather than the "common herd," shapes history.

[4]Benjamin Disraeli (1804–81) was the first Earl of Beaconsfield; a novelist, member of Parliament,and intimate friend of Queen Victoria, he served twice as the Prime Minister of England. Léon Gambetta (1838–82); Count Helmuth Von Moltke (1800–1891).

[5]Benjamin Franklin (1706–90). Bayard Taylor (1825–78) was a journalist, poet, novelist, and travel writer, now best known for his translation of Goethe's *Faust* (1870–71). In 1882, he was a widely recognized poet, the "laureate of the Gilded Age." Elihu Burritt (1810–79) enjoyed the sobriquet of "the learned blacksmith" because he was a self-educated linguist, journalist, pacifist lecturer, and travel writer.

[6]Chesnutt paraphrases the opening line of the first essay in *The American Crisis* series (1776) written by Thomas Paine (1737–1809) in support of the American Revolution.

[7]Ulysses S. Grant (1822–85). Cornelius Vanderbilt (1794–1877) developed a shipping line and railroad system, accumulating a $100,000,000 estate. Alexander T. Stewart (1803–76) established in 1862 the first department store in the United States and then developed it into the largest retail enterprise of the kind in the world—sold in 1896 to John Wanamaker (1835–1922).

[8]James C. Flood (1826–89) and William S. O'Brien (1826–78) met in San Francisco in 1849, after the gold rush had begun. They opened a saloon frequented by stockbrokers, entered the brokerage business themselves, gained control of Nevada mines, and were soon multimillionaires. The bank they formed became Wells Fargo.

[9]Horace Greeley (1811–72).

[10]Douglass wrote three autobiographies: *Narrative of the Life of Frederick Douglass, an American Slave* (1845), *My Bondage and My Freedom* (1855), and *Life and Times of Frederick Douglass* (1881; expanded version, 1892).

[11]The comparison of Douglass with Demosthenes is intended not only to suggest that Douglass was one of the greatest speakers in history but that both were equally significant as opponents of oppression: Demosthenes, in his Philippics, urged Athenians to action against the expansionist and anti-democratic Philip of Macedon (382–336 B.C.).

[12]*Othello*, 3.3.373.

[13]Rutherford B. Hayes (1822–93) served as U.S. president from 1877 to 1881.

[14]Chesnutt originally wrote "bright yellow color," a then-commonplace way of describing a relatively fair mulatto.

[15]Chesnutt heard Douglass speak in behalf of presidential candidate James A. Garfield and against the Democratic hegemony in North Carolina, transcribing the speech for publication as "Why Should the South Be Solidly Democratic?" in a weekly newspaper published by the Republican State Committee, the *Raleigh Signal*, 7 October 1880, 2. Douglass therein referred to the other speech he delivered earlier in the day at the Raleigh fairgrounds: "I came here" not to make a political speech but "to address the colored people on the subject of agriculture, and the means of their elevation." Chesnutt heard both speeches on the same day.

[16]The anecdote intended as comical is keyed to the mulatto status of Douglass.

[17]Ecclesiastes 7:10.

[18]The source text reads "1821"; this newspaper failed in 1830, and Greeley went to New York in 1831.

[19]Perseverance conquers all obstacles.

[20]William Henry Harrison (1773–1841), elected U.S. President in 1840.

[21]*What I Know of Farming* (1871). While Greeley won the second prize for turnips at the New York State Fair in 1854, he is not known to have published a monograph on turnip-culture.

[22]Whitelaw Reid (1837–1912) was a journalist who wrote on the Civil War and the South during the Reconstruction; a selection of his articles was published in *After the War* (1866). He became managing editor of the *New York Tribune* in 1869 and, after Greeley's death, controlled it until 1905.

Methods of Teaching

Speech to the North Carolina State Teachers Educational
Association, Raleigh, N.C., 23 November 1882

The term *education*, in its narrowest and most generally accepted use, signifies merely the training of the intellect, and the acquiring of those first principles of knowledge which are taught in our schools and commonly supposed to be the best preparation for the work of life. A broader and better definition of its meaning is, the drawing out or unfolding of all the faculties of intellect, body and conscience or the moral sense, in a harmonious and well-balanced development, giving to each faculty its due proportion of training, regarding no one attribute of the man as superior, but holding each to be supreme in its sphere, and all equally necessary to a perfect whole.[1]

Taking this meaning of the word, a perfect theory of education must rest upon, 1st, a perfect mental philosophy; 2d, a perfect physiology; 3rd, a perfect system of ethics; and, 4th, a right conception of the true end of existence. These four parts would constitute a perfect anthropology, or science of the whole man. That we have them all, few would be willing to affirm; and until we have them, we must be content with imperfect theories and imperfect methods. While we cannot look upon modern methods of culture as perfect, we can with justice believe that they have partaken of the general advance of civilization. "History," it has been said, "is philosophy teaching by example";[2] and the student will find this truth as applicable to the history of education as to government, or arts, or morals, or any department of life.

In primitive ages education was purely physical. Men taught their sons to hunt and fish and gather the fruits of the forest. Later they learned to till the soil, to tend flocks and herds, to make clothing and tents, and to fashion rude pottery. Moral instruction was given at a very early period, and, as we learn from Holy Writ, the domestic affections,—the duties of parents and children, and of husband and wife,—and a simple form of monotheism, were inculcated from the creation of man.[3] A rude, symbolic worship, including burnt offerings and sacrifices was known to the sons of Adam.[4] The Patriarch was prophet, priest, and king,[5] and without doubt his children were instructed by him in the duties of these offices.

With the growth of civilization, man's wants became more numerous and diversified. Politics had to be studied in order that rulers might govern well; military science, in order that wars might be successfully carried on; and in every department of life, each new need called for a new class of workers to supply it.

This knowledge was of course very crude, and the methods of acquiring it purely experimental. Men learned war on the battle-field, and not at military schools; they learned theology in the temple, not at the seminary; they learned architecture with the rule and the compass, and not in industrial and polytechnic schools. This method of learning had its advantages, which, somehow or other we cannot even now secure by any other but the same old methods. "*Iter longum per præcepta est,*" says Seneca, "*breve et efficax per exempla,*" the road is long by precept, but short and efficacious by example.[6]

Learning then, in primitive ages, was chiefly, if not entirely, for its practical value. Useless learning is, indeed, not desirable at any time; but it remained for the men of another age to discover that truth is valuable in itself, and to devote themselves to learning, simply for the love of truth and the desire to find it out. This intellectual revolution took place in Greece. The Athenian philosophers are the first who merit the title of Teachers, and the influence of their philosophy is felt in every department of science down to the present day. They were the first to realize that education is not merely a preparation for life, but an integral part of it; that development is the highest duty and privilege of man, and that whatever promotes development is valuable—is indeed invaluable in a system of education.

Socrates, of all the Grecian philosophers, has the greatest claim to the title *educator*. It was his plan to draw out truth by questioning and analogies. His method is still in use among teachers, and is known as the Socratic, or drawing-out method. Socrates exerted a powerful influence on Greek thought, and broke the power of the Sophists, a school of false philosophers, whose theories had long enslaved the Greek intellect, and his mind went out beyond the limit of material things, and caught glimpses of the power and goodness of the one true God; as a traveller sees through intervening mists the majestic outline of a distant mountain. Socrates was in advance of his age, and paid the penalty with his life.[7]

Plato, "the broad," the pupil of Socrates, was the first to lay down a theory of education. In his *Republic* and *Laws* he sets forth a complete scheme of an ideal government, in which the children are the property of the State whose duty it was to educate them.[8] He believed infancy the most important period of life, as the impressions then made were never effaced. The studies he used to cultivate the mind were arithmetic, geometry, philosophy, music, rhetoric, declamation, poetical composition, the principles of taste, and morals.

The "foremost man of all the Greeks" was Aristotle, the pupil of Socrates, and tutor of Alexander the Great. Aristotle was the founder of the Peripatetic school of philosophy.[9] He taught dialectics, physical science, philosophy, politics, ethics, and rhetoric. His vast learning attracted pupils from all parts of the world, and his philosophy soon superseded that of all former teachers and held undisputed sway over the intellectual world for twenty centuries. Aristotle was the first to reduce dialectics or logic to a science. He invented the syllogism, the magic key which has unlocked so many of the mysteries of mind and matter. His treatise of *Politics* contained a theory of education which was a further development of the doctrines of his master Plato.

But perhaps Aristotle rendered the greatest service to the intellectual world, not by his original researches, but by his labors in another direction. He was an intellectual architect. He systematized learning. He gathered up the scattered fragments of science and fitted them together into a harmonious whole. He was among philosophers what Shakspeare was among poets, and Napoleon among generals.[10] So rounded and complete did his system seem, that nineteen centuries later, when Scheiner, a German student of astronomy, informed his master that he had seen spots on the sun, he was dismissed as follows: "I have read Aristotle's works from end to end many times, and I assure you I do not find anything in them similar to that which you mention. Go, my son, tranquilize yourself; be assured that what you take for spots are the faults of either your glasses or your own eyes."[11]

Aristotle gave instruction in the form of lectures, which he delivered while walking in a pleasant grove near Athens, called Academia.[12] He was accompanied in these walks by his pupils who took notes and propounded queries—very much after the fashion in which instruction is given in the higher scientific and professional studies at the present day.

With the death of Aristotle the race of great philosophers disappeared. There were schools of philosophy and dialectics at Alexandria and Athens for several centuries later, but they added nothing material to the sum of human knowledge.

The Roman Empire added little to the purely intellectual progress of mankind. Its influence was distributive, rather than productive. The empire was almost entirely under the sway of the Greek learning, which was spread throughout its borders. In agriculture and jurisprudence the Romans made great progress, and by the patronage of the best emperors, many great literary works were given to the world. The emperor Marcus Aurelius, the Stoic philosopher, wrote on educational topics and established schools for orphans.[13]

The next great influence felt in the world of learning was that of Christianity, which for many years lighted up the declining glory of Rome. The early church produced many great men among the early fathers, but the growth of the papal system soon caused ignorance and superstition to settle like a nightmare over the face of Europe and brought on the period of a thousand years of mental and moral stagnation known as the Dark Age. During this period the study of the classics was discontinued in the schools; theology, church history, and the scholastic philosophy were the principal subjects of study; and learning was confined almost entirely to the priesthood. Men lived, and studied, and died—and left the world no better than they found it.

With the discovery of America and the invention of the art of printing, a ray of light broke upon the intellectual darkness of Europe. The Protestant Reformation, pioneered by Martin Luther, was the next step toward the light.[14]

Under the policy of the Roman Church—its policy to-day—the masses were kept in ignorance. The Bible was held to be "strong meat, not fit for babes."[15] It was therefore kept from the common people, and read by the priests only. When Luther in his famous theses proclaimed the right of the masses to read the Scriptures, it was a necessary corollary that they must be taught in order to know how to read them.[16] He discarded the scholastic philosophy, and insisted on the development of thought and the culture of the reasoning powers by new methods. By means of his teachings and those of his friend Melanchthon,[17] Protestant Germany soon recognized the right of the whole people to be educated, and the German states began the work of teaching them. This is the corner-stone of the modern theory of education. The right of the masses to be taught, and, *a fortiori*, the duty of the State to teach them.

The greatest influence exerted on the intellectual world after the revival of learning was produced by the Inductive Philosophy of Lord Bacon.[18] Hitherto the schools of Europe had taught the scholastic philosophy, a debased form of Aristotelianism, devoted chiefly to the discussion of silly quibbles, theories of moral perfection, and attempts to solve questions which from their very nature were insoluble. It was a stationary, or rather a stagnant philosophy. "The chief peculiarity of Bacon's philosophy," says Macaulay, "seems to us to have been this—that it aimed at things altogether different from those which his predecessors had proposed to themselves. Two words form the key to the Baconian doctrine—utility and progress. The ancient philosophy disdained to be useful, and was content to be stationary."[19] The end which Bacon proposed to gain from his philosophy, "was the multiplying of human enjoyments and the mitigating of human sufferings." The Baconian philosophy considered nothing that conduce to this end unworthy of it. It advanced into every department of knowledge; and by a careful observation of natural phenomena, and a careful tracing of effect to cause, it sought to increase the sum of human learning.

The impetus given to education by these great events—the Reformation, the discovery of the art of printing, and the introduction of the Baconian philosophy, was attended by the rise of multitudes of teachers and systems of teaching. With these begin what may be called Modern Methods of Teaching.

The first of these schools was that of the classicists, who revived[20] the study of the Latin and Greek classics which had fallen into disuse during the Dark Age. Wolfgang Ratich,[21] a distinguished classicist, introduced a new method of teaching languages. The greatest of this school of educators was Bishop John Amos Comenius, of Holland, who in his *Janua* and *Methodus Novissima* taught languages and science by a new method.[22] Though his method has been abandoned, yet its influence is still felt in the educational systems of Northern Europe.

The school of Pietists embraced such men as Fenelon, Spener, and Francke. In the purity of their lives and the loftiness of their aims they remain to this day unsurpassed. Fenelon advocated female education, Francke established Orphan Asylums and probably the first Normal School ever established.[23]

The Humanists were a school of educators who insisted on a more thorough study of the classics, or humanities as they were called. Heyne the philologist, Jean Jacques Rousseau, and the philosopher John Locke belonged to this school.[24] Philanthropinism, a school led by John Bernhard Basedow, of Germany, was also popular among many teachers.[25]

The man who has exerted the most influence on the education of the race within the last hundred years is J. H. Pestalozzi, of Switzerland.[26] To him we are indebted for the best theory of education that has yet been given to the world; and his system, with various modifications, forms at the present day the foundation of the educational systems of Europe and America.

Pestalozzi was not what would be called a successful man—especially in

America, where success is measured by dollars and cents. His life was a series of failures. He taught his own method but indifferently, and every enterprise he undertook seemed doomed to failure. But "he builded better than he knew,"[27] and initiated a great educational movement which in other hands accomplished all that he claimed for it.

Pestalozzi adopted the premise laid down at the beginning of this paper— that education should be based on mental philosophy. The labors of Kant, Locke, and Dugald Stewart, in metaphysics, had opened the way,[28] and it remained only for him to devise methods for the development of each mental faculty in the order of its natural growth. He taught,

> that education should proceed according to the laws of nature; that it was the duty of the teacher to assist this by exciting the child to self-activity, and rendering him only a limited degree of assistance; that progress should be slow and gradual, but uninterrupted, never passing to a second topic till the first is fully understood; that the memory and the understanding should not be unduly cultivated, but all the faculties developed in harmony; that the peculiarities of every child, and of each sex should be carefully studied in order to adapt instruction to them; that the elements of all knowledge were Form, number and Language, and that these elements should be taught with simplicity and thoroughness; that the art of observing should be acquired and the perceptive faculties well developed; that every topic of instruction should become an exercise for the reflective powers; that mental arithmetic, geometry, and the arts of drawing and modeling objects of beauty, were all important exercises for training, strengthening and disciplining the mind; that the laws of language should be developed from within, and the exercises in it made not only to cultivate the intellect, but to improve the affections; that vocal music should be taught in schools, not by note, but by a careful study of the element—any principles of music; that the Socratic method was not suited to young minds, and that in the early stages of instruction, dictation by the teacher and repetition by the scholar is preferable, and, at a more advanced stage, the giving out of problems by the teacher, to be solved by the pupil without assistance; that religious instruction should begin with the mother, the filial feelings of the child should be first cultivated, and directed toward God, and that formal religious instruction should be reserved to a later period, when the child can understand it; that despotic and cruel government in schools was improper, but that mutual affection between pupil and teacher was a better incitement to intellectual activity than prizes or other stimulants to emulation; and, finally that the exercise of the senses and the thorough cultivation of the physical powers were of very great importance to the complete development of the child.

Such was the theory of Pestalozzi. The defects of his system were, that while it quickened the intellect, it neglected the memory, and imparted too little useful knowledge. Modern methods of teaching are all based upon the Pestalozzian theory, with such modifications as have been suggested by experience and more advanced knowledge.

Jacotot, a Frenchman, who lived from 1740 to 1780, in his system of teaching, gave more exercise to the memory than Pestalozzi.[29] He required his pupils to memorize each lesson, and at the first recitation he explained the difficulties; at the next recitation the lesson was repeated, and the pupils explained it themselves. He claimed that in this way they learned more and acquired a greater command of language than by the Pestalozzian method. His system is still followed by many teachers and possesses some excellent features.

The Method of Sagan was taught by Felbiger, an Austrian Bishop, and is the system now employed in the public schools of Austria.[30] It regards everything taught from a purely practical or utilitarian point of view. Classes were taught by the simultaneous system, or that of reciting in classes. It was further supplemented by frequent examinations to test the progress of the pupils. The principal defect in this system is, that it cultivates the intelligence at the expense of the memory, and does not allow sufficient room for the pupil's individuality— regarding him as a mere machine—just as a soldier is regarded in the army—as a part of a system, to the utter disregard of his individuality. The graded schools of our day, with their rigid classification and frequent examinations, are based on the method of Sagan.

The monitorial system, or the plan of using advanced pupils as teachers of the lower grades, was introduced by Joseph Lancaster, an Englishman and a Quaker.[31] The theory is that the pupil, being more on an intellectual level with his companions, can better make the lesson clear to their understandings than a teacher who is far in advance of them. This system was for a time very popular in this country and in England, but it is now generally abandoned, except when adopted, occasionally, from motives of economy. In my own experience I have found it to work poorly. The more advanced a teacher is, the better he can teach the simplest branches. The recognition of this fact has caused some of the Northern cities to raise the pay of primary teachers to level with that of teachers of the higher branches; and it has even been suggested that the best teachers be assigned to the primary grades.

The Pestalozzian theory has been most minutely developed in practice by Friedrich Froebel, of Germany, who was born in 1782 and died in 1852. Froebel was the inventor of the kindergarten, a system for educating very young children, which has been very popular in Germany for many years. The kindergarten is a systematized course of object lessons which is begun with the child at the age of three or thereabouts, and continued till its mind is sufficiently matured to begin the usual course of study pursued in the schools. It is based on the Pestalozzian principle that the elements of all knowledge are Form, Number and Language. It is devoted mainly to the development of the perceptive faculties, which are most active in youth. Children are taught color by means of colored balls; they are taught form by drawing, modeling, etc.; language is developed by a careful system of questioning; counting is taught; and rhythm and harmony are cultivated by means of movement exercises and vocal music. The discipline is mild and home-like; and the efforts of the teacher are directed to furnish the mind of the child, in its most active period, employment which will please, instruct and develop it. The system as taught by Froebel included twenty gifts, or sets of materials. The first gift consists of colored balls for teaching color; the second of a sphere, a cube, and a cylinder for teaching form, the third, fourth, and fifth, of blocks for building; the seventh, eighth and ninth, of staffs and rings for designing or laying figures; the tenth, materials for drawing; the eleventh, of materials for card perforating; twelfth, materials for embroidering; thirteenth, materials for paper-cutting; the fourteenth, fifteenth, sixteenth, and seventeenth, of slats for braiding or interlacing; the eighteenth, of materials for paper-folding; the nineteenth, materials for peas-work; the twentieth, materials for modeling in clay or plaster.[32] Very few *kindergarten*, however, employ all the occupations above-mentioned.

This system, with various additions and modifications, is taught in many schools throughout the country, and in a few in our own State. For developing the perceptive faculties it is better than any but the best home training; and it is an excellent preparation for school work. There are many teachers in Germany, and some in America, who were pupils of Froebel himself; and schools for the training of kindergartner can be found in most of our large cities.

There has been for some years a discussion as to whether the classics, which since the revival of learning have held the foremost place in the curricula of our higher institutions of learning, are the best medium of intellectual culture. The argument in favor of the classics is, that they have been taught so long that our whole literature is pervaded with classical knowledge, or language formed from Greek and Latin roots, that every branch of science and philosophy is filled with classical allusions; and that the treasures of ancient literature can be better understood and appreciated in the original than in any translation; and that, aside from these important considerations, the experience of centuries has shown them to be the best means of cultivating taste, memory, and language. The argument against the classics is that they are studied mainly for intellectual culture; and that the same degree of intellectual culture could be secured, and more useful knowledge imparted by the study of mathematics, the sciences, and the modern languages. The German States, to their glory be it said, the first in every educational movement, have established schools of both classes. The *Gymnasien* teach the classics and the higher mathematics; the *Realschulen* teach the science, mathematics and the modern languages, to the exclusion of classical studies. A careful comparison of results is being made, but the experiment is not yet completed. The presumption lies with the classical school, and is sustained by the prejudice of centuries; the burden of proof lies with the *Realschule*, and only the most positive and unequivocal proofs of the superiority of the latter can destroy the prestige of classical learning. It is my opinion that in this, as in most things, there is a golden mean, which can be attained by a judicious combination of the two methods.

Normal schools are a natural outgrowth of the modern theory of education. The history of the gradual development of Normal schools, and the discussion of their utility would easily furnish material for a paper of much greater length than this. Normal schools were first established in Germany, as early as 1705, by Augustus Herman Francke, formerly mentioned as a member of the Pietistic school. The first Normal school established in this country was in Massachusetts, and was opened in 1839.[33] The establishment of Normal schools in any community is evidence of the advancing position of the teacher's profession in public estimation. The people recognize the claims of the profession, and schools are established to train teachers, as lawyers, doctors, and members of other professions are trained. Indeed, so many are the improvements introduced in discipline and methods of instruction, so intellectual is the activity in pedagogical circles, that a teacher must have special preparation to attain to anything like eminence in his profession.

Another evidence of the growing activity in the profession is the rapid increase, during late years, of the number of educational journals. By the discussion of methods, and the spread of information on educational topics, these journals supply a want long felt among teachers. One can no more hope to keep abreast of the times in educational science without a good paper of this class, than he can hope to understand politics without a good newspaper.

Methods of Discipline are attracting no small share of attention among educators of our day. The general tendency, in theory and practice, is toward greater mildness in discipline. The old *régime* of the rod and the ferule is still fresh in our memory. The fiction of the last generation is full of realistic and thrilling portrayals of the barbarities practiced, in the name of discipline, in public and private schools. Dotheboys Hall, in Dickens' *Nicholas Nickleby*, is no great exaggeration of the system of terrorism carried on by English teachers even so late as Dickens' own day.[34] But there has been a great revulsion in popular sentiment, which has resulted in the abolition of corporal punishment in many schools, and its restriction, in others, to a few grave offenses against discipline. The doctrine of moral suasion, or the appeal to the conscience of the pupil, has in many cases been carried out with the best results. In other instances it has proved a conspicuous failure—leading one to the conclusion that the best method would be a combination of the two—or as a distinguished American educator expresses it, moral suasion well whipped in. For pupils of advanced years and standing corporal punishment should be discarded entirely, and incorrigible children should be dismissed, or sent to reform schools. There is in the school system of Cleveland, Ohio, a School for Refractory Children, to which all the "hard cases" of the other schools are sent. The fear of being sent to this school places a wholesome restraint on the pupils of the other schools. With respect to rules, I find in my own experience that the best system of discipline is that which secures the best government with the fewest rules—the maximum of government with the minimum of rules.[35]

Among the experiments in this direction, the system of discipline adopted by Col. Parker in the school at Quincy, Mass., and carried on by his successor, Superintendent Brown, is not the least interesting.[36] "It includes," says the *New*

England Journal of Education,

> a large freedom from the usual restraints of school exercises; free use of illustrative objects in instruction; the attempt to draw out the ideas of the children in order to improve and develop them; the practice of requiring the children to set down these ideas on the blackboard in their view, that all may see whether they are correct and full, or whether they need amendment; and with all this a large amount of practical elementary work in reading, writing, spelling, map-making and the like. The school is made to resemble in its liberty a family busied in educational work.

This system seems to be a return to the original Pestalozzian method, and is said to work well. A curious innovation in French public schools is the introduction of school savings-banks.[37] These are conducted by the teachers, who receive deposits and issue certificates for them, payable on demand, under certain conditions. This system is making rapid progress in France. It is claimed that it teaches the children economy and forms business habits. There were in France in 1871, 24,273 school savings-banks, in which the deposits amounted to 6,228,560 francs, or about one and a quarter million dollars. In Germany the large majority of teachers condemn the system as unpedagogical—as not being properly the work of the school, but of the family, and as adding too much to the already overcrowded curriculum of the public schools.

There has been, within a few years, a marked change of sentiment with reference to college government. In most schools the faculty are responsible for the discipline as well as the instruction. A few peculiar modes lately introduced will indicate the prevailing tendency.

The Illinois State University organized a students' government in 1870. A committee of the older students, assisted by the President, drew up a constitution and by-laws, which were adopted by the students. This constitution provided for the election of a president, vice-president, secretary, and treasurer by the students, and the appointment of a marshal and three judges by the President. The law-making power was vested in the general assembly of the students, the President having an absolute veto. Laws were made for the preservation of order in the buildings; against gambling and drinking; against injury to college buildings—the rules usually made by the faculty of an institution. The penalties consisted of fines varying from five cents to five dollars. Several cases were turned over to the faculty, who retained full power to suspend or expel.

Two or three years later, the growth of the university, with other modifying circumstances, made some changes in the form of government necessary. All legislative power is vested in a senate of twenty-two, elected by the general assembly of the students. Amendments to the constitution are proposed in the senate, but must be adopted by the general assembly of the students. There is a senate chamber and court-room fitted up for the purpose; and trials, elections, etc., are carried on according to the usual forms.

In Amherst College, the whole marking system has been abolished. There is an assignment of rank in the awarding of diplomas, but the old scale of 100, with its first, second and third classes, etc., has been abolished entirely. When a student enters he signs the rules of the College. This is regarded as a contract to which he is a party. His membership depends on his good conduct. Any violation of the rules is regarded as a violation of contract. He violates the contract, and it ceases to be binding. There is no expulsion, or vote of censure, but he simply ceases to be a member of the school.

These methods, explained at greater length in the Report of the Commissioner of Education, 1880, are really only a return to old methods. Trotzendorf, of Silesia, Germany, who lived in the latter part of the sixteenth century,[38] was the first teacher who we know to have committed the government of his pupils to themselves, organizing them into a court or senate, to decide on the offences committed and the punishment deserved; in his system, the senate was composed of pupils whose behavior, for a month previous, had been most exemplary. He also first introduced the monitorial system, which was afterwards developed by Joseph Lancaster and others.

In Wellesley Female College, Mass., the system of written examinations has been abolished, on the ground that they are no true test of scholarship, and are unduly exciting and exhausting to the pupils.

The changes made in our labor system by the organization of trades and labor unions, have brought the subject of industrial education into a prominence which it has never before attained, though it has been discussed for many years. The systematic attempt of labor unions to limit the number of workmen in order to keep up the price of labor, has almost caused the disappearance of apprenticeship, and threatens to leave the next generation without skilled workmen. In the South, the old generation of artisans is dying out, and there are none to take their places. In many Southern towns it is impossible to get fine work done; and at the North, the best stone-masons, painters, and house-decorators are of foreign birth. Such a state of affairs is alarming, and the establishment of industrial schools urged as a remedy. As a concession to this feeling, the use of tools has been introduced in some of the Massachusetts public schools; and industrial drawing in many schools throughout the country. There are industrial departments at Hampton Institute, Va., at the Carlisle Indian school, Penn., and in various other institutions; and there are about fifty schools which make a specialty of industrial training.[39] There is no doubt that this class of schools will increase in numbers and importance in the near future. "Without doubt," says Dr. Philbrick, in a paper on "Technical Education," "the best Pedagogical authority is everywhere overwhelmingly opposed to the idea of annexing the workshop to the common school, and in favor of insisting on a sound and thorough general education as the most truly practical preparation for life."[40] While this is true, I think that by a careful selection of studies, such as may discipline the mind, and at the same time teach the principles underlying all technological work—such studies, for instance, as drawing, geometry, applied mathematics, etc., and the establishment of separate industrial courses of training, to be taken up after leaving the common school—we can do much in this direction without materially encroaching upon the time given to purely intellectual culture in our schools. In the revised school law of North Carolina, drawing was omitted from the studies in which teachers are examined. This is a retrograde movement. We advance but slowly—let us "hold fast to that which is good."[41]

There is no special system of teaching generally followed in the United States. Our methods are a confused jumble of different methods, occasionally a judicious combination of methods; and in too many cases are distinguished by a total absence of method. The paucity of information on educational subjects leaves most teachers ignorant of the labors of great educators. The recent introduction of Normal Schools into our country has not given time for a careful teaching of systems. The low estimation in which the profession of teaching is held, and the poor remuneration offered to teachers, has not had a tendency to draw the best informed men to the profession. Our best institutions generally pursue an eclectic system, which is in most cases left to the choice of the individual teacher, and judged by its fruits.

A perfect system of education must be based, as I remarked before, on a perfect anthropology. There is no lack of activity in the discussion of theories, and all over the civilized world there is a healthy interest developing in educational science. "All Roads lead to Rome,"[42] and every subject discussed, new methods proposed, will help the cause forward. Men will more fully appreciate the value of learning, and the importance of correct methods of imparting it. The world is yet in its infancy and a thousand years hence our knowledge will seem as crude, our methods as imperfect as those of the middle age appear to us. *Sursum corda!*[43] my fellow workers! The perfect school, and the perfect teachers will yet exist, if not in this world, in a higher sphere, where the stores of infinite knowledge will be placed at our disposal, and we shall have an eternity in which to learn them.

~

SOURCE: "Methods of Teaching," *Minutes of the North Carolina State Teachers Educational Association* (Raleigh: Baptist Standard Print, 1883), 5–13. The 23–24 November 1882 conference program in this publication cited the title "Modern Methods of Teaching"; but the title of the published version of the speech itself, which is not limited in focus to the modern era, is here retained. On the same day, 23 November, Chesnutt also delivered another, no longer extant paper, "The Importance of Organization."

[1]Chesnutt here articulates conventional nineteenth-century educational theory, that a child's intellect, body, and moral state should receive equal attention.

[2]The ultimate source of this quotation is the *Antiquities of Rome* by Dionysius of Halicarnassus (c. 40–8 B.C.).

[3]Genesis 3:16–20.

[4]Genesis 4:3.

[5]Jesus is described as prophet, priest, and king by Samuel Medley (1738–99) in "I Know That My Redeemer Lives," *Hymns* (1785).

[6]Lucius Annaeus Seneca (c. 4 B.C.–65 A.D.), *Epistles of Lucilius*, 6, section 5.

[7]Socrates (469?–399 B.C.), as described by Plato (427?–347 B.C.), was a philosopher

dedicated to the discovery of absolute truth and its ethical corollaries. In his dialogues Plato pictured the Sophists as opposed to him: they were less metaphysically oriented, seeing truth and moral law as human inventions or merely consequences of social custom. Socrates was condemned to death for allegedly having corrupted Athenian youths by his teachings.

[8]*The Republic* and *The Laws* are two of Plato's 35 dialogues.

[9]Aristotle (384–22 B.C.) was Plato's student and the tutor of Alexander (356–23 B.C.). Contrary to Chesnutt's description below, he established his Lyceum (rather than "Academia") in a grove near Athens, where his "Peripatetic school of philosophy" derived its name from the *peripatos*, or covered walkway, in which he lectured to his students while walking with them. The term denotes both the method of teaching and Aristotelianism.

[10]William Shakespeare (1564–1616); Napoleon Bonaparte (1769–1821).

[11]Christoph Scheiner (1573–1650) was a Professor of Hebrew and Mathematics at the Jesuit University at Ingolstadt, Bavaria. The story related by Chesnutt is told in a similar manner by Robert Grant (1814–92) in his *History of Physical Astronomy from the Earliest Ages to the Middle of the Nineteenth Century* (1852).

[12]See n. 8.

[13]Marcus Aurelius (121–80).

[14]Martin Luther (1483–1546).

[15]Chesnutt may be recalling Hebrews 5:12–14.

[16]Luther, challenging Roman Catholic orthodoxy, nailed his "Ninety-five Theses" to the door of All Saints' Church in Wittenburg on 31 October 1517.

[17]Philipp Melanchthon (1493–1560)—misspelled "Melancthon"—was an ally of Luther who wrote the Augsburg Confession (1530), the Lutheran creed.

[18]Sir Francis Bacon (1561–1626) challenged the supremacy of Aristotelianism's deductive method of reasoning, as it had been developed by Scholastic thinkers.

[19]This and the next quotation are derived from Macaulay's *Lord Bacon* (1837). This volume positions Bacon as the father of the "scientific method" of inductive reasoning.

[20]Emended is the source text reading "received."

[21]Wolfgang Ratich or Ratke (1571–1635) incorporated Baconian principles into language instruction, assuming that experimentation was more profitable than rote learning.

[22]John Amos Comenius (1592–1670) was the author of *Janua Linguarum Reserata* (1631) which propounds a new plan for language instruction by means of using parallel lists of vernacular and Latin vocabulary. Emended is "*Sanna*," rather than *Janua*, in the source text. *Didactica Magna* (1657) is a collection of his writings; it includes *Linguarum Methodus Novissima*.

[23]Pietism, a German movement of the late seventeenth century, emphasized emotional religious experience, study of the Bible, and dedication to living a Christ-like life. François de Salignac de la Mothe-Fénelon (1651–1715) was a French theologian who advocated the education of women. Philipp Jakob Spener (1635–1703) was a German educator who expounded his Pietistic views in *Pia Desideria* (1675) and influenced August Hermann Francke (1663–1727), a Professor of Greek and Hebrew at Friedrich University in Halle, Germany. Francke is best known for translating Pietistic principles into action, founding at least four more schools than Chesnutt notes.

[24]Christian Gottlob Heyne (1729–1812) was an educator who served as curator at the library of Göttingen University. Jean Jacques Rousseau (1712–78) published *Emile* in 1762, portraying the sensitive and potentially creative mind of the young person in

such a way that it revolutionized European educational thought. John Locke (1632–1704), philosopher and social theorist, opposed the concept of education as the mere acquisition of fact. All favored the provision of the means of a broadly liberal education that was exploratory in nature.

[25]Johann Bernhard Basedow (1723–90)—misspelled "Bosedow" in the source text—translated Rousseau's theory into action, motivated by the concept that children should be taught sympathetically and with the goal of stimulating the development of their naturally occurring interests. In 1774 he founded a school, the "Philanthropinum" or "place of human love."

[26]Johann Heinrich Pestalozzi (1746–1827).

[27]Ralph Waldo Emerson, "The Problem" (1840).

[28]Immanuel Kant (1724–1804), German philosopher; Dugald Stewart (1753–1828), Scottish philosopher. Like Kant, Locke and Stewart developed epistemological theories. How the three contributed to Pestalozzi's thought was undoubtedly explained in the book or article that Chesnutt consulted; but, as with the description of Pestalozzi that immediately follows and the subsequent quotation from the *New England Journal of Education*, Chesnutt's source has not proven identifiable.

[29]Jean-Joseph Jacotot (1770–1840, rather than 1740–80, and misspelled "Jacotab" in the source text) developed a "universal teaching method" promulgated in his *Enseignement Universel* (1823).

[30]Johann Ignaz von Felbiger (1724–88) was the abbot of the Augustinian monastery at Sagan, Silesia, before being appointed General Director of the School System of the Austrian States in 1774. Influenced by the Prussian Protestant *Realschule* model emphasizing a non-classical curriculum, teacher education, and uniform instruction, he employed the ideas he had developed at Sagan to reform the schools in the Austrian empire.

[31]Though it was in practice before he developed the method extensively, Joseph Lancaster (1778–1838) popularized the "monitorial" or "mutual" approach to educational instruction, which emphasized the joint efforts of teachers and peer tutors.

[32]The omitted sixth gift, like gifts 3–5, involved blocks which, when assembled properly, formed a single cube. "Peas-work" involved applying concepts of points (resembling peas), lines, and surfaces by drawing them.

[33]In 1837, Massachusetts organized the first state board of education in the United States, with Horace Mann (1796–1859) as its secretary. Mann appealed to Edmund Dwight (1780–1849) who donated $10,000 to create schools for the training of teachers, the first of which were chartered in 1839 at Lexington and Barre.

[34]In this 1838–39 novel by Charles Dickens (1812–70), the title character is sent to Dotheboys Hall, where he and his classmates are cruelly abused by the headmaster.

[35]Possibly an adaptation from Emerson's essay "Politics" (1844): "The less government we have, the better—the fewer laws, and the less confided power."

[36]Francis Wayland Parker (1831–1902), Superintendent of the Board of Education in Quincy, Massachusetts, in 1873–80, was influenced by the German educational theorist John Frederick Hebart (1776–1841). Hebart emphasized the development of "inner freedom" or moral character. Parker implemented many of Hebart's ideas in the "Quincy Movement" which stressed experiential learning. Brown is likely to have been Moses True Brown (1827–1900), a professor at Tufts University who succeeded Parker after the latter became the Superintendent of the Boston public schools.

[37]First introduced in Germany in 1820, school savings banks programs appeared in France as early as 1834 but would not be instituted in the United States until 1885.

[38]Valentin Trotzendorf (1490–1556).

[39]Hampton Normal and Agricultural Institute was founded in 1868, twelve years before Tuskegee Institute, which also emphasized industrial education. The Carlisle Indian School was formed in 1879.

[40]John Dudley Philbrick (1818–86) preceded Francis Parker as the Superintendent of the Boston public schools.

[41]1 Thessalonians 5:21.

[42]Jean de la Fontaine (1621–95), "Le Juge Arbitre, l'Hospitalier, et Le Solitaire," *Fables Choisies Mises en Vers* (1693).

[43]"Lift up your hearts" is proclaimed by the priest during the Roman Catholic mass (conducted in Latin in Chesnutt's time).

Things to Be Thankful For

Essay published in *The Social Circle Journal*, October 1886

If you are rich, be thankful that you are spared the narrow cares of poverty.

If you are poor, be thankful that you are not exposed to the temptations of wealth.

If you are dull, be thankful that you are not one of those conceited fellows who think they know everything.

If you are ugly, be thankful that beauty is but skin deep.[1]

If your friend is lucky, and makes much money by speculation, thank heaven that you earn your living honestly.

If your fellow clerk gets promoted, you should be thankful that you at least, don't owe your advancement to favoritism or partiality.

If you break your arm, be thankful that you did not break your leg.

If you break your leg, be thankful that your head is still whole.

If you break your neck, be thankful that you have at least finished your journey through the barren desert of life.

If you recover from a severe illness, be thankful that you are spared to your friends a little while longer.

If your husband dies, be thankful that you are yet young enough to catch another.

If your wife runs away with another man, be thankful that you have at last found her out.

If you meet with a narrow escape in a railroad accident, be thankful that a special providence preserved you, although twenty or thirty better men lost their lives.

If you are fat, be thankful that you can keep warm in cold weather.

If you are lean, be thankful that you can keep comfortable when the thermometer is in the nineties.

If you have no place to sleep nights, be thankful that the streets are well lighted.

If you are sent to the workhouse, be thankful that you have steady employ-ment.

If you have no money, no home, no reputation, no prospects,—be thankful that you at least have life, and while there is life there is hope.[2]

In short, as St. Paul puts it, "in everything give thanks."[3] You can scarcely get into a condition where you cannot conceive of something worse, and by looking at the bright side of things, you will always find something to be thankful for.

↫

SOURCE: "Things to Be Thankful For," *The Social Circle Journal* (Cleveland, O.), 18 (October 1886), n.p., signed "Uncle Solomon." A clipping of this essay appears in one of Chesnutt's scrapbooks at the Fisk University Library.

[1]John Davies (1565?–1618), *A Select Second Husband* (1606).
[2]John Gay (1683–1732), "The Sick Man and the Angel," *Fables* (1727).
[3]1 Thessalonians 5:18.

Advice to Young Men

Essay published in *The Social Circle Journal*, November 1886

Marriages are getting to be such common, every-year affairs in Cleveland, that I think it might be well to lay down a few rules for the guidance of young men who may be contemplating matrimony. These rules are based on experience,—the ex-perience of other people. I made up my mind to get married some years ago, but haven't had time yet. Every man ought to get married. It is a duty which he owes to himself and to humanity. A married man is a happier man and a very much better citizen than the lonely and selfish bachelor who has nobody to care for, and no-body to care for him. But as marriage is a serious matter, one should be careful to avoid mistakes, and a careful observance of the following rules will prevent a great many serious blunders:

1. Marry early and often. The wisest man that ever lived was perhaps the most striking example of the application of this rule that history affords.[1] Brigham Young and the Mormon elders are far behind him, though they have done the best they could under the circumstances, and deserve credit.[2] In fact it is difficult to see how they could support their families without credit.

There may be difficulties in the practical application of this rule at the present day, but by a frequent change of name and residence, and an occasional resort to the divorce courts, an energetic person can accomplish a good deal.

2. But though early marriages are advisable, it is never too late to marry. M. de Lesseps, the distinguished French engineer, married a blushing school-girl after he

had reached the mature age of sixty-eight. This industrious young woman has since presented this vigorous old man with six pledges to their affection. (This item will be news to you if you have not read it before.)[3]

3. Always marry for money. If you cannot find a woman with hard cash, at any rate be sure and pick out one who can make money if occasion should require it. If you should feel a call to preach, if you should adopt literature for a profession, or if a patriotic zeal should draw you into politics, your heart will be lighter, and you can attend to your public duties better when you know that you will get your regular meals, and that the money necessary to keep up the family will be provided by your thrifty spouse. Some men find music teachers, a good investment; others have been successful with milliners and dressmakers; but perhaps the safest thing for a prudent man is a good laundress. The man who marries a first-class laundress need never want bread. In fact I am now hesitating between a Euclid Avenue heiress and a washerwoman with a large business.

4. Beware of widows—including grass widows.[4] Knowledge is power.[5] Women who know too much are not apt to make good wives. If you marry a tender young creature, whose heart is full of the illusions of youth, and who regards all men as angels, it will be easy to form her to your tastes, and she will get accustomed to your habits without difficulty. You can convince her of the inestimable advantages which you derive from Freemasonry, and she will then be willing to sit up till two o'clock on lodge nights without a murmur. She can be taught to like tobacco smoke, and to believe that you eat cloves for your health.

5. If possible, always marry an orphan. The laws of this country are still crude and imperfect, and in spite of all our boasted nineteenth century civilization, it is still a crime to murder a mother-in-law. By marrying an orphan you will be spared this temptation.

6. If you find it difficult to follow all or any of these rules, you can keep on the safe side by remaining single. Most of our young men seem anxious to keep on the safe side.

꩜

SOURCE: "Advice to Young Men," *The Social Circle Journal* (Cleveland, O.), 18 (November 1886), 1, signed "Uncle Solomon." A clipping of this essay appears in one of Chesnutt's scrapbooks at the Fisk University Library.

[1]Solomon, who had "seven hundred wives, princesses, and three hundred concubines," 1 Kings 11:3.

[2]Brigham Young (1801–77) was the second president of the Church of Jesus Christ of the Latter-day Saints. Young, who had twenty-seven wives, and other Mormons believed polygamy divinely ordained.

[3]Ferdinand Marie de Lesseps (1805–94) was a French diplomat and designer of the plan for the building of the Suez Canal. He remarried at 64 and fathered 12 children, after the death of his first wife, who gave birth to five.

[4]A woman either separated or formally divorced from her husband.

[5]Adaptation of Francis Bacon's statement in *Novum Organum* (1620): "Knowledge and human power are synonymous."

An Inside View of the Negro Question

Essay written c. 10 January 1889

"Is the Negro contented and prospering? There are actually millions of citizens wanting to know," says Mr. Cable in a recent number of the *Forum*;[1] and it is to these inquiring millions that this paper is addressed, in order that they may see the Negro question from the Negro's standpoint. The gentlemen who so loudly assert that the relations of the white and colored races at the South are harmonious, that the Negro vote is cast without hindrance and honestly counted, and that the Negro is contented and happy, are the same men who thirty years ago maintained the essential righteousness of slavery, and assured the world that the Negro was contented and happy in bondage, and could not exist at all in the United States except in a state of servitude. Their wish was father to the thought: the correctness of their views in regard to the contentment of the slaves may be gauged by reading the records of the Underground Railroad,[2] and time has abundantly falsified their predictions as to the disastrous results of emancipation. And their opinions of to-day are no more correct than their views of thirty years ago. The Negro is *not* contented; and while he has made great progress during the twenty-five years of his freedom, he is not prospering in that degree which the enjoyment of the full measure of citizenship would have made possible to him. The Negro knows that even in a large part of the territory covered by the old free States his rights are grudgingly conceded, and often require the aid of special legislation to enforce them; and that in the greater part of the area of the old slave states his political rights are practically nullified, and his civil rights not only universally disregarded, but denied in theory. He sees a powerful faction using all the advantages derived from a superb political organization, from wealth, from the habit of command, from high and assured social position, from skill in literary composition and the arts of debate, engaged in a desperate struggle to perpetuate in a free government and in the nineteenth century, a system of caste of which he is the victim, and to keep him for an indefinite period in a position of hopeless inferiority. He hears it solemnly asserted that the exercise of his right to vote means destruction to our political institutions; that the recognition of his right to decent and equal treatment in public institutions, in hotels, on railroads and steamboats, and in places of public amusement, means the demoralization and ultimate destruction of the social fabric. To argue that under such conditions the Negro is contented would be an insult to even the most limited intelligence which his detractors can concede to him.

To the Negro, then, there is a most serious Negro problem, and in the nature of things, this problem must present itself to him in a somewhat different light from that in which it is seen by the white people of this country. To a white man it may be a question of personal prejudice, a question of political expediency, a question of conscience, a question of abstract justice, a question of wise statesmanship—

any one, in fact, of a hundred questions. But to the man of Negro blood it is all of these, and more than these: It is to him the question of life itself. White men think about the Negro question when their attention is called to it, and as one of numerous questions arising out of the varied relations of man to man and of man to nature; with the Negro it is always present, and all other questions are dwarfed in its contemplation. It is his staple of conversation; he writes of scarcely anything else; his hopes, his fears, his affections, his zeal—all the powers of his being, are centered upon the question of his own future. He has no glorious past on which to rest his claim for consideration or to sustain him under the burden of present wrong; to the future he looks for all that life may offer him. The manner in which the question of his rights is decided in the United States will determine for him whether he shall be a patriot, or whether the peace and safety of the republic shall be menaced by the presence within its borders of a large and increasing portion of its population who have no share in its glory and no respect for its institutions. It will largely determine for him whether Christianity is or is not a failure. It is indeed hard for thinking men and women to look without disgust upon a religionism which makes a brave show of obedience to the Divine command to love God, and at the same time entirely ignores the companion precept, "Thou shalt love thy neighbor as thyself."[3] To the Negro, therefore, there will always be a Negro question, until there is equality of right and privilege for him in every relation of life; and then, if as a race he survive the attainment of this position, there will remain to him the question of what record he shall make in history, and what he shall do to remove the reproach which centuries of inferiority have placed upon him.

But what does the Negro think about the Negro question which addresses itself to the white people of the United States at the present moment? The question has been clearly and concisely stated in a recent number of the *Forum*,[4] by Mr. Cable, himself a native of the extreme South and a scion of the old slave aristocracy, who having broken his idols (if indeed he ever worshipped them) is able, from his long residence in the South, to appreciate the position of the Negro more clearly, perhaps, than Northern men who have not possessed equal opportunities for observation. "Shall the Negro," says Mr. Cable in substance, "individually, enjoy equally with the white man, individually, the full measure of an American citizen's public rights?" That is the Negro question in a nutshell, so far as it can be a question for legislation or concerted public action.

The discussion of this question has brought out a great flood of argument, in which some of the leading men and ablest writers of the country have taken part. Some of them, writing from a Southern standpoint, have tried to dodge the issue; others have met it boldly, have answered it with an emphatic negative, and have striven to justify their position; still others have admitted the abstract justice of the demand, have tried to compromise the case, and ask for more time. No Southern white writer claims that the Negro enjoys these public rights on Southern soil. Northern writers look at the subject from as many different points of view: some sympathize with the Negro, some with the Southern whites; some are despairingly pessimistic, while others are full of hope. But to the thinking Negro there are several things which narrow this problem down to a very simple one.[5]

1. The Negro knows what he wants. He wants an equal share in all public benefits, and an equal right to share in the exercise of every public function. He wants the right, or rather the opportunity, to cast his vote unmolested, for the candidate of his own choice, to have that vote honestly counted, and accepted, equally with the votes of other citizens, as expressive of the will of the people. He wants to enjoy the right to accommodation in hotels and on public conveyances, and in places of public amusement; he wants an equal share in the benefits of public schools and colleges and asylums; and he wishes to be permitted to enjoy these rights equally and in common with other citizens. He demands the repeal of all laws on the statute-books of Northern or Southern States, which in any way limit or qualify his rights, or that recognize any distinctions of race or color; and of all contract or labor laws, and all harsh and oppressive penal laws which, while ostensibly applicable to all citizens alike, are in reality aimed at his liberties. He simply asks, in other words, from the States, the rights which the Constitutional amendments were intended to secure to him, and which are conceded in theory and practically recognized in nearly all the Northern and Western States. And in his opinion he asks for as little as a self-respecting people could ask for in this age of the world. The intelligent Negro would spit upon any final settlement of his status which offered him less than this.

2. The Negro does not ask for social equality with white people; that is to say, he does not ask for admission into private white society. The fear of intimate personal contact with the Negro on terms of equality seems the greatest bugbear to the Southern people in the discussion of the Negro question. They are afraid that Southern society will be "Africanized." Absurd fear, if it really exists at all! No right is more zealously guarded by our constitutions and laws than the right of a man to be supreme within the walls of his own house. The much-dreaded "miscegenation," so freely condoned by a former generation of white people when it was the result of unbridled license, and so loudly condemned by the present generation, when there is a possibility that it may some day receive the sanction of law, never was and never will be possible without the consent of the white people. If, as some Southern writers argue, Senator Eustis for example, Nature has fixed between the white and black races an antagonism which prevents any possibility of assimilation, there is surely no ground for this fear that equal rights for the Negro means the pollution of the pure Caucasian stream which courses through the veins of Southern white people.[6] Nature has a way of making her laws distinct, and of enforcing them. That the Negro can contemplate with perfect satisfaction the indefinite duration of a prejudice which condemns him to social inferiority, and the withholding of those privileges which are conceded to him in every other civilized country, is hardly natural. But he is quite willing to leave to time and to the operation of natural laws the question of his reception into private white society; he recognizes in every man an inalienable right to select his own associates. He can ask,

however, that there be no legal barriers to his social advancement, and that these matters be left entirely to nature and to social convention.

3. The Negro believes in the righteousness of his cause. The most of what he asks for has already been decreed to him by the[7]

* * *

citizenship. If they do fear it, he regards it as a craven fear; the "all-pervading, all-conquering Anglo-Saxon race"[8] surely ought not to tremble for its pre-eminence in a system of society which is founded on equal justice to all men.

4. The Negro believes that *now* is the time to settle this question. Southern writers want "time" for its settlement. They look forward with comparative equanimity to a period in the dim and distant future, when the rights of colored people will be respected; in fact, they are rather fond of referring to such a period—it serves to distract the imaginative mind from the serious problem of the present. But such talk is mere idle words. If a man's son were in danger from disease, or his daughter from dishonor, he would not wait for time to check the one or ward off the other. Time was to have settled the slavery question. Time *did* settle it, but at what cost of blood and treasure, of human woe, and of arrested national development! Every moment that this question of the Negro's rights remains unsettled, involves not only the happiness of seven or eight millions of the citizens of the Union, but the fair fame and prosperity and glory of the nation. The Negro sees no insurmountable difficulty in its settlement. He does not believe that the Southern State governments would go to pieces if his vote were counted; indeed, he does not believe they could be much worse than they are now. He has always been willing and anxious for intelligent white cooperation and leadership. Even the much abused, and not always justly abused carpet-baggers, are a shining example of this very fact. The Southern white people stood sullenly aloof, and threw every possible obstacle in the way of good government by their former slaves. The Negro, newly enfranchised, and finding no aid or guidance from those who, under a free government, should have been his natural leaders, availed himself of such assistance as the moment offered. The Negro has a tender place in his heart for the carpet-bagger: he came to the once despised slave, and to the still scorned and hated freeman, like a ray of light through the outer darkness; he treated the Negro like a man, and guided his footsteps, not always wisely, alas! in the untried path of citizenship.[9] But the Negro to-day is not the Negro who came out of bondage. The grave has closed over more than half of those above whose backs cracked the whip of the slave-driver. The millions poured out by the philanthropic North for the maintenance of colored schools and churches, and the other millions spent by the Southern States for educational purposes, have not been fruitless. The acquisition of property, amounting in the State of Georgia alone to upwards of twelve millions of dollars has created for the Negro a powerful personal interest in economical government; he has profited by past experience, and knows that his own welfare is bound up in that of the commonwealth. And while

he will ever remember with grateful kindness all that was good in his old friend the carpet-bagger, he would not invite him back to power. Henceforth when the Negro vote is cast, it will be cast for such white men, rooted in Southern soil, as recognize the rights of the Negro, and are not afraid to express their convictions; and for such colored men as are qualified, by nature and by training, for leadership. If the Negro made great mistakes, if he should still make occasional blunders, he has only to point to his white fellow-citizens for precedents innumerable.

The Negro does not believe that all colored men should have become the equals of the better class of white men, or even of the average white man, before they are allowed to enjoy their rights. The Declaration of Independence does not say that all white men are created free and equal; it does not say that all men who can read and write are created free and equal. It lays down as the first maxim of free government the right of all men to life, liberty and the pursuit of happiness. For one hundred years and more the United States has held out this boon of equal rights to the people of every nation, and has freely conceded it to the very off-scourings of European society. Twenty-five years of even the imperfect freedom which people of color have enjoyed in this country must surely have produced some hundreds of thousands who are capable of properly appreciating the responsibilities and wisely exercising the duties of citizenship. To say that these men must be deprived of their rights because others of their complexion have not reached that point of development is simply outrageous: it takes away the very greatest incentive to effort. The theory that the intelligent colored man is the rare exception that proves the rule that the Negro is ignorant, vicious and degraded, is ripe for explosion. The good, the wise, the great, are the exceptions among all peoples. The slave-holding aristocracy which ruled the South and domineered over the country before the war, was but a small portion of the white people of the South; behind it lay the vast, inert, illiterate, and poverty-stricken mass of poor whites of that section. A race has a right to be judged by its best men. It is high time that this man of straw, the ignorant, degraded Negro who came out of slavery, always painted at his worst, should be knocked down, and something better set up in his place as the typical American Negro. There is no white man who does not know a Negro, ten Negroes, who have made some progress along the road to learning, or wealth, or self-respect, or all these; and so many exceptions ought certainly to overturn a rule which was not even correct in the first place.

5. To the Negro, the solution of this problem is simple. It does not consist in deporting the swarming black millions of the South to some particular portion of this country, or to some other country, and leaving them there alone, to learn as well as they can with their poverty and ignorance, the lesson of civilization. The Negro does not believe in any theory of race antagonism which will prevent the two races in the South from ever assimilating. He does not particularly desire a further admixture of races than has already taken place; but he scouts as absurd the argument, which, after the marriage of a white person and a person one eighth Negro has been made a penal offense, solemnly points to the fact that the races do

not intermarry as proof that they can never assimilate by marriage. But even if no other marriage of a white person and a colored person ever took place in the United States, that would be no reason why the two races should not dwell together peacefully. The Jews do not intermarry with the children of Japheth to any great extent, yet they live and flourish among them.[10] Even in those portions of the North where the public rights of colored people have never been denied, or have long since been substantially assured, marriages between white and colored persons are rare, and by no means popular among the people of either race.

One reason why the Negro question will never be settled by any colonization scheme, is that the Southern whites need the Negro: their harsh contract laws, establishing a sort of praedial slavery in the agricultural districts; their stringent laws against emigrant soliciting;—are the plainest kind of evidence that they are very anxious to retain the Negro in their midst. And, again, the Negro needs the white people. The colored people are poor, and dependent upon their labor for subsistence. By the unrequited toil of two centuries they have helped to make the country what it is, and they have a right to enjoy such advantages as a well-developed civilization may offer them. They have a right to share in the public benefits which are derived from the taxation of accumulated wealth. They have a right, and a sore need, to acquire those refinements of thought and conduct which will find their most natural habitat in highly developed communities. And they have a right to these things, not as charity, but as something which their labor rendered possible—which they themselves helped to produce.

Another obstacle to any such scheme would be met in the greed of white men. It is almost impossible for the government to keep intact for Indian reservations a few thousand square miles of land in the Western States. The white race is forcing its way into Africa, the home of the black race, and is overrunning every spot of the globe, not already fully occupied, which is available for human habitation. It would break its record if it permitted any desirable part of the world to be long monopolized by another race. This theory of colonization would hardly be worthy of refutation, but for its periodical recurrence, even in the mouths of the Negro's friends: its simplicity is alluring, but it is utterly and hopelessly impracticable.

The Negro question so far as the Southern States are concerned, cannot be settled by leaving the Negro, in the language of Senator Eustis, "to rely implicitly upon the magnanimity of his white fellow-citizens of the South to treat him with the justice and generosity due to his unfortunate condition."[11] The Negro is willing to forget the past, and to regard his condition as not unfortunate, except as the present injustice of his white fellow-citizens makes it so. He has no faith in their magnanimity where his rights are concerned. He does not want their magnanimity; he wants simple justice. He does not want his "due" of justice to be measured by this mythical magnanimity; he does not want a black "justice," as there was a black "freedom" before the war; he wants a man's justice, a man's chance in life. He wants no more of the magnanimity which has filled the statute-books of the Southern States with laws imposing degrading distinctions upon men of his blood, to the fourth generation removed; the magnanimity which proposed and supported the Glenn Bill, superior in infamy to the Dred Scott decision;[12] the magnanimity which, goaded by the "conscience which makes cowards of us all,"[13] magnifies every protest of outraged manhood into a "race war" or a "Negro insurrection," and thereby tries to justify the oppression of the colored race. The Negro asks to be saved from this magnanimity. When Southern white men have rendered justice to the Negro, if they then feel inclined to show their generosity by making some amends to him for past injustice, they will not find him ungrateful.

The Negro question cannot be settled by fixing an educational qualification for voters. It is extremely improbable that any such law will ever be put into operation in any Southern State; and it can hardly be supposed that peace and harmony between the two races in the South would be promoted by a law which is deliberately and avowedly aimed at the Negro vote, and which would never be dreamed of if the Southern Republican vote were a white vote.[14] The very root of this whole evil lies in the class treatment of the Negro, and any such legislation would only intensify the galling sense of wrong under which he rests, and add fuel to the smouldering flame of discontent which is not yet brave enough nor strong enough to express itself in terms which would command a hearing. The Negro reads and travels. He knows that such a law would be an anomaly in modern legislation. He knows that manhood suffrage was from the beginning the settled policy of the Nation, and that local exceptions have gradually conformed to the rule.

* * *

question. How can it be settled?

The return of the Republican party to power in national politics affords a means for securing honest elections at the South. The power of Congress to regulate Congressional and Presidential elections is ample and well-defined. Once let perfect freedom of the ballot prevail in these elections, and honesty in local elections will not be long in following. It will not be so easy to suppress the Negro vote a second time. That the moral influence of the National administration is very great is evident from the almost feverish anxiety exhibited by the whites of the South in regard to the policy of the incoming administration.[15]

* * *

fined by law, and these laws are only nullified by public opinion: and it is at the bar of *public opinion* that the Negro presents his plea for justice. He asks that public opinion express in unmistakable terms its disapproval of laws which restrict his rights, and of customs which override the laws by which his rights are recognized. The Northern people cannot wash their hands of this matter; they cannot stand off and say: "We have given the Negro his rights at the North; we can't do anything with the South." There was never a greater mistake. What defeated the Glenn bill? Nothing under heaven but the outspoken public opinion of the North. The South is morbidly sensitive of Northern criticism; it will resort to any degree of concealment and dissimulation to avoid it. And in the united and aggressive public opinion of the North the Negro sees his chief hope for the speedy and peaceful recognition of his public rights at the South.

Another factor in the solution of this question is the slow growth of a healthy public opinion at the South, in favor of justice and equity in the treatment of the Negro. This Southern white movement is not entirely philanthropic. The Negro is not the only sufferer from the anomalous condition of things in the old Slave States, and it requires no argument to show that the rights of the white people are largely circumscribed by laws and customs directed primarily at the Negro. Only a few days ago the editor of a South Carolina Democratic newspaper denounced as outrageous the ejection of a colored traveller from a sleeping-car.[16] Such men as Dr. Haygood,[17] standing midway between the Northern and Southern ideas of the Negro, and advancing slowly in the right direction, have a following which though small, is constantly growing in numbers and in influence. These men know the needs of the Negro, and are gradually learning to recognize his capabilities; and in the course of time they will see that his needs can best be satisfied and his capabilities best developed by granting him strict and impartial justice.

The Negro himself will do something toward the settlement of this question. The Silent South will find speech.[18] The Negro is learning his strength, and the next step in the line of progress is to learn how to utilize it. But the Negro also knows his weakness: he knows that in the United States his race stands in the proportion of one to eight or ten of the white race. He is well aware that he could never hope to lift himself one step higher in the world if the fifty millions of white people in the United States were so to decree. He knows that he can not hope to succeed in this battle for his rights without the sympathy and cooperation of the vast majority of the white people all over the country and he will adopt no policy that would alienate from him this support; he will not draw the dagger nor brandish the torch: such manifestations, if any occur, will be merely local, and temporary, and provoked by white people. But the Negro will insist upon his rights, and will if needs be, die in the attempt to exercise them, and in defense of them, and he will endeavor to do this in such a manner that the world will applaud instead of condemn. Another Presidential election will see the Negro vote organized and united all over the country, on the basis of securing to colored men their rights in the United States.

6. The Negro believes in the ultimate success of his cause.[19] That faith in God which survived the dark days of slavery, will not forsake him in this the dawn of his liberty. He believes in the Republican party, and that it will do something, perhaps haltingly, perhaps imperfectly, but yet something, to improve his condition. He believes that the balance of public opinion is rapidly turning to his side. He sees the country waking up to the importance and gravity of the situation. He sees the question of his rights rapidly dwarfing every other subject of public discussion. He sees the dawn of a new school of literature dealing with the Negro as a man, with hopes and passions and aspirations as other men. He sees the best and ablest men

of the time, men foremost in statesmanship, in war, in literature, in the church, es-
pousing his cause, urging him to action, and predicting for him a bright and happy
future. He sees men of great wealth, such as Mr. Hand and Mr. Slater, literally
pour out their millions to improve his opportunities for education.[20] He sees the
great religious organizations of the North refuse to compromise with wrong, or to
unite with Southern churches which still treat him wrongfully or discourteously.
Twenty-five years of agitation brought about the downfall of slavery, with which
was bound up a complex social system and the wealth and power of half the Nation. Twenty-five years of freedom have obtained for the Negro at the North
nearly all that he can ask for: every year has seen some relic of slavery dropped
from the statute-books of some Northern State, and other laws passed to protect
him from the prejudices of a still bigoted minority. Every year has seen the horizon
of life broaden for him. The only things which retard his progress at the South are
the selfishness of a certain class of politicians who desire to keep up race antagonisms for the purpose of perpetuating their own lease of power, and a race prejudice, which, though as yet virulent and uncompromising, begins to show signs of
weakening. The South is not altogether satisfied with itself now, and with the
spread of education, and of the true spirit of Christianity, it will soon be entirely
unwilling to merit the reproach of being in the matter of human rights the most
backward and most illiberal corner of the civilized world.

~

SOURCE: Two incomplete typed drafts of this essay at the Fisk University Library.
Pages of an authorially revised draft and a later-completed version that was sent to, edited by, and returned by George Washington Cable have been conflated for the purpose
of reconstructing, as far as is possible, the text of "An Inside View" that Chesnutt
mailed to Cable on 10 January 1889. Not adopted are the suggested revisions in Cable's
hand. After 30 January, Chesnutt produced a further revised typed text in light of Cable's comments and alterations, retitling it at his suggestion "The Negro's Answer to the
Negro Problem." So few pages of this final form of the essay survive that it is impossible
to create even a partial reconstruction.

[1]George Washington Cable (1844–1905), a Louisiana-born short story writer, novelist, essayist, and lecturer, had become a vociferous critic of Southern racism by the
time that Chesnutt made his acquaintance in Cleveland on 21 December 1888. Adopting the role of a mentor, he suggested that Chesnutt offer the "insider's" view on the
"Negro Problem," the result of which was the present essay, which, in a revised form no
longer extant, Cable unsuccessfully attempted to place for publication at *Forum* and
Century. The question posed by Cable that Chesnutt quotes appeared in "A Simpler
Southern Question," *Forum*, 6 (December 1888), 392–403. Cable was responding to
Louisiana's U.S. Senator James B. Eustis (1834–99), who had recently declared that in
"the South to-day [the Negro] is happy, contented, and satisfied. The reason is that
there is always a demand for his labor, and that his wants, cares, anxieties, and aspirations are very limited. In these respects the Negroes have every advantage over every
other laboring class in the world" ("Race Antagonism in the South," *Forum*, 6 [Octo-
ber 1888], 144–54). The main points of Eustis's essay, however, were that African
Americans are innately inferior and that whites will never tolerate the "Negro supremacy" in Southern political life that the North attempted to establish following the Civil

War. Eustis's point of view was anticipated by South Carolina's U.S. Senator Wade Hampton (1818–1902) in "What Negro Supremacy Means," *Forum*, 5 (June 1888), 383–95, to which Cable also refers in his essay.

[2]Reference to *The Underground Rail Road* (1872) by William Still (1821–1902).

[3]Leviticus 19:18 and Matthew 19:19.

[4]Chesnutt's repetition here of the phrasing in the first sentence of "An Inside View"—"in a recent number of the *Forum*"—appears in the remnants of both his initial draft and the version sent to Cable.

[5]Canceled here in the initial draft is an outline specifying the six points that Chesnutt develops below: "1. He knows what he wants; and in that connection, 2. He does not ask for social equality with white people; 3. He knows that his cause is just, and that its justness is recognized before the great tribunal of the world; 4. He believes that *now* is the time to settle this question; 5. The means of its solution are simple; 6. He is confident of the ultimate success of his cause. And the remainder of this paper will be devoted to defining briefly the position of intelligent, educated colored men, who are the rightful spokesmen of their race, upon these propositions." It is assumed that Chesnutt did not alter the sequence of points treated in the typescript sent to Cable; and this arrangement has guided the editors when reconstructing its text below.

[6]Chesnutt refers to Eustis's essay, "Race Antagonism" (see n. 1). Eustis did not raise the specter of miscegenation when advancing his argument in his essay.

[7]A continuation of this passage was not located. Below the asterisks, the text immediately appearing was identified as the conclusion of Chesnutt's third point because, on the same page, the fourth point is initiated. That is, Chesnutt's development of the third point does not survive, though—as will be seen—it appears that he addressed the subject of "white supremacy" and dismissed the notion of a desire for "Negro dominance" from serious consideration. (See, however, "The Future of the Negro.")

[8]In "What Is a White Man?" Chesnutt tentatively attributes this phrase to Henry W. Grady (1850–89), the *Atlanta Constitution* part-owner and spokesman for the "New South" who had delivered a widely reported white supremacy speech, "The South and Its Problems," at the Texas State Fair in Dallas in October 1888.

[9]Following the Civil War numerous Northerners moved to the South not only to exploit economic opportunities made possible by its depressed economy but to participate in the Federal government's Reconstruction plan for the region. Chesnutt's friend, novelist and journalist Albion W. Tourgée (1838–1905), for example, was an Ohioan carpet-bagger who, after the Civil War, practiced law and engaged in business in North Carolina, became a judge, and played a significant role in the design of a new constitution for that state. Positively viewed by some because they assisted in the political empowerment, economic advancement, and education of former slaves, carpet-baggers were seen by others as self-aggrandizing interlopers who collaborated with equally corrupt or incompetent African Americans in the misgovernance of Southern whites. Chesnutt was critical of the group in "The Future of the Negro."

[10]That is, Jews infrequently marry gentiles. Shem (representing Israel or the Jews), Ham, and Japheth (representing the Indo-European) were the sons of Noah responsible for repopulating the world after the Great Flood (Genesis 9:19).

[11]Here and in the derisive references to Southern "magnanimity" immediately below, Chesnutt focuses on Eustis's "Race Antagonism" (see n. 1), which concludes: "If [the Negro's] lot is to continue to be one of inferiority, rather than appeal to the political favoritism of the federal government, or to the partisan sympathies of Northern philanthropists, as he has done in the past, he should rely implicitly upon the magnanimity of his white fellow-citizens of the South, to treat him with the justice and generosity due to his unfortunate condition."

[12]In 1857 the decision of the U.S. Supreme Court in Scott v. Sandford, 19 Howard 393, was that the slave Dred Scott, who claimed his freedom because of his residence on "free soil" in Missouri, was not in fact a citizen but another's property; and, not being a citizen, he could not sue for his liberty in a Federal court. The unsuccessful Glenn Bill, also referred to by journalists as the Teachers Chain-Gang Bill, was submitted to the Georgia legislature by W. C. Glenn of Dalton, Ga., in 1887. It stipulated segregation in all of the educational institutions of the state. Teachers continuing to instruct African Americans and whites in mixed groups would be liable to one or more of these punishments: a fine of $1,000.00; imprisonment for no more than six months; chain-gang labor for no more than 12 months.

[13]*Hamlet*, 3.1.83–85.

[14]Well beyond the turn of the century, the African-American vote was overwhelmingly Republican; thus, Chesnutt implies here, white Democrats had a political reason for effecting disfranchisement. The Democrat counter-argument at this time was that Republicans were championing the African American and ignoring more pressing issues of national concern in order to secure his vote; see Georgia Governor Alfred H. Colquitt (1829–94), "Is the Negro Vote Suppressed?" *Forum*, 4 (November 1887), 268–78.

[15]In January 1889, Benjamin Harrison (1833–1901), a Republican, was inaugurated President of the United States, succeeding Democrat Grover Cleveland (1837–1908). Chesnutt here reiterates the Republican complaint that Cleveland was elected only because the African-American vote in the South was suppressed in 1884. Suppression was again observed in the South during the November 1888 election; see the editorial "A Southern Policy," *Independent*, 41 (2 February 1889), 235.

[16]On 17 December 1888, the Reverend T. H. Lee was traveling by train from Lincoln University, Oxford, Pa., to a black Presbyterian church in Augusta, Ga. He entered the sleeper car at Atlanta and was approached by a group of whites who told him, "There's a car for your sort of people in the front and you will have to go there." He complied, taking a seat "in the colored people's car." The treatment given this "inoffensive and decently behaved person" was termed "an unreasonable thing and an outrage" in "*Nigger in the Sleeper!*" Columbia, S.C., *Daily Register*, 20 December 1888, 2. See also the more heated denunciation of the whites who abused Lee in "Facts from Georgia," *New York Age*, 5 January 1889, 2.

[17]Atticus G. Haygood (1839–96) was a Methodist Episcopal minister and President of Emory College (1875–84) who became an agent of the Slater Fund for the education of African Americans in 1883 (see n. 20). Author of *Our Brother in Black* (1881) and *Pleas for Progress* (1889), he replied to Eustis's *Forum* article (see n. 1) in "Senator Eustis on the Negro Problem," published in the Christian and editorially pro–African American *Independent*, 40 (8 November 1888), 1425–27. Contra Eustis, he argued that "the Negro question" is a national rather than regional concern; that Northern philanthropic efforts to "educate the Negro into Christian citizenship" have been successful and their continuance is essential; that race antagonism is not the inherent and insuperable condition Eustis alleges it to be; that African Americans have made "marvelous" progress since their emancipation; and that "the most significant" shortcoming in Eustis's article is a demonstrated lack of faith in "God's providence" and trust in "the conservative and saving influences of the Christian religion." Haygood's spirited reaction to Eustis became the subject of a "symposium" of essays entitled "Shall the Negro Be Educated or Suppressed?" *Independent*, 41 (21 February 1889), 225–27.

[18]"The Silent South" was the title of a collection of essays on racism in the South published by Cable in 1885.

[19]In the initial draft of the essay, Chesnutt did not place here the number 6. Here is stated, however, the sixth point identified in his outline; see n. 5.

[20]John F. Slater (1815–84) was a New England manufacturer who established in 1882 a fund, named after him, dedicated to providing a Christian education to African Americans in the South. Daniel Hand (1801–91) was a New Englander who moved to the South when he was 18 and became a very successful merchant; in 1888 he created the Hand Education Fund for Colored People, which used the income from his contribution of over one million dollars to educate African Americans.

What Is a White Man?

Essay published in the *Independent*, 30 May 1889

The fiat having gone forth from the wise men of the South that the "all-pervading, all-conquering Anglo-Saxon race" must continue forever to exercise exclusive control and direction of the government of this so-called Republic, it becomes important to every citizen who values his birthright to know who are included in this grandiloquent term. It is of course perfectly obvious that the writer or speaker who used this expression—perhaps Mr. Grady of Georgia—did not say what he meant.[1] It is not probable that he meant to exclude from full citizenship the Celts and Teutons and Gauls and Slavs who make up so large a proportion of our population; he hardly meant to exclude the Jews, for even the most ardent fire-eater would hardly venture to advocate the disfranchisement of the thrifty race whose mortgages cover so large a portion of Southern soil. What the eloquent gentleman really meant by this high-sounding phrase was simply the white race; and the substance of the argument of that school of Southern writers to which he belongs, is simply that for the good of the country the Negro should have no voice in directing the government or public policy of the Southern States or of the nation.

But it is evident that where the intermingling of the races has made such progress as it has in this country, the line which separates the races must in many instances have been practically obliterated. And there has arisen in the United States a very large class of the population who are certainly not Negroes in an ethnological sense, and whose children will be no nearer Negroes than themselves. In view, therefore, of the very positive ground taken by the white leaders of the South, where most of these people reside, it becomes in the highest degree important to them to know what race they belong to. It ought to be also a matter of serious concern to the Southern white people; for if their zeal for good government is so great that they contemplate the practical overthrow of the Constitution and laws of the United States to secure it, they ought at least to be sure that no man entitled to it by their own argument, is robbed of a right so precious as that of free citizenship; the "all-pervading, all conquering Anglo-Saxon" ought to set as high a value on

American citizenship as the all-conquering Roman placed upon the franchise of his State two thousand years ago. This discussion would of course be of little interest to the genuine Negro, who is entirely outside of the charmed circle, and must content himself with the acquisition of wealth, the pursuit of learning and such other privileges as his "best friends" may find it consistent with the welfare of the nation to allow him;[2] but to every other good citizen the inquiry ought to be a momentous one. What is a white man?

In spite of the virulence and universality of race prejudice in the United States, the human intellect long ago revolted at the manifest absurdity of classifying men fifteen-sixteenths white as black men; and hence there grew up a number of laws in different states of the Union defining the limit which separated the white and colored races, which was, when these laws took their rise and is now to a large extent, the line which separated freedom and opportunity from slavery or hopeless degradation. Some of these laws are of legislative origin; others are judge-made laws, brought out by the exigencies of special cases which came before the courts for determination. Some day they will, perhaps, become mere curiosities of jurisprudence; the "black laws" will be bracketed with the "blue laws," and will be at best but landmarks by which to measure the progress of the nation. But to-day these laws are in active operation, and they are, therefore, worthy of attention; for every good citizen ought to know the law, and, if possible, to respect it; and if not worthy of respect, it should be changed by the authority which enacted it. Whether any of the laws referred to here have been in any manner changed by very recent legislation the writer cannot say, but they are certainly embodied in the latest editions of the revised statutes of the states referred to.

The colored people were divided, in most of the Southern States, into two classes, designated by law as Negroes and mulattoes respectively. The term Negro was used in its ethnological sense, and needed no definition; but the term "mulatto" was held by legislative enactment to embrace all persons of color not Negroes. The words "quadroon" and "mestizo" are employed in some of the law books, tho not defined; but the term "octoroon," as indicating a person having one-eighth of Negro blood, is not used at all, so far as the writer has been able to observe.

The states vary slightly in regard to what constitutes a mulatto or person of color, and as to what proportion of white blood should be sufficient to remove the disability of color. As a general rule, less than one-fourth of Negro blood left the individual white—in theory; race questions being, however, regulated very differently in practice. In Missouri, by the code of 1855, still in operation, so far as not inconsistent with the Federal Constitution and laws, "any person other than a Negro, any one of whose grandmothers or grandfathers is or shall have been a Negro, tho all of his or her progenitors except those descended from the Negro may have been white persons, shall be deemed a mulatto." Thus the color-line is drawn at one-fourth of Negro blood, and persons with only one-eighth are white.

By the Mississippi code of 1880, the color-line is drawn at one-fourth of Negro blood, all persons having less being theoretically white.

Under the *code noir* of Louisiana, the descendant of a white and a quadroon is white, thus drawing the line at one-eighth of Negro blood. The code of 1876 abolished all distinctions of color; as to whether they have been re-enacted since the Republican Party went out of power in that state the writer is not informed.

Jumping to the extreme North, persons are white within the meaning of the Constitution of Michigan who have less than one-fourth of Negro blood.

In Ohio the rule, as established by numerous decisions of the Supreme Court, was that a preponderance of white blood constituted a person a white man in the eye of the law, and entitled him to the exercise of all the civil rights of a white man. By a retrogressive step the color-line was extended in 1861 in the case of marriage, which by statute was forbidden between a person of pure white blood and one having a visible admixture of African blood. But by act of legislature, passed in the spring of 1887, all laws establishing or permitting distinctions of color were re-pealed. In many parts of the state these laws were always ignored, and they would doubtless have been repealed long ago but for the sentiment of the southern counties, separated only by the width of the Ohio River from a former slave-holding state.[3] There was a bill introduced in the legislature during the last session to re-enact the "black laws," but it was hopelessly defeated; the member who introduced it evidently mistook his latitude; he ought to be a member of the Georgia legislature.

But the state which, for several reasons, one might expect to have the strictest laws in regard to the relations of the races, has really the loosest. Two extracts from decisions of the Supreme Court of South Carolina will make clear the law of that state in regard to the color line.

> The definition of the term mulatto, as understood in this state, seems to be vague, signifying generally a person of mixed white or European and Negro parent-age, in whatever proportions the blood of the two races may be mingled in the indi-vidual. But it is not invariably applicable to every admixture of African blood with the European, nor is one having all the features of a white to be ranked with the de-graded class designated by the laws of this state as persons of color, because of some remote taint of the Negro race. The line of distinction, however, is not ascertained by any rule of law. . . . Juries would probably be justified in holding a person to be white in whom the admixture of African blood did not exceed the proportion of one-eighth. But it is in all cases a question for the jury, to be determined by them upon the evidence of features and complexion afforded by inspection, the evidence of reputation as to parentage, and the evidence of the rank and station in society oc-cupied by the party. The only rule which can be laid down by the courts is that where there is a distinct and visible admixture of Negro blood, the individual is to be denominated a mulatto or person of color.[4]

In a later case the court held: "The question whether persons are colored or white, where color or feature are doubtful, is for the jury to decide by reputation, by reception into society, and by their exercise of the privileges of the white man, as well as by admixture of blood."

It is an interesting question why such should have been, and should still be, for that matter, the law of South Carolina, and why there should exist in that state a condition of public opinion which would accept such a law. Perhaps it may be attributed to the fact that the colored population of South Carolina always outnumbered the white population, and the eagerness of the latter to recruit their ranks was sufficient to overcome in some measure their prejudice against the Negro blood. It is certainly true that the color-line is, in practice as in law, more loosely drawn in South Carolina than in any other Southern State, and that no inconsiderable element of the population of that state consists of these legal white persons, who were either born in the state, or, attracted thither by this feature of the laws, have come in from surrounding states, and, forsaking home and kindred, have taken their social position as white people. A reasonable degree of reticence in regard to one's antecedents is, however, usual in such cases.

Before the War the color-line, as fixed by law, regulated in theory the civil and political status of persons of color. What that status was, was expressed in the Dred Scott decision.[5] But since the War, or rather since the enfranchisement of the colored people, these laws have been mainly confined—in theory, be it always remembered—to the regulation of the intercourse of the races in schools and in the marriage relation. The extension of the color-line to places of public entertainment and resort, to inns and public highways, is in most states entirely a matter of custom. A colored man can sue in the courts of any Southern State for the violation of his common-law rights, and recover damages of say fifty cents without costs. A colored minister who sued a Baltimore steamboat company a few weeks ago for refusing him first-class accommodation, he having paid first-class fare, did not even meet with that measure of success; the learned judge, a Federal judge by the way, held that the plaintiff's rights had been invaded, and that he had suffered humiliation at the hands of the defendant company, but that "the humiliation was not sufficient to entitle him to damages." And the learned judge dismissed the action without costs to either party.[6]

Having thus ascertained what constitutes a white man, the good citizen may be curious to know what steps have been taken to preserve the purity of the white race. Nature, by some unaccountable oversight having to some extent neglected a matter so important to the future prosperity and progress of mankind. The marriage laws referred to here are in active operation, and cases under them are by no means infrequent. Indeed, instead of being behind the age, the marriage laws in the Southern States are in advance of public opinion; for very rarely will a Southern community stop to figure on the pedigree of the contracting parties to a marriage where one is white and the other is known to have any strain of Negro blood.

In Virginia, under the title "Offenses against Morality," the law provides that "any white person who shall intermarry with a Negro shall be confined in jail not more than one year and fined not exceeding one hundred dollars." In a marginal note on the statute-book, attention is called to the fact that "a similar penalty is not imposed on the Negro"—a stretch of magnanimity to which the laws of other states are strangers. A person who performs the ceremony of marriage in such a case is fined two hundred dollars, one-half of which goes to the informer.

In Maryland, a minister who performs the ceremony of marriage between a Negro and a white person is liable to a fine of one hundred dollars.

In Mississippi, code of 1880, it is provided that "the marriage of a white person to a Negro or mulatto or person who shall have one-fourth or more of Negro blood, shall be unlawful"; and as this prohibition does not seem sufficiently emphatic, it is further declared to be "incestuous and void," and is punished by the same penalty prescribed for marriage within the forbidden degrees of consanguinity.

But it is Georgia, the *alma genetrix* of the chain-gang, which merits the questionable distinction of having the harshest set of color laws. By the law of Georgia the term "person of color" is defined to mean "all such as have an admixture of Negro blood, and the term 'Negro,' includes mulattoes." This definition is perhaps restricted somewhat by another provision, by which "all Negroes, mestizoes, and their descendants, having one-eighth of Negro or mulatto blood in their veins, shall be known in this State as persons of color." A colored minister is permitted to perform the ceremony of marriage between colored persons only, tho white ministers are not forbidden to join persons of color in wedlock. It is further provided that "the marriage relation between white persons and persons of African descent is forever prohibited, and such marriages shall be null and void." This is a very sweeping provision; it will be noticed that the term "persons of color," previously defined, is not employed, the expression "persons of African descent" being used instead. A court which was so inclined would find no difficulty in extending this provision of the law to the remotest strain of African blood. The marriage relation is forever prohibited. Forever is a long time. There is a colored woman in Georgia said to be worth $300,000—an immense fortune in the poverty stricken South. With a few hundred such women in that state, possessing a fair degree of good looks, the color-line would shrivel up like a scroll in the heat of competition for their hands in marriage. The penalty for the violation of the law against intermarriage is the same sought to be imposed by the defunct Glenn Bill for violation of its provisions; i.e., a fine not to exceed one thousand dollars, and imprisonment not to exceed six months, or twelve months in the chain-gang.

Whatever the wisdom or justice of these laws, there is one objection to them which is not given sufficient prominence in the consideration of the subject, even where it is discussed at all; they make mixed blood a *prima-facie* proof of illegitimacy. It is a fact that at present, in the United States, a colored man or woman whose complexion is white or nearly white is presumed, in the absence of any knowledge of his or her antecedents, to be the offspring of a union not sanctified by law. And by a curious but not uncommon process, such persons are not held in the same low estimation as white people in the same position. The sins of their fathers are not visited upon the children,[7] in that regard at least; and their mothers' lapses from virtue are regarded either as misfortunes or as faults excusable under the circumstances. But in spite of all this, illegitimacy is not a desirable distinction, and is likely to become less so as these people of mixed blood advance in wealth and social standing. This presumption of illegitimacy was once, perhaps, true of the majority of such persons; but the times have changed. More than half of the colored people of the United States are of mixed blood; they marry and are given in marriage,[8] and they beget children of complexions similar to their own. Whether or not, therefore, laws which stamp these children as illegitimate, and which by indirection establish a lower standard of morality for a large part of the population than the remaining part is judged by, are wise laws; and whether or not the purity of the white race could not be as well preserved by the exercise of virtue, and the operation of those natural laws which are so often quoted by Southern writers as the justification of all sorts of Southern "policies"—are questions which the good citizen may at least turn over in his mind occasionally, pending the settlement of other complications which have grown out of the presence of the Negro on this continent.

⌐

SOURCE: "What Is a White Man," *Independent*, 41 (30 May 1889), 5–6.

[1] Henry W. Grady. Chesnutt as ironically used the same epithet in "An Inside View of the Negro Question," without citation of its source. Chesnutt appears not to have been wryly making a point when suggesting that Grady was "perhaps" the originator; rather, he seems to have been uncertain whether Grady in fact originated the phrase. It will be found in none of his collected writings.

[2] As in "An Inside View of the Negro Question," Chesnutt is responding to James B. Eustis's argument that the Southern whites are the African Americans best friends and can be relied upon to make the appropriate political decisions for their present welfare and future improvement as a people.

[3] Kentucky.

[4] State v. Davis, S.C. 2 Bailey 558 (1831).

[5] The status was that of a non-citizen who could not claim a citizen's civil rights.

[6] Chesnutt appears to have read "He Had No Redress," *New York Times*, 26 January 1889, 3. In July 1887, the Reverend Robert McGuinn paid the first-class fare, boarded the *Mason L. Williams*, seated himself for dinner, and refused to leave the table when requested to do so. The food was then taken to another table, where his fellow passengers relocated themselves. Claiming that he was threatened by these passengers, he debarked and filed a libel suit against the owners and the captain of the ship. The holding in McGuinn v. Forbes *et al.*, 37 F 639 (1889), was that he should have enjoyed the same accommodations as the others but that public sentiment in such a situation must be acknowledged. Further, the carrier should not be compelled to experience financial loss in order to combat such a sentiment.

[7] Exodus 20:5.

[8] Matthew 22:30.

Some Uses and Abuses of Shorthand

Speech to the Ohio Stenographers' Association,
Cleveland, O., 28 August 1889

The invention of phonography deserves to rank, and does rank, in the minds of those who know its uses, with the great inventions of the nineteenth century; along with the steam engine, the telegraph, the sewing machine, the telephone. Not indeed so potent is its influence on the welfare of humanity as some of these, it is yet unquestionably one of the great mental triumphs which are the pivotal events of civilization.

Phonography is something more than a labor-saving invention. Its greatest value—its most important use—is as a conservator of thought. In one sense it may be said to have been born out of due season. In these days, when oratory is on the decline, from one reason or another, perhaps not a great deal of permanent value would be lost by reason of the inability of reporters to take down congressional debates or political harangues. But in those periods of the world's history when oratory was a fine art, when men studied it as they do law or medicine, or chemistry; when speech took the place of printing; when the career of a statesman, the success or failure of a party, the fate of a nation, might depend upon a single speech, and often an extemporaneous one at that; when Athens rang with the eloquence of Demosthenes, of Pericles; when Plato discoursed to his disciples of the nature of existence; when Socrates talked of the unknown God—phonography would have laid the world under a debt of gratitude which no homage could have paid.

In one of the books of the New Testament, we are told that if all the sayings of Jesus were written down, the world would not contain the books.[1] The passage is obviously a figure of speech. But when we read the matchless Sermon on the Mount,[2] and the parables in which the Founder of Christianity emphasized the religion of humanity—the doctrines of peace, and mercy and love—we could well wish that there might have been in the multitude a clever youth whose stylus could have recorded more of his teachings. We are told that Cicero's orations[3] were reported by a shorthand writer. From the handful of them that have come down to us as models of eloquence, we can easily imagine the wealth of diction, of argument, of illustration, which were lost in the fierce, white heat of the Roman politics of that epoch. If my friend Davies or Pomerene,[4] or any one of the distinguished reporters who have honored our city by their attendance here, could have had a stand in the forum, a little to the front or at one side of the rostrum, and could have taken down the words of the orator in the Pitman phonography[5] (I use the words generically) with a fountain pen, on red-lined paper, and could have handed down to posterity a fair typewriter transcript of his notes, the fame of

Cicero would have rested on a broader basis, and the world would have been the richer.

But, perhaps, after all, it is better for the reputation of those illustrious ancients that so little of their work has been preserved. What has come down to us is of the best—at least we know nothing better, and can indeed conceive of nothing better. Suppose that, alongside of Demosthenes' *De Corona*,[6] we could have, in the same volume, the speech which he might have made to a howling mob of Athenian patriots just after getting up from a banquet at which he had imbibed too freely of the flowing bowl. Suppose too, for instance, that the reporter had not submitted his transcript for revision next morning, but had published it verbatim in the Athenian *Leader* or *Plaindealer*; and that when the cornerstone of the Acropolis or the Parthenon[7] was laid, a copy of the paper had been deposited along with the usual mementoes; and suppose further, that in the zeal for learning and the reverence of antiquity, which characterize the present epoch, we had pulled the building to pieces to see how it was built, and discovered this relic of the past, the fame of Demosthenes might have been put in serious jeopardy. Perhaps it is well enough too, that there were no stenographers in those days; for a discriminating posterity might not have been able to tell how much of the reported speech was the orator's and how much the stenographer's. Perhaps even yet some Ignatius Donnelly may arise to challenge the authorship of Demosthenes' oration, but the tongue of scandal can not say that they were written by his stenographer.[8]

As a set-off, therefore, to its usefulness as a conservator of thought, it may be said that the art of shorthand promotes diffuseness in writing and speaking, with a corresponding loss of strength and directness. Not only more letters are written, but longer letters. Bills of exceptions in court cases stretch out to an inordinate length. The man who is too lazy to write, is often too lazy to stop talking. Even in my own limited experience I have written out a transcript of 1,300 typewritten pages of testimony, and this number doubtless has been exceeded by any experienced stenographer here. I know of but one way in which stenographers can correct this tendency, and that is by making the prices of their work so high that those who employ them will consider the value of conciseness. The stenographer may lose folios, but he will get more for them.

Another use of shorthand is its effect, shared by the press, in checking the utterances of public speakers—political speakers, preachers, lawyers, all men who earn their living by the sweat of their tongues.[9] When the impassioned orator, thrilling with anger or zeal, feels burning words of sarcasm, invective, recrimination, rising to his lips, his eyes happen to fall on the stenographer, who alone, perhaps, in all that vast audience, sits calm and cool—mentally, (sometimes he is uncomfortably warm physically), and the orator feels the words grow cold upon his lips. "There's that confounded reporter," he says, "and every l—, every mistake of fact I may fall into, every grammatical slip, every mixed metaphor I make, he will dish up in his paper to-morrow. I am here in a free trade district, anxious to make votes. Next week I shall be in a protection county, and how can I straddle the tariff with an opposition reporter chained to my ankle?" This is the way he is apt to feel, unless he is a man of resources, who can "smile, and smile, and he be a villain,"[10] in which case he will calmly deny in one place what he said in another, and ascribe reported discrepancies to the carelessness or ignorance of the stenographer. Many a poor shorthand writer has had to answer for more sins than Mr. Dana's office cat.[11]

There are other reasons to which are partly due the decline of oratory, yet still we must perceive that in the check that shorthand, supplemented by the press, places upon rash and inconsiderate utterance from platform and pulpit, and at the bar; it promotes truth and justice, and thereby is of positive moral benefit to humanity.

Another use of short-hand—and this is a personal, not a public use—is as a stepping-stone. Upon that subject I do not wish to say much, if anything. It has been treated at much length and with great ability by President Dickinson, of the New York Association, in a paper read at a former meeting of that association. He took the ground that shorthand offers no career to a man of high intellectual gifts and acquirements, but that to such it might serve as a stepping-stone to some pursuit which would give more play to the exercise of the higher mental faculties, and larger rewards in the way of wealth and fame. Perhaps to a man of genius this would be true; there are callings in which a man of equal ability and attainments can earn more with the same or less labor. And to those who aspire to distinction, to fame, the career of Dickens, of Sumner, of some less distinguished but well known men, of Theo. Tilton,[12] of our own ex-Gov. Hoadley, of Chief Justice Fuller,[13] offer shining examples of the use of shorthand as a stepping-stone. But the abuse, or rather the mistaken idea I wish to refer to in this connection, is the attempt to make of short-hand a step-ladder. How many eager students are toiling over their pot-hooks[14] beside smoky kerosene lamps in country cottages; how many eager students, dazzled by brilliant advertisements, are learning shorthand in three months, perhaps by mail, with the expectation of graciously accepting a lucrative situation, which a public hungering for stenographers will thrust upon them!

Of course no member of this Association has any such notices. We have all doubtless learned by sad experience, that there is no royal road to skill and success in shorthand, or *through* shorthand. What the business, or the profession, if you prefer the term, offers to a young man, is, first, an art which he can learn from a textbook, unaided. Of course, not every one could learn it thus; but every one with sufficient intelligence to become a skillful stenographer, can, I venture to say, if he have the necessary industry, master the art without a teacher. I would not advise any one thus to study it who can obtain competent instruction, but it can be so learned, and learned better without a teacher than any other art I know of that offers equal rewards. Then again, the art once thoroughly acquired, the stenographer need never be out of employment. The time may come when it will be difficult for a stenographer to make a living, but very few good ones are at present out of employment.

These misconceptions with regard to shorthand are not without their influence, and it is not a good influence upon the shorthand business. If the public have their eyes greeted every time they open a newspaper, with an advertisement in boldface type, offering to teach shorthand in three months, is it surprising that after a time they begin to think lightly of a business which can be learned so easily, and that they murmur at paying high prices for such work? And it is these tyros, these neophytes, who dream of gold harvests, who see in shorthand, the wonderful lamp which will put at their command the treasures of the world—it is these who talk most about shorthand; they learn its history from their text-books, they expatiate to their neighbors and friends upon its advantages, modestly allude to the wonderful progress they themselves are making, and speak in tones of awe of the wonderful success which some acquaintance has achieved. The consequence is that people of good, hard sense, form a low estimate of the business; young people of vivid imagination, and too often with no other intellectual equipment, rush to the business colleges and shorthand schools, and are turned out by battalions upon a suffering public.

I would not discourage the aspiring student; I would have him see in his profession an honorable, useful and fairly paid pursuit, in which, if he be moderate in his desires, he may reasonably hope for success. I have no word of blame for the teachers who spend their lives and find their vocation in teaching the magic art; they are worthy of their hire.[15] But I do insist that the idea that shorthand is a stepladder, a short cut to heights which only industry and perseverance can attain in any pursuit, is a mistaken one, and that no candid man will endeavor to convey such an impression of it to the student or inquirer. For my part, I would not, from selfish motives, discourage a young person from entering the profession. But I would say to him frankly, that only by hard work and faithful practice, can he obtain even a fair degree of proficiency in the stenographic art, and that only by years of practice and experience can he hope to become competent to meet well the requirements of the more difficult kinds of reporting.

I do not think there will be any question among us that we should endeavor to maintain and elevate the character of the profession by which we live. Let us then strive to emphasize the higher uses of shorthand, to correct such abuses as can be corrected, and disseminate correct ideas with regard to the true requirements of the art. And by presenting to the communities in which we may live the spectacle of capable, trustworthy successful business men, we shall the more easily win all the prizes that our profession can at present offer, and smooth the pathway of those who will follow us.

↜

SOURCE: "Some Uses and Abuses of Shorthand," *Proceedings of the Fifth, Sixth and Seventh Annual Sessions of the Ohio Strenographers' Association* (Cincinnati, O.: The Wrightson Printing Company, 1890): "Proceedings of the Seventh Annual Session . . .

August 27 and 28, 1889," 37–41. The convention was held at the Forest City House, Cleveland, O., and Chesnutt gave this speech on 28 August.

[1]John 21:25.

[2]Matthew 5–7.

[3]Marcus Tullius Cicero (106–43 B.C.), Roman philosopher, statesman, and orator.

[4]Henry J. Davies and Julius G. Pomerene were Cleveland stenographers and business partners in the 1880's; Chesnutt would be Pomerene's partner in 1892.

[5]Sir Isaac Pitman (1813–97) created a shorthand transcription system based upon phonographic, rather than orthographic, principles. His brother Benjamin "Benn" Pitman (1822–1910) founded the Phonographic Institute in Cincinnati, O., in 1853.

[6]In 330 B.C., Demosthenes defended his reputation in the face of charges against his character and patriotism made by Aeschines (389–314 B.C.), a supporter of Philip of Macedon and his as-tyrannical son, Alexander. *De Corona*, or *On the Crown*, has been acknowledged since ancient times as an oratorical masterpiece.

[7]The Acropolis is the fortified height, or citadel, of ancient Athens; the Parthenon is an Athenian temple.

[8]Ignatius Donnelly (1831–1901) was the author of *The Great Cryptogram* (1888) and *The Cipher in the Plays and on the Tombstone* (1899), both of which advanced the thesis that Sir Francis Bacon was the actual author of Shakespeare's plays.

[9]Adaptation of Genesis 3:19.

[10]*Hamlet*, 1.5.109.

[11]Charles A. Dana (1819–97) had been the editor of the New York *Sun* since 1868, and the primary rule governing this newspaper was "be interesting." The running joke in his editorials was that dull news, much of it relating to politicians, did not appear in print because his cat had a voracious appetite for matter of the kind.

[12]Theodore Tilton (1835–1907) was a prominent anti-slavery and pro-woman suffrage lecturer who became the editor of the *Independent* (1856–71); he was a novelist and poet as well.

[13]George Hoadley (1826–1902) served as Ohio's governor in 1883–85; Melville W. Fuller (1833–1910) began his term as Chief Justice of the U.S. Supreme Court the previous year, 1888.

[14]Chesnutt refers thus to students practicing phonography, "pot hooks" indicating the "s"-shaped figures, or curls, that modify the spelling and meaning of signs.

[15]Luke 10:7.

A Multitude of Counselors

Essay published in the *Independent*, 2 April 1891

The colored people of this country are just now passing through a trying period in their history, a history full of trying situations—a dark and gloomy record, with only here and there a flash of light. Even now they are scarcely in the twilight of their liberties. All over the country they are the victims of a cruel race prejudice, the strength and extent of which none but cultivated, self-respecting colored people can rightly apprehend. It pervades every department of life—politics, the schools, the churches, business, society—everywhere, tho not always in the same degree. There is actually no single locality in the United States where a man avowedly connected by blood with the Negro race can hold up his head and feel that he is the recognized equal of other men (in the broad sense of the term), or where he is not taught to feel every day of his life that he is regarded as something inferior to those who were fortunate enough to be born entirely white. Colored people who think have long since recognized that in the more intimate and personal relations of men, society can have but one opinion, and that the Negro is under the ban of society. They feel that as long as any considerable part of the United States denies them any right or any privilege, something will be lacking to the completeness of their citizenship everywhere else in the United States.

But it is a far cry from slavery—from the Dred Scott decision—to the time when the ghost of negrophobia will be laid. Sufficient unto the day is the evil thereof:[1] and the crying evil of to-day is the outrageous manner in which the colored people of the South are deprived of the elementary rights of citizenship—the right to the protection of life and limb, the right to trial when accused of crime, the right to assist in the choice of their rulers and the making of their laws, and the right to equal treatment on railroads and in places provided for the accommodation of the traveling public. These are not social privileges; they are public rights, to which these people are entitled under the law. There are other rights of which they are deprived, but which they have not chosen to assert; but the manifest disposition on their part to claim and exercise the rights enumerated, has stirred the Negro-hating spirit of the South to the dregs, and given occasion for a series of outrages within the last month which is without a parallel in number or malignity since the downfall of the Ku Klux organization,[2] if the disbanding of that organization after complete success in the object sought by it can be called a downfall.

Mr. George W. Cable advises the colored people to unite and by every peaceable means—by word, by voice, by pen, to forward their own cause.[3] One writer advises the colored people to emigrate to Mexico or South America, another tells them not to yield their tardily acknowledged birthright, but to work out their salvation in the United States. A writer prominently identified with the cause of the colored people advises them to forget the fact that they are Negroes, and to endeavor to feel that they are simply men and citizens. One counselor advises them to emigrate largely from the South, and thus relieve that section of the strain caused by the fear of Negro majorities. Another advises them to stay in the South and retain their majorities, on the theory that a bird in hand (even if the hand is shackled) is worth two in the bush.[4] One friend finds a specific for every race trouble in the division of the colored vote; another, many others in fact, see no hope for the Negro except in the supremacy of the Republican Party; they believe, in the language of Frederick Douglass, that to the Negro "the Republican Party is the ship; all else is the ocean." Judge Tourgée openly predicts a guerilla warfare of races, and can only advise the colored people to defend themselves in an uneven and hopeless conflict.[5]

When the colored man has read with hopeful eagerness the conflicting advice which his friends have given him, he is apt to reach the conclusion that his counselors are as much in the dark as to what is best for him to do, or as to what will be the outcome of his presence in the United States, as he himself is.

From one point of view scarcely any of the courses proposed are practicable for the ten million colored people in the United States, or any considerable proportion of them, to follow. Take, for instance, a wholesale emigration of the colored people to South America, or Mexico. It is questionable whether they would be welcomed in any such mass. The expense of transportation, the loss of time, the withdrawal of so many laborers, would cost the country as much as the late War, and would be infinitely more injurious to the South than they at one time imagined the loss of their slaves to be. No such movement has been known in history; the exodus of the Hebrews from Egypt, the expulsion of the Moors from Spain, the flight of the Tartar tribe which De Quincey has immortalized,[6] would be mere preparatory sketches for such a gigantic movement of population. When it is considered that it has taken four hundred years of immigration and a century of unparalleled national growth, to give the United States a population of sixty millions, the preposterousness of colonizing the whole colored population of the United States is apparent, even supposing no other obstacle than mere numbers in the way of it. A wholesale emigration to any State or Territory is open to similar objections, and to the still stronger one that no State or Territory capable of supporting a large population would be left to the exclusive occupation of the colored people. The lesson of Oklahoma is recent enough to demonstrate this.[7] It is not at all likely that even Africa will be left to the Negro; it is not, indeed, desirable that it should be left entirely to him. But supposing every obstacle to such an emigration removed, the Southern whites would not let the colored people go.[8] This modern Pharaoh, "the white South," is quite as obdurate as his Egyptian prototype. The Negro problem seems to worry the people of Georgia more than those of any other State; and yet the laws of Georgia, to say nothing of public opinion, are such as to render it absolutely impossible for any organized movement for emigration to be successfully carried out.[9] Cheap, abundant and easily managed, white labor is not so readily procured that the Southern white planters would take their chances of getting along without colored labor. The Negroes must, as a mass, remain in the South. A more practicable emigration, that of the Southern whites, who are more able to go, strange to say, does not seem to meet with much favor in their eyes, and yet, if, as they are so fond of asserting, it is impossible for the two races to live together on terms of equality, this is more likely to be the ultimate outcome.

The division of the colored vote is equally impracticable. The whites do not, at present, desire it on such terms as they could get it, that is, the recognition of the Negroes' rights under the law. It could be easily effected on that basis; but that any considerable number of colored people in the face of the torrent of vilification and abuse, to say nothing of physical outrage, to which they are subjected, should support the party which at the South justifies and at the North excuses such a course toward them, it is difficult to see; they do not do it, and will not do it. A colored editor in New Orleans, who turned Democrat, for the reason, as he asserts, that he thought the condition of his race would be improved by such changes of politics, and another in Ohio who forsook his party for similar reasons, have both returned recently to the Republican Party; even patriotism, or venality, or whatever their motive may have been, could not resist the arguments of the past month.[10] They have declared that the lives and liberties of their people are above every other consideration, and that there is neither prospect nor hope for the preservation of either in the Democratic Party. It is joined to its idols, the bigotry and lawlessness of the Bourbon Democracy of the South.[11]

That the colored people will ever inaugurate anything that could be seriously called a race war, is not likely. They have the experience of the past to warn them. Never but once in history have they come out victorious in such a struggle, and the conditions under which they were successful in San Domingo are not apt to be repeated.[12] Even supposing them equal in numbers and intelligence to the Southern whites, they know from painful experience that the spirit of slavery is not dead at the North, but that in the event of any widespread conflict, Southern whites would be re-enforced by their sympathizers at the North. The people who are characterized as "ignorant, degraded and brutal," know quite enough to appreciate the lessons of the draft riots in New York, the Cincinnati riots, and the active Copperheadism of the War period.[13]

That the colored people can improve their condition by a general organization, like that of the Irish National League for instance, is hardly possible.[14] The recent troubles in Mississippi grew out of an attempt to organize a colored Farmers' Alliance. If a peaceful organization for industrial protection is discouraged in so emphatic a way—by the estimated murder of at least a hundred colored people, among them the leaders of the organization—what kind of reception would a similar political organization meet?

The advice that colored people should have nothing to say in the prevailing discussion is doubtless intended in the best possible spirit. The writer who gave it is evidently friendly to those whom she would advise. But it is asking too much of poor human nature. Perhaps white people, with centuries of culture behind them, have reached that point of self-control where they could endure in silence such indignities and wrongs as are heaped upon the Negro—tho no such fact is apparent from the study of their history. Indeed, the fact that they have always loved liberty, have spoken and fought to maintain it, is the noblest characteristic of the English-speaking race. The colored people were denied the right to fight for their freedom until the rebellion was substantially over, but that they should now be denied the right to speak for themselves, that they should continue to be the passive bone of contention between North and South, is asking them to be false to Nature, false to humanity, false to every tradition of human liberty.

But since the colored people can do none of these things, what can they do? Perhaps, after all, these conflicting and impracticable opinions can be reconciled in such a manner as to avoid confusion, and thus, after all, to lead to safety.

For instance, if the colored people cannot emigrate *en masse*, they can gradually spread over the country. The advantages of such dispersion are obvious. It would hasten the ultimate assimilation of the two races, which would be quickest where race prejudice is weakest. It would keep the colored people in touch with their friends, who are most numerous at the North where colored people are fewest—not, indeed, as the Southern whites assert, because they know least about the Negro, but because slavery and proscriptive laws and the supposed exigencies of partisan politics have not benumbed their consciences, or warped their love of liberty. The descendants of the Puritans, who direct the public sentiment of the North and West, would, if confronted with such a condition, find some other method than assassination and disfranchisement to counteract the alleged dangers of Negro ascendancy. There is already a large movement of colored people toward the North. But unfortunately for those who remain, it is a movement of the younger and more aspiring element, who can find in the North larger opportunities for development. For in spite of the assertive Southern white people and their apologists, race prejudice at the North does not entirely prevent colored people from climbing up into the higher walks of life. The writer of this article lives in a city where there are about five thousand colored people—about one in fifty of the population. And he is not guessing when he says there is no colored man in the city qualified to follow any special pursuit requiring special knowledge, who cannot, by reason of race prejudice, find employment at it; and with few exceptions, no pursuit which he cannot, for that reason, qualify himself to follow. With such a state of public opinion, which is true of a large part of the North, it is not strange that young colored people should leave the South. Their departure will better their own condition, and, after all, the progress of any race is dependent on the advancement of individuals. One Vanderbilt, one Stewart, one Depew, one Edison,[15] one leader in any department of human endeavor, would do more to enlarge the opportunities of colored people than double the same aggregate of wealth, or talent, or labor, scattered among a hundred or a thousand of them.

If they cannot combine all over the South for the purpose of securing their rights they can in certain localities. They can at the North. By a proper organization of their voting strength, which in many localities and in half a dozen States constitutes the balance of power, they can compel the local recognition of such rights as are still denied them, and force upon the attention of Congress and the Administration the condition of their brethren at the South. The whole machinery of the Government was once put in motion to procure the return of fugitive slaves;[16] it is strange that the combined wisdom of Congress cannot devise some plan whereby the Constitution will be a shield rather than a sword to these struggling millions.

The colored people will instigate no race war. But when they are attacked, they should defend themselves. When the Southern Negro reaches that high conception of liberty that would make him rather die than submit to the lash, when he will meet force with force, there will be an end of Southern outrages. The man who will offer a personal indignity to another who has not injured him, is a tyrant and a coward, and will not continue a conflict with no odds in his favor. History is full of inspiration, and of illustrious example, for the defenders of liberty. The memory of those who die for liberty is cherished; the names of tyrants become the synonyms for all that is basest in human nature.

The colored people can speak out for themselves, and ought to whenever they can safely do so. The right of free speech is as sacred to a freeman as any other right, for through it he sets in motion the agencies which secure his liberty. Whether or not he can exercise his rights is not to the point; he should nevertheless assert them. The Declaration of Independence was not the cool utterance of a nation secure in its position; it was the indignant remonstrance of an outraged, disorganized people; and coming from the heart it went to the heart, and not only inspired Americans to heroic effort, but enlisted the sympathy and admiration of lovers of liberty the world over. Rash and intemperate expression on the part of colored people, where the consequences can easily be foreseen, is to be deplored. But a just self-respect requires that they should let the world know that they are not "dumb, driven cattle,"[17] but that they know, and know better than any one else can, the extent to which they are oppressed and outraged. If the colored people of the South could voice in one cry all the agony of their twenty-five years of so-called freedom, the whole world would listen, and give back such an indignant protest as would startle this boasted land of the free into seeing itself, for a moment at least, as others see it[18]—as a country where prejudice has usurped the domain of law, where justice is no longer impartial, and where the citizen deprived of his rights has no redress.

⌒

SOURCE: "A Multitude of Counselors," *Independent*, 43 (2 April 1891), 4–5, datelined "Cleveland, O." The title is derived from Proverbs 11:14 or 24:6.

[1]Matthew 6:34.

[2]The Ku Klux Klan was dissolved by a proclamation from its Grand Wizard, General Nathan Bedford Forrest (1821–77), in March 1869.

[3]"What Shall the Negro Do?" *Forum*, 5 (August 1888), 627–39.

[4]While this expression appears to have been a commonplace one by 1891, Chesnutt may be indicating his familiarity with its use in *Don Quixote de la Mancha* (Part 1, 1605; Part 2, 1615) by Miguel de Cervantes (1547–1616).

[5]*An Appeal to Caesar* (1884).

[6]Thomas De Quincey (1785–1859), "The Revolt of the Tartars; or, Flight of the Kalmuck Khan and His People from the Russian Territories to the Frontiers of China." Available in collections of De Quincey's writings, this piece initially appeared in *Blackwood's Edinburgh Magazine*, 42 (July 1837), 89–137.

[7]On 22 April 1889 President Benjamin Harrison opened approximately 1,800,000 acres of the recently acquired Indian lands in the Oklahoma Territory for settlement, and the resulting "land rush" was widely reported.

[8]Exodus 9:1.

[9]In the Georgia state legislature was a Committee on Emigration that considered petitions for permission to emigrate, frequently to Africa. These requests were routinely denied.

[10]Chesnutt alludes to efforts by Democrats to disfranchise Southern blacks.

[11]"Bourbon," originally referring to royalists determined to restore the monarchy after

the French Revolution, was the epithet for Southern whites who succeeded in reestablishing much of the antebellum status quo after the Reconstruction ended.

[12]Pierre Dominique Toussaint L'Ouverture (1743–1803), born a slave in Haiti, led an uprising against the French planters and colonial administrators. In 1801 his forces gained control of the island, expelling Spanish slave masters from Santo Domingo as well.

[13]A three-day draft riot began on 13 July 1863 in New York City when opponents of conscription into the Union Army burned buildings and assaulted blacks. Over 1,000 people were killed or wounded, and more than 50 buildings were destroyed. On 28 March 1884 a riot broke out in Cincinnati when a white man, William Berner, was given a lighter sentence than a mulatto, Joseph Palmer, for the same crime, the murder of their employer, William Kirk. The state militia had to be called upon to restore order. Copperheads, or Peace Democrats, were Northern supporters of the Confederate States.

[14]The Irish National League was formed in Dublin on 17 October 1882 by Charles Stewart Parnell (1846–91) and others who opposed British rule and favored self-government in Ireland.

[15]Chauncey DePew (1834–1928) was an attorney, railroad executive, and U.S. Senator (1899–1911); Thomas Alva Edison (1847–1931) was an internationally famous inventor.

[16]Reference to the consequences of the Fugitive Slave Law (1850).

[17]Henry Wadsworth Longfellow, "A Psalm of Life."

[18]Robert Burns (1759–96), "To a Louse," *Poems* (1786).

Some Requisites of a Law Reporter

Speech to the Ohio Stenographers' Association, Dayton, O., 25 August 1891

The requisites of a law reporter, in my opinion, may be broadly classified as natural and acquired.

The natural qualifications requisite for a successful law reporter are easily disposed of. Quickness of apprehension—the ability to "catch-on" quickly—is one; a reporter must understand, superficially at least, what is going on, and he has no time to study it out. Good hearing is another. When one is listening merely to understand, one word or sentence explains another; but when listening to record, each word, at least each sentence, must explain itself, and therefore must be heard distinctly. Quickness of movement is equally essential; the reporter who takes down correctly a rapid cross-examination has not a second to lose. His work must be even. The regularity of the piston stroke of an engine would hardly be sufficient to characterize it; it must be rather the steady flow of a stream of water, which pauses only when the initial pressure is interrupted.

A cool head, an even temper, as much modesty as is consistent with a proper self-respect, are other requisites which may be classed as natural, though they may be more or less influenced by education.

The things I have mentioned are requisite in order to write shorthand, after having learned it. In order to learn it, even in the abstract, with no reference to any special application, two things are necessary—patience and perseverance. Perhaps the first generation of law reporters, who acquired the art painfully and without other instruction than the text books afforded, needed more patience in unravelling difficulties than the generation who are receiving instruction in well conducted schools. But perseverance is necessary in any case. One cannot acquire, in a few brief weeks, the ability to record accurately in unaccustomed and abbreviated signs the language which it has taken 20 years to learn to speak and write in longhand with average correctness. Any instance cited to the contrary is a phenomenon.

The acquired requisites of a law reporter are more numerous. We must bear in mind the duties of a law reporter; that he is expected to take down correctly and write out intelligibly whatever takes place in a court of justice. The proceedings of a court in one year, in the present age of commercial and scientific activity, are likely to embrace, in one of our great cities, a large part of the field of human knowledge. To be thoroughly at home in this work, to do it easily and well, a reporter should know everything. Perhaps my claim may seem too broad and I ought to specify. For instance:

I. *A good law reporter should be an accomplished linguist.* Not only should he be thoroughly acquainted with the principal languages of Europe, but with the chief dialects, for he does not know at what moment he may be called upon to report the testimony of a German, a Frenchman, a Pole, a Dutchman, a Russian, or a Spaniard. Perchance the witness will testify in what he intends for English, which will be plentifully interlarded with words and phrases of his mother tongue. If he disclaims a knowledge of English an interpreter is needed, and it is convenient for the reporter to act in that capacity. It adds to the dignity and importance of the profession. Languages are sometimes very much modified by a new environment. Take the following gem for an example of what German, for instance, may become in the United States:

> John Miller, welcher de bes gekhnownter Citizen von seine Ward ist, un seit de bloody fourth mit Intschein 33 geronnt hat, ist gestern nacht beinah auf de sport naufgagangen, because er die light extinguishen wollt bei de gas ausblasen. Wenn er seinen Kopf level gehalten hatte, konnte so etwas nicht happen. Glucklicherweise war Dr. Schnabenheiser an died Hand und mit einer Elektrisir Maschine ist Mr. Miller fur seine fellow-citizens gesaved worden. In die zuckerhaftige nach-und-nach sollte Mr. Miller carefuller sein und nicht mit die ward bummers die Districkt roth painten wollen und somit nicht geuscht nach Haus kommen zu Hahnekrah.[1]

The reporter who could struggle successfully with this specimen of transplanted German would certainly have to be a linguist of remarkable powers. I fear that mixed languages would affect the reporter unaccustomed to them somewhat as mixed drinks are popularly supposed to affect the uninitiated. I heard a few years ago of a Chautauqua phonographer who could report foreign languages with no previous acquaintance with them, so marvelous a mastery had he obtained of his art. I have not heard of him lately. I suppose he is dead; in fact, I hardly see how he could expect to live long.

II. *The successful law reporter should be thoroughly versed in medical sci-*

ence. Large numbers of law suits are concerned with personal injuries and their resulting complications. In order to report such cases a reporter should be familiar with anatomy, physiology, hygiene, *materia medica* and therapeutics. I would suggest a three years' course in medicine as an excellent and almost indispensable preparation for law reporting. No stenographer could take down the following paragraph, taken at random from a medical work, without some previous knowledge of the subject. It is a description of the course of the facial nerve, which gives expression to the countenance:

> The nerve passes forwards and outwards upon the crus cerebelli, and enters the internal auditory meatus with the auditory nerve. At the bottom of the meatus it enters the aquaeductus Falliopii, and follows the serpentine course of that canal through the petrous portion of the temporal bone from its commencement at the internal meatus to its termination at the stylo-mastoid foramen. It is at first directed outwards towards the hiatus Falliopii, and divides behind the ramus of the inferior maxillary into the temporo-facial and cervico-facial branches. As it emerges from the stylo-mastoid, it sends a twig to the pneumo-gastric, another to the glosso-pharyngeal nerve, and communicates with the carotid-plexus of the sympathetic with the great auricular branch of the cervical plexus and with the auriculo-temporal branch of the inferior maxillary nerve in the parotid gland.

Or this simple passage:

> The great or deep cardiac plexus (*plexus magnus profundus*) is situated in front of the trachea at its bifurcation. It is formed by the cardiac nerves derived from the cervical ganglia of the sympathetic, and the cardiac branches of the recurrent laryngeal and pneumo-gastric.

Let the reporter who thinks he knows everything struggle with a few pages of similar matter, and his opinion of his powers may be slightly modified.

III. *The successful law reporter should be a thorough scientist.* He should be proficient in electricity, chemistry, mechanics and civil engineering. He should know the difference between a chlorate and a chloride. When an electrical expert casually remarks that "the conductivity of an electrolyte is proportional to the sum of the oppositely directed velocities of the anion and cation," or that "there is a remarkable relation between the migration constants and the conductivities of extremely dilute solutions containing electrochemically equivalent amounts of haloid or oxygen salts," the competent reporter should have the words at his fingers' ends, and be sufficiently well informed on the subject, to know, when he reads it, whether he has it right or not.

IV. *A successful law reporter should know how to spell.* Those who think this statement an anti-climax should pause and reflect that the man who knows how to spell must know all the rest, and that good spelling is the last accomplishment of the cultivated. A good speller, in a scholarly sense, should know how to spell not only the words he is familiar with, but those he has never heard; he should be thoroughly acquainted with the principles which govern the derivation and formation of technical and scientific terminology.

V. *A good law reporter should be a lawyer.* A majority of the leading reporters of the country, perhaps, have read law. Others, by long experience, are fairly good theoretical lawyers, without any systematic course of reading. In the reporting of charges or opinions, a sufficient knowledge of law to be able to get citations correctly, and to know when a proposition of law is correctly stated, is almost absolutely necessary to an accurate law reporter.

VI. *A knowledge of English grammar is essential to a successful law reporter.* If a distinguished lawyer or a learned judge uses such an expression as this, for instance: "If the witness had of saw the defendant,"—and it is not an uncommon thing for distinguished counsel and venerable judges to make mistakes of that kind—the reporter should be able to write what the judge meant to say. A knowledge of grammar is of vastly more importance to the reporter than to the judge or the lawyer. They deal with ideas, or ought to; the reporter is chiefly concerned with words.

I might go on, perhaps at great length to tell what a successful law reporter should be. I might say that he should be a gentleman, for he must expect to get most of his employment from among gentlemen, who, very naturally, will prefer to deal with gentlemen. It is not necessary to define the meaning of the word "gentleman" to this audience. A successful reporter must have tact. He must be a good collector. He should know how to take care of money when he gets it. I think that it would add very much to happiness and length of life if every professional reporter had some fad or hobby outside of his profession. The reporter's work does not call into play to any great extent the higher faculties of the mind. Memory and exactness are his main intellectual tools, even if he should acquire every branch of knowledge which has been suggested for his equipment. It is true that a certain grade of reporters have to draw on their imagination, have even to exercise their judgment at times, in deciding what is the best thing with which to fill up a *hiatus* in a report; but this exercise is denied to the skilled reporter, who gets what is said.

An avocation of some kind—music, art, literature, something which calls into play a different set of faculties than his daily work demands—will preserve his mental balance and virility and keep him from falling into a rut from which he cannot extricate himself. A Chicago stenographer is a distinguished amateur astronomer. Several stenographers of my acquaintance are of an inventive turn of mind. There are certain kinds of "fads" which, however, it is well to avoid. It does not help a reporter any to be a valiant trencher-man or an expert at poker, or to have too wide an acquaintance with the various liquids which are prepared and sold for the refreshment of the thirsty.

One qualification which I was about to overlook, but which some members of the profession might deem important, though, perhaps, a secondary consideration, is the ability to write shorthand rapidly and correctly, and to read it back readily. Indeed, upon second thoughts, I suspect this is the first requisite of a successful law reporter. All the learning of the ages—the linguistic accomplishments of a Cardinal Mezzofanti[2] or an Elihu Burrit; the scientific attainments of a Darwin, a Faraday,[3] an Edison; the legal learning of a Blackstone or a Story[4]; even the wisdom of Solomon, the genius of a Raphael[5] or a Shakespeare—will not avail you to report a case if you do not know how.

Perhaps some one may think I have set too high a standard for the law reporter, higher than there is any reasonable probability of his reaching. If so, I think it is better to err on the safe side; better to know too much than too little; better not to attempt what you cannot do well. "Hitch your wagon to a star," said Emerson,[6] and let me add, if you never reach the star, you can at least keep your wagon tongue up out of the mud.

↫

SOURCE: "Some Requisites of a Law Reporter," *Proceedings of the Eighth and Ninth Annual Conventions of the Ohio Stenographers' Association* (Cleveland, O.: The F. W. Roberts Co., [1891]): "Ninth Annual Convention . . . Proceedings," 64–70. The convention was held at the Phillips House, Dayton, O. on 25 and 26 August 1891, and Chesnutt delivered his speech on 25 August.

[1]The anecdote reads: "John Miller, who is the best-known citizen of his ward, and since the bloody fourth has run with Intschein 33[,] was almost done in by the game last night because he wanted to extinguish the light by blowing out the gas. If he had kept a level head such a thing could not have happened. Fortunately Dr. Schnabenheiser was at hand and Mr. Miller was saved for the benefit of his fellow-citizens with an electrical device. In the sweet bye and bye Mr. Miller should be more careful and not wish to paint the town with the bums of his ward nor seek to come home with them at dawn." "Intschein" is not a German word, though schein signifies a certificate or document as well as a flash or light. It is possible that an inebriated Mr. Miller was a lamplighter who maintained 33 street lamps and made the mistake of attempting to extinguish one by blowing it out. If Mr. Miller was not a lamplighter, the joke remains the same: the alcohol-suffused breath of this man who was "painting the town" was ignited by the flame.

[2]Linguist Giuseppe Mezzofanti (1774–1849) was a professor at the University of Bologna; and, in 1833, he became the chief keeper of the Vatican Library.

[3]Charles Darwin (1809–82) was an English naturalist who developed a theory of evolution based upon the principle of natural selection; Michael Faraday (1791–1867) was an English physicist and chemist famous for his pioneering studies of the nature of electricity.

[4]Sir William Blackstone (1723–80) was an English jurist who wrote the monumental four-volume *Commentaries on the Laws of England* (1765–69); Joseph Story (1779–1845) was a Harvard law professor appointed to the U.S. Supreme Court (1811–45).

[5]Raphael (1483–1520) was a major artist of the Italian Renaissance whose works set longstanding standards for painting in the naturalistic manner.

[6]"Civilization," *Society and Solitude* (1870).

Resolutions Concerning Recent Southern Outrages

Essay published in the *Cleveland Gazette*, 4 June 1892

WHEREAS, The only legitimate object and use of any government is to protect its citizens in the enjoyment of life, liberty and the pursuit of happiness;[1]

WHEREAS, The colored people of the United States, by their[2] conduct in the pursuits of peace and their bravery and courage upon the battlefield in every period of their country's need, have thrice earned their citizenship;[3]

WHEREAS, In the Southern states of this Union, citizens of this Republic, whose only crime is that they contain in their veins African blood, not only are constantly proscribed in the just and equitable pursuits of life, denied equal access to railway coaches, shut out from public inns and places of amusement, and[4] in many other ways oppressed and persecuted, but are daily and mercilessly, without any legal or moral justification, whipped, shot, hung, burnt at the stake, mutilated and flayed alive;

WHEREAS, All our cries of distress and petitions sent up to the governing power of this Union have evoked no active interference in our behalf, nor even an investigation by any legally constituted authority of any one of these notorious outrages on law and conscience;[5]

WHEREAS, These abuses are daily becoming more numerous and wickedly unblushing, with no apparent prospect of aid from the national or state governments in the near future. Therefore, recognizing the fact that there is a higher power and a higher law,

Be it resolved by the colored citizens and their friends of the City of Cleveland, O., in conference assembled, that in this emergency and dire distress we lift our eyes and our hearts in supplication to Almighty God, the maker and ruler of all nations, and ask Him to stretch forth His omnipotent arm in our defense.[6]

Resolved, That we now take up the cry of the children of Israel of old and our fathers in the bonds of slavery, in that same southland, and while we exclaim "O Lord, how long," yet still we pray to Him for deliverance.[7]

Resolved, That it is with profound gratitude that[8] we note the decided stand in behalf of our oppressed brethren in the South taken by the Methodist Episcopal Church in its late General Conference at Omaha,[9] and we appeal to all other ecclesiastical bodies, to the labor assemblies, the Grand Army of the Republic, and all fraternal organizations based upon the principle of the fatherhood of God and the brotherhood of man, to emulate its example and to lend their aid and sympathy to this cause.

Resolved, That we earnestly invite and appeal to all good citizens and God-fearing men and women who favor justice and abhor all injustice and oppression, to aid us by their prayers, and in every other lawful and consistent way, to stop the horrible butcheries and oppression[10] of colored citizens in the South, and we demand as American citizens the enactment of proper laws and that our chief executive and the judges of our federal Courts do so construe the Constitution and laws of this land as to protect all citizens at home as well as abroad.

Resolved, That a copy of these resolutions be furnished to the press of this city, and that copies of the same be forwarded to our senators and members of Congress.

~

SOURCE: The source text is included in "Fittingly Observed," *Cleveland Gazette*, 4 June 1892, 1. It has been emended in light of an undated and untitled typed draft at the Fisk University Library. As with "Resolutions Concerning the Recent Election," Chesnutt composed the resolutions for a group of black Clevelanders who would negotiate a final version to be presented at St. John's A.M.E. Church during a day of prayer, reflection, and protest on 31 May 1892. Ohio State Senator John P. Green (1845–1940), chair of the resolutions committee, read the collectively revised text which was approved by those in attendance. It is assumed that Chesnutt, accepting the role of collaborative author, sanctioned the final version that was published—to which the present title has been given. Substantive variants from the typed draft are recorded in the annotations.

[1]Declaration of Independence (1776).

[2]The draft does not include "by their."

[3]The American Revolution, the War of 1812, and the Civil War.

[4]The draft does not include "and."

[5]The draft reads "conscience, and" without a completion of the sentence. The source text reads "conscience, and supplication to God"; and it is assumed that this represents a typographical error.

[6]Psalms 121:1 and Isaiah 5:25.

[7]Psalms 90:13

[8]The draft does not include "that."

[9]On 17 May 1892, the General Conference of the Methodist Episcopal church passed a resolution decrying violent discrimination against African Americans, who constitute both "an important portion of the membership of the Church and of the citizenship of the nation"; further, the Conference called on the "religious and secular press of the entire country to unite . . . in denouncing the wrongs and cruelties [specified in the resolution], and in efforts to secure equality and justice in the enactment and enforcement of humane and righteous laws" ("General Conference Proceedings," *Christian Advocate*, 8 June 1892, 7).

[10]The draft reads "oppressions."

Competition

Speech to the Ohio Stenographers' Association, Columbus, O., 31 August 1892

It is a business proverb that "Competition is the life of trade."[1] The unsuccessful reporter is prone to say that competition is the death of shorthand. But I think that a little reflection will show that the first statement is the true one, and that a healthy competition promotes the efficiency of the shorthand art. In any competition experience teaches that some one must go to the wall. Every day we see men fail in something they have rashly or unadvisedly undertaken. Men are slow to learn that ambition is not ability, that the desire to do a thing is not necessarily a sign of fitness for it. The conservatories of music are full of young women who have all the ambitions, all the qualifications for great singers—

except voices. In politics, for every victory there is a defeat for some one. Every congressman represents a defeated opponent and a dozen unsuccessful aspirants to the office.

I have in my pocket a letter from a young man who tells me he has a "purfic krays" to learn shorthand, and wants my aid and advice and all through it he spells "and" *a-n*, and "to" *t-o-o*, and other words with an equal disregard to conventional rules. It is a clear case of misplaced ambition. This young man may study shorthand, but he will not be qualified to practice it. But he will not hurt the business. Competition will step in and crowd him out. He will, perhaps, take to running an elevator and working on a street-car, or perhaps collecting monthly payments of a subscription book agency. And he will always say, when he meets a stenographer whom he knows: "I was once a stenographer. I could write 300 words a minute and run the typewriter blindfold. But competition crowded me out. Competition has killed the shorthand business." And perhaps he will be mean enough to add: "So many of these women coming in have killed the business."

But what a mistake it will be! The business will not be dead. There will be more stenographers and better ones than ever. The good stenographers will all be making a living, and people will be looking for more good stenographers.

This, then, is the great benefit of competition—it weeds out the incompetent. And should any competent stenographer complain? A poor stenographer generally loses a customer every time he reports a case or takes a dictation; the good stenographer gains one. The result is that the inefficient reporter has no regular clientage, and is dependent on chance for the crumbs which fall from the full tables of the competent. The good stenographer has all he can do, and wishes he could be in three places at once.

The competition of the ladies seems to be a bugbear which frightens a good many male reporters. I take the broad, manly ground that if I cannot compete with the women I am willing to retire. In fact I think, with all due respect to the ladies, that I should want to get out of a calling in which I could not do equally as well as the ladies. I would think them better adapted to the work, and I would not wish to follow a career in which nature had disqualified me for high success. I think him a poor man who is thus frightened off by female competition. Given equal skill, why should a woman get more business than a man? The ladies are better looking, I admit that, and I am glad for the sake of humanity that they are; I am afraid ours would be a homely race if men set the standard of beauty. But looks don't report cases as our reverend friend so clearly indicated in his address to-day,[2] nor make up bills of exceptions, nor write letters, nor report conventions—and these things after all are what shorthand is for. Men have the advantage of greater physical strength, more endurance. They have generally the advantage of better business training. There is a prejudice against women in business which men do not meet. Men can go to places, hear things, and even say things without reproach, which would be held unbecoming in a woman; I don't know why this should be, but it is nevertheless true.

So I think any big hearted men, in fact any man at all, can afford to put aside the bugbear of female domination, and admitting the ladies to our ranks, extend to them every professional courtesy and abide by the result. If the gray mare is the better horse,[3] let her win the race and take the stakes. All hail to our sisters of the pen and the typewriter, who already form so important a part of our Association and of our profession, and who are destined in the freedom which the future has for man, to win still brighter laurels!

But competition does not only operate for good by weeding out the incompetent. It also raises the standard of skill and intelligence. It is in the nature of things that no two men shall be in all respects equal as our brother Pomerene so clearly showed us in his address this afternoon,[4] and these natural inequalities are intensified and enlarged by conditions of training, by opportunities for culture, and by the application of natural endorsements.

This being so, of any two stenographers one must possess some qualities that the other lacks, and one as a rule must be better qualified to succeed as a stenographer than the other. The best set the standard, and all the others strive to reach it—perhaps unconsciously, but none the less actually. Where there is but one stenographer in a community he can write as he pleases, and no one knows whether any one else can do any better. If he cannot read his notes, it is popularly believed that no one can read shorthand notes back readily. If he fails to keep his engagements it is supposed to be a characteristic of shorthand writers. If he takes to drink or other vices it is ascribed to the influence of shorthand; and it is gravely asserted that all shorthand men are cranks. Their faults are overlooked as the eccentricities of genius.[5] In fact, I think the tendency on the part of the multitude in small towns to hang over the back of the stenographer's chair in open-mouthed wonder, indulging in occasional remarks of admiration and incredulity, has a tendency to make some stenographers eccentric. They get so accustomed to being gaped at that they begin to feel like celebrities—somewhat like I imagine a paroled murderer or a reformed horse-thief would feel. They swell around the court houses like they own them, and look down upon the legal profession with a lordly scorn, or with a fine contempt mingled with profound pity, and if in the course of time the bucolic mind becomes accustomed to the winged art and ceases to wonder, these members of our craft feel it necessary to keep up the public interest by vagaries of conduct which serve to attract attention. I have heard of these fellows, but I am glad none of them belongs to our Association.

But where there is competition this sort of thing does not exist. For lawyers, like ordinary mortals, want the most they can get for their money, and they prefer the man who is most skillful, who is promptest, most trustworthy, and most gentlemanly.

It is this spirit of competition which has given birth to our wonderful civilization; which has heaped up colossal fortunes, which has built our great systems of interstate and international communication; which has developed our vast mineral and agricultural resources and built up our great manufactories. It is competition which has produced our excellent typewriting machines, and our wonderful operators who almost excel the speed of stenography itself on the rattling keys. Competition has brought up the standard of speed to a very high figure, and thereby has abbreviated the forms and lessened the labor of the reporter. Competition then is useful. And even if it sometimes causes you temporary inconvenience, it is philosophy to make a virtue of necessity,[6] and to acquiesce in what you cannot help. For competition is unavoidable. The young come forward upon the field of action while the old are still alive. The young must live, and so they compete with the old. The old have skill and reputation and judgment. The young have energy and boundless hope. There is room for both and their interests need not conflict.

But by competition I do not mean a cut-throat struggle for supremacy; I do not mean a resort to unworthy methods. I would not want a dollar which I had put myself in the way of earning by decrying a worthy competitor. I think the most desirable way, in fact the only absolutely safe way to succeed, is on one's own merits, and not on the weaknesses of others. The latter reminds one of the ladder of rotten spokes. It will not support you if a better man enters the field. It is like climbing a pyramid of skulls, such as are said to attest the powers and the cruelty of the Dahomey Chiefs.[7] Of course, no one can hope to reach the absolute in shorthand any nearer than in art or science or any branch of human effort. Excellence is always comparative, but I should prefer the excellence which is compared with the best, rather than that which is good *only*, as compared with what is worse. I would rather be a *good* stenographer than to merely be "the best there is," because the latter term might mean very little, whereas the former has a well defined significance. No one can object to the kind of competition that is based on merit, that is open and above board in its methods.

I have been speaking of shorthand not chiefly as an art, but as a business, as a vocation. But there are certain conditions under which there is, in a business sense, but little room for competition. For instance, the laws of supply and demand and of the survival of the fittest[8] do not operate so directly or to the same extent where stenographers are salaried appointees as where there is free competition. And, for my part, I think that the efficiency and the standing of the profession are enhanced when it depends for its existence upon its own efforts, so to speak. Given an equal amount of shorthand work to be done, I think it will be better done and more profitably when paid for by fees than by a salary. Perhaps the chief advantage in having official stenographers is that it increases the quantity of work, and provides a *certain* mode of payment. But a salary too often has an enervating effect. A lazy salaried man does only work enough to keep his place. A diligent man has no incentive to special exertion. The men who rule in the world of art, of literature, in the learned professions, in business, do not work for salaries. Of course we cannot all choose in these matters; we must take things as we find them. But now and then we can choose. And if we could get large enough salaries I do not know that I should object to them.

Let us all, then, join hands in the effort to encourage honorable competition. Let each one of us try to set such a standard of skill, of business methods, of character, or all-round excellence, in fact, as will make those who are inferior to us strive to catch up, and those who are in advance of us bestir themselves to keep the lead. Thus we will benefit ourselves and our patrons, provide better for those dependent upon us, elevate our calling in the eyes of the world, and fulfill the duty which our reverend friend made so clear to us this afternoon, the obligation which conscious existence imposes upon every one, and which alone proves one's right to live—the duty of doing something and doing it well, the duty of making the best of himself and his powers. Then life will be to us not a bloody battlefield, not a stormy sea, not a barren desert, not a vale of tears;[9] but it will be a fertile and well-watered garden where the brightest flowers and the most luscious fruits will fall to those who have earned the right to them.

⤙

SOURCE: "Competition," *Proceedings of the Tenth Annual Convention of the Ohio Stenographers' Association* (Cleveland, O.: [Buel & Hubbell Print], 1893): 25–33. The convention was held at the Hotel Chittenden, Columbus, O., on 30 and 31 August 1892, and Chesnutt delivered his speech on 31 August.

[1]This adage is quoted and acknowledged as an old saw by Mason Long (1842–1903) in *The Life of Mason Long, the Converted Gambler* (1878).

[2]Presbyterian minister Francis E. Marsten (1855–1915) of Columbus, O., spoke at the conference, and Chesnutt offered a brief response for the Association, thanking Marsten and the city of Columbus for courtesies extended.

[3]John Heywood (1497–1580), *Proverbs* (1546).

[4]Julius G. Pomerene delivered the Presidential Address.

[5]The phrase "eccentricities of genius" is Mr. Pickwick's in Charles Dickens's *The Pickwick Papers* (1837).

[6]Paraphrase of *Richard II*, 1.3.278–79

[7]Benin, formerly Dahomey, is a western African country that was legendary for its repressive rule. Chesnutt is referring to a monarchical state in which past kings were honored annually by human sacrifices. Editorially emended is the source text's reading, ". . . the powers and the cruelty of the kinds of Dahomey Chiefs." Chesnutt may also have intended as the final reading ". . . cruelty of the kings of Dahomey."

[8]Chesnutt here uses the evolutionary term coined by Herbert Spencer (1820–1903). His familiarity with Spencer's thought would be more fully measured in 1898 when he wrote "The Gray Wolf's Han't" for 1899 publication in *The Conjure Woman*. At its beginning the character John reads to his wife from the "Instability of the Homogeneous" chapter of Spencer's *First Principles* (1862, chapter 13; 1867 and thereafter, chapter 19).

[9]Robert Browning (1812–89), "Confessions" (1864).

Why I Am a Republican

Speech delivered in the autumn of 1892

Gentlemen:—

After the many eloquent and able orators, and the many experienced and successful politicians who have addressed you, I do not think of anything new or particularly interesting which I can hope to bring to your notice to-night. If I cannot thrill you with oratory, or enlighten you by superior wisdom, I can at least exercise the right so dear to every American citizen, the right of free speech, and use this opportunity to tell you why I am a Republican. I suspect my reasons are yours, and while we may not all agree as to their relative importance, I think that among them all there ought to be at least one conclusive reason why every good citizen should be a Republican, some reason which will convince every Republican that he is in the right party.

1. I am a Republican because my father was one. A poor argument it may be said. I could not expect this argument to convince anyone else. But as time goes on and I see more clearly the superiority of our party, I thank the old man for saving me the necessity of changing my politics, as I should otherwise have had to do; for, I cannot imagine how I could have remained a Democrat after arriving at years of discretion.

2. I am a Republican because the Republican party is the party which seeks to protect home industries from ruinous foreign competition. Free trade is a pretty theory. Supposing it were adopted; for a time we could buy many things cheaper than we do now. Then when some of our workshops and factories were shut down, and in the rest wages had been reduced to the European or still worse the Asiatic level, our foreign friends, having no competition to fear from us, would put up their prices, and we would have more to pay and less to pay it with.[1] I do not believe in free trade as the embodiment of commercial evil; I do not believe that of itself it has horns and a tail and cloven feet. I do not believe that protection is a panacea for every commercial ill. I can easily imagine a time when complete freedom of trade will be desirable for all nations. But that time is not now, nor is it likely to be for a hundred years.[2] By the policy so wisely conceived and so ably executed by the Hon. James G. Blaine, may his fame grow ever brighter, we are able by means of reciprocity to gain the advantages of commercial freedom and at the same time to avoid the evils of absolute free trade.[3]

3. I am a Republican because the Republican party by this policy of protection renders possible a high degree of intelligence and a wise diversification of our industries. I cannot believe that a purely agricultural people, or people engaged in merely mechanical pursuits can be so intelligent or enterprising as a people among whom there is a considerable diversity of interests and employ-

ments. I have read somewhere a story of a country where the people are so constituted that when they cease to exercise any bodily or mental function, the faculty or the member thus neglected loses in time its power to act. The man who sits loses the power to walk; his limbs become weak and shrivelled. The man who merely walks loses all muscular power in his arms. The man who works at night loses the power to see by day. We are familiar with this principle, though not in so exaggerated a form. And we can imagine a country—in fact we see plenty of examples of them—so closely identified with some pursuit that if by some sudden disaster that pursuit is interfered with, ruin stares it in the face.[4]

4. A fourth reason why I am a Republican is because the Republican party has always advocated a liberal system of public internal improvements. Under the fostering influence of government aid our great railroad system and interstate waterways have been pushed in almost a generation to an extent and completeness which is the wonder of the world. A network of great trunk lines spans the continent and gives employment to hundreds of thousands. Our great lakes teem with Commerce. Our navigable rivers are kept open. Our harbors are filled with ships of all nations. The ambitious and the enterprising poor of all countries flock to our shores, and help to develop our resources, and foreign capital flows in vast amounts to seek investment here.[5]

Of course with these blessings some evils creep in. But the wise foresight of the Republican party has endeavored in the past and can be trusted in the future to counteract these evils. Witness the alien pauper immigration and the alien contract laws.[6]

5. I am a Republican because it is the party of a sound currency. The financial policy of the nation, as established and maintained by the Republican party since the war is almost ideal in its excellence. It may be said of Secretary Chase, an Ohio man, with even greater force than it was said by Edward Everett of Alexander Hamilton, that like Moses in the wilderness, "he touched the rock of public credit, and abundant streams of revenue burst forth."[7] And I believe that the National Banking system and the gold standard are so firmly seated that the attacks of free silver men and rag money and wild cat bank demagogues cannot avail to disturb them.[8] And I am proud to belong to the party which has produced such finance policy-makers as Secretary Chase and the Hon. John Sherman.[9] These men have never got to be president; but they will be remembered for their public services when future generations will have to turn to musty, worm-eaten encyclopedias to find out who Franklin Pierce and Millard Fillmore and Andy Johnson and Grover Cleveland were.[10]

6. I am a Republican because I love my country, and I do not think it safe to trust her interests to the Democratic party. I do not think that either its principles or its *personnel* are fit to govern this country. It is the party of many followers and few leaders. The Republican party in nominating candidates finds it difficult to choose because of the multitude of good men who would honor office rather than be honored by it. The Democratic party finds it difficult to discover

anyone to nominate for high office. The Democratic party is a party of large promises and small performance. By a peculiar combination of circumstances the Democrats this year have had an immense majority in the House of Representatives.[11] They professed to believe that free trade was the *summum bonum* of statesmanship. What have they done to promote it? They cursed the McKinley bill as the Jonah that would sink the ship of State. What attempt have they made to throw it overboard?[12] They abused the last Congress[13] as wasteful and extravagant, and then made appropriations vastly in excess of those of the last session. They boast of being the people's party, the party of the poor, and what have they done to lighten the burden of poverty which it seems must needs fall on some of us? It is the party which was willing to see the Union destroyed, which opposed the abolition of slavery, an institution that kept 3,000,000 of the poor in bondage and subjected free men to the competition of unpaid labor. And when the slaves were freed it resisted every effort to enlarge their liberties. It raises its hands in holy horror at any attempt on the part of the Republican party to preserve the purity of the ballot, and its high-priest Father Grover prates pragmatically of the disasters that would result from a free vote and a fair count.[14]

7. I am a Republican because the Republican party is the party of grand achievements and glorious traditions. The French it is said worship glory, and the pages of their history are bright with it. I despise that mean and vulgar soul which never thrills with pride at great deeds, which denies a due meed of honor to great men. The glory of our country is bound up in the history of the Republican party. What achievement of prince or king can compare with the emancipation and enfranchisement of 3,000,000 bondsmen? What European war was ever so far reaching in its results, so beneficent to humanity as the heroic struggle which preserved and perpetuated the unity of this nation? Gaze into the magic mirror of history and a long line of great spirits rise up and pass before you. Lincoln the emancipator, the martyr, Grant the hero, whose deeds of arms excited the wonder of the Generals of the world and brought the war to a successful termination. Greeley, Seward, Chase, Sumner, Sherman, Sheridan—I might go on naming them for an hour.[15] Their deeds are ours, their fame is safe in our keeping. We cherish their memories—and our children may perhaps find a place for their monuments. I must confess that I prefer this glorious parchment to the ragged, soiled, and faded sheet of foolscap upon which are recorded the failures and mistakes of the Democratic party.

8. Lastly, I am a Republican because of what I expect the Republican party to do in the future. We have laid the foundations of greatness; we have seen its walls rise in stately magnificence. But we have yet to add the towers, and clean up the debris around this splendid structure. We must maintain the protective system, our financial system. Other evils will grow up, and the nation must look to the Republican party to remedy them. But in my humble opinion there is at present one evil which must be remedied and that right speedily. I refer to the

almost universal corruption of the ballot and denial of the suffrage to large numbers of citizens in the Southern States.

I suppose it is a unique spectacle in history, the present state of political affairs in the South. There are countries where the right of suffrage is restricted, where there are privileged classes, where the rich oppress the poor under cover of law. But this is perhaps the only country in the world where a large class of the population, in many instances a majority, are deliberately and systematically denied the exercise of fundamental rights which by the Constitution and the laws are theirs. There is no excuse for it. We are pointed to the carpet-bag era as a specimen of what Negro domination of the South would mean. A comparison of figures will show that half a dozen defaulting Democratic State Treasurers have stolen more money than all the carpet-bag governments put together. Under the carpet-bag governments men accused of crime, whether white or black, were sure of a fair trial.

Under the present Democratic *régime* a colored man accused of almost any crime is liable to be executed without judge or jury. More men have been lynched in the South in the last year of enlightened, civilized Democratic rule, than during the entire carpet-bag era. That is one glory of that epoch. During those brief years the country was free and men in the South were equal before the law. They never were before and they never have been since, and they will not be in this generation unless the strong outstretched arm of the government is invoked to compel the execution of the laws. The Republican party will not have accomplished its mission until it shall have brought about the reign of law in all this fair land; until it shall have made this a free country both in name and in fact, both South as well as North; until liberty and intelligence and law and order and prosperity and happiness shall prevail within our boundaries. And future generations, looking back upon the history of our country, shall see in the history of the Republican party of the 19th Century the most glorious epoch of our country's progress. Life would be too short, Mr. Chairman and fellow citizens, to tell you why I am not a Democrat. But these are a few of the reasons why I am Republican, and why I think every good citizen ought to be a Republican.

⤚

SOURCE: Untitled and undated typed text at the Fisk University Library. References to the contemporary political situation indicate that the 1892 presidential election pitting the incumbent Benjamin Harrison against Democrat Grover Cleveland was close at hand.

[1]Chesnutt is articulating the protectionist Republican hostility to low tariffs and is, consequently, criticizing the position of Grover Cleveland, who had served as President in 1885–89 and would be elected again in 1892 as Republican Benjamin Harrison was concluding his term.

[2]Chesnutt here made a parenthetical note in his typescript, indicating related topics on which he might extemporize: "Climate. Standard of living, of education. Expense of living, Rate of wages etc."

[3]Republican James G. Blaine (1830–93) was the Secretary of State during Harrison's presidency (1889–93). In the high, protective tariff context resulting from passage of the McKinley Tariff Act (1890), Blaine enjoyed considerable bargaining power when arranging reciprocal tariff arrangements with Latin American countries that were beneficial to U.S. interests: that is, these countries lowered their duties on imported American products in exchange for adjustments of the tariff on the raw materials they shipped to the United States.

[4]Chesnutt again made a parenthetic note on how he might illustrate his point: "The South and Manchester. South ruined by want of market; Manchester for want of cotton."

[5]Since 1861, two Democrat and six Republican administrations (including Harrison's through the summer and fall of 1892) had overseen the development of a U.S. transportation infrastructure facilitating domestic and foreign travel and commerce.

[6]If Chesnutt meant alien pauper immigration laws rather than alien pauper immigration itself, he was thus referring to the Immigration Act of 1882, whose principal sponsors were New York Republican Congressmen Warner Miller (1838–1918) and John Van Voorhis (1826–1905). It was passed during the Republican administration of President Chester A. Arthur (1881–85). In the Immigration Act of 1891, restrictions against pauper immigrants and those likely to become dependent upon public assistance were made tighter; passed during the Republican administration of Benjamin Harrison, it too was originated by party members such as Senator Henry Cabot Lodge (1850–1924) of Massachusetts and Representative William D. Owen (1846–1906) of Indiana. With regard to the "alien contract laws," the 1891 act also reinforced the 1885 Contract Labor Act providing that those foreigners with prearranged work contracts could be barred from entry into the United States

[7]Republican Salmon P. Chase (1808–73) was Abraham Lincoln's Secretary of the Treasury; that he secured the passage in 1863 of the National Bank Act, creating a national banking system with a single currency that was not replaced until 1913, is the stabilizing achievement by Chase on which Chesnutt focuses. Edward Everett (1794–1865) was a Unitarian minister, professor of Greek literature, editor of the *North American Review*, Secretary of State, U.S. Senator from Massachusetts, and renowned orator. The eulogy concerning Alexander Hamilton (1755–1804), George Washington's Secretary of the Treasury and a proponent of high tariffs protecting "infant industries," relates to his advocacy of a centralized, national banking system, modeled upon the Bank of England. The originator of the encomium, however, was Daniel Webster (1782–1852) rather than Everett: "He smote the rock of the national resources, and abundant streams of revenue gushed forth. He touched the dead corpse of the Public Credit, and it sprung upon his feet" ("Speech at a Public Dinner at New York," 1831). Webster's biblical allusion is to Exodus 17:6.

[8]From its beginning, the United States had a bi-metallic standard. That is, any gold or silver offered to it was purchased and then turned into coins. The ratio was fixed at a 16:1 value of silver to gold. When large new deposits of silver were discovered in the West, the price of silver dropped dramatically. In 1878 a free-silver bill, the Bland-Allison Act, was passed by Congress to ensure that the government would buy no less than $2,000,000 and no more than $4,000,000 worth of silver monthly and convert it into dollars. In 1890 the Sherman Silver Purchase Act forced the government to buy massive amounts of silver monthly and to issue treasury notes and silver certificates ("rag money") which could be redeemed in gold. "Wild cat" banks were state banks chartered in the West before the 1863 National Bank Act. With little capital, they issued notes that they were not able to redeem.

[9]John Sherman (1823–1900) was a Republican who represented Ohio in the U.S.

House of Representatives and Senate. A fiscal conservative, he served as the chairman of the Senate Finance Committee during the Reconstruction Era, as Rutherford B. Hayes's Secretary of the Treasury (1877–81), and, much later, as William McKinley's Secretary of State (1897). In this sentence, "such finance policy-makers" originally read "such finances." Chesnutt circled "e" and drew a line through "s"—indicating that he noted the typographical error. He did not, however, provide the replacement reading to which the text is here emended.

[10]Fillmore (1800–1874) was a Whig, and the other three presidents were Democrats. As though to prove his point, Chesnutt misspelled "Fillmore" as "Filmore."

[11]This statement by Chesnutt is the primary reason for an 1892 dating of this speech. The 1890 election resulted in the Democrats' gaining 75 seats in the House, this giving them an "immense" majority: 321 Democrats, 88 Republicans, and 14 with other affiliations. The "lame duck" period between the election and the seating of the 52nd Congress was approximately 14 months; and so it did not convene until 7 December 1891. The first session adjourned on 5 August 1892; the second session did not begin until 5 December 1892. Since Chesnutt refers below to what the Democrats did and did not do during the first session, and does not refer to the events of the second session, he made the present speech after August and before the November 1892 election. In the 53rd Congress, the Democrats maintained their majority in the House and assumed control of the Senate; but the House majority was not the "immense" one gained in the 1890 election, and so Chesnutt cannot have been referring to it.

[12]The McKinley Tariff Act is the "Jonah" (see Jonah 1:4–16).

[13]The 51st, in which Republicans were in the majority.

[14]Republicans had submitted to Congress bills effecting federal supervision of elections, in the hope of thwarting the voter registration laws of the states that disfranchised African Americans and ensured Democrat victories in the South. For the Republican point of view, see William E. Chandler (1835–1917), "National Control of Elections," *Forum*, 9 (August 1890), 706–18. The perspective of the Democrats who opposed such legislation was succinctly articulated by Alabama Senator John T. Morgan (1824–1927), "Federal Control of Elections," *Forum*, 10 (September 1890), 23–36. Chesnutt here made a parenthetical note regarding "Inconsistency, Alabama election"—and he apparently extemporized at this point on the disparity between the number of African Americans there who might have voted and the number of those who actually did in a recent election.

[15]Horace Greeley was one of the founders of the Republican Party (1854) and a radical abolitionist. William H. Seward (1801–72) was the Whig governor of New York State. An abolitionist, he became a Republican in 1855 and served as Abraham Lincoln's Secretary of State, as well as Democrat Andrew Johnson's. Charles Sumner became prominent in abolitionist circles when, in 1849, he argued before the Supreme Judicial Court of Massachusetts in Roberts v. City of Boston, 5 Cushing (Massachusetts) 198, against the "separate but equal" doctrine upon which segregation in schools was based. From 1851 through the rest of his life, he was a U.S. Senator representing Massachusetts and a prominent Republican intent on minimizing Southern political power during the Reconstruction and maximizing Northern control of national legislation—this resulting in the Reconstruction Acts, which were in part intended to "punish" the South for its rebellion, and the Fourteenth and Fifteenth Amendments. Chesnutt, consistently seeing the federal intervention in Southern affairs as an ethical imperative, viewed Sumner as a paragon of righteousness; see "The Disfranchisement of the Negro." John Sherman may again be referred to by Chesnutt here; but, given his next reference to Sheridan, he may have in mind General William Tecumseh Sherman

(1820–91), John's elder brother. Philip H. Sheridan (1831–88) was a distinguished Union Army general who frustrated Robert E. Lee's retreat from Appomattox in 1865 and thus forced his surrender and the termination of the Civil War. After the war, he served as the head of the military departments governing the South.

Liberty and the Franchise

Essay written c. 1899

Some thirty-odd years ago a great civil war was fought in this country, the only constructive result of which, beyond the pomp and circumstance,[1] the misery and horrors of war, and the resulting mountain of debt, was the abolition of slavery and the enfranchisement of the colored people. If it be said that the Union was saved, it will be remembered that from the Northern point of view the Union had never been destroyed, but merely threatened. The great fact that stood out before the world as the outcome of the war was the abolition of slavery and the elevation of the colored race to the plane of citizenship.

And it is well enough to remember, in these reactionary days, that the game was considered worth the candle. Lincoln's highest title to fame has been that of the Great Emancipator. A great party was born and reared on the doctrine of equality before the law, and for ten years the Federal Government lent the force of its arms to maintain that doctrine, and for ten years or so longer lent its influence to maintain the rights of the enfranchised people in an atmosphere hostile to their liberty and progress.

Of late years, however, the zeal of the Northern people for humanity as embodied in the colored people of the South has apparently cooled. We are told by a large portion of the Republican press that the enfranchisement of the Negroes of the South was a grave mistake, an act of ill-advised generosity, of hysterical enthusiasm, the baleful effects of which are apparent, and that the Negro would have been much better without the ballot than with it.

Are these things true? Are the principles which guided the really great men who brought this country through the most dangerous crisis in its history any less correct or operative now than they were then? If enfranchisement was a mistake, was not the abolition of slavery a mistake? If these people are to be governed without their consent, and taxed without representation, their condition will be perilously near to that of slavery. Only yesterday a writer has put forth the astonishing prediction that in another generation slavery, characterized thirty years ago as the sum of all villainies, would be recognized as the ideal relation of capital and labor. It is unnecessary to say that this proposition emanated from the New South.

Another theory that prevailed for some time after the war, and the faint echo of which can still be heard in the columns of some backwoods paper in Maine or Vermont or Massachusetts, was that humanity was the test of liberty and opportunity, and that the Negro was a man, and capable of progress along all lines, commensurate only with his individual capacity. On this theory philanthropic people of the North poured out their wealth to establish schools, first for primary instruction, later for the higher education of these people, and sent some of their best blood to teach and train the emancipated race in institutions of higher learning.

One other belief that is evident from a perusal of ante- and post-bellum literature was that the colored people were the victims of a cruel oppression, which crushed every aspiration toward manhood, and which had been deliberately and advisedly exercised for generations, in order that they might more easily be held in subjection. At the same time it was argued that a people who endured hardships, as many of them did, according to the records of the Underground Railroad, that they might be free; who bore themselves so well toward their hereditary oppressor during the trying period of the Civil War; and who fought so nobly on the battlefield, were worthy of liberty and opportunity.

All these things were believed, and for a time were acted upon, as the history of the country will show. Colored men were clothed with the ballot and for a few brief years were protected in its exercise. For a much longer period they have exercised it under difficulties, but still sufficiently to give them, until within the last five years, some representation in the legislatures of all or nearly all the Southern States, and with the exception of one or two terms, in Congress.

At present, after the lapse of thirty years, there seems to be taking place a reaction in public sentiment. The Negro, according to the prevailing tone, from a patient and respectful servitor, has become a bestial villain, whom it is dangerous to meet alone. The Negro soldier, it is admitted, will fight, when led by white officers, but not otherwise. As a regular he is amenable to discipline; as a volunteer he is turbulent and unruly. As a scholar, he is a failure, and since the safety and interest of society require that he be not idle, he must be taught to work, but only with his hands. As a politician and a voter the horrible example of the reconstruction period and the shocking condition of Hayti are shaken before the eyes of the American people,[2] and they are told to behold what the South would come to if the Negroes were permitted to vote.

Reflection on this state of things leads to one of two conclusions: either the past generation were wrong—Garrison, Phillips, Sumner, Lincoln, Seward, Greeley and the rest of the great men of the heroic period of our history; or they were right, and public opinion is being led astray by false guides. That the men of the past were right and that the results have proved it, is the firm belief of the writer. That public opinion is being guided in the wrong direction, and deliberately and intentionally so, the writer is also fully persuaded. That the people who so industriously disseminate their anti-Negro arguments believe them, is quite likely; and if so, they have the courage of their convictions. That they believe them is no evidence whatever of their truthfulness. They are the same people who preached the essential righteousness of slavery, and as yet at least, the rest of the world is against them.

To demonstrate the first proposition, that the men we have been taught to revere were right, and not a set of self-deluded enthusiasts, look for a moment at the results, as they have been under unfavorable conditions, and as they might have been under more favorable conditions. A people, like a horse in a race, should be judged by its handicap. That the colored race in this country has made wonderful progress, creditable alike to itself and to humanity, no unprejudiced person would deny. If the result is not what we might have wished or hoped, let us place the blame where it belongs, and give credit where credit is due. And if the American people are to stand still and see this race, clothed with liberty at such a fearful cost, robbed, by the Southern States, of its shadow as well as its substance, let them at least see the nature of the crime and the spirit that incites to it.

First as to the nature of the Negro. Several hundred colored men and women and children—not even babes at the breast were spared—have been put to death by unlawful mobs during the past two or three years, most of them because they or their relations or friends, were charged with or suspected of certain crimes mainly criminal assault, or murder, or attempted murder, or office-holding, or being black. It will be apparent to any one who follows these reports that they emanate from sources hostile to the colored race, and that those who write them, even when pretending to tell the truth about these matters, invariably give them a coloring most prejudicial to the victims. In most of these cases suspicion is equivalent to a charge, a charge is equivalent to a conviction, and an execution follows post-haste, sometimes so rapidly that the participants do not stop long enough to be sure they have the man who is suspected. And while comparisons are odious, it is submitted whether burning a man alive or mutilating him is not equally as horrible a crime as violating a woman's person. One is the perversion of a very natural instinct, and is not unknown in the most highly civilized communities; the other is pure, unadulterated savagery. The one should be severely punished; the other is apparently not possible in any Christian country except the United States. The charge of bestiality against the race may therefore, in the light of the past, and considering the source of the charge, be dismissed as at least not proven. As in all these discussions the white people of the South are presumed to represent the embodiment of all the virtues, comparisons of course would be out of the question.

As to the higher education, in any natural order of development no race can be all hewers of wood and drawers of water,[3] builders of houses or makers of bricks. The Southern theory is that the colored people must be kept a separate and distinct race. A race must have leaders, and a healthy progress demands that these leaders be of their own blood and thus in a position to sympathize with their aspirations; who are in the ship with them, to sink or swim with them, and whose fate is, in some measure at least, bound up with theirs. The reader can judge for himself whether the colored race in the South are likely to find such leaders among the Southern white people, or whether, however much disposed some individuals might be to assume such a role, they would find it possible to do so. Northern white men have played the part with great results, but always with sacrifices, which no man in a Christian country should be asked to make; and they have never been permitted to do all that they would. Witness the withdrawal of the State appropriation from Atlanta University because the white teachers would not yield the right to teach their own children in the school with their colored pupils;[4] also the white men who led the Negro vote in North Carolina, and who paid for it by their expulsion from the State a few months ago.[5]

If, then, leaders in church and school and other walks of life are essential to any true progress, and these leaders must be drawn from the colored race, it must have the higher education that it may produce them. That the money spent in giving this education has not been wasted is a matter beyond question. The race has preachers of character, eloquence and talent for organization, of which the statistics of their churches are the best evidence. Most colored schools of the country, of all grades, are taught by colored teachers. Every Northern university has pupils of color; and men of the race are contributing, in increasing volume, to the best literature of the day. Races should be judged by their best and not by their lowest, and a people who can produce a Frederick Douglass during slavery and a Booker Washington, a Tanner and a Dunbar[6] within 30 years after emancipation, is worthy of the higher education.

But the great ground upon which the disfranchisement of the colored race is urged, is its failure to exercise the franchise wisely; and the awful examples are the reconstruction period and the spectacle of Hayti. With reference to Hayti, how many of those who quote it know anything at all about its recent history? I simply refer to the recent work of Robert Thomas Hill, of Tennessee on Cuba, Porto Rico and the West Indies. To summarize his statements in regard to Hayti, of which he speaks from personal knowledge,—in spite of the absolute lack of sympathy or association or commendation of any advanced nation for a hundred years, Hayti today is the most promising of the West Indies, shows larger trade balances than any other of the islands, has good standing in the diplomatic world, good credit, and is making substantial progress in civilization.[7] And it may be well to reflect in this connection, that there have been more presidents assassinated in the United States in thirty-five years than in Hayti, and more political murders in North and South Carolina last year than during the past five years in the black republic. I challenge any advocate of white supremacy to dispute this proposition.

The reconstruction period is in itself a subject for a volume, and more than one has been written concerning it. When the worst has been said of it, there are some things in its favor. The worst things to be said of it are that it loaded several states with debt, and that the politicians stole some of the money. Grant the charge. The Southern States were impoverished, and the sources of revenue impaired. No government could have built railroads or other public improvements without drawing on the public credit. Bribery and corruption is not unknown in the Northern States. There have been at least two senators from Ohio in the last fifteen years who owed their election to notorious bribery. The Tweed ring in New York City stole more money than the combined peculations of the reconstruction period.[8] So notorious has become bribery and corruption in politics that it is proposed to elect senators by the people because of the ease with which legislatures can be bought up. If the franchise is to be taken away from the poor and the ignorant in the South because they do not use it wisely, folk say that there are other places where the axe can be laid to the root[9] with profit. That the enfranchisement of the Negroes humiliated the whites was not regarded, thirty years ago, as any objection to it; in fact, it was considered that they got off easy. That the colored people would be humiliated by taking the franchise away from them does not seem to have occurred to any apologist of this bare-faced robbery. These difficulties attending enfranchisement were as apparent when it was given as they are now, but the danger of leaving half the population of the South without representatives in any law-making tribunal seems to have been lost sight of. If it be admitted that it was a mistake to give the Negro the ballot thirty years ago, it will be a crime to take it away from him to-day.

On the other hand, the reconstruction had some good features. Life was secure; there were no lynchings and burnings, and men charged with crime were tried by the courts and punished or acquitted as the testimony warranted. All men were equal before the law. The free school system was established, and the township form of government. Under the system of "white supremacy" now in vogue, murder and lynching abound, repressive and degrading legislation against the Negro is the order of the day, the civil rights which have heretofore been largely denied the colored race by mere force of custom and prestige and judicial decision, are now being steadily taken away from him by legislative enactment, until soon his boasted liberty, so dearly bought, so freely bestowed, so nobly maintained for a few brief years will have faded away like a vision of the night.[10]

No one can deny the situation in the Southern States is deplorable. That it must sooner or later be corrected is certain. That, like slavery, the future of the colored race is a problem for the whole nation, must soon be admitted. That the Southern white people alone cannot be trusted to solve it with justice to the colored man, may, in the light of the past and the present, be safely assumed.

It is well, in dealing with an evil, to get, if possible, at the root of it. And the root of this evil, it must be apparent to the most casual observer, is the race prejudice, not unknown at the North, but which hovers over the South like a nightmare, warping all judgments, darkening counsel, and confusing all standards of right and wrong, of justice and equity. Consciously or unconsciously, all conduct is affected by this consideration. Southern legislatures devote a large part of their time, now as before the Civil War, to devising ways and means to keep the Negro down. As one of the wisest and most progressive men of the South once said in substance, the white people of the South have stooped so long to the old Negro in the dust that they have never been able to rise to the full stature of manhood. Their thoughts by day, their dreams by night,[11] are haunted by the fear that in some distant future one of their remote descendants may contain a drop of Negro blood. Hence such drastic legislation as that by which in Georgia a few days since a colored man and a white woman were sentenced to a fine of $3,000.00 and three years in the chain gang for the crime of being husband and wife. By virtue of this same prejudice railroads must have double equipment; there must be a dual school system, at enormously additional expense. People of mixed blood, no matter how white, must be classed as black; to hold an office is a crime punishable with death. Instead of a harmonious forward movement of the whole people, there is the constant friction of opposing elements. Scorn and contumely on the one side foster fear and hatred on the other, and as the colored people rise in the scale of life, they come in contact with the whites at more different points, each new one of which contacts is the signal for a new manifestation of an old prejudice. If an illustration is needed, look at the attitude of the Southern press and the Southern people toward colored regiments and colored officers in the recent war.[12]

This is the root of the whole evil. The Constitution of the United States proclaims in spirit if not in words, equality before the law. Before the Civil War this was construed to apply to white men, but the 13th, 14th and 15th Amendments make it perfectly clear that it applies to all white and colored men born or naturalized in the United States. The white people of the South have declared, as they did once before to their sorrow, that they are superior to the Constitution, and that the Negro shall not vote. The Federal Government, which confessedly has power to interfere, says nothing, does nothing, and we are all apparently agreed, that the Constitution, like the rest of the laws, can be ignored when it seems difficult to enforce it. There is absolutely no recourse for the colored man who is denied his rights. If the Supreme Court be suggested, it may be replied that it stands by the doctrine of the Dred Scott decision, which was scotched and not killed by the Civil War, and that, at present, at least, no more disastrous course could be pursued by the colored race than to carry their wrongs to the Supreme Court of the United States. They have rights, when they go there, that have been violated; when they leave, they are likely to have no rights at all. The history of the Civil Rights Bill and the Mississippi franchise amendment are plain reading.[13]

Why has the North permitted itself to be persuaded that the great men of the past were wrong, and why do they stand idly by and let the fruits of their labors become ashes on the lips of those whom they meant to benefit?

There are several reasons. They are absorbed in money getting. They are annexing distant territories and freeing new peoples.[14] Their zeal for liberty and humanity has yielded to the persistent activity of the Southern white people, who never cease for a moment to urge with tongue and pen that they are justified in their oppression—their suppression—of the colored race. The same thing took place before the war. They never rested until they could shackle their slaves and march them under the shadow of Bunker Hill monument.[15] They will never cease trying to force their prejudices on the Northern people in the same way. Through their influence most benefit societies and fraternities, most organizations for sport or pleasure, deny colored men from membership; hotels in the North refuse them accommodation. They labor unceasingly with voice and pen to shut out colored men from the light of opportunity, and to degrade the Negro race and all connected with it, however remotely, to a permanent condition of servitude and subordination only less tolerable than slavery itself. There may be, indeed there are, some Southern men who deplore these things and would be willing to give the Negro an even chance; but they either do not live in the South, leaving it sometimes involuntarily—or they prudently refrain from saying what they think.

That the South will succeed in this new work of reconstruction seems at present more than probable. That having done so at home, they will seek to force their system on the North, for the sake of the example is to be expected. That they will succeed permanently is not probable, for liberty, though temporarily eclipsed by arrogance or greed, is a vital instinct in the human heart, and this country cannot now permanently remain any more than formerly, half slave and half free.[16] But while we are going back to the foot of the hill to work slowly up again to the ideals we are abandoning, let us at least face the truth honestly, and for any error we may make, lay the blame at the foot of our own prejudices, which will not permit us to see any good in more than two or three colored men at a time out of eight or ten millions.

⤸

SOURCE: Undated typed text at the Fisk University Library. Two references by Chesnutt to himself as the "writer" suggest that this was intended as an essay. Internal references to recent events suggest the composition of the essay in 1899.

[1]*Othello*, 3.3.354.

[2]Political instability resulting from frequent *coups d'état* in Haiti was popularly viewed as proof of the incapacity of blacks for self-governance.

[3]Joshua 9:21.

[4]In September 1887 the Georgia House Committee on Education passed the "Calvin Resolutions" directing the Governor to withhold the annual appropriation of $8,000 to the university if it did not agree to teach blacks only. Atlanta University did not comply.

⁵Reference to the consequences of the November 1898 election in North Carolina, specifically in Wilmington.

⁶Booker T. Washington (1856–1915), founder, head, and principal fund raiser for the Tuskegee Institute; Henry Ossawa Tanner (1859–1937), expatriate American painter living in France; Paul Laurence Dunbar (1872–1906), poet and novelist.

⁷Chesnutt left spaces for the first and middle names of Robert Thomas Hill (1858–1941), as well as his place of origin. Hill's *Cuba and Porto Rico, With the Other Islands of the West Indies; Their Topography, Climate, Flora, Products, Industries, Cities, People, Political Conditions, Etc.* (1898) commends Haiti for its educational system, its financial solvency, and its international relations. But his complimentary descriptions are sometimes more backhanded than Chesnutt indicates, e.g., "It may be said to their credit that they have shown a wish to acquire little homes from their savings, and that they give many signs of a desire to rise above their racial debasement." Thomas also opines that Haitians show a "low degree of culture," and he characterizes the government as "despotic." Here and in later writings in which Chesnutt quotes and paraphrases authorities on the conditions in the Caribbean, Central America, and South America, he downplays or elides negative comment on groups of subsaharan descent.

⁸Chesnutt is probably referring to U.S. Senators from Ohio Henry B. Payne (1810–96), a Democrat who served from 1885 to 1891, and Marcus Alonzo Hanna (1837–1904), a Republican who served from 1897 to 1904. Both were accused of bribery to secure political favors. Democrat U.S. Senator William M. Tweed (1823–78) was a corrupt New York political boss who ruled the Tammany Hall organization for nearly three decades.

⁹Matthew 3:10.   ¹⁰Job 33:15.
¹¹I Kings 3:5.   ¹²The Spanish American War, 1898.

¹³The Civil Rights Act of 1866 nulled the Dred Scott decision by conferring citizenship to all who were born in the United States. The "Civil Rights Cases" of 1883 resulted in the U.S. Supreme Court's holding that the Act was an unconstitutional invasion of states' rights. The Mississippi amendment or "Second Mississippi Plan" of 1890 effected the disfranchisement of blacks. It was unsuccessfully challenged in the U.S. Supreme Court in Williams v. Mississippi, 170 U.S. 213 (1898).

¹⁴The Spanish American War resulted in the "freeing" of countries under Spanish rule such as Cuba. It also marked the advent of extra-continental imperialistic expansionism, and commercial interests were in part responsible for the consequent American presence in Puerto Rico and the Philippines. Chesnutt may also have had in mind the annexation of Hawaii and the establishment of a protectorate in Samoa.

¹⁵On 17 June 1775, Americans were defeated by British troops at Bunker Hill, in Charlestown, Mass. Chesnutt ironically refers to the spectacle of slavery in Massachusetts, and perhaps that state's compliance with the 1850 Fugitive Slave Law, in the environs of this site symbolizing the struggle for freedom.

¹⁶When nominated for election to the U.S. Senate on 16 June 1858, Abraham Lincoln declared, "A house divided against itself cannot stand. I believe this government cannot endure permanently half slave and half free."

Literature in Its Relation to Life

(The Relation of Literature to Life)

Speech to the Bethel Literary and Historical Association,
District of Columbia, 21 November 1899

When your good president asked me to address the Bethel Literary and Historical Association sometime during the present season, my first impulse was to
speak upon some phase of the great problem that concerns us all so much, and
that should concern all good citizens, who have the prosperity and happiness of
the country at heart—the problem of our own troubled present and our somewhat uncertain future. This feeling of mine was not due altogether to the
thought that the subject might interest you, but to the fact that I myself was full
of it, and would thus have an opportunity to pour into attentive and appreciative ears the thoughts that have sometimes oppressed me; for personally my lot
has been cast for many years in a part of the country where the more acute
forms of the race question do not exercise the public mind, and where those
phases of it which do exist must be fought with deeds rather than with words.

This then was my first thought—to relieve my mind on the Race problem.[1]
But it was suggested to me, and very wisely, I suspect, that I could hardly hope
to say anything new on the subject, since it had been discussed here from every
point of view, by experts of every shade of opinion. And then I recalled the
things I had read in the papers of recent years,—the glowing periods of the optimist, who, having just been appointed to a place in one of the departments,[2]
sees the race standing, only a few months or years hence, on glory-crowned
heights—in fact rather looks upon himself as the pioneer who has already
reached the pinnacle of prosperity. I remembered having read somewhere the
views of the philosophic pessimist, who sees no future for his race in this country except in the sacrifice of their dearest and fundamental rights to the rapacity
of others, while they content themselves with the husks of citizenship and resign
themselves to live always or for an indefinite period, in the byways[3] of civilization. I recalled too the oft-reiterated views of the reverend gentleman who
would banish ten millions of people from the land of their nativity and send
them back to barbarism, in search of rights which are guaranteed to them by the
Constitution of their own country.[4] I remembered also the politic utterances of
the wise and justly distinguished educator who knows so well what not to say,
and who steers his craft so skilfully that even adverse winds waft it toward its
goal;[5] who by his tact and wisdom has charmed more money out of the pockets
of good people than any other man of his race ever did, and has applied it to the
betterment of the colored people in the place and along where its need is perhaps

the most immediately imperative. I had in mind, too, the mild protests of some of the devoutly inclined, who would sit down and wait for God to lift them out of the slough of despond;[6] and the fulminations of our good friends who would like—if they dared,—to smite the Amalekites hip and thigh,[7] but who wisely keep away from dangerous places, and work off their energy and indignation in slashing newspaper articles. And then I thought about the restriction of the franchise, and the nullification of the war amendments, and race prejudice, and the lynching epidemic, and manual training, and the higher education, and the prevalence of consumption, the death rate, the percentage of crime and of illegitimacy—the whole sad story of hard conditions and the evils that grow out of them; and then I picked up your programme of exercises for the year, and saw that it covered all these subjects I have mentioned and all other conceivable subjects with reference to the race problem. When I had considered all these things, while I still felt a lingering suspicion that the last word had not been said, I was not at all sure that I could say it, so I thought it the part of prudence for me to talk about something else, especially since I had been warned of the fate of certain rash spirits who have ventured from time to time to bring specious arguments or bad logic before this society.

Having thus reluctantly retired from the precipice on the edge of which I tottered and hovered, it occurred to me that there are certain broad views of life that are, after all, more important to men and women, as human beings, and citizens of the world, than even the serious matters of lynch law and the franchise;—for only a fraction of mankind vote under even the most liberal governments,—women, children, the disqualified—and only a fraction of a very small fraction of the population are lynched in even the least enlightened parts of our country. These things are important, after all, only as they bear on life and its opportunities. It is perhaps well for all of us, sometimes, to get out of our own narrow rut, so far as we can, and to look out upon the world about us, even if we must look through prison bars, and view the world and mankind in their broader aspects—as something not merely for to-day or tomorrow, but for all time. When we turn back, as we can through the medium of books, to the dawn of history, and follow its course down to our own time, the troubles of any one individual or any one race dwindle into comparative insignificance; and when we look around us and see the forces of progress in operation on every hand, imagination pictures for us a future for which the troubles of to-day are but a brief apprenticeship.

And therefore, as one of these broader views, which include all mankind, and make no distinctions of time or place or caste or creed, I am going to speak to you of the relation of Literature to Life. Life is the great fact of the universe. Faith would teach us that it is not the ultimate fact, but it is the most obvious and immediately important fact. Thoughtless men, in good health, sometimes belittle life. "Life is a jest" wrote the poet Gay for his own epitaph, "and all things show it. I thought so once and now I know it."[8] Godly men, whose minds are fixed on eternity, speak slightingly of this earthly existence. Tis a vale of tears, a career of pain and sorrow; its pleasures are but sin and shame, with the shrouded figure of death casting its shadow everywhere. Philosophers, by long pondering over the real and imaginary evils of mundane existence, are led to regard it as a weary burden. "Unless suffering," says Schopenhauer, in beginning his *Studies in Pessimism*, "is the direct and immediate object of life, our existence must entirely fail of its aim. It is absurd to look upon the enormous amount of pain that abounds everywhere in the world, and originates in needs and necessities inseparable from life itself, as serving no purpose at all and the result of mere chance. Each separate misfortune, as it comes, seems no doubt to be something exceptional; but misfortune in general is the rule."[9] My notion of the matter is that since the Creator thought enough of the life here below to fit up a world for it, we ought to treat it with some little consideration, and since I like to believe that God is good, I would not for a moment think that he merely put us here to torture us for seventy or eighty years, on the mere chance of our being able to so overcome our weaknesses as to merit happiness in another world. I shall prefer to think he meant us to be happy here as well, and therefore I shall waste no time in arguing the proposition that life is real[10] and valuable. The poet Browning agrees with me on that—which speaks well for him—

> "How good is man's life—the mere living! How fit to employ
> All the heart and the soul, and the senses forever in joy!"[11]

Whatever the argument of priest or philosopher, the fact remains that each individual of us does set a very high value on the few years of conscious existence of which he is certain on this earth. "All that a man hath"—now as in the days of Job—"all that a man hath will he give for his life."[12] All the institutions of society are organized to prolong and promote it, and men are continually combating by all the resources of knowledge, the forces of nature which are adverse to life. Why discuss the desirability of life to a city full of doctors and hospitals? Nature has taken elaborate precautions for the perpetuation of the species, and all life shrinks from annihilation. That now and then some tired soul shuffles off this mortal coil,[13] or men go out to shoot one another to death, does not alter the fact that broadly speaking, each individual loves his life well enough to cling to it under any burden of misery or disgrace or suffering that may weight it down—loves it well enough to do everything for it except perhaps to take proper care of it. Especially need I not try to prove the value of life to a people whose ancestors, or many of them, endured for more than two hundred years the hardships of American slavery, by common consent the worst form of that hoary iniquity that had ever cursed the earth.

> "The meanest and most loathed worldly life
> That age, ache, penury, and imprisonment
> Can lay on nature, is a paradise
> To what we fear of death."
> *Measure for Measure*. Act III. Sc. 1.[14]

Now, as over against *this* life, we have had set for us the life to come, and history, I am afraid, teaches that our good friends the preachers, who have done so much for us, have in magnifying the life to come, at least in past ages, neglected this world unduly; and while they were building up an elaborate system of hells and heavens and purgatories beyond, have permitted castes and creeds to work untold horrors among men on earth; while they paved the streets of heaven with gold, they left men to wade through earthly mud; while angels soared through the skies, tired men and women trudged on foot, or rode on the backs of weary beasts. But men finally waked up to the importance of the life here, and now we have steam and electricity and improved sanitation, and professions of human equality—I presume we shall work around to the fact of it in due course of time. Our good ministers however, do not let us forget the other life, which it is well we should not be unmindful of. But after we have heard all the sermons and read all the books, when sickness comes to us, and death threatens, all the delights of heaven fade into insignificance before the touch of solid earth and the sight of four plastered walls. Your yearning is not for the streets of gold, but for the asphalt pavement. You prefer the street-cars to the wings of the morning. The sound of a familiar voice is sweeter than the music of the celestial choir; you would rather feel the touch of a loved hand than the sustaining arms of the angels as they waft your soul to glory. One ray of sunlight is worth more to you than the splendid radiance of the heavenly city. Such is the law of life. Whether a boon or a burden, a blessing or a curse, we cling to it, and thus we seek, and should seek, to make of it, for ourselves and others, the best that it is capable of becoming.

It is of the relation of literature to this life that we thus love and cherish, and ought to value and take care of, that I am going to speak to you briefly to-night.

I have given some considerations on the character of life, and I think before I go further it would be well for us to fix in our minds some measurably adequate conception of what is embraced in the term "literature." Dictionaries, which contain the tools that work upon the raw material of thought to make literature, are good places in which to seek definitions, and I will give you one from a dictionary: Literature is—

> The written or printed productions of the human mind collectively, especially such productions as are marked by elevation, vigor, and catholicity of thought, by fitness, purity and grace of style, and by artistic construction.
>
> Literature, in its narrowest and strictest sense, belongs to the sphere of high art, and embodies thought that is power-giving, or inspiring and elevating, rather than merely knowledge-giving (excluding thus all purely scientific writing); catholic, or of interest to man as man (excluding writings that are merely technical, or for a class, trade, profession or the like, only); esthetic in its tone and style (excluding all writings violating the principles of correct taste); and shaped by the creative imagination, or power of artistic construction (excluding all writings that are shapeless or without organic unity).

When you study that definition you will see why it is difficult to write a book worthy of a place in literature, and why the world is always ready to honor the man who writes a good book.

"Literature" this definition goes on, "may be divided into (1) Oratory, where the representation is for the effect on another mind; (2) Representative discourse, where it is for the sake of the theme itself, a good story for instance; (3) Poetry, where it is embodied in beautiful form, for the sake of the form."[15]

Now, all that is said much better than I could have said it. My own notion of it, before I looked up the clean-cut and comprehensive definition I have read to you, was that the term Literature should include all that body of writings of which form constitutes an important element, and which, by virtue of their form, in addition to their other claims upon the attention, are likely to be preserved for some length of time because of the pleasure men derive from reading them.

"By literature," says Dean Stanley, who is a good authority, for he has helped to make literature, "I mean those great works that rise above professional or commonplace uses, and take possession of a whole nation or a whole age."[16]

Now, you will observe the elementary condition of literature—it must be *written*—the word itself means that first of all. Your hearts and mine have doubtless thrilled many a time with noble thoughts, as we listened to inspiring music or moving eloquence, or witnessed some dramatic masterpiece interpreted by a great artist. We have felt epic poems as we stood by the sounding sea and watched the great waves roll in over the boundless reach of the ocean; or as we stood upon some mountain height and seemed to gaze down upon all the kingdoms of the earth. What poems of sentiment have throbbed rhythmically through our hearts, as with some loved one by our side we have wandered through sylvan solitudes, and felt what old Omar Khayyám said so beautifully—

> With you along the strip of herbage strewn,
> That just divides the desert from the sown,
> Where name of slave and sultan is forgot—
> And peace to Mahmud on his golden throne!
>
> A book of verses underneath the bough,
> A jug of wine, a loaf of bread, and thou
> Beside me singing in the wilderness,
> Oh, wilderness were paradise enow![17]

But inspiring moods, and exalted sentiments, are but the raw material of literature. As the glow of the sunset must be transferred to canvas in order that it may not perish, so these fine thoughts must be clothed in worthy words before they become available for the use of the rest of mankind. The "mute inglorious Miltons"[18] do not move the world. Only when our best thoughts have passed laboriously, and painfully for the most part, through the loom of language, and have been submitted to the gauge of rhyme or reason, or both, and have been put into such shape that they will convey to the wayfaring man something of the same impression that they made upon the mind that first conceived them—then and only then do they rise to the dignity of literature.

Now, having thus tried to bring your minds into harmony with my own on what life is, and on what literature consists of, I shall try to suggest some few of the respects in which literature is related to life.

Literature may be viewed in two aspects—as an expression of life, past and present, and as a force directly affecting the conduct of life, present and future. I might call these the subjective and objective sides of literature—or, more lucidly, the historical; and the dynamic, the forceful, the impelling. History is instructive, and may warn or admonish; but to this quality literature adds the faculty of persuasion, by which men's hearts are reached, the springs of action touched, and the currents of life directed.

I think perhaps the most obvious of these relations of literature to life is the historical. Literature is an expression of life. As another has tersely said, "The literature of any age is but the mirror of its prevalent tendencies."[19] Would you know a nation, read its books.

* * *

have left to the world? Of Egypt we learn much by her well-nigh imperishable monuments, but how many of these, alas! we cannot fathom. Who built the Sphinx, and why? The riddle is no nearer solved than when Cadmus sought to guess it.[20] A whole library of books have been written on the pyramids, but even yet we do not know just why they were built. Tombs of kings, and kings of tombs we know they are, but if they had an esoteric purpose we shall in all probability never fathom it;—for the Egyptians left no literature, in the sense in which we use the word, and there are great gaps in the meager records that we have of this ancient empire, the cradle of civilization. In our own land vast earthworks, scattered through the Mississippi valley, reveal the passage of a race-wave that once flowed over the country. What epics the mound-builders sung, what lives they led, what arts they possessed, we do not know. If they learned aught that could benefit mankind, posterity has never profited by it, for they left no literature. Of the more advanced civilizations of Peru and Mexico we are but little more enlightened. Whether in their lives or their thoughts there was aught to instruct or to inspire, we can never tell—for the few rude records they left were not a literature.

How different it was in Israel and Greece and Rome! We have the life of every little cross-roads judge in Israel, of every petty king who ruled, and only when the tribes were dispersed, the greater part of them leaving no books, is the continuity of their history broken. With their records before us, we can compare their history with our own, and find out whether history really only repeats itself or whether the race has made substantial progress toward ideal perfection . . . .[21]

⌒

SOURCE: Incomplete typed text at the Fisk University Library. This speech before the Bethel Literary and Historical Association, District of Columbia, was given on 21 November 1899. The subtitle in parentheses was added in Chesnutt's hand.

[1]In an undated draft of a letter to the president of the Bethel Literary and Historical Association, William H. Richards (1856–?), Chesnutt described the present paper as one that he might deliver. He also proposed three other topics, two of which dealt with the race problem: "New Wine in Old Bottles," focusing on "the difficulty of putting the new liberties of the colored race in the old forms of slavery race prejudice [sic]"; and "The New American," a "discussion of the present make up of the American people and a prophecy as to the future." See Letters, ed. McElrath and Leitz, 135–36.

[2]That is, departments of government.

[3]The typescript reads "alleys (byways)." It is assumed that Chesnutt, in a draft, replaced the former word with the latter, and that his typist mistranscribed the revision.

[4]Prior to the Civil War, abolitionists proposed the return of slaves to their native lands; after the war both those sympathetic to and those antagonistic toward African Americans repeatedly addressed the same solution to the race problem. In the previous sentence Chesnutt describes the view of a black pessimist. It is likely that he here continues to refer to an African American's perspective and thus may be alluding to A.M.E. minister Henry McNeal Turner (1834–1915). Turner was famous not only as one of the most energetic promoters of African colonization in the late nineteenth century but as the first African American to be commissioned (in 1863) as chaplain for black soldiers in the Union army. He also served two terms in the Georgia state legislature (1868–72).

[5]Concerning Booker T. Washington, Chesnutt originally used another figure of speech in the typescript: "trims his sails—and I use the word by way of sincere admiration for his skill, and not by way of criticism—who trims his sails."

[6]John Bunyan (1628–88), Pilgrim's Progress (1678).

[7]In Judges 15:8, Samson smites the Philistines hip and thigh, rather than the Amalekites; the Amalekites figure as the enemies of Israel much later in Biblical history.

[8]John Gay, English poet and playwright; "My Own Epitaph" is inscribed on his monument in Westminster Abbey.

[9]Arthur Schopenhauer (1788–1860), German philosopher; a selection of his reflections on various topics, first published in 1851, was translated into English and collected in Studies in Pessimism (1890). Chesnutt quotes from the initial essay, "On the Sufferings of the World."

[10]Henry Wadsworth Longfellow, "A Psalm of Life" (1838).

[11]"Saul" (1855).

[12]Job 2:14.

[13]Hamlet, 3.1.66–68.

[14]One of the less well-known plays by Shakespeare, lines 129–32. Misquoted is "weariest" as "meanest."

[15]That a contemporaneous "dictionary" offered such an extensive definition is unlikely. Chesnutt appears to have consulted a more specialized, unidentified reference work. The beginning of the quotation is preceded by a "1" in the typed text, indicating that the primary definition is first offered. Since the "1" is not followed by a "2" or "3," it has been editorially excised.

[16]The "Dean" Chesnutt may be quoting is Arthur P. Stanley (1815–81), an Oxford Professor of Ecclesiastical History, the Dean of Westminster from 1864 to 1881, and a prolific author who wrote mainly on religious topics.

[17]Edward FitzGerald (1809–83), The Rubáiyát of Omar Khayyám (1859).

[18]Thomas Gray (1716–71), "Elegy Written in a Country Churchyard" (1750).

[19]While the source of this statement has not been determined, the notion that literature is a mirror of the prevalent tendencies of an age was a commonplace one in the nineteenth century. It is rooted in the notion that art "imitates" or holds the mirror up to life.

[20]Cadmus, a Greek mythological figure, was the founder of the city of Thebes, located on the Nile River in present-day central Egypt. Neither his story nor that of Oedipus includes an attempt to guess the origin of the Sphinx structure; Oedipus, however, did correctly interpret the riddle posed by the mythological figure called the Sphinx.

[21]Having treated only the beginning of his first main point—that literature records the histories of nations and their cultures as well as describes the human condition—Chesnutt very likely continued in this vein and then went on to treat the other points that he had identified for his audience: that literature should have a reform purpose, and that it is capable of contributing mightily to social amelioration because of its power over the imagination and intellect. In the draft of his letter to William H. Richards (see n. 1), Chesnutt provided another indication of the probable content of the remainder of his paper: he related that in this presentation he would discuss "literature as a reflection of life as it is, as a warning of life as it should not be, and as an example and inspiration of life as it ought to be."

On the Future of His People

Essay published in the *Saturday Evening Post*, 20 January 1900

Doctor Washington may be considered, in relation to education, as the prophet of the practical. For instance, the volume before us—*The Future of the American Negro*[1]—indulges in no flights of fancy, no gilded speculations about the condition of the American Negro generations hence; indeed, the author frankly dismisses the question as one that does not now much concern him. Though he is hopeful of his race, and believes in the ultimate triumph of the forces of progress which in the end make for justice, the future of the Negro which he discusses is that of to-morrow, as growing out of the conditions of yesterday and to-day; and as he believes in getting the foundations of an argument, as well as of an education, properly laid, he gives to the present a large part of his attention.

This volume is chiefly devoted to Mr. Washington's theory of the industrial education of the Negro, and is a logical and forceful presentation of the views he has so long endeavored to propagate, and has carried out with such marked success at Tuskegee. The magnitude and seriousness of the problem confronting the South—for it is chiefly in its Southern aspects that Mr. Washington discusses the future of the Negro—are clearly perceived by the author. Being a diplomatist as well as a philosopher, he does not dwell unduly upon race prejudice, which is the most obvious and to some minds the most serious feature of the Negro problem. The point he emphasizes is that the low esteem in which the colored race is held is largely due to the Negro's poverty, his ignorance of the immediate means to overcome it, and his lack of thrift and enterprise. Making due allowance for discouraging conditions, he sees in the Negro a great amount of undeveloped energy, which, if wisely directed along the lines of most obvious need and of least resistance, will vastly simplify the problem of his elevation. In industrial education, carried on side by side with mental training, and perhaps given for a time the greater emphasis, Mr. Washington finds the entering wedge by which his people can work their way into the body politic in a higher sense than they have hitherto been able to do.

A very casual perusal of this volume will convince the thoughtful reader that there is much in it that will apply, with almost equal force, to the white people of the South as well as to the black, and, in some measure, as well to the North as to the South. The overcrowding of the learned professions; the "stepping stone" system of never learning to do anything thoroughly, because you are always expecting to have something better to do very soon; the lack of scientific agricultural training; the need of trades' schools to replace the old and moribund apprenticeship system and offset the tyranny of trades' unions—are not confined to the Afro-American people. If Mr. Washington, with his system of education, can get the masses of his race started in life on a broad industrial foundation, with ample room for the upward development of those who have ability and opportunity for yet higher things, he will do them a great service. If, in addition, his views, so clearly set forth in this well-written book, receive proper recognition as an important contribution to the general subject of popular education, Doctor Washington will have conferred a benefit upon the people of the entire country.

The book is in all respects worthy of the attention of thoughtful minds, and is sure to be widely read.[2]

⌒

SOURCE: "On the Future of His People," *Saturday Evening Post*, 172 (20 January 1900), 646.

[1]The title of Booker T. Washington's 1899 book is editorially inserted here. It originally appeared as a footnote indicating that it was published by Small, Maynard and Co.

[2]Chesnutt was twice invited to review this work; see also "A Plea for the American Negro."

A Plea for the American Negro

Essay published in *The Critic*, February 1900

Mr. Booker T. Washington has secured so strong a hold upon the public attention and confidence that anything he has to say in his chosen field is sure to command the attention of all who are interested in the future of the American Negro. This volume,[1] which is Mr. Washington's first extended utterance in book form, cannot fail to enhance his reputation for ability, wisdom, and patriotism. It is devoted to a somewhat wide consideration of the race problem, avoiding some of its delicate features, perhaps, but emphasizing certain of its more obvious phases. The author has practically nothing to say about caste prejudice, the admixture of the races, or the remote future of the Negro, but simply takes up the palpable problem of ignorance and poverty as he finds it in the South, and looking neither to the right nor the left, and only far enough behind to fix the responsibility for present conditions, seeks to bring about such immediate improvement in the condition of the Negro, and such a harmonious adjustment of race relations, as will lay the foundation for a hopeful and progressive future for the colored people. The practical philosophy of the book is eminently characteristic; it fairly bristles with the author's individuality.

As might be expected, much of the volume is devoted to discussing the importance of industrial education for the Negro, of which the author is the most conspicuous advocate. Himself a product of the Hampton school, Mr. Washington is a living example of the value of such institutions; and his own school at Tuskegee has demonstrated how much the condition of an ignorant and untrained people may be improved by teaching the trades and useful arts along with adequate mental and religious training.[2] The argument for industrial education is not based upon any theory of inferiority of the Negro, which is beside the question, but upon the manifest conditions under which he must seek his livelihood. Since manual labor of some kind offers the line of least resistance for the mass of the race in the struggle for existence, it is imperative that as many as possible of them qualify themselves, by becoming skilled laborers, to get as much as possible out of it. The soundness of the argument cannot be gainsaid, and there is no doubt that the extension of this system of education will be an important contribution to the settlement of our most important civic problem. There need be no fear that thereby the race will be deprived of the higher education, for the field for schools of all kinds is unlimited. There are many men to whom perhaps a trade would not provide an adequate career—Mr. Washington, for instance; there is perhaps no man who is the worse for knowing one. It is not likely that any large number of colored men are overburdened with knowledge of law, medicine, or divinity, but every one familiar with the subject will agree that there are entirely too few handicraftsmen among them. No race can play any worthy part on the world's stage which can bring to it only a few indifferent professional men and a vast mass of servants and day-laborers. It is to the building up of a substantial middle-class, so to speak, that industrial education and the lessons of industry and thrift inculcated by Mr. Washington are directed. He insists, somewhat rigidly, on the rational order of development, and is pained by such spectacles as a rosewood piano in a log schoolhouse, and a Negro lad studying a French grammar in a one-room cabin. It is hardly likely that Mr. Washington has suffered very often from such incongruities, and some allowance should be made for the personal equation of even a Negro lad in the Black Belt. Abraham Lincoln came out of a one-room cabin, and it would hardly have been a serious misfortune for him to have had a knowledge of French, or even the piano. The world is wide, and the ambitious Negro lad might move to some part of it where his knowledge of French or music would prove a very useful acquirement.[3]

Mr. Washington is a pioneer in another field. He has set out to gain for his race in the South, in the effort to improve their condition, the active sympathy and assistance of the white people in that section. This is perhaps a necessary corollary to his system of education, for it is in the South that he advises the Negroes to stay, and it is among their white neighbors that they must live and practise the arts they acquire. If Mr. Washington succeeds in this effort, he will have solved the whole problem. But he has undertaken no small task, and realizes it, and while hopeful, does not permit himself to be too optimistic. The student of history and current events can scarcely escape the impression that it is the firm and unwavering determination of the Southern whites to keep the Negro in a permanent state of vassalage and subordination. Lynching and other barbarities practised upon the colored race may be mere local ebullitions of feeling; but disfranchisement by popular vote, and discriminating and degrading laws passed by the Legislatures, can hardly be called anything else but expressions of general public opinion. It is difficult to think of these things as evidences of friendship. The lines of caste in the South are being drawn tighter and tighter, and with every forward step the Negro takes, in certain directions at least, he but enlarges the area of the prejudice which he must encounter.

It is to be hoped that Mr. Washington may convince the South that the policy of Federal non-interference, which seems to be the attitude of the present and several past administrations, places a sacred trust upon the South to be just to the Negro. But the whole nation is so directly responsible for present conditions, and the general welfare is so deeply involved, that the settlement of this problem can neither honestly nor safely be left entirely to the South. The South is poor, and needs the financial aid of the North, by giving which the North would gain the right to speak, if it did not have a higher right; the South is ignorant and backward and prejudiced, and needs the superior knowledge and progressive spirit of the North. There are many wise and able men in the South, but they are not the controlling element where the Negro is concerned, by their own testimony, and they need to have their hands held up by the North. It is idle to speak of taking the Negro or the

Negro question out of politics, for politics is the proper arena for the discussion and settlement of great public questions. There can be no safety for the rights of the citizen who is without friendly representation, and there is no more important and far-reaching field for enlightened statesmanship than the future of the American Negro.

There will undoubtedly be a race problem in the United States, with all its attendant evils, until we cease to regard our colored population as Negroes and consider them simply as citizens. Ignorance and poverty and immorality exist in all countries, and can be dealt with independently of questions of color. But so long as we have laws determining, by standards of race or complexion, whether or not a man shall vote, where he shall eat or sleep or sit, where he shall be taught and what; and so long as we have social customs fixing, by the same standards, what trade he shall follow, what society he shall be received in, what position he shall be permitted to attain in life, just so long will the race question continue to vex our republic. How long such laws and customs will persist in the United States it were idle to speculate—probably for a long time, with variations according to latitude, and a gradual relaxation everywhere. In the meantime, if the work led by Mr. Washington shall succeed in promoting better conditions, either by smoothing over asperities; by appealing to the dormant love of justice which has been the crowning glory of the English race—a trait which selfishness and greed have never entirely obscured; or by convincing the whites that injustice is vastly more dangerous to them than any possible loss of race prestige, Mr. Washington will deserve, and will doubtless receive, the thanks of the people of this whole nation.

The closing sentence of the volume suggests its scope: "The education and preparing for citizenship of nearly eight millions of people is a tremendous task, and every lover of humanity should count it a privilege to help in the solution of a great problem for which our whole country is responsible."

Mr. Washington is doing his part, to which this volume is a notable contribution, and other lovers of humanity are not neglecting theirs. The American people are justly proud of their growing strength and prestige; they cannot devote them to a better use than to go manfully to work and get rid of this black nightmare that threatens the welfare and happiness of the whole country. The race problem can be settled, but it has grown to too great proportions to be permanently disposed of along any other lines than those of equal and exact justice, let the ultimate consequences be what they may.

↩

SOURCE: "A Plea for the American Negro," *The Critic*, 36 (February 1900), 160–63. This essay was introduced in an editorial headnote thus: "[Mr. Chesnutt is particularly well equipped for the writing of Mr. Washington's book. By birth he belongs in part to the race of which it treats, and by education, in pedagogy and the law, he brings sympathy and intelligence to bear upon the subject. Mr. Chesnutt is the author of two books of striking merit, 'The Conjure Woman' and 'The Wife of his Youth,' both published by Messrs. Houghton, Mifflin & Co. He is now delivering lectures on the negro problem throughout the country. A biographical sketch of Mr. Chesnutt, by Miss Carolyn Ship-man, will be found in THE CRITIC for July, 1899.—Eds. CRITIC.]"

[1]For the second time, Chesnutt is reviewing Washington's *The Future of the American Negro*. (See "On the Future of His People" for the first, less polemical review.) The title and the publisher—Small, Maynard and Co.—were originally cited in a footnote.

[2]Washington began his remarkable rise, "up from slavery," at Virginia's Hampton Institute, which emphasized manual labor skills education, basic intellectual attainments, and proper personal deportment in a Christian spiritual environment. It provided the model for his Tuskegee Institute.

[3]One of the persistent criticisms of Washington articulated by sophisticated African Americans of the time was that he did not give proper emphasis to "higher education." In *The Souls of Black Folk* (1903), W. E. B. Du Bois (1868–1963) produced the best-known attack of the kind. What was particularly irritating was Washington's penchant for anecdotes illustrating as ludicrous the intellectual pretensions of individuals who had not yet learned the basics for survival and progress in the socioeconomic sphere. Unfortunately, his illustrations also grated upon more accomplished and advanced individuals such as Chesnutt. As a young man in Fayetteville, N.C., Chesnutt studied, among other languages, French; and he did learn to play the piano and organ.

The Future American

What the Race Is Likely to Become in the Process of Time

Essay published in the *Boston Evening Transcript*, 18 August 1900

The future American race is a popular theme for essayists, and has been much discussed. Most expressions upon the subject, however, have been characterized by a conscious or unconscious evasion of some of the main elements of the problem involved in the formation of a future American race, or, to put it perhaps more correctly, a future ethnic type that shall inhabit the northern part of the western continent. Some of these obvious omissions will be touched upon in these articles; and if the writer has any preconceived opinions that would affect his judgment, they are at least not the hackneyed prejudices of the past—if they lead to false conclusions, they at least furnish a new point of view, from which, taken with other widely differing views, the judicious reader may establish a parallax that will enable him to approximate the truth.

The popular theory is that the future American race will consist of a harmonious fusion of the various European elements which now make up our heterogeneous population. The result is to be something infinitely superior to the best of the component elements. This perfection of type—no good American could for a moment doubt that it will be as perfect as everything else American—is to be brought about by a combination of all the best characteristics of the different

European races, and the elimination, by some strange alchemy, of all their undesirable traits—for even a good American will admit that European races, now and then, have some undesirable traits when they first come over. It is a beautiful, a hopeful, and to the eye of faith, a thrilling prospect. The defect of the argument, however, lies in the incompleteness of the premises, and its obliviousness of certain facts of human nature and human history.

Before putting forward any theory upon the subject, it may be well enough to remark that recent scientific research has swept away many hoary anthropological fallacies. It has been demonstrated that the shape or size of the head has little or nothing to do with the civilization or average intelligence of a race; that language, so recently lauded as an infallible test of racial origin is of absolutely no value in this connection, its distribution being dependent upon other conditions than race. Even color, upon which the social structure of the United States is so largely based, has been proved no test of race. The conception of a pure Aryan, Indo-European race has been abandoned in scientific circles, and the secret of the progress of Europe has been found in racial heterogeneity, rather than in racial purity. The theory that the Jews are a pure race has been exploded, and their peculiar type explained upon a different and much more satisfactory hypothesis. To illustrate the change of opinion and the growth of liberality in scientific circles, imagine the reception which would have been accorded to this proposition, if laid down by an American writer fifty or sixty years ago: "The European races, as a whole, show signs of a secondary or derived origin; certain characteristics, especially the texture of the hair, lead us to class them as intermediate between the extreme primary types of the Asiatic and Negro races respectively."[1] This is put forward by the author, not as a mere hypothesis, but as a proposition fairly susceptible of proof, and is supported by an elaborate argument based upon microscopical comparisons, to which numerous authorities are cited. If this fact be borne in mind it will simplify in some degree our conception of a future American ethnic type.

By modern research the unity of the human race has been proved (if it needed any proof to the careful or fair-minded observer), and the differentiation of races by selection and environment has been so stated as to prove itself. Greater emphasis has been placed upon environment as a factor in ethnic development, and what has been called "the vulgar theory of race," as accounting for progress and culture, has been relegated to the limbo of exploded dogmas. One of the most perspicuous and forceful presentations of these modern conclusions of anthropology is found in the volume above quoted, a book which owes its origin to a Boston scholar.

Proceeding then upon the firm basis laid down by science and the historic parallel, it ought to be quite clear that the future American race—the future American ethnic type—will be formed of a mingling, in a yet to be ascertained proportion, of the various racial varieties which make up the present population of the United States; or, to extend the area a little farther, of the various peoples of the northern hemisphere of the western continent; for, if certain recent tendencies are an index of the future it is not safe to fix the boundaries of the future United States any-where short of the Arctic Ocean on the north and the Isthmus of Panama on the south.[2] But, even with the continuance of the present political divisions, conditions of trade and ease of travel are likely to gradually assimilate to one type all the countries of the hemisphere. Assuming that the country is so well settled that no great disturbance of ratios is likely to result from immigration, or any serious con-flict of races, we may safely build our theory of a future American race upon the present population of the country. I use the word "race" here in its popular sense—that of a people who look substantially alike, and are moulded by the same culture and dominated by the same ideals.

By the eleventh census, the ratios of which will probably not be changed mate-rially by the census now under way, the total population of the United States was about 65,000,000, of which about seven million were black and colored, and something over 200,000 were of Indian blood. It is then in the three broad types—white, black and Indian—that the future American race will find the material for its formation. Any dream of a pure white race, of the Anglo-Saxon type, for the United States, may as well be abandoned as impossible, even if desirable. That such future race will be predominantly white may well be granted—unless climate in the course of time should modify existing types; that it will call itself white is reasonably sure; that it will conform closely to the white type is likely; but that it will have absorbed and assimilated the blood of the other two races mentioned is as certain as the operation of any law well can be that deals with so uncertain a quantity as the human race.

There are no natural obstacles to such an amalgamation. The unity of the race is not only conceded but demonstrated by actual crossing. Any theory of sterility due to race crossing may as well be abandoned; it is founded mainly on prejudice and cannot be proved by the facts. If it come from Northern or European sources, it is likely to be weakened by lack of knowledge; if from Southern sources, it is sure to be colored by prejudices. My own observation is that in a majority of cases peo-ple of mixed blood are very prolific and very long-lived. The admixture of races in the United States has never taken place under conditions likely to produce the best results but there have nevertheless been enough conspicuous instances to the con-trary in this country, to say nothing of a long and honorable list in other lands, to disprove the theory that people of mixed blood, other things being equal, are less virile, prolific or able than those of purer strains. But whether this be true or not is apart from this argument. Admitting that races may mix, and that they are thrown together under conditions which permit their admixture, the controlling motive will be not abstract considerations with regard to a remote posterity, but present interest and inclination.

The Indian element in the United States proper is so small proportionally—about one in three hundred—and the conditions for its amalgamation so favor-able, that it would of itself require scarcely any consideration in this argument. There is no prejudice against the Indian blood, in solution. A half or quarter-breed, removed from the tribal environment, is freely received among white peo-ple. After the second or third remove he may even boast of his Indian descent; it gives him a sort of distinction, and involves no social disability. The distribution of the Indian race, however, tends to make the question largely a local one, and the survival of tribal relation may postpone the results for some little time. It will be, however, the fault of the United States Indian himself if he be not speedily amal-gamated with the white population.

The Indian element, however, looms up larger when we include Mexico and Central America in our fields of discussion. By the census of Mexico just com-pleted, over eighty per cent of the population is composed of mixed and Indian races. The remainder is presumably of pure Spanish, or European blood, with a dash of Negro along the coast. The population is something over twelve millions, thus adding nine millions of Indians and Mestizos to be taken into account. Add several millions of similar descent in Central America, a million in Porto Rico, who are said to have an aboriginal strain, and it may safely be figured that the In-dian element will be quite considerable in the future American race. Its amalgama-tion will involve no great difficulty, however; it has been going on peacefully in the countries south of us for several centuries, and is likely to continue along similar lines. The peculiar disposition of the American to overlook mixed blood in a for-eigner will simplify the gradual absorption of these Southern races.

The real problem, then, the only hard problem in connection with the future American race, lies in the Negro element of our population. As I have said before, I believe it is destined to play its part in the formation of this new type. The process by which this will take place will be no sudden and wholesale amalgamation—a thing certainly not to be expected, and hardly to be desired. If it were held desir-able, and one could imagine a government sufficiently autocratic to enforce its be-hests, it would be no great task to mix the races mechanically, leaving to time merely the fixing of the resultant type.

Let us for curiosity outline the process. To start with, the Negroes are already considerably mixed—many of them in large proportion, and most of them in some degree—and the white people, as I shall endeavor to show later on, are many of them slightly mixed with the Negro. But we will assume, for the sake of the argu-ment, that the two races are absolutely pure. We will assume, too, that the laws of the whole country were as favorable to this amalgamation as the laws of most Southern States are at present against it; i.e., that it were made a misdemeanor for two white or two colored persons to marry, so long as it was possible to obtain a mate of the other race—this would be even more favorable than the Southern rule, which makes no such exception. Taking the population as one-eighth Negro, this eighth, married to an equal number of whites, would give in the next generation a population of which one-fourth would be mulattoes. Mating these in turn with white persons, the next generation would be composed one-half of quadroons, or persons one-fourth Negro. In the third generation, applying the same rule, the en-tire population would be composed of octoroons, or persons only one-eighth Negro, who would probably call themselves white, if by this time there remained any particular advantage in being so considered. Thus in three generations the pure whites would be entirely eliminated, and there would be no perceptible trace of the blacks left.

The mechanical mixture would be complete; as it would probably be put, the white race would have absorbed the black. There would be no inferior race to domineer over; there would be no superior race to oppress those who differed from them in racial externals. The inevitable social struggle, which in one form or another, seems to be one of the conditions of progress, would proceed along other lines than those of race. If now and then, for a few generations, an occasional trace of the black ancestor should crop out, no one would care, for all would be tarred with the same stick. This is already the case in South America, parts of Mexico and to a large extent in the West Indies. From a Negroid nation, which ours is already, we would have become a composite and homogeneous people, and the elements of racial discord which have troubled our civil life so gravely and still threaten our free institutions, would have been entirely eliminated.

But this will never happen. The same result will be brought about slowly and obscurely, and, if the processes of nature are not too violently interrupted by the hand of man, in such a manner as to produce the best results with the least disturbance of natural laws. In another article I shall endeavor to show that this process has been taking place with greater rapidity than is generally supposed, and that the results have been such as to encourage the belief that the formation of a uniform type out of our present racial elements will take place within a measurably near period.

‸

SOURCE: "The Future American," *Boston Evening Transcript*, 18 August 1900, 20, emended in light of a typed text at the Fisk University Library which was produced after the 1900 publication. The subsequent headlines in the *Transcript* read thus:

———

A Perfect Type Supposably to Be Evolved—
Some Old Theories of Race that Are Exploded—
The Ethnic Elements on Which
the Fusion Must Be Based

———

IN THREE ARTICLES—ARTICLE I.

———

[1] In a parenthetical note, Chesnutt cited his source as "Professor Ripley's 'Races of Europe,' page 457; New York, 1839." William Z. Ripley (1867–1941) delivered the lectures on which his monograph was based at the Lowell Institute in 1896; *The Races of Europe: A Sociological Study* was published by D. Appleton and Company in the United States in 1899, rather than 1839.

[2] Chesnutt alludes to American expansionist tendencies following the outbreak of the Spanish American War in 1898.

The Future American

A Stream of Dark Blood in the Veins of the Southern Whites

Essay published in the *Boston Evening Transcript*, 25 August 1900

I have said that the formation of the new American race type will take place slowly and obscurely for some time to come, after the manner of all healthy changes in nature. I may go further and say that this process has already been going on ever since the various races in the Western world have been brought into juxtaposition. Slavery was a rich soil for the production of a mixed race, and one need only read the literature and laws of the past two generations to see how steadily, albeit slowly and insidiously, the stream of dark blood has insinuated itself into the veins of the dominant, or, as a Southern critic recently described it in a paragraph that came under my eye, the "domineering" race. The Creole stories of Mr. Cable and other writers were not mere figments of the imagination; the beautiful octoroon was a corporeal fact; it is more than likely that she had brothers of the same complexion, though curiously enough the male octoroon has cut no figure in fiction, except in the case of the melancholy Honoré Grandissime, f. m. c.; and that she and her brothers often crossed the invisible but rigid color line was an historical fact that only an ostrich-like prejudice could deny.[1]

Grace King's "Story of New Orleans" makes the significant statement that the quadroon women of that city preferred white fathers for their children, in order that these latter might become white and thereby be qualified to enter the world of opportunity.[2] More than one of the best families of Louisiana has a dark ancestral strain. A conspicuous American family of Southwestern extraction, which recently contributed a party to a brilliant international marriage, is known, by the well-informed, to be just exactly five generations removed from a Negro ancestor. One member of this family, a distinguished society leader, has been known, upon occasion, when some question of the rights or privileges of the colored race came up, to show a very noble sympathy for her distant kinsmen. If American prejudice permitted her and others to speak freely of her pedigree, what a tower of strength her name and influence would be to a despised and struggling race!

A distinguished American man of letters, now resident in Europe, who spent many years in North Carolina, has said to the writer that he had noted, in the course of a long life, at least a thousand instances of white persons known or suspected to possess a strain of Negro blood.[3] An amusing instance of this sort occurred a year or two ago. It was announced through the newspapers, whose omniscience of course no one would question, that a certain great merchant of Chicago was a mulatto. This gentleman had a large dry goods trade in the South, notably in Texas. Shortly after the publication of the item reflecting on the immaculateness of the merchant's descent, there appeared in the Texas newspapers, among the advertising matter, a statement from the Chicago merchant characterizing the rumor as a malicious falsehood, concocted by his rivals in business, and incidentally calling attention to the excellent bargains offered to retailers and jobbers at his great emporium. A counter-illustration is found in the case of a certain bishop, recently elected, of the African Methodist Episcopal Church, who is accused of being a white man. A colored editor who possesses the saving grace of humor, along with other talents of a high order, gravely observed, in discussing this rumor, that "the poor man could not help it, even if he were white, and that a fact for which he was in no wise responsible should not be allowed to stand in the way of his advancement."

During a residence in North Carolina in my youth and early manhood I noted many curious phases of the race problem. I have in mind a family of three sisters so aggressively white that the old popular Southern legend that they were the unacknowledged children of white parents was current concerning them. There was absolutely not the slightest earmark of the Negro about them. It may be stated here, as another race fallacy, that the "telltale dark mark at the root of the nails," supposed to be an infallible test of Negro blood, is a delusion and a snare, and of no value whatever as a test of race. It belongs with the grewsome superstition that a woman apparently white may give birth to a coal-black child by a white father. Another instance that came under my eye was that of a very beautiful girl with soft, wavy brown hair, who is now living in a Far Western State as the wife of a white husband. A typical case was that of a family in which the tradition of Negro origin had persisted long after all trace of it had disappeared. The family took its origin from a white ancestress, and had consequently been free for several generations. The father of the first colored child, counting the family in the female line— the only way it could be counted—was a mulatto. A second infusion of white blood, this time on the paternal side, resulted in offspring not distinguishable from pure white. One child of this generation emigrated to what was then the Far West, married a white woman and reared a large family, whose descendants, now in the fourth or fifth remove from the Negro, are in all probability wholly unaware of their origin. A sister of this pioneer emigrant remained in the place of her birth and formed an irregular union with a white man of means, with whom she lived for many years and for whom she bore a large number of children, who became about evenly divided between white and colored, fixing their status by the marriages they made. One of the daughters, for instance, married a white man and reared in a neighboring county a family of white children, who, in all probability, were as active as any one else in the recent ferocious red-shirt campaign to disfranchise the Negroes.[4]

In this same town there was stationed once, before the war, at the Federal arsenal there located, an officer who fell in love with a "white Negro" girl, as our Southern friends impartially dub them. This officer subsequently left the army, and carried away with him to the North the whole family of his inamorata. He married the woman, and their descendants, who live in a large Western city, are not known at all as persons of color, and show no trace of their dark origin.

Two notable bishops of the Roman Catholic communion in the United States are known to be the sons of a slave mother and a white father, who, departing from the usual American rule, gave his sons freedom, education and a chance in life, instead of sending them to the auction block. Colonel T. W. Higginson, in his *Cheerful Yesterdays*, relates the story of a white colored woman whom he assisted in her escape from slavery or its consequences, who married a white man in the vicinity of Boston and lost her identity with the colored race.[5] How many others there must be who know of similar instances! Grace King, in her "Story of New Orleans," to which I have referred, in speaking of a Louisiana law which required the public records, when dealing with persons of color, always to specify the fact of color, in order, so far had the admixture of races gone, to distinguish them from whites, says: "But the officers of the law could be bribed, and the qualification once dropped acted, inversely, as a patent of pure blood."

A certain well-known Shakspearean actress has a strain of Negro blood, and a popular leading man under a well-known manager is similarly gifted. It would be interesting to give their names, but would probably only injure them. If they could themselves speak of their origin, without any unpleasant consequences, it would be a handsome thing for the colored race. That they do not is no reproach to them; they are white to all intents and purposes, even by the curious laws of the curious States from which they derived their origin, and are in all conscience entitled to any advantage accompanying this status.

Anyone at all familiar with the hopes and aspirations of the colored race, as expressed, for instance, in their prolific newspaper literature, must have perceived the wonderful inspiration which they have drawn from the career of a few distinguished Europeans of partial Negro ancestry, who have felt no call, by way of social prejudice, to deny or conceal their origin, or to refuse their sympathy to those who need it so much. Pushkin, the Russian Shakspeare, had a black ancestor.[6] One of the chief editors of the London *Times*, who died a few years ago, was a West Indian colored man, who had no interest in concealing the fact.[7] One of the generals of the British army is similarly favored, although the fact is not often referred to. General Alfred Dodds, the ranking general of the French army, now in command in China, is a quadroon.[8] The poet, Robert Browning, was of West Indian origin, and some of his intimate personal friends maintained and proved to their own satisfaction that he was partly of Negro descent. Mr. Browning always said that he did not know; that there was no family tradition to that effect; but if it could be demonstrated he would admit it freely enough, if it would reflect any credit upon a race who needed it so badly.

The most conspicuous of the Eurafricans (to coin a word) were the Dumas family, who were distinguished for three generations.[9] The mulatto, General Dumas, won distinction in the wars under the Revolution. His son, the famous Alexandre Dumas *père*, has delighted several generations with his novels, and founded a school of fiction. His son, Alexandre *fils*, novelist and dramatist, was as supreme in his own line as his father had been in his. Old Alexandre gives his pedigree in detail in his memoirs; and the Negro origin of the family is set out in every encyclopædia. Nevertheless, in a literary magazine of recent date, published in New York, it was gravely stated by a writer that "there was a rumor, probably not well founded, that the author of *Monte-Cristo* had a very distant strain of Negro blood." If this had been written with reference to some living American of obscure origin, its point might be appreciated; but such extreme delicacy in stating so widely known a fact appeals to one's sense of humor.

These European gentlemen could be outspoken about their origin, because it carried with it no social stigma or disability whatever. When such a state of public opinion exists in the United States, there may be a surprising revision of pedigrees!

A little incident that occurred not long ago near Boston will illustrate the complexity of these race relations. Three light-colored men, brothers, by the name, we will say, of Green, living in a Boston suburb, married respectively a white, a brown and a black woman. The children with the white mother became known as white, and associated with white people. The others were frankly colored. By a not unlikely coincidence, in the course of time the children of the three families found themselves in the same public school. Curiously enough, one afternoon the three sets of Green children—the white Greens, the brown Greens and the black Greens—were detained after school, and were all directed to report to a certain schoolroom, where they were assigned certain tasks at the blackboards about the large room. Still more curiously, most of the teachers of the school happened to have business in this particular room on that particular afternoon, and all of them seemed greatly interested in the Green children.

"Well, well, did you ever! Just think of it! And they are all first cousins!" was remarked audibly.

The children were small, but they lived in Boston, and were, of course, as became Boston children, preternaturally intelligent for their years. They reported to their parents the incident and a number of remarks of a similar tenor to the one above quoted. The result was a complaint to the school authorities, and a reprimand to several teachers. A curious feature of the affair lay in the source from which the complaint emanated. One might suppose it to have come from the white Greens; but no, they were willing that the incident should pass unnoticed and be promptly forgotten; publicity would only advertise a fact which would work to their social injury. The dark Greens rather enjoyed the affair; they had nothing to lose; they had no objections to being known as the cousins of the others, and experienced a certain not unnatural pleasure in their discomfiture. The complaint came from the brown Greens. The reader can figure out the psychology of it for himself.

A more certain proof of the fact that Negro blood is widely distributed among the white people may be found in the laws and judicial decisions of the various States. Laws, as a rule, are not made until demanded by a sufficient number of specific cases to call for a general rule; and judicial decisions of course are never announced except as the result of litigation over contested facts. There is no better index of the character and genius of a people than their laws.

In North Carolina, marriage between white persons and free persons of color was lawful until 1830. By the Missouri code of 1855, the color line was drawn at one-fourth of Negro blood, and persons of only one-eighth were legally white. The same rule was laid down by the Mississippi code of 1880. Under the old *code noir* of Louisiana, the descendant of a white and a quadroon was white. Under these laws many persons currently known as "colored," or, more recently as "Negro," would be legally white if they chose to claim and exercise the privilege. In Ohio, before the Civil War, a person more than half-white was legally entitled to all the rights of a white man. In South Carolina, the line of cleavage was left somewhat indefinite; the color line was drawn tentatively at one-fourth of Negro blood, but this was not held conclusive.

"The term 'mulatto'," said the Supreme Court of that State in a reported case, "is not invariably applicable to every admixture of African blood with the European, nor is one having all the features of a white to be ranked with the degraded class designated by the laws of the State as persons of color, because of some remote taint of the Negro race. . . . The question whether persons are colored or white, where color or feature is doubtful, is for the jury to determine by reputation, by reception into society, and by their exercises of the privileges of a white man, as well as by admixture of blood."[10]

It is well known that this liberality of view grew out of widespread conditions in the State, which these decisions in their turn tended to emphasize. They were probably due to the large preponderance of colored people in the State, which rendered the whites the more willing to augment their own number. There are many interesting color-line decisions in the reports of the Southern courts, which space will not permit the mention of.

In another article I shall consider certain conditions which retard the development of the future American race type which I have suggested, as well as certain other tendencies which are likely to promote it.

⤿

SOURCE: "The Future American: A Stream of Dark Blood in the Veins of the Southern Whites," *Boston Evening Transcript*, 25 August 1900, 15, emended in light of a typed text at the Fisk University Library produced after the 1900 publication. The remainder of the headlines read thus:

———

Some Examples of the Mixing Process—
"Colored Men" Whose Color is Imperceptible—
A Curious Incident Near Boston—
Strange Family Histories

IN THREE ARTICLES—SECOND ARTICLE

———

[1]Cable sympathetically focused upon those of mixed racial background in works such as *Old Creole Days* (1879), *The Grandissimes* (1880), and *Madame Delphine* (1881).

[2]Grace King (1852–1932) was a New Orleans author distinguished by her "local color" descriptions and realistic analyses of conditions in Louisiana. The "Story of New Orleans" to which Chesnutt refers is *New Orleans: The Place and the People* (1895), wherein King describes the *gens de couleur* who viewed blacks as their inferiors and made fine distinctions about the worth of individuals on the basis of the degree to which they were white.

[3]Tourgée was the U.S. Consul at Bordeaux, France, at this time.

[4]Democrat Wade Hampton and his supporters forced the abdication of South Carolina Governor Daniel H. Chamberlain (1835–1907), a Republican, in 1877. Hampton's followers were the "red shirts," and the epithet is thus applied by Chesnutt to all white supremacists.

[5]Thomas Wentworth Higginson (1823–1911), a Unitarian minister and fervid abolitionist, was an ardent lecturer who advocated equal rights for African Americans. His autobiographical *Cheerful Yesterdays* was published in 1898.

[6]Alexander Pushkin (1799–1837), poet and novelist. See also "The Literary Outlook of Colored Men in Literature," n. 1.

[7]The journalist to whom Chesnutt refers is Barbadian Sir William Conrad Reeves (1821–1902). He was not one of the London *Times*'s chief editors but did serve as a London correspondent for the Barbados press while studying law.

[8]Alfred A. Dodds (1842–1922).

[9]See "Alexander Dumas" and "Race Ideals and Examples," wherein Chesnutt describes the accomplishments of the Dumas family at length.

[10]Chesnutt earlier treated these distinctions in "What Is a White Man?"

The Future American

A Complete Race-Amalgamation Likely to Occur

Essay published in the *Boston Evening Transcript*, 1 September 1900

I have endeavored in two former letters to set out the reasons why it seems likely that the future American ethnic type will be formed by a fusion of all the various races now peopling this continent, and to show that this process has been under way, slowly but surely, like all evolutionary movements, for several hundred years. I wish now to consider some of the conditions which will retard this fusion, as well as certain other facts which tend to promote it.

The Indian phase of the problem, so far at least as the United States is concerned, has been practically disposed of in what has already been said. The absorption of the Indians will be delayed so long as the tribal relations continue, and so long as the Indians are treated as wards of the Government, instead of being given their rights once for all, and placed upon the footing of other citizens. It is presumed that this will come about as the wilder Indians are educated and by the development of the country brought into closer contact with civilization, which must happen before a very great while. As has been stated, there is no very strong prejudice against the Indian blood; a well-stocked farm or a comfortable fortune will secure a white husband for a comely Indian girl any day, with some latitude, and there is no evidence of any such strong race instinct or organization as will make the Indians of the future wish to perpetuate themselves as a small and insignificant class in a great population, thus emphasizing distinctions which would be overlooked in the case of the individual.

The Indian will fade into the white population as soon as he chooses, and in the United States proper the slender Indian strain will ere long leave no trace discoverable by anyone but the anthropological expert. In New Mexico and Central America, on the contrary, the chances seem to be that the Indian will first absorb the non-indigenous elements, unless, which is not unlikely, European immigration shall increase the white contingent.

The Negro element remains, then, the only one which seems likely to present any difficulty of assimilation. The main obstacle that retards the absorption of the Negro into the general population is the apparently intense prejudice against color which prevails in the United States. This prejudice loses much of its importance, however, when it is borne in mind that it is almost purely local and does not exist in quite the same form anywhere else in the world, except among the Boers of South Africa, where it prevails in an even more aggravated form; and, as I shall endeavor to show, this prejudice in the United States is more apparent than real, and is a caste prejudice which is merely accentuated by differences of race. At present, however, I wish to consider it merely as a deterrent to amalgamation.

This prejudice finds forcible expression in the laws which prevail in all the Southern States, without exception, forbidding the intermarriage of white persons and persons of color—these last being generally defined within certain degrees. While it is evident that such laws alone will not prevent the intermingling of races, which goes merrily on in spite of them, it is equally apparent that this placing of mixed marriages beyond the pale of the law is a powerful deterrent to any honest or dignified amalgamation. Add to this legal restriction, which is enforced by severe penalties, the social odium accruing to the white party to such a union, and it may safely be predicted that so long as present conditions prevail in the South, there will be little marrying or giving in marriage[1] between persons of different race. So ferocious is this sentiment against intermarriage, that in a recent Missouri case, where a colored man ran away with and married a young white woman, the man was pursued by a "posse"—a word which is rapidly being debased from its proper meaning by its use in the attempt to dignify the character of lawless Southern mobs—and shot to death; the woman was tried and convicted of the "crime" of "miscegenation"—another honest word which the South degrades along with the Negro.

Another obstacle to race fusion lies in the drastic and increasing proscriptive legislation by which the South attempts to keep the white and colored races apart in every place where their joint presence might be taken to imply equality; or, to put it more directly, the persistent effort to degrade the Negro to a distinctly and permanently inferior caste. This is undertaken by means of separate schools, separate railroad and street cars, political disfranchisement, debasing and abhorrent prison systems, and an unflagging campaign of calumny, by which the vices and shortcomings of the Negroes are grossly magnified and their virtues practically lost sight of. The popular argument that the Negro ought to develop his own civilization, and has no right to share in that of the white race, unless by favor, comes with poor grace from those who are forcing their civilization upon others at the cannon's mouth;[2] it is, moreover, uncandid and unfair. The white people of the present generation did not make their civilization; they inherited it ready-made, and much of the wealth which is so strong a factor in their power was created by the unpaid labor of the colored people. The present generation has, however, brought to a high state of development one distinctively American institution, for which it is entitled to such credit as it may wish to claim; I refer to the custom of lynching, with its attendant horrors.

The principal deterrent to race admixture, however, is the low industrial and social efficiency of the colored race. If it be conceded that these are the result of environment, then their cause is not far to seek, and the cure is also in sight. Their poverty, their ignorance and their servile estate render them as yet largely ineligible for social fusion with a race whose pride is fed not only by the record of its achievements but by a constant comparison with a less developed and less fortunate race, which it has held so long in subjection.

The forces that tend to the future absorption of the black race are, however, vastly stronger than those arrayed against it. As experience has demonstrated, slavery was favorable to the mixing of races. The growth, under healthy civil conditions, of a large and self-respecting colored citizenship would doubtless tend to lessen the clandestine association of the two races; but the effort to degrade the Negro may result, if successful, in a partial restoration of the old status. But, assuming that the present anti-Negro legislation is but a temporary reaction, then the steady progress of the colored race in wealth and culture and social efficiency will, in the course of time, materially soften the asperities of racial prejudice and permit them to approach the whites more closely, until, in time, the prejudice against intermarriage shall have been overcome by other considerations.

It is safe to say that the possession of a million dollars, with the ability to use it to the best advantage, would throw such a golden glow over a dark complexion as to override anything but a very obdurate prejudice. Mr. Spahr, in his well-studied and impartial book on *America's Working People*, states as his conclusion, after a careful study of conditions in the South, that the most advanced third of the Negroes of that section has already, in one generation of limited opportunity, passed in the race of life the least advanced third of the whites.[3] To pass the next third will prove a more difficult task, no doubt, but the Negroes will have the impetus of their forward movement to push them ahead.

The outbreaks of race prejudice in recent years are the surest evidence of the Negro's progress. No effort is required to keep down a race which manifests no desire nor ability to rise; but with each new forward movement of the colored race it is brought into contact with the whites at some fresh point, which evokes a new manifestation of prejudice until custom has adjusted things to the new condition. When all Negroes were poor and ignorant they could be denied their rights with impunity. As they grow in knowledge and in wealth they become more self-assertive, and make it correspondingly troublesome for those who would ignore their claims. It is much easier, by a supreme effort, as recently attempted with temporary success in North Carolina, to knock the race down and rob it of its rights once for all, than to repeat the process from day to day and with each individual; it saves wear and tear on the conscience, and makes it easy to maintain a superiority which it might in the course of a short time require some little effort to keep up.[4]

This very proscription, however, political and civil at the South, social all over the country, varying somewhat in degree, will, unless very soon relaxed, prove a powerful factor in the mixture of the races. If it is only by becoming white that colored people and their children are to enjoy the rights and dignities of citizenship, they will have every incentive to "lighten the breed," to use a current phrase, that they may claim the white man's privileges as soon as possible. That this motive is already at work may be seen in the enormous extent to which certain "face bleachers" and "hair straighteners" are advertised in the newspapers printed for circulation among the colored people. The most powerful factor in achieving any result is the wish to bring it about. The only thing that ever succeeded in keeping two races separated when living on the same soil—the only true ground of caste—is religion, and as has been alluded to in the case of the Jews, this is only superficially successful. The colored people are the same as the whites in religion; they have the same standards and mediums of culture, the same ideals, and the presence of the successful white race as a constant incentive to their ambition. The ultimate result is not difficult to foresee. The races will be quite as effectively amalgamated by lightening the Negroes as they would be by darkening the whites. It is only a social fiction, indeed, which makes of a person seven-eighths white a Negro; he is really much more a white man.

The hope of the Negro, so far as the field of moral sympathy and support in his aspirations is concerned, lies, as always, chiefly in the North. There the forces which tend to his elevation are, in the main, allowed their natural operation. The exaggerated zeal with which the South is rushing to degrade the Negro is likely to result, as in the case of slavery, in making more friends for him at the North; and if the North shall not see fit to interfere forcibly with Southern legislation, it may at least feel disposed to emphasize, by its own liberality, its disapproval of Southern injustice and barbarity.

An interesting instance of the difference between the North and the South in regard to colored people, may be found in two cases which only last year came up for trial in two adjoining border States. A colored man living in Maryland went over to Washington and married a white woman. The marriage was legal in Washington. When they returned to their Maryland home they were arrested for the crime of "miscegenation"—perhaps it is only a misdemeanor in Maryland—and sentenced to fine and imprisonment, the penalty of extra-judicial death[5] not extending so far North. The same month a couple, one white and one colored, were arrested in New Jersey for living in adultery. They were found guilty by the court, but punishment was withheld upon a promise that they would marry immediately; or, as some cynic would undoubtedly say, the punishment was commuted from imprisonment to matrimony.

The adding to our territories of large areas populated by dark races, some of them already liberally dowered with Negro blood, will enhance the relative importance of the non-Caucasian elements of the population, and largely increase the flow of dark blood toward the white race, until the time shall come when distinctions of color shall lose their importance, which will be but the prelude to a complete racial fusion.

The formation of this future American race is not a pressing problem. Because of the conditions under which it must take place, it is likely to be extremely slow—much slower, indeed, in our temperate climate and highly organized society, than in the American tropics and sub-tropics, where it is already well under way, if not a *fait accompli*. That it must come in the United States, sooner or later, seems to be a foregone conclusion, as the result of natural law—*lex dura, sed tamen lex*—a hard pill, but one which must be swallowed. There can manifestly be no such thing as a peaceful and progressive civilization in a nation divided by two warring races, and homogeneity of type, at least in externals, is a necessary condition of harmonious social progress.

If this, then, must come, the development and progress of all the constituent elements of the future American race is of the utmost importance as bearing upon the quality of the resultant type. The white race is still susceptible of some improvement; and if, in time, the more objectionable Negro traits are eliminated, and his better qualities correspondingly developed, his part in the future American race may well be an important and valuable one.

⤚

SOURCE: "The Future American: A Complete Race-Amalgamation Likely to Occur," *Boston Evening Transcript*, 1 September 1900, 24, emended in light of a typed text at the Fisk University Library produced after the 1900 publication. The remainder of the headlines read thus:

———

The Indian Will Fade into the White Population
as Soon as He Chooses—Legal and Social Barriers
to Absorption of the Negro Element Must Give Way
—The Process is Going on Rapidly

BY CHARLES W. CHESNUTT

*Author of "The Wife of His Youth," "The
Conjure Woman," etc.*

IN THREE ARTICLES—THIRD ARTICLE

[1]Matthew 24:38.

[2]Chesnutt refers to the American presence in countries ruled by Spain prior to the Spanish American War.

[3]Charles B. Spahr (1860–1904), in *America's Working People* (1900), extensively treated the condition of African Americans in the workplace.

[4]The November 1898 election in North Carolina saw the restoration of power to the Democrats and the defeat of the "fusion" candidates, Republicans and Populists who had appealed to African Americans by extending their civil rights. The Wilmington race riot of 10 November was a result of the hotly contested elections; another was a curtailment of the rights of African Americans in the months that followed. Chesnutt interpreted the Wilmington situation in *The Marrow of Tradition* (1901).

[5]That is, lynching.

Introduction to Temple Course Reading

Speech to the "Temple Course" Participants, Tifereth Israel
Temple, Cleveland, O., 15 November 1900

It is often said, by disappointed people and their friends, that a prophet is not without honor save in his own country and in his own house.[1] There is, often, however, a very good reason for this, for more than one prophet, especially those of the self-appointed order, deserve little honor, either at home or abroad. The people at home, knowing the man, know this—those abroad have yet to find it out. As a Cleveland man, I certainly ought to be very proud of the audience here to-night, especially since I understand that attendance upon these lectures is not compulsory, even to ticket holders.[2] The relation of a speaker to an audience before which he appears for the first time, always suggests to me those three of the cardinal virtues of which we generally speak together.[3] The mere presence of the audience by no means implies entire faith in the speaker's powers; it is, however, a sign that they hope to be entertained, and that they may be willing, if need be, to throw the mantle of charity over the speaker's shortcomings. It is a great thing to have such an audience with you, but it makes one shudder to think what might happen if they should turn against you.

I am reminded, in this same connection, of a little story which I might tell you before I start in on my own, from which I intend to read to you. I would like to inquire whether there is a clairvoyant in the audience?[4] I imagine, then, from your silence that there is no one here who possesses the faculty of seeing Evil, with a capital E—the pure, unadulterated article. We generally see it mixed with good, but I think perhaps our nearest conception of abstract Evil would be obtained by putting a capital D in front of the word, which would introduce us to an old acquaintance. Of course I mean nothing personal by this remark. In the Southern States, however, where most of my own stories are located, there are people who possess this faculty. Two colored men—as I'm going to read stories about colored people, it may be well enough to start off with one of the same sort—two colored men in a Southern city are discussing this power of seeing Evil, which one of them claims to possess, and he is giving the other an instance of its exercise:

"You know dat ole hanted house down yander by de creek?" he asked, "whar datman wuz kill' three er fo' yeahs ago, an' whar nobody ain' live' sence?"

"Yes."

"Well, 'bout a yeah ago I wuz walkin' 'long Main Street, an' I run 'cross two gent'emen stan'in' on de cawner; an' one of 'em wuz sayin' ter de yuther, 'I'll bet five dollahs dey ain' narry man in dis town w'at'll stay in dat hanted house all night.' I spoke up, an says I, 'I knows a man, Majah, w'at'll stay in dat hanted house all night.' 'Who'de man,' sezee, 'who's de man?' '*I'm* de man,' sez I, 'you gimme de five dollahs, an' *I'll* stay dere all night. Day ain' no ha'nt livin' w'at kin skeer *me*. I sleeps in graveyards by prefe'nce. *I'm* hant-proof, *I* is.'

"Well, he gimme a dollah in advance, an' 'long 'bout nine er-clock I tuck a lamp an' went down ter de old hanted house. I went in, sot my lantern down on de table, looked all roun' de room ter see dat dey wan't nuthin' dere and dat de winders wuz all fastened, an' den I shet an' lock' de do' an' barred it tight. W'en I got thoo wid de do' I turn' roun',—an' dere wuz a big black cat walkin' roun' on 'is tiptoes in de middle er de flo', wid his tail curled up over his back.

"I looked at de black cat, an' he looked at me, but I wanted dem other fo' dollahs, so I went over ter de table an' sot down. I had n't mo' d'n teched de cheer befo' dere wuz dat black cat settin' up on de table, wid his tail curled all roun' de lamp! I dunno how he got dere, but dere he wuz!

"'Good ev'nin',' sez de black cat.

"'Good ev'nin', suh,' says I.

"Den de black cat lean' over to'ds me, an' sezee, in a low, myste'ious voice, 'Dey ain' nobody hyuh but you en me, is dey?'

"'N-n-n-o,' sez I, 'an' quick as I kin git *outer* hyuh, dey ain' gwineter be nobody hyuh *but you!*'"

There's nobody here but you and I to-night, but I hope we shall be able to keep together a little longer than the ha'nt-proof man and his embodiment of Evil.

My programme this evening will consist of extracts from my own writings, which are referred to in the little circular which has been distributed among the audience.[5] Several years after the Civil War, when I was about nine years old, my father, who had lived some time in Ohio and had spent several years in helping to save the country, moved to North Carolina, the State of his birth, taking me with him.[6] As a result, I spent the most impressionable years of my life in the picturesque old town of Fayetteville, which I have attempted to describe faithfully in my novel, *The House Behind the Cedars*. It was a community a hundred years behind the times, made up of people of all colors and all degrees of ignorance and superstition, and numbering only a small upper stratum among the enlightened. In that primitive town every graveyard was alive with ghosts, and every vacant house was ha'nted—and I don't recall any haunt-proof men. All sorts of old odds and ends of superstition prevailed—remnants of Scotch and English witchcraft, rubbing elbows with obscure survivals of Indian legend and African folk-lore. Conjurers and witches were not mere chimæras of the imagination, but existed here and there in the living flesh, in the person of some ancient Negro or wrinkled poor-white woman. I received from this old town, only a week ago, a letter, written just before election day, in which my correspondent informed me that the community was exercised by a prediction of one of these gifted old women, who had dreamed a dream in which she had seen a great tidal wave sweeping over the country, upon the crest of which floated—William Jennings Bryan![7]

It occurred to me, long, long ago, that I might take some of these quaint superstitions, dress them in some rags of fancy and that the result might perchance interest or amuse those choice spirits who read books. This I endeavored to do in the volume entitled *The Conjure Woman*,[8] from which I shall take my first number this evening. It is written in the character of an Ohio man who moves South for his wife's health. To the old plantation which they buy is attached, by a sort of squatter right, an old colored man, formerly a slave of the proprietor. The Northern settler employs this relic of the past as coachman, and from time to time he tells the kind-hearted Northern man and his sympathetic wife many remarkable tales of the times "way back yander nefo' de wah." The stories, as a rule, relate to the doings of Old Aunt Peggy, the Conjure Woman.

The first story in this volume relates how the gentleman became acquainted with Julius, whom he finds seated on a log eating grapes out of his hat, when the gentleman goes to inspect the old plantation. Julius learns the purpose of the white folks' visit, and advises the gentleman not to buy the vineyard.[9]

⌐⌐

SOURCE: Typed text dated "Nov. 15, 1900," at the Fisk University Library. The Temple Course was a lecture series conducted by Moses J. Gries (1868–1918), rabbi of Cleveland's Tifereth Israel Temple from 1892 to 1917; this "speech" is an introduction to a series of readings from his own works that Chesnutt performed.

[1]Matthew 13:57. Here, and below in his references to St. Paul's epistles and to Satan, Chesnutt does not register awareness of the sponsorship of his presentation.

[2]Chesnutt originally wrote ". . . here to-night. (Near the doors.) Nevertheless, I trust I shall feel better at the end of my lecture than I do at the beginning. The relation . . . ." That is, he originally planned to direct attention to members of his audience who were near an exit and to allude waggishly to the possibility of their slipping out unobserved.

[3]St. Paul specifies these cardinal virtues: "And now abideth faith, hope, charity, these three; but the greatest of these is charity," 1 Corinthians 13:13.

[4]Chesnutt here canceled the sentence that immediately followed: "I used to live next door to one, and I did n't know that there might be another in this seventh city in the United States."

[5]Chesnutt's publisher, Houghton, Mifflin & Co., provided him with printed advertisements for his books, which he distributed at readings and lectures. *The House Behind the Cedars*, mentioned by Chesnutt below, was published less than a month before.

[6]Born in 1833, Andrew Jackson Chesnutt served with the Union Army, apparently as a teamster. After the Civil War, in 1866, he returned to Fayetteville, N.C., where he lived until his death in 1921.

[7]Bryan (1860–1925) was a Democrat defeated by William McKinley (1843–1901) in both the 1896 and the 1900 presidential elections. A spokesman for the common man whose sobriquet was "The Great Commoner," he was opposed not only by Republicans but by those in the middle and upper middle class with an interest in preserving the status quo.

[8]Chesnutt's first book, published in 1899.

[9]Chesnutt here added by hand "p. 11," referring to the pagination of *The Conjure Woman* and indicating the point in his short story "The Goophered Grapevine" at which he would begin reading. The other "extracts" read by Chesnutt were from "Sis' Becky's Pickanniny" and "The Passing of Grandison."

The White and the Black

Essay published in the *Boston Evening Transcript*, 20 March 1901

After attending the Negro conference at Tuskegee, which has been fully described in your columns, I paid a visit to Atlanta University, of which institution I was the guest for several days.[1] The contrast, in some respects, between Tuskegee and Atlanta was very striking. In the one, the busy note of industry was predominant; in the other, an air of scholastic quiet pervaded the grounds and the halls. Perhaps the weather, which was unusually cold for Atlanta, had some effect in restraining the natural exuberance of youth. The difference, it seemed to me, however, lay deeper. Atlanta avowedly stands for the higher education. If it be granted that the majority of the Negroes must work with their hands, like the majority of all other races, and that manual training will best prepare them to work effectively, it is none the less true that, abandoned as they are by the Southern whites, in church, in school and in social life, they need leaders along these lines—picked men and women, in whose training special stress has been laid upon the highest ideals of manhood and womanhood, upon culture of mind, character and manners. This school, which is under the charge of New

England people, has, in its externals, a completeness of detail which is not apparent in some other Southern schools. While there is nothing fine about it, nothing superfluous, there is a neatness and an attention to little things that makes bareness seem mere simplicity. The teaching force, which is mainly white, has been supplemented by the addition of several colored teachers, men and women of high culture, who do not lower the average. The most conspicuous of these is Dr. W. E. B. Dubois, whose studies in sociology have won him a wide reputation.[2] The group of schools at Atlanta devoted to the education of colored youth have been a powerful lever for the elevation of this neglected race, and it is sincerely to be hoped that no zeal for other forms of training will lead them to suffer. The Negroes of the South need all sorts of training; the South is not able to give it unaided, even if those in power were willing to do so, and they are not over-enthusiastic. The North has a twofold interest: it insisted upon keeping the South in the Union; it has, therefore, a family interest. Another consideration is that under prevailing conditions in the South, many people of color will, in time, prefer to live at the North, and the better prepared they are for citizenship, the less difficulty will the North have in their assimilation. For instance, from the town of Wilmington, N.C., since the "revolution," as the white people call it, or the "massacre" according to the Negroes,[3]—it was really both—over fifteen hundred of the best colored citizens have left the town. Most of these have sought homes farther North. It is a curious revival of ante-bellum conditions. The Negroes in the South are not yet free, and social odium at the North is deemed, by many, preferable to the same thing at the South, with oppressive and degrading legal enactments superadded.

I have said that the Southern Negro is not free. The same may be said of the Southern white man, for the laws which seek the separation of the races apply to him as well—but with a very material difference. Society is divided into horizontal strata, with the white man on top. One can endure, with considerable equanimity, restrictions which make him superior whether he will or no. The brunt of the separation falls upon the Negro, but the white man does not escape.

For instance, on leaving Washington, D.C., the capital of a nation, by the constitution of which all men are equal before the law one is confronted in the Southern Railway Depot with signs in the cars labelled respectively "White" and "Colored." The passenger is supposed to take his seat according to his complexion. If he does not he is sure to be called to order in a short time. The law, however, does not really become effective until the train has crossed the river into Virginia, the old-time mother of presidents and breeder of slaves. She has lost her first preeminence; the existence of these laws shows with what tenacity she clings to the other. But, nevertheless, the American citizen, white or black, who has travelled all over the North and West, with only the private consciousness that his color affected his citizenship, is met at this gate to the Sunny South with a classification which puts a legal stamp upon the one as superior, upon the other as inferior. A white man is never allowed to forget that he is white; lest he forget, a large sign is fastened at either end of the car, keeping him constantly in mind of the fact. A colored man is not permitted to cherish any illusions as to equality; if he should endeavor for a moment, in his temporary isolation, to forget this fact and all it implies, that sign in large white letters keeps him sternly admonished of the fact that between him and mankind not of his own color, or some variety of it, there is a great gulf.

I could almost write a book about these laws, their variations, their applications and curious stories that one hears continually concerning them. When first adopted there was some pretence made of furnishing equal accommodations for the different classes of passengers; but as soon as the Supreme Court of the United States had affirmed the validity of this class of legislation, the pretence of equality was practically dropped.[4] It could not be otherwise. With society thus divided, horizontally, the two classes of travellers were not equal in numbers, in appearance, in means or in any other way. Most of the colored travellers are poor, many of them uncouth and passively submissive to the inevitable. That they should be treated with equal courtesy or be given equal comfort and consideration would be contrary to human nature. The Negro coach is invariably the less comfortable of the two and the less ornate. It is always in the least desirable portion of the train. A colored passenger often does not know where he must sit. He is shifted around from compartment to compartment to suit the convenience of the traffic. The conductor of a train has the power of an autocrat. He nods his Jove-like head, corrugates his high Caucasian brow and the Negro seldom argues, because there is no use in doing so.

"How long," I asked a Virginia conductor, "has this Jim Crow car system been in operation?"

"Since 1st July," he answered.

"Does it work all right?"

"Oh, yes."

"Do the colored people object to it?"

"No, they don't mind it. Some of them kicked a little at first—a nigger likes to show off, you know, put on a little airs; but I told 'em it was the law, and they would have to submit, as I had to. Personally I don't mean to take any chances: I've been hauled up in court once, or threatened with it, for not enforcing the law. I'd put a white man out of the colored car as quick as I'd put a nigger out of this one."

"Do you ever," I asked, "have any difficulty about classifying people who are very near the line?"

"Oh, yes, often."

"What do you do in a case of that kind?"

"I give the passenger the benefit of the doubt."

"That is, you treat him as a white man?"

"Certainly."

"But suppose you should find in the colored car a man who had a white face, but insisted that his descent entitled him to ride in that car: what would you do then?"

"I'd let him stay there," replied the conductor, with unconcealed disgust, which seemed almost to include the questioner who could suppose such a case. "Anyone that is fool enough to rather be a nigger than a white man may have his choice. He could stay there till h_ll froze over for all I'd care."

This reminds me of an incident which happened recently, down in North Carolina, where the conductor had no doubt, but afterward wished he had. On passing through the white car he saw a dark woman sitting there, whom he promptly spotted as colored, and upon whom he pounced with the zeal of a newly promoted man.

"You will have," he said abruptly, "to go into the other car."

"Why so?"

"This car is for white people only."

"I am white."

The conductor smiled incredulously. He knew a Negro when he saw one. "Come on," he said: "my time is valuable. I'll have the porter bring your valise."

The woman submitted. At her destination her son, a palpably and aggressively white man, was at the station to meet her. Upon seeing his mother alight from the Negro car, assisted by a colored porter—conductors in the South, on railroad or street cars, seldom or never assist colored women—the son demanded an explanation, which, when forthcoming, elicited from him a flood of language not suitable for newspaper publication. The next day suit was brought against the railroad company for $25,000 damages. It is to be hoped that judgment may be recovered. The more expensive this odious class legislation, so inconsistent with free institutions, can be made, the sooner it will be ended.

The same system prevails everywhere. There are separate waiting-rooms at the railway stations. If there is any choice of location the Negro always gets the worst room, and it is seldom so well lighted or clean. The signs usually read: "Waiting Room for White People," "Waiting Room for Colored People." In a certain town in North Carolina they read: "Ladies' Waiting Room," "General Waiting Room." No people of color are admitted to the ladies' waiting room. A colored lady, if she enter the station at all, must wait in the general waiting room, where white men and colored men smoke freely. In Atlanta the signs read: "Colored Waiting Room." "Waiting Room for Ladies and Gentlemen." It must be borne in mind that in the South the terms "gentleman" and "lady" are reserved, so far as public use of them is concerned, exclusively for white people. As a rule, only a white woman who is entirely beneath consideration is ever referred to as a "woman." The amount of ingenuity which a Southern newspaper will exercise to speak well of a colored man—they often speak well of individuals—without calling him "Mr." is very curious to study. He is cheerfully dubbed "Bishop," or "Dr.," or "Rev.," or "Professor," but the little prefix "Mr." is reserved exclusively for gentlemen—i.e., white men. It is the stamp of Vere de Vere.[5]

The separate system extends by law to schools, and by social custom to everything else. Two races who must live side by side are taught from infancy that they are essentially different and must not meet in any relation but that of master and servant, or superior and inferior. If the facts conformed always to the theory, the situation might be tolerable. But they are not even distinct races; the colored people certainly are not a distinct race. Many of the latter are persons of education and refinement, who have travelled at the north and in Europe, and who resent bitterly this attempt to degrade them permanently, by law, into a hopelessly inferior caste. That they are often silent proves nothing: they must live, or think they must, and the Negro who talks too much holds his life by uncertain tenure in the Southern States. Then, too, their self-respect prevents them from saying a great deal to outsiders. A man of color who is treated in the North as a citizen, in Europe as a gentleman, does not like to tell strangers that at home he is a pariah and an outcast.

Of the expense to society this system entails, I will not speak: it is easily imaginable. Of the loss to the colored people, who are thus thrown back upon themselves and Northern philanthropists for that leadership which would naturally, under healthful conditions, come in large part from the white people of the community, there is no room to speak. Of the jealousy, the distrust, the deep-seated hatred which such conditions inevitably tend to promote, the less said, perhaps, the better.

There are other things in the South, of which we read in the newspapers, which do not tend to promote good citizenship. There are many good men in that section who will tell you, with a glance over the shoulder to see that no one else is within hearing, that they quite agree with you that the lynchings and burnings and discriminating franchise laws are all wrong, and that the best people do not approve of them. But the best people are evidently not in control, and make no public expression of their disapproval. Let us hope that they may some time pluck up courage to do the right, and assume the leadership to which by character and culture they are entitled. It will be better for the South and for the Negro, who is a large part and perhaps the most distinctive part of the South, when the white man of the South has obtained his freedom.

I cannot close this article without some reflections suggested by a book recently published, *The American Negro*, by William Hannibal Thomas of Everett, Mass.[6] Mr. Thomas has lived in Ohio, in Georgia, in South Carolina, and elsewhere. I have recently been in all these States, and find a universal disposition everywhere to let Massachusetts claim him: she is, perhaps, better able to bear the burden than any other State. This book, being in large degree unquotable, and, consisting as it does, of five or six hundred pages of defamation of a race with which he admits close kinship, it is difficult to pick out particular passages. Suffice it to say that it denies the Negro intellect, character, and capacity for advancement. With my own eyes I have seen, upon revisiting places which I knew eighteen or twenty years ago, that the colored people are acquiring property, in large amounts. Most of it, so far, is in the shape of farms, homes and churches; too much of it, perhaps, is tied up in churches, where a smaller number of these would suffice, for, thrown back largely upon the churches for social life, there are too many splits and dissensions. By the same token, some of the preachers might be better employed. But that many of them are earnest, God-fearing men, working zealously for the uplifting of their people, and serving them with profit to their moral and religious life, I can give personal testimony. I can say frankly that I was agreeably surprised to find the progress that was apparent on every hand—in culture, in character, in the accumulation of property, and in the power of organization. The recent reaction against the Negro is traceable to this very fact. At each forward step the Negro comes in contact or competition with the white man at some new point. The result is a new friction, with a consequent ebullition of race prejudice.

Mr. Thomas's statements concerning the womanhood and the youth of his race, confute themselves by overstatement. I can truthfully say that during a month spent in the South, mainly among colored people, I found no evidence to support his views. The value of his book lies entirely in the character of the writer, his truthfulness, his judgment, and his means of observation; for it is backed up by no statistics.

⌐

SOURCE: *"The White and the Black," Boston Evening Transcript*, 20 March 1901, 13. The remainder of the headlines read:

By Charles W. Chesnutt.
Author of "The Wife of His Youth"

[1]Chesnutt visited Tuskegee Institute and Atlanta University in mid-February 1901. See "A Visit to Tuskegee," nn. 1 and 6.

[2]Du Bois taught economics and history at Atlanta University from 1897 to 1910.

[3]Reference to the 10 November 1898 race riot there and the consequent establishment of a local white supremacist régime.

[4]Plessy v. Ferguson, 163 U.S. 537 (1896) interpreted the Fourteenth Amendment to establish the "separate but equal" concept legitimizing such discriminatory acts.

[5]Alfred Lord Tennyson (1809–92), "Lady Clara Vere de Vere" (1842), a poem that focuses on caste distinctions of the kind Chesnutt has just described.

[6]See Chesnutt's review of this work, "A Defamer of His Race."

A Visit to Tuskegee

Essay published in the *Cleveland Leader*, 31 March 1901

My approach to Tuskegee was not propitious. I had taken a train at Wilmington, N.C., which, according to a handsome folder, with a beautiful map, decorated with broad red lines, and an alluring time table, was to make connection at Atlanta with a train for Montgomery, Ala., by which Tuskegee was to be reached.[1] For some reason or other the train for Montgomery left Atlanta fifteen minutes before our train arrived, resulting in a wait of half a day for a local train by which I reached my destination at 9 o'clock at night instead of at 9 in the morning. This, however, was not the end of my troubles.

Arrived at Chehaw, the little station from which a five-mile railroad runs twice a day to the town of Tuskegee, the train from the south, due at about the same time, was found to be two or three hours late, and the Tuskegee train would not go until it came in. The prospect of waiting in this lonesome place for several hours, on a raw, damp evening, with no place in sight where food or drink might be procured, was not agreeable. Several gentlemen bound, like myself, for Tuskegee, proposed that we walk. I suggested that we offer substantial inducements to the train conductor to take us over and return for the delayed train. We figured that it was worth about fifty cents to run the diminutive engine and one rickety car five miles and back, but the engineer, who seemed the man in charge, proved obdurate, and even an offer of $2.50 did not move him. We, therefore, decided to walk the five miles, which we did, after procuring a lantern to light our way along the railroad track.[2] We beguiled ourselves during the journey with speculations[3] as to the value of the railroad. It is five miles long, is capitalized at $40,000, and pays 25 to 50 per cent in dividends, which is not surprising when one considers that the fare for the five miles is fifty cents. It is curious that this profitable property has thus far escaped exploitation at the hands of the professional promoter.

It is but fair to say, however, that my experience was an unusual one, and that passengers direct from the North, traveling by through trains, can make the passage comfortably and directly, and will be well rewarded for their pains.

Tuskegee was a revelation, as it must be to anyone upon the first visit. I was hospitably entertained at Mr. Washington's own handsome house, and in the morning was taken in charge by Mr. Palmer,[4] one of the attachés, who piloted me about the place. In the afternoon I was under the guidance of Mr. Max Bennett Thrasher, who has adopted Tuskegee as his special literary property. He has written a book about Tuskegee, and was able to show it to me from the standpoint of an experienced observer, who had made the school and its work a special study.[5]

There were a number of Northern visitors present on this day, which was the day before the conference,[6] and the unanimous verdict among them was that Tuskegee, to be appreciated, must be seen. One who comes and sees, is conquered.[7] It is not a school in the ordinary sense of the word, but a great industrial university; for, while mental training is not neglected, and care is obviously taken to obtain for the teaching force the best product of the Northern schools, the industrial feature is kept well to the front, and most emphasis laid upon it. It was apparent, too, in the various workshops that something more than a mere superficial smattering of manual training was imparted, and that a student who wished to acquire any art or trade taught could, if he remained long enough, learn it with sufficient thoroughness to qualify himself as an expert workman. There are many, of course, who come and go, but the boy who has learned only to saw a plank, to drive a nail, to make a joint, has increased his social efficiency to just that extent, and the girl who has learned how to do plain sewing and make good bread has vastly increased her value as a wife and a mother. The practical air of the place is an inspiration in itself. The student workers build the houses in which they live, and make the bricks with which to build them. The boys make the shoes and clothes they wear. The girls make the dresses and trim the hats which deck them out so neatly. The furniture for the whole community is made on the grounds, and the surplus handiwork finds a ready sale in the country and towns roundabout. I was shown, in addition to handsome cases of samples made for exhibition purposes, a large filing case in process of construction which had been ordered for the county court house near by.

The work is done, too, on a scale which impresses the imagination. Dairying and butter making are taught with the aid of sixty or seventy fine Jersey cows, requiring model stables and expert attention to keep them in order. There are large farms, truck patches, bee hives, poultry houses, sawmills, and planing mills, a foundry, a machine shop, a dress-making establishment, model kitchens, a millinery department, a laundry, and other things too numerous to mention. Everything seems to be moving smoothly to its appointed end. In fact, so vivid is the impression made by a visit to the various departments that one is swept off his feet, as it were, and feels for the moment that industrial education is the only education worthy of consideration for colored people, or people of any other sort. And while sober reflection reveals what is needed beyond, one is entirely convinced that Mr. Washington has discovered the tremendous importance, to a struggling people, of a branch of education which has been sadly neglected, and which[8] will prove a powerful lever for their uplifting.

One of the most interesting features of Tuskegee is that it is entirely officered and administered, locally, by colored men and women. The names of several white men appear on the board of trustees, however, and the school is, of course, run mainly by the money of good white people. Mr. Washington has accomplished a remarkable feat in finding, and inducing to live in Alabama, so large a number of capable colored men and women. That they do not go there for the loaves and fishes[9] entirely is evident; for they are not extravagantly paid, and are certainly hard worked. But Mr. Washington has succeeded in inspiring them with his own hopefulness, which sees a bright future for his people, his own philosophy, which makes the best of a hard situation, and his own enthusiasm, which never seems to falter. Tuskegee is a colored institution, through and through. It has a sort of swing to it which is in a way characteristic of the race.

The present writer does not believe in the wisdom of the separation of the races which prevails in the Southern States, and thinks that it is carried to an extreme which is not only short-sighted, expensive, and troublesome, but which, to an outsider, borders upon the ridiculous.

But Mr. Washington, accepting the situation as inevitable, for the time being at least, has adopted the theory of letting the race develop along characteristic lines. They are permitted to sing extempore "spiritual" songs; marching, counter-marching, and military drill, in which the students take a very evident pleasure, are made a feature of the work. The co-operation and presence of leading colored men is eagerly sought, and a spirit of race pride and self-respect is sedulously cultivated. All this results in a sense of freedom, an independence of bearing, a courtesy and consideration toward one another, a respect for the authority of superiors of their own race, which is extremely gratifying to the thoughtful visitor.

It was my privilege to attend during my brief stay at Tuskegee a session of the Tuskegee Conference, which is held annually for the benefit of the colored farmers in the black belt. The exercises began at 10 o'clock and lasted until 3, but throughout were of very great interest. Mr. Washington made a characteristic address, full of hope and encouragement, and impressing upon his audience the value of patience, industry, thrift, character, and property. Most of the time was taken up by speeches of the farmers, who gave their experience for the benefit of the rest.

For instance, Tillman Vines, of Tallapoosa, Ala., old and black and rugged, made a rattling good speech, characteristic of the old-time Negro. He gave his name, his postoffice address, stated that he was born a slave and was the father of fourteen children, twelve of whom were living. His youngest child, four years old, was able, he proudly averred, to count a hundred. "When I was a young man," he said, "I couldn't count a hundred and my wife couldn't count at all." He now owns over five hundred acres of land and owes no man anything. The colored people in his neighborhood own 5,000 acres. He acknowledged, in a naive way, one bit of sharp practice in the course of his life, which very palpably suggested the rabbit and the fox of the plantation stories. When he began to appreciate the need of education he went to his own people and told them he wanted their aid to build a school house, which, in their new zeal for learning, they eagerly promised. Then he went to "old Mars Ben," to whom he "use ter b'long," and told him he wanted the land to build a "church house." "Mars Ben," who saw no objection to the Negroes having religion, gave the land. "I call 'im Mars Ben," explained the orator, "beca'se I wuz bawn his'n; he raise'

me." This double-dealing was made good by using the new structure for both
purposes. "We helt church in de new building Sunday, an' opened school a-
Monday."

Green Weldon, a very dark man from Butler country, said that he was so
impressed by what he saw of the improvement of his people that he was "mos'
skeered"—he hardly knew what to say. He had started out in life with the idea
of having something. Having got a little land and a little money he had felt too
rich, and had spent most of his time riding on the railroad. By neglecting his
business he lost everything. He took a fresh start and now owns 350 acres of
land, all paid for. He sells meat and corn and lard to the best white and black
people in the settlement, has a good house with five rooms, and has built a
three-room house for his son. "A man with a bad heart," he said, with wisdom
worthy of Solomon, "don't live—he just stays here; and if you have a good heart
the Lord will let you prosper." His houses, he stated, had been built by a carpenter of his own color. When asked the length of the school term in his district, he
replied that it was four months. "We needs he'p down dere on de school question. I come mighty nigh totin' eve'y school dat comes dere, an' I come mighty
nigh totin' de church, too. I built two school houses down dere. My boy is got
pretty good learnin', an' my gal is got ter come right here, she sho' is!"

Joseph Strickland, a fine looking, well-dressed, and very black man, said to
be the most successful colored farmer in Bullock county, advised the Negro
farmers to work six days in the week; the most money, he said, was taken away
from them on Saturdays, when they were wasting their time in town. Mr.
Strickland confesses to thirty-two mules and five horses, a steam grist mill, corn
mill, and cotton gin. He owns 660 acres of land, and leases 2,000 acres besides.
He believes that no man can make a successful farmer without a good wife, and
admits that before he got where he is now, his wife plowed a two-mule team. He
has 300 men in his employment, and can take the place of any one of them at a
minute's notice. He has 5,000 pounds of well-cured meat in his smoke houses,
uses 225 bushels of corn every month to feed his stock, and raises the corn. Mr.
Strickland is not without a vein of sentiment in his very excellent make-up. He
still has the old mule he started with, and would not take $250 for her. He raises
260 bales of cotton a year. His neighborhood has a five-months' school, and a
good teacher.

Another speaker thought that the future of the Negro lay in his being able to
make money, so that the North and the South would want to trade with him. "I
want every man," he said, "that ain't did nothin', to come here an' hear about
the fellow that done somethin'." He modestly admitted that he owned not only
land, but money (I was informed that he was a stockholder in a bank) and was
glad to say that other men in his community were waking up. "If you go forward," he said, "somebody else in that community is gwine ter spread his wings
an' fly up along of you."

Another speaker observed:

Dis yer is one er de bes' countries in de worl'. You kin go mighty nigh naked; up in the No'the'n States they've got to wear de bes' goods de worl' ever made—we kin wear one garment fer eight mont's in de year, an' live. If you ever git de slothful people out er dis country, an' git de No'the'n people ter ownin' it, you're gwine ter have hard wo'k ter keep up wid 'em. We better git dis lan' while we kin git it cheap, an' befo' de No'the'n man begins ter crowd us.

Mr. Daniels, of Elmore county, was of a somewhat pessimistic disposition. He owned 193 acres of land, and thought there was about a thousand acres in his country owned by colored people and paid for, "if I make no mistake," he added cautiously. There was a time, he said, when land could have been bought for $1.25 an acre, which cannot now be had for less than fifteen dollars. He maintained, however, that some of the colored people wouldn't have land if it were given to them. A sharp cross-examination at the hands of Mr. Washington showed, however, by comparison with conditions ten years ago, that substantial progress had been made. When asked about the churches and the preachers, the speaker replied:

I'm a little off on the preachers for the last ten years. They ought to teach the people that they need homes here. Our preachers save it all for over yonder in the other world. We want to get something in this world. I think people have got as much right to a home here as to a home in heaven. They are getting around to that now, however, and I can hear 'em striking at it away off.

When asked the curious and suggestive question as to whether the morals of the ministers were improving, he replied that he thought they were.

There were many other speakers along the same line. Henry Thomas, of Tallapoosa county, told how he had acquired a thousand acres of land. After the war he went to work for his old master—his "ole boss," he called him, who wanted to see the people he used to own have something, and who encouraged him to save and invest his money. First he bought forty acres of land. Having a keen commercial instinct, he bought and sold and saved, and got more land. His idea was, however, that a small farm, well cultivated, with money in the bank, was better than too much land.

Joe Harris said: "I own 320 acres of land and a cottin gin, which white people patronize. If any one hears that Joe Harris says something, they believe it. I can order yards of bagging, and I will get it, with the money or without. The white people in my county have been friends to me, and have led me up to where I am."

Mr. McKinnie, from Coosa county, knew only one man owning land that ever went to the penitentiary from his county, and public opinion was with him, only a false report had been made to his disadvantage. Colored people in Coosa owned 10,000 acres of land; for one stretch of six miles there was not a single white family.

One of the best speeches of the day, which was entirely unexpected by the management, was made by "the boss colored farmer of Talladega county," as he described himself—his name has escaped my memory and I do not find it in my notes.

His address was illustrated by neatly prepared samples of farm products he produced from a satchel which he took with him upon the stage, and which made Mr. Washington a little fearful, at first, lest the speaker might have something to sell which he was seizing a convenient opportunity to advertise. Most of the speakers had been apparently full-blooded Negroes, but this one was a yellow man, with straight hair.

All these speeches were interesting and inspiring. They proved that former slaves, without any education in letters, could work, could save, could prosper under conditions which were not favorable to the highest or quickest development. If they could succeed, better taught men, other things being equal, should easily excel them. The speeches were pervaded by a shrewd business sense, a keen appreciation of the humorous side of things, and many of them not without a certain degree of child-like vanity. They had done well, these men, and knew it, and wished to have proper credit for it. But the finest thing about it all was the spirit of charity which filled these knotted and gnarled old men, whose lives had been spent with the sun and the soil. They stood up for their own race, but were full of good will for all men. What Tuskegee has done for them can be seen in part, but the rest may be imagined. It has furnished them a center of thought, of interest, of communication, of light: a place where they can come once a year, meet in friendly intercourse, and exchange views and experiences, a place to which they will naturally think of sending their children for instruction. The speakers, of course, were picked men; if every Negro farmer in Alabama were as prosperous as some of them, there would be small need of Tuskegee. But the most, even of those who come, are still poor men, who come, often at a sacrifice, to seek knowledge and inspiration. The influence of these meetings does not stop with those in immediate attendance. Each visitor, upon his return home, spreads the leaven among his neighbors who were too poor to go—and the mass of the farm laborers are still desperately poor, and need all the help which enlightened philanthropy can give them. The conference idea, too, has spread beyond Tuskegee, and similar meetings are being held at other points in the South, with like encouraging results.

Following the speeches came an interesting exhibition of stereopticon views, showing the contrasts between the homes of the colored people ten years ago and now. A strong "set of declarations" was then adopted, emphasizing the objects of the conference, *viz.*: To encourage the buying of land, getting rid of the one-room cabin and the abuse of the mortgage system, the raising of food supplies, building better school houses, the lengthening of the school term, and the securing of better teachers and preachers, the doing away with sectarian prejudice, the improvement of the moral condition of the masses, and the encouragement of friendly relations between the races—in all of which, the declarations state, progress is constantly being made by the masses throughout the South.

To one who is interested in the Southern situation, a visit to Tuskegee is well worth what it costs to go there.

↬

SOURCE: "A Visit to Tuskegee," *Cleveland Leader*, 31 March 1901, 19, emended in light of two typed texts at the Fisk University Library, one of which may have been produced after the publication of the essay (as was the case with the three in the "Future American" series).

[1]Chesnutt left Cleveland for a Southern lecture tour on 6 February 1901. On 14 February he read from his stories in Wilmington, N.C.; he did the same on 19 February at Tuskegee, 21 February in Birmingham, 22 February in Atlanta, and 25 February in Charlotte, N.C.

[2]Emended here and in eight other instances is a peculiar line-arrangement in the source text that is not seen elsewhere in Chesnutt's manuscripts or publications. A compositor used to creating intratextual section heads for articles in newspaper-columns appears to have been responsible for a line-break that read thus: ". . . our way along / THE RAILROAD TRACK. / We beguiled the journey . . . ." The effects produced thus are solely visual, that is, ornamental; and Chesnutt's conventional method of developing paragraphs is restored.

[3]Emended is the reading, "We beguiled the journey by speculations . . . ."

[4]John H. Palmer joined the faculty in 1894 as assistant superintendent of industries and served as business agent (1898–99) before becoming the registrar.

[5]Max Bennett Thrasher (1860–1903), an administrator at Tuskegee, was the author of *Tuskegee: Its Story and Its Work* (1900).

[6]The tenth annual Tuskegee Negro Conference, 20–21 February 1901, focused on the accomplishments of African-Americans and means of further improving their condition. Nationally known black leaders in attendance included W. E. B. Du Bois; Bishop Henry McNeal Turner; Bishop Evans Tree (1853–1920); Isaiah Benjamin Scott (1854–1931), an educator who served in 1893–96 as the president of Wiley College in Marshall, Tex., was the editor of the *Southwestern Christian Advocate*, and was at one time the only African-American bishop of the Methodist Episcopal Church; and Benjamin Tucker Tanner (1835–1923), former editor of the *Christian Recorder* and a bishop of the A.M.E. church. Chesnutt read his story "Hot-Foot Hannibal" in the chapel the evening before the conference commenced. For another account of the conference, see Max Bennett Thrasher, "The Tuskegee Negro Conference," *Outlook*, 67 (2 March 1901), 484–87.

[7]Adaptation of "I came, I saw, I conquered," attributed to Julius Caesar.

[8]The words, "has been sadly neglected, and which," do not appear in the typed texts.

[9]That is, a free meal; see John 6:5–14.

A Defamer of His Race

Essay published in *The Critic*, April 1901

The first thought that strikes the reader of this atrocious book is, how did a reputable publishing house ever permit itself to become parties to its publication?[1]. The answer probably is that the readers of the publishing house knew nothing about the colored race beyond what they read in the newspapers, and therefore took it for granted that a colored man, who claimed to be a lawyer and ex-member of a legislature, would know all about his own people.[2] It seems never to have occurred to them that a man might be all that, and yet be unworthy of credit, nor do they seem to have inquired into the antecedents of the author of a book the value of which must rest almost solely upon the writer's character, for the book is almost wholly an expression of opinion, with no statistics to support it, but based entirely upon the claimed knowledge and experience of the writer. That a reputable publishing house should have issued such a book against any other considerable class of people without such preliminary investigation is incredible.

The present reviewer during a recent extended tour of the Southern States, under circumstances which threw him mainly among the better class of the colored people, has taken pains to ascertain as far as possible the past record of Mr. Thomas, and is obliged to say that he has not heard anywhere one good word concerning him. The writer has conversed with colored bishops, college professors, and others, men of substance and character, who have known this man during his variegated career, and they are all unanimous in the statement that the book faithfully represents the man.[3] The only parallel example to this book was one written some years ago by a renegade Jew, in which all the worst slanders against this oppressed people were gathered from the obscure and musty folios of ancient libraries, and dished up in a paper-covered volume for the delectation of the nineteenth century. It must have been a satisfaction to the chosen people to note that within a year the author of the book was sent to the penitentiary for forgery, and that a year or two later the publishing house failed disastrously. This may have been a logical *non sequitur*, but it was poetic justice. Mr. Thomas may continue to escape this fate, but if it be any satisfaction to him to know that he has not a single friend or well-wisher among the whole eight or ten millions of his own people, he may rest content that such is emphatically the case.

So much for the man, if it be possible to separate the man from the book. The present reviewer once wrote a story in which a Negro was transformed into a tree, and the tree sawed up into lumber, and built into a house, which was ever afterwards haunted by the spirit of the unfortunate victim of an untoward fate.[4]

The parallel between Thomas and this tree-man is obvious. He has transformed himself into white paper and black ink—he is a mulatto by blood—and has bound himself into a book. Nevertheless, it may be possible, by an effort, to consider the book as a separate thing.

In the first place, it is not a well-written book. That it has a certain amount of ability is beyond question; but it lacks consecutiveness. It would seem to have been compiled from a scrap-book, into which the author had pasted for twenty years or more every newspaper clipping that he had seen anywhere to the discredit of the colored race. A peculiarity of the book which bears out this view is his employment of the word "freedman," a term which is not now in common use as descriptive of the colored people, as it was twenty years ago. A full average generation has elapsed since the abolition of slavery, and fully three fourths of the colored people of the present day are free born, as a comparison of their numbers now and at the close of the Civil War will demonstrate. Mr. Thomas has great fluency of language—a fondness for big words is supposed to be a trait of his race. A good command of a large vocabulary is a valuable accomplishment, and, if it be a race trait, one which may be judiciously cultivated to the enrichment of literature; but it is painfully apparent here and there that Mr. Thomas's thought has been swept away by the current of his own eloquence. One must sometimes fish long in this turbid pool to catch a minnow.

The Negro has suffered a great deal, in the public estimation, from loose and hasty generalizations with reference to his intelligence, his morals, his physical characteristics, and his social efficiency. But not the worst things said about him by his most radical defamers, all put together, could surpass in untruthfulness and malignity the screed which this alleged reformer has put forth under his publisher's imprint. The slanders against the womanhood of his race are so vile as to confute themselves by their mere statement. There are several passages in the book, reflecting on the morals of colored youth, which ought to bar the volume from circulation in the United States mails. They are false on the face of them. No individual could possibly know that they were true, and they are utterly abhorrent to human nature and human experience. To believe them, one must read the Negro out of the human family. If they are the fruit of this author's observation, one shudders to contemplate the depths of vice which he has fathomed.[5]

His characterization of colored preachers is also unjust. That there are many such preachers who might be otherwise employed with more profit to society may well be admitted; but that there are among them many good men, faithful to their trust, earnestly striving to uplift their people, and with encouraging results, is apparent to any one who will take the trouble to inquire.[6] The greatest preacher of America did not escape calumny, if he avoided sin.[7] Human character is a compound of good and evil. For aught we know, Judas Iscariot was a very good apostle before he betrayed his Master; we know that Benedict Arnold was a gallant soldier who had served his country well before he betrayed her.[8] But here the parallel between these men and this author fails, for what good thing Thomas had ever done for his people before he dealt them this traitorous blow is not of record among the traditions of his people, nor in the archives of the South Carolina Legislature of which he claims to have been a valuable member. That membership in that body should be set forward by a writer and accepted by a publisher as a certificate of moral character, is the most curious feature of this whole remarkable performance.

Among the glimmerings of reason which here and there may be found in this book, is the statement that the colored people are deprived of social stimulus because the white people will not associate or intermarry with them. Granted. But with what face could any one ask a race with any self-respect, any pride of its past, any hope for its future, to consort with such moral and mental degenerates as Thomas has sought in this book to make of his own people?

The strongest argument against the Negro suggested by this book is the existence of the book itself. As one of a race which has but just begun to win a hearing in the forum of letters, the author might have found a different theme. If the book were truthful, it would be without excuse as coming from such a source. But being false, as the book essentially is, it is all the more worthy of condemnation. That a man of color should write such a book is almost enough to make out his case against the Negro.

<hr>

SOURCE: "A Defamer of His Race," *The Critic*, 38 (April 1901), 350–51. An editorial headnote introduced this essay: "[Mr. Charles W. Chesnutt, the writer of this review, speaks freely and forcibly of the man who has defamed his race. Mr. Chesnutt, who is himself allied by blood to the Negro race, is also a writer of wide reputation. He knows his subject thoroughly and speaks not only with feeling, but with the facts at his finger-ends.—EDS. CRITIC.]"

[1]The full title of the 1901 volume reviewed is *The American Negro: What He Was, What He Is, and What He May Become, A Critical and Practical Discussion*. An asterisk originally followed "atrocious book," directing the reader to a footnote reading: "'The American Negro.' By William Hannibal Thomas. The Macmillan Company. $2.00."

[2]William Hannibal Thomas (1843–?).

[3]Chesnutt conducted a full-scale investigation of Thomas and circulated reports of his findings later in 1901 and in 1904, vividly describing and documenting the unsavory past of a scoundrel lucky to have avoided imprisonment. See *Letters*, ed. McElrath and Leitz, 198–209.

[4]"Po' Sandy," *The Conjure Woman* (Boston: Houghton, Mifflin, 1899), 36–63; originally published in *Atlantic Monthly*, 51 (May 1888), 605–11.

[5]Thomas declared that it is "impossible" to find males or females above the age of 15 who have not had "actual carnal knowledge"; that marriage is no barrier to sexual indulgence for males or females; that 90 percent of African-American women are "lascivious by instinct and in bondage to physical pleasure"; and that the youths of the race masturbate frequently.

[6]Thomas alleged that "preachers and laity" vie with each other in the use of rum and other intoxicants.

[7]The Reverend Henry Ward Beecher (1813–87) defended himself against a widely publicized adultery charge in 1847. He was acquitted, but his good name was never fully restored.

[8]Arnold (1741–1801), after serving with distinction, abandoned the American cause and served the British during the Revolutionary War against England.

Superstitions and Folk-Lore of the South

Essay published in *Modern Culture*, May 1901

During a recent visit to North Carolina, after a long absence, I took occasion to inquire into the latter-day prevalence of the old-time belief in what was known as "conjuration" or "goopher," my childish recollection of which I have elsewhere embodied into a number of stories.[1] The derivation of the word "goopher" I do not know, nor whether any other writer than myself has recognized its existence, though it is in frequent use in certain parts of the South. The origin of this curious superstition itself is perhaps more easily traceable. It probably grew, in the first place, out of African fetichism which was brought over from the dark continent along with the dark people. Certain features, too, suggest a distant affinity with Voodooism, or snake worship, a cult which seems to have been indigenous to tropical America. These beliefs, which in the place of their origin had all the sanctions of religion and social custom, became, in the shadow of the white man's civilization, a pale reflection of their former selves. In time, too, they were mingled and confused with the witchcraft and ghost lore of the white man, and the tricks and delusions of the Indian conjurer. In the old plantation days they flourished vigorously, though discouraged by the "great house," and their potency was well established among the blacks and the poorer whites. Education, however, has thrown the ban of disrepute upon witchcraft and conjuration. The stern frown of the preacher, who looks upon superstition as the ally of the Evil One; the scornful sneer of the teacher, who sees in it a part of the livery of bondage, have driven this quaint combination of ancestral traditions to the remote chimney corners of old black aunties, from which it is difficult for the stranger to unearth them. Mr. Harris, in his Uncle Remus stories, has, with fine literary discrimination, collected and put into pleasing and enduring form, the plantation stories which dealt with animal lore,[2] but so little attention has been paid to those dealing with so-called conjuration, that they seem in a fair way to disappear, without leaving a trace behind. The loss may not be very great, but these vanishing traditions might furnish valuable data for the sociologist, in the future study of racial development. In writing, a few years ago, the volume entitled *The Conjure Woman*, I suspect that I was more influenced

by the literary value of the material than by its sociological bearing, and therefore took, or thought I did, considerable liberty with my subject. Imagination,
however, can only act upon data—one must have somewhere in his consciousness the ideas which he puts together to form a connected whole. Creative talent, of whatever grade, is, in the last analysis, only the power of rearrangement—there is nothing new under the sun.[3] I was the more firmly impressed
with this thought after I had interviewed half a dozen old women, and a genuine
"conjure doctor;" for I discovered that the brilliant touches, due, I had thought,
to my own imagination, were after all but dormant ideas, lodged in my childish
mind by old Aunt This and old Uncle That, and awaiting only the spur of imagination to bring them again to the surface. For instance, in the story, "Hot-foot
Hannibal,"[4] there figures a conjure doll with pepper feet. Those pepper feet I regarded as peculiarly my own, a purely original creation. I heard, only the other
day, in North Carolina, of the consternation struck to the heart of a certain dark
individual, upon finding upon his doorstep a rabbit's foot—a good omen in itself perhaps—to which a malign influence had been imparted by tying to one
end of it, in the form of a cross, two small pods of red pepper!

Most of the delusions connected with this belief in conjuration grow out of
mere lack of enlightenment. As primeval men saw a personality behind every
natural phenomenon, and found a god or a devil in wind, rain, and hail, in
lightning, and in storm, so the untaught man or woman who is assailed by an
unusual ache or pain, some strenuous symptom of serious physical disorder, is
prompt to accept the suggestion, which tradition approves, that some evil influence is behind his discomfort; and what more natural than to conclude that
some rival in business or in love has set this force in motion?

Relics of ancestral barbarism are found among all peoples, but advanced
civilization has at least shaken off the more obvious absurdities of superstition.
We no longer attribute insanity to demoniac possession, nor suppose that a
king's touch can cure scrofula.[5] To many old people in the South, however, any
unusual ache or pain is quite as likely to have been caused by some external evil
influence as by natural causes. Tumors, sudden swellings due to inflammatory
rheumatism or the bites of insects, are especially open to suspicion. Paralysis is
proof positive of conjuration. If there is any doubt, the "conjure doctor" invariably removes it. The credulity of ignorance is his chief stock in trade—there
is no question, when he is summoned, but that the patient has been tricked.

The means of conjuration are as simple as the indications. It is a condition of
all witch stories that there must in some way be contact, either with the person,
or with some object or image intended to represent the person to be affected; or,
if not actual contact, at least close proximity. The charm is placed under the
door-sill, or buried under the hearth, or hidden in the mattress of the person to
be conjured. It may be a crude attempt to imitate the body of the victim, or it
may consist merely of a bottle, or a gourd, or a little bag, containing a few rusty
nails, crooked pins, or horsehairs. It may be a mysterious mixture thrown sur-

reptitiously upon the person to be injured, or merely a line drawn across a road or path, which line it is fatal for a certain man or woman to cross. I heard of a case of a laboring man who went two miles out of his way, every morning and evening, while going to and from his work, to avoid such a line drawn for him by a certain powerful enemy.

Some of the more gruesome phases of the belief in conjuration suggest possible poisoning, a knowledge of which baleful art was once supposed to be widespread among the imported Negroes of the olden time. The blood or venom of snakes, spiders, and lizards is supposed to be employed for this purpose. The results of its administration are so peculiar, however, and so entirely improbable, that one is supposed to doubt even the initial use of poison, and figure it in as part of the same general delusion. For instance, a certain man "swelled up all over" and became "pieded," that is, pied or spotted. A white physician who was summoned thought that the man thus singularly afflicted was poisoned, but did not recognize the poison nor know the antidote. A conjure doctor, subsequently called in, was more prompt in his diagnosis. The man, he said, was poisoned with a lizard, which at that very moment was lodged somewhere in the patient's anatomy. The lizards and snakes in these stories, by the way, are not confined to the usual ducts and cavities of the human body, but seem to have freedom of movement throughout the whole structure. This lizard, according to the "doctor," would start from the man's shoulder, descend to his hand, return to the shoulder, and pass down the side of the body to the leg. When it reached the calf of the leg the lizard's head would appear right under the skin. After it had been perceptible for three days the lizard was to be cut out with a razor, or the man would die. Sure enough, the lizard manifested its presence in the appointed place at the appointed time; but the patient would not permit the surgery, and at the end of three days paid with death the penalty of his obstinacy. Old Aunt Harriet told me, with solemn earnestness, that she herself had taken a snake from her own arm, in sections, after a similar experience. Old Harriet may have been lying, but was, I imagine, merely self-deluded. Witches, prior to being burned, have often confessed their commerce with the Evil One. Why should Harriet hesitate to relate a simple personal experience which involved her in no blame whatever?

Old Uncle Jim, a shrewd, hard old sinner, and a palpable fraud, who did not, I imagine, believe in himself to any great extent, gave me some private points as to the manner in which these reptiles were thus transferred to the human system. If a snake or a lizard be killed, and a few drops of its blood be dried upon a plate or in a gourd, the person next eating or drinking from the contaminated vessel will soon become the unwilling landlord of a reptilian tenant. There are other avenues, too, by which the reptile may gain admittance; but when expelled by the conjure doctor's arts or medicines, it always leaves at the point where it entered. This belief may have originally derived its existence from the fact that certain tropical insects sometimes lay their eggs beneath the skins of animals, or even of men, from which it is difficult to expel them until the larvae are hatched. The chico or "jigger" of the West Indies and the Spanish Main is the most obvious example.

Old Aunt Harriet—last name uncertain, since she had borne those of her master, her mother, her putative father, and half a dozen husbands in succession, no one of which seemed to take undisputed precedence—related some very remarkable experiences. She at first manifested some reluctance to speak of conjuration, in the lore of which she was said to be well versed; but by listening patiently to her religious experiences—she was a dreamer of dreams[6] and a seer of visions—I was able now and then to draw a little upon her reserves of superstition, if indeed her religion itself was much more than superstition.

"W'en I wuz a gal 'bout eighteen or nineteen," she confided, "de w'ite folks use' ter sen' me ter town ter fetch vegetables. One day I met a' ole conjuh man name' Jerry Macdonal', an' he said some rough, ugly things ter me. I says, says I, 'You mus' be a fool.' He did n' say nothin', but jes' looked at me wid 'is evil eye. W'en I come 'long back, dat ole man wuz stan'in' in de road in front er his house, an' w'en he seed me he stoop' down an' tech' de groun', jes' lack he wuz pickin' up somethin', an' den went 'long back in 'is ya'd. De ve'y minute I step' on de spot he tech', I felt a sha'p pain shoot thoo my right foot, it tu'n't under me, an' I fell down in de road. I pick' myself up an' by de time I got home, my foot wuz swoll' up twice its nachul size. I cried an' cried an' went on, fer I knowed I'd be'n trick' by dat ole man. Dat night in my sleep a voice spoke ter me an' says: 'Go an' git a plug er terbacker. Steep it in a skillet er wa'm water. Strip it lengthways, an' bin' it ter de bottom er yo' foot'.' I never didn' use terbacker, an' I laid dere, an' says ter myse'f, 'My Lawd, wa't is dat, w'at is dat!' Soon ez my foot got kind er easy, dat voice up an' speaks ag'in: 'Go an' git a plug er terbacker. Steep it in a skillet er wa'm water, an' bin' it ter de bottom er yo' foot.' I scramble' ter my feet, got de money out er my pocket, woke up de two little boys sleepin' on de flo', an' tol' 'em ter go ter de sto' an' git me a plug er terbacker. Dey didn' want ter go, said de sto' wuz shet, an' de sto' keeper gone ter bed. But I chased 'em fo'th, an' dey found' de sto' keeper an' fetch' de terbacker—dey sho' did. I soaked it in de skillet, an' stripped it 'long by degrees, till I got ter de en', w'en I boun' it under my foot an' roun' my ankle. Den I kneel' down an' prayed, an' next mawnin de swellin' wuz all gone! Dat voice wus de Spirit er de Lawd talkin' ter me, it sho' wuz! De Lawd have mussy upon us, praise his Holy Name!"

Very obviously Harriet had sprained her ankle while looking at the old man instead of watching the path, and the hot fomentation had reduced the swelling. She is not the first person to hear spirit voices in his or her own vagrant imaginings.

On another occasion, Aunt Harriet's finger swelled up "as big as a corn cob." She at first supposed the swelling to be due to a felon. She went to old Uncle Julius Lutterloh, who told her that some one had tricked her. "My Lawd!"

she exclaimed, "how did they fix my finger?" He explained that it was done while in the act of shaking hands. "Doctor" Julius opened the finger with a sharp knife and showed Harriet two seeds at the bottom of the incision. He instructed her to put a poultice of red onions on the wound over night, and in the morning the seeds would come out. She was then to put the two seeds in a skillet, on the right hand side of the fire-place, in a pint of water, and let them simmer nine mornings, and on the ninth morning she was to let all the water simmer out, and when the last drop should have gone, the one that put the seeds in her hand was to go out of this world! Harriet, however, did not pursue the treatment to the bitter end. The seeds, once extracted, she put into a small phial, which she corked up tightly and put carefully away in her bureau drawer. One morning she went to look at them, and one of them was gone. Shortly afterwards the other disappeared. Aunt Harriet has a theory that she had been tricked by a woman of whom her husband of that time was unduly fond, and that the faithless husband had returned the seeds to their original owner. A part of the scheme of conjuration is that the conjure doctor can remove the spell and put it back upon the one who laid it. I was unable to learn, however, of any instance where this extreme penalty had been insisted upon.

It is seldom that any of these old Negroes will admit that he or she possesses the power to conjure, though those who can remove spells are very willing to make their accomplishment known, and to exercise it for a consideration. The only professional conjure doctor whom I met was old Uncle Jim Davis, with whom I arranged a personal interview. He came to see me one evening, but almost immediately upon his arrival a minister called. The powers of light prevailed over those of darkness, and Jim was dismissed until a later time, with a commission to prepare for me a conjure "hand" or good luck charm, of which, he informed some of the children about the house, who were much interested in the proceedings. I was very much in need. I subsequently secured the charm, for which, considering its potency, the small sum of silver it cost me was no extravagant outlay. It is a very small bag of roots and herbs, and, if used according to directions, is guaranteed to insure me good luck and "keep me from losing my job." The directions require it to be wet with spirits nine mornings in succession, to be carried on the person, in a pocket on the right hand side, care being taken that it does not come in contact with any tobacco. When I add that I procured, from an equally trustworthy source, a genuine graveyard rabbit's foot, I would seem to be reasonably well protected against casual misfortune. I shall not, however, presume upon this immunity, and shall omit no reasonable precaution which the condition of my health or my affairs may render prudent.

An interesting conjure story, which I heard, involves the fate of a lost voice. A certain woman's lover was enticed away by another woman, who sang very sweetly, and who, the jilted one suspected, had told lies about her. Having decided upon the method of punishment for this wickedness, the injured woman watched the other closely, in order to find a suitable opportunity for carrying out her purpose; but in vain, for the fortunate one, knowing of her enmity, would never speak to her or remain near her. One day the jilted woman plucked a red rose from her garden, and hid herself in the bushes near her rival's cabin. Very soon an old woman came by, who was accosted by the woman in hiding, and requested to hand the red rose to the woman of the house. The old woman, suspecting no evil, took the rose and approached the house, the other woman following her closely, but keeping herself always out of sight. When the old woman, having reached the door and called out the mistress of the house, delivered the rose as requested, the recipient thanked the giver in a loud voice, knowing the old woman to be somewhat deaf. At the moment she spoke, the woman in hiding reached up and caught her rival's voice, and clasping it tightly in her right hand, escaped unseen, to her own cabin. At the same instant the afflicted woman missed her voice, and felt a sharp pain shoot through her left arm, just below the elbow. She at first suspected the old woman of having tricked her through the medium of the red rose, but was subsequently informed by a conjure doctor that her voice had been stolen, and that the old woman was innocent. For the pain he gave her a bottle of medicine, of which nine drops were to be applied three times a day, and rubbed in with the first two fingers of the right hand, care being taken not to let any other part of the hand touch the arm, as this would render the medicine useless. By the aid of a mirror, in which he called up her image, the conjure doctor ascertained who was the guilty person. He sought her out and charged her with the crime which she promptly denied. Being pressed, however, she admitted her guilt. The doctor insisted upon immediate restitution. She expressed her willingness, and at the same time her inability to comply—she had taken the voice, but did not possess the power to restore it. The conjure doctor was obdurate and at once placed a spell upon her which is to remain until the lost voice is restored. The case is still pending, I understand; I shall sometime take steps to find out how it terminates.

How far a story like this is original, and how far a mere reflection of familiar wonder stories, is purely a matter of speculation. When the old mammies would tell the tales of Br'er Rabbit and Br'er Fox to the master's children, these in turn would no doubt repeat the fairy tales which they had read in books or heard from their parents' lips. The magic mirror is as old as literature. The inability to restore the stolen voice is foreshadowed in the *Arabian Nights*, when the "Open Sesame" is forgotten.[7] The act of catching the voice has a simplicity which stamps it as original, the only analogy of which I can at present think being the story of later date, of the words which were frozen silent during the extreme cold of an Arctic winter, and became audible again the following summer when they had thawed out.

$\backsim$

SOURCE: "Superstitions and Folk-Lore of the South," *Modern Culture*, 13 (May 1901), 231–35.

[1]In addition to those that appeared in *The Conjure Woman*, five other stories of the

kind had seen periodical publication by 1901: "Dave's Neckliss," *Atlantic Monthly*, 64 (October 1889), 500–508; "A Deep Sleeper," *Two Tales*, 11 March 1893, 1–8; "Lonesome Ben," *Southern Workman*, 29 (March 1900), 137–45; "A Victim of Heredity; or Why the Darkey Loves Chicken," *Self-Culture Magazine*, 11 (July 1900), 404–9; and "Tobe's Tribulations," *Southern Workman*, 29 (November 1900), 656–64.

[2]*Uncle Remus: His Songs and Sayings* (1881) included a portion of the total output of such tales by Joel Chandler Harris (1848–1908).

[3]Ecclesiastes 1:9.

[4]Included in *The Conjure Woman*.

[5]The King of England was alleged to have the power of curing scrofula—a tissue condition predisposing one to tuberculosis, lymphatism, glandular swelling, and respiratory distress—by his touch. Samuel Johnson suffered from this disability; see "Who and Why Was Samuel Johnson?"

[6]Deuteronomy 13:1.

[7]See Richard Burton (1821–90), ed. and trans., "The History of Ali Baba," *Arabian Nights* (1885–88).

The Negro's Franchise

Essay published in the *Boston Evening Transcript*, 11 May 1901

I have been asked by the *Transcript* to express any thoughts which may occur to me upon the very interesting and thoughtful address of Dr. Donald of Trinity Church, delivered at the dedication of Dorothy Hall, Tuskegee Institute, and published in a recent number of the *Transcript*, and in which the speaker expresses certain views with regard to the future of the Negro and the value of the franchise in connection therewith.[1] As the subject is one of vital importance, perhaps a few reflections upon certain points brought out by Dr. Donald by one who, like himself, is groping for light upon this vexed problem, may not be out of place nor without interest to your readers.

It is indeed a compliment to be considered worthy of commenting upon what Dr. Donald has said. Every word that he says about the work done at Tuskegee I can heartily indorse, and I have been there to see. It is a great institution, a monument to enlightened philanthropy, guided and directed by the genius of a remarkable man, whose diversified talents and unselfish devotion to a cause have long since won the cordial recognition of the American people in all parts of the country. I do not believe that anywhere else in the world can be found so inspiring an example of the capabilities of a race long despised and held incapable of grasping the opportunities or exercising the privileges of an advanced civilization.

But in the conclusion which Dr. Donald and some other good friends of the colored race seem to have reached, or to which they seem to have been forced by recent events, that education for awhile take the place of the franchise, so far as the Negro is concerned, I cannot for a moment concur. Dr. Donald's address was delivered to an audience of colored students in Alabama, and while an ideal one for that latitude, it is a question whether it should be accepted in Boston as a solution of the race problem. Nothing has seemed more astounding to me than the manner in which the people of the North have passively permitted themselves to be persuaded by the South that the enfranchisement of the freedmen was a colossal blunder. To my mind it was one of the finest acts of statesmanship ever recorded. It was the righting of a great wrong: had it been logically and consistently followed up by appropriate legislation, as the Constitution amendment provided, it would long since have been acquiesced in by the Southern whites. That the white South should approve it was not to be expected; that they should condemn it was to be looked for; that they should seek to overthrow it, and, failing in that, to circumvent it, was not at all unnatural. But that the North should unconcernedly submit to the nullification, within thirty years, of a large part of the results of the Civil War, has been to me not only a matter of profound sorrow, but of astonishment equally great. With all the criticisms of reconstruction, so common in our day and time, no one has yet suggested a better plan to confirm the freedom of the slaves. The bestowal of the franchise was a choice between difficulties, which those upon whom the responsibility rested had to meet. They chose what seemed to them best, in view of all the circumstances. Their critics, who, in the light of subsequent events, condemn their action, have as yet suggested no alternative which would have promised better—even in the light of subsequent events. The thirteenth, fourteenth and fifteenth amendments mark the most glorious onward step in the cause of human liberty that history discloses—a past generation recognized this fact, and future generations will echo their verdict. The franchise was not extorted by the sword, in the hands of the oppressed, as the French peasant won it, nor forced, like Magna Charta, from the reluctant hand of a sovereign. It was a generous gift, freely bestowed, in response to an impulse of conscience and humanity, which was no less strong because it happened to coincide with what was deemed wise politics. Instead of regretting this deed and slurring the memory of those who did it, it should be held as the crowning glory of our history.

The thirteenth amendment abolished slavery. The fourteenth and fifteenth amendments sought to confer civic equality. It seemed as clear then as it seems to the writer now, that the one without the other was a myth—the shadow without the substance. There is no tenable half-way ground between servitude and freedom. That a man's master is the community rather than some one individual improves the situation but very slightly; it really leaves the slave without the protection which the personal interest of the master might have given. Henry Clay, a consistent defender of slavery, once said that to emancipate the Negro from chattel slavery would be merely to make him the slave of society.[2] If the Negro is to be deprived of every substantial guarantee of his rights and left to the mere caprice of those endowed with superior rights, this malign prophecy is likely to be fulfilled. At no time has this been more clearly apparent than since the practical disfranchisement of the Negroes in several of the Southern States. Without the ballot, with no direct representation in any law-making body, their rights are mere paper rights. With society divided on the color line, into two castes, the one laboring under the fear that the other may one day attain equality with it, the other sullen and resentful under the deprivation, by fraud or indirection, of rights solemnly conferred, earned in many cases upon the battle field, and inherent, as they have been taught to believe by their Northern mentors, in mankind, it is idle to dream that strict justice toward the weak may be looked for at the hands of the strong. Irresponsible power was the curse of slavery. Men endowed with it could not be just if they tried. Such a consummation would be contrary to human nature. Even though one man or several men in a Legislature should be animated by the noblest sentiments, if the interests, real or imaginary, of the majority were opposed to justice, justice would not prevail. Corporations, it is said, have no souls; it may be said with equal truth that a Legislature has no conscience. We are often told of the good masters who flourished in the days of slavery—and they were not myths in all instances—who sometimes showed their appreciation of faithful service by manumitting their slaves. Toward the end of the slavery régime manumission was forbidden by legal enactment. What then would have been the condition of the slave who, relying on his master's good will and kindly intentions, had let slip a good opportunity to escape from bondage? His case would have been that of the Negro of today, who, relying upon the friendship and good will of the Southern whites, should consent or submit without protest to the deprivation of so fundamental a right as the franchise, which, by the way, in most parts of the country, any ignorant foreigner may have for the asking.

The position of the Negro is anomalous. There are in the United States quite as many ignorant and poor white people as there are Negroes. No one has sought to deny these the right of suffrage. Even in Massachusetts, so often held up as the example of a restricted franchise State, the law which imposed the restriction deprived no one of the franchise who possessed it already.[3] The door of opportunity is open wide to every one of these millions who may aspire to learning, to wealth, to civic honors, to social recognition. The Negro is by reason of his color denied these things which come to others as a matter of course. For let no friend of the Negro deceive himself: the ability to read and write will not let the Southern white man contemplate with equanimity the possible political and social equality of the Negro. It is the opinion of more than one close observer that the advancement of the Negro in education is the real moving cause of the present reaction against his enfranchisement. When every Negro has learned to read and write, unless the Constitutional guarantees of his liberty are maintained, some other means will be sought to preserve intact the power and prestige of the white race. There must be a total revolution of Southern sentiment toward the Negro before equality of learning, intelligence, or ability, will make the Southerner content to share equally with his darker fellow-citizens the benefits of citizenship. Such an equality, even in the distant future, is not at all the Southern idea. Such an equality, if the Negro be worthy at all of consideration, he should never cease to seek, through education, through thrift, through industry, through agitation, and in every other honorable way. The desire for liberty, like the hope of the human race for immortality, is the best proof that it should exist.

There are many white men in the South who think themselves the friends of the Negro. There are some who would concede to him every right which a white man enjoys. I myself have met and talked with such a man within three months, who proved his faith by his works. But they are in the small minority. As a separate caste, it is the white community, and not the individual, with which the Negro's rights are concerned, and the sentiment of the white community toward the Negro is to be found in its laws. I have little faith in the friendship of a man who would condemn me, by law, to social obloquy; who would make it unlawful to sit at table with me; who, by law, would refuse me lodgings at an inn; and who would drive me, by law, into a separate car upon a railroad train, into a separate compartment of a street-car; who would make it a penal offence to marry me, to the ninth generation inclusive; who drives me to Boston, or to the schools supported by Boston's money, to get the higher education which the State supplies freely to white young people. These are not signs of friendship. There are many Southerners and a class of Northerners who affect to believe that the North dislikes the Negro as much as or more than the South. Compare the laws of Massachusetts with those of Georgia, and the Negro will not hesitate for a moment as to where his best friends live. If by circumstances the Negroes at the North are mainly condemned to servitude, the majority of them are in no better case at the South. There are more colored men and women earning their living in the higher walks of life in Boston today than in Atlanta, which has many times the colored population of Boston.

Dr. Donald's advice to the Negroes is excellent. If it were any one else than he I might say that the Negro has been surfeited with advice—that if he had less advice, and a little more consideration, a little wider opportunity, he would have made a better showing. But Dr. Donald has followed the word by the deed, as his presence at Tuskegee and his well-known interest in the welfare of the race disclose; a member of his congregation, I assume, built the hall which he went to Alabama to dedicate. From his point of view the immediate, pressing need of the Negro is to qualify himself to meet the requirements of the new suffrage laws which restrict the franchise. He must learn to read, i.e., get education, presumably in the schools. The South has never been friendly to popular education; it was an exotic introduced by the hated carpet-bagger, and more than one Southerner would be glad to see the whole system abolished. The New England theory of the public school system, that it is supported by the whole community, for the good of the whole community, has never taken root in the South. According to the Southern notion, free education is a gratuity, and when given to the Negroes, a gratuity bestowed by the whites upon the blacks, who do not rightfully appreciate their own opportunity or the kindness of the whites. All taxes are held to be paid by white men, because the money passes through their hands. That the tenant, when he pays the rent, pays the taxes, is a theory that has never yet found lodgment in the Southern consciousness. Since the disfranchisement of the Negroes in certain States, strenuous efforts have been made to reduce the relative amounts appropriated for the education of Negro youth. To the credit of the South they have so far failed, as far as the law is concerned. The same end is sometimes obtained by indirection. In the State of Georgia, with a law providing for a pro rata division of the school fund between the two races, the colored schools, which enroll 48 per cent of the school population, receive but 20 per cent of the school funds.[4] Such a result is inevitable, law or no law, where the whole power of the State is in the hands of one faction, or one caste, whose interests are felt to be antagonistic to another not in power. The colored people can no more expect equal educational facilities where they have no representation, which the franchise alone can give, than they can expect equal accommodations in the separate cars which are set aside for them in the South. To take away the franchise from the Negro, with the present unsympathetic attitude of the South toward his aspirations, is to rob him of liberty, of which it has always been the mark and crown.

It is not at all safe to assume that the fourteenth and fifteenth amendments cannot be repealed. There is a powerful minority already demanding their repeal, led by the same master minds who have engineered the recent discriminating legislation in the South. If they continue to have their way in the future as in the past, one need be surprised at nothing. With the fourteenth and fifteenth amendments repealed, the thirteenth may as well be abrogated.

Dr. Donald very wisely says that the Negro must strive to understand the social, industrial and political conditions of his day and nation. How is he to understand them, deprived of all participation in them? He cannot acquire the knowledge of these things merely by living among the white people. If so, he would not be ignorant and socially inefficient at the end of 300 years of the slavery which it is claimed did so much for him. Barred out, by theft of the franchise, from any participation in government; barred out by industrial jealously from factories and workshop; barred out by race prejudice from office and counting-room, where is he to acquire this knowledge? A few may learn these things, theoretically, in the schools, but they are but a drop in the bucket compared with the millions who might learn them, if permitted, in the work of life. Missionary work is needed with the Southern whites. The Negro could do a great deal more and learn a great deal more than he has opportunity for. He must learn, it is said, self-respect, self-reliance and love of struggle. Undoubtedly. He will need them all. The struggle for existence will be harder for him than for a

white man. This is no theory, but to colored men a concrete fact. He will find it
hard to learn self-respect in a school where scorn and contempt is the portion of
his race. Men are looked down upon according to their weakness. The Negro,
even with a franchise which he cannot exercise, is feared, lest he may some time
learn to use it; those who are feared are in some degree respected and their rights
not wantonly disturbed. The Negro without the franchise is helpless either in
fact or in theory, and is despised still more for his weakness. Scorn is a poor
school in which to learn self-respect.

The advice that the Negro devote himself to the upbuilding of character, the
acquirement of education, the accumulation of wealth, is sound advice for any
people. But the implication, and in the case of a recent sermon by Dr. Parkhurst,
the direct statement that it would be better for the Negro to stop agitating the
question of his rights and his wrongs,[5] is one with which I beg to take issue.
There is a place for everything and a time for everything under the sun.[6] The Negro of the South does not say, publicly, a great deal about rights or his wrongs;
he does not dare to be too outspoken. On the contrary, some of the things written by colored men in the effort to please the whites are profoundly depressing.
Nor does it follow that because one man, who occupies a conspicuous position
in connection with one line of effort, does not seek to promote some other, he
does not consider the other of vital importance. Mr. Washington, whose absten-
tion from politics is cited by Dr. Donald as an example to be followed, has undertaken a great educational work and carried it on with wonderful success—
and adjectives are not misplaced in speaking of it. To have accomplished this in
the South was incompatible with political activity. There is no high political career anywhere in the United States for a man of color. But to draw from his diplomatic silence, where to speak might easily alienate the sympathies of the progressive Southern whites, whose moral support he needs in order to enhance the
usefulness of his work, the inference that he regards nothing else but industrial
education as of importance to his people, is unfair to the reputation for wisdom
which he so deservedly has won. The place for the Negro to get money and education is wherever his lot may be cast; for some, perhaps for most, the better
field may lie in the Southern States. The place for the Negro and his friends to
agitate the question of his rights is in the North, where he can exercise freedom
of speech and secure a hearing. The South is sensitive to Northern opinion.
Southerners fill the Northern magazines with articles in which they seek to win
the sympathy of the North to themselves and alienate it from the Negro. The
Negro should let no right, great or small, go by default. He is either a citizen or
not a citizen, and our laws and the theory of our government recognize, so far,
no halfway ground. He should endeavor to see that his own case be not taken to
establish a precedent for a curtailed citizenship. If he be a citizen, then he should
be entitled, as an individual, without regard to his race or color, to every right
that any man enjoys by virtue of his citizenship. And it should not be left to individual white men to say whether or not he shall enjoy them. It should be the part

of society, represented by government, to see that he enjoys them. If the Supreme Court of the United States had sustained the war amendments, instead of emasculating them in half a dozen decisions, the Negro would have been much farther along the path of progress. If the white South could have been made to understand that the war amendments would be enforced they would long since have accommodated themselves to the new order, and have secured by fair means the ascendancy they have at length obtained by the high hand. The Negro can secure education and wealth, can learn self-reliance and self-respect, and do this all the better, while clinging to the elective franchise. Its value to him may be measured by the frantic efforts which have been made to deprive him of it. He needs the friendship of the Southern whites; but the best fruit of friendship is justice and fair play, and a friendship without these is of no real value. To obtain these he still needs the sympathy and moral support of the North.

Where a Negro should live depends upon the individual. For some colored men the North offers opportunities which the South does not; for others the South offers greater material benefits. But so long as the traditions of the past remain, and until the North has changed much more than it has, the Negro will feel that the North is more friendly to his aspirations than the South.

I do not regard the Negro's cause as hopeless, nor do I underestimate the difficulties which he must face. He has reserve powers which have not been fully appreciated. I believe that even under the present Southern theory of a separate and distinct race which must work out its own destiny in as wide a separation from the whites as is practicable, the Negro will slowly but surely rise. But to my mind the best thing is the right thing, the fine thing. I will leave it to the diplomats to establish a *modus vivendi*. My solution of the race problem is an old cry, replete with historic significance. It has been wrought out in blood in other lands; it may quite as easily be enforced by peaceful means: "Liberty, Equality, Fraternity";[7] liberty to all, on equal terms; equality to every man as soon as he shall have won it—nay, more, for every man at all times equality with those who are no wiser or better than he; fraternity, for only with this can equality or true friendship exist.

∽

SOURCE: "The Negro's Franchise," *Boston Evening Transcript*, 11 May 1901, 18. Below the title appeared these headlines:

———

A RIGHT HE MUST STRUGGLE TO MAINTAIN

———

Mr. Charles W. Chesnutt Takes Issue with Dr.
Donald's Tuskegee Address—The Thirteenth
Amendment of Little Value Without the
Fourteenth and Fifteenth—The Negro
Must Continue to Appeal to the
North for Help—A Stirring
Article

———

Chesnutt's essay closed with the dateline "Cleveland, O., May 8."

[1]Elijah Winchester Donald (1848–1904) was the Rector of Trinity Church, Boston; his dedication address was aptly summarized in the headlines appearing in the *Boston Evening Transcript*, 1 May 1901, 24:

FRANCHISE IS NOT ALL

———

THE REAL FUTURE OF THE NEGRO LIES IN EDUCATION

———

Dr. Donald Advises the Black Man Not to Declaim
Fiercely Against Unjust Disfranchisement by
Their States, but to Train Themselves for
Citizenship—The North Not the Place for
the Southern Negro

That is, he did not condone disfranchisement but articulated the perspective of Booker T. Washington, Charles H. Parkhurst (1842–1933), and numerous other sympathetic commentators on "The Negro Problem": that African Americans should now give priority concern to upbuilding character, acquiring education, and accumulating property and wealth—rather than insisting upon the franchise.

[2]Henry Clay, a Whig, was a U.S. Senator from Kentucky who earned the sobriquet of "The Great Compromiser" because of his dedication to preserving the union by means of negotiating agreements between North and South on the territorial extension and limitation of slavery.

[3]In 1901, three states outside the South—Massachusetts, Connecticut, and California—restricted suffrage by an educational test: those requested to do so had to demonstrate to officials that they could read and write.

[4]Two years later when presenting the same datum in "The Disfranchisement of the Negro," Chesnutt acknowledged W. E. B. Du Bois as his information source. Du Bois was the preeminent authority on statistical data concerning blacks in both the North and South. Although Chesnutt and he had not met by 1901, their correspondence appears to date from, at the latest, 1898.

[5]Parkhurst was, in 1901, one of the most visible members of the New York City clergy because of his relentless and successful attacks on Tammany Hall political corruption. Recently returned from a religious conference in Winston-Salem, N.C., he delivered a sermon at the Madison Square Presbyterian Church, where he had served since 1880; he declared that the "closer one comes to the actual situation [in the South], the more one must feel that the less the negro talks about his civic rights under the Constitution, particularly the right of suffrage, the better it will be for him, and the sooner he will attain to all the rights that justly belong to him." Giving the Negro the right to vote, he opined, was "one of those blunders that it is not easy to escape from after . . . it is committed." In closing, he focused on federal funding for education as a remedy, and he lamented the absurdity of millions of dollars being spent in the Philippines while black and white Southern children languished in poverty and ignorance ("Relations of North and South," *New York Times*, 29 April 1901, 7).

[6]Paraphrase of Ecclesiastes 3:1.

[7]The French national motto, first used by the leaders of the French Revolution.

Charles W. Chesnutt's Own View of His New Story, *The Marrow of Tradition*

Essay published in the Cleveland *World*, 20 October 1901

I have been asked to make for this page a brief summary of the motive and chief points of my forthcoming novel, *The Marrow of Tradition*.[1] The primary object of this story, as it should be of every work of fiction, is to entertain; and yet it belongs in the category of purpose novels,[2] inasmuch as it seeks to throw light upon the vexed moral and sociological problems which grow out of the presence, in our Southern states, of two diverse races, in nearly equal numbers.

The title of the book fairly embodies the theme, which is an attempt to picture, through the medium of dramatic narrative, the atmosphere in which these problems must be worked out—an atmosphere of which the dominant note is Tradition.

Tradition made the white people masters, rulers, who absorbed all the power, the wealth, the honors of the community, and jealously guarded this monopoly, with which they claimed to be divinely endowed, by denying to those who were not of their caste the opportunity to acquire any of these desirable things.

Tradition, on the other hand, made the Negro a slave, an underling, existing by favor and not by right, his place the lowest in the social scale, to which, by the same divine warrant, he was hopelessly confined.

The old order has passed away, but these opinions, deeply implanted in the consciousness of two races, still persist, and *The Marrow of Tradition* seeks to show the efforts of the people of a later generation to adjust themselves in this traditional atmosphere to the altered conditions of a new era.

There is no subject of more vital interest to the student of history or of life than the upward struggle of a race, as there is no issue of greater importance to the nation than a right settlement of the race problem.

As to the story, it must speak for itself. It has several threads of interest, the chief incidents being concerned with the fate of the child of a proud old family related by an unacknowledged tie to the family of a colored doctor. The father of the child leads a reactionary political movement against the Negro, while the doctor is at the head of an enterprise for the education and uplifting of his people. There is a crime, followed by a threatened lynching. There is an episode of injury and revenge, another of wrong and forgiveness.

Among the characters are a typical old "mammy," a faithful servant who is willing to die for his master and an ideal old aristocrat who practically sacrifices his life to save that of his servant. The incidents of the race riot described in the story were studied from two recent outbreaks of that kind—one in Wilmington, N.C., and the other in New Orleans.[3]

The political element of the story involves a fair statement, I believe, of the course and the underlying motives of the recent and temporarily successful movement for the disfranchisement of the colored race in the South, and particularly in North Carolina, where there was less excuse for it than in any other state where it has been carried through.

There is a love story with a happy ending. The book is not a study in pessimism, for it is the writer's belief that the forces of progress will in the end prevail, and that in time a remedy may be found for every social ill.

It may interest the readers of my previous books to learn that *The Marrow of Tradition* admits of an ending which is at the same time consistent with the canons of good art and satisfying to the emotions.

↬

SOURCE: "Charles W. Chesnutt's Own View of His New Story, *The Marrow of Tradition*," Cleveland *World*, 20 October 1901, "Magazine Section," 5.

[1]When this essay appeared, *Marrow* had already been published: copyright registration and deposit occurred on 14 and 17 October 1901, respectively. An advance copy was mailed to Chesnutt by Houghton, Mifflin & Co. on 17 October.

[2]"Purpose novel," or "novel of purpose," was a term used frequently by literary critics of the turn of the century, indicating that a work was a thesis-driven, didactic one. When used, the connotation was most often negative: art had been sacrificed for the sake of polemic. Chesnutt appears to have understood this; and, in first stressing his intention to "entertain," he appealed to a traditional definition of the function of art, to delight as well as instruct.

[3]The Wilmington and New Orleans riots occurred in 1898 and 1900.

Obliterating the Color Line

Essay published in the Cleveland *World*, 23 October 1901

The recent Roosevelt-Washington episode has contributed considerably to the gayety of nations and might be allowed to pass without further comment were it not in some of its bearings a vitally significant incident.[1]

The American people are prone to generalization. When the great majority of the Negroes in the South were slaves all Negroes were practically so counted. We class the whole colored race as Negroes, when only the glance of an eye is required to show that many of them are partly of white blood. We lump them all together, after our usual large, careless manner, and since the great majority of them are of low estimate, it is inevitable that the minority must suffer from such a state of things.

Whether Mr. Washington should eat a meal at the White House was no great thing; but that the President of the United States should, consciously or unconsciously, give the nation an object lesson in fairness, in courtesy, and in fundamentally wise statesmanship, is an important matter.

There is something radically wrong about a free republic where any class of citizens is entirely foreclosed from any avenue of advancement, and there is something inspiring in the thought that for every strong man there is a clear way open to the top.

We sometimes underestimate the influence of little things; there is no more powerful factor than sentiment in the conduct of human affairs.

The attitude of the President's Southern critics is not a pleasing one. It savors of narrowness and illiberality, and would seem to indicate an antipathy to the Negro solely because of his color, and not because of his condition.

The South has been very tenderly dealt with of recent years. It has been allowed, without serious protest on the part of government or public opinion, to override the federal constitution and disfranchise most of the Republican voters in the South, and to build up a body of laws which mark the colored people in their midst as a distinct and inferior caste.

They ought to be reasonably satisfied with this control of their own affairs and not try to dictate who shall be the dinner guests of Northern people.

This is a united country, and is going to remain so, but that united country will not necessarily consist entirely of the Southern states.

It is gratifying to note, however, that some Southerners disapprove this hostile criticism of the President, and it is to be hoped that, sometime or other, there will be such a division of public opinion in the South on political and race questions as will relieve the North of any wearing responsibility.

It will be noted, too, that the President has appointed another Southern Democrat to office since this incident occurred.[2] Possibly the matter may yet be amicably arranged. The Negroes are good trenchermen, the Southern whites are fond of power. They may be induced to consent that the colored folks may have all the dinners, on condition that they themselves have all the minor offices.

⌒

SOURCE: Unsigned editorial in Cleveland *World*, 23 October 1901, 4. Chesnutt identified it as his in his "Miscellaneous Writings" scrapbook at the Fisk University Library and made one alteration in the pasted-down clipping: in the last sentence of the text—which originally read "the offices"—he added "minor" in ink.

[1]On 16 October 1901, Booker T. Washington dined with President Theodore Roosevelt (1858–1919) at the White House. Since this was viewed as a sign of social equality being granted an African American, not only Southern periodicals but those with national distribution gave attention to the event for weeks.

[2]Thomas Goode Jones (1844–1914), former governor of Alabama (1890–94), had received a federal judicial appointment to the Middle and Northern Districts of Alabama.

Pussy Meow: The Autobiography of a Cat, by S. L. Patteson

Essay published in *Modern Culture*, November 1901

This little volume[1] is a welcome addition to the list of books which within the last few years have done so much to interpret animal life and bring it within the pale of human sympathy. The author frankly states that *Pussy Meow* seeks to do for the cat what *Black Beauty* did for the horse and *Beautiful Joe* for the dog;[2] and even without this admission the book is very obviously written with a purpose. This, however, does not detract from its interest, but merely furnishes an additional reason why it should be read. Another element of interest lies in a very pleasant introduction by Mrs. Sarah K. Bolton, the well-known author, herself a devoted friend and champion of dumb animals.[3]

Pussy Meow is written in the form of an autobiography, and the illusion is well sustained throughout. A kitten, who lives in a pleasant garden, ventures through the gate into the outer world. A dog chases her so far that she is unable to find her way back. This is the beginning of a varied career, in which she experiences most of the joys and sorrows incident to the life of a cat. She goes to sleep in a strange yard, from which she is driven out with stones by a bad boy. She is rescued by a kind lady, who rebukes the boy and provides the kitten with a home. Here she forms the acquaintance of other kittens, and finds herself in clover. The household includes a kind mistress, a good boy, and a friendly dog. In this ideal home, which Pussy Meow finds a sort of cat's paradise, she has many pleasant adventures which are narrated in her autobiography. Interesting children of the neighborhood figure extensively in the story, and help to give the incidents a pleasant variety. Incidentally there is much valuable information conveyed with regard to the proper treatment of cats.

Mrs. Patteson's style is simple and direct, as becomes the form in which the subject is treated. One of the most pleasing features of the book is a profusion of handsome half-tone photographs of the author's cats; the illustrations alone are worth the price of the book. While *Pussy Meow* will appeal to all lovers of dumb animals, it will prove particularly pleasing to the young, who live closer to nature than their elders. It will make an admirable gift book for which it ought to be in large demand.

⤸

SOURCE: "Pussy Meow: The Autobiography of a Cat, S. L. Patteson," *Modern Culture*, 14 (November 1901), 261. Signed "C. W. C."

[1]As was indicated in a footnote that has been editorially excised, *Pussy Meow*, by Susanna Louise Patteson (1853–1922), was published in Philadelphia by George W. Jacobs and Company. It was also published in Cleveland by Burrows Brothers the same year, 1901.

[2]Anna Sewell (1820–78), *Black Beauty* (1877); Marshall Saunders (1861–1947), *Beautiful Joe, An Autobiography* (1894).

[3]Sarah Knowles Bolton (1841–1916), author of *The Present Problem: A Temperance Story* (1874) and *Our Devoted Friend, The Dog* (1901), was a prolific author and social reformer. Her preface to *Pussy Meow* explains how the tale was conceived: "In the fall of 1895, while the National Convention of the S.P.C.A. was in session in Cleveland, a group of people stood in the assembly room one day discussing *Black Beauty* and *Beautiful Joe*. One expressed the hope that as the horse and dog had now secured a public hearing, some one would be willing to undertake the same for the cat. That same evening Pussy Meow began writing her story. Its only object is to breathe out the joys, the sorrows, and the longings of a misunderstood and much maligned fellow-creature, and to secure for her the consideration which humanity owes to the dumb."

The Free Colored People of North Carolina

Essay published in the *Southern Workman*, March 1902

In our generalizations upon American history—and the American people are prone to loose generalization, especially where the Negro is concerned—it is ordinarily assumed that the entire colored race was set free as the result of the Civil War. While this is true in a broad, moral sense, there was, nevertheless, a very considerable technical exception in the case of several hundred thousand free people of color, a great many of whom were residents of the Southern States. Although the emancipation of their race brought to these a larger measure of liberty than they had previously enjoyed, it did not confer upon them personal freedom, which they possessed already. These free colored people were variously distributed, being most numerous, perhaps, in Maryland, where, in the year 1850, for example, in a state with 87,189 slaves, there were 83,942 free colored people, the white population of the state being 515,918; and perhaps least numerous in Georgia, of all the slave states, where, to a slave population of 462,198, there were only 351 free people of color, or less than three-fourths of one per cent., as against the about fifty per cent. in Maryland. Next to Maryland came Virginia, with 58,042 free colored people, North Carolina with 30,463,[1] Louisiana with 18,647 (of whom 10,939 were in the parish of New Orleans alone), and South Carolina with 9,914. For these statistics, I have of course referred to the census reports for the years mentioned. In the year 1850, according to the same authority, there were in the state of North Carolina 553,028 white people, 228,548 slaves, and 27,463 free colored people. In 1860, the white population of the state was 631,100, slaves 331,059, free colored people, 30,463.

These figures for 1850 and 1860 show that between nine and ten per cent. of the colored population, and about three per cent. of the total population in each of those years, were free colored people, the ratio of increase during the intervening period being inconsiderable. In the decade preceding 1850 the ratio of increase had been somewhat different. From 1840 to 1850 the white population of the state had increased 14.05 per cent., the slave population 17.38 per cent., the free colored population 20.81 per cent. In the long period from 1790 to 1860, during which the total percentage of increase for the whole population of the state was 700.16, that of the whites was 750.30 per cent., that of the free colored people 720.65 per cent., and that of the slave population but 450 per cent., the total increase in free population being 747.56 per cent.

It seems altogether probable that but for the radical change in the character of slavery, following the invention of the cotton-gin[2] and the consequent great demand for laborers upon the far Southern plantations, which turned the border states into breeding-grounds for slaves, the forces of freedom might in time have overcome those of slavery, and the institution might have died a natural death, as it already had in the Northern States, and as it subsequently did in Brazil and Cuba. To these changed industrial conditions was due, in all probability, in the decade following 1850, the stationary ratio of free colored people to slaves against the larger increase from 1840 to 1850. The gradual growth of the slave power had discouraged the manumission of slaves, had resulted in legislation curtailing the rights and privileges of free people of color, and had driven many of these to seek homes in the North and West, in communities where, if not warmly welcomed as citizens, they were at least tolerated as freemen.

This free colored population was by no means evenly distributed throughout the state, but was mainly found along or near the eastern seaboard, in what is now known as the "black district" of North Carolina. In Craven county, more than one-fifth of the colored population were free; in Halifax county, where the colored population was double that of the whites, one-fourth of the colored were free. In Hertford county, with 3,947 whites and 4,445 slaves, there were 1,112 free colored. In Pasquotank county, with a white and colored population almost evenly balanced, one-third of the colored people were free. In some counties, for instance in that of Jackson, a mountainous county in the west of the state, where the Negroes were but an insignificant element, the population stood 5,241 whites, 268 slaves, and three free colored persons.

The growth of this considerable element of free colored people had been due to several causes. In the eighteenth century, slavery in North Carolina had been of a somewhat mild character. There had been large estates along the seaboard and the water-courses, but the larger part of the population had been composed of small planters or farmers, whose slaves were few in number, too few indeed to be herded into slave quarters, but employed largely as domestic servants, and working side by side with their masters in field and forest, and sharing with them the same rude fare. The Scotch-Irish Presbyterian strain in the white people of North Carolina brought with it a fierce love of liberty, which was strongly manifested, for example, in the Mecklenburg Declaration of Independence, which preceded that at

Philadelphia;[3] and while this love of liberty was reconciled with slavery, the mere prejudice against race had not yet excluded all persons of Negro blood from its benign influence. Thus, in the earlier history of the state, the civil status of the inhabitants was largely regulated by condition rather than by color. To be a freeman meant to enjoy many of the fundamental rights of citizenship. Free men of color in North Carolina exercised the right of suffrage until 1835, when the constitution was amended to restrict this privilege to white men. It may be remarked, in passing, that prior to 1860, Jews could not vote in North Carolina. The right of marriage between whites and free persons of color was not restricted by law until the year 1830, though social prejudice had always discouraged it.

The mildness of slavery, which fostered kindly feelings between master and slave, often led to voluntary manumission. The superior morality which characterized the upper ranks of white women, so adequately protected by slavery, did not exist in anything like the same degree among the poorer classes, and occasional marriages, more or less legal, between free Negroes or slaves and poor white women, resulted in at least a small number of colored children, who followed the condition of their white mothers. I have personal knowledge of two free colored families of such origin, dating back to the eighteenth century, whose descendants in each case run into the hundreds. There was also a considerable Quaker element in the population, whose influence was cast against slavery, not in any fierce polemical spirit, but in such a way as to soften its rigors and promote gradual emancipation. Another source of free colored people in certain counties was the remnant of the Cherokee and Tuscarora Indians, who, mingling with the Negroes and poor whites, left more or less of their blood among the colored people of the state. By the law of *partitus sequitur ventrem*,[4] which is a law of nature as well as of nations, the child of a free mother was always free, no matter what its color or the status of its father, and many free colored people were of female Indian ancestry.

One of these curiously mixed people left his mark upon the history of the state—a bloody mark, too, for the Indian in him did not passively endure the things to which the Negro strain rendered him subject. Henry Berry Lowrey was what was known as a "Scuffletown mulatto"—Scuffletown being a rambling community in Robeson county, N.C., inhabited mainly by people of this origin. His father, a prosperous farmer, was impressed, like other free Negroes, during the Civil War, for service upon the Confederate public works. He resisted and was shot to death with several sons who were assisting him. A younger son, Henry Berry Lowrey, swore an oath to avenge the injury, and a few years later carried it out with true Indian persistence and ferocity. During a career of murder and robbery extending over several years, in which he was aided by an organized band of desperadoes who rendezvoused in inaccessible swamps and terrorized the county, he killed every white man concerned in his father's death, and incidentally several others who interfered with his plans, making in all a total of some thirty killings. A body of romance grew up about this swarthy Robin Hood, who, armed to the teeth, would freely walk into the towns and about the railroad stations, knowing full well that there was a price upon his head, but relying for safety upon the sympathy of the blacks and the fears of the whites. His pretty yellow wife,[5] "Rhody," was known as "the queen of Scuffletown." Northern reporters came down to write him up. An astute Boston detective who penetrated, under false colors, to his stronghold, is said to have been put to death with savage tortures. A state official was once conducted by devious paths, under Lowrey's safeguard, to the outlaw's camp, in order that he might see for himself how difficult it would be to dislodge them. A dime novel was founded upon his exploits. The state offered ten thousand, the Federal government, five thousand dollars for his capture, and a regiment of Federal troops was sent to subdue him, his career resembling very much that of the picturesque Italian bandit who has recently been captured after a long career of crime.[6] Lowrey only succumbed in the end to a bullet from the hand of a treacherous comrade, and there is even yet a tradition that he escaped and made his way to a distant state.[7] Some years ago these mixed Indians and Negroes were recognized by the North Carolina legislature as "Croatan Indians," being supposed to have descended from a tribe of that name and the whites of the lost first white colony of Virginia. They are allowed, among other special privileges conferred by this legislation, to have separate schools of their own, being placed, in certain other respects, upon a plane somewhat above that of the Negroes and a little below that of the whites.

I may add that North Carolina was a favorite refuge for runaway slaves and indentured servants from the richer colonies north and south of it. It may thus be plainly seen how a considerable body of free colored people sprang up within the borders of the state.

The status of these people, prior to the Civil War, was anomalous but tenable. Many of them, perhaps most of them, were as we have seen, persons of mixed blood, and received, with their dower of white blood, an intellectual and physical heritage of which social prejudice could not entirely rob them, and which helped them to prosperity in certain walks of life. The tie of kinship was sometimes recognized, and brought with it property, sympathy and opportunity which the black did not always enjoy. Many free colored men were skilled mechanics. The State House at Raleigh was built by colored workmen, under a foreman of the same race. I am acquainted with a family now living in the North, whose Negro grandfather was the leading tailor in Newbern, N.C. He owned a pew on the ground floor of the church which he attended, and was buried in the cemetery where white people were laid to rest. In the town where I went to live when a child, just after the Civil War,[8] nearly all the mechanics were men of color. One of these, a saddler by trade, had himself been the owner, before the war, of a large plantation and several slaves. He had been constrained by force of circumstances to invest in Confederate bonds, but despite this loss, he still had left a considerable tract of land, a brick store, and a handsome town residence, and was able to send one of his sons, immediately after the war, to a Northern school, where he read law, and returning to his native state, was admitted to the bar and has ever since practiced his profession. This was an old free family, descended from a free West Indian female ancestor. For historical reasons, which applied to the whole race, slave and free, these families were, before the war, most clearly traceable through the female line.[9]

The principal cabinet-maker and undertaker in the town was an old white man whose workmen were colored. One of these practically inherited what was left of the business after the introduction of factory-made furniture from the North, and has been for many years the leading undertaker of the town. The tailors, shoemakers, wheelwrights and blacksmiths were men of color, as were the carpenters, bricklayers and plasterers.

It is often said, as an argument for slavery, by the still numerous apologists for that institution, that these skilled artisans have not passed on to the next generation the trades acquired by them under, if not in, slavery. This failure is generally ascribed to the shiftlessness of the race in freedom, and to the indisposition of the younger men to devote themselves to hard work. But the assumption is not always correct; there are still many competent colored mechanics in the South. In the town of which I have spoken, for instance, colored men are still the barbers, blacksmiths, masons and carpenters. And while there has been a falling off, partly due to the unsettled conditions resulting from emancipation and inseparable from so sudden and radical a change, another reason for it exists in the altered industrial conditions which confront mechanics all over the country, due mainly to the growth of manufactures and the increased ease and cheapness of transportation. The shoes which were formerly made by hand are now manufactured in Massachusetts and sold, with a portrait of the maker stamped upon the sole, for less money than the most poorly paid mechanic could afford to make them for by hand. The buggies and wagons, to produce which kept a large factory, in the town where I lived, in constant operation, are now made in Cincinnati and other Northern cities, and delivered in North Carolina for a price prohibitive of manufacture by hand. Furniture is made at Grand Rapids, coffins in one place, and clothing in still another. The blacksmith buys his horseshoes ready made, in assorted sizes, and has merely to trim the hoof and fasten them on with machine-made nails. The shoemaker has degenerated into the cobbler; the tinner merely keeps a shop for the sale of tinware; the undertaker merely embalms the dead and conducts funerals, and tombstones are sold by catalogue with blanks for the insertion of names and dates before delivery. In some of the new industries which have sprung up in the South, such, for instance, as cotton-milling, Negroes are not employed. Hence, in large part through the operation of social forces beyond any control on their part, they have lost their hereditary employments, and these have only in part been replaced by employment in tobacco factories and in iron mines and mills.

The general decline of the apprenticeship system which has affected black and white alike, is also in some degree responsible for the dearth of trained mechanics in the South. Even in Northern cities the finer grades of stone-cutting, bricklaying, carpentry and cabinet work, and practically all the mosaic and terra-cotta work and fine interior decorating, are done by workmen of foreign birth and training.

Many of the younger colored people who might have learned trades, have found worthy employment as teachers and preachers; but the servile occupations into which so many of the remainder have drifted by following the line of least resistance, are a poor substitute for the independent position of skilled mechanic. The establishment, for the colored race, of such institutions as Hampton and Tuskegee, not only replaces the apprenticeship system, but fills a growing industrial want. A multiplication of such agencies will enable the "free colored people" of the next generation, who now embrace the whole race and will number some ten millions or more, to regain these lost arts, and through them, by industry and thrift, under intelligent leadership, to win that equality of citizenship of which they are now grasping, perhaps, somewhat more than the shadow but something less than the substance.

⌒

SOURCE: "The Free Colored People of North Carolina," *Southern Workman*, 31 (March 1902), 136–41.

[1]Chesnutt cites the 1860 census figure.

[2]1793.

[3]Although there is no record of a 20 May 1775 declaration of independence from British rule by Mecklenburg County citizens, the State of North Carolina now recognizes its historicity.

[4]That is, the status of the offspring is recognized as that of the mother rather than the father.

[5]At the turn of the century, light-skinned mulattoes were frequently referred to as "yellow," e.g., Frederick Douglass and Booker T. Washington. Such is Chesnutt's epithet in *The House Behind the Cedars* for some young women darker than the very fair African-American heroine.

[6]The "Italian bandit" (in the sense of outlaw rather than robber) was Giuseppe Musolino (1875–1956). Irenaes Prime-Stevenson describes his history in "An Italian Brigand of To-day," *Independent*, 53 (8 August 1901), 1844–48: this Calabrian peasant accidently became involved in a quarrel in his father's wine shop; two men turned on him with their knives; one of them was later discovered dead; and Musolino was convicted on evidence subsequently shown to be false. Escaping from prison, he assassinated those who testified against him. He then killed those who had made his fiancée unhappy; broken-hearted and sneered at by many in her village, she died during his imprisonment. He was viewed by his compatriots as a victim rather than a criminal, and as a heroic figure, righting many wrongs suffered by men and women like himself. His apprehension was reported in "Italian Brigand Musolino Captured," *New York Times*, 17 October 1901, 1.

[7]Lowrey (1846?–72?) was a member of what is now known as the Lumbee Tribe. The book about Lowrey (Lowry, Lowrie, or Lowery) to which Chesnutt alludes may be Mary C. Norment's *The Lowrie History as Acted in Part by Henry Berry Lowrie, the Great North Carolina Bandit* (1895; originally published in 1875).

[8]Fayetteville, N.C.

[9]That is, the children were most often reared by and remained affiliated with their

mothers rather than fathers. This is illustrated in the genealogical data concerning Chesnutt's ancestry presented by Frances Richardson Keller in *An American Crusade: The Life of Charles Waddell Chesnutt* (1978). The "historical reasons" are illuminated in "What Is a White Man?" as well as in the description of the personal history of the heroine's unmarried mother, Molly Walden, in *The House Behind the Cedars*.

The Disfranchisement of the Negro

Essay published in *The Negro Problem*, 1903

The right of American citizens of African descent, commonly called Negroes, to vote upon the same terms as other citizens of the United States, is plainly declared and firmly fixed by the Constitution. No such person is called upon to present reasons why he should possess this right: that question is foreclosed by the Constitution. The object of the elective franchise is to give representation. So long as the Constitution retains its present form, any State Constitution, or statute, which seeks, by juggling the ballot, to deny the colored race fair representation, is a clear violation of the fundamental law of the land, and a corresponding injustice to those thus deprived of this right.

For thirty-five years this has been the law. As long as it was measurably respected, the colored people made rapid strides in education, wealth, character and self-respect. This the census proves, all statements to the contrary notwithstanding. A generation has grown to manhood and womanhood under the great, inspiring freedom conferred by the Constitution and protected by the right of suffrage—protected in large degree by the mere naked right, even when its exercise was hindered or denied by unlawful means. They have developed, in every Southern community, good citizens, who, if sustained and encouraged by just laws and liberal institutions, would greatly augment their number with the passing years, and soon wipe out the reproach of ignorance, unthrift, low morals and social inefficiency, thrown at them indiscriminately and therefore unjustly, and made the excuse for the equally undiscriminating contempt of their persons and their rights. They have reduced their illiteracy nearly 50 per cent. Excluded from the institutions of higher learning in their own States, their young men hold their own, and occasionally carry away honors, in the universities of the North. They have accumulated three hundred million dollars worth of real and personal property. Individuals among them have acquired substantial wealth, and several have attained to something like national distinction in art, letters and educational leadership. They are numerously represented in the learned professions. Heavily handicapped, they have made such rapid progress that the suspicion is justified that their advancement, rather than any stagnation or retrogression, is the true secret of the

virulent Southern hostility to their rights, which has so influenced Northern opinion that it stands mute, and leaves the colored people, upon whom the North conferred liberty, to the tender mercies[1] of those who have always denied their fitness
for it.

It may be said, in passing, that the word "Negro," where used in this paper, is
used solely for convenience. By the census of 1890 there were 1,000,000 colored
people in the country who were half, or more than half, white, and logically there
must be, as in fact there are, so many who share the white blood in some degree, as
to justify the assertion that the race problem in the United States concerns the welfare and the status of a mixed race. Their rights are not one whit the more sacred
because of this fact; but in an argument where injustice is sought to be excused because of fundamental differences of race, it is well enough to bear in mind that the
race whose rights and liberties are endangered all over this country by disfranchisement at the South, are the colored people who live in the United States to-day,
and not the low-browed, man-eating savage whom the Southern white likes to set
upon a block and contrast with Shakespeare and Newton[2] and Washington and
Lincoln.

Despite and in defiance of the Federal Constitution, to-day in the six Southern
States of Mississippi, Louisiana, Alabama, North Carolina, South Carolina and
Virginia, containing an aggregate colored population of about 6,000,000, these
have been, to all intents and purposes, denied, so far as the States can effect it, the
right to vote. This disfranchisement is accomplished by various methods, devised
with much transparent ingenuity, the effort being in each instance to violate the
spirit of the Federal Constitution by disfranchising the Negro, while seeming to respect its letter by avoiding the mention of race or color.

These restrictions fall into three groups. The first comprises a property qualification—the ownership of $300 worth or more of real or personal property
(Alabama, Louisiana, Virginia and South Carolina); the payment of a poll tax
(Mississippi, North Carolina, Virginia); an educational qualification—the ability
to read and write (Alabama, Louisiana, North Carolina). Thus far, those who believe in a restricted suffrage everywhere, could perhaps find no reasonable fault
with any one of these qualifications, applied either separately or together.

But the Negro has made such progress that these restrictions alone would perhaps not deprive him of effective representation. Hence the second group. This
comprises an "understanding" clause—the applicant must be able "to read, or
understand when read to him, any clause in the Constitution" (Mississippi), or to
read and explain, or to understand and explain when read to him, any section of
the Constitution (Virginia); an employment qualification—the voter must be
regularly employed in some lawful occupation (Alabama); a character qualification—the voter must be a person of good character and who "understands the duties and obligations of citizens under a republican [!] form of government" (Alabama). The qualifications under the first group it will be seen, are capable of exact
demonstration; those under the second group are left to the discretion and judg-

ment of the registering officer—for in most instances these are all requirements for registration, which must precede voting.

But the first group, by its own force, and the second group, under imaginable conditions, might exclude not only the Negro vote, but a large part of the white vote. Hence, the third group, which comprises: a military service qualification—any man who went to war, willingly or unwillingly, in a good cause or a bad, is entitled to register (Ala., Va.); a prescriptive qualification, under which are included all male persons who were entitled to vote on January 1, 1867, at which date the Negro had not yet been given the right to vote; a hereditary qualification (the so-called "grandfather" clause), whereby any son (Va.), or descendant (Ala.), of a soldier, and (N.C.) the descendant of any person who had the right to vote on January 1, 1867, inherits that right. If the voter wish to take advantage of these last provisions, which are in the nature of exceptions to a general rule, he must register within a stated time, whereupon he becomes a member of a privileged class of permanently enrolled voters not subject to any of the other restrictions.

It will be seen that these restrictions are variously combined in the different States, and it is apparent that if combined to their declared end, practically every Negro may, under color of law, be denied the right to vote, and practically every white man accorded that right. The effectiveness of these provisions to exclude the Negro vote is proved by the Alabama registration under the new State Constitution. Out of a total, by the census of 1900, of 181,471 Negro "males of voting age," less than 3,000 are registered; in Montgomery county alone, the seat of the State capital, where there are 7,000 Negro males of voting age, only 47 have been allowed to register, while in several counties not one single Negro is permitted to exercise the franchise.

These methods of disfranchisement have stood such tests as the United States Courts, including the Supreme Court, have thus far seen fit to apply, in such cases as have been before them for adjudication. These include a case based upon the "understanding" clause of the Mississippi Constitution, in which the Supreme Court held, in effect, that since there was no ambiguity in the language employed and the Negro was not directly named, the Court would not go behind the wording of the Constitution to find a meaning which discriminated against the colored voter;[3] and the recent case of Jackson W. Giles, brought by a colored citizen of Montgomery, Alabama, in which the Supreme Court confesses itself impotent to provide a remedy for what, by inference, it acknowledges *may* be a "great political wrong," carefully avoiding, however, to state that it is a wrong, although the vital prayer of the petition was for a decision upon this very point.[4]

Now, what is the effect of this wholesale disfranchisement of colored men, upon their citizenship? The value of food to the human organism is not measured by the pains of an occasional surfeit, but by the effect of its entire deprivation. Whether a class of citizens should vote, even if not always wisely—what class does?—may best be determined by considering their condition when they are without the right to vote.

The colored people are left, in the States where they have been disfranchised, absolutely without representation, direct or indirect, in any law-making body, in any court of justice, in any branch of government—for the feeble remnant of voters left by law is so inconsiderable as to be without a shadow of power. Constituting one-eighth of the population of the whole country, two-fifths of the whole Southern people, and a majority in several States, they are not able, because disfranchised where most numerous, to send one representative to the Congress, which, by the decision in the Alabama case, is held by the Supreme Court to be the only body, outside of the State itself, competent to give relief from a great political wrong. By former decisions of the same tribunal, even Congress is impotent to protect their civil rights, the Fourteenth Amendment having long since, by the consent of the same Court, been in many respects as completely nullified as the Fifteenth Amendment is now sought to be. They have no direct representation in any Southern legislature, and no voice in determining the choice of white men who might be friendly to their rights. Nor are they able to influence the election of judges or other public officials, to whom are entrusted the protection of their lives, their liberties and their property. No judge is rendered careful, no sheriff diligent, for fear that he may offend a black constituency; the contrary is most lamentably true; day after day the catalogue of lynchings and anti-Negro riots upon every imaginable pretext, grows longer and more appalling. The country stands face to face with the revival of slavery; at the moment of this writing a federal grand jury in Alabama is uncovering a system of peonage established under cover of law.[5]

Under the Southern program it is sought to exclude colored men from every grade of the public service; not only from the higher administrative functions, to which few of them would in any event, for a long time aspire, but from the lowest as well. A Negro may not be a constable or a policeman. He is subjected by law to many degrading discriminations. He is required to be separated from white people on railroads and street cars, and, by custom, debarred from inns and places of public entertainment. His equal right to a free public education is constantly threatened and is nowhere equitably recognized. In Georgia, as has been shown by Dr. Du Bois, where the law provides for a pro rata distribution of the public school fund between the races, and where the colored school population is 48 per cent. of the total, the amount of the fund devoted to their schools is only 20 per cent.[6] In New Orleans, with an immense colored population, many of whom are persons of means and culture, all colored public schools above the fifth grade have been abolished.

The Negro is subjected to taxation without representation, which the forefathers of this Republic made the basis of a bloody revolution.[7]

Flushed with their local success, and encouraged by the timidity of the Courts and the indifference of public opinion, the Southern whites have carried their campaign into the national government, with an ominous degree of success. If they shall have their way, no Negro can fill any federal office, or occupy, in the public service, any position that is not menial. This is not an inference, but the

openly, passionately avowed sentiment of the white South. The right to employment in the public service is an exceedingly valuable one, for which white men
have struggled and fought. A vast army of men are employed in the administration
of public affairs. Many avenues of employment are closed to colored men by
popular prejudice. If their right to public employment is recognized, and the way
to it open through the civil service, or the appointing power, or the suffrages of the
people, it will prove, as it has already, a strong incentive to effort and a powerful
lever for advancement. Its value to the Negro, like that of the right to vote, may be
judged by the eagerness of the whites to deprive him of it.

Not only is the Negro taxed without representation in the States referred to,
but he pays, through the tariff and internal revenue, a tax to a National government whose supreme judicial tribunal declares that it cannot, through the executive arm, enforce its own decrees, and, therefore, refuses to pass upon a question,
squarely before it, involving a basic right of citizenship. For the decision of the Supreme Court in the Giles case, if it foreshadows the attitude which the Court will
take upon other cases to the same general end which will soon come before it, is
scarcely less than a reaffirmation of the Dred Scott decision;[8] it certainly amounts
to this—that in spite of the Fifteenth Amendment, colored men in the United
States have no political rights which the States are bound to respect. To say this
much is to say that all privileges and immunities which Negroes henceforth enjoy,
must be by favor of the whites; they are not *rights*. The whites have so declared;
they proclaim that the country is theirs, that the Negro should be thankful that he
has so much, when so much more might be withheld from him. He stands upon a
lower footing than any alien; he has no government to which he may look for protection.

Moreover, the white South sends to Congress, on a basis including the Negro
population, a delegation nearly twice as large as it is justly entitled to,[9] and one
which may always safely be relied upon to oppose in Congress every measure
which seeks to protect the equality, or to enlarge the rights of colored citizens. The
grossness of this injustice is all the more apparent since the Supreme Court, in the
Alabama case referred to, has declared the legislative and political department of
the government to be the only power which can right a political wrong. Under this
decision still further attacks upon the liberties of the citizen may be confidently
expected. Armed with the Negro's sole weapon of defense, the white South stands
ready to smite down his rights. The ballot was first given to the Negro to defend
him against this very thing. He needs it now far more than then, and for even
stronger reasons. The 9,000,000 free colored people of to-day have vastly more to
defend than the 3,000,000 hapless blacks who had just emerged from slavery. If
there be those who maintain that it was a mistake to give the Negro the ballot at
the time and in the manner in which it was given,[10] let them take to heart this reflection: that to deprive him of it to-day, or to so restrict it as to leave him utterly
defenseless against the present relentless attitude of the South toward his rights,
will prove to be a mistake so much greater than the first, as to be no less than a

crime, from which not alone the Southern Negro must suffer, but for which the nation will as surely pay the penalty as it paid for the crime of slavery. Contempt for law is death to a republic, and this one has developed alarming symptoms of the disease.

And now, having thus robbed the Negro of every political and civil *right*, the white South, in palliation of its course, makes a great show of magnanimity in leaving him, as the sole remnant of what he acquired through the Civil War, a very inadequate public school education, which, by the present program, is to be directed mainly towards making him a better agricultural laborer. Even this is put forward as a favor, although the Negro's property is taxed to pay for it, and his labor as well. For it is a well settled principle of political economy, that land and machinery of themselves produce nothing, and that labor indirectly pays its fair proportion of the tax upon the public's wealth. The white South seems to stand to the Negro at present as one, who, having been reluctantly compelled to release another from bondage, sees him stumbling forward and upward, neglected by his friends and scarcely yet conscious of his own strength; seizes him, binds him, and having bereft him of speech, of sight and of manhood, "yokes him with the mule" and exclaims, with a show of virtue which ought to deceive no one: "Behold how good a friend I am of yours! Have I not left you a stomach and a pair of arms, and will I not generously permit you to work for me with the one, that you may thereby gain enough to fill the other? A brain you do not need. We will relieve you of any responsibility that might seem to demand such an organ."

The argument of peace-loving Northern white men and Negro opportunists that the political power of the Negro having long ago been suppressed by unlawful means, his right to vote is a mere paper right, of no real value, and therefore to be lightly yielded for the sake of a hypothetical harmony, is fatally short-sighted. It is precisely the attitude and essentially the argument which would have surrendered to the South in the sixties, and would have left this country to rot in slavery for another generation. White men do not thus argue concerning their own rights. They know too well the value of ideals. Southern white men see too clearly the latent power of these unexercised rights. If the political power of the Negro was a nullity because of his ignorance and lack of leadership, why were they not content to leave it so, with the pleasing assurance that if it ever became effective, it would be because the Negroes had grown fit for its exercise? On the contrary, they have not rested until the possibility of its revival was apparently headed off by new State constitutions. Nor are they satisfied with this. There is no doubt that an effort will be made to secure the repeal of the Fifteenth Amendment,[11] and thus forestall the development of the wealthy and educated Negro, whom the South seems to anticipate as a greater menace than the ignorant ex-slave. However improbable this repeal may seem, it is not a subject to be lightly dismissed; for it is within the power of the white people of the nation to do whatever they wish in the premises—they did it once; they can do it again. The Negro and his friends should see to it that the white majority shall never wish to do anything to his hurt. There still stands, before the Negro-hating whites of the South, the specter of a Supreme Court which will interpret the Constitution to mean what it says, and what those who enacted it meant, and what the nation, which ratified it, understood, and which will find power, in a nation which goes beyond seas to administer the affairs of distant peoples, to enforce its own fundamental laws; the specter, too, of an aroused public opinion which will compel Congress and the Courts to preserve the liberties of the Republic, which are the liberties of the people. To wilfully neglect the suffrage, to hold it lightly, is to tamper with a sacred right; to yield it for anything else whatever is simply suicidal. Dropping the element of race, disfranchisement is no more than to say to the poor and poorly taught, that they must relinquish the right to defend themselves against oppression until they shall have become rich and learned, in competition with those already thus favored and possessing the ballot in addition. This is not the philosophy of history. The growth of liberty has been the constant struggle of the poor against the privileged classes; and the goal of that struggle has ever been the equality of all men before the law. The Negro who would yield this right, deserves to be a slave; he has the servile spirit. The rich and the educated can, by virtue of their influence, command many votes; can find other means of protection; the poor man has but one, he should guard it as a sacred treasure. Long ago, by fair treatment, the white leaders of the South might have bound the Negro to themselves with hoops of steel. They have not chosen to take this course, but by assuming from the beginning an attitude hostile to his rights, have never gained his confidence, and now seek by foul means to destroy where they have never sought by fair means to control.

I have spoken of the effect of disfranchisement upon the colored race; it is to the race as a whole, that the argument of the problem is generally directed. But the unit of society in a republic is the individual, and not the race, the failure to recognize this fact being the fundamental error which has beclouded the whole discussion. The effect of disfranchisement upon the individual is scarcely less disastrous. I do not speak of the moral effect of injustice upon those who suffer from it; I refer rather to the practical consequences which may be appreciated by any mind. No country is free in which the way upward is not open for every man to try, and for every properly qualified man to attain whatever of good the community life may offer. Such a condition does not exist, at the South, even in theory, for any man of color. In no career can such a man compete with white men upon equal terms. He must not only meet the prejudice of the individual, not only the united prejudice of the white community; but lest some one should wish to treat him fairly, he is met at every turn with some legal prohibition which says, "Thou shalt not," or "Thus far shalt thou go and no farther." But the Negro race is viable; it adapts itself readily to circumstances; and being thus adaptable, there is always the temptation to

> "Crook the pregnant hinges of the knee,
> Where thrift may follow fawning."[12]

He who can most skillfully balance himself upon the advancing or receding wave of white opinion concerning his race, is surest of such measure of prosperity as is permitted to men of dark skins. There are Negro teachers in the South—the privilege of teaching in their own schools is the one respectable branch of the public service still left open to them—who, for a grudging appropriation from a Southern legislature, will decry their own race, approve their own degradation, and laud their oppressors. Deprived of the right to vote, and, therefore, of any power to demand what is their due, they feel impelled to buy the tolerance of the whites at any sacrifice. If to live is the first duty of man, as perhaps it is the first instinct, then those who thus stoop to conquer[13] may be right. But is it needful to stoop so low, and if so, where lies the ultimate responsibility for this abasement?

I shall say nothing about the moral effect of disfranchisement upon the white people, or upon the State itself. What slavery made of the Southern whites is a matter of history. The abolition of slavery gave the South an opportunity to emerge from barbarism. Present conditions indicate that the spirit which dominated slavery still curses the fair section over which that institution spread its blight.

And now, is the situation remediless? If not so, where lies the remedy? First let us take up those remedies suggested by the men who approve of disfranchisement, though they may sometimes deplore the method, or regret the necessity.

Time, we are told, heals all diseases,[14] rights all wrongs, and is the only cure for this one. It is a cowardly argument. These people are entitled to their rights to-day, while they are yet alive to enjoy them; and it is poor statesmanship and worse morals to nurse a present evil and thrust it forward upon a future generation for correction. The nation can no more honestly do this than it could thrust back upon a past generation the responsibility for slavery. It had to meet that responsibility; it ought to meet this one.

Education has been put forward as the great corrective—preferably industrial education. The intellect of the whites is to be educated to the point where they will so appreciate the blessings of liberty and equality, as of their own motion to enlarge and defend the Negro's rights. The Negroes, on the other hand, are to be so trained as to make them, not equal with the whites in any way—God save the mark![15]—this would be unthinkable!—but so useful to the community that the whites will protect them rather than lose their valuable services. Some few enthusiasts go so far as to maintain that by virtue of education the Negro will, in time, become strong enough to protect himself against any aggression of the whites; this, it may be said, is a strictly Northern view.

It is not quite clearly apparent how education alone, in the ordinary meaning of the word, is to solve, in any appreciable time, the problem of the relations of Southern white and black people. The need of education of all kinds for both races is wofully apparent. But men and nations have been free without being learned, and there have been educated slaves. Liberty has been known to languish where culture had reached a very high development. Nations do not first become rich and learned and then free, but the lesson of history has been that they first become free and then rich and learned, and oftentimes fall back into slavery again because of too great wealth, and the resulting luxury and carelessness of civic virtues. The process of education has been going on rapidly in the Southern States since the Civil War, and yet, if we take superficial indications, the rights of the Negroes are at a lower ebb than at any time during the thirty-five years of their freedom, and the race prejudice more intense and uncompromising. It is not apparent that educated Southerners are less rancorous than others in their speech concerning the Negro, or less hostile in their attitude toward his rights. It is their voice alone that we have heard in this discussion; and if, as they state, they are liberal in their views as compared with the more ignorant whites, then God save the Negro!

I was told, in so many words, two years ago, by the Superintendent of Public Schools of a Southern city that "there was no place in the modern world for the Negro, except under the ground." If gentlemen holding such opinions are to instruct the white youth of the South, would it be at all surprising if these, later on, should devote a portion of their leisure to the improvement of civilization by putting under the ground as many of this superfluous race as possible?

The sole excuse made in the South for the prevalent injustice to the Negro is the difference in race, and the inequalities and antipathies resulting therefrom. It has nowhere been declared as a part of the Southern program that the Negro, when educated, is to be given a fair representation in government or an equal opportunity in life; the contrary has been strenuously asserted; education can never make of him anything but a Negro, and, therefore, essentially inferior, and not to be safely trusted with any degree of power. A system of education which would tend to soften the asperities and lessen the inequalities between the races would be of inestimable value. An education which by a rigid separation of the races from the kindergarten to the university, fosters this racial antipathy, and is directed toward emphasizing the superiority of one class and the inferiority of another, might easily have disastrous, rather than beneficial results. It would render the oppressing class more powerful to injure, the oppressed quicker to perceive and keener to resent the injury, without proportionate power of defense. The same assimilative education which is given at the North to all children alike, whereby native and foreign, black and white, are taught side by side in every grade of instruction, and are compelled by the exigencies of discipline to keep their prejudices in abeyance, and are given the opportunity to learn and appreciate one another's good qualities, and to establish friendly relations which may exist throughout life, is absent from the Southern system of education, both of the past and as proposed for the future. Education is in a broad sense a remedy for all social ills; but the disease we have to deal with now is not only constitutional but acute. A wise physician does not simply give a tonic for a diseased limb, or a high fever; the patient might be dead before the constitutional remedy could become effective. The evils of slavery, its injury to whites and blacks, and to the body politic, were clearly perceived and acknowledged by the educated leaders of the South as far back as the Revolutionary War and the Constitutional Convention, and yet they made no effort to abolish it. Their remedy was the same—time, education, social and economic development;—and yet a bloody war was necessary to destroy slavery and put its spirit temporarily to sleep. When the South and its friends are ready to propose a system of education which will recognize and teach the equality of all men before the law, the potency of education alone to settle the race problem will be more clearly apparent.

At present even good Northern men, who wish to educate the Negroes, feel impelled to buy this privilege from the none too eager white South, by conceding away the civil and political rights of those whom they would benefit. They have, indeed, gone farther than the Southerners themselves in approving the disfranchisement of the colored race. Most Southern men, now that they have carried their point and disfranchised the Negro, are willing to admit, in the language of a recent number of the Charleston *Evening Post*, that "the attitude of the Southern white man toward the Negro is incompatible with the fundamental ideas of the republic."[16] It remained for our Clevelands and Abbotts and Parkhursts to assure them that their unlawful course was right and justifiable, and for the most distinguished Negro leader to declare that "every revised Constitution throughout the Southern States has put a premium upon intelligence, ownership of property, thrift and character."[17] So does every penitentiary sentence put a premium upon good conduct; but it is poor consolation to the one unjustly condemned, to be told that he may shorten his sentence somewhat by good behavior. Dr. Booker T. Washington, whose language is quoted above, has, by his eminent services in the cause of education, won deserved renown. If he has seemed, at times, to those jealous of the best things for their race, to decry the higher education, it can easily be borne in mind that his career is bound up in the success of an industrial school; hence any undue stress which he may put upon that branch of education may safely be ascribed to the natural zeal of the promoter, without detracting in any degree from the essential value of his teachings in favor of manual training, thrift and character-building. But Mr. Washington's prominence as an educational leader, among a race whose prominent leaders are so few, has at times forced him, perhaps reluctantly, to express himself in regard to the political condition of his people, and here his utterances have not always been so wise nor so happy. He has declared himself in favor of a restricted suffrage, which at present means, for his own people, nothing less than complete loss of representation—indeed it is only in that connection that the question has been seriously mooted; and he has advised them to go slow in seeking to enforce their civil and political rights, which, in effect, means silent submission to injustice.[18] Southern white men may applaud this advice as wise, because it fits in with their purposes; but Senator McEnery of Louisiana, in a recent article in the *Independent*, voices the Southern white opinion of such acquiescence when he says: "What other race would have submitted so many years to slavery without complaint? *What other race would have submitted so quietly to disfranchisement?* These facts stamp his [the Negro's] inferiority to the white race."[19] The time to philosophize about the good there is in evil, is not while its correction is still possible, but, if at all, after all hope of correction is past. Until then it calls for nothing but rigorous condemnation. To try to read any good thing into these fraudulent Southern constitutions, or to accept them as an accomplished fact, is to condone a crime against one's race. Those who commit crime should bear the odium. It is not a pleasing spectacle to see the robbed applaud the robber. Silence were better.

It has become fashionable to question the wisdom of the Fifteenth Amendment. I believe it to have been an act of the highest statesmanship, based upon the fundamental idea of this Republic, entirely justified by conditions; experimental in its nature, perhaps, as every new thing must be, but just in principle; a choice between methods, of which it seemed to the great statesmen of that epoch the wisest and the best, and essentially the most just, bearing in mind the interests of the freedmen and the Nation, as well as the feelings of the Southern whites; never fairly tried, and therefore, not yet to be justly condemned. Not one of those who condemn it, has been able, even in the light of subsequent events, to suggest a better method by which the liberty and civil rights of the freedmen and their descendants could have been protected. Its abandonment, as I have shown, leaves this liberty and these rights frankly without any guaranteed protection. All the education which philanthropy or the State could offer as a *substitute* for equality of rights, would be a poor exchange; there is no defensible reason why they should not go hand in hand, each encouraging and strengthening the other. The education which one can demand as a right is likely to do more good than the education for which one must sue as a favor.

The chief argument against Negro suffrage, the insistently proclaimed argument, worn threadbare in Congress, on the platform, in the pulpit, in the press, in poetry, in fiction, in impassioned rhetoric, is the reconstruction period. And yet the evils of that period were due far more to the venality and indifference of white men than to the incapacity of black voters. The revised Southern constitutions adopted under reconstruction reveal a higher statesmanship than any which preceded or have followed them, and prove that the freed voters could as easily have been led into the paths of civic righteousness as into those of misgovernment. Certain it is that under reconstruction the civil and political rights of all men were more secure in those States than they have ever been since. We will hear less of the evils of reconstruction, now that the bugaboo has served its purpose by disfranchising the Negro. It will be laid aside for a time while the nation discusses the political corruption of great cities; the scandalous conditions in Rhode Island; the evils attending reconstruction in the Philippines, and the scandals in the postoffice department—for none of which, by the way, is the Negro charged with any responsibility, and for none of which is the restriction of the suffrage a remedy seriously proposed. Rhode Island is indeed the only Northern State which has a property qualification for the franchise!

There are three tribunals to which the colored people may justly appeal for the protection of their rights: the United States Courts, Congress and public opinion.

At present all three seem mainly indifferent to any question of human rights under the Constitution. Indeed, Congress and the Courts merely follow public opinion, seldom lead it. Congress never enacts a measure which is believed to oppose public opinion;—your Congressman keeps his ear to the ground. The high, serene atmosphere of the Courts is not impervious to its voice; they rarely enforce a law contrary to public opinion, even the Supreme Court being able, as Charles Sumner once put it, to find a reason for every decision it may wish to render; or, as experience has shown, a method to evade any question which it cannot decently decide in accordance with public opinion.[20] The art of straddling is not confined to the political arena. The Southern situation has been well described by a colored editor in Richmond: "When we seek relief at the hands of Congress, we are informed that our plea involves a legal question, and we are referred to the Courts. When we appeal to the Courts, we are gravely told that the question is a political one, and that we must go to Congress. When Congress enacts remedial legislation, our enemies take it to the Supreme Court, which promptly declares it unconstitutional."[21] The Negro might chase his rights round and round this circle until the end of time, without finding any relief.

Yet the Constitution is clear and unequivocal in its terms, and no Supreme Court can indefinitely continue to construe it as meaning anything but what it says. This Court should be bombarded with suits until it makes some definite pronouncement, one way or the other, on the broad question of the constitutionality of the disfranchising Constitutions of the Southern States. The Negro and his friends will then have a clean-cut issue to take to the forum of public opinion, and a distinct ground upon which to demand legislation for the enforcement of the Federal Constitution. The case from Alabama was carried to the Supreme Court expressly to determine the constitutionality of the Alabama Constitution. The Court declared itself without jurisdiction, and in the same breath went into the merits of the case far enough to deny relief, without passing upon the real issue. Had it said, as it might with absolute justice and perfect propriety, that the Alabama Constitution is a bold and impudent violation of the Fifteenth Amendment, the purpose of the lawsuit would have been accomplished and a righteous cause vastly strengthened.

But public opinion cannot remain permanently indifferent to so vital a question. The agitation is already on. It is at present largely academic, but is slowly and resistlessly, forcing itself into politics, which is the medium through which republics settle such questions. It cannot much longer be contemptuously or indifferently elbowed aside. The South itself seems bent upon forcing the question to an issue, as, by its arrogant assumptions, it brought on the Civil War. From that section, too, there come now and then, side by side with tales of Southern outrage, excusing voices, which at the same time are accusing voices; which admit that the white South is dealing with the Negro unjustly and unwisely; that the Golden Rule has been forgotten; that the interests of white men alone have been taken into account, and that their true interests as well are being sacrificed. There is a silent white South, uneasy in conscience, darkened in counsel, groping for the light, and willing to do the right. They are as yet a feeble folk, their voices scarcely audible above the clamor of the mob. May their convictions ripen into wisdom, and may their numbers and their courage increase! If the class of Southern white men of whom Judge Jones of Alabama, is so noble a representative, are supported and encouraged by a righteous public opinion at the North, they may, in time, become the dominant white South, and we may then look for wisdom and justice in the place where, so far as the Negro is concerned, they now seem well-nigh strangers. But even these gentlemen will do well to bear in mind that so long as they discriminate in any way against the Negro's equality of right, so long do they set class against class and open the door to every sort of discrimination, there can be no middle ground between justice and injustice, between the citizen and the serf.

It is not likely that the North, upon the sober second thought, will permit the dearly-bought results of the Civil War to be nullified by any change in the Constitution. So long as the Fifteenth Amendment stands, the *rights* of colored citizens are ultimately secure. There were would-be despots in England after the granting of Magna Charta; but it outlived them all, and the liberties of the English people are secure. There was slavery in this land after the Declaration of Independence, yet the faces of those who love liberty have ever turned to that immortal document. So will the Constitution and its principles outlive the prejudices which would seek to overthrow it.

What colored men of the South can do to secure their citizenship to-day, or in the immediate future, is not very clear. Their utterances on political questions, unless they be to concede away the political rights of their race, or to soothe the consciences of white men by suggesting that the problem is insoluble except by some slow remedial process which will become effectual only in the distant future, are received with scant respect—could scarcely, indeed, be otherwise received, without a voting constituency to back them up,—and must be cautiously made, lest they meet an actively hostile reception. But there are many colored men at the North, where their civil and political rights in the main are respected. There every honest man has a vote, which he may freely cast, and which is reasonably sure to be fairly counted. When this race develops a sufficient power of combination, under adequate leadership,—and there are signs already that this time is near at hand,—the Northern vote can be wielded irresistibly for the defense of the rights of their Southern brethren.

In the meantime the Northern colored men have the right of free speech, and they should never cease to demand their rights, to clamor for them, to guard them jealously, and insistently to invoke law and public sentiment to maintain them. He who would be free must learn to protect his freedom. Eternal vigilance is the price of liberty.[22] He who would be respected must respect himself. The best friend of the Negro is he who would rather see, within the borders of this republic one million free citizens of that race, equal before the law, than ten million cringing serfs existing by a contemptuous sufferance. A race that is willing to survive upon any other terms is scarcely worthy of consideration.

The direct remedy for the disfranchisement of the Negro lies through political action. One scarcely sees the philosophy of distinguishing between a civil and a political right. But the Supreme Court has recognized this distinction and has designated Congress as the power to right a political wrong. The Fifteenth Amendment gives Congress power to enforce its provisions. The power would seem to be inherent in government itself; but anticipating that the enforcement of the Amendment might involve difficulty, they made the supererogatory declaration. Moreover, they went further, and passed laws by which they provided for such enforcement. These the Supreme Court has so far declared insufficient. It is for Congress to make more laws. It is for colored men and for white men who are not content to see the blood-bought results of the Civil War nullified, to urge and direct public opinion to the point where it will demand stringent legislation to enforce the Fourteenth and Fifteenth Amendments. This demand will rest in law, in morals and in true statesmanship; no difficulties attending it could be worse than the present ignoble attitude of the Nation toward its own laws and its own ideals— without courage to enforce them, without conscience to change them, the United States presents the spectacle of a Nation drifting aimlessly, so far as this vital, National problem is concerned, upon the sea of irresolution, toward the maelstrom of anarchy.

The right of Congress, under the Fourteenth Amendment, to reduce Southern representation can hardly be disputed. But Congress has a simpler and more direct method to accomplish the same end. It is the sole judge of the qualifications of its own members, and the sole judge of whether any member presenting his credentials has met those qualifications. It can refuse to seat any member who comes from a district where voters have been disfranchised; it can judge for itself whether this has been done, and there is no appeal from its decision.[23]

If, when it has passed a law, any Court shall refuse to obey its behests, it can impeach the judges. If any president refuse to lend the executive arm of the government to the enforcement of the law, it can impeach the president. No such extreme measures are likely to be necessary for the enforcement of the Fourteenth and Fifteenth Amendments—and the Thirteenth, which is also threatened—but they are mentioned as showing that Congress is supreme; and Congress proceeds, the House directly, the Senate indirectly,[24] from the people and is governed by public opinion. If the reduction of Southern representation were to be regarded in the light of a bargain by which the Fifteenth Amendment was surrendered, then it might prove fatal to liberty. If it be inflicted as a punishment and a warning, to be followed by more drastic measures if not sufficient, it would serve a useful purpose. The Fifteenth Amendment declares that the right to vote *shall not* be denied or abridged on account of color; and any measure adopted by Congress should look to that end. Only as the power to injure the Negro in Congress is reduced thereby, would a reduction of representation protect the Negro; without other measures it would still leave him in the hands of the Southern whites, who could safely be trusted to make him pay for their humiliation.

Finally, there is, somewhere in the Universe a "Power that works for righteousness,"[25] and that leads men to do justice to one another. To this power, working upon the hearts and consciences of men, the Negro can always appeal. He has the right upon his side, and in the end the right will prevail. The Negro will, in time, attain to full manhood and citizenship throughout the United States. No better guaranty of this is needed than a comparison of his present with his past. Toward this he must do his part, as lies within his power and his opportunity. But it will be, after all, largely a white man's conflict, fought out in the forum of the public conscience. The Negro, though eager enough when opportunity offered, had comparatively little to do with the abolition of slavery, which was a vastly more formidable task than will be the enforcement of the Fifteenth Amendment.

‿

SOURCE: "The Disfranchisement of the Negro," *The Negro Problem* (N.Y.: James Pott & Co., 1903), 79–124; printed in "September, 1903" (copyright page); published *circa* 16 September when a copy of the bound volume was sent to Chesnutt. The text has been emended in light of Chesnutt's corrections in his copy of the galley proof, at the Library of the Western Reserve Historical Society.

[1]Proverbs 12:10.

[2]Sir Isaac Newton (1642–1727), English mathematician and scientist.

[3]In Williams v. Mississippi, the U.S. Supreme Court ruled in 1898 that Mississippi's voter registration requirements, including the demonstration of the ability to comprehend a portion of the state constitution of 1890, did not violate the Fifteenth Amendment since they did not deny to anyone the right to vote because of race or color; that is, they "do not on their face discriminate between the races, and it has not been shown [by the plaintiff] that their actual administration was evil, only that evil was possible under them." Williams was appealing his criminal conviction on the grounds that his jury was wrongly composed: jurors were chosen from a list of registered voters; African Americans were deliberately excluded from the list; and thus his jury was without authority.

[4]In the galley proof and the published essay, the reference is to "Jackson vs. Giles"; but Jackson W. Giles, the Montgomery Alabamian not permitted to register as a voter, was the plaintiff and E. Jeff Harris *et al.* were the defendants. At issue was Giles's being prevented from registering in 1902, prior to 1 January 1903 when new state constitutional requirements (concerning literacy, regular employment, and property ownership) would become effective. The U.S. Supreme Court decision described by Chesnutt was rendered in Giles v. Harris, 189 U.S. 475, submitted without oral argument by Wilford H. Smith on 24 February 1903 and decided on 27 April. The statement to which Chesnutt alludes reads: "Apart from damages to the individual [Giles had claimed financial losses as well as the deprivation of his rights under the Fourteenth and Fifteenth Amendments], relief from a great political wrong, if done, as alleged, by the people of a state and the state itself, must be given by them or by the legislative and political department of the government of the United States." After the publication of "The Disfranchisement," Giles, once more represented by Smith, again approached the U.S. Supreme Court, with as little success. After oral argument on 5 January 1904, it decided on 23 February that it did not have the "right to review the action of the state court," and it cited its previous decision as having already made clear the "great difficulty of

reaching the political action of a state through remedies afforded in the courts, state or Federal" (Giles v. Teasley, 193 U.S. 146).

[5]See "Peonage, or the New Slavery."

[6]Two years earlier, Chesnutt first used this datum provided by W. E. B. Du Bois; see "The Negro's Franchise," n. 4.

[7]The statement "Taxation without representation is tyranny" has been attributed to colonial lawyer, activist, and patriot James Otis (1725–83). He wrote "No parts of His Majesty's dominions can be taxed without their consent" in his *Rights of the Colonies* (1764).

[8]That is, slaves are not citizens and cannot exercise the rights of citizens.

[9]The number of members of the U.S. House of Representatives that a state could elect was then determined by its number of adult males, i.e., those qualified to vote. Disfranchisement had, however, not resulted in the diminution of any state's representation, as Chesnutt notes below. See also n. 23.

[10]Even among sympathetic white Northerners this had become a commonplace point of view expressed in liberal periodicals. Chesnutt here makes the first of several oblique and direct references to Booker T. Washington's perspective on this matter. Immediately prior to the publication of "The Disfranchisement," Chesnutt energetically initiated an epistolary debate with Washington on this subject. See *Letters*, ed. McElrath and Leitz, 181–83 and 185–91. See also his comments after the publication of "The Disfranchisement," 194–98.

[11]Shortly after the passage of the Fifteenth Amendment in 1870, discussion of its repeal was initiated in earnest in the South, and the possibility was frequently alluded to as disfranchisement became more widespread. In 1900 at a Montgomery, Ala., conference on the race problem attended by Booker T. Washington, the desirability of repealing the amendment was the subject of debate; and Chesnutt corresponded with Washington concerning what had transpired, requesting more information about the conference than could be found in the periodicals available to him. See *Letters*, 147–48.

[12]*Hamlet*, 3.2.66–67.

[13]Oliver Goldsmith (1730?–74), *She Stoops to Conquer* (1773).

[14]Adaptation of the proverb "Time heals all wounds."

[15]*Henry IV, Part 1*, 1.3.56.

[16]Chesnutt did not begin to write "The Disfranchisement" before 5 February 1903, and he mailed the manuscript to his publisher on June 16. Thus, when it appeared in print in mid-September 1903, the reference to a "recent number" of the Charleston *Evening Post* was considerably dated. The statement quoted—which is not a criticism of Southern whites—appeared in "First Principles," 4 April 1903, 3. This was one of many editorials criticizing President Roosevelt's appointment of African-American physician William D. Crum (1859–1912) as Collector of Customs at the Port of Charleston. While this editorial was not dedicated to the franchise issue, numerous others made clear the pro-disfranchisement attitude of this newspaper; see, for example, "Fifteenth Amendment Dead," 30 April 1903, 3, and "Make a Clean Sweep of It," 5 May 1903, 3. Further, an untitled editorial (11 May 1903, 3) praised the liberal-minded minister Charles H. Parkhurst for publicly lamenting the enfranchisement of the African American; it opined that this Northerner sympathetic to the African-American cause "has for once . . . become really rational."

[17]Former U.S. President Grover Cleveland was a Democrat, and during both of his terms (1885–89 and 1893–97) the disfranchisement movement headed by Southern Democrats proceeded unopposed by him. More specifically, Chesnutt appears to refer to a speech he made on 14 April 1903. Cleveland proclaimed the failure of suffrage as a means of uplifting African Americans to an appropriate level of responsible citizenship.

Southern Negrophobes were delighted; a *New York Sun* article on Cleveland's remarks was gleefully reprinted as "The Burden Bearers" in the relentlessly anti-franchise Charleston, S.C., *Evening Post*, 20 May 1903, 3. Like The Reverend Charles H. Parkhurst who came to regret that African Americans had been give the right to vote (see "The Negro's Franchise," n. 5), Lyman Abbott (1832–1927) was a reform-minded minister who did not see African-American suffrage as the immediate, first-priority concern that it was for Chesnutt. Like Booker T. Washington, whose *Up from Slavery* (1901) he serialized in the politically liberal magazine he edited, *Outlook*, Abbott focused on the ways Southern blacks could obtain the right to vote by properly educating themselves and proving themselves both socially and economically qualified to exercise the franchise. Particularly galling to Chesnutt was Abbott's "The Race Problem," *Outlook*, 73 (14 March 1903), 607–10, in which it was suggested that white Southerners were best qualified to manage their region's affairs. It declared that, at "no time since the Civil War has the eventual solution of the race problem seemed to us so hopeful as it seems to-day"; Abbott was convinced that Southerners "are trying to solve this problem on principles consonant with justice and freedom." See *Letters*, 181, where Chesnutt criticizes Abbott for this stance. The "most distinguished Negro leader" to whom Chesnutt refers is Booker T. Washington.

[18]In *Up from Slavery*, Washington made both of these points: "I cannot help feeling that it would have been wiser if some plan could have been put in operation which would have made the possession of a certain amount of education or property, or both, a test for the exercise of the franchise . . . to apply honestly and squarely to both the white and black races"; and, "I believe it is the duty of the Negro . . . to deport himself modestly in regard to political claims, depending upon the slow but sure influences that proceed from the possession of property, intelligence, and high character. . . . I think that the according of the full exercise of political rights is going to be a matter of natural, slow growth, not an over-night, gourd-vine affair."

[19]Samuel D. McEnery (1837–1910), "Race Problem in the South," *Independent*, 55 (February 1903), 424–30. The clarification in brackets of "his" is Chesnutt's.

[20]Charles Sumner was an abolitionist not given to compromises when high moral principle was at stake, and—after the Civil War while continuing to serve in the U.S. Senate—he remained as radical when legislatively ensuring full civil rights for African Americans in the South.

[21]John R. Mitchell (1863–1929) was the editor of the *Richmond* (Va.) *Planet*. A frequent critic of the U.S. Supreme Court, he expressed this opinion in "Another Decision," 2 May 1903, 4.

[22]While this statement has often been attributed to Thomas Jefferson, there is no record of his having spoken or written it. Chesnutt is most likely making a conscious quotation of one of his abolitionist heroes, Wendell Phillips, who made this declaration before the Massachusetts Antislavery Society in an address entitled "Public Opinion" on 28 January 1852.

[23]The Fourteenth Amendment provides that the number of a state's representatives in Congress shall be reduced in proportion to the number of adult male citizens denied the right to vote. The "more direct method" of dealing with states in which disfranchisement has occurred is provided in article 1, section 5, of the U.S. Constitution: "Each House shall be the Judge of the Elections, Returns and Qualifications of its own Members. . . ."

[24]U.S. Senators were not directly elected until the Seventeenth Amendment was ratified in 1913.

[25]"God is a power not ourselves that makes for righteousness," Matthew Arnold (1822–88), *Literature and Dogma* (1873).

The Race Problem

Speech delivered in 1904

The problem which I am asked to discuss before you this afternoon is no new one. It began with the introduction of the first black slave into the British Colonies of North America. Never was human inconsistency attended with graver historical consequences than when Negro slavery was weakly and wickedly permitted to gain a firm foothold in a nation consecrated to liberty, the great bulk of whose population had fled far across the ocean to escape a far milder tyranny than to which they now condemned some thousands, destined, in the course of time, to become many millions, of their fellow men.

In its earlier development slavery could have been suppressed. Several colonies made a feeble effort to keep it out; slavery was forbidden, for instance, by the charter of Georgia.[1] There was no lack of warning of its bad morals, its menace to the safety and civilization of the nation. Washington recognized and deplored its evils; Jefferson pointed them out as clearly.[2] The debates in the Constitutional Convention which formed the first Constitution of the United States set out cogently the reasons why, humanly slavery should not be tolerated;[3] and the Constitution itself was a compromise with an acknowledged evil.[4] And while the South was most guilty, and bore the brunt of the burden, and suffered most severely both from the institution and its consequences, the sin was truly a national one, for which the nation has paid the penalty—is still paying it by steady installments. It has been paid in blood and treasure—read the statistics of the Civil War. 1,000,000 men killed and disabled to save the Union which slavery menaced—the life of one strong, white man for every three black men, women and children held in bondage.[5] 10,000 million dollars to free 3,000,000 million slaves—or $3,000.00 apiece for slaves who could have been bought in the open market, before the war began, for a fraction of the money![6] To say nothing of the enormous annual expenditure for pensions.

The Nation has paid for this sin in the retardation of national development. The South, with its delightful climate, should have been the garden spot of the Nation. On the contrary it is in little better than a semi-barbarous condition. The energies of the white people, which should be devoted to the promotion of good government, to the development of science, art, letters, are expended in the main in the promotion of schemes to prevent the rise of the Negro—as before the war they were devoted to the maintenance of slavery. Immigration shuns the South. The poorest European immigrant knows instinctively that there he will find neither money, nor education, nor larger liberty; and he prefers the severe Canadian winters, the harsh climate of our lake region, the bleakness of the wind-swept prairies to a more pleasant climate, because he does not care to live in communities where life is held cheap, where labor is despised, and where the opportunities for education are limited. I do not ignore the fact that there are good men in the South, and that some of them are making splendid efforts to improve present conditions especially in the matter of education. That freedom of speech is growing in the South is the most hopeful sign in a rather dreary outlook. Professor Sledd, Trinity College.[7] Judge Jones of Alabama. Old man Simpson.[8]

These are timely utterances, and invaluable as offsetting the ravings of the Tillmans, Vardamans, Dixons and others who have of late conducted so strenuous a campaign against the rights of colored men.[9] In the debasement of the fine ideals of "liberty, equality and fraternity" the Nation is still paying the penalty for slavery. And lest we should be at all vainglorious, there come such incidents as this lamentable affair in our own state, and the recent similar occurrences in Illinois and in Delaware, to warn us that our hands are not clean;[10] that as the North in earlier days compromised with evil, yielded to the urgent voice of the slaveholder, and permitted slavery to grow until it threatened national unity; so now, since it has sat passively and watched the legal degradation of a race, it must also share the punishment. If your son or your daughter should "go wrong," as the phrase is, you would bow your head in shame; nor would you accept, as any palliation of the offense, the excuse that others had done as bad or worse. What good citizen of Ohio, then, or what white man or woman proud of the race's achievements, can feel anything but humiliated at the spectacle of five hundred white men engaged in a brutal and unlawful murder? One black murderer—, five hundred white murderers, you can figure the ratio yourselves, and to whom it is favorable.

If I should discuss this problem before a colored audience, I should not need to tell them that their race is made the victim of injustice, for, it is part of their daily life. I should not need to tell them that their race, in spite of many obstacles has made rapid progress in wealth, in education, in a healthy unity of action, and in the development of capable leaders. These things they know, better than you could. They do not see, as do you, in considering their race, an occasional barber, or waiter, or bootblack, or much more rarely, a clerk or teacher or professional man and beyond these, through the mists of the daily press dispatches, a vast mass of besotted ignorance, steeped in crime. They view their people as a whole. They have a large and active newspaper press of their own, of which you know nothing. Several magazines. They know that the violent criminal is the rare exception among *them*, as among all peoples. When a Negro is lynched, they are not entirely dependent upon the associated press dispatches for their information concerning the event. When a Negro is lynched for the murder of a white man, they are apt to know *why* the white man was killed, and that the facts often justify the killing, by the rude code of ethics prevalent in the South. Even a black man might justly protect his wife or daughter, or defend his own life. I should not need to inflame their passions by recounting their wrongs; I should urge them to patience, and perseverance; to the manly and persistent as-

sertion of their rights in the proper place and at the proper time, and to the cultivation of a cheerful hope that all will be yet for the best. I should ask them to
believe that the great majority of white people wish them well, or at least wish
them no harm, and should cite to them the lives they have devoted to the service
of teaching, and the money they have spent in their elevation. But I am not addressing an audience of colored people, and I think there are other considerations to which your attention should be called.

(Your duty in the premises.)

I think it is safe to assume that you are all here because you realize that there
is something wrong about the national attitude toward the Negro, and that as
good citizens and as Christian men and women, you are anxious to know the
right, in order that you may the more effectively do it. I know, too, that your
minds are clouded by a multitude of diverse opinions; nor am I sanguine enough
to hope that they are entirely free from prejudice—and by that I mean the influence of ancestral tradition and current opinion. I know that able arguments are
presented every day by forceful writers, entirely of your own blood, to convince
you that the white race was ordained to overrun and rule the whole earth, and
that those who would resist them are flying in the face of Providence. I know
that ministers of Christ preach the gospel of human degradation, and justify it
by the necessity of preserving the white race to the world;—and that politicians
preach the same doctrine, from the necessity of preserving the world to the
white race. There are those who assure you, with solemn earnestness, that there
is no race problem, and that the Southern whites are the best friends of the Negro. Some assure you that education is the only remedy for existing evils, and
others that education only accentuates them.

And yet, in spite of all this diversity of view and forcefulness of argument, I
am convinced that you are anxious to know the right, and are groping about in
this cloud of conflicting opinions, in search of it.

I have said that I should try to impress upon you *your* duty, or the fact that
you have some duty in this matter, and it may not be amiss to recapitulate,
briefly, a few events which must, it seems to me, bring this duty home to you.
Events follow so thick and fast that I can mention only the more recent. Within
a few months the state of Kentucky has aimed a fatal blow at the usefulness of
Berea College.[11]

Governor Vardaman (Mississippi) elected on a platform of hostility to Negro education.[12] "Booker Washington should not vote." Maryland legislature
passed disfranchising measure; no excuse.[13]

Also passed Jim Crow car law.[14]

The Supreme Court has twice declined to interfere with Southern disfranchisement, holding itself powerless to enforce the Constitution.[15]

Two Negroes burned in Mississippi.[16] One rescued at a cost stated to be
$250,000.00. Another burned in Arkansas. Bishop Brown formerly of Cleve-
land lectures in Boston.[17] Culminating horror of the Springfield lynching. All di-

rected against the Negro. That these things suggest a serious evil no one will dispute. An occasional crime might be attributed to an epidemic. To say there is no remedy for them is to relinquish civilization, to give up religion, and to relapse into barbarism—black barbarians at one end, white barbarians at the other—hating one another merely because they are different and seeking one another's blood.

The popular reformer is he who presents a ready remedy; just as the quack who can cure headache in one minute, or consumption in three months, or the divine healer who thinks away an abscess or a broken leg. But for a deep seated constitutional evil, whether of the physical body or the body politic, there is no nostrum. The race problem is one which is easily susceptible of inadequate treatment. An eloquent representative of a colored school in the South appears before you and paints a moving picture of ignorance and squalor, which may be remedied by a contribution to his school. You are moved by the appeal. You take out your purse; you contribute according to your means or the strength of your emotion; and you go home with the comfortable feeling that you have done your duty and met your entire responsibility.

But it is apparent that a problem which ramifies through the whole social fabric—which involves the painful and difficult problem of race, of blood—which reaches questions of labor, and popular education, and social movement, the distribution of wealth, can not be settled by a few great schools for Negroes or even a wide-spread use of the spelling-book among black and white alike. The people who lynch Negroes at the North are presumably educated—if our school system means anything and in our Southern communities the best citizens are said to be active in these extra-judicial executions. The kind of education needed must strike its roots deeper. It belongs really in the higher realms of thought—in the field of religion and philosophy. This problem requires for adequate treatment the exercise of all the virtues. The enlightened pagans of the ancient world recognized four conditional virtues—Wisdom, Justice, Temperance, Courage. To these St. Paul added a glorious trinity in Faith, Hope and Charity. Jesus himself, in his philosophy of life, blessed the virtues of poverty of spirit, of hunger and thirst after righteousness, of mercy, of meekness, and of purity of heart.[18]

To rightly solve this problem which is thrusting itself upon us we need all the virtues.

Pardon me, then if I suggest a few respects in which you who are here present can do some thing now to bring about correct conditions in regard to these questions.

1. Try to think wisely and logically, banishing from your minds as far as possible any preconceived notions which are not consistent with the probability. When you read anything that is written or hear anything that is said upon these subjects, do not accept it off-hand, without examination; but weigh it in the light of history and experience, and then make up your mind in the light of

all that you have learned and reasoned out. Nothing is so dangerous as a half-truth, and on no subject are there more half-truths in circulation. A lie may be denied; a half-truth is much more subtle. If you will take an isolated group, or perhaps some particular community, it is easy to prove that all the women of any race are unchaste, that all the men are dishonest, that the whole human race is degenerate. You remember the traveler who looked out of the car window and saw a red-haired man and his two sons standing on the platform. He turned to his notebook and made the minute. "The people of this town have red hair." While he was writing, the train moved past a hundred people with black and yellow hair whom he did not see at all.

2. Cultivate justice, remembering that the hope of humanity still lies in the doctrine of the equality of all men before the law. Let no man's color or condition influence you to his injury. Justice is the root of civilization, as Peace is its flower. The Golden Rule is a safe guide. Do unto others as you would have them do unto you. If you could for a moment put yourself in the place of a black or brown man who thinks and feels and has studied history, you might be able to see what you would like others to do to you, and see whether your conduct comes up to the test. If you would do this, read that beautiful book *The Souls of Black Folk* (Du Bois).

3. Cultivate a little poverty of spirit. I presume that by the term is meant meekness. I have not, so far, said anything to you about the great and glorious race to which you belong. I do not need to flatter you; history tells of its wonderful achievements. But beware of attributing to yourself too much of the credit for this wonderful progress. Subtract from Anglo-Saxon civilization what it borrowed from Egypt, a Negroid country; from Arabia and Syria, from Greece and Rome—art, letters, philosophy, religion, government, and what would be left? Subtract from the wealth of the white world that which was inherited from past generations, and what would be left?

Colored people are sometimes charged with having little race pride. Race pride can only be founded on achievement, and the race has not been in a position, as yet to achieve a great deal. Pride of birth, if it carry with it a sense of responsibility and incitement to noble deeds, may be very valuable. But while looking down loftily upon the poor Negro who cannot disown or deny his origin, it would be well enough to remember, now and then, the peasant ancestor who packed his belongings in a handkerchief and braved the horrors of a voyage but little more comfortable than that of the middle passage[19] of the slave in order that they might find here a refuge from oppression. I have sometimes thought that a little Negro blood might not be a bad thing for that very reason—it promotes a humility which prevents us from doing injustice through pride and vainglory. *Memento mori—memento originis.*[20]

Exalt humanity above race. The most diverse races resemble in more things than they differ. Stanley.[21]

Respect for human life and human rights is the end and aim of civilization.

Color is an accident, humanity is a God-given attribute. We have carried the distinction between races so far that it has become wellnigh ludicrous, except for its serious consequences. In the South race is made a fetish. The whole fabric of society is regulated by it. Politics. Schools. Churches. Cars. Steamers. Hotels. Elevators. Telephones. Not quite reach the point of certain South African cities where natives are not permitted to walk upon the sidewalks. Negroes protect themselves in the matter of street cars. Reaching the national capital. Mount Vernon.

4. You must feel your responsibility. This problem is your problem. Your religion is on trial, and your civilization is at stake. You have the power of numbers. You have command of the world's accumulated resources, you control the avenues of human advancement. Men of your race, in open defiance of the Constitution, and with the acquiescence of your press and pulpit and Congress, have robbed the Southern colored people of all political power. The wisdom, the necessity of conferring the right of suffrage upon them is made clear by the article by Honorable Carl Schurz in *McClure's Magazine* for January.[22] The argument which influenced the really great statesman of a generation ago is even more forcible to-day, as it deals with the rights of the people who have a generation of liberty, and who see their rights taken away by arguments which were pushed aside even when they were slaves but just emerged from bondage. In the North their numbers are not great. They did not inherit the wealth of ages, nor even the fruits of their fathers' toil. They have scarcely begun to tap the store-houses of knowledge. But God is no respecter of persons; before him is neither bond nor free nor black nor white.[23] Before him you must give account for your dealings with those less fortunate. Upon you lies the responsibility of correcting the evils which your absorption in other things has permitted to grow up until they knock at your doors and threaten your civilization, as slavery threatened it a generation ago.

Our Supreme Court, in passing upon the disfranchisement cases to which I have referred, has said that the remedy for the conditions complained of in the South, is political rather than judicial. I do not follow the distinction. Political action can only result in the enactment of laws, which it is the province of Courts to enforce. I think what the Supreme Court means to say is that its function is to interpret and enforce the will of the people, and that it will not enforce a law which, though approved when made, has since become obnoxious. If this be true, then there remains but one method by which these wrongs can be righted—the creation of a wholesome public opinion which will demand political action. Every argument for the debasement of the Negro to-day, did duty in the strenuous days before the war, until an aroused and righteous public opinion swept them aside and destroyed the institution, and embodied certain great principles in a Constitution which I think will yet be held to mean what it says, which is, in effect, that before the law, the foundation of our liberties, as before God our Creator, there shall be no respect of persons. Courts, Congresses, Governors, Presidents, merely follow public opinion. This then is your high privilege and your solemn duty; to help make public opinion. If public opinion demand justice and fair play for all men—which it certainly does not in the United States to-day—then Courts and Congresses will exert themselves to secure justice and fair play for all men. Until that time, the strong will continue to oppress the weak, the rich will eat the poor, and the forces of selfishness will prevail over those of righteousness.

I have said very little about the Springfield lynching. I know that you share with me the horror and indignation of such a spectacle within the border of our commonwealth. This is an incident, as indeed as are all others like it, which might well be considered with no references to the question of race, were it not for the fact of the many similar things with which it is correlated, and the further fact that they are directed almost entirely against colored men. White criminals are not burned or otherwise lynched. But your duty here is concerned with something more important than the matter of race. Our laws are defied, our state disgraced, our civilization besmirched. Public officials have proved recreant to their duty. Our militia has traitorously turned its back upon its plain duty. Let us not neglect ours, which is equally plain. We should demand of our Governor and of those who execute our laws that they punish those who have thus disgraced us and reduced us a long way toward the level of Alabama or Mississippi. We should make our condemnation of mob murder so strong that not only will punishment be meted out to the guilty—and the cowardly sheriff is but little less guilty than the murderous mob—but we should make our condemnation so emphatic that any man who again feels tempted to join a mob, may see hanging over his head the shadow of the gallows. The South you can reach directly only through a distant Congress, to which you send only a few members, and which sits in a Southern community. Ohio is your own state; it is the place where your lives must be lived, where your children will be born and reared. Shall it maintain its reputation as a liberty loving, law abiding commonwealth, with just and liberal laws equitably administered; or shall our cities be at the mercy of any mob which may see fit to make some other man's sin an excuse for unleashing its own brutal passion? I know what your choice is of these alternatives, and I have no doubt that you perceive the only way of making it effective.

And finally, do not underestimate the persistence of evil. Some sins are like the head of Hydra, lopped off, only to spring forth again tenfold;[24] or like the roots of a tree which, after the trunk is cut down only await favorable conditions to project a new growth above the surface. I believe that modern theology has wellnigh abolished the personal devil; but it has not yet eradicated from human nature the tendencies which have been associated with that interesting personality. We had supposed that slavery and polygamy, a generation ago our twin relics of barbarism, had been eradicated from our midst. Yet at this moment our newspapers are filled with the revelation of conditions in Utah which show that plural marriage still flourishes in one of our sovereign states,[25] and the Courts of the United States have frequently been called upon during the past year to try cases of peonage, another form of slavery, now flourishing in many Southern communities. It will not do for us to sit down and do nothing in the pleasing hope that time will right every wrong, and the comfortable belief that civilization moves always steadily forward in a direct line. Far from it. After Greece and Rome we had the night of the Middle Ages. Each generation has a right to happiness, and the life of man is very fleeting. Eternal vigilance is the price of liberty—now as always. Civilization is earned at the sacrifice of self for the good of the whole.

You ladies have husbands and brothers and sons. If you see to it that every one of them shall condemn outspokenly every defiance of law; that they shall denounce every proposed violation of civic honor; that they shall uphold correct ideals of the sacredness of humanity and of human rights; that they shall be patient with the weak, charitable toward the unfortunate; that they shall insist upon just laws, applicable to all men alike and enforced impartially,—you will have done your duty and both you and they will be worthy of your heritage. Upon no other basis can a nation be truly great.

↩

SOURCE: Undated typed text at the Fisk University Library. Before which organization Chesnutt spoke is not known. But the text indicates that the audience was white and female; that the state in which the address was given was Ohio and the city or town was very likely close to Lake Erie; that Mississippi Governor Vardaman had recently given his January 1904 inauguration speech; and that the lynching that occurred at Springfield, O., on 7 March 1904 was fresh to memory, as was the 12 March approval of a disfranchisement referendum by the Maryland state legislature.

[1]Issued by George II (1683–1760) on 27 January 1732, the charter establishing Georgia as a proprietary colony granted absolute authority to twenty-one trustees, of whom the most famous was James Edward Oglethorpe (1696–1785), with no provision for a colonial legislature. On 9 January 1735, they approved a statute prohibiting slavery.

[2]The attitudes of both were not so amenable to easy description as Chesnutt implies. Most historians support Chesnutt's contention that Washington engaged in slavery only reluctantly; he was the only founding father who provided in his will for the manumission of his slaves. Jefferson viewed slavery as certain to lead to catastrophic consequences; but, as much as he disapproved of it, he both recognized the unlikelihood of its being abolished in his time and viewed as unrealistic the hopes of those who called for a radical alteration of the status quo in slavery-based economies.

[3]Many delegates at the 25 May–17 September 1787 Constitutional Convention, who themselves owned slaves but felt the institution was morally reprehensible, condemned slavery. For example, George Mason (1725–92) was a wealthy Virginia delegate and experienced legislator who organized opposition to the newly drafted U.S. Constitution. He refused to sign it without a bill of rights and a formal denunciation of slavery.

[4]Chesnutt may be referring to the "three-fifths" compromise which, once it was accepted by Southern representatives at the Constitutional Convention, became Article I, Section 2. It defines the apportionment of representation for individual states as a func-

tion of population, specifying that "three-fifths" the number of "all other Persons" (non-whites but excluding Native Americans) were to be added to the "Number of free Persons" in a state in order to determine a state's population. Or, he may have in mind the compromise that resulted in Article 1, Section 9, which prohibited the importation of slaves to the United States after 1808.

[5]According to statistics published by the U.S. Civil War Center, 970,227 soldiers died in battle or were wounded on both sides during the Civil War.

[6]This estimate doubles the cost of the Civil War, which the U.S. Civil War Center considers to have been $5.2 billion in 1865.

[7]Professor Andrew Sledd (1870–1939) taught Latin not at Trinity College but at Emory College (1898–1902) and Greek at Southern University in Greensboro, Alabama (1903–4). When the University of Florida was chartered in 1904 by the legislature, Sledd became its first president, returning to Emory—by then a university—in 1914 as a professor of New Testament and librarian of the Theological Department. Chesnutt may have read Sledd's article "The Negro: Another View," *Atlantic*, 90 (July 1902), 65–73. While it begins by admitting that "the negro belongs to an inferior race," it advocates the recognition of "fundamental rights" that should be enjoyed by all African Americans.

[8]Jeremiah ("Sockless Jerry") Simpson (1842–1905), a Kansan, was a well-known Populist and member of the U.S. House of Representatives whose slogan was "Equal rights to all, special privileges to none."

[9]Benjamin R. Tillman (1847–1918) served as Governor of South Carolina (1890–94) and as U.S. Senator (1894–1918). "Pitchfork Ben" was a white supremacist who advocated property and educational requirements for voting, called for the repeal of the Fifteenth Amendment, and justified lynching in cases of rape. James K. Vardaman (1861–1930) was a Mississippi state legislator and the successful 1904 gubernatorial candidate. His primary constituency comprised agriculturalists and poor whites; and he, too, was a well-known white supremacist. Thomas Dixon, Jr. (1864–1946), was a Baptist minister, lecturer, and novelist. His *The Leopard's Spots* (1902) was diametrically opposed in its point of view on blacks to Chesnutt's *The Marrow of Tradition*, published the previous year; he was the preeminent anti–"Negro Dominance" novelist at this time.

[10]A race riot in Springfield, O., culminated in the lynching of African-American Richard Dickinson on 7 March 1904. He had allegedly killed a white politician. Similar incidents had occurred on 23 July 1903 in Danville, Ill., and on 22 June 1903 in Wilmington, Del.: I. D. Mayfield, suspected of murder, was hanged; George White, suspected of rape and murder, was burned at the stake.

[11]House Bill 25, passed on 12 March, declared illegal the integration of the student body in any Kentucky school. Berea, long an integrated college, was seeking to have the law rendered null. The Kentucky Court of Appeals would view the law as constitutional in October 1906 (Berea College v. Commonwealth, 123 Ky. App. Ct. 209). Chesnutt discusses the U.S. Supreme Court's upholding of the decision in "The Courts and the Negro."

[12]On 19 January 1904, as the newly elected governor of Mississippi, Vardaman delivered an inaugural address in which he reiterated a theme of his campaign: that blacks should not be allowed to govern whites and that black children should not receive education comparable to that of white children.

[13]By 12 March 1904, both houses of the Maryland state legislature had approved a disfranchisement referendum to be voted on at the next general election.

[14]In 1904, Maryland adopted Article 27, Section 510, of its statutes, legalizing racial segregation in public conveyances.

[15]See "The Disfranchisement of the Negro," nn. 3 and 4.

[16]In Doddsville, Miss., on 7 February 1904, a posse burned at the stake Luther Holbert and his wife, holding both responsible for the death of a white landlord, a black tenant farmer, and four other African Americans.

[17]The Right Reverend William Montgomery Brown (1855–1937), Episcopal Bishop of Arkansas, had recently made sensational statements in support of lynching, reported in "The Week," *Nation*, 78 (25 February 1904), 140–41: "I extenuate the offense of lynching, for it is the only remedy for attacks on women"; "the South is obliged to lynch because women would not appear in court"; and "lynchers are justified in the sight of God, because lynching is a form of self-protection."

[18]Matthew 5:3–11.

[19]The crossing of the Atlantic Ocean from Africa.

[20]Remember that one must die—remember that one is born. Chesnutt thus fashions a Latinate restatement of the biblical adage, "for dust thou art, and unto dust shalt thou return," Genesis 3:19.

[21]Explorer Sir Henry Morton Stanley (1841–1904) traveled extensively on several continents, but best known is his exploration of Africa. *Through the Dark Continent* (1878) displays the tolerance and empathy called for by Chesnutt.

[22]"Can the South Solve the Negro Problem?" *McClure's Magazine*, 22 (January 1904), 259–75. Carl Schurz (1829–1906) was a German-born Civil War veteran, adviser on Reconstruction policy, politician, journalist, and newspaper editor. While some of his points of view may now be considered racist, he was known in Chesnutt's time for his sympathetic attitude toward African Americans.

[23]See "The Future of the Negro," n. 20, and Galatians 3:28..

[24]The second of Hercules's "twelve labors" was to slay the Hydra, a nine-headed snake. He found that one of the heads was immortal and that, when any one of the remaining eight was severed, two new ones appeared in its place.

[25]The Church of Jesus Christ of Latter-day Saints declared polygamy no longer an officially sanctioned practice on 6 October 1890. Thereafter it neither accepted nor endorsed plural marriage among its members, excommunicating those who persisted.

Peonage, or the New Slavery

Essay published in the *Voice of the Negro*, September 1904

Something more than a year ago the country was startled by the announcement that numerous indictments had been made in the Federal Court for the District of Alabama, for the crime of peonage. The dictionary failed to disclose the exact nature of this novel offense, but the facts stated in the news despatches made it clear that human slavery, with its most revolting features, was openly practiced, under color of local law, and in violation of a Federal statute, in certain remote districts of the South. The machinery of the crime was simple. By conspiracy between the officers of the law—justices and constables, mostly white men of the baser sort—and heartless employers, all white men—ignorant and friendless

Negroes were arrested on trumped up charges, fined to the full limit of harsh laws, sold at hard labor, worked under armed guards, cruelly flogged and kept in this worse form of slavery long after the fine and costs imposed upon them had been worked out.

By the efforts of the Department of Justice, at the suggestion of Federal Judge Jones of Alabama,[1] one of President Roosevelt's appointees, and at the personal instance of the President himself, it was ascertained and made known that this iniquitous system of involuntary servitude was flourishing widely and had been practiced for years in the "black belt" of Alabama and adjoining States, and was spreading to the upland counties. Convictions followed the indictments; many of the guilty were punished, and warning was given that the Federal Government would no longer tolerate this state of things. The State press acknowledged the existence of the evil, and declared that owing to local conditions and feeling upon the race question, the Federal Government alone was competent to deal adequately with it. So general was the condemnation of this new slavery that not even the morbid and diseased politics of the Southern States could find in it a political issue. There are still some indictments pending, but the crime, as far as can be seen at present, is no longer safe.

Now, why was this evil permitted to grow up? It was due, in the first place, to perfectly natural causes, and would have happened almost anywhere under like conditions. Nothing is slower than social movements. A form of government may be radically changed and laws easily enacted without modifying for a long period thereafter the social customs, the habits of thought, the feelings, in other words the genius, of a people. The labor system of the South had grown upon a basis of slavery, under which the black laborer worked for the benefit of the white masters, receiving as his hire merely the simplest necessaries of life; this not only by law but with the warrant of Scripture. Had not St. Paul written, "Servants, obey your masters"?[2] That a people who still retained to their former slaves the relation of employers, should immediately and cheerfully pay them a fair wage for their labor, was highly improbable. That there were just men who paid the market price is true enough, but the market price was inadequate. Fifteen dollars a month for a farm laborer who has to "find" himself,[3] is not a liberal wage. This is far more than the average Negro laborer receives.

Under the renting system, the crop mortgage laws leave the laborer but little more than a slave to the soil, while at its worst the Southern labor system presents peonage, or the new slavery. The old habit of making the Negroes work for the white people for their board and clothes has in large measure survived. Enough Negroes have risen above this level to present a remarkable average of industrial progress, but the majority are still subject in one way or another to the old rule.

This continuity of social custom is sufficient in part to account for the survival of slavery in some modified form. When to this is added the temptation of greed and cunning to take advantage of poverty and ignorance, it is not strange that peonage should exist. Taking into account the artificial solidarity of the white South on all questions relating to the rights of the Negro and in all matters between white and black, it is easily seen why the State Courts were inadequate to cope with the evil. The individuals who bribe constables and justices to arrest ignorant and friendless Negroes and sentence them to servitude, are the same men who, in a more northern latitude, would exploit imported foreign work-men in factories and sweatshops, or immature white children in the cotton mills, and bribe legislatures and city councils to betray the rights of the people and grind the faces of the poor in the interest of their own selfish greed.

The only sure preventive of the recurrence of slavery in some other form is the development of the Negro. No one will seek to rob those whom he knows are abundantly able to defend themselves. But pending this slow development which is to result from greater learning and growing thrift and larger liberty, just laws impartially administered can curb the greed of evil men. If this impar-tial enforcement of law does not come from within it must be sought without. The time is not far distant when there will exist among Southern white men a body of thought which will demand justice for Southern black men. They will not all agree as to what that justice shall consist of, and their views on the sub-ject will enlarge as the years go by, but they will demand, first and unanimously, fair play in the courts and just treatment of the labor upon which the prosperity of the South depends. When this influence is strong enough, the South may safely be left to wash its own dirty linen; but in the meantime it is in the hands of unfriendly white men, and it has been left to the Federal Government, under the administration of President Roosevelt, to expose this peonage iniquity and stretch out the long arm of the Nation to punish and prevent it. There is such a thing as national citizenship, and there should be lodged in the power of the government the right to protect it. This question of peonage, involving as it does the simplest and most fundamental elements of citizenship, has an important bearing on the attitude of colored voters in the presidential campaign. The Democratic party has nominated for President an able candidate, upon a plat-form in some respects admirable. There is no reason to believe that Judge Parker[4] would personally be anything but friendly to the colored race and just in his dealings with colored men. The National Republican party has of late done little to protect the rights of the Negro, and its platforms and policies, given over to a rampant commercialism and dreams of empire, no longer ring true to its old ideals. No colored voter owes the present Republican party anything. But he does owe to Theodore Roosevelt who stands for the open door of opportunity his unqualified support. When a Negro votes in the coming Presidential elec-tion, it should be with an eye single[5] to the future welfare of his race. This ought to be synonymous with the welfare of the Republic; if it is not so in every par-ticular, it is surely not the Negro's fault. He is quite willing to ignore questions of race, in politics and elsewhere, whenever the white people see fit to do so.

The Negro cannot trust the Democratic party on the vital questions of his rights. The Southern Democracy, where lies the main strength of the party, is frankly hostile to his rights and would if possible limit them still more. Thinking colored men can only view with apprehension the prospect of a cabinet dominated by the Gormans, Tillmans, Vardamans, or others of their kind.[6] With all its shortcomings the Republican party, by virtue of its traditions, and in view of the large Northern colored vote, cannot afford to be actively unfriendly to the Negro. It might be still more indifferent and still be the lesser of the two evils.

But the chief reason why colored men who vote will support the Republican ticket in the coming campaign lies in the personality of the candidates. President Roosevelt and his appointees in the Federal Courts have made a strong effort to break up the new slavery ere it became firmly established, and in many other ways the President has endeavored to stem the tide of prejudice, which, sweeping up from the South, has sought to overwhelm the Negro everywhere; and he has made it clear that he regards himself as the representative of all the people. The influence of the executive is greater in the nation than ever before. The opponents of President Roosevelt criticise him as impulsive; his impulses are friendly toward the colored race. He is said to be impolitic in his attitude upon the race question; his impolicy in that regard has been in the line of justice and generosity. We have nothing to hope for from the national Democratic party; its success in the present campaign would be a menace to our liberty. With four more years of a courageous and friendly executive, the South will have time for a sober second thought on its attitude towards the Negro; the Southern party friendly to human rights will have time to grow, and the colored race will be stronger to resist oppression, and to press its claim for justice at the hands of the party it supports.

⌒

SOURCE: "Peonage, or the New Slavery," *Voice of the Negro*, 1 (September 1904), 394–97.

[1]Thomas G. Jones.

[2]Colossians 3:22.

[3]The one-word quotation is from a poem, "The Absent-Minded Beggar" (1899), written by Rudyard Kipling (1865–1936) and set to music the same year by Sir Arthur Sullivan (1842–1900). Chesnutt seeks to bring to mind these two lines: "He's an absent-minded beggar, and his weaknesses are great— / But we and Paul must take him as we find him."

[4]Alton Brooks Parker (1852–1926) served as Chief Justice of the New York State Court of Appeals from 1897 to 1904. In 1904 he was the Democrat candidate for the U.S. presidency. A conservative representing an alternative to Theodore Roosevelt's progressivism, Parker was decisively defeated in the election.

[5]Matthew 6:22.

[6]Arthur P. Gorman (1839–1906) began his fourth term as a U.S. Senator from Maryland in 1903. A Democrat, in 1890 he successfully recruited Republicans favoring a silver standard for the U.S. currency to defeat the Force Bill intended to establish federal supervision of elections. Chesnutt thus views him as representative of those determined to disfranchise African Americans.

For Roosevelt

Essay published in the *Cleveland Gazette*, 22 October 1904

I am unable to conceive how any Negro voter in the United States, who has the interests of his race at heart, can support the Democratic national ticket in the approaching election.[1] No one would more readily than I concede the advantage which it would be to the Negro in the United States to have the vote of his race so divided that no partisan question could be raised in respect to it. There has been a time, perhaps, when such a division was at least possible, had the Negro voters been mere calculating machines, and not men of flesh and blood, with a lively memory of past benefits and a very natural resentment for past injuries. But, whatever may be said of the past, the present is certainly no time to go following after strange political gods.[2]

It is a great pity that Negro men should not feel free to choose their political party in the same way as other voters do. There would doubtless be some pronounced difference of opinion among them on the questions, for instance, of Philippine independence, and the course of the administration in respect to the Panama Canal; the question of trusts; and the question of a protective tariff; the relations of capital and labor. These are real, vital issues, which closely concern the national prosperity, and which every good citizen ought to consider carefully and seek in each case the right conclusion. But vital as these questions are, they fade into insignificance beside the issue of Negro rights—human rights—which the Democratic party has injected into this campaign, and which it has put to the front in every recent state election.

The strength of the Democratic party lies in the Southern states, from which any Democratic candidate for president must receive the bulk of his support. The Democratic South is frankly and aggressively hostile to Negro rights. A vote for Parker and Davis is a vote to give Tillman and Vardaman and Graves and Williams and those whom they represent, a right to be heard in the councils of a Democratic administration.[3] It is not easy to believe that a president, however well intentioned or well grounded in correct political principles he may be, could remain uninfluenced by those to whom he owes his election. The Negroes, poor, disorganized, disfranchised, comparatively few in number,—are not without their influence in the Republican party; is it conceivable that the powerful and aggressive Southern majority of the Democratic party would be without a strong, if not even a commanding influence, in a Democratic administration? And is it conceivable that in view of the anti-Negro legislation of the past ten years, and of the violent utterances of the recognized spokesmen of the Southern democracy, that their influence would be anything but actively and virulently hostile to the political and civil rights, the proper ambitions, and the higher aspirations of the Negro race?

The Republican party has been lukewarm in regard to the rights of the Negro, but it has not antagonized them in any instance, except in the case of the curious fungus growth known as the "Lily White" Republican of the Southern states,[4] which has received small encouragement under the present administration. Many Negroes still serve the government in its various departments, and the Republican party, however it may have fallen behind in practice, has never abandoned the theory of equality before the law. Moreover, the Republican party is the Negro's party, and by retaining his standing as a vital element of it, he can command in some small degree its influence for his protection.

So much for the parties.

But the Negro finds another reason for voting for the Republican ticket, in the personality of its presidential candidate. President Roosevelt has declared in clear[5] terms that he is in favor of equal citizenship and equal opportunity for all men in the United States, and he has in many instances proved his faith by his works. The most violent criticism to which he has been subjected has been because of his fair and friendly attitude toward the Negro. The man with one drop of black blood who would vote against him, and to place the destinies of this nation for four years to come in the hands, or even subject to the direct influence, of the horde of Negro-burning, Negro-hating, Negro-disfranchising and "Jim Crow"-ing Democratic politicians of the South, is, not to mince words, both an ingrate and a fool.

~

SOURCE: This essay may have been of greater length when it was first published in an issue of the *New York Age* that has not survived. The source text is a subsequent publication in another African-American weekly: "For Roosevelt," *Cleveland Gazette*, 22 (October 1904), 1. The remainder of the headlines, the dateline, and the introduction read:

———

AND THE REPUBLICAN PARTY,
AS USUAL, AND SOME
GOOD REASONS

———

Why This is the Position of the Loyal
Afro-American—Charles W. Chesnutt,
Esq., States the Case, Concisely
and Plainly—Read It Carefully
and Thoughtfully.

———

New York City.—The following appeared in a recent issue of the *Age* and ought to, for an obvious reason, prove exceptionally interesting to *The Gazette's* readers in Cleveland and throughout Ohio:

[1]President Theodore Roosevelt—completing the assassinated William McKinley's term in 1904—was the Republican candidate for the U.S. presidency. In November he would defeat conservative Democrat Alton B. Parker, as well as the Socialist Party candidate, Eugene V. Debs (1855–1926).

[2]Genesis 35:2. For decades the advice proffered to African Americans was that they should not allow any political party to take their vote for granted, but should use it to exact the aid of the one that offered them the best terms. That the black vote was overwhelmingly Republican was seen as one of the reasons that the "solid South" Democrats dismissed African Americans as a group whose rights and needs should be taken into consideration by them.

[3]Former U.S. Senator for West Virginia Henry G. Davis (1823–1916) was the Democrat nominee for the vice-presidency. John Temple Graves (1856–1925) was a Georgian journalist and politician whose 1889 eulogy for the late white supremacist Henry W. Grady made him so popular that he became a professional lecturer. He became a well-known advocate of deporting African Americans to Africa; and his animosity would be widely viewed as one of the factors contributing to the 1906 race riot in Atlanta. John Sharp Williams (1854–1932), a Mississippian, served in the U.S. House of Representatives and the Senate; in 1904 he was a powerful Democrat who influenced his party's platform, championing the ideology of the conservative faction.

[4]"Lily White" Republicans sided with Democrats, breaking rank with Republicans who were not antagonistic to African-American interests.

[5]Emended is the source text reading "in terms."

The Literary Outlook

Speech given at a banquet honoring Booker T. Washington,
Cleveland, O., 13 January 1905

Mrs. Chairman, Ladies and Gentlemen:

In the few moments at my command this evening I shall discuss the subject assigned to me from its point of special interest to us as a people. Colored men in literature are not unknown in other lands, and in the instances where they have achieved fame it has been of a high and enduring kind. To mention merely a few of them, just a few months ago the people of Russia celebrated the centenary—the one hundredth anniversary of the birth—of their famous poet, Alexander Pushkin, known as the Russian Shakespeare. Pushkin's grandfather was first a slave, later an officer at the court of Peter the Great. He married a woman of noble blood, and his descendants belonged therefore to the aristocracy of Russia. Pushkin was a poet as well as a prose writer of rare genius, and his considerable body of literary work would doubtless have been greatly augmented had he not died immaturely in a duel fought at the age of thirty-eight.[1] One of his grandchildren is the wife of a Russian Grand Duke.

Perhaps the most distinguished French literary family, the Dumas family, as you must all know, was of Negro extraction.[2] General Dumas, a hero of the revolutionary wars, was the mulatto son of a French marquis; his son became Alexander Dumas, the elder, the author of *The Count of Monte-Cristo*, *The*

Three Musketeers, and a great body of romantic fiction, of which he might be called the founder.

His son, Alexander Dumas the younger, shone in the same field, and is ranked as one of the two or three best dramatists of the nation which has produced most of the dramatic work of Europe. It was my privilege, upon a visit some years ago to Paris, to visit the graves of these distinguished men and to see their statues in bronze and marble in the public places of that great city, the center of art and taste.

Crossing the ocean to our own country, our friend Mr. Daniel Murray, of the Library of Congress, has compiled a list of 2,000 volumes written by colored writers.[3] Many of these of course are of little merit from a literary standpoint. From another point of view, the least of them is not without value. For literature, after all, is but an expression of life. Men write books as the trees put forth leaves, in obedience to the creative instinct. The humblest of these pamphlets, brought out upon obscure printing presses in the days of oppression, voicing the woes of the slave, the yearnings of the captive spirit, has a value, to the sympathetic spirit, all its own. But many of the last have been well worthy of consideration.

As far back as the Revolutionary period, Phyllis Wheatley, the poet, a slave girl brought from Africa, and reared in a New England household, wrote verses which won the respect and admiration of the cultured people of her day, including even the great Washington himself, who did not scorn to address a courteous letter of compliment to a lowly black girl.[4]

But a few years later Benjamin Banneker, a learned Negro and a civil engineer by profession, wrote an *Almanac*, in an age when almanacs were works of trained mathematicians and not mere drugstore advertisements—a work which brought him to the attention of Thomas Jefferson, President of the United States, by whom he was employed to assist in the engineering work of laying out the city of Washington. I may remark in passing that Mr. Banneker had the honor of dining at the table of President Jefferson more than a hundred years ago, when slavery still overshadowed the land, more than a hundred years before our distinguished guest this evening, by accepting a similar invitation from another president, so disturbed the equanimity of a nation in which slavery has been for a generation abolished.[5]

A generation later the immortal Frederick Douglass, in his *Autobiography*, added a work of enduring interest to the annals of the slavery epoch. Nearer our own day, Mr. William Still prepared an interesting record of the labors of the underground railroad; the brilliant but erratic George W. Williams contributed to the country's literature a painstaking and copious history of the Negro race.[6]

Not however till our own day can colored men be said to have pruned their wings for flight in the upper realms of literary effort. Of the few who have essayed this, Mr. Paul Laurence Dunbar was among the first to spring a full fledged poet into the literary arena. His lyrics are read with pleasure in thousands of American households and have won him an enduring place among the poets of America. With my own efforts in the field of imaginative literature you are doubtless more or less familiar—and I might say, since I receive a royalty upon every copy sold, that they ought to be in every library. Dr. Du Bois, who has the brain of a philosopher combined with the soul of a poet, has contributed a history of the African slave trade to the Harvard Historical Series, and has prepared many statistical works upon the life and progress of the Negro in America, and his latest work, *The Souls of Black Folk*, has been widely read, as voicing the aspirations of an oppressed but aspiring people.

And last but not least, our distinguished guest, Dr. Washington, has added to his other talents, that of authorship. His autobiography, *Up From Slavery*, is numbered as among the most interesting of the class of volumes known as human documents which record the lives of great men. Already it has been translated into eight foreign languages, and other lands seek in its direct, simple, forceful style, inspiration and aspiration for the humble toward better things.

My time will not permit me to go into greater detail, or I might mention many others who have written wisely & well.[7] As I have said, literature is an expression of life. And as the life of our people grows broader and deeper and higher, so its literature will expand and become riper and finer and more enduring. And in due time, and that I trust not long hence, works of men of Negro blood shall by common consent be ranked among those books which represent the finest fruit of American civilization.

~

SOURCE: Untitled typed text at the Fisk University Library. Chesnutt gave this speech at Cleveland's Woodliff Hall on 13 January 1905 during a banquet honoring Booker T. Washington. The event was sponsored by two of the city's prominent literary clubs, the Minerva Reading Circle and the Friday Study Club. An edited version of this speech appeared in "Dr. Booker T. Washington Banqueted," *Cleveland Journal*, 21 January 1905, 1. This publication was derived from a copy of the source text, which was prepared as a press release that began thus: "Mr. Charles W. Chesnutt spoke upon 'The Literary Outlook' as follows:—" "Literary Outlook" is here adopted as the title in light of both this introduction to Chesnutt's remarks and the specification of the same title in "'Nigger' Stories!" *Cleveland Gazette*, 21 January 1905, 1.

[1]Pushkin's maternal great-grandfather, Abram Petrovich Hannibal (1697–1781), was Abyssinian, i.e., Ethiopian; by his own admission, he went to Russia of his own free will and not as a slave. He was a favorite of Peter the Great (1672–1725) and was given an engineering post in the army. Pushkin claimed that his aristocratic ancestry could be traced over six hundred years.

[2]See "Race Ideals and Examples" and "Alexander Dumas," in both of which Chesnutt describes in detail the Dumas family.

[3]Daniel Alexander Payne Murray (1852–1925), Assistant Librarian at the Library of Congress (1881–1923), compiled a *Preliminary List of Books and Pamphlets by Negro Authors for Paris Exposition and Library of Congress* (1900).

[4]Phillis Wheatley (c. 1753–84), the author of *Poems on Various Subjects, Religious and Moral* (1773), was purchased by Boston merchant John Wheatley (?–1778) in 1761 and reared in his household. After the publication of "To His Excellency General

Washington" in *Pennsylvania Magazine* in April 1776, she was invited to visit Washington at Cambridge, Mass.

[5]Benjamin Banneker (1731–1806), a self-taught mathematician and astronomer, was a scientific assistant in the 1791 survey of the Federal Territory. That year he sent Thomas Jefferson, then Secretary of State, a copy of his first almanac, *Benjamin Banneker's Pennsylvania, Delaware, Maryland and Virginia Almanack and Ephemeris, for the Year of Our Lord, 1792; Being Bisextile, or Leap-Year, and the Sixteenth Year of the American Independence, Which Commenced July 4, 1776.* Jefferson replied cordially and helped him find the position described by Chesnutt.

[6]George Washington Williams (1849–91), lawyer, historian, and Ohio state representative, published in 1882 his *History of the Negro Race in America from 1619 to 1880.*

[7]*Othello*, 5.2.340.

Race Prejudice

Its Causes and Cures

Speech to the Boston Literary and Historical Association,
Boston, Mass., 25 June 1905

Mr. President, ladies and gentlemen:—

Before approaching my subject this evening I wish to express my appreciation of the invitation to address this society. It is a privilege to stand before so cultivated and thoughtful an audience in this the most intellectually advanced city of our land, and it is an honor to be numbered among those who have addressed this body.[1]

I saw it stated the other day, that "the Negro writes only about his rights and his wrongs, and occasionally a little pastoral poetry." I thought the remark very clever, and very nearly true. But the same time that my eye fell upon this gem of criticism, I read an editorial by Mr. Fortune in the *New York Age,* in which he expressed his disgust with the race subject, and his wish that the thought of the colored people might be set free to seek expression along other lines of intellectual effort and achievement.[2] I had often felt the same regret. But I observed that after writing this paragraph of protest, our friend Mr. Fortune proceeded to dash off three or four columns of red hot race editorials. And so, following his example I am going to take one phase of the old familiar subject as my theme. There is so much that has not been said upon it, and so much that ought to be said, that even pastoral poetry seems at times like wasted effort.

I may just as well, before I seek to find the causes and cure of race prejudice, state briefly my views upon this question of race. I do not believe that the current notion of race has any logical or scientific ground, or that it is, in its essence, a matter of very much importance; as a *fact* it is extremely important, or we should not spend our time here today discussing it. We speak of superior and inferior races, and measure their relative capacity by their contributions to human learning or human progress. Finding one group of people, inhabiting a favorable locality, which has been able by virtue of this favorable environment, to acquire wealth and the arts of civilization we speak of it as superior; and finding another group which under different conditions has lagged behind in the march of civilization, we call it an inferior race. And yet we have the highest scientific authorities for believing that if the conditions had been reversed for a few generations or a few centuries, the results would equally have been reversed; the most favored race would have been the superior race, the less favored the inferior. This difference in races, superficial and inconstant—for races rise and fall and ebb and flow—is very different from the deep-seated, essential, almost geological differences of which we hear so much that many of us have come to believe them, and to accept the purely fictitious lines and cleavages between races as something fixed and eternal. Virchow, an eminent European ethnologist, in writing upon this subject of race, says, in language that recalls the spirit of the old Boston abolitionists—I wish there might be a St. Gaudens monument to every one of them!—this great and great-hearted man says: "If I survey the history of mankind I cannot help believe that all men are in truth brothers and sisters. Our longing ought to be toward that unifying toleration from which our artificial differences have alienated us."[3]

We scarcely need science to teach us a thing so obvious as the unity of mankind—the brotherhood of man. Consider for a moment the distribution of the human family and how insensibly each variety shades into the next. Begin for instance in equatorial Africa, the home of the pure Negro, the progenitor of our own colored people. To the north of these, after several intervening links, lie the Sudanese, not casually distinguishable from the Congo Negro in color or in quality of hair, but a somewhat more shapely people and with a somewhat finer cast of features, and a more warlike spirit. Still further northward lie the Moors, black people still, with nostrils somewhat higher and narrower and hair which has become wavy instead of kinky. And when we reach the Mediterranean shore we find the Arab and the Berber, still further removed from the equatorial type. The Congo Negro placed side by side with the indigenous North African would show a pronounced deviation, yet at no time on the journey northward would the traveler have been able to draw the exact line between one type and the other, so closely related are they, and so widely have they overlapped and commingled along the edges of their various habitats.

Crossing the Mediterranean Sea at Gibraltar for instance, where there is the least break in the chain, we find the swarthy Spaniard, dark originally, still further darkened by the Moorish strain. The Frenchman of the south of France is also a person of dark complexion, and with the dark or brick-red Italian and

Portuguese types we are familiar. Advancing northward, the color gradually fades out until it reaches, in Northern Europe the fair-skinned, fair-haired type, which has furnished the ancestry of most of the people of the United States. This change of color has been accompanied in its northern progress, by other modifications of type, due to differences in climate, to the influence of different religions and forms of government, which as they encouraged or retarded mental and economic development have reacted upon the mental and physical characteristics of the people. A similar journey from eastern Asia to western Europe would show in much the same manner a gradual change of type, beginning with the brown Malay or slant-eyed Mongolian, and ending, as in the other case, with the fair-skinned, fair-haired European type. This change is not uniform, of course, for there have been great historical shiftings of population, which have interfered with natural development, but it is sufficiently uniform to establish, as did our northward journey from Central Africa, the essential unity of the human race. And the strongest proof of man's essential unity is that nowhere has nature placed any impassable barrier between men. Nature does not permit the crossing of the lower forms of life; but wherever the races of men come in contact they mingle their blood. Not all the laws men can enact, not all the forces of social prejudice, are able to prevent it entirely, and great parts of the world are peopled with mixed races. I shall recur to this point later on in my remarks.

Now, I think it very important to have established this principle of the unity of mankind; to have determined that the differences, the sometimes very marked differences between certain varieties of mankind, are not so radical and deepseated as they sometimes seem, but are, after all, merely superficial, and due to circumstance, to conditions, to environment, and therefore subject to modification from the same causes. I wish you could keep this in mind, for it is in these superficial differences that I shall seek the causes of race prejudice, or race antagonism, or race feeling, or whatever you may call it; and it is in the modification, or softening or removal of these differences, by the operation of a different environment, that I shall seek the remedy. For whatever its source may be, the prejudice is a very real and vital evil, which must be cured before we can hope, for ourselves or for our children, or our children's children, to enter into the full enjoyment of those rights to which by virtue of our humanity and our citizenship we are justly entitled.

Let us see now, while we are digging our way to the root of this matter, how this prejudice which we are to consider manifests itself, and it involves, I think you will agree with me, the whole race problem. For if the element of race prejudice were removed from our national life, there would be an end to the race problem, even though other conditions should remain exactly as they are. Grave questions there would be, of poverty, of ignorance, and of other things; but the Negro would have no special grievance. What then are the conditions of this problem?

I shall pass over its historical development and state briefly in what it consists today. And while what I shall say is in principle applicable to every part of the world where diverse races meet, I shall confine my argument in the main to our own South. For North and South have, in principle and in practice, diverged so widely upon this question that Northern and Southern conditions really present separate problems, and if the same problem, certainly widely separate phases of it. North and South are growing, doubtless will continue to grow, nearer in feeling upon this and most other questions, and we hope that when they are in perfect harmony it will be wiser and more liberal thought that will prevail. However that may be, the North now is at least a century in advance of the South in its attitude toward the Negro.

In the Southern states, where the race problem is most acute, the population is about three-fifths white and two-fifths colored. In some communities the populations vary largely. In the western counties of the states which border on the Appalachian Mountains, the colored population is very slight, not greater perhaps than in our Northern cities; while in the coast counties of the same states, it sometimes exceeds the white population. In South Carolina and Mississippi the colored outnumber the whites, and in the last census Louisiana, formerly preponderantly colored, now shows on paper a slight white majority. In the black belt the colored population is very dense, running as high in places as 20 Negroes to one white person. The people of Negro descent in the South alone number something over 7,000,000.

These millions are practically voteless. They cannot send one of their own number to speak for them in the National Congress, nor can they enjoy the election of a friendly white man to that body; nor is there in Congress a single representative from the Southern States who would speak for them in that body from the Negro point of view, or even from the Northern white point of view. Nor have they any share in the local government of those states of which they constitute even a majority of the population. Their civil rights are materially restricted. In many places they do not have the equal protection of the law. For some crimes they are denied the right of trial, and for most offenses are punished with unmerciful severity. Every effort has been made by the Southern state governments to force them into a distinct and inferior class, recognized and maintained by law. Their children must attend separate schools, and they are not admitted to State institutions of higher learning. They must travel in different cars upon the public highways and seek entertainment at different inns. They must sit in separate waiting rooms at railroad stations, and are rigorously set aside by themselves in places of public entertainment. They are everywhere treated with the scorn and contempt which men are only too apt to feel for those who are stamped by law as their inferiors. Even the church of God, who is no respecter of persons, the church of Christ the Jew, the friend of publicans and sinners,[4] closes its doors to men of dark complexion, and the white ministers of that church refuse to sit in synods and presbyteries and conventions for a few days in the year with their darker brethren, to consult together for the advancement of Christ's kingdom. This has resulted in a state of feeling between the two races which is extremely unhealthful, and which becomes more so as the colored people advance. The situation has grown tense and unnatural, and therein lies its danger. This race discrimination in the United States is attracting worldwide attention, and Mr. James Bryce, the distinguished English publicist, who recently revisited this country, has thus expressed himself upon this subject: "This attitude of social aloofment and exclusiveness is compatible in a person of good breeding and kindly nature, with courteous treatment of the individual colored man. But in the case of persons who do not possess these qualities, it destroys any sort of friendliness."[5] I scarcely need say that perhaps nowhere in the world, and certainly not in our own country, are the majority of the people courteous and well bred. Good breeding is a heritage of culture. The many are swayed by their feelings, and most powerfully by their prejudices, which they make no effort to conceal.

I do not think I have overstated conditions in the South; I have seen them stated much more vividly. I am aware that all generalizations are faulty—including this one. There are many honorable individual exceptions and there is even a small class of Southerners who deprecate the present system; but I have stated, I think, the general attitude and I need not dwell longer upon it to this audience.

Now, having before us these conditions, and desiring to change them; and having established the fact that they do not grow out of any such essential and fundamental differences as would justify their treatment by any other rule of morals than that which would apply between men of the same color, let us consider for a brief space what are the real underlying causes which created the prejudice lying at the base of the problem—the substructure, so to speak, of the whole edifice.

This prejudice grew out of an accumulation of differences, any one of which, alone, was sufficient to create a certain antagonism. The Negro slave who was brought from Africa to the United States differed from the typical man of the dominant class in a number of ways. They differed physically. The one was black, and the other white. The one had constituted for poets and sculptors the ideal of beauty and of grace. The other was rude and unpolished in form and feature. The one possessed the arts of civilization and the learning of the schools; the other, at most, the simple speech and rude handicrafts of his native tribe, and no written language at all. The one professed the most enlightened of all religions, the other had been sunk in the grossest heathenism. The one was native, or, if not indigenous, had driven back the native Indian and was master of the soil, while the other was frankly alien and counted equally with the soil as the subject of ownership. The one was master, the other slave; the one rich, the other poor, possessing not even himself.

This accumulation of superficial differences brought into play antagonism measured by the sum of that engendered by each. There was the contempt of the instructed for the ignorant, the contempt of the fair and comely for the black and homely, the contempt of the master for the slave; the scorn of the Christian for the heathen; the contempt of the native for the foreigner, of the citizen for the alien, of him who speaks a language fluently for him who speaks it brokenly or corruptly. Such was the combination of differences, with their resulting antagonisms, which the Negro had to face in the long struggle for equality stretching through the centuries in front of him, though at that time perhaps neither he nor his masters ever thought of it, seeing no further than men are apt to see beyond their own immediate environment.

These, then, were the causes of race prejudice. We have stated, already, its results, as embodied in present day conditions. Where lies the remedy? It lies in the removal of these antagonisms by the removal of the causes which gave rise to them.

The instinct of antagonism—the prejudice—will disappear just as characteristics that called it into play are modified. In other words, as the structure was built up, beam by beam, stone by stone, so must it be torn down, stone by stone, beam by beam. If any one has come here today hoping that I might by a higher inspiration, have hit upon some instantaneous remedy for race prejudice, he will go away disappointed. There is no magic wand which we can wave and make it vanish in a night. There is no panacea we can take and cure it with so many bottles, at a reduced price in quantities.

Assuming then that this doctrine is correct, and that as the causes which produce a condition are modified, so the condition resulting from these causes will change, let us see how this rule has worked out in the past, before we apply it to the present. As our time is brief, and as historical comparisons can only be made by periods, let us pass over 250 years of colonial and national development, and see to what extent the differences out of which the race problem grew had been modified during that period—at the period just before the Civil War.

In language the Negroes were one with the whites. They spoke nothing but English, corruptly or ungrammatically in most cases, but there was no longer any barrier of alien speech between them. The heathen religions had entirely disappeared; perhaps proportionately as many Negroes professed the Christian faith as whites. And if slavery had not produced exalted moral standards, the reproach of heathenism at least could not be brought against them, and there were many pure souls who followed in the footsteps of the meek and lowly Saviour, which has always been easier for Lazarus than for Dives.[6] The one was master and the other slave; except that there had grown up in many States a large class of free colored people. In Maryland there were more free colored people than slaves. The one was citizen, and the other, if not alien, was still not citizen and had no right which the other was bound to respect. The physical type had been greatly changed, though not uniformly. A constant infusion of white blood, permitted by the customs of slavery, had left its impress upon the black race. In some typical Southern cities, like New Orleans for instance, and Charleston, it was difficult for the casual traveler to draw the line of race in the people he met upon the streets. And while the great masses of the black field hands in the rural districts still retained almost unchanged, the physical characteristics of their ancestors, there had come into existence a race of mixed bloods, and these, seeping downward through the blacks had in varying degree begun to attack and modify the original African. The two races had thus been brought closer together at many points, and the antagonism between them should have been in large degree, and really was in some degree, essentially less than at any earlier period.

The Civil War by a violent change of political conditions removed some others of these differences. No longer were they master and slave, but all men were alike free. All were made voters and were therefore theoretically equal citizens, and laws were passed intended to fix these changed conditions. Thus radically, were swept away (in theory at least) several of the barriers which separated these two peoples. The whites were still in the main instructed, the blacks in the main ignorant. The whites were still the rich, the blacks the poor, although the war by depriving them of their slaves, by its enormous expense, and by its destruction of the economic system of the South, had largely closed up the gap between great wealth upon the one hand and absolute poverty upon the other. The social differences—the control of the social organism, the habit of command, the pride of race and of authority, still remained with the whites and in due time easily reasserted itself.

And now, forty years having elapsed since the Civil War, in what respect has this problem been modified by a still further softening of the lines of difference between the two peoples which make up the population of the South?

There has been a political reaction in the South, but I shall not dwell upon it. It is temporary, and will in due time pass away; for the Constitution still stands, and will not be changed. Its principles are as vital to the liberties of white men as to those of black. Freeman and citizen is the Negro and freeman and citizen will he remain. Physically there has been no great change. Indeed, with the passing of slavery and the better moral conditions resulting from the advancement of both races, there has been certainly less illicit intermixture of the races than theretofore, and Southern laws have forbidden intermarriage. The old Adam has not, however, been entirely put away, and the old customs still survive in some degree, with the old results.[7] But another change has been taking place, which, if it has not brought the Negro materially nearer to the white in color, has at least removed him, on the average, farther from the ancestral type. The tremendous quantity of mixed blood has, in the general evolution of the race been diffused within its own limits, and there has been a wide and gradual change of type in this respect. The number of mulattoes pure and simple may have declined. The number of cross breeds between the mulatto and black has largely increased, and this new type, were there no future admixture of white blood, would in time become fixed, for there is no Negro immigration to modify it from the other side.

For other reasons, as well, the physical type of a large part of the colored people has improved. They have been better fed and better clothed. With limited opportunities, they have had at least boundless hopes. These gradually improving conditions have left their impress in a gradual softening of crudities, a gradual refinement of type. People who can hold up their heads and feel that they are men and women and free citizens do not drag their dull way through life like fettered slaves.[8] Men who read and think show it in their faces. The face is the index of the mind, and a brightly illumined soul may shine through a dark face. The same process which makes in two or three generations, out of stupid European peasants, leaders of men, is making, out of the slaves of a generation ago, men and women who will, in themselves and their children, contribute their full share to the future greatness of the nation and of humanity.

In general enlightenment they have advanced tremendously. They have reduced their illiteracy one-half since the Civil War. They have 27,000 men and women employed as teachers. They use the English language well enough to be able to conduct, in it, several hundred newspapers, and several monthly magazines (some of which are very well edited) and the writings of a respectable and increasing number of colored men and women find ready acceptance for publication.

Beginning their careers with no educated leaders, 2500 young colored men and women have graduated from good colleges since the Civil War. We are told sometimes that much money has been wasted in seeking to give them the higher education. But can this be true? They are thrown back largely upon themselves for all sorts of social leadership. The color line, and the unfriendly feeling fostered by it requires them to find their own teachers and preachers, and encourages them to produce their own doctors and lawyers and social leaders. There are, roughly speaking, ten millions of them. Five millions more have died since the war. Fifteen million divided by 2500 gives 6000. One educated leader to 6000 people is not a large proportion. To lead the white people as many are turned out from our colleges every year as there have been colored men in a generation.

Now, I might run through the whole gamut of differences with which I started out, to show you that this people, leaving slavery with nothing, have accumulated three or four hundred millions worth of property, that their style of living and their standards of culture have improved in ever greater proportion. In the matter of wealth, let us take the statistics for one State alone. In 1903 the colored people of Virginia owned 1,000,000 acres of land, out of the total of 26,000,000 acres in the State. In the report of the Auditor of State for 1904, they are shown to possess 1,277,571 acres, having risen in one year from the ownership of 1 acre in 26 to that of 1 in 20. If their thrift holds out, and it ought to increase, and if no restriction is placed upon their right to acquire land, it will be only 20 or 30 years before they will own land in proportion to their numbers. In the same State their farm property is assessed at $8,000,000, their town property at $6,500,000, and their personal property at $5,000,000, to say nothing of church, hospital, Y.M.C.A. and other buildings for eleemosynary work, not taxed, but which bring their personal property up to the respectable total of $23,000,000.

In religion and in morals they have made great progress. Their race church societies include 300,000 members, and own $40,000,000 of church property; and they send missionaries to Africa and the West Indies, and are causing some uneasiness in British South Africa because their preachers are charged with preaching the dangerous doctrine of "Africa for the Africans," to the apprehended disturbance of imperial politics. It would be an amusing repetition of history if the American Negroes, barred from political power in their own country, should follow the example of the Irish and seek it in another continent. I know that the quality of Negro religion is much decried, and no doubt much of it is open to criticism; but whoever asserts, whether he be a renegade mulatto from Boston, or a renegade Northerner from Arkansas;[9] whether he be a Southern Negro-hater or Northern dough-face,[10] that the Negro has made no gain in morals, states that which is not true;—whether his motive be hatred, or malice, or whether it be grounded in mere ignorance, the statement is not true.

So, as I have tried to show, our savage has become civilized, our heathen a Christian, our foreigner a native, our slave a citizen, our Negro a man of mixed blood, our pauper a property-owner. *Why, then, has not the prejudice grown less?* Why does it even seem, in some ways, to have become more pronounced?

I might answer that it *has* grown less, and might easily prove it, here in Massachusetts, or anywhere in the North; and I might show, I think, that it had diminished as these differences had grown less pronounced. It has not diminished uniformly, because the race has not been modified uniformly. The individual who has lost one of these differences may retain some of the others in a very pronounced degree, and the prejudice will not entirely disappear until they have all disappeared or ceased to be regarded as important.

In the South, where race feeling has gone to such lengths that it would be farcical if it were not tragical, race prejudice has not been left to the operation of natural laws, but has been deliberately and designedly stimulated for political purposes.

Another reason why the progress of the Negro has not resulted in a proportionate decrease of prejudice, is that it has not yet gone far enough to overcome the inertia, the dead weight, of preconceived opinions. Notice the strain with which a team of horses starts a loaded wagon, and the ease with which they draw it while in motion over a good road. Forty years have been barely sufficient to start the Negro's wagon. Great social movements always drag. Human society, which is only organized human nature, is governed by two opposing principles—that of progress and that of conservatism; the one holds society to-gether, the other makes improvement possible. A false system becomes estab-lished; the interests of many, the tranquility of most, are involved in it, and to a large number any radical change would threaten disaster. It is a tremendous thing to uproot a popular belief. How many of us still cherish a pet superstition! Slavery existed long after the essential moral and economic evils of the system were clearly recognized. Old and discredited beliefs, entrenched by privilege and power, still keep their grip upon large masses of mankind. Russia is still gov-erned by "divine right" and struggling in the effort to shake off a belated des-potism which has led her armies and navies to defeat at the hands of a despised enemy.[11]

This natural conservatism is rooted in many things: in habit—we keep on doing injurious things because others do them; wear standing collars when we would feel better and look better in low ones, wear hard hats when soft ones would be much more comfortable, wear tight shoes to make our feet look small. We go to church, some of us, long after the spiritual impulse has ceased to draw us thither. And, by the same token, the Negro and his blood are slighted because it is the custom. And this custom, like other beliefs, persists even after its basic causes have disappeared. Who knows why 13 is considered an unlucky number, Friday an unlucky day, to break a mirror a presage of misfortune? Long after the light of reason and education has flooded the dark corners of the mind, these childish superstitions linger. Is it likely that so deeply rooted a prejudice as that under which we labor will be easily let go; a prejudice rooted in the strongest and at the same time the weakest of human passions,—the vanity which needs but the slightest suggestion to make one man think himself better than another?

Had I the time, I could make this point clear from the history of this very question. It was necessary, before race prejudice attained its full growth, to overcome some well settled principles. The white people who settled this coun-try began their career here with a distinct prejudice in favor of freedom, so much so that when a slave became a freeman, he became endued with the rights of a freeman. In North Carolina, as late as 1830, free men of color could vote, and could marry white women. White people had a prejudice in favor of their own blood, even when diluted. Nearly every Southern State had its laws or judicial decisions fixing the degree at which persons of mixed blood might cease to be Negroes and claim the rights of white men. It was only when the growing value of the cotton industry made slavery more profitable; and when the agitation against the system made it a national political issue which the forces of greed and ambition rallied to support, that slavery reached its highest point—long af-ter it was really tottering to its fall. And so let us hope that the very reaction which confronts us in the South, may be but the last instinctive rallying of the old forces in a desperate effort to maintain the old conditions against the ad-vance of inevitable change. It may be in part successful, may seem for a time entirely successful. But the axe has been laid to the root. Race prejudice may survive for a while after its causes have been removed, but in the end it must go, as its mother, slavery went.

But it has not yet gone, and hence we are here to-day, I to speak, and you to listen, and I hope as well to speak. And for the remainder of my time I wish to consider how we may best remove these differences which gave rise to this prejudice, in order that the prejudice itself may as speedily as possible disappear. For with the prejudice will go the problem. We should miss the problem, if it were settled in our time. It has furnished for several generations a bone of political contention. It brought on the Civil War. It has resulted, in our own day, in bringing our Constitution and laws into something very much like contempt; and it has caused the perpetration of horrors which put the Middle Ages to the blush. It is the stock in trade of most Southern politicians and of our own race leaders and race journalism. It has inspired much literature, good, bad, and indifferent. We should miss it, as we would an old sore, or chronic rheumatism, or any other affliction that occupied our thoughts and influenced our lives. We should miss it, but we would try to worry along without it, and seek our careers in other fields of intellectual activity,—even if we should only write more pastoral poetry. Perhaps if we wrote more, we might write better. We should miss it, but we shall be glad to have it go.

Now then, how are we going to get rid of it—for ourselves as far as may be, and for our children and our children's children? Having seen with our eyes and by the study of history what changes time *can* make, what remains to be done to complete this adjustment to our environment? Keeping up for a moment the fiction of a distinct race, which we have accepted so readily, where do we stand in comparison with the white race, who constitute the main feature of our environment, and with whom we must live in harmony and unity, in order to live wholesomely and happily?

Language and religion, as elements of antagonism, have disappeared. Some of us might use the language better, and might have more religion without being at all too good for this world; but no one, I imagine, dislikes the Negro for his language or his faith. The relation of master and slave no longer exists, though that of employer and servant is still very imperfectly adjusted, and the customs of slavery die hard, requiring the strong arm of the federal government to destroy them.

Of the differences which remain, a vital one is that of education—or rather, of the social efficiency which grows out of training. So important and fundamental is this question that it has for the moment overshadowed every other element of the race problem, from the standpoint of both white man and Negro. A people in a low state of social efficiency, living apart, in a country of their own, and avoiding international complication, might live in fair comfort and happiness. Every people has passed through such a stage, and many have not yet emerged from it. In the same way a people in a high state of social efficiency,

living in a land by themselves, may maintain a high standard of civil and political liberty and of ethical conduct. But mingle the two, and the least efficient are
forced backward and downward, and liberty and morals languish. The weak
and inefficient cannot compete with the strong; and liberty and justice cannot
prevail in presence of the constant temptation to take unfair advantage of
weakness and ignorance. And it is immensely significant and hopeful that in the
discussion of this problem, all good men, whatever their color and however they
may differ in other ways, are agreed that education, training in the arts of life is
a primary element of any attempted or possible solution.

The matter of education, too, is important to us as a means as well as an end,
for with the temporary closing of other avenues, much of the best thought of our
ablest men has been directed toward it. It is no justification, but at least a consolation for exclusion from some other walks of life, that the talents of colored
men have found a healthy outlet and a worthy career in this important and useful and not overcrowded field. Much progress has been made. We say, with
pardonable pride, that the colored people have reduced their illiteracy from one
hundred to forty-eight per cent. But let us not deceive ourselves. Let us, in this
little heart-to-heart home talk, be directly honest with ourselves. What does that
reduction mean? It means, by the conditions of the federal census of 1900 that
fifty-two per cent. of the colored people can read and write. As I remember the
method of enumeration, does it really mean more than fifty-two per cent. of
those examined answered, or some one answered for them, that they could read
and write? What was the test, or was there any? The percentage is based on the
population of ten years old and upwards, which, of colored people, was in
1900, 5,664,975. Out of a white population of 12,000,000 in the Southern
states, 88.3 per cent. are returned as literate. But does that mean that the 52 per
cent. of the colored are as well educated as the 88 per cent. of the whites? I think
you would not maintain it. The scholars, the thinkers, the people who direct the
government, the industries, the various functions of the state, are, in the main,
white people of superior education; not only can they read and write, but they
can do a great deal more. Among other things, they can figure. I scarcely know
whether I dare make an illustration at this point, but they have mastered the old
formula with which I dare say most of us are familiar:

> Nought's a nought, a figger's a figger,
> All for the white man and none for the—other fellow.

So with the matter of teachers. In 1900 there were 21,267 colored school teachers. Their value as a comparative test of literacy depends upon the length of time
they teach during the year, and the quality of instruction which they give, which
is measured by the grade of the schools in which they teach. Mere numbers are
no fair test.

So with clergymen, of whom we have 15,528 colored as compared with
94,437 whites. What is their relative degree of education, morality, and zeal for

the cure of souls? This is the test of their influence, much more than their number. We speak with just pride of the number of our business men, but, in the census statistics, the grocer with a $200 stock counts as much as the grocer with a
$200,000 stock; the bank with $10,000 capital counts the same as the bank
with $1,000,000 capital; therefore the number of colored grocers or bankers as
compared with the number of white men engaged in the same occupation, is not
an accurate test. It may be much like a school census in Annapolis, Md., would
be, which gave the number of colored and white children respectively in attendance at the public schools, and neglected to state that the white schools were
open ten months in the year and the colored schools but ten weeks.

To close this gap so as to compete with the whites in social efficiency the
colored people must be, relatively, *as well* educated; their teachers must be relatively of as high a grade, and their schools open as many months a year; their
grocers must have relatively as large stocks, their banks relatively as large a
capital and volume of transactions. The mere raising of percentages in quantity
without a corresponding advance in quality does not by any means eliminate
the difference.

Whatever can be done, by organization, or by individual effort, to dignify
labor, to make it more efficient, and thereby to increase its rewards and increase
the number of those who employ and lessen that of those who serve, is an advantage to our people, and whoever helps this cause forward is their benefactor.
We should not permit ourselves, in our impatience of results, in our just resentment of well-known wrongs, to forget the noble philanthropy which has given
so freely and fully both of money and of lives toward the education of the Negro
in the South. Without them his lot would have been much harder.

As to the kind of education which the colored people in their present condition, need most, you all recall, no doubt, the old story of the shield which hung
across the roadway, in front of a castle which two knights in armor were approaching from different directions. One knight maintained that it was gold,
and the other that it was silver. After the fashion of their age, they set their
lances and fought for their opinions, until they were both unhorsed—and when
they were carried into the castle to have their wounds dressed, they discovered
that both were right,—one side of the shield was gold and the other silver. Our
rival advocates of different sorts of education have sometimes reminded me of
this story.

I think that some of the confusion of mind upon this subject may be cleared
up by stopping to think of the definition of Education. I have already spoken of
it as training for social efficiency or usefulness. The ideals of the past, the literature of education, have been based upon the idea of education as intellectual
training, pure and simple, with a small sprinkling, perhaps, of moral precepts,
and a little religious instruction, which the democratic spirit has viewed with
suspicion. But in our own day the definition of education has been enlarged to
take in the whole field of preparation for the duties of life. The great mass of

men have always, and must, in all probability, always, earn their living by the labor of their hands;[12] and that these hands must be trained, that that living may be comfortable, and may leave some margin of earnings to save, is a vital necessity for any people who hope to register progress; and that there must be institutions to teach the trades and handicrafts is well-nigh imperative, owing to the decline of the apprenticeship system and the selfish tyranny of many labor unions. And will any one pretend to say that this necessity among our people has been fully met, or more than merely begun upon? An institution like Hampton or Tuskegee, in every Southern State, for another generation, would not meet the need of the Negro for training in the arts of life.

But this is not all. I have said, earlier in my remarks, that the colleges of this country had graduated in all some 2,500 colored men and women as leaders for a total of 15,000,000 people—one to 6,000. (There are towns in the U.S. where there is one saloon to every 30 or 40 people.) Were there no color line, the need for higher education would be no less vital, of course, to the gifted individual, but it would be less imperative for the public welfare; for in every Southern community there are trained white men who could furnish the needed leadership. But there is a color line, deep and dark, and wide, across which few dare as yet to cross, and our Southern brethren are thrown back upon ourselves[13] for all sorts of leadership. And from the necessities of the case, from their own greater handicap, and the harder and longer path which they must traverse to attain equality, they need even wiser and better leadership than white men need. To supply this need we shall want all the higher education that can be supplied by Southern colored colleges, and by the Northern universities which are free to all, without regard to color. A Fisk or an Atlanta in every Southern State, for a generation to come, would be none too many, nor would it even then have met to the full the demand for trained teachers and preachers and engineers and architects and professional men for the healthy and diversified development of a people which, a generation hence, is likely to be 30 millions—a population as large as that of the U.S., at the outbreak of the Civil War. And already, I think, we have begun to develop this superior leadership.

I have sometimes doubted, however, whether the attempt to teach everything in one institution would not result in the weakening of all. I question whether the influence of Harvard College, even in its small days, would have been strengthened by the addition of a horse-shoeing department.

As to how education should be provided for the young, I believe it should be primarily a function of the State; that next to national safety, the preservation of order, and the equal enforcement of just laws, education is the highest function of the State. I am not sure that, though not more obvious, it is not more important than any of these, since with it all of these can be the more certainly assured, and without it any of them is difficult of accomplishment. And I need not argue to this audience that so far as the State assumes to exercise this function, it should apply it to all alike. The state has always, in the North, and, since the Re-

construction governments established the principle, in the South, assumed the
duty of furnishing the simpler elements of learning. It has also assumed to some
extent, the responsibility for the higher education, and will doubtless, in time,
take over the whole field of education. If a man is to be trained, at the expense of
the State, for a carpenter, or a blacksmith or a bricklayer, it should be because
nature or inclination has fitted the individual for such work, and not because
some theorist assumes that a person of certain complexion or antecedents could
do nothing else, or find nothing else to do. If the state provide the higher education for its youth, it should be open to those who are qualified to receive it to the
public advantage; and the test should be the aptitudes of the student, and not
any consideration of color or caste. Any theory of education based on the assumption that one class is destined to rule and another to serve is repugnant to
our political system, repugnant to justice, and repugnant to human liberty. Let
men rule or serve as their talents, not their color, may dictate. We seldom choose
a horse for color, but for strength or endurance or speed. Why choose our leaders less intelligently? The percentage of illiteracy in the Southern States is so
high, and those states so poor, relatively, and their system of separate schools so
expensive, that it is yet an open question whether the nation ought not to take
up the matter of Southern education for whites and blacks alike. We might well
ask whether we have not a duty to perform at home before we spend the nation's money in carrying the blessings of civilization to distant and alien peoples.
By what color of reason do we spend our own money in teaching science to the
Filipinos when a great portion of our own population, white and colored, cannot read or write? Duty, to say nothing of charity, at least *begins* at home.[14]

When private philanthropy enters the field of education, it is its privilege to
direct the expenditure of its gifts. And that kind of education is likely to be most
eloquent for the moment, which has the ablest or most eloquent or most polite
advocate. The most popular thing may not be ideally the perfect thing, or the
best thing, but it is likely to be a good thing; and time and the operation of natural forces, will bring about, in due course, a healthy readjustment. So much for
education. I have spoken rather at length upon it, because it is, for the moment
the leading "race" issue.

Poverty is still a characteristic of the Negro. We justly pride ourselves upon
the property accumulated by the colored people since the Civil War. They were
not entirely penniless at the date of emancipation, for there was in the country a
considerable population of free people of color who, in the aggregate, possessed
a considerable amount of property. But in the main their three or four hundred
million dollars of accumulations are the fruits of freedom. It is a respectable sum
and shows a high percentage of progress. But we must remember that the man
who today having nothing, shall tomorrow possess one dollar, has increased his
wealth—how many fold? As many as you like, for one dollar is ten times, one
hundred times, one thousand times, one million times more than nothing, as the
fancy may dictate. But when day after tomorrow a man has earned another

dollar and possesses two, he has merely doubled his wealth, and with each succeeding dollar the ratio becomes smaller. The second dollar has increased his
wealth 100 per cent.; the hundredth dollar increases it only one per cent. We
must not be misled by these superficial ratios of advancement, in estimating real
progress, any more than we shall permit ourselves to be misled, in estimating the
quality of mankind, by superficial physical differences. To illustrate, I find by
the figures of the census of 1900 that Negroes are reported as owning in whole
or in part one hundred and eighty-six thousand farms, out of a total of
5,739,657 farms in the U.S., or one farm in thirty-one. If we stopped there this
would not be a bad showing. But pursuing our investigation a little further we
find that the acreage of these Negro farms amounts to 15,827,030 acres out of a
total acreage of farm lands of 841,201,546, or only one acre in fifty-three. Not
quite so good a showing. Going a step further, we find the value of these farms
owned by them reported at $177,915,476, out of a total value of farm lands in
the United States of $20,439,906,164, or $1.00 in $133.00.

Now, I need not argue with you that in order to bring up the colored farmer
to the economic position of the white farmer he must own one farm in every
eight instead of one in every thirty-one, or four times as many farms as he now
possesses; these farms to contain one acre in every eight instead of one in every
fifty-three, or about seven times as many acres as they now contain, and these
farms to be worth one-eighth of the entire farm valuation of the country, or seventeen times as much as their present value.

We are loosely credited with property to the value of three hundred to
four hundred millions of dollars. It is a very respectable sum, and would make
half a dozen white men fairly well to do—it would make one white man very
rich. There are several families in New York who could buy out the whole
colored race and have money to spare. The aggregate wealth of the nation in
1900 was given by the Bureau of Statistics as $94,300,000,000. We have the
$300,000,000; they have the $94,000,000,000. Dividing the $94,000,000,000
among the whites, they are worth an average of $1446 apiece. Dividing the
$300,000,000 among the colored people gives them an average of $30.00
apiece. I need not argue with you that before the Negro shall have attained
financial equality with the white he must possess one dollar in every eight instead of one in every three hundred, or 39 times as much as he now possesses.
Does the outlook seem overly hopeful? Is it likely that with such a fearful
handicap to overcome he can hope in any measurable time, as a *separate* and
distinct class, to close up this gap?

But there are other things no less important and fundamental than education
and property. We have ceased, before the law, to be aliens, and have become
citizens. But we are often spoken of, and, because of the persistence of prejudice
long after its causes have disappeared, we exist, very largely, in the public consciousness, as aliens still. To remove this disparity, our equality of civil and political rights must be established. The Constitution must be respected. Our na-

tional laws must be made to conform to it, so that whatever test be applied to the suffrage, to the right to hold office, to any civil function whatever, must be applied to all men alike. Personally I believe in manhood suffrage; I scarcely see, under our system, how anything else is compatible with justice and freedom. In some way, and what other way is possible except by the ballot? every sane man, not in prison, who contributes by his labor to the wealth of the community, should have a voice in the selection of those who make and administer the laws. If he cannot read and write and explain the Constitution, he needs protection all the more, and should be taught. If he does not own a certain amount of property, he pays rent, and the rent pays the tax, and if he be not allowed to vote, he is taxed without representation.[15] I have sometimes thought, however, that some qualification of character or education might be, not unwisely, required for holding office. The progressive debasement of state and municipal legislatures, not to mention the occasional black sheep in the National Congress, suggests that in some way a higher standard must be sought. But whatever the law shall be, wherever men's rights are fixed by law, those laws should apply equally. In the army and navy, and in all branches of the public service, entrance and promotion should be governed by fitness and that alone, as is already the rule in the civil service. Discriminating laws which classify men and fix their rights and opportunities by race or color are utterly abhorrent to the spirit of liberty, and nothing more astonishes me than that a free people should so long have tolerated them, in violation of the plain letter and obvious spirit of their Constitution.

Laws there must be for the protection of the weak and ignorant; and the laws already in existence must be enforced. We have justly charged the Supreme Court with undue timidity in passing upon questions involving the rights of the Negro; but there are signs of a growing change in this regard. And death or retirement is likely ere long to make changes in the personnel of the Court which will presumably be for the advancement of liberal ideas. There have been two recent Circuit Court decisions, one from Arkansas and one from Alabama, either one of which, if affirmed, will produce far-reaching changes in the relation between the Federal and State judicial systems. It is the primary right of a State to protect its citizens in their right to inherit, purchase, sell, lease, hold and convey real and personal property; and in his right to make and execute, or enforce contracts. But U.S. District Judge Jacob Trieber has held, in an Arkansas case, now pending on appeal in the Supreme Court, that where any of these rights are denied because of race or color they fall under the 13th Amendment, and thereby under the provisions of section 1 of the Civil Rights Act of April, 1866. In concluding his opinion the Court said:—

> Congress has the power, under the provision of the 13th Amendment to protect citizens in the enjoyment of those rights which are fundamental and belong to the citizen, if the deprivation of these rights is solely on account of his race or

color, as a denial of such rights is an element of servitude within the meaning of that amendment.[16]

The case of Riggins vs. The United States, decided by Judge Jones of Alabama, was a case where the U.S. District Court took cognizance of a lynching case and indicted three white men for lynching a Negro, named Horace Maples, charged with murder and in the custody of the sheriff at the time. A writ of habeas corpus was sued out, and denied by Judge Jones, who held that Maples had a right to a fair trial, and that when denied it or unable to secure it, because of his color, the case came under the 13th Amendment and was one for the Federal Courts. The Court said in its opinion:

> Whether or not Maples, a Negro citizen, had the right, privileges or immunity under the Constitution and laws of the United States to be free from lawless violence at the hands of white men, intending on account of his race to prevent his enjoyment of civil equality before the law, as is enjoyed by white citizens, depends upon the proper construction of the Thirteenth Amendment and valid legislation under it.

Judge Jones proceeded in the particular case before him to say that

> Whatever may be said of any other murder of a Negro by white men, it is undeniable when a Negro is taken by white men from the custody of the State authorities, when he is being held for trial on accusation of crime against State laws, and put to death to prevent his having such trial, because of race hostility, that the manifest result, as well as intent of such act, is to deprive him, because of his race, of the enjoyment of the civil rights accorded by law to white freemen.[17]

And now, in closing this already too long address, I reach the last and most difficult of these differences which hold us apart from our fellow-citizens and give rise to that antagonism of hostile feeling which we call race prejudice. I refer to the still strongly marked difference, in physical characteristics—in other words, the difference in color, or in "race," as we use the term. I have shown how this difference has been modified. I can look down into this audience and see how, in three or four generations, it has, with certain individuals and groups, almost entirely disappeared. Should it disappear entirely, race prejudice, and the race problem, would no longer exist. The question is, do we wish this difference to disappear, or do we wish to perpetuate it? And in discussing this question, we must dismiss the personal point of view, for so far as we are individually concerned, the leopard cannot change his spots, or the Ethiopian his skin, nor can a man by thinking add one cubit to his stature.[18] Nor is it the matter of the next generation. But it is a matter of vital interest to our grandchildren and our great-grandchildren—and we ought not to forget, in our discontent at our own wrongs, our duty towards those who will come after us—and the principle involved is essential to our own personal rights, and important to the future of our political system.

We have had preached to us of late a new doctrine—that of Race Integrity. We must so glory in our color that we must zealously guard it as a priceless heritage. Frankly, I take no stock in this attitude. It seems to me a modern invention of the white people to perpetuate the color line. It is they who preach it, and it is *their* racial integrity which they wish to preserve. They have never been unduly careful of the purity of the black race. I can scarcely restrain a smile when I hear a mulatto talking of race integrity, or a quadroon dwelling upon race pride. What they mean is a very fine thing, and a very desirable thing, but it is not at all what they say.

For why and to what good end, should we wish to perpetuate this disastrous difference? Ashamed of it we need not be; we are men, created of the same clay, by the same God. I certainly am not ashamed of the blood, of any of the blood, which courses in my veins. I myself came by it honestly, as the word is conventionally used; and had I not, I should still have owed it to the laws established by nature and by God long before man began to interfere with and often to obstruct the laws of nature. But of what should we be proud? Of any inherent superiority? We deny it in others, proclaiming the equality of man. Of any great achievement? We are still in the infancy of achievement, and the showing we can make is not by comparison with others, but by contrast with our own less fortunate past; and while it should encourage us to greater efforts, it should promote humanity instead of pride. We complain because others judge us by our worst; and yet we ourselves are too prone to compare ourselves with ourselves, to look down rather than up, backward rather than forward. What we have done merely marks the inevitable advance of a people surrounded by many things which stimulate to advancement. We have made greater progress than any people has ever made in the same period of time; but we have had larger opportunities—limited as they have been—and while some of us have been cruelly hampered by lack of opportunity, I think we will all admit, here in the privacy of our own family circle, that the mass of us have not taken the fullest advantage of the opportunities we have enjoyed.

Every other people who come to this country seek to lose their separate identity and to become Americans, with no distinguishing mark. For a generation they have their ghettoes—their residence quarters, their churches, their social clubs. In the second generation, when the differences of language and creed and culture and social custom have been modified, they still retain a sentimental interest in these things. In the third generation they are all Americans, and seldom speak of their foreign descent. They enter fully and completely, if they are capable, and worthy, into the life of this Republic. Are we to help these white people build up walls between themselves and us, between our children and theirs? to fence in a gloomy back yard for our descendants to play in? This nation, with the War Amendments, threw that theory overboard, when it established the theory of the equality of all men—before the law. These Northern States repudiated it when they abolished all discriminating laws, and threw open the public schools and places of travel and entertainment to all alike. The Southern States, in attempting to emphasize the line of race are simply trying to do what is impossible; and I, for one, do not wish to encourage them for one moment, by accepting their views any further than they can compel their acceptance by superior force. Their whole system is wrong. Their whole policy of race separation is illogical and unjust and must sooner or later fall by its own weight. Nor will race prejudice entirely disappear until distinctions based upon color shall have disappeared, or at least until all of us, white and colored, shall have resolutely shut our eyes to differences of color, and shall have learned to judge men's rights by their humanity, to respect and honor them according to their talents. The fates of all the people in our land, are hopelessly bound up together, for they must live in the same communities, and they must be governed by the same body of laws. I ask you to dismiss from your mind any theory, however originated, or however cherished, that there can be built up in a free country, two separate sorts of civilization, two standards of human development. The familiar argument that the white race represents a thousand years of development to every hundred of the Negro's, and that therefore the Negro must patiently wait his thousand years to be equal of the whites, is a self-refuting fallacy. For, at the end of the thousand years, unless the whites ceased to develop, the gap between them would be just as great.

I dwell upon this subject of race purity because it is the latest argument for the oppression of the Negro in the South; and being made, it must be met. I not only believe that the admixture of the races will in time become an accomplished fact, but I believe that it will be a good thing for all concerned. It is already well forward, and events seem to be paving the way to embrace the Negro in the general process by which all the races of mankind are being fused together here into one people. Millions of foreigners of various types are pouring into the country. Our native white stock—and by native I mean those who have reached or passed the third generation of assimilation—is scornful of the Negro blood. But by what token can alien Italians, Portuguese and Slavs of Europe, turn up their noses at the free-born citizens of a free country? Nor do they. Perhaps, in the economy of Divine Providence, they are sent over here to help us solve our problems by furnishing a bridge with which to span the race chasm. Who knows? The ways of God are past finding out;[19] and it may be safely said that the laws of man can only hinder or delay but cannot in the end defeat them.

The fusion of races which is in process here is going on all over the world. Quatrefages quotes another great ethnologist, I forget the name for the moment, as stating more than 30 years ago that one person in 60 in the whole world was born of one white European and one colored parent.[20] Since that was written white Europeans have swarmed into Africa, leaving their own women behind them. White Americans have overflowed into Asia and the islands of the sea,[21] and the ratio of race admixture has steadily increased. In our own land mixed bloods are numbered by the million. We may hide our heads in the sand, like the ostrich, and call them Negroes, but slowly and surely the races are passing through the crucible of change. If thereby some may lose, the majority will gain; and the spirit of democracy seeks the welfare of the majority, seeing in it, after all, the happiness of the whole. Nor will nature, in its beneficence, permit the process to be so rapid as to bring disaster. For a long time, and perhaps for all time, the white race will be secure in its ancient seats. What is it here, after all, but a recent tenant, who moved in a century or so ago? Asia will be for the Asiatics; who can doubt it, in the light of recent events?[22] One can scarcely conceive of tropical Africa as anything else than preponderantly black. Whatever is good in purity of type will be preserved to the world so long as it is of use to the world. But wherever the races meet, there will be, in a mixed race, a link to bind them into a common humanity and a greater efficiency. And in our own land, where all the races meet, will be tried first the experiment of what humanity, pure and simple, without regard to distinctions of race, can accomplish for the glory of God and the advancement of mankind. For we are all one people; we are all men and women. We should insist upon our birthright. Why worry about what we shall be called, or what we shall call ourselves? It is enough that we are men and citizens and Americans; I think it might be well if we never called ourselves, or encouraged others to call us, anything else.

I know that the matter of mixed races is a somewhat difficult one to discuss, but it is in my opinion the very marrow of the race problem. And I think I hardly need say now, after having said so much, that by a solution for this problem I do not mean an easy or speedy arrangement or compromise which will make life tolerable for the colored people of to-day. That is important. No man can live his life but once, and it is limited, so far as our definite knowledge goes, to some seventy or eighty years or less of conscious existence. If any of us ever existed before, we did not know it; and if any of us shall live hereafter, as I trust we may, it will be under conditions a knowledge of which has not been vouchsafed to us. Each one of us is entitled to the full use of his brief hour in the search for whatever good thing life has to offer. I say all honor to the practical men, who seek to make friends of those who have not been friendly, and Godspeed to their efforts, wherever these do not involve the sacrifice of any vital principle. And I doubt, after all, whether a vital principle can be sacrificed;—the very fact that it is a vital principle must make it prevail in the end. It may be obscured, but is never extinguished. But in my discussion of race prejudice I am seeking the long-time remedy, which will kill the prejudice so that it will stay dead, and not "bob up serenely" in some new place the day after the funeral. In this connection, I wish I had time to direct your thought for a moment to some recent utterances on this subject from the pen of a former governor of the island of Jamaica[23] and for 20 years connected officially with the government of that British dependency, where the experiment of a white and black and colored community has been carried on for several generations—two generations since the abolition of slavery in the West Indies. In our country it is assumed that where there are few Negroes, as in Massachusetts, they may safely be allowed equality of rights; but where there are many they must be sternly repressed, or anarchy and misrule and social disintegration and damnation and race degeneration and destruction, and a whole lot of other evils beginning in "dis" and "de" will inevitably result. This evidence to the contrary comes from a sea-girt island where the experiment has had a fair opportunity to work out, and where the white population is not more than one in forty, or even less than that.

There is a considerable class of mixed African and European descent, who largely supply the artisans and tradesmen of the community, and very many of them are landowners and planters, many are overseers and bookkeepers on estates, clerks, lawyers, doctors, office holders and a large part of the clergy of all the Protestant denominations are drawn from this class. Some of them are magistrates and several hold important positions under the government. According to their professional position they associate with the white residents on precisely the same terms as persons of pure European extraction, and the same would be the case with any person of pure African blood who should rise to a like position. Mr. Olivier admits that there is some color prejudice in Jamaica and other West Indian colonies, but it does not appear on the surface and is unquestionably diminishing. Twenty years of experience convinces him that there is no support for the sweeping generalization by which it is claimed that the mixture of races results in weakness and degeneration. He finds that the graded mixed class in Jamaica helps to form an organic whole of the community and save it from that sharp cleavage between two distinct races. And he considers that a colony of black, colored and white people has far more organic efficiency and far more promise in it than a colony of black and white alone. "The Negro in Jamaica," he says,

> has thus far been raised, and a freedom of civic mixture between the races has been made tolerable by the continuous application of the theory of humanity and equality, and equal claim of the black with the white to share, according to personal capacity and development in all the inheritance of humanity. Perfect equality in the law courts and in the constitution, whatever the law or the constitution may be, takes away the sting of race difference, and if there is race inferiority it is not burdened with an artificial handicap. Whatever mob prejudices may dictate, statesmen and educated observers cannot fail to recognize that the allegation of inequality, of insuperable race differences and degradation is a sin against light that cannot fail to aggravate the disorders already distracting the South.

He goes on:

> The color line is not a rational line, the logic neither of words nor of facts will uphold it. If adopted it infallibly aggravates the virus of the color problem. The more it is ignored and forgotten, the more is that virus attenuated. It is not possible either as a working political formula, or as an anthropological theorem, to justify the generalization that there is any political or human function for which colored persons are disqualified because of their African blood.

And he says in closing:

My comparison of conditions in the Republic and in the West Indies has brought me to the conviction that no solution of color difficulties can be found except by resolutely turning the back to the color line and race differentiation theory. If the race differentiation formula is held to it will doubtless in time bring about civil war. If statesmen face in the contrary direction I do not say that they will immediately attain civil peace, but I believe that they will be traveling the only road toward it.

And so say I, and so I think we must all agree.

And now to close, may I venture a prophecy? There are many who see the world through smoked glasses, and who view this problem of race solely from the pessimistic point of view. I think for my own part that it is in a healthy process of solution, which, by sticking closely to correct principles and by acting upon them when the opportunity offers, we can help to further. Looking down the vista of time I see an epoch in our nation's history, not in my time or yours, but in the not distant future, when there shall be in the United States but one people, moulded by the same culture, swayed by the same patriotic ideals, holding their citizenship in such high esteem that for another to share it is to entitle him to fraternal regard; when men will be esteemed and honored for their character and talents. When hand in hand and heart with heart all the people of this nation will join to preserve to all and to each of them for all future time that ideal of human liberty which the Fathers of the Republic set out in the Declaration of Independence, which declared that all men are created equal, the ideal for which Garrison and Phillips and Sumner lived and worked; the ideal for which Lincoln died, the ideal embodied in the words of the Book which the slave mother learned by stealth to read, with slow-moving finger and faltering speech, and which I fear that some of us with our freedom and our culture have forgotten to read at all:—the book which declares that "God is no respecter of persons, and that of one blood hath He made all the nations of the earth."[24]

↬

SOURCE: Untitled typed text at the Fisk University Library. This speech was delivered before the Boston Literary and Historical Association in Parker Memorial Hall on 25 June 1905. The title was cited in "All the News from Boston," *New York Age*, 29 June 1905, 1—written by a correspondent who heard both Chesnutt's speech and another "on the negro question" by Professor Richard R. Wright, Sr. (1853–1947), President of the State Industrial College of Georgia (1891–1921). Not present in the typed texts are two statements made by Chesnutt that were recorded in the correspondent's commentary. First, he "announced that an ambulance might be required to take his remains from the building after his utterances. But there was no occasion for the ambulance. . . . The only dissenting voice was that of the editor of a local paper, who was not backed by any other speaker." (William Monroe Trotter [1872–1934], the editor of the Boston *Guardian*, a black weekly, was present.) Second, Chesnutt "quoted from John Stuart Mill [1806–73] that 'The attempt to deduce national characteristics from so-called peculiarities of race is one of the most vulgar of all historical explanations.'" An abbreviated version of the speech was subsequently published under the same title in *Alexander's Magazine*, 1 (July 1905), 21–26. Excerpts were presented in "Chesnutt Sees Prejudice's Finish," *New York Age*, 6 July 1906, 6.

    ¹The compliment is not a *pro forma* one: Chesnutt viewed Boston as the seat of

American intellectual vitality, ethical rigor, and cultural dynamism. The Boston Literary and Historical Association was an organization devoted to the stimulation and enhancement of intellectual life among African Americans in the Boston area.

[2]Timothy Thomas Fortune (1856–1928) worked for several newspapers before he established *New York Freeman* in 1884, which became in 1887 the *New York Age*. Much less militant than Booker T. Washington's nemesis, William Monroe Trotter, and a long-term supporter of Washington, Fortune made the point Chesnutt describes in "Dearth of Afro-American Writers," *New York Age*, 20 April 1905, 2.

[3]Rudolf Virchow (1821–1902) was a German anatomist, physiologist, and anthropologist. Augustus Saint-Gaudens (1848–1907) was an Irish-born American sculptor famous for his renderings of historically significant individuals.

[4]Matthew 11:19.

[5]James Bryce (1838–1922), an English historian, diplomat, and later the ambassador to the United States (1907–13), began to observe American society in 1870 and, in 1888, published his frequently reprinted *American Commonwealth*. Chesnutt refers to his latest U.S. visit, during which he delivered a series of lectures on "Law and Its Relation to History" at Columbia University (10–21 October 1904). Bryce updated his *Commonwealth* interpretations in "America Revisited: The Changes of a Quarter-Century," *Outlook*, 79 (25 March 1905), 733–40; (1 April 1905), 846–55. In the second installment, he made the statement quoted by Chesnutt, doing so in light of his description of the Southerner's "supreme duty (as they call it) of preventing sexual relations between the races." He went on, in the same sentence, to observe that "one need not be surprised that the relations of the two races show little improvement since 1876, when the Northern troops were withdrawn from the South." Indeed, one of his "ablest informants" had opined that relations were actually worse.

[6]In Luke 16:19–31 is the parable of Lazarus, a beggar who suffers on earth and consequently enjoys bliss in heaven. A rich man, Dives, neglects his religious duty to help Lazarus, dies, and experiences torment in hell.

[7]Adam, like Eve, committed the "original sin," and their descendants are as prone to sinful behavior. That is, the likeness of "old Adam" is to be seen in all.

[8]Chesnutt echoes William Cullen Bryant (1794–1878), whose poem "Thanatopsis" (1821) similarly advises readers to abandon dreary, "quarry-slave" attitudes.

[9]The renegade mulatto is William Hannibal Thomas, author of *The American Negro*. The renegade Northerner is Bishop William Montgomery Brown.

[10]A dough-face was a Northerner who sided with the South during the Civil War.

[11]Reference to the Russo-Japanese War (1904–5).

[12]Psalms 128:2.

[13]In the abbreviated version of the speech published in *Alexander's Magazine*, "themselves" is the reading. It appears that, when addressing African American intellectuals in the Boston area, Chesnutt instead referred to his audience and himself as a "leadership" already in place—upon which the less sophisticated depend. During his visit to the area, Chesnutt interacted with the Atlanta University Committee, which engaged in fund-raising; "ourselves" may have been a means of reminding his listeners that they had a leadership obligation to which there was an economic dimension.

[14]"Charity begins at home," Sir Thomas Browne (1605–82), *Religio Medici* (1643).

[15]Chesnutt is referring to education, property, and poll tax requirements for voting, which he explains in "The Disfranchisement of the Negro."

[16]U.S. District Court Judge Jacob Trieber (1853–1927), in United States v. Morris *et al.*, 125 F. 322, ruled on 9 October 1903 against the claim that the white defendants should not have been indicted for conspiring "to injure, oppress, and intimidate certain citizens of the United States, of African descent" by refusing to lease land to them—"a

right alleged to be guaranteed to them by the thirteenth amendment to the Constitution of the United States" and the 1866 Civil Rights Act. He concluded that the African-American Arkansans' civil rights appeared to have been violated and that the white appellants should be tried for this act of racial discrimination.

[17]On 24 October 1904, U.S. District Judge Thomas G. Jones concluded in *Ex parte Riggins*, 134 F. 404 (not "Higgins," as Chesnutt misnamed him), that the civil rights guaranteed Maples by the U.S. Constitution, and particularly his right to due process as an alleged murderer, appeared to have been violated and that the conspirators who hanged him on 7 September 1904 should not be released from Alabama's Madison County jail but stand trial.

[18]Jeremiah 13:23 and Matthew 6:27.

[19]Romans 11:33.

[20]Armand de Quatrefages de Breau (1810–92) published his lectures on "The Natural History of Man" in *Popular Science Monthly*. In the first installment—1 (May 1872), 61–75—and in the first chapter of the 1875 book with the same title, he defines "species" in terms of the fecundity of unions between its members and the contrary consequences of unions between members of different ones. Arguing against the notion that Caucasians, Negroes, and Mongolians comprise discrete species, and for the conclusion that they merely represent races within the same species, he observes the high fertility of cross-breeders. He points out that, in the modern era, "already one-seventieth of the total population of the globe are mixtures, resulting from the cross of the whites with indigenous peoples" outside of Europe. More dramatic evidence will be seen in South America where one-quarter of the inhabitants, and in some regions one-half, are "cross-breeds."

[21]So reads Chesnutt's typescript, and clarification is not offered in the *Alexander's Magazine* publication, wherein the passage does not appear.

[22]Chesnutt again refers to the Russo-Japanese War and the inability of a European power, Russia, to establish hegemony in the Far East. At this time President Roosevelt was bringing the two countries together to negotiate the Treaty of Portsmouth, which was accepted by both on 29 August 1905 and signed four days later.

[23]Sydney H. Olivier (1859–1943), "White Man's Burden at Home," *International Quarterly*, 11 (April 1905), 2–23.

[24]See "The Future of the Negro," n. 20.

Age of Problems

Speech to the Cleveland Council of Sociology, Cleveland, O., November 1906

We live in an age of social unrest—indeed every age is an age of unrest, an age of transition. If science has taught us anything, it is that constant movement, incessant change, is the law of life. There is no longer any firm earth, no longer any eternal hills. The movement may be fast or slow, as the vibrations are short or long, but it is constant. And the human race, and human institutions are so firmly in the grip of this law as are the most distant stars or the tiniest molecules.

And change involves, always, readjustment, and readjustments create problems. Every age has its problems. Some are continuing problems—as for instance the problems of poverty, of vice, of crime—they grow out of the fundamental functions of life—to sustain itself and to reproduce itself. Other problems are temporary, and peculiar to the day or the year or the generation. Our Race Problem seems to lie somewhere between the two. It is not unsolvable, but it is difficult, and we shrink from the application of the remedy. I think I see the remedy, I am sure I foresee the difficulty of its application.

PRESENT STATUS OF PROBLEM.

(Incident on steps of News Office: "Chasing a nigger." "It was my own idea.")[1] This incident in one of the advanced stages of the Race Problem, in one of the advanced communities of this country, roughly typifies the present status of the Race Problem. One eighth of the population of this country stand to the rest distinctly in the position of a despised and oppressed race. Disfranchised, to such an extent that from the eleven states where the majority of them dwell there comes not one friendly voice to represent them in Congress. The governor of one state, whose Negro population is vastly in excess of the white, can find nothing better to say of the majority of the people who pay his salary than to predict their extermination.[2] The governor of another State, where the Negro males of voting age are 153,000 in excess of the whites, has made an unholy reputation by stirring up race hatred at home and in Congress, and by wandering about the North, defaming, for one hundred dollars a night, the constituents and the constitution, to support and defend which he is paid a salary.[3] He is recently quoted as saying, apropos of the Atlanta atrocity, that the Southern people should go ahead and settle this race problem in their own way, regardless of what might be said by all the Yankees between Cape Cod and hell.[4] There are a good many Yankees, at varying distances, between Cape Cod and hell, but I think he will find, if he crowds this question too far, that the majority of them are not on his end of the road. We are to have this "statesman" here to instruct our school teachers, I believe, sometime this winter.[5] I have yet to learn whether he will appear with his pitchfork in his character as licensed mountebank, or as a teacher of the popular Southern brand of political morals and civic righteousness. The colored people are denied the equal protection of the laws, they are "jim-crowed" from the old Mason and Dixon's line southward, in schools, and hotels, on trains and steamboats, on street cars and in waiting rooms, and there is a vigorous tendency to extend this discrimination northward. They get a square deal nowhere. A few years ago, a judge of the Common Pleas Court in this city, wishing to make an example, selected the case of a colored woman who had lured a white man, who followed her with an amorous intent, into an alley, where she relieved him of his roll, some few dollars. Mrs. Chadwick, who stole millions, and left a trail of tragedy behind her, received a shorter sentence.[6] Even the President of the United States, the apostle of the Square Deal, wishing to make an example, discharged, without honor, a whole battalion of colored troops, under circumstances which the press of the country unanimously, so far as I have followed the comment, condemn as unjust and unfair.[7] Every one who wishes to can make an example of the man who has no friends. (Story: Pitch into the Jews.) And even when the Negro gets justice, it is rarely tempered with mercy.

But enough of this phase of the subject—which is not a hopeful phase, unless one go upon the theory that the darkest hour is just before dawn.[8] (Story: Old black woman and children.)

Carl Schurz, in an illuminating paper on this subject, published some three years ago in *McClure's Magazine*,[9] said:

> This is evidently a political and social condition which cannot continue to exist without constant and most unwholesome irritation and restlessness. Such as it is, it cannot possibly be permanent. The colored people will be incessantly disturbed by the feeling that they are unjustly deprived of their legal rights and have become the victims of tyrannical oppression. The most thoughtful and self-respecting among the whites will be ashamed of that state of things, and dissatisfied with themselves for tolerating it. The reckless among the white population, the element most subject to the passions fomented and stirred by a race-antipathy, and most responsive to the catch-phrases of the demagogue, will understand it as a justification of all the things done to put down the negro, and as an incitement to further steps along the same line.
>
> And here is the crucial point: *There will be a movement either in the direction of reducing the negroes to a permanent condition of serfdom—the condition of the mere plantation hand, "alongside of the mule," practically without any rights of citizenship—or a movement in the direction of recognizing him as a citizen in the true sense of the term. One or the other will prevail.*

A superficial glance at present conditions would seem to indicate that the first of these movements is well under way. Fortunately the antidote is found near the poison, and I am going to show, if I can, in my search for hopeful phases, that the other movement has begun.

EQUALITY THE ONLY SOLUTION.

Nor in my search for a solution of this problem am I going to make any stops at way stations. I am going straight to the heart of it: There is but one solution to the race problem in the United States, and that is to grant the Negro *equality*. I do not speak of something which is to be achieved. Men achieve liberty; they achieve civilization. The equality of which I speak is that of which in the language of the Declaration of Independence, all men are created. It is the equality which is freely conceded between white man and white man. It is the right to share fairly and equitably in the use of the earth, which is our common mother, our common inheritance, our common grave. It is the right of the Negroes the world over because of their humanity. It is their right in this land if such a basis of right were needed, because of their nativity. Here they were born and their fathers for more generations than most of the white people who are trying to crowd them off the earth. And they are entitled to this simple elemental right by the Constitution of the United

States. I shall not quote it; some of you are lawyers and officeholders who have sworn to support it; some of you are teachers who assume to teach it. If it was intended to mean anything in its amended form, it was intended to define citizenship and establish the equality of the citizens without regard to race or color.

This equality is frankly denied in all the Southern States, and I may add, is but feebly maintained in many parts of the North.

SOUTH THE ONLY OBSTACLE TO SOLUTION.

It is the white South alone which stands in the way of the solution of the Race Problem—and it stands squarely in the middle of the road. (I might add that it stood there once before, and got so badly bumped by the car of progress that it has not yet recovered.) The North has long ago followed the Constitution and recognized the doctrine of equality. The manner in which it has of late years leaned back upon the question is traceable solely to the Southern influence.

Mr. H. G. Wells, the eminent English writer recently visiting this country, speaks of the very obvious lack of any settled opinion upon this subject in the North and West.[10] "The quality of the discussion," he says,

> is variable, but upon the whole pretty low. We English, a century ago, said all these things of the native Irish. If there is any trend of opinion at all in this matter at present, it lies in the direction of a generous decision on the part of the North and West to leave the black more and more to the judgment and mercy of the white people with whom he is locally associated. This judgment and mercy points, on the whole, to an accentuation of the colored man's natural inferiority, to the cessation of any other educational attempts than those that increase his industrial usefulness, to his industrial exploitation through usury and legal chicanery, and to a systematic strengthening of the social barriers between colored people of whatever shade and the whites.

HOW SOUTH JUSTIFIES OPPRESSION.

The South, of course, seeks to justify its oppression of the Negro and its denial of constitutional right and the democratic principle of equality.

"We cannot," they declare, "concede the Negroes political equality, because, if granted, it will lead to every other kind of equality. With political equality they would demand civil equality. With civil equality they would seek social equality. The purity of our race would be contaminated. Our civilization would be destroyed."

"Why," one asks, "would all these direful consequences ensue?"

"Because," is the answer, "the Negroes are ignorant. They are criminal. They are lustful. They are fundamentally and hopelessly inferior. And they are unreasonably aspiring. They will not accept the inevitable. Only by the strong hand of repression can they be kept in their proper position of subordination."

There is the whole argument. And when I have indicated a few of its inconsistencies, exposed a few of its hypocrisies, and corrected a few of its honest mistakes, there will be little of it left.

In doing this I am going to cite as authorities, various white men, experts, who know their subjects, and cannot be suspected of any prejudice in favor of the Negro. And the fact that I shall be able to do this by their words is one of the most helpful phases of the problem.

IGNORANCE OF THE NEGRO.

Upon the ignorance of the Negro I shall spend but a moment. Ignorance is a matter of school and schoolhouses and experience in life. The Negro with the aid of the white North, and a saving remnant of the white South, has made great strides in education. The colored people have reduced their illiteracy by one half in one generation. Could one ask a better showing? I am in a position to know that young men and women of color sometimes make incredible sacrifices for the sake of an education. The records of our colleges are replete with honorable examples. Nor has their learning been in vain. They are found in the ranks of all the professions, and in every branch of economic endeavor—where they are not barred by race prejudice. Let me quote another paragraph from Carl Schurz which covers not only this subject, but the excuse which is given for the harsh and unjust labor laws of the South—the charge that the Negroes will not work:

> Negro suffrage is plausibly objected to on the ground that the great bulk of the colored population of the South are very ignorant. This is true. But the same is true of a large portion of the white population. If the suffrage is dangerous in the hands of certain voters on account of their ignorance, it is as dangerous in the hands of ignorant whites as in the hands of ignorant blacks. To remedy this, two things might be done: to establish an educational test for admission to the suffrage, excluding illiterates; and, secondly, to provide for systems of public instruction so as gradually to do away with illiteracy, subjecting whites and blacks alike to the same restrictions and opening to them the same opportunities. This would be easily assented to by the Southern whites if the real or the principal objection to negro suffrage consisted in the ignorance of the black men. It is also said "that education unfits the negro for work." This is in so far true as it makes many negroes unwilling to devote themselves to the ordinary plantation labor, encouraging them to look for work more congenial to their abilities and tastes, and sometimes even seducing them to live upon their wits without work. But the same, then, is true in regard to white men. The increasing disinclination of young white persons to walk behind the plow or attend to the milking of cows in the solitude of farm life, and the spreading among them of the desire to enjoy a pleasanter existence and to do easier and finer work in the cities, which we observe all around us in the North, with no little anxiety as to what it may at last lead to, is no doubt largely attributable to the natural effects of popular education. But if here, at the North, the question were asked whether for this reason popular education should be restricted to the end of increasing the fitness and taste for farm work among our people, there would hardly be an audible voice of assent.
>
> That the evil of ignorance as an active element on the political field presents a more serious and complicated problem in the South than in the North cannot be denied, for the mass of ignorance precipitated into the body politic by the enfranchisement of the blacks is so much greater there than here. But most significant and of evil augury is the fact that with many of the Southern whites a well-educated col-

ored voter is as objectionable as an ignorant one, or even more objectionable, simply on account of his color. It is therefore not mere dread of ignorance in the voting body that arouses the Southern whites against the colored voters.

CRIMINALITY OF THE NEGRO.

Great stress is laid of late, in excusing mob violence in the South, upon the increasing criminality of the Negro. I shall not inquire whether murder is worse than rape, whether therefore the white mob which murders a rapist is not more criminal than he. I merely suggest that it has lately been discovered that the increase of crime—including this one, in this country has been appallingly great and appallingly general. The Negroes are the lower class of the South, and in this class everywhere the criminals are mostly found. The crimes of Negroes are emphasized by the newspapers, which find them good copy, mainly because of the crimes of riot and mob murder which accompany or follow them. To illustrate the conscious or unconscious hypocrisy of the I-am-holier-than-thou charge that Negroes are unduly addicted to the crime of rape, I call attention to the fact that on the very day on which, in Atlanta, four Negroes were charged with criminal assaults on white women—not one of the charges has since been verified as a case of rape, and in only one did a Negro so much as lay his hand upon a white woman, resulting in a carnival of violence and murder done upon the persons of admittedly innocent and even unsuspected colored men, and women—on that same day in the city of Chicago, twenty-three men were fined, imprisoned or remanded for trial, in the police court of that city, for assaults upon white women and girls. This was a one day's record. There are 40,000 Negroes in Atlanta, 46,000 Negroes in Chicago. Of the 23 miscreants not one was a Negro. In the city of Cleveland, last month, there were seven cases of criminal assault by the police court records, and the number of such crimes during the past year was shocking to say the least. These crimes are not exploited in the newspapers, for very good sociological and psychological reasons. Similar crimes of Negroes are, and very often for very low and indefensible reasons. Race prejudice is popular, to cater to it is profitable. (Case in my own knowledge, little girl in police court.) White womanhood has been outraged, is outraged every day; but there are no riots, no violence. The law considers the cases, weighs them, more or less carefully, leans to mercy rather than to severity, remembering the weakness of the flesh; gives the accused the benefit of the doubt, bearing in mind the difficulty and uncertainty of evidence in such cases.

All of which leads to the serious question, "Is there really in the South any such exaggerated respect for white womanhood before which all other laws must give way, or is it founded purely upon race and caste hatred?" I yield to no one in my respect for womanhood (and I don't judge it by its color either), but I have never yet been able to see why the virtue of a woman is more valuable than the life of a man. In Atlanta, or any other large city in the South—or in the North, for that matter, you will find there the usual number of lupanars,[11] where for a pecuniary consideration, white men may satisfy their lusts upon the bodies of young and of-

ten beautiful women of their own race. For twenty-five cents, in any city, an ignorant, half-trained, wholly unrestrained youth of any race may go, night after night
and watch a half-naked white woman often young and beautiful, disport herself
before the footlights, with suggestive leer and gesture, and befoul her own lips and
their imaginations with risqué song and foul innuendo. Surely the exalted respect
for women—which burns men alive for looking at them, is either badly out of balance or else it is a mere pretense. I quote the writer in the *Atlantic Monthly*, who
signs himself "Nicholas Worth."[12] He was a Southerner, one of the enlightened
who had lived long at the North. Like the Colonel in my novel *The Colonel's
Dream*,[13] he went back to his old home to build up the waste places, to heal the
wounds of slavery and of war.

"We had," he says,

> come to the Mount of Hope, and the prospect was fair in our upland South. We
> were freeing our old King (cotton) from the fetters of slovenly work and poor land
> and primitive manufacture, and we were regaining our own liberties,—prosperity,
> right training, free thought. A man was a man, white or black. We had our own
> ways of life to which custom and convenience had shaped us. But we were men who
> lived without bitterness and hatred. Under the fairest land I suppose, if one could
> dig deep enough, volcanic fires are somewhere smouldering.
>
> The hard pressed political machine was even to loose volcanic fires if it could
> thereby save itself. And the machine was not now run by the old colonels; for they
> were nearly all gone to their eternal rest, or to the half-way house of state pensions.
> Men of my own generation—some younger than I—were come into political man-
> agement. They had seemed to us hitherto to be commonplace lawyers without cli-
> ents, editors of newspapers that did not yield a profit, hangers-on to legitimate in-
> dustry. They were not thought to be burdened with convictions, nor had they re-
> ceived credit for sleepless vigilance in "saving society." But suddenly they assured us
> that they were its most zealous guardians, and they came forth with social and po-
> litical convictions, which, they declared, they would stand for to the death! . . .
>
> The Negro was a savage, a brute, a constant menace. Educate him? Then you
> only make him more cunning for evil. He must be put down, and kept down.
>
> The political expression of this crusade was a disfranchising amendment. But
> the oratorical expression of it became a cry of race-hatred. Men whose faithful
> servants were negroes, negroes who had shined their shoes in the morning and
> cooked their breakfasts and dressed their children and groomed their horses and
> driven them to their offices, negroes who were the faithful servants and constant
> attendants on their families,—such men spent the day declaring the imminent
> danger of negro "equality" and "domination." "We must put them out of politics
> once and forever." The old Colonels had been more frank when they said, "What
> are our niggers for but to win elections with?" This was an election that must be
> won. The governorship and a senatorship were at stake.
>
> And the volcanic fires were found. The race-difference became in many minds a
> fierce race-hatred. There is no way to know how many crimes were provoked by
> this outburst of race-feeling. But every crime, little or big, that was committed was
> described again and again, and commented on. The newspapers became unreadable
> by decent women. Conversation ran to criminal talk. The political orators talked
> crime. The redcoats of the ku-klux era reappeared. Negroes were threatened and in-
> timidated. Even the pulpit took up the cry, "Our homes must be saved!"

Of course there were protests; but they came too late. Many men who under-stood the insincerity of it all, and saw the harm that it was doing,—for such a cru-sade provokes the very evils that it cries out against, and all other evils of social dis-order,—such men declared their objection. But they had feeble voices, because they spoke late. The volcano was in eruption. It was too late to say that there was no vol-cano.

And right here, I think, is the saddest and the most sinister effect of the denial of equality—it poisons the fountains of sympathy, and renders friendship impos-sible. The very essence of friendship is equality—and sympathy is merely *fellow* feeling. Patronage there might be, and condescension and sincere benevolence on the one hand, deference and gratitude on the other, but friendship, no—it is too noble a word to be profaned by such a use.

There I shall leave the question of Negro crime, and especially the usual crime. God knows the Negroes are human—they are very human, and many of them very weak. They need restraint, and guidance, but they need justice and friendship and sympathy far more.

INFERIORITY OF THE NEGRO.

The Negro it is said, is inferior, fundamentally inferior, so radically differenti-ated in evolutionary development that it will require ages of upward struggle to bring him up to the level of the whites in intellect, in morals, or social efficiency.

The race we are told, has never produced a Newton, a Shakespeare, a Milton, a Galileo, a Copernicus.[14] Well, what of that? The white race throughout all its ages of opportunity, with all that it has borrowed from dead and forgotten prehis-toric races whose color no one knows, in command, throughout the historic ages, of all the enginery of progress, has produced but *one* Shakespeare, *one* Milton, *one* Copernicus, *one* Galileo, *one* Newton. And these men were so preeminently the flower of all humanity, that no race or nation claims them—no one thinks of them as great Englishmen, or great Italians or whatever they may be, but simply as great men. We think of them as we do of Jesus—not as Jesus the Jew, son of Joseph and of Mary, but as Jesus the Son of Man, or the Son of God. I shall not cite instances of famous men, of more or less Negro blood, who would at least refute the theory that Negro blood *per se*, is a badge of any sort of inferiority. I might mention a goodly number of those in our own land who in the forty years which measure their period of opportunity, have lifted their heads above the level of mediocrity: There are 25 or 30 living men who are counted worthy of enrolment in the few thousand names recorded in the current number of the well-known handbook, *Who's Who in America*. (Tanner, Du Bois, Washington, the Bishops, Scott, Bowen, Fortune, Dunbar.)[15]

Dr. Franz Boas, a professor of Columbia College, has made a notable contri-bution to this discussion in a recent article, "The Negro and the Demands of Mod-ern Life,"[16] discussing the subject from a purely scientific side—the ethnic and ana-tomical side. His conclusions are most interesting and most hopeful:

He discusses the obvious physiological differences between the white and black races—the differences in pigmentation in hair, in shape of the head and features, and in the development of the nervous system, and concludes with this statement: "As it is, almost all we can say with certainty is that the differences between the average types of the white and the Negro that have a bearing upon vitality and mental ability are much less than the individual variations in each race.

This result is, however, of great importance, and is quite in accord with ethnological observations. A survey of African types exhibits to our view cultural achievements of no mean order. To those unfamiliar with the products of native African art and industry a walk through one of the large museums of Europe would be a revelation. None of our American museums has made collections that exhibit in any way worthily this subject. The blacksmith, the woodcarver, the weaver, the potter, these all produce ware original in form, executed with great care and exhibiting that love of labor and interest in the results which is apparently so often lacking among the Negroes in our American surroundings. No less instructive are the records of travelers, reporting the thrift of the native villages, of the extended trade of the country and of its markets. The power of organization as illustrated in the government of native states is of no mean order and when wielded by men of great personality has led to the foundation of extended empires. All the different kinds of activities that we consider valuable in the citizens of our country may be found in aboriginal Africa. Neither is the wisdom of the philosopher absent. A perusal of any of the collections of African proverbs that have been published will demonstrate the homely practical philosophy of the Negro which is often of sound feeling and judgment.

It would be out of place to enlarge on this subject, because the essential point that anthropology can contribute to the practical discussion of the adaptability of the Negro is a decision of the question how far the undesirable traits that are at present undoubtedly found in our Negro population are due to racial traits, and how far they are due to social surroundings for which *we* are responsible. To this question anthropology can give the decided answer that the traits of African culture as observed in the aboriginal home of the Negro are those of a healthy primitive people with a considerable degree of personal initiative, with a talent for organization, and with considerable imaginative power; with technical skill and thrift. Neither is a warlike spirit absent in the race, as is proved by the mighty conquerors who overthrew states and founded new empires, and by the courage of the armies that follow the bidding of their leader. There is nothing to prove that licentiousness, shiftless laziness, lack of initiative, are fundamental characteristics of the race. Everything points out that these qualities are the result of social conditions rather than of hereditary traits.

It may be well to state here once more, with some emphasis, that it would be erroneous to assume that there are no differences in the mental make-up of the Negro race and of other races, and that their activities should run in the same lines. On the contrary, if there is any meaning in correlation of anatomical structure and physiological function, we must expect that differences exist. There is, however, no evidence whatever that would stigmatize the Negro as of weaker build, or as subject to inclinations and powers that are opposed to our social organization. An unbiased estimate of the anthropological evidence so far brought forward does not permit us to countenance the belief in a racial inferiority which would unfit an individual or the Negro race to take his part in modern civilization: We do not know of any demand made on the human body or mind in modern life that anatomical or ethnological evidence would prove to be beyond the powers of the Negro.

The best observers of foreign races in all parts of the world who have had opportunity to come into intimate contact with individuals of the tribes they visited, and who have shared their joys and sorrows, furnish us with data which show with ever-increasing clearness the sameness of the fundamental traits of the human mind in all the races that exist at present and in all forms of culture that are found in our times; they bring before our eyes the intellectual powers of primitive man, and his ethical and esthetic standards. At the same time becomes apparent the overwhelming influence of tradition, the unreasoning adherence to forms of thought and action that have once been established—not only in primitive culture, but even in the most advanced types of civilization.

There is nothing in the present status of the African and American Negro that cannot be adequately explained on this basis. The tearing away from the African soil, and the consequent complete loss of the old standards of life which were replaced by the dependency of slavery and by all it entailed, followed by a period of disorganization and by a severe economic struggle against heavy odds, are sufficient to explain the inferiority of the status of the race without falling back to the theory of hereditary inferiority.

In short, there is every reason to believe that the Negro when given facility and opportunity will be perfectly able to fill the duties of citizenship as well as his white neighbor. It may be that he will not produce as many great men as the white race, and that his average achievement will not quite reach the level of the average achievement of the white race, but there will be endless numbers who will be able to outrun their white competitors, and who will do better than the defectives whom we permit to drag down and retard the healthy children of our public schools.

ASPIRATIONS OF THE NEGRO.

"The Negroes," says our Southern apologist for suppression, "are unreasonable. They aspire to equality. They are not satisfied to remain in that state of subordination to which God in his wisdom has obviously been pleased to call them." Aspire! of course they aspire! Are they not benefited, and through them society, by their aspiration? Who does not despise the willing slave? Not only do they aspire to equality—they aspire to distinction. (Ms. on my desk, Pullman porter; seven years writing, seven years to find a publisher.) One may smile, but an unfulfilled aspiration is better than none, and, by the way, that is not the first unpublished Ms. I have read, and not from the hands of colored men either. He would be cruel indeed that would deprive any man of aspiration. It is a cheap commodity—it is about all that is left to the Negro in many parts of this land. Do not at least deprive him of his moon. Let him reach up toward it, and by and by when his arms have grown longer, he will grasp it, and other men, in another age, who never saw the bruised and shackled stumps, which he first lifted up, will never think to question his possession!

RACE PURITY.

And now I wish, for a moment to attack the fetish of Race Purity. And I want to do it seriously, and even solemnly—I wish to show no disrespect to other men's gods, or seek to convert them to any other faith except by reason. And if I fail, I will accept as far as I must, their judgment. I know quite well that the difference in color and physical characteristics is the main stumbling block in the path of equality. There is a tendency in nature toward the preservation of types, even toward the preservation of varieties, and society tends to accentuate this tendency, especially when it involves the perpetuation of privilege. But every student of Darwin knows that all progress in nature comes through departure in types.[17] History shows us that the most virile and progressive races have always been mixed races, and that races which interbreed too closely are sure to degenerate. But whatever may or may not be most desirable, more or less mixture of blood would seem to be inevitable where different races come in contact, and no system of social discouragement has ever proved sufficient to prevent it. In the treaty ports of China and Japan, and in India, the Eurasians number many thousands; perhaps the most eminent English author of the day has a slight strain of Hindoo blood on his mother's side.[18] Africa has many white men, few white women, and many mulattoes. Whole sections of our own continent are inhabited by mixed races. (Specify.) By the census of 1890 there were one million perhaps half or more than half white returned; of the remainder of the so called Negroes, at least half have a strain more or less large, of white blood. And when a class of people reaches a million in number, its existence is no longer a theoretical matter; it is an accomplished fact which must be reckoned with. Taking our nation in the raw, and finding in its present population the ingredients of our future race, ours is a mixed race already—combined of every variety of mankind under the sun. Some are taken with a wry face—the Negro is a hard pill to swallow. The Chinese we have sought to keep out—the Negro is too big to throw up.

On this subject I wish to quote a gentleman who has lived many years in the British West Indies, where this race problem has been worked out to a practical and peaceful conclusion:

(Quote Olivier, *Int. Quar.*)[19]

* * *

RACE CONSCIOUSNESS.

But I fear I have overrun my time. I had wished to mention, as a hopeful phase of the Race Problem, that the Negro is beginning, under pressure, to find himself, to become conscious of the tremendous power latent in nine or ten millions of human beings: They are beginning to resent oppression. By concerted effort they have well nigh bankrupted a number of the street railroads in the South which jim-crow them. They killed at least one white man, in the Atlanta riot.[20] They have by protest and concerted action prevented the presentation in Philadelphia, Chicago and elsewhere of Dixon's infamous play, *The Clansman*.[21] They are boycotting, in South Carolina, the planters who lynch or oppress them. They are declining to work without fair wages. In many cities they are wisely dividing their vote. In other words, they are learning, not at the end of several thousand additional years of evolution, but now, today, the use of the machinery of society. They are beginning to regain those powers possessed by the forefathers in Africa, of which our system of slavery deprived them.

And in spite of surface indications to the contrary, they are making friends.

CONDEMNATION OF RIOTS.

Another hopeful phase is the unanimous and almost savage condemnation which the press of the North and generally of the South heaped upon the city of Atlanta for the recent riot there, and the clear perception of the real causes which led up to it, throwing the onus clearly upon the Southern whites.

WORLD-WIDE REVOLT.

Another hopeful phase is the revolt of oppressed peoples the world over. Russia is in the throes of a struggle for equality. Persia demands a representative government. China is in transition. Japan has found herself, and demands equality for her people in America. The Zulus have been subdued. The Indians are on the warpath. Every point gained for liberty and equality anywhere is a point for liberty and equality everywhere.

A WORD OF WARNING.

A most helpful phase of opinion is suggested by the following significant utterance in a recent editorial in the *New York Times*, commenting upon some of Senator Tillman's incendiary utterances:[22]

* * *

FORAKER.

This is refreshing and helpful talk. And even an Ohio Senator has seen the light, and *apropos* of the race troubles, Senator Foraker recently said:[23]

* * *

LIBERTY PARTY IN THE SOUTH.

I have always believed that the colored people in this country would never have a square deal until a party favorable to human equality grew up among the white people of the South. I wish I had time to indicate the signs which point to the growth of such a party. I should have liked to quote from Professor Bassett of Trinity College, N.C., who says in the *South Atlantic Quarterly*, for October 1903:[24]

* * *

CONCLUSION.

When by the growth of Southern opinion, aided by friendly criticism from without, these fair words have been transmuted into actions,[25] the race problem will be settled. It will at least be lifted to a level where its solution may be left there, as it is at the North already, to time and the operation of beneficent social forces.

I wanted to quote from ex-Congressman Fleming's recent address before the Alumni Society of Georgia State University, in June of this year.[26] The Constitution, he says, will never be changed to limit the rights of the Negro. The problem, he says, can never be settled except upon lines of honesty and justice. And the strength of the hope that lies in these utterances rests in the fact that men do not stand alone. Each has a following. Professor Bassett has a magazine and a subscription. Mr. Fleming is the leader of a party. One is a professor in a college for white young men. The other was the orator at a college function. I cannot better close this long and discursive paper, in which I have said so much and left so much unsaid, than in the language of this same Mr. Fleming: (Quote Fleming) . . . .[27]

SOURCE: Incomplete and undated typed text at the Fisk University Library. Lacking are five quotations read by Chesnutt when he delivered this speech to the Cleveland Council of Sociology. References to the Brownsville Affair and to a planned Cleveland speech by Senator Benjamin R. Tillman indicate a dating of early November 1906.

[1]The nature of the anecdote related by Chesnutt is not known. Recent issues of local newspapers do not include a report on an incident of the kind.

[2]Mississippi's Governor James K. Vardaman.

[3]Former Governor Benjamin R. Tillman was at this time a U.S. Senator from South Carolina. The *New York Times*, in an editorial entitled "The Negroes and the South" (12 October 1906, 8), chastised him for his "burst of savage fury" at a meeting of African Americans in New York City: "When his reason is not submerged by his passions he is capable of good counsel. But the vein of coarseness and brutality in him shocks and revolts all the decency of the American people whenever he gives it expression. And he has never made a more cynical or a more revolting exhibition of it than in his recent outbreak about the race question in the South. It simply disqualified him to be heard with respect or even with patience upon the subject."

[4]Tillman declared on 7 October 1906 in Augusta, Ga., that the white men of the South should do all that was necessary to maintain white supremacy, regardless "of all the Yankees between Cape Cod and hell" ("Race War Is Coming, Says Senator Tillman," *New York Times*, 8 October 1906, 1). Tillman's main point was that the Atlanta race riot triggered on 22 September by an alleged assault upon a white woman would pale into insignificance when compared with the bloody conflicts between blacks and whites that were inevitable in the North and the South: lynching had not discouraged the rape of white women; and the African American had not yet learned that he must forswear all social and political ambitions, as well as the hope for racial amalgamation. Even when acknowledging that all African Americans were not troublesome, he was inflammatory: "The superior race should protect many millions of innocent negroes from

false teachers and bad leaders, who are rapidly driving the whites to a desperation that means race war that can only result in the destruction of the weaker race."

[5]Tillman was scheduled to speak in a "teachers' lecture course" in Cleveland on 19 December 1906. By 3 November, the *Cleveland Journal* reported protest; by 17 November, the lecture had been canceled.

[6]Mrs. Cassie L. Chadwick was indicted by a grand jury in Cleveland on 21 February 1905 for aiding and abetting two bankers in Ohio and New York who had embezzled funds. Chadwick was found guilty and sentenced to a prison term of ten years.

[7]African-American soldiers of the Twenty-fifth U.S. Infantry stationed at Fort Brown near Brownsville, Tx., were charged with firing over 100 rifle shots on the night of 3 August 1906, killing one citizen and wounding a police officer. When none would admit to any connection with the incident, President Theodore Roosevelt decided on 5 November 1906 to "discharge without honor" 160 of the soldiers.

[8]William Carew Hazlitt (1834–1913), *English Proverbs and Proverbial Phrases* (1882).

[9]"Can the South Solve the Negro Problem?"

[10]H. G. Wells (1866–1946), "The Future in America," *Harper's Weekly*, 50 (14 July–6 October 1906); Chesnutt quotes from the installment in the 15 September 1906 issue, 1317–19. See also the book with the same title (1906): chapter 12 in the American printing and 13 in the English.

[11]Brothels.

[12]"Autobiography of a Southerner Since the Civil War," *Atlantic Monthly*, 98 (July–October 1906), 1–12, 157–76, 311–25, 474–88. Nicholas Worth was the pseudonym of North Carolinian Walter Hines Page (1855–1918).

[13]Published in 1905.

[14]Galileo Galilei (1564–1642), Italian astronomer and physicist, is most famous for having supported the theory that the earth revolves about the sun, which was propounded by Polish astronomer Nicolas Koppernik or Copernicus (1473–1543).

[15]*Who's Who in America* was published biennially, beginning in 1899, by Albert Nelson Marquis of Chicago. The 1906–7 edition included Bishop Benjamin Tucker Tanner, his eldest son Henry Ossawa Tanner, W. E. B. Du Bois, Booker T. Washington, Isaiah B. Scott, Methodist clergyman and educator John Wesley Edward Bowen (1855–1933), T. Thomas Fortune, and Paul Laurence Dunbar. The reference to "Bishops" is not to a surname but to African-American bishops.

[16]This article appeared in *Charities and the Commons*, 15 (7 October 1905), 85–88. Boas (1858–1942) was a German-born anthropologist who taught at Columbia from 1896 to 1942.

[17]Darwin focuses on the effects of variation within species in both *On the Origin of Species* (1859) and *The Descent of Man* (1871).

[18]Chesnutt is perhaps speculating thus about Rudyard Kipling.

[19]Sydney H. Olivier, "White Man's Burden at Home."

[20]When the police fired into a crowd, an African American returned fire, killing one officer; two other whites also lost their lives.

[21]This novel was given dramatic adaptation and performed for the first time on 22 September 1905 in Norfolk, Va. It was a sell-out in almost every Northern and Southern city in which it played. Its performances in Philadelphia and Chicago were halted because of rioting.

[22]In all likelihood, Chesnutt read from an editorial in the *New York Times*, 27 November 1906, 8. Therein Senator Tillman's claim that the black race is "naturally inferior" was assailed as being "as shallow as it is brutal."

[23]In "That Atlanta Massacre," *Cleveland Gazette*, 6 October 1906, 2, U.S. Senator from Ohio Joseph D. Foraker (1846–1917) was quoted: "The situation at Atlanta is too shocking, too uncivilized, barbaric and un-American to be discussed calmly and dispassionately."

[24]Emended is Chesnutt's misidentification of John Spencer Bassett (1867–1928) as Professor "Barnes." Bassett was a Professor of History at Trinity College in North Carolina (1893–1906) and Smith College (1906–28), and he edited the *South Carolina Quarterly* (1902–5). He appears to have been the author of the unsigned article "Stirring Up the Forces of Race Antipathy," 2 (October 1903), 297–305. Having admitted his own prejudice against African Americans, he laments the way in which white politicians have exacerbated inter-racial tensions for the sake of maintaining Democratic rule in the South. He is opposed to the caste mentality resulting in the "philosophy" that blacks must be kept in their "place": "We ought to remember that such an ideal is neither scientific nor charitable. The 'place' of every man in our American life is such [a] one as his virtues and his capacities may enable him to take. Not even a black skin and a flat nose can [justify] caste in this country."

[25]Emended to "actions" is "words."

[26]Chesnutt canceled a reference to a lack of time in which to do so.

[27]William Henry Fleming (1856–1944) was a Georgia Democrat who had served in the U.S. House of Representatives from 1897 to 1903. It is likely that he spoke against repeal of the Fifteenth Amendment. Georgia State University was not formed until 1913; Fleming may have instead spoken before a group at the University of Georgia or the State Industrial College of Georgia.

Rights and Duties

Speech to the Bethel Literary and Historical Association,
District of Columbia, 6 October 1908

... With each forward step the Negro has aroused some latent antagonism. Once the colored people all lived in mostly alleys and low marshy places which white people avoided; when one of them would buy a house in a better locality, and he was touching the tender pocket nerve of his white neighbors, a new source of antagonism was developed. Once they were mostly glad to eat, at the white man's back door, the leavings of the white man's table. But when a dignified government official or a dapper department clerk or a daintily attired school teacher, with a dollar to spare, would enter a Washington restaurant to eat, in a public place amid agreeable surroundings, a palatable meal, the nerve of racial exclusiveness was touched and a new source of antagonism developed. I need not multiply instances. And with the means and the leisure of enjoying came the capacity for feeling, and with each recurring repulse came a sense of wrong and outrage. I cannot overstate the difficulty and complexity of these questions, so important as bearing upon the very inner life of a people. I don't think that any white person has ever begun to appreciate the heart burnings that have grown out of the separate car and other segregation laws which disgrace our Southern states. These things were bad enough when grounded in custom. Then one had at least a fighting chance. They are infinitely worse when founded on law, from which there is no escape except through a long and expensive fight in the courts, with a doubtful outcome. Indeed, one sometimes wishes it were doubtful, the chances are so much one way.

This is our problem today; now, how is it to be solved? And how can we help to solve it? For the solution is not wholly in our hands, as the problem is not wholly our own. How does it involve our rights and how our duties?

What is it then that we want and can help bring about? It is equality—equality of rights, equality of opportunity. These are fundamental, they mean a great deal. They mean a great deal. They mean more than we even think they mean. They mean a fair field in which the individual citizen may run the race of life. And mark you, I say the individual citizen. The whole curse of the race situation lies in the class feeling which complicates it. Once teach men to look upon other men and judge other men by some other standard than that of race or color, and all the other difficulties will vanish like mist before the sun. Every effort to segregate and to stamp as different or inferior a class of people redounds to the injury of the class less fortunate. The Negro cannot compete with the white people, as a class. As individuals they can make such a showing as their deserts may qualify them for. Temporarily, here and there, in the face of conditions which cannot be gainsaid and which it will take a long time to alter, it seems necessary to maintain certain separate institutions for the two races, in the South of course, since in the North the principle of democracy does not permit them. But they foster the spirit of caste. While it is true they open up careers for many who might otherwise find the struggle of life more difficult, this is often at the expense of those whom they serve, since they force into prominence now and then people who are not qualified to render the service undertaken. Our children should be taught by those people best qualified to teach them. Our pulpits should be filled by men whose character and whose training fit them to preach the gospel. Our doctors, to whom we entrust our lives; our lawyers, to whom we look for protection of our property; our law-makers and judges, in whose hands is the safeguarding of our rights and our liberties, should be the best men, not of any particular class, but in the community. And we all instinctively recognize this fact, and when we have a medical or a legal case, we are very apt to seek the man who we think can save our life or our property, and questions of race loyalty are apt to receive a rude setback when they interfere with things which we consider more vital.

How simply and how easily these difficulties would resolve themselves if men looked upon one another as man upon man and if they did not think and speak, as they do in a large part of this country, in terms of black and white. What would become of the Negro, or rather of the Negroes, for with such a state of things we would have no Negro, but only a number of people more or less colored—what would become of these people under such a condition of affairs? They would find their proper level in society as inevitably as water seeks its level. No man would be promoted and no man would be denied promotion because of his color. Some men perhaps would occupy positions of less authority and influence than they do now. Many would, on the other hand, rise in life. Those who were worthy would be honored and trusted, not as Negroes but as men; those who were unworthy or inefficient, would gravitate naturally and properly to the lower places. No man with an overweening ambition, beyond his powers, could deceive himself with the reflection that it was the prejudice of others and not his own shortcomings which relegated him to inferiority.

And what dreadful consequences could flow from the adoption of this principle by the America people as a rule of conduct in the intercourse of the people who make up our mingled population, composed as it is of the people of all races and all degrees of civilization? Take the government of the Southern states. Would Negroes dominate? With no prejudices to push them aside and solidify them into antagonism against the whites, they would no longer vote as a class, but as individuals. They would be subject to the same influences which move other voters. And I challenge any one to point to any quarter of the globe where under conditions such as I speak of, ignorance and inefficiency conduct and administer government. The pen is mightier than the sword;[1] the brain is stronger than the bludgeon. Under such a condition, those best qualified ought to rule, it is better for the interests of all concerned that they should rule; but they should rule with the consent of the governed, they should depend upon them for their power, and in that event the governed would see to it that their rights and their interests were respected.

Under such a state of things every man's rights would be respected. Men would treat one another with the courtesy and consideration due to them. All social questions would take care of themselves in a natural manner. Men would not seek society for which they were not qualified, nor would courtesy or respect or honor be denied to any man because of his race or color. That is what equality means. We hear men speak of different kinds of equality. They are willing to concede the Negro *this* kind of equality, but deny him *that* kind of equality. There is but one kind of equality, as there is but one kind of truth. We cannot classify equality as we do eggs—eggs, fresh eggs, strictly fresh eggs. It means an equal chance for every man and it denies to other men any more right to consider a man's pedigree, unless he chooses to bring it up himself, than it would to inquire of one's private affairs in other particulars. It would be as discourteous to refer to the fact that your father was a slave as it would be to recall the incident that some other man's father was hanged. It was no disgrace of course to be a slave, it is no disgrace to be the son of a slave. It may have been a disgrace to be hanged; it is no just reproach that a man should be the son of one who had met with such an accident. In the ideal state of affairs of which I speak, delicacy would lead one to refrain from mentioning either fact. The man whose father was hanged would like to forget the circumstance but never can; it is not necessary for the man whose father was a slave to direct the attention of others to that fact. Indeed, I think it would be well to let them forget it, now and then, nevertheless, though this will perhaps be difficult so long as they bear the badge of it upon their faces.

There are those, I know, who cherish the dream of a great Negro people in the United States, who shall make a mark upon the page of history. It is as well to dismiss this dream—it is an idle dream. Under the condition of which I speak, the only condition under which you can secure your rights and your liberties and this free opportunity for upward movement of which I have spoken, there will no longer be a Negro race in the United States. Men of color there will be in large numbers. They will marry and perpetuate their own kind. But what opportunity will they have to lay the foundations of a nation or a great people? They may accumulate wealth, but wealth is often a source of weakness rather than of strength; without the power to defend it, it may render the possessor a prey of the rapacious. Where will the Negro as a class in the United States be permitted to acquire that experience in government and statecraft in affairs which will develop a class efficiency along these lines? What state in our Union will turn itself over to the Negro exclusively to test the racial capacity for government? The experiment was tried once, of course under conditions which negatived the possibility of any correct inference from the result, which was no true test of what the capacity of the educated Negro might be.[2] But assuming all that we could claim for the capacity of the Negro, what state will be turned over to him to try his hand upon? Over what large expanse of territory will he be permitted to build up systems of education and economics? Nowhere in the wide world, even in his native continent of Africa today, except perhaps in Abyssinia, a Negroid country, and in Hayti and Liberia, which are not brilliant examples of successful administration, has the Negro absolute control of all departments of society. It is his fate for a long time in the future to live in contact with the white race. He will not have the opportunity to develop a civilization of his own. Nor does he need to. In common with all mankind, he is the heir of the ages. The civilization of Europe was borrowed from Asia and Africa. Modern civilization was founded upon the ruins of ancient systems. Much of the wealth of the world was created in past generations. Our laws in large part are those of ancient Rome, and our language is largely composed of its fragments. Our religion is that of Palestine. Our art is but a feeble copy of that of ancient Greece. Why should the Negro be excluded from his inheritance. He is entitled to share in it upon the same terms as the rest of mankind. He will never get his share as a separate race, segregated by the prejudices of others and by his own prejudices.

And now, at the close of my address, I begin to reach the subject of which I set out to speak. Two movements within the colored race have been discovered and labeled. One is said to insist upon rights, the other upon duties and responsibilities.[3] They are contrasted in such a way as to seem antagonistic. The leaders of the one side or the other are set over against one another as those who in order to advance and emphasize their end of the argument, must seem to decry and minimize the other. I am going to close my eyes to the obvious and insist that this is not true;

that both of these movements are so absolutely necessary to the welfare and happiness and the progress of the Negro that a man is a fool who could see any antagonism between them. And if there is any antagonism between men, it is due entirely and regrettably to those human weaknesses from which, unfortunately, we cannot entirely purge ourselves. Rights and duties. What are our rights and what are our duties?

Some of them are the natural rights of man: the right to life, which once given should be ours to retain until we voluntarily relinquish it, or it is terminated in the course of nature. The right of personal liberty, unless it be forfeited by some violation of a just law. The right, involved in this, to sell one's labor in the best available market. And the rather vague, but highly important right covered by the term "the pursuit of happiness," the right not of an equal share in the products of social effort,—that would be pure socialism, and we do not want that, except as a last resort—but an equal opportunity to share, in accordance with fitness or effort or effectiveness. That is the kind of equality we are entitled to by natural and I think by legal right in this country. That is democracy, and our government is nominally, and except so far as the Negro question has modified it, is practically a democracy. No just man will deny that every human being should, somewhere, have a right to develop the best that is in him, to move freely and hopefully and uprightly in the consciousness that he is in his own place. There can be no other school for patriotism; to the extent that men are denied these natural rights their love of country, which ought to be the keystone of liberty, is undermined and weakened; instead of a bulwark of strength to the nation, they become a source of internal weakness. I sometimes wonder what sort of patriots the colored people of this country will be if the present movement toward their segregation is carried to its logical extreme.

But experience has taught that these fundamental rights are not secure in the hands of the mass, unless in some way the power of the people can be brought to bear against the few, who by superior strength, or cunning, might otherwise seek to destroy liberty and, by monopolizing them, make the rights of others into privileges for themselves. Hence the invention of the ballot, and the gradual extension of the suffrage. Hence the establishment of courts of justice. These rights and these immunities are guaranteed by the Constitution, and I believe that any fair interpretation of that document will find this to be true.

The difficulty of course lies in their adaptation, their enforcement. Only a few years ago was overturned, in our Southern States, an economic and social system entirely different from this; a system under which had grown up all the antagonisms of which I have already spoken. The system was destroyed, in theory; and a new one laid down. But human nature was not changed, nor were habits and customs greatly altered.

I need not tabulate the Negro's rights. They are the natural rights of all men. They are embodied in our Constitution, in plain language or in the clearest implication. But we can never win this battle on the Constitution alone. For legal rights we must of course appeal to this tribunal. But the great fight for equal rights must be fought in the court of conscience. It rests upon the great fundamental principle of the equality of *man*. Not, mark you, the equality of men, or even of races. Our Supreme Court once held in an important case that the Constitutional amendments were not intended to wipe out distinctions of race.[4] Any just distinctions, any real distinctions of race, could not be wiped out by Constitutions or anything else, their sources lie deeper than human enactment. But legal and civil differences based upon race and having their warrant only in convenience and prejudice and selfishness and privilege, were intended by the Constitution to be wiped from our governmental policy. If they were not they ought to have been, and we should plead for the larger interpretation; we should impress upon every court that it is a court of conscience as well as a court of law.

The one thing which prevents the practical application of this principle of equality is our system of color caste. I think it is the duty of this government to seek by every means in its power to eliminate this most dangerous thing, not only for the protection of the rights of the Negro, but those of all other citizens. Once admit the right to classify people by any rule and limit or regulate their rights by that classification, and we are on the verge of a system which will paralyze our liberty. The people of this country could much better bear all the evils which the most rabid Negro-baiter could predict, than to see any kind of caste system established in this country. A striking illustration is immediately to our hand. Within a comparatively few years a strong prejudice has developed in this country against the Jews. Had the principle of human equality and equal rights been maintained since the Civil War, this would not have been possible. But the ease with which the Negro has been segregated has rendered it easy for another unpopular class to be subjected to the same treatment. And if this evil is accepted as a natural and proper thing, there will soon be other classes against which the majority will feel free to discriminate.

Our government has been derelict in their maintenance of this doctrine. It has been recognized in large measure. In fact, so far as the Southern States are concerned, the administrative department of the Federal Government is almost the sole bulwark of the Negro's political rights. By virtue of its authority he is still permitted to hold a few good Federal offices and a large number of minor positions in the Federal service. The Civil Service rules, in the minor places, have been measurably well observed, thousands of colored men are earning their living in the postoffice and other governmental departments. But hand in hand with this the government has fostered race discrimination. By what principle are Negro soldiers formed into black regiments?[5] Is it a matter of esthetics, because they look better when all of the same complexion? Is it a sop to army pride and class exclusiveness? Do they fight any more efficiently? Has not this segregation in one instance which has become historical, led to a state of misunderstanding—I like to believe that it was a case of misunderstanding, which has stirred from center to circumference the mass of the Negroes of this country, has shaken old faiths, has loosened old ties, and has forced the question of the Negro's political life home upon the minds, not to say the conscience, of the entire United States. Had these Negro soldiers been scattered among the various regiments of the country, there never could have been a Brownsville affair. It would have been impossible to raise a race question, or to inject one into the situation.

But we should always keep this in mind—and I say this from the practical side: the Negro is not entitled to any more rights than are other men. It is well to keep this point in view. If he is to have equality with the white man, he must accept it subject to the white man's tests. He must not aspire to honor or to office unless he is qualified, equally qualified with the white aspirant. I have a friend whom I have heard argue that representing in his own person the best of the colored race, and standing at the head of the class—I am expressing no opinion about his modesty or whether other people would agree with him in his estimate of his own worth— he was therefore entitled to consider himself the equal of those who occupied a similar position among the white race. Such fallacies of argument will have to go under the rule of human equality. All men are not equal; they vary in strength, in wisdom and comeliness, in energy and in many other ways. And when the Negro demands equality he must accept it with the possibility that it may mean inferiority. Whether or not it does will depend upon the individual. We shall all be apples, shaken in a basket; the biggest will come to the top, be they black or white. That kind of freedom the Negro should be willing to accept—it is the best he will ever get—and that sort of equality the white man ought to be willing to concede, without any great fear that he may lose any large part of his present advantage. He has a golden opportunity to do a fine thing at a very small sacrifice. For we must accept the fact that considered as a class the Negroes are far behind the whites and except in rare instances will remain so under the most favorable conditions.

Now, the curse of the whole situation lies in the policy of segregation—it is a policy in the South and has become by force of example a movement in the North. The doctrine of equal rights, if maintained inviolate, would in time overcome the social prejudices which interfere with its application; but the enactment of discriminating laws interrupts the course of nature and poisons the stream at its fountain. The Negro is not responsible for these laws; he did not make them; he was not consulted; they were enacted against his protest and to his injury. Our government condones them on some theory of necessity or convenience or exercise of the police power. They are a source of greater irritation than the robbery of the suffrage. They are said to be intended to prevent clashing between the races. They create more bad blood on the part of colored people than they prevent irritation on the part of the white.

I might multiply examples. I think we are all agreed that the Negro is entitled to the right of suffrage, upon the same terms as those upon which other men possess it, and I for one am a believer in manhood's suffrage. Any man of sound mind and legal age should have some voice in his government. The vast mass of men are unfit to govern personally; scarcely any man is so imbruted that he is not capable in some form or other of expressing an opinion about those who should govern him. Our Southern disfranchising constitutions, pretending to base the suffrage upon education and property, and dodging their own pretenses by bare-faced grandfather clauses and other expedients which some time or other will be laughed at, are unworthy of consideration. Accepting the principle that the suffrage should be restricted, present conditions in the South simply amount to this, that when you restrict the suffrage of the Negro you absolutely eliminate him from any political influence whatever. I speak of present conditions. There is a stirring among the dry-bones;[6] changes may take place in the near future which will correct this wrong. But it can only be corrected entirely when Negroes cease to have any political interests which are adverse to or different from those of other citizens.

I hear a great deal about the right to education of various kinds. The right to education is a matter of mutual contract. Public education is a modern invention, reaching its highest development in two modern nations, America and Germany, not to mention Switzerland. It is in effect applied socialism. Society as a whole, in view of the resulting benefit to society from a high level of intelligence and social efficiency, assumes the expense of educating the young. Now, the Negro's right to education is exactly the same as that of every other man. As to the kind of education which he should have, that is for society to decide. But the young should be educated as individuals and not as races or classes. The vast majority of the colored people will remain for a long time hewers of wood and drawers of water. They will make their living along the lower levels of life and they can dwell there with profit and with honor to themselves. For all that could be asked of a man is to do the best that he can and do it worthily. There will be an increasing number of those who are qualified by nature to adorn the higher walks of life and render higher service to the public. These should have exactly the same opportunities for education that white youth similarly qualified would enjoy. Here again comes in the evil of race segregation. There is a limit to the resources which society can devote to public education. The taxpayer can never be lost sight of. There is a general movement certainly in our own country toward directing education to those ends which will produce the largest results. To take a people who by virtue of their circumstances are confined in the mass to lowly pursuits, and establish schools for their average, is necessarily to condemn their brighter minds to inferior studies and inferior pursuits. This is the result of a policy of segregation and is only another proof that this policy is wrong in principle and must sooner or later be changed or prove disastrous in results.

And I will sum up this question of rights by saying, as I have said before that the Negro is entitled to all the rights that other men are.

Now, white people, those who are worth while, recognize these principles as clearly as you do. They are the basis of their civilization. They have won them on many a hard-fought battlefield; they won them for themselves long ago, and for you when the Constitutional amendments and the enfranchisement act became the law of this country. They give various reasons, most elaborate and sometimes very specious arguments for denying their application to colored men. My friend Prof. Du Bois calls these reasons lies, plain lies, dictated by selfishness and greed. Now, men do not like to be called liars, and the use of harsh language often tends to stir up antagonisms which only make the matter worse. It is better perhaps to make a man discover and feel for himself that he is lying, than to charge him too directly with the fact. Men are swayed by self-interest. A man may enjoy a privilege so long that he believes it to be a right; the whole struggle for human liberty has been fought against privileged classes. And yet a cursory study of history will show that the battle against privilege has always been fought most effectively by those who were among the privileged classes. Jesus was a Jew, one of the chosen people; he destroyed Judaism. Martin Luther was a monk; he led the forces of the Reformation. The leader of every great cause has been one who, had he chosen, might have entrenched himself behind the barriers of privilege and turned his talents to its perpetuation. It is to the unselfish labors of white men that the Negro owes such liberty as he enjoys today. It is to the sense of justice as well as to the enlightened self-interest of white men that he must look in large part for whatever he shall enjoy of liberty and opportunity in the future. He must convince them that his interests are theirs; and he must second this argument by the appeal to justice and humanity and charity. He must try to lead the white man out of the category of adversary and put him in that of friend.

Now, I know you will say that this is easier said than done; that the white man, in fixing the relations of the races, has not consulted the Negro. But there are things which you can do, and things which you can refrain from doing. And that brings us to the subject of duties.

And now, what are his duties? I should say that duties are dependent upon rights, without rights there can be no duties. What were the duties of a slave? He was not a citizen and therefore he had no civic duties. He was denied the institution of marriage and the control of his family; hence he had no domestic duties. For a long time there were those who denied him a soul; one of these fossils was dug up, like the skeleton of a plesiosaurus out in Missouri a year or two ago and published a book entitled, *Is the Negro a Beast?*[7] Without a soul of course he could have no duty to God. The only duty taught him was to obey his master.

Thus it will be seen that duties are dependent upon rights. And therefore the first duty that a man owes to himself and to his children is to assert, to maintain, to defend his rights by every means within his power. It is often said, with some show of force, that the Negro is absolutely helpless at this angle of his career; that his future lies entirely in the hands of the whites. This is not strictly true, for several reasons. The white people have the power, it is true, to reenslave the Negro. They have the power to annihilate the whole colored race. Assuming *equality* of strength and cunning, there are still eight or nine white men to every Negro, and in the present condition of the races I think the eight or nine would have the best of any conflict. Their own number might be slightly reduced, but the others could be destroyed entirely.

But this will never be. It is inconceivable. No one has ever suggested it. The first enemy that the white man would confront if such a proposition were attempted would be himself. He would first have to destroy his civilization, abandon his religion, cast aside all his ideals. He would destroy everything which has given European civilization its proud preeminence in the history of the world. So, on the other hand, the Negro cannot maintain his rights by the strong hand. Now and then an individual can defend his person from violence, his property from seizure. But this battle is to be fought in the arena of reason and in the courts of justice. The appeal must be made to ethics, to justice and to the interests of the whole community, of which the Negro forms after all but a small part.

And now, having performed this first duty, having secured our rights or set out upon that path, what are our other duties? I hardly need to specify. We have a thousand schools pressing them upon us. We have a white people calling our attention to them. We have our most powerful persuasive and popular leaders insisting upon them. Our wives and children are impressing upon us every day our duty to provide them with the necessaries and the luxuries of life; ten thousand preachers are impressing upon us our duty to God and to the Church and threatening us with the pains and penalties of damnation if we fail in either. The tax collector regularly, without fail, calls our attention to the duty which we owe to the state. Just before every election the campaign orator reminds us of our duty to the Republican party and touches very lightly upon the duty of the Republican party to us. The sheriff, the jail, the chain gang, the penitentiary, the torch and the shotgun forcibly impress upon us our duty to our fellow man. All these duties have grown out of our rights. It is a glorious privilege to perform them and they are the things that have made nations great; that have made men worth while. I cannot conceive of any antagonism between rights and duties. I am glad to lend my feeble aid in whatever way I can to any movement designed to protect the one, to advance the other. The needs of this people are too great, their case too hard, for divisions within their own ranks; for fine distinctions which have no real existence. If we need anything it is to work in harmony and no matter along what lines, to the same great end, the uplift of a great people, the sweeping away of this cloud of prejudice, the obliteration of those lines of demarcation which prevent them from becoming in every proper and desirable sense an integral and worthy part of a still greater people. God speed the day when all men in this great land, regardless of race, color or condition, can join hands and move forward to one common goal of prosperity and happiness and worthy living!

♋

SOURCE: Untitled, undated, and incomplete typed text at the Fisk University Library. "Rights and Duties"—referred to in Chesnutt's 9 October 1908 letter to his son Edwin (Fisk University Library)—was read before the Bethel Literary and Historical Association, in the District of Columbia, on 6 October 1908. How the speech was initiated has not been determined; the surviving portion appears to begin *in medias res*.

[1]Edward Bulwer-Lytton, *Richelieu* (1839).

[2]Chesnutt alludes to the negative impression made by black legislators during the

Reconstruction, particularly in South Carolina where their alleged dishonesty and incompetence gave rise to a dramatic white backlash.

[3]Chesnutt wrote in the margin "D. B." (for W. E. B. Du Bois) and "BTW" (for Booker T. Washington).

[4]Plessy v. Ferguson (1896).

[5]Following the Civil War, Congress organized four all-black regiments: the Twenty-fourth and Twenty-fifth Infantry, and the Ninth and Tenth Cavalry. While the War Department formed four more volunteer regiments during the Spanish-American War, each composed solely of African-Americans, these latter units never became part of the regular army. The Brownsville affair of 1906 was the most recent reminder of discrimination against blacks in the military.

[6]Ezekiel 37:3–6.

[7]In 1901 Charles Carroll (1849–?) published *The Negro a Beast*, the subtitle of which discloses its lurid theme: "or In the Image of God: the Reasoner of the Age, the Revelator of the Century! The Bible as it is! The Negro and His Relation to the Human Family! The Negro a beast, but created with articulate speech, and hands, that he may be of service to his master—the White man. The Negro not the Son of Ham. Neither can it be proven by the Bible, and the argument of the theologian who would claim such, melts to mist before the thunderous and convincing arguments of this masterful book." Responding to Carroll, William Gallio Schell published the same year the work with the title given by Chesnutt, *Is the Negro a Beast?*

The Courts and the Negro

Speech delivered c. 1908

The function of courts in the organization of modern society is to protect rights,—to pass upon disputes between man and man or between the individual and the State; and then, by their mandate, to set in motion the arm of the executive to prevent or punish a wrong or to enforce a right. Obviously if this great power be not rightly exercised, if it be swayed by prejudice or class interest, justice will not be done.

The rights of citizens of the United States are embodied in constitutions and statutes. But these, at best, are mere declarations of principles, which, in the complex and shifting nature of society, it is left for courts to apply to the particular instance. And in so doing courts often give to constitutions and statutes constructions which have the effect of greatly enlarging or narrowing their scope and sometimes, as I shall show, of even altering the whole course of government on matters of the most vital consequence. If public opinion acquiesce in these interpretations, they remain the law; if not, the legislature assumes to correct them by new statute, and the process is thus begun all over again. Nowhere, in the history of our jurisprudence, has this power of courts been more strongly exerted than in the matter of Negro rights, and nowhere has it been more swayed by prejudice and class interest. We are taught, and properly taught, to hold our courts in high respect. As a rule this is not difficult. But courts are made up of human beings. Under wigs and gowns and titles and deferential formulas, judges are simply men, and subject, as other men, to every human frailty. I shall endeavor to trace, of course in an inadequate and sketchy way and subject to correction by those better informed in the principles and practice of the law and the progress of our jurisprudence, the history of Negro rights as affected by the decisions of the Supreme Court of the United States. This can be done most effectively by reference to a few leading cases. For the Court rarely reverses itself, and has followed the prevailing public opinion so closely, in its interpretation of the Constitution and laws applying to the Negro, that its decisions have seldom been disturbed by legislative enactment.

The historic antebellum cause was, of course, the Dred Scott decision. Dred Scott was returned to slavery, and citizenship of the United States was denied to Negroes, thus repealing so far as it applied to them, Article 4 Section 2 of the Constitution: "The citizens of each State shall be entitled to all privileges and immunities of citizens of the several States." Of this decision the venerable Justice Harlan said, in his dissenting opinion in the Civil Rights Cases (109 U.S.):[1] "It is said that the case of Dred Scott vs. Sandford overruled the action of two generations, virtually inserted a new clause in the Constitution, changed its character, and made a new departure in the workings of the federal government." Thus vast and portentous is the power resting in the hands of nine men who hold their office for life and are directly responsible to no one. This decision was purely a political one and deserved the outburst of indignation which greeted it and did so much to bring about the ultimate abolition of slavery.

How different was the attitude of Lord Mansfield in the parallel English case![2] A Negro who had been in England was sought to be returned to a British colony as a slave. He claimed his freedom. Lord Mansfield might have made a similar ruling to that of the Supreme Court, with much better warrant, for there was no written constitution to restrain him, and by custom Negro slaves had often been brought into England by their masters and returned to the colonies. But the English jurist seized his opportunity to recognize a principle which enlarged human rights. The Supreme Court chose to give a narrow and strained interpretation of the law and thereby restrict human rights.

I think it is exceedingly unfortunate for the Negro that the seat of government should be located in the South. Inevitably the administration, the courts, the whole machinery of government takes its tone from its environment. The influence of social life upon government is well known—it has always been the power behind the throne. The fate of nations has more often been settled in clubs and parlors than in courts and parliaments. The influence of Southern customs and Southern caste which is and always has been enthroned at Washington, has colored the attitude of presidents and congressmen and judges toward the Negro. To men living in a community where by law all men are denied the suffrage, it does not seem such an enormity that the Negro elsewhere should be left without it. To men living in a community where service and courtesy in public places is in large measure denied the Negro, there seems no particular enormity in separate car laws and similar iniquities. Had the capital of this nation been left at Philadelphia or established in Boston or New York, the Negro would long since, in my opinion, have had his rights enlarged and recognized. Justice Mansfield lived in a free country. Justice Taney lived in Maryland,[3] and the Supreme Court sat in Washington.

The Dred Scott decision, with all its implications, remained the law until it was overturned by revolution, and the effort made to fix, by the Constitution, the rights of the colored race to equal citizenship. Certainly the language of the amendments is plain enough to bear that interpretation; and certainly that was the intent of those who drew them and promoted their passage. But they were, after all, mere statements of principles, not difficult of application in the North, but involving social revolution in the South. It was necessary to embody them in federal and state statutes, and then, in order to render them effective, to enforce their application.

The Thirteenth Amendment abolished slavery and by implication extended to the former slaves the rights as well as the status of free men. The Fourteenth Amendment extended citizenship of the United States in terms to all persons born or naturalized in the country and subject to its jurisdiction; forbade the making or enforcement of any law which abridged the privileges or immunities of citizens or which should deprive any person of life, liberty or property without due process of law or deny to any person within its jurisdiction the equal protection of the laws.

One of the earliest federal statutes intended to carry into effect the principles of the Thirteenth and Fourteenth Amendments was the Civil Rights bill of 1866, by which were fixed the rights of Negroes in the courts, their right to contract, to sue, to be parties, to testify, and their full and equal benefit of all laws and proceedings for the security of persons and property as is enjoyed by white citizens. In general these rights have been respected, so far as statutes and Supreme Court decisions are concerned, although the right to contract in marriage, and certain other rights, have been limited under the principle of police power in the State.

In the case of Virginia vs. Rives, 100 U.S. 313 (1879)[4] it was held by the Supreme Court:

> The Fourteenth Amendment was ordained to secure equal rights to all persons, and extends its protection to races and classes, and prohibits any state legislation which has the effect of denying to any race or class, or to any individual, the equal protection of the laws. The plain object of this amendment, as well as of the statutes enacted prior thereto, was to place the negro race, with respect to its civil rights, upon the same level with the white. They made the rights and responsibilities, civil and criminal, of the two races exactly the same.

Such a statement would seem both comprehensive and conclusive. But a moment of reflection will show that it is neither. What constitutes race? When are rights equal or unequal? What is a denial of the equal protection of the laws? What are civil rights? What are civil and criminal responsibilities, and when are they the same, and exactly the same?

The answers of the Supreme Court to these questions, as they have come up, generally in cases based on the Fourteenth Amendment, have fixed, for the present at least, the legal status of colored citizens.

When it became clear that in the former slave states civil rights, as Charles Sumner and the men of his school defined them, were to be denied the Negro in spite of the Fourteenth Amendment, the Civil Rights Act of 1875 was enacted. It was not long before numerous cases involving this law were presented to the Supreme Court, and in 1883 (109 U.S.) five cases were considered together.[5] By the opinion of the Court, sections 1 and 2 of the civil rights act were held unconstitutional, section 1 giving full and equal enjoyment to all citizens of the accommodations of inns, public conveyances and places of public amusement, and section 2 providing a penalty. It was held that these things were subject to regulation by the State only and that Congress had no power to legislate except as to State action which is subversive of the fundamental rights specified in the amendment, and that therefore the Fourteenth Amendment had no application. In this case Justices Bradley[6] and Harlan filed dissenting opinions. Justice Harlan based his argument upon Article IV., Section 2, of the Constitution, heretofore quoted, and maintained that no State could deny privileges and immunities to colored persons on the ground that they were extended only to whites, and that the majority opinion, to the effect that the nation, in the absence of State laws, adverse to such rights and privileges, might not interfere for their protection and security, is a denial to Congress of the power by appropriate legislation to enforce one of the provisions of the Fifteenth Amendment. And quoting what I have already said in reference to the effect of the Dred Scott decision in changing the character of the Constitution, he expressed the fear that the decision in the Civil Rights Cases would mark the opening of an era in which the rights to freedom and American citizenship cannot receive from the nation efficient protection. These were prophetic words.

In the course of the opinion of the Court, Justice Bradley said, very truly:

> When a man has emerged from slavery and by the aid of beneficent legislation has shaken off the inseparable concomitants of that state, there must be some stage in the progress of his elevation when he takes the rank of a mere citizen, and ceases to be the special favorite of the law, and when his rights as a citizen or a man are to be protected in the ordinary modes by which other men's rights are protected.

There is nothing to indicate, except the well known facts of the situation, whether or not this perfectly correct statement was made with jocular intent. Certainly there is such a stage, but it was obvious then that the Negro had not yet reached it. And Justice Harlan further says: "The opinion proceeds upon grounds entirely too narrow and artificial. I cannot resist the conclusion that the substance and spirit of the recent amendments to the Constitution have been sacrificed to a subtle and ingenious verbal criticism."

In the Civil Rights decision the Court did not hold that the things complained of were not deprivations of rights, but merely that they were not attributable to any action of the State. For it is the *State* which is prohibited by the Fourteenth Amendment from denying to any person within its jurisdiction the equal protection of the laws, and this amendment has been held not violated until the denial of the rights has some State sanction or authority. I do not recall whether this argument was made or not, but why would it not have been a good one, in that case, and in cases which are made under civil rights laws of the Northern States? Railroad companies are creatures of the State. Whatever powers they exercise are derived from the State and to that extent they are the agents of the State, and the State is responsible for their acts. Similar reasoning would apply to inns and common carriers, labor unions and other bodies, either chartered by the State or enjoying special benefits by statute or by common law.

But to my mind the most important and far reaching decision of the Supreme Court upon the question of civil rights is that in the case of Plessy vs. Ferguson, a case which came from Louisiana in 1895. (163 U.S., 537.) The opinion is a clear and definite approval of the recognition by State laws, of color distinctions, something which had theretofore been avoided in civil rights cases. It establishes racial caste in the United States as firmly as though it were established by act of Congress. To the opinion Mr. Justice Harlan dissented with his usual vigor, and Justice Brewer[7] did not hear the argument or participate in the decision. The Court cited the passage quoted by me from a former decision:

> The Fourteenth Amendment was ordained to secure equal rights to all persons, and extends its protection to races and classes, and prohibits any State legislation which has the effect of denying to any race or class, or to any individual, the equal protection of the laws, and made the rights of the two races exactly the same.

And then the Court stabbed in the back, and to death, this ideal presentment of rights, in the following language, and threw its bleeding corpse to the Negro,—the comprehensive Negro, black, brown, yellow and white—the plaintiff in that case, which involved the separate car law of Louisiana, was seven-eighths white and showed no sign of the darker blood—as that court's definition of his civil status:

> But in the nature of things it [the Fourteenth Amendment] could not have been intended to abolish distinctions based upon color or to enforce social, as distinguished from political, equality, or a commingling of the two races upon terms unsatisfactory to either. If the two races are to meet on terms of social equality, it must be the result of natural affinities, a mutual appreciation of each other's merits and a voluntary consent of individuals. When the government, therefore, has secured for each of its citizens equal rights before the law and equal opportunities for improvement and progress, it has accomplished the end for which it was organized, and per-

formed all the functions respecting social advantages with which it is endowed. Legislation is powerless to eradicate racial instincts or to abolish distinctions based upon physical differences. If the civil and political rights of both races be equal, one cannot be inferior to the other civilly or politically. If one race be inferior to the other socially, the Constitution of the United States cannot put them upon the same plane.

A statute which implies merely a legal distinction between the white and colored races—a distinction which is founded in the color of the two races and which must always exist so long as men are distinguished from the other race by color—has no tendency to destroy the legal equality of the two races or reestablish a state of involuntary servitude.

When it was suggested in the argument that to sustain such discriminating laws might justify separate cars for people with red hair or aliens, or require people to walk on different sides of the street, or require colored men's houses to be in separate blocks, the Court in the opinion, said that such regulations must be reasonable. And the Court held: "In determining the question of reasonableness, it is at liberty to act with reference to the usages, customs and traditions of the people, with a view to the promotion of their comfort and the preservation of the public peace and good order."

It is obvious where this leaves the Negro, and it is difficult to see where the 14th Amendment has any application.

The opinion in Plessy vs. Ferguson is, to my mind, as epoch making as the Dred Scott decision. Unfortunately, it applies to a class of rights which do not make to the heart and conscience of the nation the same direct appeal as was made by slavery, and has not been nor is it likely to produce any such revulsion of feeling.

Another extract from the opinion makes one wonder whether the Court was merely playing with the subject:

> We consider the underlying failure of the plaintiff's argument to consist in the assumption that the enforced separation of the races stamps the colored race with the badge of inferiority. If this be so, it is not by reason of anything found in the act itself, but solely because the colored race chooses to put that construction upon it.

I presume that hanging might be pleasant if a man could only convince himself that it would not be painful, nor disgraceful, nor terminate his earthly career. It is perhaps true that some Negroes—I suspect very few people of mixed blood—have seemed to accept this reasoning. But I have never been able to see how a self-respecting colored man can approve of any discriminating legislation. To do so is to condone his own degradation, and accept an inferior citizenship. If discrimination must of necessity be submitted to, it should meet no better reception than silence. Protest were better still.

I need not suggest the far-reaching effect of this decision. The colored people of the South have been, it would seem, as completely segregated as the business of daily life will permit. Perhaps the lowest depths of race hatred have not been sounded, but a more humiliating, insulting and degrading system is hardly conceivable under even a nominally free government. And under Plessy vs. Ferguson there is no reason why any Northern State may not reproduce in its own borders the conditions in Alabama and Georgia. And it may be that the Negro and his friends will have to exert themselves to save his rights at the North.

The latest, and since Plessy vs. Ferguson, the most serious blow delivered by the Supreme Court to Negro rights—it was in fact a restriction of the rights of white men, and involved the Negro only indirectly—is that of Berea College vs. Kentucky (1908). A recent statute of Kentucky forbade the receiving of both white and Negro races as pupils for instruction in any institution of learning. (Ky. Acts 1904, ch. 85, page 181.) Berea College was indicted and fined for a violation of this statute. The case was appealed to the Kentucky Court of Appeals. (123 Ky. 209, 94 S.W. 623.) There were other sections of the statute, some of which the court found unconstitutional; but it affirmed the judgment below, sustaining the constitutionality of the section upon which it was based, the principal ground of the decision being that the original charter of Berea College had been conditioned upon the right of the legislature to revoke or alter it, and that the statute of Kentucky was in effect an amendment of the charter which did not defeat or substantially impair the object of the grant, the object of the grant being "to give instruction to all who might apply, and promote the cause of Christ." The Supreme Court of the United States accepted the decision of the Kentucky Court on the ground that the judgment being a non-federal ground, fairly construed, sustained the decision, and that the decision by a State court of the extent and limitation of the powers conferred by the State upon one of its own corporations is of a purely local nature. The Court did not consider the statute as a whole, but only the section above referred to.[8]

Justice Harlan, dissenting, said:

> In my judgment the Court should directly meet and decide the broad question presented by the section. It should adjudge whether the statute, as a whole, is or is not unconstitutional, in that it makes it a crime against the state to maintain or operate a private institution of learning where white and black pupils are received, at the same time, for instruction. . . . I am of opinion that in its essential parts, the statute is an arbitrary invasion of the rights of liberty and property guaranteed by the Fourteenth Amendment against hostile state action, and is, therefore, void.

Since this decision Berea College, the attitude of which in the matter was scarcely heroic, though perhaps justified by the law of self-preservation, has set aside certain moneys and promoted the collection of a fund to establish a school which should provide for colored students the advantages formerly offered by Berea College, and since then the Jim Crow annex of that institution has been dodging injunctions and protests, seeking a place to lay its woolly head and to rest its tired feet. All honor to Justice Harlan. There is no more inspiring spectacle than this grand old man, ever steadfast to right and justice, fighting unwearyingly, never yielding, and almost always defeated, for the principles which were so dearly bought by the Civil War. I know nothing with which to compare it except the staunchness of the *New York Evening Post* and the *Independent*, which, with a few individuals, amid all the ruck of concession and compromise have kept alight the torch of liberty against the day when in the language of the decision in the Civil Rights Cases, the Negro shall "take the rank of a mere citizen . . . and when his rights as a citizen or a man are to be protected in the ordinary modes by which other men's rights are protected"—the time when the colored race shall have gained sufficient strength to protect itself, or until the democratic spirit now so nearly dead in the nation shall have become again a vivifying flame. I hope they may live to see the day.

THE RIGHT TO VOTE.

The Fifteenth Amendment provided that "the right of citizens of the United States to vote shall not be denied or abridged by the United States, on account of race, color or previous condition of servitude," and Congress was given power in the Amendment to enforce by appropriate legislation its provisions.

The right of colored men to vote on equal terms with white men as provided by the Fifteenth Amendment, has never been denied in terms by any State, but in effect disfranchisement is general throughout the South. A few individuals are permitted to vote, but the race is disfranchised; and the race, and not the individual, is the social unit. It was easily within the power of the government to strangle the movement for disfranchisement at its birth. It would have been as easy for the Department of Justice to work up a case involving disfranchisement, as it was to work up the recent cases against peonage, and to have them taken to the Supreme Court in the ordinary course. And the Court might have held, as it did in cases involving the right to sit on juries, that the action of State officers charged with the execution of the law was as much a violation of the Constitution as an act of the legislature.[9] But on the contrary, it took the narrow view, and held that so long as the State did not discriminate in terms against Negroes as such, there was no violation of the constitutional provision,—though in effect it might disfranchise the race.

In the case of Giles vs. Harris (189 U.S. 475), where a Negro was refused the right to register, the Court did not find that a wrong had not been done, but, assuming, for the sake of the argument that the facts claimed were true and that the Constitution had been disregarded, declared itself impotent to enforce any mandate it might make in that behalf and referred the plaintiff to Congress for relief. To this decision Justices Brewer, Brown[10] and Harlan dissented. Other cases have been before the Court, but it has steadily refused to face the main issue and has entrenched itself behind a hedge of technicalities. It will require, in all probability, some such extreme measure as that proposed, the other day, in Maryland, to force a decision; and there are those who have so little confidence in the majority of the Court as at present constituted, where similar questions are involved, as to be glad the question was not put up to them until there is some greater assurance of an effective public demand to back up a right decision. There is little more that the States can do, within the limit of the Fourteenth Amendment as now construed, to further defeat Negro rights. For the Supreme Court to repeal, by judicial construction, the uniform application of the Fourteenth and Fifteenth Amendments, would be a calamity indeed.

⌒

SOURCE: Undated typed text at the Fisk University Library. Two versions of the text of this speech are extant. The source text is the expanded one, signed by Chesnutt and emended in his hand. The reference to the U.S. Supreme Court decision concerning the segregation of Berea College indicates that Chesnutt delivered this speech after 9 November 1908. This may be the autumn 1908 address given to a Niagara Movement conference at Oberlin, O., noted by Helen Chesnutt in *Charles Waddell Chesnutt* (1952).

[1] 109 U.S. 3 (1883). John Marshall Harlan (1833–1911) was known as the "great dissenter" during his U.S. Supreme Court tenure (1877–1911), in part because of his positions on civil rights.

[2] Sir James Mansfield (1733–1821) was an attorney who ascended to the position of Lord Chief Justice of the Court of Common Pleas (1804–14). He adjudicated the case of Somerset v. Steuart (12 Geo. 1772 K.B.), which came before the King's Bench in 1771. James Somerset, a slave who had run away from his master upon their arrival in England, was detained in irons aboard ship; Mansfield issued a writ of *habeas corpus*, commanding the ship's captain to appear before him. The captain related that Somerset's owner, Virginian Charles Steuart, had placed him in his custody for the voyage to Jamaica, where he was to be sold. Mansfield gave his decision on 22 June 1772: the condition of slavery, he asserted, was "so odious, that nothing could be suffered to support it but positive law. Whatever inconvenience, therefore, may follow from the decision, I cannot say this case is allowed or approved by the law of England; and therefore the black must be discharged."

[3] Roger B. Taney (1777–1864) was Chief Justice of the U.S. Supreme Court in 1836–64. He was born on a tobacco plantation in southern Maryland.

[4] Chesnutt miscited "Rives" as "Reeves."

[5] The Civil Rights Cases referred to earlier; see n. 1.

[6] Joseph P. Bradley (1813–92) was an Associate Justice of the U.S. Supreme Court (1870–92).

[7] David Josiah Brewer (1837–1910) was an Associate Justice of the U.S. Supreme Court (1889–1910).

[8] Berea College v. Kentucky, 211 U.S. 26 (1908).

[9] See "Peonage, or the New Slavery" and "The Right to Jury Service."

[10] Henry Billings Brown (1836–1913) was an Associate Justice of the U.S. Supreme Court (1890–1906).

Lincoln's Courtships

Essay published in the *Southwestern Christian Advocate*, 4 February 1909

A great man is in a way a human document, and whatever concerns his life is of interest, if not all of equal importance; and, since a man's life is a unit, it cannot be properly viewed, or his character correctly estimated, without a knowledge of it all or its most important phases.

Mr. Lincoln was a very human person, all sides of whose nature were developed, though perhaps not equally, and in the matter of love and courtship his experience was very interesting and perhaps unusual. He was not a handsome man, and was deficient in some of those charms of manner which make men attractive to women. His stature and strength, however, his energy and ambition, and a certain frank sincerity, a longing for sympathy and encouragement, rendered him in his youth not only popular with men, but equally attractive to the other sex.

His first love affair of which there is any record was that with Anne Rutledge,[1] a slender, blue-eyed blonde, nineteen years old, a very lovely and universally admired and generally fascinating girl, of South Carolina descent, whose father kept the village tavern at New Salem, Illinois, where Lincoln had moved from the farm. Miss Rutledge had been engaged to another man, who went away and did not return. Lincoln was postmaster and to him she went every day for the letters which came so rarely and finally not at all. He became interested in her sorrow, and sought after a while to comfort her, with the result that she promised to marry him. But she could not banish her love for the other man; memories, doubts and fears, and a tender conscience, lest she might have misjudged her absent lover, preyed upon her mind, and shortly after her betrothal to Lincoln, she was taken ill and died. Her death was a great shock to Lincoln, and it is said that the melancholy which was so conspicuous in his disposition, dates from the time of this bereavement. This is the most touching and romantic of Lincoln's love affairs.

But when one is young, nature abhors an empty heart. In time Mr. Lincoln recovered from his grief sufficiently to look around for some other object upon which to bestow his affections. Some two years before the death of Anne Rutledge, he had made the acquaintance of Miss Mary Owens, of Kentucky, who had come to New Salem to visit her sister, a Mrs. Abell.[2] She remained in New Salem four weeks, after which she returned to her Kentucky home. Some three years later, and about a year after Anne's death, Mrs. Abell went on a visit to Kentucky, and before leaving, laughingly suggested to Lincoln that she would bring her sister back with her if Lincoln would marry her. He replied, in the same strain, that he would. He remembered Miss Owens as a tall, slim, handsome, witty and vivacious girl, liberally educated and considered wealthy.

But alas! the first interview dissipated some illusions on both sides. The lady had grown stout—distressingly stout. Some of her roses had fled; she was now twenty-eight, a year older than Lincoln, and the difference, not so apparent when he had first known her, had become more pronounced with the passing years. Nor is it likely that he was all that her imagination had pictured him. He was a diamond in the rough, and the speech and manners of the Illinois frontier did not compare favorably with the more polished graces of Kentucky society. They both seemed to have taken the promise to Mrs. Abell seriously, and were soon absorbed in a formal courtship—formal in more ways than one, since it seems to have been singularly lacking in warmth. Indeed, Lincoln was never a very ardent wooer. He debated with himself and with his friends whether he should marry Miss Owens, and when he finally made his marriage proposal, it was couched in the form of a letter, and was more like a legal document than the outpouring of a loving heart. He set out very frankly his circumstances and his shortcomings, which he feared might prevent his finding favor in the lady's eyes. The lady, who seems to have been equally practical, accepted his view of himself and declined his proposal. She was known to have stated, in substance, years afterwards, that Mr. Lincoln was not in her social class, and that the marriage would probably have resulted unhappily. Neither of them seems to have suffered from their disagreement. Miss Owens made a presumably happy marriage with another man. And Mr. Lincoln was frank in congratulating himself upon his escape. One of his letters on this subject throws some side lights upon his character—his conscientiousness, his sense of humor, and the homely directness which characterized all his speech and actions. He dwells upon his disappointment upon Miss Owens' changed appearance, and continues:

> But what could I do? I had told her sister that I would take her for better or worse, and I made it a point of honor and conscience to stick to my word, especially if others had been induced to act upon it, which in this case I had no doubt they had; for I was now fairly convinced that no other man on earth would have her, and hence the conclusion that they were bent on holding me to my bargain.

And in another letter he says, speaking of his rejection: "I was mortified, it seemed to me, in a hundred different ways. My vanity was deeply wounded by the reflection that I had so long been too stupid to discover her intentions, and at the same time never doubting that I understood them perfectly, and also that she whom I had taught myself to believe nobody else would have, had actually rejected me with all my fancied greatness. And to cap the whole, I for the first time began to suspect that I was really a little in love with her."

There was a period of several years following the affair with Miss Owens, during which we know nothing of Lincoln's love affairs. He was now past thirty, and had begun to make a reputation as a writer and speaker, and was gaining a foothold in politics, when he met his fate in the person of Miss Mary Todd,[3] of Springfield, Illinois. She was twenty-one years old, came of a good family, had been well educated and was a social favorite. Her portraits do not show her to have been beautiful, but she possessed many social graces, by the standards of the community, and an imperious disposition which compelled a certain amount of respect and admiration. She was distinctly Mr. Lincoln's superior from a social point of view.

Mr. Lincoln, though he found the society of ladies attractive, and seems to have paid attentions to quite a number of them at this period of his life, seems always to have shrunk from the ultimate step. This was no less true with Miss Todd than it had been in the case of Miss Owens. After a courtship lasting a twelve-month they became engaged. Shortly after his engagement he fell into a panic, and without any lovers' quarrel or unpleasantness of which there is any record, he told the lady that he did not love her. She did not prove, however, so reasonable as Miss Owens; perhaps she was more in love. She burst into tears; Mr. Lincoln was moved by her distress, caught her in his arms and kissed her. This was accepted by both as a renewal of their engagement, and things continued upon their old footing.

The wedding day was fixed for January 1st, 1841, and the usual preparations were made and the guests invited and the supper spread. But while Lincoln had been susceptible to the shafts of Cupid, he seems to have had a singular disinclination for the noose of Hymen. The lady waited, the guests came, but the bride-groom came not.[4] Messengers were sent out to search for him, but in vain. Finally the guests departed, the lights were put out, and the lady went to bed with broken heart and shattered nerves. Some biographers deny this episode, but none of them ignores it, and the weight of evidence seems in favor of its correctness.

Mr. Lincoln seems to have suffered not less than the lady. A constitutional melancholy, which dated from his unfortunate love affair with Anne Rutledge, laid stronger hands upon him after the fiasco of his wedding with Miss Todd. He very wisely left Springfield and remained away some time. His conduct in connection with this affair has been much criticized. It only bears out the proposition that no man can be uniformly great or wise or strong—even the sun has spots upon it; and, after all, a man's conduct in so intimate a personal matter cannot be rightly judged unless one could put himself exactly in another's place. Mr. Lincoln's friends said that at this time he was indeed scarcely himself; his melancholy was at times so profound as to leave him scarcely responsible for his actions. Indeed, Miss Todd's friends put his failure to appear upon this ground.

But both his affections and those of Miss Todd had been too deeply engaged to be lightly broken. Through the mediation of a friend they were brought together,[5] and about two years later they were quietly married. Those who care to look up in the libraries the biographies of Lincoln, will find that some interesting social events took place in the society where they moved, at about that time, which assisted in their reconciliation. But not even yet had Mr. Lincoln recovered from his gloom, and he is said to have acted very singularly on the evening of the cere-mony—that from his manner he might have been attending a funeral rather than a wedding. There is no doubt that the lady was ambitious and took, more or less, she and her friends, the initiative in the affair. But she made him a faithful and af-fectionate wife, and he was never known to express any subsequent regrets. They lived together happily enough, and her ambition and energy undoubtedly contributed to his advancement.

During the twelve years which followed his marriage, Mr. Lincoln lived at Springfield, practiced the profession, and was active in politics, serving one term in Congress.[6] Upon his election to the presidency,[7] his wife and he were suddenly transferred from the simple social life of the still undeveloped West to a city where society had long been dominated by Southern aristocracy tempered by New England culture. Mr. Lincoln was absorbed in affairs of tremendous import, and had little time to cultivate social amenities. Mrs. Lincoln, in spite of her many amiable qualities, was at a disadvantage compared with other ladies in Washington society and was not always popular. But the married life of Mr. Lincoln and the story of his family is not within the scope of the subject upon which I have been asked to write, and I shall therefore leave it to some other pen.

One might see, in Mr. Lincoln's mental attitude toward the important question of marriage, a forecast of his position with regard to most of the great questions which came to him for solution during the Civil War. A full appreciation of all the difficulties involved, and yet a strong sense of what was right and what duty demanded—both elements were present in every instance.

↬

SOURCE: "Lincoln's Courtships," *Southwestern Christian Advocate*, 43 (4 February 1909), 10, datelined "Cleveland, Ohio." Here, and in the speeches focused on Lincoln, a principal information source is *A Short Life of Abraham Lincoln* (1902) by John Nicolay (1832–1901).

[1](1813–35).
[2]Owens (1808–77); Mrs. Elizabeth Abell (1804–?). Chesnutt and Nicolay both misspell Abell as "Able."
[3](1818–82).
[4]Matthew 25:6.
[5]The friend was Mrs. Simeon Francis (1793–1873), wife of the Whig editor of the *Sangamo Journal* published in Springfield, O.
[6]Lincoln served in the Thirtieth Congress, 1846–48.
[7]He was elected President in 1860.

The Right to Jury Service

Speech delivered c. 1910

The attitude of the Supreme Court with reference to jury service by colored citizens has been more liberal and perhaps above criticism.[1] While it has held that

> A colored citizen, party to a trial involving his life, liberty or property, cannot claim, as matter of right, that his race shall have representation on the grand or petit jury,

and while a mixed jury in a particular case is not, within the meaning of the Constitution, necessary to the equal protection of the laws, it is a right to which he is entitled that, in the organizing of the grand jury and in the selection of jurors to pass upon his life, liberty or property, there shall be no exclusion of his race and no discrimination against them because of their color,[2]

in Strauder vs. West Virginia, 100 U.S. (1879), it was held:

That the law of West Virginia limiting to white male persons twenty-one years of age, citizens of the State, the right to sit upon juries was a discrimination which implied a legal inferiority in civil society, which lessened the security of the rights of the colored race and was a step toward reducing them to a condition of servitude.[3]

This case it will be seen refers to State action by statute.

Adopting a more liberal policy with reference to this right than it has adopted in case of civil rights, or the right to vote, it has extended its definition of State action as follows:

Whenever by any action of a State, whether through its legislature, through its courts, or through its executive or administrative officers, all persons of the African race are excluded, solely because of their race or color, from serving as grand jurors in the criminal prosecution of a person of the African race, the equal protection of the laws is denied to him, contrary to the 14th amendment of the Constitution.[4]

The same rule has been recognized as applying to petit jurors. I do not see why by parallel reasoning, a white man could not with equal justice complain of the exclusion from the jury of all persons of the African race. It might easily be that the case might involve collaterally, a question of race prejudice, in which (even) the exclusion of Negroes from the jury would work a hardship upon a white defendant.

In Thomas vs. Texas, decided in November, 1908,[5] a colored man convicted of murder, appealed to the court of criminal appeals of the State on a motion to quash the indictment and special venire drawn in the cause on the ground of race prejudice and inadequate representation of race rights on grand jury and petit jury. Both motions were denied. The Supreme Court of the United States, to which the case was taken on writ of error, held that the question of discrimination was one of fact, the decision of which by the State court is conclusive on the federal Supreme Court, on writ of error, unless so grossly wrong as to amount to an infraction of the federal Constitution. It was not contended that the laws of Texas in that behalf are themselves discriminating, and the Texas court had held that the facts in the case did not prove discrimination.

The general effect of all these decisions is that "What the accused is entitled to demand under the Constitution of the United States is, that in organizing the grand jury as well as in the impanelling of the petit jury, there shall be no exclusion of his race and no discrimination of them, because of their race or color." (200 U.S.)[6]

That the Supreme Court has the power to enforce its mandate where its own dignity is attacked or its power denied is apparent in the recent case of Shipp, where a Tennessee Sheriff and other citizens won local glory and honor and a jail sentence for permitting the lynching of a colored man convicted of a crime, whose case was pending before the Supreme Court upon a writ of error involving a Constitutional question.[7] I think we may regard the *right* of a Negro to representation on juries as firmly settled. The exercise of the right will of course remain largely subject to local conditions.

It will be clear, it seems to me, that this extreme sensitiveness of our highest court to a reactionary public opinion, this juggling of words, this hesitancy to face the real questions involved in cases before it, is in itself due to disfranchisement. With any adequate representation of the Negro in Congress and in the administrative and judicial departments of the government, the Supreme Court would have found new arguments and would more often have leaned toward the broad than the narrow view. Had it not, Congress itself would have acted, and had there been any reluctance, the executive has the right from time to time, in the course of nature, to change the constitution of the Court. But it is inconceivable that the Court would resist a righteous demand thus backed up, and what that court decided, inferior courts would ultimately be obliged to follow.

So much for the rights of colored persons as defined by law. Their practical enforcement is a very different problem. The machinery of justice is complicated, at least manifold, and the law's delays are proverbial. When crimes are charged there must be a presentment to the grand jury. It does not require a great deal of evidence to induce an indictment against even a white man; it is enough to show probable cause which oftentimes is rebutted without difficulty. How easy it is to indict a man who belongs to a race which is classed as criminal, thus establishing a presumption of crime from the mere fact of race! The case must then be heard before a judge, always a white man—there are I believe a few inferior magistrates of color in some of the border States—in the election of this judge the Negro who comes before him for trial has had no voice, in his future choice or defeat men of that race can have no share. From the judge the jury must take the law, and if, as we have seen highest courts are not immune to public prejudice, what else could be expected from courts not sitting in that high serene atmosphere, but close to the ground and exposed to every vagrant wind of local prejudice or passion?

As I have shown, the Supreme Court has endeavored to safeguard the Negro's right to be represented on juries, at least where a colored person is a party. But with the machinery of state and county governments in the hands of those hostile to Negro equality, the right is largely an empty one and can only be invoked at great expense and with great delay. On the other hand it can be easily seen that if colored men were drawn on juries which must pass upon the rights of white men, white men on juries would be much more careful in passing upon the rights of colored men.

When, in a criminal case, an adverse verdict is rendered, in most states and in most cases the judge fixes the punishment. And I am willing to declare, here and now that on the average, scarcely anywhere in the United States does the Negro convicted of crime get the same justice as white men under similar circumstances.

With the best intentions in the world the judge is a product of his environment, and, in certain respects, can no more help his prejudice against the Negro than any thoughtful man of color can resist a feeling of distrust and apprehension when a Southern Democrat is selected for the President's cabinet or for a judge of the Supreme Court. The best that the Negro can expect, even at the North, is justice; he rarely gets mercy.

In effect, the white man in court, opposed to a Negro, stands in the position of one of a privileged class, to which those controlling the machinery of justice belong, and in courts, as elsewhere, the privileged classes get the benefit of their privilege. Doubtless gentlemen here who live in the South can give concrete illustrations. It is sufficient for me to state the general principle.

The growth of race prejudice, aside from any immediate question of personal advantage, but viewed merely in the light of a class consciousness, is the most sinister feature of the whole race conflict in the United States.[8] With caste firmly established, how can any man escape it? The civil and political rights of the Negro in the North have always reflected in some degree his condition at the South. His "social privileges," since the Supreme Court has distinguished them from civil rights, are increasingly regulated in the North by the customs of the Southern states. Some of those customs would be amusing if it were not for their underlying seriousness. A case was on trial in a South Carolina court, in which a white man was called as a witness. In testifying he referred to a colored man, a party to the suit, as "Mr. Jones." "Stop," thundered the Court, "I allow no man to call a negro 'Mister' in my court." Jones was called as the next witness. He was asked among other things, what relation if any he sustained to the preceding witness, the white man. Jones replied, "He works for me." The master was Jones, the servant was Mister.

I do not know whether the learned judge of New York who decided a case in the Supreme Court last year, to which a Negro was a party, had ever heard of this case or not, but certainly the spirit which underlay it had percolated to the North, when he ruled, in reducing the amount of a verdict granted in a case of assault, that the plaintiff was a colored man and therefore could not feel as much humiliation under given conditions as though he were a white man. The decision I believe was subsequently reversed, with what amounted to a judicial reprimand from the upper court to the judge of the court below. This judge belongs in the same class with a judge in Oklahoma who the other day, discovering a colored man in the panel, announced to the white men on the jury, with the usual disregard of courtesy and humanity so often manifested by white men in their dealings with men of a different color, that since the laws of Oklahoma discouraged social equality, he would not insult them by requiring them to sit upon the jury with a Negro; and the Negro was discharged from the jury, solely on account of his color—the Fourteenth Amendment and the decisions of the Supreme Court to the contrary notwithstanding. In cheering contrast was the action of that judge in this city[9] who, the other day, upon objection by a white juryman that he was from the South and objected to serving upon jury with a Negro, promptly discharged the white man for the whole term, with the statement that a man with such sentiments was not fit to serve upon any jury.

And in a case tried recently in North Carolina, of which I have knowledge, a colored man, a doctor with a considerable practice which he attended to with the assistance of an automobile, was called as a witness—he was not a party but merely a witness. At the close of his testimony a white man was put on the stand to prove that Doctor _____ was a very good Negro and that he would believe him under oath. To a lawyer this was an amusing reversal of the ordinary rule as to credibility.

I have reached, I suspect, the limit of the time I ought to take, and cannot perhaps speak further without exceeding the limit of the subject assigned to me. But I cannot close this paper without a brief reflection upon the effect of disfranchisement upon the *morale* of colored citizenship. As a little incident in point I was speaking one day with a New York comedian of color, who commented, with a laugh which was not entirely jocular, upon the desire expressed by the members of his company, when touring the country, to get back to the "Great White Way." "And there's scarcely a place of amusement," he said, "or of public entertainment on Broadway, from 14th to 45th street, where they would be given decent service, if served at all." Their interest was purely academic, as the Negro's interest is bound to become, and increasingly so, if the present tendency continues, in every national ideal. Why, for instance, should a Negro have any enthusiasm about an army in which he can have no honorable preferment, the uniform of which not only does not command respect but is likely to provoke to insult? Under the present laws of Georgia a Negro soldier in the United States army is not permitted to wear his uniform more than forty-eight hours except he be on duty; and a colored regiment must wander from army post to army post in search of a place where local opinion will permit it to perform its duties without hostility and insult. What enthusiasm can he feel for a navy in the service of which he cannot get beyond the wardroom, for a national game in which he cannot play?[10] What zeal can he feel about a national drama, a national art, when those who judge his product see first his color and then his work?

When Samuel Coleridge-Taylor, the eminent English composer, who by the way, is a mulatto, and to use the language of the South, takes after his black father, was in Washington a few years ago to conduct a concert at which was produced his *Hiawatha Trilogy*, a great musical convention was in session at Washington.[11] Had Mr. Coleridge-Taylor been a white man he would doubtless have been made the lion of the occasion. Being a colored man his presence in the city was absolutely ignored by the convention.

How can a Negro defend and cherish a democratic ideal which excludes him in large measure from its benefits? On what basis can he build the "race pride" which is invoked to make him acquiesce in segregation, when the mere fact of identification with a certain race denies him his rights, ostracizes him socially and exposes him to oppression and insult? A sinister development of the race situation is the segregation of the colored race in sympathy and the growth among them of prejudice against white people. The old, genial Negro, whose teeth were so constantly exposed in contrast with his dark skin that their whiteness has become a racial synonym—the companion of the old black mammy to whom our Southern friends proposed to erect a monument[12]—is rapidly giving place to the man of guarded if not morose face, who sees in every white man a possible enemy, and who, like the man from Missouri, has to be shown,[13] step by step, and is never quite convinced, feeling that somewhere he will reach the dead line where familiarity becomes presumption, and beyond which the most friendly white man, North or South, will, if only from the instinct of social self-preservation, either not wish or dare to go. How can the educated Negro take the interest which he should in the great political and social movements of the nation, when, by force of circumstances, all his thoughts, his energies, his hopes, his fears, are centered upon the problem of his own racial status in the nation?

The Negro who is anxious to vote one way upon a question, is constrained to support a party or a policy which his better judgment condemns, because to vote the other way is to strengthen the hands of his enemies. Thus prejudice begets prejudice, hate begets hate, there is no true friendship, and there is fertile soil for anarchy. I have seen the mulatto referred to, somewhere, as anti-social. It would be a calamity, in some national crisis which required the united front of all the people to defend the national interests or the national honor, to find the whole colored race divorced in sympathy from the white and in a position to welcome any change, no matter what, in the hope that it might turn out a change for the better.

To combat the present tendency, and to restore the recognition of manhood rights in the United States, is likely to prove a long and difficult task, unless some emergency should arise to stir the dormant conscience of the nation.

Carl Schurz wrote, in 1904:

> There will be a movement either in the direction of reducing the negroes to a permanent condition of serfdom—the condition of the mere plantation hand, "alongside the mule," practically without any rights of citizenship—or a movement in the direction of recognizing him as a citizen in the true sense of the term. One or the other will prevail.[14]

Which movement is now in progress, or are they both? I think they are; but one is a slow sociological development, and the other a consuming fire of race hatred. Unless something can be done to stem its progress the Negro is likely to be reduced to at least a "temporary" condition of serfdom, as he has been "temporarily disfranchised." And from that slough he could never lift himself by his own bootstraps, and the sordid tragedy of slavery would all have to be gone over.

When a class is wronged, some other man or class profits thereby, perhaps not in the long run, but for the time being. A man or a class may enjoy a privilege so long that it seems a God-given right. The struggle for liberty against privilege has often been waged most effectively by those who were among the privileged classes. A Jew founded Christianity. A monk led the forces of the Reformation. A priest of the English Church was the founder of Methodism, and Mr. Carnegie tells us that the steel industry does not need the tariff.[15] The logical minded aristocrats of France encouraged the new philosophy of the rights of man, coquetted with Franklin and the encyclopedists, and having lost faith in the divinity of their privileges, let themselves fall an easy prey to the Revolution.[16] Slaveholders were the first abolitionists. White men fought and died to free the slaves. And you white men, leaders of thought, realizing, as you must, that the Negro should have his rights, for the ultimate good of all, that he is denied them in ever increasing measure, for the present interest of a class, and that though he were wise as Solomon he can never secure them by himself alone, because, if for no other reason, of his disparity of numbers, are here to consider how it is possible to stem the tide of proscription and race hatred, to the end that the Negro may be saved for useful citizenship and the democratic ideal be preserved for white men, until the time when there shall be no question of race or color in fixing, either by law or custom, a man's place in the nation, and when all citizens shall work together for the good and glory of the commonwealth. May that time come sooner than we anticipate. No price would be too great to pay for it.

⁓

SOURCE: Undated typed text at the Fisk University Library. There are two typed versions; the source text is the one revised in Chesnutt's hand. Identification of the audience and the dating of the speech depend upon allusions to recent events and his reference to both "this" city and "New York"—neither of which alternate readings was canceled. A specific reference to New York need not have been made when Chesnutt spoke if the editors are correct in concluding that he was in New York City on 13 May 1910 and addressing the second annual conference of the National Negro Committee.

[1]Chesnutt apparently offered prefatory remarks about the U.S. Supreme Court's attitudes concerning other matters, and thus the comparison with which the text begins.

[2]Neal v. Delaware, 103 U.S. 370 (1880), quoted in Wood v. Brush, 140 U.S. 278 (1891).

[3]Chesnutt quotes not from Strauder v. West Virginia, 100 U.S. 303, but from Plessy v. Ferguson, which in 1896 restated the holding in Strauder.

[4]Carter v. Texas, 177 U.S. 442 (1900).

[5]212 U.S. 278 (1908).

[6]Martin v. Texas, 200 U.S. 316 (1906).

[7]Chesnutt miscited "Schipp" in referring to U.S. v. Shipp, 214 U.S. 386, for which a decision was reached on 24 May 1909.

[8]In the margin, Chesnutt reminded himself to read from an attached clipping. How he made the transition is not indicated, but the clipping makes it clear that he read from a reprinting of a quotation of H. G. Wells that appeared in "Race Prejudice," *Independent*, 62 (14 February 1907), 381–84. It reads, "I am convinced myself that there is no more evil thing in this present world than Race Prejudice; none at all. I write deliberately—it is the worst single thing in life now. It justifies and holds together more base-

ness, cruelty and abomination than any other sort of error in the world. Thru its body runs the black blood of coarse lust, suspicion, jealousy and persecution and all the darkest poisons of the human soul."

[9]Emended is "this New York/city."

[10]Major league baseball.

[12]Chesnutt again derides this quite serious proposal in "The Negro in Present Day Fiction." By 1910, fund raising for the monument had begun in earnest; there was a Black Mammy Memorial Institute in Athens, Ga. See "Old Black Mammy," *New York Age*, 12 May 1910, 4.

[13]Congressman Willard D. Vandiver (1854–1931) originated the "Show me" state slogan in 1899: "I am from Missouri. You have got to show me."

[14]"Can the South Solve the Race Problem?"

[15]John Wesley (1703–91) is credited with founding Methodism; Andrew Carnegie (1835–1919) was a major American industrialist and, by the turn of the century, an internationally renowned philanthropist.

[16]In 1745 Denis Diderot (1713–84) began his *Encyclopédie*, which appeared in twenty-eight volumes from 1751 to 1772, with seven more volumes added by 1780; many other illustrious thinkers of the time contributed to the work, including Voltaire (1694–1778) and Rousseau.

Who and Why Was Samuel Johnson?

Speech to the Rowfant Club, Cleveland, O., 11 November 1911

Beginning somewhere about 1750, Samuel Johnson occupied in England the most conspicuous position among contemporary men of letters. He was not only the dean of English authors, as we use the term nowadays, but the dictator of the literary world, a position in which he had but two predecessors, Dryden and Pope, neither of whom, tho both were greater writers, had equalled him in extent of influence, or durability of fame;[1] and he had no successor. He had been a prolific writer, of great talent and diversified product; his acquaintance, during this period of his life was eagerly sought by people in all ranks, from Kings to beggars. His commendation would secure a publisher for a virgin manuscript, and his favorable notice and that of the little coterie of distinguished men who surrounded him, would make success for the published book. His views on morals, religion and philosophy were listened to with respect and often with veneration. He died full of years and honors and was buried in Westminster Abbey, in close proximity to the Shakespeare monument.[2] His fame has extended to our own day, not so much as writer as man. Few of us read his works, but we read his life, and quote his epigrams as recorded by his friends, and we refer to him in a semi-humorous but affectionate way, and think of him somewhat as a virtuous Falstaff or a serious Uncle Toby,[3] or compare him, perhaps, in our own minds with some local eccentric of our acquaintance, who affects long hair, or clothes of a certain cut, or carelessness about his linen or his manners. Indeed his fame may be said to be, in our own day, colloquial rather than literary. We study Shakespeare's works, but Johnson's life, and character, for while he wrote these into his books, as every writer must, there was in him so much of interest and of value that he never reduced to writing, that others found fame in writing books about him. There have been over thirty editions of Boswell's life,[4] and several abridgments, and at least half a dozen other lives. He has an honored place in every history or compendium of English literature or lives of great men, and scarcely an English critic from the greatest to the most obscure but has tried his hand at an essay on Johnson's life and works, his character and genius.

I propose, in the short time which I have at my disposal to run over very briefly the chief events in his life and then seek to discover, if I may, the basis of his fame, which is not equally obvious, with that of some other writers.

In the first place, no part of Johnson's success was due to the accident of birth. It was his good fortune, of course, to be born of a progressive race in an enlightened age, but as this was a privilege shared by 15 million other Englishmen "mostly fools," as Carlyle cynically characterized them,[5] a little later it was not a distinction worth much in a struggle for success with the other 14,999,999.

He could boast neither noble nor gentle birth. It does not hurt an author to be a lord. Bacon, Byron, Scott and Bulwer-Lytton, to mention only a few, were no better writers because they were of the aristocracy, but any possible advantage that a literary career could derive from noble birth in a nation of snobs, (*vide* Thackeray) was at least not shared by Johnson.[6] His name is one of the commonest of the vulgar; the only other Johnsons I can think of offhand, who have filled the public eye are Ben Johnson, Tom Johnson, Ban Johnson and Jack Johnson.[7] I name them chronologically in order to avoid invidious comparison. His father, Michael Johnson was of obscure extraction, his mother somewhat better born, descending from an ancient race of substantial yeomanry.[8] Michael Johnson was an unsuccessful and finally a bankrupt bookseller and stationer, and the family never rose above the lower middle class.

Nor was Johnson's fame founded upon any superior educational equipment. "His intellectual stock" says Carlyle, "was perhaps inconsiderable; the furnishings of an English school and English University; a good knowledge of the Latin tongue, a more uncertain one of Greek, this is a rather slender stock of education with which to confront the world."[9] He learned English at a dame's school, began to learn Latin in a school at Lichfield, the head of which, a Mr. Hunter,[10] used the rod vigorously and according to Johnson, unmercifully and undiscriminatingly, although Johnson gratefully ascribes to these same floggings his unusually accurate knowledge of Latin, and warmly proclaims the efficacy of the rod.

At the age of eleven he was removed to the school of Southbridge in Worcestershire, where he remained for little more than a year. The following two years he spent at home, reading much in a desultory manner without any scheme of study.

During this period he probably did much of the reading from which he derived the almost encyclopedic knowledge which distinguished him. At the age of nineteen he was entered as a student of Pembroke College, Oxford. Boswell puts his residence in Oxford at three years. An examination of the records of the College proves it to have been really about fourteen months, at the end of which he was obliged by his father's insolvency to leave Oxford without his degree.

The winter following Johnson's departure from the University, his father died, leaving him, at 22, only twenty pounds with which to begin the battle of life. He had no family or powerful friends to place him. He became usher in a grammar school, and filled for a time the position of companion in a Country gentleman's home. At Birmingham, to which city he repaired, he earned a few guineas by literary drudgery, and printed a translation of a volume called *A Voyage to Abyssinia.*[11]

And now, having no income and no prospects, as one of his biographers says, Johnson very naturally got married. The lady of his choice was old enough to be his mother, with some years to spare. He was 26 and she was 48. She was the widow of a Birmingham mercer, and her name was Eliza Porter.[12] She is described by those who knew her as very fat, with cheeks colored by paint and cordials, flimsy and fantastic in dress and affected in her manners. But Dr. Johnson seems to have loved and admired her very much and never wavered in his fidelity to his dear Letty, as he referred to her.

One attraction the lady had,—a fortune of 800 pounds. With this little capital the Johnsons opened a boys' school.[13] But Johnson was not cut out for a pedagogue. The school failed after a year and a half, one of its few pupils being David Garrick.[14] Johnson then, like many another, put his manuscripts in his pocket and went to London to seek his fortune. Garrick accompanied him on the same errand, which he achieved much sooner than Johnson, becoming the most famous actor of his age and earning large sums of money, while Johnson was still an out-at-elbows literary hack.

Johnson was probably the first English writer to owe his whole support to literature; and by literature is meant, for the most part, such drudgery as translation for booksellers. For many years he contributed to the *Gentleman's Magazine,* I believe still in existence, conducted by an enlightened and intelligent publisher by the name of Cave.[15] For the magazine Johnson wrote Latin poems in praise of Cave and Cave's friends, and Jacobite squibs, for he was a rabid Tory. He was one of the first of reporters. The art of shorthand had not been invented, or he might have spoiled his literary career by practising it. Notes were taken in the two houses of Parliament and brought to Johnson, who licked them into shape, for the *Magazine.* For a time they passed as the originals, and for this deception Johnson, at the end of life, expressed penitence, though he said that he had ceased to write them when he found that they were taken as genuine. He would not, he said, be "accessory to the propagation of falsehood."[16]

In 1742 he published his *Life of Richard Savage,* one of his Grub Street friends, a brilliant but dissipated man, with a romantic background to his history.[17] It is one of Johnson's best works and the best extant picture of the life of the struggling authors of the time.

In 1738 Johnson published his poem *London*—an imitation of the Third Satire of Juvenal, which attracted the notice of Pope, then the literary dictator of London, who predicted a future for Johnson.[18] One couplet of the poem is much quoted:

> This mournful truth is everywhere confessed,
> Slow rises worth by poverty depressed,

a touch of pessimism borne out by Johnson's own experience.

In 1749, ten years later, appeared *The Vanity of Human Wishes*, an imitation of the Tenth Satire of Juvenal. Johnson was a great Latinist, wrote much in the language, and translated largely from it. For his *London*, though it ran into two editions in as many weeks, he received ten guineas, and for his *Vanity of Human Wishes* fifteen.

In 1749 Garrick, who had become Manager of Drury Lane Theater, brought out his friend Johnson's Tragedy of *Irene*.[19] Then as now, writing for the state when successful was the most profitable kind of literary work. It was a heavy and unreadable performance, interesting, if at all, as a literary curiosity. With all his influence and friendly ardor, Garrick was only able to run it nine nights, for which Johnson received 195 pounds, 17 shillings, and 100 pounds for the copy, probably more money than he had ever had at any one time since his marriage.[20]

Meantime he had embarked upon his most conspicuous enterprise, the *Dictionary of the English Language*.[21] His plan for the *Dictionary*, he addressed, at the suggestion of Dodsley, the bookseller and writer, to Lord Chesterfield, then Secretary of State, and the great contemporary Maecenas. Lord Chesterfield gracefully acknowledged Johnson's homage and presented him with a few guineas.[22] Johnson continued during some time to call upon his patron, but being not of a personality to ornament a nobleman's parlor or table, and being repeatedly told by the porter that his lordship was not at home, discontinued his visits and began to nourish a righteous grudge for the neglect with which he was treated.

Johnson began the dictionary in 1747. He had hoped to finish it by 1750, but only gave it to the world in 1755. In the meantime he found relaxation in lighter forms of literature.

About a year after the publication of *Irene*, Johnson began the issue of short essays, similar to those of the *Spectator* and the *Tatler*, a popular form of composition in that age, under the title the *Rambler*. The *Rambler* appeared twice a week for two years, and added greatly to Johnson's reputation.[23] It was well received, and spread Johnson's fame beyond the confines of London, and though of limited circulation, established Johnson's position as a great practical moralist.

In 1752 Mrs. Johnson died. Johnson's grief was deep and lasting. For a time he was broken hearted, and plunged into work to deaden his suffering.

The dictionary came out in 1755. Johnson's tilt with Lord Chesterfield upon the occasion of its appearance is one of the most interesting episodes in literature. Chesterfield was a leader of society, was an *arbiter elegantiarum,* of his day, and himself an author and man of wit, of a type very different from that of Johnson, who expressed his opinion of him freely. "I thought," he said, "that this man had been a Lord among wits; but I find he is only a wit among lords"; and of Chesterfield's famous letters he said that they taught the morals of a harlot and the manners of a dancing master. Chesterfield returned the compliment. He describes Johnson in his *Letters,* as a

> respectable Hottentot, who throws his meat anywhere but down his throat. This absurd person, was not only uncouth in manners and warm in dispute, but behaved exactly in the same way to superiors, equals and inferiors, and therefore, by a necessary consequence, absurdly to two of the three.[24]

A comparison of these two *bon mots* leaves the balance in Johnson's favor. What Johnson said of Chesterfield was witty; Chesterfield's language is little more than abusive.

When the dictionary was ready to come out,—it had been talked about almost as much as Rostand's *Chanticleer,*[25]—Chesterfield began to get busy and try to break into the game—to speak in the vernacular. He published in the *World,*—a periodical devoted to the polite world—two articles in which were set forth the need of a dictionary and various courtly compliments describing Johnson's fitness for a dictatorship over the language;[26]—obviously what Johnson took it to mean, that Chesterfield would like to have the dictionary dedicated to him, which would blazon him to the world as a patron of literature as well as an authority upon manners. Johnson, however, was not so easily placated, and gave the noble earl a piece of his mind in a letter which first appeared in Boswell's *Life:*[27]

> My Lord,—I have been lately informed by the proprietor of the World that two papers, in which my Dictionary is recommended to the public, were written by your lordship. To be so distinguished is an honour which, being very little accustomed to favours from the great, I know not well how to receive, or in what terms to acknowledge.
>
> When, upon some slight encouragement, I first visited your Lordship, I was overpowered, like the rest of mankind, by the enchantment of your address; and could not forbear to wish that I might boast myself, *le vainqueur du vainqueur de la terre*[28]—that I might obtain that regard for which I saw the world contending; but I found my attendance so little encouraged that neither pride nor modesty would suffer me to continue it. When I had once addressed your Lordship in public, I had exhausted all the arts of pleasing which a wearied and uncourtly scholar can possess. I had done all that I could; and no man is well pleased to have his all neglected, be it ever so little.
>
> Seven years, my Lord, have now passed, since I waited in your outward rooms and was repulsed from your door; during which time I have been pushing on my work through difficulties of which it is useless to complain, and have brought it at last to the verge of publication without one act of assistance, one word of encour-

agement, or one smile of favour. Such treatment I did not expect, for I never had a patron before.

The shepherd in Virgil grew at last acquainted with Love, and found him a native of the rocks.

Is not a patron, my Lord, one who looks with unconcern on a man struggling for life in the water, and when he has reached the ground encumbers him with help? The notice which you have been pleased to take of my labours, had it been early, had been kind; but it has been delayed till I am indifferent, and cannot enjoy it; till I am solitary, and cannot impart it; till I am known, and do not want it. I hope it is no very cynical asperity not to confess obligations where no benefit has been received, or to be unwilling that the public should consider me as owing that to a patron, which Providence has enabled me to do for myself.

Having carried on my work thus far with so little obligation to any favourer of learning, I shall not be disappointed though I should conclude it, should less be possible, with less; for I have been long wakened from that dream of hope in which I once boasted myself with so much exultation, my Lord,

Your Lordship's most humble, and most obedient servant,

Sam Johnson.

For some years after the appearance of the *Dictionary* Johnson seems to have written little of importance—a sort of constitutional indolence seeming to mark the reaction from the great task of the dictionary. From 1758 to 1760 he published a set of essays called the "Idler," on the old *Rambler* plan.[29] He wrote prospectuses and corrected manuscripts and reviewed books. (Ads.) Upon the death of his mother, he wrote *Rasselas* to pay for her funeral expenses, wrote it in the evenings of a single week and received 100 pounds for it, probably the best paid of his lighter works.[30]

When George III came to the throne, after the manner of Kings he looked around for men who had achieved things worthy of honor, and recognized the profession of letters by bestowing a pension of 300 pounds a year upon Johnson for his services to literature.[31] Johnson was in real distress at the time, and the pension was very welcome. Several times, shortly preceding its bestowal, he had been in a sponging house[32] for debt. But on the tender of the pension he was confronted with a certain difficulty. He had defined a pension in the dictionary as generally understood to mean "pay given to a State hireling for treason to his country." The difficulty was surmounted however, and he accepted the pension and was duly grateful. Johnson had been a rabid Tory, and Jacobite, and while he was never called upon to do any political service with his pen his teeth were drawn and he became a very good Hanoverian, and was quite willing to drink King George's health.

With the ease and freedom from care which his pension gave him, he ceased to write except at long intervals, and then very rapidly for a time. He edited an edition of Shakespeare, not a very good one, wrote the *Lives of the Poets*, perhaps his finest work and recorded his impressions of a voyage to the Hebrides.[33] He devoted himself to his Club and to his friends, by whom he died surrounded, on December 13th, 1784, in the Seventy-fifth year of his life.[34]

In seeking to find the basis of Johnson's influence and renown, there are some things, to which, obviously, he did not owe them.

Johnson owed no part of his success to physical charms or graces.[35]

He was afflicted with the hereditary disease of scrofula, and was taken by his mother when a child to be touched by Queen Anne for the King's Evil.[36] The demon of hypochondria was always lying in wait for him and could be exorcised for a time only by hard work or social excitement. The disease had scarred and disfigured his features otherwise regular and always impressive, as is obvious from Reynolds's portrait. It had seriously injured his eyes, entirely destroying, it seems, the sight of one. He could not, it was said, distinguish a friend's face half a yard off. This defect of vision obviously closed to him the world of art; he could not appreciate a picture, a statue or a play, for the simple reason that he could not see it. To this, however, can hardly be ascribed his insensibility to music, which was even more pronounced than his dullness of sight.

He was given to queer convulsions, which amazed all beholders and were probably connected with his disease, though he and Reynolds ascribed them simply to habit. Sometimes he seemed to be obeying some hidden impulse, which commanded him to touch every post in the street, or tread on the center of every paving stone, and would return if his task had not been accurately performed.

In spite of these oddities he was possessed of physical power corresponding to his great height and massive stature, and was proficient at athletic exercises. Once he is said to have taken up a chair at the theatre upon which a man had seated himself during his temporary absence, and to have tossed it and its occupant bodily into the pit. Once at least he went out fox hunting, and though he despised the amusement, was deeply touched by the complimentary assertion that he rode as well as the most illiterate fellow in England.

The young are often told that good manners are a passport to polite society and an aid to success in life. Johnson derived no advantage from this source. His manners had never been courtly, and as the result of the privations and sufferings he endured during his earlier years in London, they became almost savage. Being too poor to buy decent clothes, he became a confirmed sloven. Until he became a pensioner and fell under the refining influence of Mrs. Thrale, his huge frame was clad in the raggedest of garments. "I have no passion," he once said, "for clean linen"; and it is to be feared that he sometimes offended more senses than one.

> Being very often hungry when he sat down to his meals, he contracted the habit of eating with ravenous greediness. Even to the end of his life, and even at the tables of the great, the sight of food affected him as it affects wild beasts and birds of prey. His taste in cookery formed in subterranean ordinaries and *à la mode* beef shops, was far from delicate. Whenever he was so fortunate as to have near him a hare that had been kept too long, or a meat pie made with rancid butter, he gorged himself with such violence that his veins swelled, and the moisture broke out on his forehead.[37]

He would consume seven or eight peaches at a sitting, and remarked once that he had never had enough wall fruit[38] to eat in his life.

He was a great tea drinker, "a hardened and shameless tea-drinker" he called himself. One of his teapots, preserved by a relic hunter, contained two quarts, and he professed to have consumed five and twenty cups at a sitting. Mrs. Thrale complained that he kept her sitting up until four o'clock in the morning making tea.

Such was the heat and irritability of his blood that he would pare his nails to the quick and scrape the joints of his fingers with a penknife until they seemed quite red and raw—one is inclined to wonder why.

Nevertheless, Johnson claimed to be a polite man. "I look upon myself" he once said to Boswell, "as a very polite man." "Every man of any education," he once said to the amazement of his hearers, "would rather be called a rascal than accused of deficiency in the graces," and upon another occasion he said, "You may observe that I am well bred to a degree of needless scrupulosity." Nor were his claims to politeness entirely unfounded. Boswell notes one occasion where, when dining with Lord Monboddo Johnson insisted on rising when the ladies left the table.[39] He always insisted upon showing ladies to their carriages through Bolt Court, and he often referred with extreme disgust to a certain footman in Paris who used his fingers in place of sugar tongs.

Johnson owed no part of his fame to wealth, either inherited or acquired. As we have seen, he wrote to live, and for a long time barely succeeded in accomplishing his purpose. He had no oppressive sense of a mission to perform. "No man but a blockhead," he said, "ever wrote except for money," and, as we have likewise seen, when he became a pensioner he ceased to write, except spasmodically. His great work, the dictionary, occupied seven or eight years of his time. For it he received 1,675 pounds,[40] out of which he had to pay the wages of seven or eight copyists, and purchase ink and paper and pens—$8,000.00 for seven years' work for as many men was a very meagre reward.

It is borne in upon us how narrow Johnson's means had been, when we read how rich he felt with his 300 pounds a year, less than the income of many a popular waiter, and only a fraction of that of a first class male cook.

A few other writers of the day were more fortunate. Addison, Congreve and Swift, during the reign of Queen Anne had made large profits and secured good places as the reward of their literary labors.[41] Pope received 8,000 pounds for his translation of Homer and for years enjoyed a large income.[42] And Hume 4500 pounds for 1 vol. of his *History*.[43] Richardson kept his dry goods shop while he wrote his novels.[44] But broadly speaking, it was the day of small things for the profession of literature.

Johnson's present day fame is not due to the greatness of his writings. They do not belong to the library of immortal works, like those of Homer, Virgil, Dante, Goethe and Shakespeare.[45] Indeed they are hardly on the second shelf of literary wares. Few people read anything of his but *Rasselas*, and perhaps the *Lives of the Poets*, and such selections from his writings as are contained in Compendiums of

English Literature. No one not suffering from an abnormally developed sense of duty could labor through his tragedy. His poetry was of the classic school, written like all the verse of his age, in the heroic couplet, iambic pentameter. The mannerism of his style is strongly marked. He himself admitted his tendency to use big words and too many of them. He preferred the abstract to the concrete, and balanced his long sentences in a monotonous rhythm, giving the appearance, sometimes borne out, of elaborate logical discrimination. But his style, though ponderous and tiresome, is perfectly clear; the reader cannot fail, at the end of the longest hunt, to bag the quarry, a respect in which the many imitations of "Johnsonese" have been sadly lacking.

His dictionary, while it was the first work worthy of the name that had been undertaken in England, could hardly be classed as literature. Johnson himself defines a lexicographer as "a harmless drudge." In his day the science of lexicography had not been invented, nor had the study of the historical development of the language or comparative philology been begun. But the dictionary brought Johnson fame and established his position firmly in the world of letters; indeed he was afterwards generally known as "Dictionary Johnson." Some of his definitions are amusing. "Oats" is defined as "a grain used in England as food for horses, and in Scotland as food for men." Windward and leeward are defined in exactly the same terms. "Grub street, the name of a street in London, much inhabited by writers of small histories, dictionaries and temporary poems; hence any mean production is called 'Grub Street.' "

He introduced not only his experiences, but his prejudices into his definitions, as may be seen by reading the definitions of Tory, Whig, Excise, as well as that of "oats" above quoted, which reflected the Doctor's prejudice against Scotchmen, with which his friend Boswell had to contend.

And now, since we have discussed some things to which Johnson did and does not owe his renown, things which were handicaps to his career, which he made in spite of them, since we have seen in some small sense what Johnson was, let us ask ourselves why he was.

To go back to his writings, while they had little lasting value, they were great by the standard of his age, and were sufficient to establish his fame in his own day. They represented a solid, honest, worthy product, and were better than those of most writers of his day. They must be accepted, therefore, as the foundation stone of his reputation.

Johnson's fame was favored, also, by the condition of literature in England when he became its acknowledged leader. It was a slack period of literary productiveness. The brilliant writers of the former generation Dryden, Addison, Fielding, Smollett, Swift, Pope, were either dead or in their dotage, or had done their best work.[46] The glorious galaxy of literary stars that were to dazzle the first half of the 19th century,—Wordsworth, Byron, Shelley, Scott, Keats, Carlyle, Tennyson, Browning, Macaulay, Thackeray, Dickens,—were not yet born, or else were in swaddling clothes.[47] Among the blind, the one-eyed man is King, and Johnson ranked as the best of his day. If there were any such as Burke or Goldsmith, for instance, whom time has given higher literary rank, they either did not realize their own quality, or modestly deferred to the man of the hour.

Johnson's fame is bound up with his friendships, and may be said to be largely due to them. No man set a higher value upon friendship than Johnson. "A man," he said to Reynolds, "ought to keep his friendship in constant repair," or he would find himself left alone as he grew older. "I look upon a day as lost," he said later in life, "in which I do not make a new acquaintance." Making new acquaintances did not involve dropping the old. The list of his friends is a long one, and includes, as it were, successive layers, superimposed upon each other, from the earliest period of his life.

By far the most celebrated of Johnson's earlier friends, was David Garrick. The two men had a sincere regard for each other, but were so widely separated by circumstances as well as by a radical opposition of temperament that any close intimacy could hardly be expected. Garrick's rapid elevation in fame and fortune seems to have produced a certain degree of envy in his old schoolmaster, who was troubled with a rather excessive allowance of human nature. He had the good old-fashioned contempt for players, characteristic both of the Tory and the inartistic mind. He asserted roundly that he looked upon players as no better than dancing dogs. "But, sir," said Bozzy "you will allow that some players are better than others?" "Yes, sir, as some dogs dance better than others."

This attitude of mind on the part of Johnson, and his freedom of expressing it sometimes led to unpleasant incidents, the most unpleasant of which was when Garrick proposed rather too freely to be a member of the Club. Johnson said that the first duke in England had no right to use such language, and said, according to Mrs. Thrale, "If Garrick does apply, I will blackball him. Surely we ought to be able to sit in a society like ours—

Unelbowed by a gamester, pimp or player![48]

Nearly 10 years afterwards, however, Johnson favored Garrick's election, and when he died, declared that the Club should have a year's widowhood. No successor to Garrick was elected during that time.

Another of Johnson's famous friends, also a member of the famous Club, was Sir Joshua Reynolds. Two other friends of Johnson's who deserve to be placed beside Reynolds, came from Ireland to seek their fortunes in London. Edmund Burke, incomparably the best writer upon political philosophy in English literature, the master of a style unrivaled for richness, flexibility, and vigor, was radically opposed to Johnson on party questions, but he had qualities which commended him even to the man who called him a "bottomless Whig," and who generally spoke of Whigs as rascals, and maintained that the first Whig was the devil. If his intellect was wider, his heart was as warm as Johnson's, and in conversation he merited the generous applause and warm emulation of his friends. Johnson was never tired of praising the extraordinary readiness and spontaneity of Burke's conversation. Burke equally admitted Johnson's supremacy in conversation. "It is enough for me," he said to some one who regretted Johnson's monopoly of the talk on a particular occasion "to have rung the bell for him."

The friendships of great men have a collective value, like the shares of a corporation. When we look upon the paintings of Sir Joshua, we always think of his friend Dr. Johnson. When we see a reference to Burke or Goldsmith or Sheridan[49] we think of the Club of which Dr. Johnson was the acknowledged head.

The Club began its meetings in February 1764 and was afterwards known as the Literary Club, or, in later years, as Johnson's Club. It was founded by Sir Joshua Reynolds, "Our Romulus" as Johnson called him. They met weekly at the Turk's Head in Gerard Street, Soho, at seven o'clock, and the talk generally continued until a late hour. The Club consisted at first of 9 members. It was afterwards increased in number and the weekly supper became a fortnightly dinner. It continued to thrive, and election to it came to be as great an honor in certain circles as election to Parliament. Some of the members elected in Johnson's lifetime were Percy of the *Reliques*, Garrick, Boswell, Fox, Gibbon, Adam Smith, Sheridan and Dr. Burney.[50] Garrick, as we have seen, was first blackballed by Dr. Johnson, and subsequently proposed by him, as were also Boswell and Charles James Fox.

Johnson had many friends among the gentler sex, and generally liked to have a mild platonic flirtation on hand. He speaks somewhere of "The endearing elegance of female friendship."[51] Nobody could pay more effective compliments than Johnson when he chose, and the many female friends who have written of him agree that he could be singularly attractive to women. They seemed to recognize the deep tenderness underlying his thoroughly masculine nature, and, for the sake of it forgave his external roughness, after the manner of their sex.

Boswell, excusing his frankness by recalling the great regard for truth which Dr. Johnson inculcated, feels called upon to say that "When J. was a young man his amorous inclinations were uncommonly strong and impetuous. He owned to many of his friends that he used to take women of the town to taverns and hear them relate their history." Boswell goes on to say that like many good and pious men, including St. Paul, Johnson was not free from propensities which were "ever warring against the law of his mind" and that in his combats with them he was sometimes overcome.[52] And then, Boswell feels called upon to warn the profane and licentious against charging Johnson with hypocrisy or laxity of principles, and argues the point, very ingeniously and convincingly, and makes Johnson out, as he was, like King David, a man after God's own heart, who sinned when too strongly tempted, yet never justified his fault, but always repented in sackcloth and ashes.[53]

In his riper years he was a social lion, frequented the parlors of fashionable ladies, and numbered among his friends many famous women, among whom a few were Peg Woffington, the celebrated actress, Fanny Burney, the author of *Evelina*, etc., afterwards Mme. D'Arblay, Hannah More, the poetess, Miss Reynolds, sister of Sir Joshua Reynolds, and herself a painter, Mrs. Montagu, a literary lady of large fortune and great liberality.[54] Boswell mentions as among Johnson's friends the Duchess of Devonshire.[55] But the most important and useful of his female friends was Mrs. Thrale, who is herself famous because of Johnson's friendship. In 1765 when Johnson was 54 years old, he met the Thrales at the home of a mutual friend. Thrale was a wealthy brewer, who had married a woman much younger than himself, of great vivacity and independence of character. She was far better educated than most women of her day, and because of a lack of sympathy on her husband's part was forced, she said, to fall back upon literature as her sole resource. One day the Thrales, calling upon Johnson, found him in a state of mental depression bordering upon despair, and carried him off to their country house at Streatham. For the next 16 years a room was set apart for him there, as well as in their house in Southwark. He passed a large part of his time with them and derived from the intimacy, most of the comfort of his later years. When Mr. Thrale died, as he did in the fulness of years, Dr. Johnson continued his friendly intimacy with the household until Mrs. Thrale, wearying of her widowhood, fell in love with, and married an Italian musician by the name of Piozzi. This greatly displeased Dr. Johnson, who wrote her a sharp letter, accusing her of treachery to her religion, her family and her fair fame.[56] This produced a coolness between them, which in spite of an ostensible reconciliation, was never quite removed. When Johnson died, Mrs. Thrale, published a book of his letters and her reflections on his life and character.[57] Boswell perhaps with a touch of professional jealousy, did not think very much of the book, and held that it maligned Johnson.

Johnson is more famous as conversationalist than as writer. He had long regarded conversation as the chief amusement, and came in later years to regard it as almost the chief employment of life; and he had studied the art with the zeal of a man pursuing a favorite hobby. He had always, as he told Sir Joshua Reynolds, made it a principle to talk on all occasions as well as he could. He had thus obtained a mastery over his weapons which made him one of the most accomplished of conversational gladiators. He had one advantage which has pretty well disappeared from modern society, and the disappearance of which has been destructive to excellence of thought. A good talker, even more than a good orator implies a good audience. Modern society is too vast and too restless to give a conversationalist a fair chance. For the formation of real proficiency in the art, friends should meet often, sit long and be thoroughly at ease. The Club, in which Johnson delighted was excellently adapted to foster his peculiar talent. His talk was full of apposite illustrations and unrivaled in keen argument, rapid flashes of wit and humor, scornful retort and dexterous sophistry. Sometimes he would fell his adversary at a blow; his sword, as Boswell said would be through your body in an instant without preliminary flourishes; and in the excitement of talking for victory he would use any device that came to hand. "There is no arguing with Johnson," said Goldsmith, quoting a phrase from Cibber, "for if his pistol misses fire he knocks you down with the butt-end of it."[58]

Johnson's retorts were fair play under the conditions of the game, as it is fair playing to kick an opponent's shins at football. But of course a man who had, as it were, become the acknowledged champion of the ring, and who had an irascible and thoroughly dogmatic temper, was tempted to become unduly imperious. Anecdotes illustrative of his ferocity abound and his best friends had all to suffer in turn. The records of his contests of this kind fill a large space in Boswell's pages. That they did not lead to worse consequences shows his absence of rancour. He was always ready and anxious for a reconciliation. There was no venom in the wound he inflicted, for there was no ill nature; he was rough in the heat of the struggle and in such cases careless in distributing blows; but he never enjoyed giving pain. None of his tiffs ripened into permanent quarrels, and he seems scarcely to have lost a friend.

Other elements of greatness in Johnson's character were numerous. He was thoroughly honest; he hated cant; he despised snobbery; he loved truth and abhorred a lie. It would have been easy for him to prostitute his talents to base uses, as did many of his contemporaries, and make a few dirty guineas by advocating principles and causes that were not his own. He stood four-square with his conscience, and took the world's thumps with courage and philosophy,—not always cheerfully, for he was a deep-dyed pessimist but without undue complaining. His great theme, running through all his writing, and the title of one of his poems was the Vanity of Human Wishes.

He was not a reformer, indeed he was an 18th century stand-patter. He stood for the established order, for virtue and morality, and never tore his hair or rent the air in screaming for reforms. But he loved his fellow men, not so much in the abstract perhaps as in the concrete. During all his life he was always willing to share his pittance with those more needy, and after he received his pension, spent more of it upon others than upon himself. While, after he made their acquaintance, most of his time was spent with the Thrales, he kept up a house on one of the narrow and gloomy courts on the North side of Fleet Street, which seems to have been more of a hospital or a menagerie than the residence of a gentleman. Among the inmates were the blind Miss Williams, several other destitute females, and an old quack doctor, who sometimes gained a few coppers or a glass of gin by bleeding or dosing coal heavers and hackney coachmen.[59] This ill-assorted collection of freaks filled out the monotony of their existence by quarreling among themselves, or with Johnson's black servant Frank,[60] and sometimes with their host himself, who they complained should set them a better table.

Dr. Johnson was a faithful Christian and Churchman—not always synonymous terms. His published prayers and meditations fill one or two volumes of his collected works, and they reveal a sincere and unaffected piety.

His conversations were made up of his views on Church and State, men and manners, books and writers, whatever was human interested him. Among other strong opinions of his, he hated slavery with a zeal which the conservative Boswell thought to be without knowledge. He combined this hatred with a hearty dislike for American independence, and recognized an anomaly which must have been apparent to everybody except Americans, and only wilful blindness could have prevented them from seeing it, when he said: "How is it that we always hear the loudest yelps for liberty amongst the drivers of negroes?"[61]

But the friend to whom Johnson's fame owes most, without whom all of his virtues, both as writer and as man, all his interesting weaknesses and peculiarities, would long since have been forgotten, was his friend Boswell.

The most informing biography of any individual would be one written by himself, provided that in it he told the truth, the whole truth and nothing but the truth. But this would be too much to hope for from poor human nature, and even the few who have pretended to complete frankness in the record of their lives have not convinced either their contemporaries or their readers of later generations of their entire frankness. So that we must take our dear wicked autobiographers, our Rousseaus and Casanovas and Cellinis, with a large grain of salt.[62] We can classify them, after a pleasantry by Dr. Van Dyke, as autobiographers or ought-not-to-be-biographers.[63] They are valuable not so much as records of useful or misspent lives, as the case may be, but as more or less faithful mirrors of the times reflected in them. But it is altogether improbable that Johnson could have written a better biography of himself than Boswell wrote of him. It has among its other merits those of frankness and truthfulness, and it was written by a friend. When Solomon wished that his enemy might write a book, it was certainly not a Life of Solomon that he had in mind.[64] This useful little Scotchman met his great friend, who despised or affected to despise Scotchmen, some time after the publication of the *Dictionary*, and thereafter made it the chief business of his life to collect the material for his famous biography. Reviewers of Boswell's *Life*, while cheerfully conceding the greatness of his work, make little of the man. Macaulay, in his famous essay, thus characterizes Boswell as an author.—

> Homer is not more decidedly the first of heroic poets, Shakespeare the first of dramatists, Demosthenes the first of orators than Boswell is the first of biographers. He has no second. He has distanced all his competitors so decidedly that it is not worth while to place them. Eclipse is first and the rest nowhere.[65]

But side by side with this superb panegyric of the book, comes with Macaulay's love of paradox, his estimate of the author; he makes him out a coxcomb and a bore, weak, vain, pushing, curious and garrulous; without reason, without wit, without humor, by nature a slave and an idolater, a parasite, who accidentally happened to cling to Johnson, and wrote his book in spite of himself.

Carlyle is equally enthusiastic about the book, and much more just in his estimate of Boswell. I think it is only fair to refute Macaulay's slander by quoting what Carlyle said about Boswell and his book:

> Boswell wrote a good Book, because he had a heart and an eye to discern Wisdom and an utterance to render it forth; because of his free insight, his lively talent, above all, his love and childlike open-mindedness. His sneaking sycophancies, his greediness and forwardness, whatever was bestial and earthly in him, are so many blemishes in his Book, which still disturb us in its clearness; wholly hindrances, not helps. Towards Johnson, however, his feeling was not Sycophancy, which is the

lowest, but Reverence which is the highest of human feelings. None but a reverent man (which so unspeakably few are) could have found his way from Boswell's environment to Johnson's; if such worship for real God-made superiors showed itself also as worship for apparent Tailor-made superiors,—the case, in this composite human nature of ours, was not miraculous, the more was the pity! But for ourselves, let every one of us cling to this last article of Faith and know it as the beginning of all knowledge worth the name: That neither James Boswell's good Book, nor any other good thing, in any time or in any place, was, is, or can be performed by any man in virtue of his badness, but always and solely in spite thereof.

As for the Book itself, questionless the universal favor entertained for it is well merited. In worth as a Book we have rated it beyond any other product of the eighteenth century: all Johnson's own Writings, laborious and in their kind genuine above most, stand on a quite inferior level to it; already, indeed, they are becoming obsolete for this generation; and for some future generation may be valuable chiefly as Prolegomena and expository Scholia to this Johnsoniad of Boswell. Which of us but remembers, as one of the sunny spots in his existence, the day when he opened these airy volumes, fascinating him by a true natural-magic! It was as if the curtains of the past were drawn aside, and we looked mysteriously into a kindred country, where dwelt our Fathers; inexpressibly dear to us, but which had seemed forever hidden from our eyes. For the dead Night had engulfed it; all was gone, vanished as if it had not been. Nevertheless, wondrously given back to us, there once more it lay; all bright, lucid, blooming; a little island of Creation amid the circumambient Void. There it still lies; like a thing stationary, imperishable, over which changeful Time were now accumulating itself in vain, and could not, any longer, harm it or hide it.

Whatever may be our estimate of the author, Boswell's Johnson will be read long after Johnson's works are forgotten, even as Shakespeare's works will be read long after the Commentaries thereon are forgotten—always excepting Rowfant Club publications!

One could spend many evenings quoting conversations from Boswell, or bright things which the good doctor said, such as his remark that "he did not believe in ghosts, but was afraid of them just the same,"—One might speak of the care with which he investigated the Cock Lane Ghost; of his tilt with Macpherson, the author of the Poems of *Ossian*;[66] of his Travels; or go critically into the merits of his writings. But Samuel Johnson lived 75 years and Boswell wrote 1200 pages and my time is limited to some thing less than one hour.

A bundle of contradictions, Johnson's virtues, and faults contribute alike to make him the hero of Boswell's epic. A fine face, ...

⌣

SOURCE: Incomplete and undated typed text at the Fisk University Library. Chesnutt delivered this speech to Cleveland's Rowfant Club, a bibliophile society, on 11 November 1911. Not a source text but a historically significant publication of this speech is *WHO and WHY was SAMUEL JOHNSON*, edited and introduced by Robert A. Tibbets (Akron, O., 1991).

[1]John Dryden (1631–1700); Alexander Pope (1688–1744).

[2]Johnson died in London on 13 December 1784; he was born in Lichfield, Staffordshire, 18 September 1709.

[3]Falstaff is a comic character in Shakespeare's *Henry IV, Parts 1 and 2* and *The*

Merry Wives of Windsor; Uncle Toby Shandy is a droll character in *Tristram Shandy* (1767) by Laurence Sterne (1713–68).

[4]James Boswell (1740–95), *Life of Johnson* (1791).

[5]"Parliaments," Pamphlet No. 6 in *Latter-Day Pamphlets* (1850).

[6]George Noel Gordon, Lord Byron (1788–1824); Edward George Earle Lytton Bulwer-Lytton, Baron Lytton (1803–73), British novelist and politician; Sir Walter Scott (1771–1832); William Makepeace Thackeray (1811–63), who attained both critical and popular success as a novelist despite his not having been born to the upper classes.

[7]Ben Johnson (1858–1950), Kentucky Congressman and lawyer; Tom Loftin Johnson (1854–1911), inventor, steel merchant, Ohio Congressman, and three-time mayor of Cleveland (1901–9); Ban Johnson (1863–1931), sportswriter, baseball executive, and founder and first president of baseball's American League in 1900; and Jack Johnson (1878–1946), first black boxer to win the world heavyweight boxing title (1908).

[8]Michael Johnson (1656–1731); Sarah Ford Johnson (1669–1759). At this point in his speech Chesnutt begins to rely on Boswell's *Life of Johnson* and *The Life of Samuel Johnson* (1789) by Sir John Hawkins (1719–89), paraphrasing frequently.

[9]Here and at the end of this speech Chesnutt quotes from Carlyle's 1832 essay on Boswell's *Life* (1831), edited by John Wilson Croker (1780–1857). See n. 65.

[10]Dame Anne Oliver (?–1731), wife of Peter Oliver (1671–1704), a shoemaker in Lichfield, operated a local village school; Rev. John Hunter (c. 1674–1741) was headmaster of Lichfield Grammar School; Johnson's teachers between Dame Oliver and Hunter included Tom Browne (1657?–1717) and Humphrey Hawkins (1667?–1741).

[11]Jerólimo Lobo (1595–1678), *Relation Historique d'Abissinie* (1728); Johnson's translation was published in 1735.

[12]Elizabeth Jervis Johnson (1689–1752), the widow of textile merchant Harry Porter (1691–1734); the Johnsons were married on 9 July 1735.

[13]At Edial, Staffordshire, near Lichfield.

[14](1717–79); his prominence in the theatrical world is described below by Chesnutt.

[15]Edward Cave (1691–1754) founded the *Gentleman's Magazine* in 1731; the periodical did not cease publication until 1914.

[16]William Guthrie (1708–70) took notes on speeches in Parliament and delivered them to Cave who, in turn, dispatched them to Johnson for final revision. Johnson began editing Guthrie's work in 1738; but, from 1741 to 1744, he reconstructed the speeches singlehandedly.

[17]Johnson's *An Account of the Life of Mr. Richard Savage*—a biography of the poet and playwright (1697–1743)—was published anonymously on 11 February 1744, a few months after Savage died in debtor's prison in Bristol.

[18]According to Boswell, Pope learned that Johnson was little known and observed that that would soon change. Juvenal (Decimus Junius Juvenalis, c. 60–c. 140) was a Roman poet who wrote sixteen satires in which he attacks both human corruption and weakness. *London* was published on 13 May 1738.

[19]Though published as *Irene* (1749), the play was produced on 6 February 1749 as *Mahomet and Irene* with Garrick in the role of Demetrius.

[20]Garrick managed Drury Lane from 1747 to 1763.

[21]Published in 1755.

[22]Philip Dormer Stanhope, Earl of Chesterfield, gave Johnson ten pounds when he forwarded his *Plan of a Dictionary* in the fall of 1747. Like Gaius Cilnius Maecenas (c. 70–8 B.C.), who was a supporter of Virgil (70–19 B.C.) and Horace (65–8 B.C.), Chesterfield was also a great literary patron.

[23]Receiving two guineas per piece, Johnson wrote all but five of the essays consti-

tuting *The Rambler*, published by Cave from Tuesday, 20 March 1750, through Saturday, 14 March 1752; like *London* and his biography of Savage, *The Rambler* appeared anonymously.

[24]Chesnutt has both condensed and altered the order of this passage taken from Chesterfield's letter to his illegitimate son, Philip Stanhope (1732–68), dated 28 February 1751, which appears in his *Letters to His Son* (1774), many editions of which would have been available to Chesnutt; even by Chesnutt's time, however, most commentators agreed that Chesterfield referred not to Johnson but to George, Baron Lyttleton (1709–73), a contemporary statesman.

[25]A play by Edmond Rostand (1868–1918), produced in 1910.

[26]Chesterfield's pieces appeared in successive issues on 28 November and 5 December 1754.

[27]Dated 7 February 1755.

[28]The conqueror of the world-conqueror.

[29]A weekly series in *The Universal Chronicle or Weekly Gazetteer*, "The Idler" was published from 15 April 1758 through 5 April 1760.

[30]*The History of Rasselas, Prince of Abissinia* (1759).

[31]George III was crowned in 1760; he granted Johnson a pension for life in July 1762.

[32]Debtors (those who "sponged" or lived on the wealth of others) were, when arrested, confined in a sponging house.

[33]*The Plays of William Shakespeare*, 8 volumes (1765); *Prefaces Critical and Biographical to the Works of the English Poets*, 10 volumes (1781); *A Journey to the Western Islands of Scotland* (1775).

[34]This Club, the 1764 creation of portraitist Sir Joshua Reynolds (1723–92), met each Monday evening at the Turk's Head in Gerard Street. It initially numbered nine members, including: Reynolds; Johnson; Johnson biographer Sir John Hawkins, a member of the earlier, Ivy Lane club; Anthony Chamier (1725–80), Under-Secretary of State from 1775 until 1780; Christopher Nugent (c. 1698–1775), physician and father-in-law of statesman and historian Edmund Burke (1729–97); Burke himself; Oliver Goldsmith (1728–74), novelist and playwright; Topham Beauclerk (1739–80), book collector and conversationalist; and Bennet Langton (1737–1801), essayist. Within a few weeks Samuel Dyer (1725–72), a translator who had been an Ivy Lane member, was admitted, as were others until the Club had thirty-five members at the time of Johnson's death.

[35]Editorially excised is the single section heading in the source text: "Personal Appearance & Characteristics."

[36]The King's Evil is scrofula, for which the touch of a monarch was believed to be a cure. Queen Anne (1665–1714) was the last sovereign who gave the touch.

[37]Hester Lynch Thrale (1741–1821) is the source of numerous anecdotes concerning Johnson. See n. 57. As Chesnutt explains much later in this speech, she was then the wife of Henry Thrale (c. 1729–81), a member of parliament and a brewer. On 25 July 1784, very much against Johnson's wishes, she married Gabriel Mario Piozzi (1740–1809), an Italian musician.

[38]Fruit trees "trained" by trimming to grow against walls produce wall fruit.

[39]James Burnett, Lord Monboddo (1714–99), Scottish judge.

[40]Boswell specifies both 1,575 and 1,675 pounds.

[41]Joseph Addison (1672–1719); William Congreve (1670–1729); Jonathan Swift (1667–1745).

[42]Pope sold his translations of the *Iliad* (1720) and the *Odyssey* (1725) by subscription at six guineas apiece.

[43]David Hume (1711–76) was a philosopher and historian whose initial volume of his *History of Great Britain* was published in 1754; by 1763 he had completed this work in eight volumes.

[44]Samuel Richardson (1689–1761), author of *Pamela* (1740–41) and *Clarissa Harlowe* (1747–48).

[45]Homer (c. tenth century B.C.); Dante Alighieri (1265–1321); Johann Wolfgang von Goethe (1749–1832).

[46]Henry Fielding (1707–54); Tobias George Smollett (1721–71).

[47]William Wordsworth (1770–1850); Percy Bysshe Shelley (1792–1822); John Keats (1795–1821); Alfred, Lord Tennyson (1809–92). Swaddling clothes were strips of cloth wrapped about a newborn's arms and legs to hold them still; see Matthew 2:7.

[48]Johnson quotes from the third of Pope's *Moral Essays* (1731–35).

[49]Richard Brinsley Sheridan (1751–1816).

[50]Thomas Percy (1729–1811), Dean of Carlisle, Bishop of Dromore, and author of a miscellany, *Reliques of Ancient English Poetry* (1765); Charles James Fox (1749–1846), statesman and well-known orator; Edward Gibbon (1737–94), historian; Adam Smith (1723–90), political economist; Charles Burney (1726–1814), musicologist.

[51]*The History of Rasselas.*

[52]Chesnutt quotes Boswell, who is quoting St. Paul in Romans 7:23.

[53]In 1 Samuel 13:14, Samuel reprimands Saul, telling him the Lord seeks another leader for his people (David), "a man after his own heart"; David does repent for his many sins but is not forgiven for the murder of Uriah (2 Samuel 11:14–27).

[54]Margaret ("Peg") Woffington (1714–60), acclaimed Irish actress and mistress to several members of London's artistic community; Frances (Fanny) Burney (1752–1840), daughter of Dr. Burney and later wife of General Gabriel Jean-Baptiste d'Arblay (1753–1818), whom she married in 1793, published her novel *Evelina* in 1778; Hannah More (1745–1833), playwright, religious polemicist, and pioneer in the education of the poor; Frances Reynolds (1729–1807); Lady Mary Pierrepoint Wortley Montagu (1689–1762), belletrist.

[55]Georgiana Spencer Cavendish, Duchess of Devonshire (1757–1806).

[56]Dated 2 July 1784.

[57]*Anecdotes of the Late Samuel Johnson* (1786).

[58]Boswell quotes Goldsmith's remark made during a gathering of Johnson's friends on 26 October 1769; according to Boswell, Goldsmith had appropriated these "witty words from one of Cibber's comedies." Colley Cibber (1671–1757) was an actor and the author of twenty comedies.

[59]At Johnson's house at No. 8 Bolt Court lived Anna Williams (1706–83), a poet first befriended by Johnson's wife. Present also were "several other destitute females," including: Elizabeth Swynfen Desmoulins (1716–86), the daughter of Johnson's godfather Samuel Swynfen (1679?–1736); Elizabeth's daughter, whom the Johnsons had taken in when her husband had unexpectedly died; and Poll Carmichael, described by Mrs. Thrale as "a Scotch wench." Another resident was Robert Levet (1705–82), an unlicensed and cantankerous surgeon.

[60]Francis (Frank) Barber (c. 1742–1801) was hired by Johnson after his wife's death on 17 March 1752. He became the chief beneficiary in Johnson's will. Mrs. Barber, *née* Elizabeth (Betsy) Ball (c. 1755–1816), was a Lincolnshire farm girl whom he married in 1773. Their first child, Elizabeth, also lived in Johnson's household. The Barbers moved soon after the child's birth, but returned following Anna Williams's death.

[61]Boswell devotes several pages to various comments by Johnson on the evils of slavery in the West Indies and the American colonies.

[62] Jean-Jacques Rousseau, *Confessions* (1782); Giovanni Giacomo Casanova (1725–98), *Memoirs* (1822); Benvenuto Cellini (1500–1571), *Autobiography* (1728).

[63] Henry Van Dyke (1852–1933), American poet and Presbyterian minister.

[64] Job 31:35. As did others of his generation, Chesnutt assumes that King Solomon wrote Job.

[65] While both Macaulay's and Carlyle's essays on Boswell's *Life* were available in several collections of writings by the time at which Chesnutt wrote this speech, the fact that he focuses only on these two reactions to Thomas Croker's edition of the *Life* suggests that he is quoting from *Macaulay's and Carlyle's Essays on Samuel Johnson* (1895). Macaulay's piece originally appeared as "Croker's Edition of Boswell's Life of Johnson," *Edinburgh Review*, 54 (September 1831), 1–38; Carlyle's was published as "Boswell's Life of Johnson," *Fraser's Magazine*, 5 (May 1832), 379–413.

[66] Johnson published "An Account of the Detection of the Imposture in Cock-Lane" in *Gentleman's Magazine*, February 1762, 81–82. James Macpherson (1736–96) produced two collections of poems, supposedly translated from the legendary third-century Gaelic poet Ossian, in 1762 and 1763, the authenticity of which Johnson and many others disputed.

Abraham Lincoln

Speech delivered c. 1912

It seemed to me not inappropriate, in this somewhat parlous and uncertain state of our rights as citizens, when I was asked to address you on a subject of my own choosing,—I say it seemed to me not unfitting to recall the memory and discuss the character of a man who believed in human equality, who during a long and active political career never failed to express his belief in words and deeds, and who had a rare and unequalled opportunity to prove it by an act of unparalleled wisdom & courage. Lincoln's life and work is an old story, thrashed out in great detail only a few years ago, on the occasion of the centenary of his birth; but his career is one which should be ever in mind of the people who were the immediate beneficiaries of his sublime action. In these days of peanut politicians posing as statesmen, the giants of the Civil War epoch loom up like mighty mountains, and we can, with a little effort look back upon them with something of the feeling that inspired those of us who are old enough to have lived through that mighty epoch.

His opportunities of education were of the most meager. The poorest black boy in any Northern and in most Southern States today has a better chance at learning than had the greatest man of the last century. He said himself that all the schooling he had in his life would not exceed a twelvemonth, and he seems to have reached the age of seventeen before he learned to write. We all know how he did his sums with a piece of charcoal on the wooden fire-shovel, by the flickering light of the pine-knot on the hearth, with the encouragement of a stepmother who was fond of him and wise enough to his superior aptitudes and abilities.[1] The greater part of his education was derived from unaided study. He was an omnivorous reader and borrowed every book in the neighborhood, and he ultimately acquired a command of terse and vigorous English which put him in the front rank of public speakers and made a few of his state papers models of forensic eloquence. What more moving, what nobler utterances can be found anywhere in literature than Lincoln's Gettysburg speech and his second inaugural.[2]

Lincoln's attitude toward slavery was never in doubt. You have all heard it maintained—you can hear anything in Washington—that Lincoln cared nothing for the Negro; that his opposition to slavery was because of its effect upon the white man, and that he abolished it merely as a war measure. This point of view is easily refuted by a reference to a few of his public utterances on the subject. While a member of the Illinois Legislature he wrote: "The institution of slavery is founded on both injustice and bad policy."[3] While a Whig member of the 30th Congress he prepared a bill for the abolishment of slavery in the District of Columbia, the Government to pay full compensation for slaves voluntarily manumitted by their owners, and prohibiting the bringing of slaves into the district or selling them out of it.

When in 1854 the repeal of the Missouri Compromise was to the fore Mr. Lincoln in opposing it: pp. 97, 106, 119, 136, and 139.[4]

Lincoln, in spite of his repugnance to slavery, was not an abolitionist. The abolitionists were fanatics, inspired fanatics, if you will, enthusiasts. But men of this type, to whom the world owes the destruction of so many abuses, are rarely distinguished by constructive statesmanship. They blaze the way, they light the fires, but when the victory is won the very qualities which made them invincible in the conflict—the zeal, the enthusiasm, the uncompromising adherence to platforms and principles, rather unfits them for the delicate adjustment of balances which is necessary after any great social change.

Like most of the free territory section of the Whig Party, Lincoln, when a young man deprecated the abolition movement as more likely to do harm than good. While maintaining the right and asserting the duty of the general government to prohibit slavery in the territories, he never questioned the constitutional right of the Slave States to maintain their peculiar institution. The Republican Party, of which he was the first president, was not founded directly on opposition to slavery, but to the extension of slavery. But as Lincoln's speeches and writings show, and as the pro-slavery South clearly saw, whoever was not with them was against them,[5] and slavery, successfully resisted anywhere, was sure, ultimately, to go down everywhere. Patiently, persistently, earnestly, throughout his whole career, but always in the open, and by fair and lawful methods, he fought the slave power; and as it grew narrower he grew broader, until finally the opportunity came to him to destroy the institution.

But though Lincoln hated slavery, combatted its extension at every point, and ultimately destroyed it, he never hated the South or Southerners. He was of their blood; he had been brought up in a State largely settled by them (quote Nicolay).[6] This feeling of pardon and sympathy played no small part, says Nicolay, in his dealings with pure problems of statesmanship. During all the time that he was sternly upholding the power of the government and crushing rebellion, he reasoned and pleaded with the anger of the South; he gave insurrection time to repent; he offered recompense to slave holders; he pardoned treason.

His great aim was to preserve the Union. To the abolitionists the Union with slavery was worse than disunion, the constitution was "an agreement with death, a covenant with hell."[7] But Lincoln had a wider vision. He was firmly convinced that the Union could not remain half slave and half free; and to maintain in its integrity a great nation throughout the whole of whose borders freedom should ultimately prevail was the larger service to liberty. There was no slavery in the North. For the North and the Republican Party to influence slavery at all, it was necessary to keep the South in the Union. So, while Mr. Lincoln was not an abolitionist, and would have saved the Union, with slavery, had the South met his temperate advances, even that would have been better for freedom than disunion, Lincoln promised himself and his God, as he said, that when the time came that he could lawfully abolish slavery he would do so.

⌐

SOURCE: Undated and untitled holograph text at the Fisk University Library. Chesnutt's reference to the observance of the centennial of Lincoln's birth "a few" years ago (1909) suggests a date of composition no earlier than 1912.

[1]Lincoln's father married his second wife, Sarah Bush Johnston, in 1819.

[2]These speeches were delivered on 19 November 1863 and 4 March 1865, respectively.

[3]Quoted in Chesnutt's source, John Nicolay's *A Short Life of Abraham Lincoln*.

[4]The source text reading—"(p. 97) (106) (119) (136) (139)"—has been emended. Chesnutt apparently read from these pages in Nicolay's *A Short Life*.

[5]Matthew 12:30.

[6]What Chesnutt quoted is not known; but the remainder of this paragraph is derived from chapter 28 of *A Short Life*.

[7]William Lloyd Garrison, resolution passed by the Massachusetts Anti-slavery Society in Boston, 27 January 1843; paraphrased is Isaiah 28:15.

The Status of the Negro in the United States

Speech delivered at the National Conference of Charities and
Corrections, Cleveland, O., 17 June 1912

The status of the Negro in the U.S., while a very concrete matter of fact, is also a
matter of opinion, depending somewhat upon the point of view. For instance, I
have seen, from the pen of a Southern writer of the vitriolic school, the statement that no white man, no matter how low or degraded, would exchange
places with any Negro, however honored or high placed. While on the other
hand, I have heard that genial optimist, my good friend Dr. Washington, say
more than once, in public, that if he could be reincarnated at the end of his present span of earthly existence, and could choose the state into which he should be
reborn, he would select that of an American Negro. He backs up his position by
the very ingenious argument that the joy of life consists in effort and in struggle,
and that to be an American Negro gives such a splendid opportunity for effort,
there is so much to overcome and so far to climb, that it brings joy to the heart of
those who love the strenuous life.[1] It would make a great deal of difference, I
imagine, which particular American Negro Dr. Washington should be born. If
he were himself again, it would not be so bad; if he were Bill Jones, who is
lynched on an unfounded charge, or Sam Johnson, who is sent to the chain-gang
for a year for shooting craps, or to the penitentiary for five years for stealing a
chicken, the case would be somewhat different. But these are mere flowers of
rhetoric, and do not prove anything. Whether every white man would echo the
Southerner's opinion I do not know; I am reasonably sure that not every Negro
would agree with Dr. Washington. Some of them are none too fond of the
strenuous life. But I think we can all agree that the Negro in the U.S. suffers under many disabilities, all of them due, directly or indirectly, to his difference of
race, either, as his enemies and detractors claim, because of deep-seated, fundamental and eternal differences which mark him off from other men, or because, as he and his friends claim and science seems to verify, of the prejudices
engendered by superficial and transitory differences which time will remove.

The word "Status" has two definitions, a broad, general one, meaning simply "state, condition," and a narrower, more technical one, which according to
the *Century Dictionary* is: "The relation fixed by law in which a person stands
towards others or the State. Different writers vary very much in the extent of
meaning implied, but in the best usage it includes liberty, citizenship, marriage,"
etc.

It is evident, therefore, that any detailed examination of the Negro's status
would involve an extended comparison with that of other elements of the
population. For example, comparing the Negro with the alien immigrant, it
might be said that the Negro's citizenship dates back only one generation, and

that his condition should be compared with that of the alien immigrant at the end of his first generation of citizenship. Another comparison, necessary to determine whether or not he has progressed, and the extent of his progress, is a comparison with his condition at former periods of his history. Several such comparisons might be made, but it is sufficient for the argument, to take his condition at the time of the abolition of slavery, and to assume what is not strictly true, but near enough so for our purpose, that at that time the Negro knew nothing of books, possessed nothing, and had no rights which white men were bound to respect. But for all practical purposes, it is sufficient, in considering the status of the Negro, to compare it with that of the white people as a whole, who constitute the other grand division of the population.

So, too, the status of the Negro could be considered under many heads—his legal, his political, his civil status, so far as these could be distinguished; his economic status, his status from the standpoint of social efficiency, his moral status, his religious status, his educational status, his social status. But these elements so commingle and overlap, that in the few minutes at my disposal I shall consider them all more or less together.

By the 13th, 14th and 15th amendments to the Constitution, the Negro became entitled to full American citizenship, with all the rights therein implied. All sophistry aside, this is the plain meaning of the war amendments. By legal, or illegal enactments in many States, with the expressed or silent acquiescence of the Supreme Court, these rights have been more or less restricted. The elemental right to select one's own employer and receive the reward of one's labor, has been interfered with by unjust contract labor laws, by peonage, by oppressive vagrancy laws, and similar expedients to restore the essential elements of slavery. The right to own and use one's property has been interfered with, by violence in many cases where a man would move into a neighborhood where his presence was not desired, and several Southern cities have undertaken to designate in what portions of their communities Negroes could reside. The right of marriage, one of the most valuable of the citizen's status, has been most flagrantly violated. In certain States the intermarriage of white persons and colored persons of as little, in Louisiana, as 1/32 of Negro blood, is made in legal terms "an infamous crime" for both parties, and punished as severely as incest and other gross offenses against morality. The right of free movement on equal terms with others, over railroad and steamboat lines, which have their existence by virtue of their public character, and are to that extent creatures and instruments of the State, has been curtailed by discriminating and offensive laws. The right of trial by jury has been interfered with by lawless mobs. The right to serve on jury, which has been firmly maintained by the Supreme Court, is evaded to a large extent. The right to bear arms is denied in many States; in no Southern State, if I am correctly informed, is there any colored militia. While the fundamental right of citizenship, upon which all other rights necessarily rest, the suffrage, the right to vote, has been and is largely denied by means of clever and unscrupulous or, to say the best of them, unjust expedients upon the legality of which it has so far proved impossible to get the Supreme Court to pass—for which, from one point of view we may be devoutly thankful, for as long as the question is not settled wrongly, there is a chance that it may be settled rightly.

Most of these discriminating laws, these denials of Constitutional rights, are found in the Southern States. In the Northern States today there is practically little or no discriminating legislation on the statute books. Such as there was has been, since the Civil War, gradually removed—the last vestige remaining in the Ohio law, the antebellum provision of the Constitution restricting the suffrage to white men, long since a dead letter, has been submitted, under the report of the Constitutional Convention, for elimination. In Ohio, which is a type in a way of all the other Northern States, and which I will use for that purpose, there is no legal discrimination against the Negro, and there is a civil rights law forbidding such discrimination, and actions are often brought under it and carried to a successful termination. And the Negro's rights are generally respected in Ohio, at least as far as can be reasonably expected in the case of a relatively small part of the population who labor under disabilities peculiar to their condition. No Negro in Ohio is denied the right to vote, and they exercise the right. Any Negro can hold office who can secure the necessary number of votes, and many do hold office. The county of Cuyahoga is always represented in the State Legislature, when the Republican party is in power in the county, by a colored member, and one legislature had two from this county; and even on one Democratic ticket within my memory a colored man was nominated for the legislature. A colored man served as a member of the city council in the last administration, and for many years there was a colored justice of the peace in this county. Colored men are represented on the police force, and there are several colored men serving on the committee appointed by Mayor Baker to represent the city of Cleveland in this conference.[2] Numerous colored men hold appointive offices in the state, of more or less value and importance. There is a colored battalion of the National Guard in the State of Ohio, as there is a regiment in Illinois.

In the State of Ohio public education is open to colored children on equal terms with whites. There are no separate schools, and in the schools colored children have equal rights and opportunities. In our schools of Cleveland colored teachers are employed. In the matter of scholarship colored pupils often distinguish themselves. It is only a few years ago that a little colored girl, at the National Educational Association meeting here, took the first prize in the spelling contest, to the great chagrin of some Southern contestants, and the same little girl was an honor speaker at the commencement of her high school last month. At the commencement exercises of West High School a colored girl was the valedictorian speaker; and the same was true of a colored youth last year at East High School. Colored girls and boys are admitted into high school societies. Such talents as they possess are given full opportunity for development, and they distinguish themselves in school life, music and athletics. This democracy of the Cleveland schools is justly regarded by those who control them and think about it as the crowning glory of this particular civil institution. The only educational institutions in the city which discriminate against people of color, so far as I know, are the Young Men's and Young Women's Christian Associations, where, I understand, a person having more than a suspicion of color, receives a very cold welcome, if any at all.

In the State of Ohio, many colored men are engaged in the successful practice of the learned professions. Preachers aside, there are in the city of Cleveland, for instance, some half dozen lawyers who earn a respectable living. Few of them have any wealthy clients; few of their own people have any important business which requires legal advice and direction, and they get their practice from the general public, without much regard to race or color. So of physicians, there are four or five in the community who live by their practice. One of them served, a year or two ago, as a school physician on the staff of the school medical examiner.[3] A number of colored men are employed in offices and in the courts as clerks and stenographers. Others are employed in factories and workshops, and some of them are foremen. And I think I can say that in the city of Cleveland a man who measured up to the accepted standards among white people for social recognition, would not be denied, at least not because of a slight infusion of Negro blood, the courtesies and amenities exchanged among ladies and gentlemen in clubs and in private life.

I have not meant to say at all, in what has gone before, that there is no race prejudice in Ohio or in Cleveland, or in the Northern States, but that the race problem is settled so far as statute law can settle it. The general principle of equality of citizenship is clearly recognized and fortified by law. What remains must be done in large part by the Negro himself, and in large part by friendly cooperation of the white people.

The status of the Negro, wherever the democratic principle has been cultivated, has shown marked improvement. Even in the South, where that principle is flouted, the Negro's material progress has been marked. The state and national census reports show a large amount of property in their possession and ownership. They have organized great churches and benefit organizations. They have developed great teachers and leaders, several of whom have achieved world-wide renown. The truth of the matter is that human nature is much the same the world over, and that when the laws are bad the people are better than the laws. The Negroes have many white friends in the South; their conception of friendship is limited, but so far as it goes it tends to the advantage and advancement of the Negro. So, on the other hand, it is possible for the laws to be better than the people. When men get together to enact laws, they are governed by principles; when they go home to live under them, they are controlled by custom, by prejudice, by self-interest, things which do not always conform to the principles in accordance with which the laws were enacted. So the South, in spite of its efforts, has not kept the Negro entirely down, nor has the North, in spite of its democracy, lifted him entirely up.

While, as I have said, colored men vote in the North, and their vote is sought and respected, yet even in the South, while their voice is negligible and they are not represented in Congress or the State legislatures, they are not entirely without political power. They still retain representation in the National Nominating Convention of their party; and we have the anomaly of people helping to select a nominee for whom they cannot cast a single electoral vote.[4] This power in the nominating convention is an important one.[5] It is probably this remnant of political power which secures to the colored race a certain number of federal appointments in the South. This, together with the Northern colored vote and that of the border States, has secured substantial recognition elsewhere at the hands of the Federal Government. Colored men hold important offices in the Federal service. There are several foreign ministers, to such countries as Hayti and Liberia, and consuls and *chargés d'affaires* in Central and South American countries. There is a consul at Tamatave, Madagascar, and another at St.-Etienne in France. There is an important federal representative at Honolulu, Hawaii, an Ohio man, by the way. There are colored officers in the U.S.A., most of them Ohio men, by the way, some of whom have risen to the rank of major. There are several colored regiments in the regular army, some of which have won distinction. There are colored assistants to U.S. District Attorneys in several cities, Boston and Washington, for instance, an assistant attorney general, and a colored collector of internal revenue in the great city of New York, an Ohio man, by the way. The Register of the Treasury and the Fourth Auditor of the Navy, and one of the judges of the Washington City Municipal Court are men of color, while there are many clerks and other employees of the same race in the various government departments. In the postal service, especially where the civil service prevails, they are largely represented.

Aside from these things, in the field of intellectual endeavor the race has made a commendable showing. It has produced poets, novelists and painters of distinction. Newspapers published by colored men number several hundred, and some of them compare very favorably with newspapers edited by white men. In music and dramatics, especially of the lighter kinds, they are well represented—I have n't time to specify.

Taking it all in all, the status of the Negro in the U.S., both actual and relative, is improving, and conditions, on the whole, are hopeful and encouraging. There are still many abuses, many wrongs, many iniquities, and these must be corrected.[6] The colored people will rise, must rise, by means of the same agencies that have uplifted other submerged classes. First and fundamentally by recognition of political rights. Then by education, to fit them to exercise those rights wisely, and to accumulate the wealth which is, however regrettably, the test of success and the source of power in this great industrial republic. Then the Negro needs a better chance in the field of labor, the opportunity for more diversified employment, a chance to rise in the pursuits he follows. The Negro needs the common man's chance. Most Negroes are common people—some of them are *very* common—and they need the common man's chance in life. The exceptional individual can take care of himself. Any man can become a poet, or an author, or an artist, if he have the divine fire—the field of high endeavor is relatively open. But the Pullman porter cannot advance in the railroad service so long as an iron wall shuts him off from anything except his menial occupation; nor can a colored man work his way up through fireman to locomotive engineer, so long as the Brotherhood of Locomotive Engineers, in the hall of whose beautiful building we now sit, and which practically controls the locomotive engineering service of the Northern and Western railroads—so long as this body and its affiliated organizations of trainmen, restrict their membership, by their constitutions, to white men only.

It is axiomatic that all social changes are slow, and that old prejudices and customs die hard. As I have said, it is easier to make a good law than to live up to it. France cut off the heads of most of its aristocrats in the Revolution, and abolished titles of nobility; and yet today, a French title, though only used by courtesy, is an exceedingly valuable social and financial asset—foolish Americans buy them at extravagant prices. The ultimate solution of the race problem in the U.S. will be no exception to this rule. The first step toward it almost disrupted and ruined the Nation, and the succeeding steps have been attended with much *Sturm und Drang*—stress and difficulty. Its ultimate success will be due to the working out of the great principles in which this great Conference finds its motive and its inspiration; the great principle which was emphasized by Judge Mack in his address at the opening meeting;[7] the great principle which has underlaid the advance of religion and civilization; the great principle upon which the future progress and happiness of mankind must depend—the great democratic ideal: to all men equal opportunity for development and usefulness and happiness, regardless of race or color or anything else but our common humanity.

⌇

SOURCE: Undated typed text at the Fisk University Library. This speech was given before the National Conference of Charities and Corrections in Cleveland's Engineers Building on the afternoon of 17 June 1912.

[1]Theodore Roosevelt first used the signature term "strenuous life" in a speech before Chicago's Hamilton Club on 10 April 1899: "I wish to preach, not the doctrine of ignoble ease, but the doctrine of the strenuous life."

[2]Newton Diehl Baker (1871–1937), the son of an antiracist Confederate physician and progressive Democrat, served as city solicitor from 1902 to 1912—during which time Tom Loftin Johnson, a nationally visible municipal reformer was mayor (1901–9). Baker, an ardent admirer of Johnson, was Cleveland's mayor in 1912–16.

[3]Chesnutt originally specified Dr. Harris G. Sherman as the examiner.

[4]Immediately following this sentence, Chesnutt originally wrote, "It has been suggested that this situation be remedied by making the representation in the convention

dependent upon the vote cast in any State or district. A juster remedy would be to enforce the constitution and permit the colored men to vote for the nominee."

[5]Referring to the Republican convention, Chesnutt originally added here: "According to the newspapers this morning the result of the contest at Chicago will depend upon the colored delegates. Let us hope that they will act wisely, and prove worthy of their responsibility."

[6]Chesnutt here canceled "It is in this field that the National Society for the Advancement of Colored People finds its greatest opportunity of usefulness. General principles always work better when they are backed up by private initiative and effort."

[7]Judge Julian W. Mack (1866–1943) of the U.S. Circuit Court of Appeals for the Seventh Circuit (1912–20) gave the opening address of the conference, sounding the note of equality for all. When he once more spoke following Chesnutt's speech, however, he proved to have been misestimated by Chesnutt. He qualified his egalitarianism by expressing support for the whites-only policy of the Y.M.C.A. and Y.W.C.A.—apparently not aware that this was a focus of black Cleveland social reformers. See the vitriolic reaction of editor Harry C. Smith (1863–1941) in "Judge Mack's Blunder," *Cleveland Gazette*, 22 June 1912, 2.

Address to the Medina Coterie

Speech to to the Medina Coterie, Medina, O., 25 March 1913

I wish to assure you, first, that I esteem it a privilege to appear before your Coterie and to say a few words in connection with your season's program, "A Year in Dixie" and to read one of my own stories which drew its own motive from conditions in that part of our country.[1] It is always a pleasure to talk to intelligent people, though in this instance the pleasure is complicated by the fact that you have apparently so covered the ground that it will be difficult for me to find anything new to say. You have discussed the geography and topography of the South, the origins of its population, its political and social history, the Civil War, agriculture, Booker Washington and Tuskegee, the South's great men, Southern literature, Southern music, and at your last meeting what is and has been the most vital and important Southern question during the course of our national history—the race problem.

Indeed, as you have doubtless discovered, the history of the South is for the most part the history of the race problem. A National institution in its scope, as was slavery, it is the peculiar institution of the South, as slavery was. The politics of the South have dealt almost entirely with it. Much of their best and most of their worst literature is founded upon it. The only Southern music, indeed the only distinctively American music, is Negro music. The South has adapted its religion to the race problem, and has created, to meet what they deem its re-

quirements, a hybrid sort of democracy, which, under the forms of free government conducts an oligarchy, which governs with small regard for the rights of
those who differ in complexion from the majority.

The Race Problem is older than the nation. When the first black savage,
shackled and trembling, was driven from the hold of the slaveship to the shore
of old Virginia, he cast upon her soil a shadow blacker than his skin, a shadow
which is not yet lifted, and at that very moment the Race Problem was born.
There were not wanting even at that day God-fearing men, who read their Bi-
bles and who had in mind the prohibition of the Mosaic Law "And he that
stealeth a man and selleth him, he shall surely be put to death,"[2] and the passage
in St. Paul's Epistle to Timothy in which men stealers are classed with "the lawless and disobedient, the ungodly and sinners, the unholy and profane, the murderers of fathers and the murderers of mothers, man slayers, liars, and perjured
persons."[3] And the first question therefore raised in the Race Problem was
whether or not Negroes were men, for, if not, then obviously these inhibitions
did not apply. The question was still unsettled when the argument was put forward that if they were men, they must have souls, and it would be serving God
to bring them to a Christian Country in order that they might be converted and
their souls saved, while their bodies incidentally worked the cotton and tobacco
of the planters. It is a quality of the English Race, as it was of the ancient Roman
people, that it values its own moral approval. The Spaniard in his career of conquest frankly fought for gold, the Frenchman for glory, the Mohamedan for the
joys of Paradise; but the English Race, when it wishes to commit an unjust action, always seeks a sop for its conscience. It steals Nations, and enslaves races,
always for their own good. Therefore they imported Negroes, or their preachers
told them they did, for the sake of the Negroes' souls—I doubt if they fooled
anybody, even themselves, but argument served.

Slavery was at first an economic status. If the slave became free, as slaves
sometimes did, in early Colonial times, freedom brought with it equal civil
rights. Freedmen could vote, could sit on juries, could bear arms, enjoy freedom
of contract, even including marriage without regard to race. But the question of
Race soon became dominant, and the rights of free colored people steadily declined until, in the Dred Scott decision, it was declared that they had no rights
which white men were bound to respect.

Another phase of the problem was the slave trade. Responding to the demands of the civilized world, led by England, the importation of slaves into the
United States was forbidden after the year 1808, although they were smuggled
in almost up to the time of the Civil War. The domestic traffic, however, still
flourished. Southern statesmanship was not always blind to the evils of slavery.
The question was a live one in the Constitutional Convention, and there was
once a movement in Virginia, somewhere in the 30s, looking toward the gradual
abolition of slavery. But the cotton gin came and furnished a powerful economic motive for the continuation of the system. Then the abolitionists entered

the arena, and by their vigorous propaganda united the forces behind slavery for its protection and extension. The slaveholders seemed to have realized, as did Lincoln, that this country could not continue to exist half slave and half free, and therefore they determined that it should be all slave. The growth of the free soil sentiment in the North was met with a determined effort to spread the institution all over the land,[4] and to extend the Nation's borders Southward to make more room for slaves. Texas was annexed as slave territory.[5] We had the fugitive slave law, the Missouri Compromise,[6] the Kansas-Nebraska imbroglio,[7] John Brown's raid,[8] the Republican party, Abraham Lincoln, the Civil War, the Emancipation Proclamation, the Freedmen's Bureau, the Constitutional amendments, Reconstruction, the Ku Klux Klan, the Restoration of the Bourbon South, the Disfranchisement of the Negro, and we are now in the midst of to-day and face to face with tomorrow. What is the present aspect of the Race Problem?

The Race Problem is primarily concerned with the status of the Negro in the United States. Of course the welfare of the white people is inextricably bound up with that of the Negro, but it is the Status of the Negro which makes the problem. The Status of the Negro in the United States, while a very concrete matter of fact, is also a matter of opinion, depending upon the point of view. For instance, I have seen, from the pen of a southern writer of the Vitriolic School, the statement that no white man, no matter how low or degraded, would exchange places with any Negro however honored or high placed. On the other hand, I have heard that genial optimist, my good friend Dr. Booker T. Washington say more than once, in public, that if he could be reincarnated at the end of the present span of his earthly existence, and could choose the state into which he should be reborn, he would select that of an American Negro. He backs up his position by the very ingenious argument that the joy of life consists in effort and in struggle, and that to be an American Negro gives such a splendid opportunity for effort! There is so much to overcome, and so far to climb that it brings joy to the heart of those who love the strenuous life. Just think how Theodore Roosevelt would have enjoyed being an American Negro! It would make a great deal of difference I imagine which particular American Negro Dr. Washington should be born. If he were himself again it would not be so bad. If he were Bill Jones, who is lynched on an unfounded charge, or Sam Johnson who is sent to the chain gang for a year for shooting craps, or to the penitentiary for five years for stealing a chicken, and farmed out to a convict contractor, the case would be somewhat different. Whether every white man would echo the Southerner's opinion I do not know. I am reasonably sure that not every Negro would agree with Dr. Washington.

But these are mere flowers of rhetoric. What are the concrete facts? There are in the United States about ten million persons of more or less remote African descent. They were not, as is often said, brought to this country against their will. They were not consulted it is true, but they came here in accordance with the laws of nature; whatever may have been the case with their ancestors, those of the present day were all born here, and if there is any place in the world where they have a right to live and to seek happiness, it is in the land of their nativity. The South owes them a great deal. They have done, through the generations, most of the labor of the South. They have created most of the wealth of the South—at one time they *constituted* most of the wealth of the South, and the South has never forgotten or forgiven the loss of that wealth. They are, in mass, except a relatively inconsiderable number of the aborigines and their descendants, the most American element of our population. A very large percentage of the white people of the country were born in other lands, and have either renounced or still owe allegiance to other sovereignties. The Negro is American born, American bred and has no other country.

Now, what are the Constitutional rights of these people? In theory and in form this is a representative government, founded upon the consent of the governed, as expressed by the ballot. By the Constitution as amended Negroes are citizens, and no state is permitted to deny or abridge the right to vote because of race or color or previous condition of servitude. As a matter of fact, the Negro in the South by force, by chicanery and by open contempt of the Constitution, has been robbed of the right to vote in any effective numbers, with the result that one-third of the Southern population—in three states a majority[9]—are without a single representative in a Congress of over five hundred members. They are without a representative in any Southern legislature, where the laws which control their daily lives, their domestic relations, their public schools and the administration of justice are enacted. They have no representation in any state government where these laws are administered, no representation in any court where their rights are passed upon—not only no direct representation by men of their own blood, but no representation by white men who owe their political existence to the colored vote. The only exception is that in some cases colored men do serve on juries. The Supreme Court has interpreted the 15th Amendment as declaratory of the Negro's right of suffrage, but has so far carefully dodged any effort to enforce that right as against hostile state legislation.

The War Amendments were intended to rescue the colored race not only from slavery, but from class tyranny and place them upon a footing of equal citizenship. In the language of Justice Miller in the slaughter house cases (16 Wall., p. 71),[10]

> No one can fail to be impressed with the one pervading purpose found in them all, lying as the foundation of each, and without which none of them would have been suggested; we mean the freedom of the slave race, the security and firm establishment of that freedom and the protection of the newly made freeman and citizen from the oppressions of those who had formerly exercised unlimited dominion over him.

But lawyers, and those who have been unfortunate enough to require their services, know that laws do not mean what they say, but what Courts say they mean. The pendulum had swung too far; mere words were not sufficient to overcome age-long prejudices and traditions. And when Congress, acting under the authority of the thirteenth Amendment, passed a civil rights law,[11] the Supreme Court, doubtless reflecting the opinion of the people, limited the act to the mere scope of the 13th Amendment, as not attempting to adjust what may be called the social rights of men and races in the community, but merely those fundamental rights which distinguish citizenship from slavery.[12] And later, when the States, responding to this invitation, passed laws discriminating against colored citizens, and one of these came before the Supreme Court, that august tribunal held, in a case from Louisiana involving the provision of separate R. R. cars for white and colored passengers, that statutes implying a legal distinction between the white and colored races, have no tendency to destroy their legal equality; and again: "If one race be inferior to the other socially, the Constitution of the United States cannot put them on the same plane," the Supreme Court thus adopting the Southern fallacy that riding in a railroad car or eating in an inn is a "social" function.[13]

Justice Harlan of Kentucky, a Lincoln appointee, and one of the few Southerners who have followed in Lincoln's footsteps, in an opinion vigorously dissenting from and protesting against this sophistry of the majority of the court,[14] said,

> In respect of civil rights, common to all citizens, the constitution of the United States does not, I think, permit any public authority to know the race of those entitled to be protected in the enjoyment of such rights. Every true man has pride of race, and under appropriate circumstances when the rights of others, his equal before the law, are not to be affected, it is his privilege to express such pride and to take such action based upon it as to him seems proper. But I deny that any legislative body or judicial tribunal may have regard to the race of citizens when the civil rights of those citizens are involved. Indeed, such legislation as that here in question is inconsistent not only with that equality of rights which pertains to citizenship, national and state, but with the personal liberty enjoyed by every one within the United States.

The Justice then reviews the purport and effect of the three amendments abolishing slavery and protecting all civil rights that pertain to freedom and citizenship, and proceeds:

> It was said in argument that the statute of Louisiana, does not discriminate against either race, but prescribes a rule applicable alike to white and colored citizens. But this argument does not meet the difficulty. Every one knows that the statute in question had its origin in the purpose not so much to exclude white persons from railroad cars occupied by blacks as to exclude colored people from coaches occupied by or assigned to white persons. Railroad corporations of Louisiana did not make discrimination among whites in the matter of accommodation for travelers. The thing to accomplish was, under the guise of giving equal accommodation for whites and blacks, to compel the latter to keep to themselves while traveling in railroad passenger coaches. No one would be so wanting in candor as to assert the contrary. The fundamental objection, therefore, to the statute is that it interferes

with the personal freedom of citizens. "Personal Liberty," it has been well said, "consists in the power of locomotion, of changing situation, of removing one's person to whatsoever places one's own inclination may direct, without imprisonment or restraint, unless by due course of law." (1 Bl. Com. 134.) If a white man and a black man choose to occupy the same conveyance on a public highway, it is their right to do so, and no government, proceeding alone on grounds of race, can prevent it without infringing the personal liberty of each. . . .

If a state can prescribe, as a rule of civil conduct, that whites and blacks shall not travel as passengers in the same railroad coach, why may it not so regulate the use of the streets of its cities and towns as to compel white citizens to keep on one side of a street and black citizens to keep on the other? Why may it not, upon like grounds, punish whites and blacks who ride together in street cars or in open vehicles on a public road or street? Why may it not require sheriffs to assign whites to one side of a court room and blacks to the other? And why may it not also prohibit the commingling of the two races in the galleries of legislative halls or in public assemblages convened for the consideration of the political questions of the day?

(Further, is this statute of Louisiana consistent with the personal liberty of citizens of the United States, or of Protestants and Roman Catholics?)

If laws of like character should be enacted in the several states of the Union, the effect would be in the highest degree mischievous. Slavery, as an institution tolerated by law, would, it is true, have disappeared from our country, but there would remain a power in the states, by sinister legislation, to interfere with the full enjoyment of the blessings of freedom; to regulate civil rights, common to all citizens, upon the basis of race; and to place in a condition of legal inferiority a large body of American Citizens, now constituting a part of the political community called by the people of the United States, for whom and by whom, through representatives, our government is administered. Such a system is inconsistent with the guarantee given by the constitution to each state of a republican form of government and may be stricken down by Congressional action, or by the courts in the discharge of their solemn duty to maintain the law of the land, anything in the constitution or laws of any state to the contrary notwithstanding.

And exactly that condition prevails at the present moment in the Southern States. Following the decision in that case, most of the Southern States proceeded to enact laws of a similar character, (specify) and a large body of citizens are thereby placed in a position of legal inferiority.

Another place where the lack of representation bears oppressively upon the Negro is in the matter of public education. The South adopted, under Reconstruction—one of the many good things to be credited to that much maligned epoch—the free public school system, and has nominally kept it up. But the South is relatively poor, and finds public education burdensome. It could not begin to compete with the rich North in this field of social activity. The average cost per capita of enrollment in the Cleveland schools last year was upwards of $55.00. It seems to a white Southerner, in view of this condition, that money spent on Negro schools is robbery of the whites, or at best a waste of money. You have all read in the newspapers, the blatant utterances of the Bleases and Tillmans of the South upon the subject.[15] The Negro, because of his lack of representation, has no voice in the distribution of the school funds, and his schools are universally neglected, and in some places there are none at all. In certain counties of some Southern states such figures as these are common: amount spent per capita on white peopled enrolled, $10.00, $12.00, $13.00, $15.00; per capita on colored enrollment $1.50, $1.33, 99 cents. The following figures are given in the Lincoln Number of the *Survey*, a conservative magazine devoted to social betterment, with which you are all doubtless familiar:[16] In Ga. the motto of which state, so given in your program, is "Wisdom, *Justice*, Moderation," colored people constitute 46 percent of the population, and receive 17.7% of the school funds; in N.C. (my own state) col. pop. 33.3%; school fund 13.6; Va. col. pop. 35.7, school funds 14.7%.

Colored teachers are paid in many places a maximum salary of $20.00 a month.[17] Colored high schools, except in the larger cities, and in some of those, are a joke. In New Orleans the colored schools were abolished above the fifth grade, although I believe the limit has since been raised by one grade. Where state aid is furnished to higher schools, the tendency has been to cut out book learning with its broadening and refining results, and to substitute a smattering of shoe-making in a world where all the shoes are made by machinery, of wagon-making where all the wagons are made by machinery, of brickmaking, where the same condition prevails. I believe in vocational training, but it should be a matter for the individual, not a race matter, an expedient to continue the colored race as merely hewers of wood and drawers of water. Most of them are condemned by circumstances to hard labor for life, and since they must work it is well that they be taught to do good work; but those who are bright enough to boss the job should have the opportunity to learn how.

Another crying evil in connection with the race problem lies in the penal systems of the South. Southern states are still semi-barbarous in their penal laws. They have capital offenses which in the Northern states are punished by short terms of imprisonment. I have seen a man sent to the workhouse for six months in Cleveland for an offense for which he certainly would have been hanged in the South, if he had not been burned alive. And where the laws admit of leniency, the Negro, at the hands of a prejudiced tribunal stands a very small chance of securing justice. I have known a colored man to be sentenced to the penitentiary for five years for drinking a pint of milk in a dairy of which he had charge. I have seen a man hanged for burglary. When the courts are so callous that a ten-year-old white lad can be sentenced to imprisonment until he comes of age for stealing a bottle of ginger-pop, as happened in Georgia the other day, and the Supreme Court lets the sentence stand, it is not difficult to imagine a Negro's chances in a Georgia court.[18]

The convict lease system, which is only slavery in a worse form, without the slave owner's incentive to at least keep his beasts of burden alive, has shortened the lives and ruined the souls of thousands of Negroes, for they are its chief victims. The fee system in the administration of criminal law, has been another instrument of oppression. I read only the other day an extract from a Southern newspaper, to the effect that it is absolutely dangerous for a Negro in certain parts of Texas to be known to have in his possession as much as fifty dollars. He was almost sure to be arrested on a trumped up charge, and by the time the constable's fees, the justice's fees and the fine were paid, the poor Negro was lucky to escape with his personal liberty.

But these miscarriages of justice, serious as they are, fade into insignificance compared with that peculiar product of American civilization, that fragrant flower of democracy, the habit of lynching and burning human beings,—by all means the most abhorrent growth of the race problem. It took its rise in the South, from which it was extended to the North, and two of the most atrocious lynchings in recent years have occurred in Ohio and Pa. respectively.[19] In no other country in the world, civilized or frankly barbarous, do such things occur. No crime which the miserable victim could commit could equal in horror the punishment. Since 1885, during which period careful statistics have been kept, 3539 people have been lynched in the U.S., many of them burned alive with tortures unspeakable. The largest number in any one year was 235 in 1902, the smallest 60 in 1906. The figure rose to 100 in 1908, was 87 in 1909, 74 in 1910, 71 in 1911, 65 in 1912.[20] Of 53 of those in 1912, Ga., whose motto is "Wisdom, Justice, Moderation"—I love that motto!—was responsible for 11, more than 1/5th. Of these 53, 50 were Negroes, three were Negro women. Southern chivalry is no respecter[21] of the sex of colored people; race has swallowed up that once proud boast of the cavalier. Of 53 lynchings in 1912 the causes assigned were: Murder 26, Rape 10, Murderous assault 2, Complicity in Murder 3, Arson 3, Insults to white women 3, Attempted rape 2, Assault and robbery 1, Race Prejudice 1—it was really the cause of them all—no cause assigned, 1. This one was probably lynched in fun. This disposes of the widespread and industriously promulgated falsehood that these extra judicial punishments—these mob murders—are only inflicted upon offenders against womanhood. Less than 1/6 of the lynchings in 1912 were even attributed to this cause.

Now, I imagine that you ladies of the Medina Coterie, in the Western Reserve, after your year's study of Dixie, appreciate the gravity of this problem, and would like to see it settled. Doubtless you are entirely willing, at least I hope you are, that colored people should have equal rights and opportunities, perhaps as an inherited attitude of mind on your part, perhaps as a matter of simple justice, of kindly feeling, of Christian brotherhood, or of sober and careful reasoning—a matter of principle. Now, all of these things are important factors in any social movement, but in the order of their importance I think the last comes first. You must get your principles straight; any reform, to be thorough and lasting, must be founded on principle. Sentiment, while a valuable weapon to bring about reform, and absolutely essential to its preservation, is not a safe basis to rest it upon—and in this particular case, since there is very little sentiment demanding it, it must depend mainly upon principles.

You must get your democratic ideal correct, which demands that you put humanity above race. The South has made a fetish of race, it has exalted it so high that it has overshadowed humanity. A man is entitled to equality of rights and opportunities because he is a man, first. Then you must revise your ideal of citizenship. Citizenship implies equality of rights. There was a time when it was a proud thing to be a citizen of a great nation. In the United States, for a large portion of the population, it means very little, or at least much less than it ought to mean. There are colored men who will not sing "America," looking upon it as as much a lie as Garrison declared the Constitution of the United States to be.

And then you must revise your definition of equality. The South confuses it in all possible ways. There is but one kind of equality. Political equality, civil equality, social equality are all mere forms of words. If there is such a thing as social equality to be considered apart from civil equality, the only proper place for its consideration is in a man's home or his club. Any rights or privileges which grow out of the general social organism, the State, should be free to all men.

When you have got your definitions correct, assuming that you are still of a mind to settle this great problem, the next step is their application. Every citizen, should have a vote, on the same terms as every other citizen, and those terms should be so fixed as not to discriminate against any class of citizens. This means that all the grandfather clauses and other qualifications devised to elimi-nate the colored vote, must be wiped out. No class of the population should be left at the mercy of another, and no qualifications of the franchise, however fair on their face, which leave half the population unrepresented in the legislature, can be fair or consistent with the democratic ideal.

Next, all discriminating laws must be wiped out. People should be allowed to travel on the same terms and in the same places as other people. If a citizen is too good to ride in a public conveyance with another he should buy an automo-bile or charter a special car. If a gentleman does not wish to stop at a hotel or eat in a restaurant with another citizen who meets the requirements of good man-ners and cleanliness and solvency, he should have his meals served in his room or rent a private house. There is always the street in which he can eat a sand-wich. If a man does not wish to live on a street with other citizens, then he should move, and if he cannot find a street which meets his wishes, there are other countries in the world to which he could emigrate. He should not ask the state to pander to his prejudices. Separate schools should be abolished. If a man's children are too good to go to school with the children of other citizens, he should send them to a private school. Or, in the South if separate schools are maintained, the school fund should be fairly and equitably divided, and the same standard of efficiency maintained.

We live in a highly organized society. There is scarcely any possible line of cleavage along which men are not organized. The trades are all organized into unions, the professions into societies, society into clubs. Equality of right and opportunity and the ordinary sense of fair play which the English race once used to boast of, demand that these organizations should be open to all qualified persons, and that race should not be a qualification. Many of the unions do not admit colored members; the most lauded of them all, held up as the ideal labor organization, the Brotherhood of Locomotive Engineers, with headquarters in Cleveland, limits its membership in terms to white men, and its affiliated organizations, the brotherhoods of locomotive firemen and trainmen, have the same limitation, and in their attempt to monopolize all labor on railroads, seek by strikes and legislation to keep colored men out of those pursuits, thus limiting their opportunity to earn a living and to contribute to the social welfare.[22]

All laws limiting the right of contract by reason of race should be abolished. The fundamental social contract, which keeps the race alive, is that of marriage. In every Northern state there is freedom of contract in this important human relation. In every Southern state intermarriage between the races is made an infamous crime, punished as is incest or other abominable offenses against good morals. Since the triumph of the Democratic party in the recent election,[23] a number of anti-marriage bills have been introduced in Northern legislatures, one in Ohio, which sought to forbid marriage between white persons and Negroes or Chinamen to the third generation inclusive, making such marriages a felony punishable with fine and imprisonment in the penitentiary. Defeated Nebraska.[24] To say nothing of the matter of right involved, such laws are morally pernicious. They put a direct premium on immorality. They deprive the victim of seduction of the only remedy which can partially reinstate her. It says to the seducer that he shall not obey the voice of conscience and seek to atone, as far as may be, for the wrong which he has done. It says to the innocent fruit of such a union, "You must rest all your life under the stigma of illegitimacy." It says to the Orientals whom we permit by thousands to enter our borders and who are not encouraged to bring their women with them, that they shall not enjoy female companionship except under the ban of the law, thus encouraging immorality. And even to those who cherish the fetish of race and who believe that, the whites being in the majority, have a right to make the laws what they please, there need be no occasion for alarm. Such unions are rare; most people prefer to mate with their own kind. The colored population of Ohio is about 2.3 per cent. of the entire number, and if every colored person were pure black and every one married a white person, the resultant admixture, when thoroughly assimilated, would contain little more than one-fiftieth of black blood, which after a few generations, could not be detected with a microscope, and there would be no more race problem as a constant temptation to injustice.

Now, when these things have been done, when correct principles have been laid down, the plain language of the Constitution enforced, discriminating laws abolished and the field of economic opportunity opened up to persons of color, all other race questions will take care of themselves. White people will no longer shrink sensitively from social contact from others who are their equals. Do not misunderstand this matter of equality. It does not alter any properly founded social standards. It does not demand that you invite your cook to your table or your coachman to your parlor. It would not demand that a Negro or anybody else be accorded any consideration to which he would not be entitled if he were white. And by the same token it means that he should not be denied any courtesy because he is not white. If you have a friend of different complexion whom you would like to invite to dine at your table or join your club, it ought to be your privilege to do so. If a person of color has talent or genius which might produce something useful to society, he should have a congenial atmosphere in which to develop it. In spite of their handicap, the colored people of the United States, where they have had a meager opportunity, have shown what exceptional talent can accomplish. (Frederick Douglass, Booker Washington, Henry O. Tanner, Paul Laurence Dunbar, Dr. Du Bois, Williams and Walker, Ernest Hogan, Braithwaite.)[25] If it were my text, I could talk to you an hour about what the Negro has accomplished since the Civil War.

As an illustration of what I mean by a congenial atmosphere, several years ago Mr. Samuel Coleridge-Taylor, the eminent English musical composer, visited Washington to conduct several concerts at which his *Hiawatha* was performed.[26] During the time of his visit to our capital city there was in session there a great convention of American musicians. In his own country on a similar occasion, he would have been an honored guest. Had he been a white man, the American musicians at Washington would have fallen all over themselves to shower attentions upon him. But he was a mulatto, and his presence was ignored.

Mr. William H. Lewis of the Boston bar, is a sufficiently able lawyer to have been the assistant attorney general of the United States, but he is not good enough to be a member of the southern-prejudice ridden American Bar Association.[27] Genius is a delicate flower, it needs sunshine and fair weather. You all know from observation, what it means to be in a position where the finger of scorn can be pointed at one. It poisons all the fountains of life, especially if one is conscious of innocence and undeserved reproach. Put yourself in the position of an educated, intelligent, sensitive person of color, made to feel at every turn of life that he is an outcast, not entitled to courtesy and consideration, and you can imagine what a deterrent or deadening effect it must have upon the mind of such a man. If you are unable to conceive it, read Dr. Du Bois's *The Souls of Black Folk*, and you may at least get a glimmering of it.

Now, how can you ladies, who do not live in the South, help to promote the reform to which I have pointed, assuming, as I do, that you believe in its urgency? Well, you can speak out when you have an opportunity, as you no doubt have done in your former discussions during the year. You can give others the opportunity, as you have given me, to express themselves upon this question. You can use your influence, when unjust laws are proposed, to defeat them—I wish you could use your votes—I am not narrow in my conception of equal rights and an equal citizenship—I believe that women ought to have the right to vote and to hold office and to do anything, so far as sex limitations permit, that men have the right to do; and I am quite sure that if women could vote, the moral level of our legislation would be appreciably raised. You have unlimited opportunities for contributing to the cause of Negro education in the South— You can support the journals which hold up the standard of human equality. The list is a long and a noble one, I can name only a few: the New York *Evening Post*, the *Independent*, the Springfield *Republican*, the *Survey*, the *Century Magazine*. There has come into existence within a few years an organization headed by a number of prominent men and women, some of them of eminent reputation, which is seeking to promote the solution of this problem—the National Association for the Advancement of Colored People.[28] It conducts a propaganda through the medium of organized local societies, of public speakers, of newspaper letters, and of its magazine, the *Crisis*, which is ably edited by Dr. W. E. B. Du Bois.[29] This movement is worthy of support and is destined to become more widely known.

In a word you can help to promote the only thing that will solve or remedy the race problem—a healthy change of public opinion that shall demand fair play for the Negro.

I want to conclude this already too long paper in the language of a writer on the same subject in the February *Survey*:[30]

> The Negro race as a whole, is capable of as fine and useful a place in our citizenship as that enjoyed by any other alien element. His sunny nature, his extraordinary imitative powers, that are as capable of a good direction as of a bad, his adaptability, his courage, his physical strength, are all characteristics that must be welded into our civilization. How, then, are we to go about the eradication of the prejudice? It is a matter primarily of individual effort, of the exercise of moral force. The logic of the situation must be brought home to each and all. We must give the Negro, whether we like him or not, a square deal. We must bring to bear the light of reason into the darkness of the self-stultification that engulfs our attitude.
>
> For two hundred and fifty years the colored race has been systematically denied its rights as men and citizens. If we reform our social attitude towards them—which is the only way on earth—and eliminate the curse of race-prejudice, we can look to the Negro to take care of himself. Let us, then, as reasonable beings take this first step, by influence, example, common sense and ceaseless agitation, to rid our country of this social and political disgrace. The cause possesses a moral basis of transcendent import, and is bound on that account to triumph in the end. The integrity of our institutions, the welfare of our political state, the trampled rights of a wronged people, cry out for justice.

↜

SOURCE: Untitled and undated typed text at the Fisk University Library. Chesnutt delivered this speech to the Medina Coterie, a women's club in Medina, O., on 25 March 1913.

[1]The club's series of lectures began on 1 October 1912 and ended on 25 March 1913 with Chesnutt's address; which of his stories Chesnutt read in conjunction with his speech is unknown.

[2]Exodus 21:16

[3]1 Timothy 1:9–10; Chesnutt rephrases the passage, elides an unnecessary second reference to menstealers, and omits the category of whoremongers.

[4]Organized during the campaign preceding the election of 1848, the Free-Soil Party opposed extending slavery into any U.S. territories ceded by Mexico following the Mexican War. It merged with the fledgling Republican Party in 1854.

[5]In 1845.

[6]The Missouri Compromise of 1820, which simultaneously admitted Maine as a free state and Missouri as a slave state in order to preserve the tenuous balance of sectional representation in Congress, may be the event Chesnutt has in mind here. His chronology, however, more likely suggests that he means the Compromise of 1850, by which California entered the Union as a free state to balance the admission of Texas, while other territories such as New Mexico and Utah were allowed to determine their status as either slave or free at such time as they became states.

[7]The Kansas-Nebraska Act of 1854 permitted residents in those two territories to decide whether they would allow slavery within their borders, giving rise to serious internal skirmishes especially in "bleeding Kansas."

[8]Originally from Ohio, radical abolitionist John Brown moved his family to Kansas in 1855 after the passage of the Kansas-Nebraska Act. See "The Future of the Negro," n. 5.

[9]Only Mississippi and South Carolina had more African-Americans than whites in 1913, though Georgia approached them with a black population of approximately 46 percent.

[10]Appointed by Lincoln as an Associate Justice in 1862, Samuel Freeman Miller (1816–90) led Court opposition to using the Fourteenth Amendment to remove businesses from governmental regulation; in the Slaughter House Cases, 16 Wallace 36, (1873) from which Chesnutt quotes, livestock butchers challenged a state law giving a monopoly of their trade to a single company. Miller's view was that the Fourteenth Amendment obtained only in cases involving civil rights.

[11]The Civil Rights Act of 1866.

[12]The Civil Rights Cases of 1883.

[13]Plessy v. Ferguson.

[14]John Marshall Harlan was appointed an Associate Justice in 1877 by President Rutherford B. Hayes and not by Lincoln. In fact, he opposed Lincoln's re-election in 1864 and attacked the Thirteenth Amendment when it was proposed. He reversed his attitude, however, after observing disturbing racist violence in his native Kentucky. A dissenter from majority court opinion in over 300 decisions, Harlan opposed the court's decision in the Civil Rights Cases as well as in Plessy v. Ferguson. Chesnutt quotes from his dissent from the holding of the latter.

[15]Coleman Livingston Blease (1868–1942) began serving the first of two terms as the Governor of South Carolina in 1911, and he would later hold office as a U.S. senator (1925–31). A confirmed "Tillmanite," Blease vigorously supported racial discrimination policies.

[16]The 1 February 1913 issue in volume 29 featured a front wrapper illustration, the head of the statue of Abraham Lincoln by Daniel Chester French (1850–1931) in Lincoln, Nebr.

[17]In 1913, Louisiana paid its African-American teachers $31.18 per month, Mississippi $30.00, and Virginia $28.38; Alabama then paid its black teachers $137 per year.

[18]On 1 March 1913, the Supreme Court of Georgia in Taylor v. Means, 139 Ga. 578 (1913), denied the petition of O. F. Taylor to have his son Ollie, then thirteen, re-

moved from the Fulton County Industrial Farm, where he had been housed for about three years after pleading guilty and being convicted of "an offense which amounted to a misdemeanor, to wit, the theft of a bottle of coca-cola, of the value of five cents."

[19]A lynching occurred in Springfield, O., on 7 March 1904; see "The Race Problem." On 13 August 1911 in Coatesville, Pa., a mob dragged Zachariah Walker from his hospital bed and burned him alive for allegedly having killed a white constable in a fight.

[20]The *Negro Year Book, 1914–1915*, differs in its figures. It notes 3,562 lynchings in the United States from 1885 through 1912; Chesnutt also seems to have erred in citing several other statistics: the largest number of lynchings, 255 rather than 235, occurred not in 1902, but in 1892, while the smallest was 64 in 1912, rather than 60 in 1906, when 72 actually occurred; his figures for 1908, 1909, 1910, and 1911 are correct, but 1912 saw 64, instead of the 65 lynchings he reports.

[21]See "The Future of the Negro," n. 20.

[22]The Brotherhood of Railroad Trainmen's national headquarters had been in Cleveland since 1899. The Brotherhood of Locomotive Engineers moved its headquarters there in 1908. The third organization to which Chesnutt refers is the Brotherhood of Locomotive Firemen and Enginemen.

[23]Woodrow Wilson (1856–1924) won the 1912 election, defeating Republican incumbent William Howard Taft (1857–1930) and Progressive Party candidate Theodore Roosevelt.

[24]Chesnutt prompted himself thus to refer to a Nebraska bill prohibiting interracial marriage that had been defeated.

[25]Entertainer and impresario George Walker (1873–1911), teamed with Egbert ("Bert") Williams (1875–1922) in the early 1890's, taking an initially unsuccessful act to fame and fortune when Koster and Bial's Music Hall, New York's premier vaudeville house, booked it. Their production of Will Marion Cook and Jessie A. Shipp's musical *In Dahomey* (1902) was the first all-black show to open in a legitimate Broadway theater. After Walker's untimely illness took him out of the act in 1909, Williams enjoyed a spectacular solo career, beginning in 1910, when he became the first black actor to receive feature billing on Broadway in *Ziegfield Follies*. Ernest Hogan, *né* Ruben Crowders (1860?–1909), was a composer, singer, and comedian. William S. Braithwaite (1878–1962) was a literary critic, poetry anthologist, and poet; his publications include *Lyrics of Love and Life* (1904) and *House of Falling Leaves, with Other Poems* (1908).

[26]In 1904.

[27]William Henry Lewis (1868–1949) was graduated from Harvard Law School in 1895. He began a successful law practice in Boston, received an appointment by Theodore Roosevelt as Assistant U.S. Attorney for Massachusetts (1903–6), became Assistant U.S. Attorney for New England (1907–11), and accepted an appointment from President Taft as Assistant Attorney-General of the United States in 1911.

[28]Organized in 1910.

[29]Du Bois served as editor from 1910 to 1934.

[30]George Packard, "A Civic Problem and a Social Duty," *Survey*, 29 (1 February 1913), 576–81.

Perry Centennial

Speech delivered at St. Andrew's Episcopal Church,
Cleveland, O., 14 September 1913

Among other reasons why we should participate with zeal and enthusiasm in this celebration, I wish to call your attention to a few facts showing the participation of colored men in the various wars in the United States.

In the Revolutionary War the value of Negroes as fighting men was early recognized by both the contending parties. The first fight in the Revolution—it was really little more than a street riot, though it is known in history as the Boston Massacre,—took place March 5, 1770, and in it four Americans were killed by members of the British garrison who were then in command of the city, one of those four being a Mulatto by the name of Crispus Attucks.[1] To Attucks, with the other three victims, was given a public funeral, the shops in Boston were closed, and all the bells in the city and the neighboring towns were rung. It is said that a greater number of persons assembled on this occasion than were ever before gathered on this continent for a similar purpose. Attucks' body and that of one of the other victims was placed in Faneuil Hall.[2] The funeral procession, headed by four hearses, formed in King Street and marched in columns six deep with a long file of coaches belonging to the most distinguished citizens, to the cemetery, where the four victims were deposited in one grave, over which a stone was placed with this inscription:

> Long as in Freedom's cause the wise contend,
> Dear to your country shall your fame extend;
> While to the world the lettered stone shall tell
> Where Caldwell, Attucks, Gray, and Maverick fell.[3]

The anniversary of this event was publicly commemorated in Boston for many years, and there is a monument to Crispus Attucks on Boston Common.[4]

At the battle of Bunker Hill, June 17, 1775, Negro soldiers stood side by side and fought bravely with their white brethren. The shot that killed Major Pitcairn of the British Marines, just as he mounted the redoubt, was fired by Peter Salem, a Negro soldier, who was in the forefront of the battle. Peter was a slave until he joined the army, since for a slave to be mustered into the army worked a practical emancipation.[5] The great American orator, Edward Everett, in his address at the unveiling of the statue of General Joseph Warren in June, 1857, did not forget to mention the colored patriot, and thus secure for his act perpetual record.[6] The speaker said, among other things:

> It is the monument of all the brave men who shared the perils of the Battle of Bunker Hill—alike of Prescott and Putnam and Warren, the chiefs of the day, and the colored man, Salem, who is reported to have shot the gallant Pitcairn as he

mounted the parapet. Cold as the clods on which it rests, still as the silent heavens to which it soars, it is yet vocal, eloquent, "in their undivided praise."[7]

Another colored soldier is referred to in the records of the general court of the Massachusetts Bay, recommending for public reward a Negro man called Salem Poor, of whom it is said that he, in the battle at Charlestown, "behaved like an experienced officer as well as an excellent soldier. We beg leave to say that in the person of this said Negro centers a brave and gallant soldier."[8]

The records of the Revolution also mention a Major Samuel Lawrence, who commanded a company whose rank and file were all Negroes, of whose courage, military discipline and fidelity, he always spoke with respect.[9] And Mr. Bancroft, in his history says, "Nor should history forget to record that in this gallant band," referring to the American army in the Battle of Bunker Hill,

> the free negroes of the country whose right to bear arms in public defence was, at that day, as little disputed in New England as are other rights. They took their place, not in a separate corps, but in the ranks with the white man; and their names may be read on the pension rolls of the country, side by side with those of other soldiers of the Revolution.[10]

At first slaves were enlisted in the Continental Army, and the British also planned to gain the blacks and induce them to take up arms against the Continentals, by promising them liberty on this condition, by which means they persuaded numbers to join them.[11] This perhaps helped the Americans to see the inconsistency of asking slaves to fight for liberty, and led to legislation by which any slave enlisted in the American Army was given his freedom. This in New England. In South Carolina, on the contrary, although some of her ablest statesmen and bravest soldiers advocated strongly in the Continental Congress and in the provincial legislature, the use of Negroes as soldiers, there was a strong and successful opposition to the measure.[12] As usual, although slavery existed throughout the country, the principal opposition to Negro soldiers came from the states where there was the least hearty and efficient support of the principles of Republican Government, and the least ability or disposition to furnish an equal or fair quota of white soldiers, among them being especially South Carolina and Georgia. In September, 1775, Gov. Rutledge of South Carolina moved in Congress the discharge of all the Negroes in the army, and he was strongly supported by many of the southern delegates, but the opposition was powerful and determined and he lost his point.[13]

General Thomas, in a letter to John Adams, says: "In the regiment at Rocksbury the privates are equal to any I served with in the last war. We have some Negroes, but I look on them in general, as equally serviceable with other men for fatigue, and in action many of them have proven themselves brave." And he adds, with reference to some white soldiers from the south, "They are as indifferent men as I ever served with, mutinous and often deserting to the enemy, unwilling for duty of any kind, exceedingly vicious, and I think the army would be as well without as with them. But to do justice to their officers, some of them are likely men."[14]

There is a great deal more interesting information in the Revolutionary archives in reference to this subject. Major General Prescott, of the British army, July 9, 1777, was captured by a valiant Negro by the name of Prince, an exploit which was much commended at the time, as its results were very important.[15] The success of the Battle of Rhode Island, August 29, 1778, was owing in a great degree to the good fighting of the Negro soldiers, who, in a black regiment under Colonel Green, distinguished themselves by deeds of desperate valor.[16] When Colonel Green was surprised and murdered near Points Bridge, New York, May 14, 1781, his colored soldiers heroically defended him till they were cut to pieces, and the enemy reached him over the dead bodies of his faithful Negroes. There is no record of the exact number of colored men enlisted in the Continental Armies but undoubtedly it was very large.[17] A Hessian officer wrote that there was "No regiment to be seen in which there were not negroes in abundance."[18] In 1783 the State of Virginia passed an act securing the freedom of all slaves who had served in the army.[19]

The War of 1812, between the United States and Great Britain, took place during the administration of President Madison.[20] War was declared in 1812 and peace was made in 1815. Ill-feeling between the two nations had been growing for several years. The British were supposed by the Americans to have secretly encouraged the famous Indian chief, Tecumseh, of Ohio, in a plot to drive the white settlers out of the west, this plot terminating in the Battle of Tippecanoe where General Harrison defeated the Indians.[21] There were also charges made by a man named Henry that the English Government in Canada had employed him to endeavor to persuade the New England States to withdraw from the Union and join themselves to Canada.[22] England was at this time at war with France, and greatly in need of seamen, and English vessels persisted in stopping our ships, taking American seamen out of them and forcing them, under the sting of the lash, to enter her service and fight her battles. Her excuse was that she seized men who were British subjects and who had deserted and entered our service. This was true in some cases, but England made no discrimination, but took any able-bodied sailor she fancied. Thousands of our citizens had been kidnapped, and England refusing to stop these acts of violence, Congress declared war in the summer of 1812, and with a hurrah for "Free Trade and Sailors' Rights" the war began.[23]

A large part of the war was fought in Ohio. General William Hull was ordered to march from Urbana, Ohio, to Detroit, with a view to attacking Canada, and if all went well, to annex it. The attempt was a failure.[24] But though we were beaten on land we were wonderfully victorious at sea. England, who called herself mistress of the seas had a navy of a thousand war ships, the Americans had twelve. One of the most famous battles of the war was that between the *Constitution*, Captain Isaac Hull, and the British Man of War *Guerrière*, August 19th, 1812, in which the *Constitution* defeated the *Guerrière* and reduced her to a shattered, helpless, sinking wreck in twenty minutes.[25] Captain Hull won twelve out of fifteen of such battles. The *Constitution* was taken to Boston, almost unhurt, and was henceforth known as "Old Ironsides" and remained in the Navy Yard until I think a few years ago, when it was cut up.[26]

On September 10, 1813, Commodore Perry gained a great victory at Put-in-Bay, on Lake Erie, the event which we are celebrating in Cleveland, which is the latest of the Lake cities to participate in this celebration.[27] Perry, with nine vessels built from green timber cut in the wilderness back of them, captured a British fleet carrying more guns and more men. Before the fight began he hoisted a flag over his vessel—the *Lawrence*, bearing the words, "Don't give up the ship."[28] During the battle the *Lawrence* was literally cut to pieces and her decks covered with dead and dying men. Perry saw that if he persisted in staying on the *Lawrence* he must be defeated. Taking his little brother, a boy of twelve, with him, he jumped into a boat and ordered the crew to pull for the *Niagara*.[29] It was a perilous undertaking. The British shot broke the oars to pieces, and young Perry's cap was torn with bullets, but the boat reached the *Niagara* and Perry gained the battle. Then, on the back of an old letter he wrote his famous dispatch to General Harrison,—"We have met the enemy, and they are ours."[30] That victory gave us control of Lake Erie and the British abandoned Detroit.

The next year, 1814, the American forces gained the battle of Chippewa in Canada, July 5, and later won the battle of Lundy's Lane, July 25th, near Niagara Falls. August 24th, 1814, the British, who had blockaded all our ports along the Atlantic Coast and had plundered and burned a number of towns, entered Washington. President Madison fled in one direction; Mrs. Madison, filling her work bag with silver spoons, snatched from the table, fled in another.[31] The President's dinner, which had just been served, was captured and eaten by the enemy. The torch was applied, and the Capitol, the President's house, and other public buildings were burned. A few weeks later a British force from Canada invaded northern New York by way of Lake Champlain and fought a battle with Commodore Macdonough in Plattsburgh Bay. The British were defeated and the invasion from Canada checked.[32] The British next attacked Baltimore, with the same force and fleet that had taken Washington, and bombarded Fort McHenry all day, September 13th, 1814, and the following night. When the sun rose next morning our flag was still there, and the British had sailed down Chesapeake Bay. It was on this occasion that Francis Scott Key, of Baltimore, wrote, *The Star Spangled Banner*.[33] He was a prisoner on board of an English Man of War. All night long he watched the bombardment of the Fort. By the flash of the guns he could see our flag waving over it. In the morning, when the mist cleared away, he found it was still there, and expressed his delight in the song, which he hastily wrote in pencil on the back of an old letter.

Jackson's[34] victory at New Orleans, in which, as I shall tell you in a minute, colored soldiers played a conspicuous part, was the final battle of the war which had now lasted over two years. The British determined to strike a tremendous blow at New Orleans, which, if successful, might give them a foot-hold on the Mississippi. Ten thousand picked men under Sir Edward Pakenham made the attack January 8, 1815.[35] General Jackson defended the approach to the city with fortifications made of banks of earth and logs and cotton bales, and with just half as many men as the British commander, most of them inexperienced in war. In less than half an hour after the fight began Pakenham was killed and the enemy had suffered so severely that they gave up the battle. This ended the war. Great Britain had already made peace with our commissioners at Ghent, in Belgium, December 24, 1814, but owing to the slow speed of sailing vessels and the fact that telegraphy had not been invented, the news did not reach us until several weeks after Jackson's victory.

An examination of the historical data on the War of 1812, shows that one in six or eight of the men who fought under Perry on the Great Lakes were colored men. Captain (afterwards Commodore) Perry complained to Commodore Chauncey about the quality of the men sent him, saying that they were "a motley set, blacks, soldiers and boys," but that he was "pleased to see anything in the shape of a man."

This letter called forth a sharp reply from Commodore Chauncey, in which he said:

> Regret that you are not pleased with the men sent you, for to my knowledge a part of them are not surpassed by any seamen we have in the fleet; and I have yet to learn that the color of the skin, or the cut and trimmings of the coat can affect a man's qualifications or usefulness. I have nearly fifty blacks on board of this ship, and many of them are among my best men.[36]

Perry found the Negroes to be all that Commodore Chauncey had represented them. He spoke highly of their bravery and good conduct. "They seemed," he said, "to be absolutely insensible to danger." Other commanders of the American fleet join in this testimony to the fighting qualities of the colored seamen.

Negroes were solicited and welcomed as soldiers, also, in the War of 1812, and fought equally as well on land as on sea. An act of the legislature of the State of New York, passed October 24, 1814, authorized the raising of two regiments of free men of color by voluntary enlistment, to serve for three years, and any able-bodied slave who might enlist with the consent of his master or mistress was to be rewarded with manumission upon his discharge. It will be remembered that Jefferson Davis, toward the close of the Civil War, made a similar proposition for the use of Negroes in the Confederate Army, but the plan was rejected by the Confederate Congress.[37] Nearly three hundred thousand colored men fought in the Union Army, and their record at Petersburg and Fort Wagner speaks for itself.[38]

President Andrew Jackson, commanding the United States forces in Louisiana during the War of 1812, invited the free colored inhabitants of that State to enlist in the United States Army in the following proclamation:

> Headquarters, Seventh Military District, Mobile
> September 21, 1814.

> To the Free Colored Inhabitants of Louisiana.
> Through a mistaken policy, you have heretofore been deprived of a participation in the glorious struggle for national rights in which our country is engaged. This no longer shall exist.
> As sons of freedom, you are now called upon to defend our most inestimable blessing. As Americans, your country looks with confidence to her adopted children for a valorous support, as a faithful return for the advantages enjoyed under her mild and equitable government. As fathers, husbands, and brothers, you are summoned to rally around the standard of the Eagle, to defend all which is dear in existence.
> Your country, although calling for your exertions, does not wish you to engage in her cause without amply remunerating you for the services rendered. . . .
> To every noble-hearted, generous freeman of color volunteering to serve during the present contest with Great Britain, and no longer, there will be paid the same bounty, in money and lands, now received by the white soldiers of the United States, *viz.* one hundred and twenty-four dollars in money, and one hundred and sixty acres of land. The non-commissioned officers and privates will also be entitled to the same monthly pay, and daily rations, and clothes, furnished to any American soldier.
> On enrolling yourselves in companies, the Major-General Commanding will select officers for your government from your white fellow-citizens. Your non-commissioned officers will be appointed from among yourselves.
> Due regard will be paid to the feelings of freemen and soldiers. . . . As a distinct, independent battalion or regiment, pursuing the path of glory, you will, undivided receive the applause and gratitude of your countrymen.
> To assure you of the sincerity of my intentions, and my anxiety to engage your invaluable services to our country, I have communicated my wishes to the Governor of Louisiana, who is fully informed as to the manner of enrollment, and will give you every necessary information on the subject of this address.
> Andrew Jackson, Major-General Commanding.
> (*Niles' Weekly Register*, vol. vii, p. 205.)[39]

Three months afterwards, on the 18th of December 1814, General Jackson reviewed the troops, white and colored, in New Orleans. At the close of the review, one of his aides read Jackson's famous address to the troops which contributed so powerfully to enhance their enthusiasm, and which the survivors of the army never forgot. Part of it was addressed directly to the colored troops and was as follows:

> To the Men of Color.—Soldiers! From the shores of Mobile I collected you to arms,—I invited you to share in the perils and to divide the glory of your white countrymen. I expected much from you; for I was not uninformed of those qualities which must render you so formidable to an invading foe. I knew that you could en-

dure hunger and thirst, and all the hardships of war. I knew that you loved the land of your nativity, and that, like ourselves, you had to defend all that is most dear to man. But you surpass my hopes. I have found in you, united to these qualities, that noble enthusiasm which impels to great deeds.

Soldiers! The President of the United States shall be informed of your conduct on the present occasion; and the voice of the Representatives of the American nation shall applaud your valor, as your General now praises your ardor. The enemy is near. His sails cover the lakes. But the brave are united, and, if he finds us contending among ourselves, it will be for the prize of valor, and fame its noblest reward. (*Niles' Weekly Register*, vol. vii, pp. 354–346.)

⌒

SOURCE: Holograph and typed text at the Fisk University Library. This speech was given at Cleveland's St. Andrew's Episcopal Church on 14 September 1913, as part of the local commemoration of the victory of the U.S. naval forces over the British on Lake Erie during the War of 1812. Principal sources of information used by Chesnutt were: *History of the Negro Race* (1882) by George Washington Williams; and *The Black Phalanx* (1888) by Joseph Thomas Wilson (1836–91). Portions of this speech were printed in "Negroes to Walk in Perry's Parade," Cleveland *Plain Dealer*, 8 September 1913, 3, and in the "Social and Personal" column of the *Cleveland Gazette*, 20 September 1913, 3.

[1]Attucks (1723–70) was a runaway Massachusetts slave of twenty years who had become a seaman.

[2]The bodies of Attucks and another sailor, James Caldwell, lay in state at Faneuil Hall because, unlike the others killed in the massacre, they were not related to anyone in Boston.

[3]Samuel Gray was a local ropemaker; Samuel Maverick was an apprentice turner who actually died the next morning; a fifth casualty, Patrick Carr, was a leatherworker who died nine days after the conflict.

[4]On 14 November 1888, John Fiske (1842–1901), historian and evolutionary idealist, delivered the dedicatory address at the monument, while Irish-American poet John Boyle O'Reilly (1844–90) composed "Crispus Attucks" for the occasion. It reads, in part: "And honor to Crispus Attucks, who was leader and voice that day: / The first to defy, and the first to die, with Maverick, Carr, and Gray."

[5]John Pitcairn (1722–75), a British officer popular with his own troops and local Bostonians alike, had served earlier as second in command at the battles of Lexington and Concord on 19 April 1775. Peter Salem (1750–1816), like Attucks, had been a slave in Framingham, Mass., but was freed to join the Continental Army as a member of the First Massachusetts Regiment.

[6]On 17 June 1857, at a dedication ceremony for a statue of Major General Joseph Warren (1741–75), a hero at Bunker Hill, Everett spoke movingly about Warren's self-sacrifice, as well as about the debt owed to others who had died in the battle (*Inauguration of the Statue of Warren by the Bunker Hill Monument Association* [1857]). A Harvard graduate and physician, Warren sent Paul Revere (1735–1818) and William Dawes (1745–99) on their famous rides to warn citizens against approaching British troops.

[7]William Prescott (1726–95), who fortified Breed's Hill the night before the battle, retired from active duty in 1775; Israel Putnam (1718–90), a leader in various colonial wars during which he rose steadily in rank, had been appointed major general just before the battle at Bunker Hill.

[8]Salem Poor (1747 or 1758–?) served at Bunker Hill, Valley Forge, and White Plains; although fourteen officers on 5 December 1775 signed a petition citing Poor's bravery and it was read into the record of the General Court of Massachusetts on 21 December 1775, he never received a commendation. The petition included the statement Chesnutt quotes.

[9]Samuel Lawrence (1759–1827), a corporal in the Minute Men in Groton, Mass., alerted his fellows to the British presence in the area and marched with them to Cambridge, where on 20 April 1775 he was promoted to the rank of major; he served at Bunker Hill and other battles before retiring to resume farming in 1778.

[10]George Bancroft (1800–1891), *History of the United States from the Discovery of the American Continent* (1837).

[11]John Murray, Earl of Dunmore (1732–1809), royal governor of Virginia until 1776, issued on 7 November 1775 a proclamation which freed slaves who joined the British Army.

[12]Opposition to manumission ran high throughout the colonies at this time, Washington himself temporarily refusing to allow more slaves to enlist since they could not serve unless they had been freed.

[13]*History of the Negro Race* notes that Edward Rutledge (1749–1800), signer of the Declaration of Independence and governor of South Carolina (1798–1800), made his proposal to the Second Continental Congress on 26 September 1775.

[14]John Thomas (1724–76), letter dated 24 October 1775.

[15]Major General Richard Prescott (1725–88) had been previously captured by Americans; this second time he was not exchanged until nearly a year later, on 6 May 1778. Scholars have advanced two separate identities for "Prince": either Prince Whipple, who enlisted in Maryland and served under General William Whipple (1730–85); or Jack or Tack Sissons (c. 1743–1821), one of three African Americans known to have helped capture Prescott.

[16]Christopher Greene (1737–81) commanded the First Rhode Island Regiment.

[17]Generally accepted is the approximate figure of five thousand.

[18]Both the identity of this "Hessian officer" and the occasion of his comment remain elusive. According to Jack D. Foner in *Blacks and the Military in American History* (1974), a Baron von Closen, upon observing the American troops passing in review at Yorktown, wrote: "Three-quarters of the Rhode Island regiment consists of Negroes, and that regiment is the most neatly dressed, the best under arms, and the most precise in its maneuvers."

[19]Passed on 20 October 1783. Editorially excised here is the superfluous "(War of 1812)."

[20]James Madison (1751–1836) was President in 1809–17.

[21]Fought on 7 November 1811 in what is now Indiana, the Battle of Tippecanoe resulted in crushing defeat for the Shawnees led by Lalawethika (1768?–1837), brother of the chief Tecumseh (1768?–1813) who died 5 October 1813, at the battle of the Thames, also won by General William Henry Harrison.

[22]An Irish adventurer, John Henry (1776?–1820?) had been sent as a British spy to Boston in 1809, by then governor-general of Canada, Sir James Henry Craig (1748–1812).

[23]President Madison issued a declaration of war on 18 June 1812, after Congress had so advised him, voting 79–49 in the House and 19–13 in the Senate in favor of war. The slogan "Free Trade and Sailors' Rights," a summary of the major causes of the war in the minds of many people, became so popular in the navy that James Lawrence (1781–1813), unsuccessful but valiant hero in the defense of Boston, flew a flag bearing

these words as the ensign of his ship *Chesapeake* when in battle with the British ship *Shannon* on 1 June 1813.

[24]Directed to invade Canada, William Hull (1753–1825) instead surrendered Detroit on 16 August 1812 without offering much resistance to the British; a young Martin Van Buren (1782–1862) successfully prosecuted him for treason.

[25]Isaac Hull (1773–1843) defeated the British *Guerrière* under the command of Captain James Richard Dacres (1788–1853) off the coast of Cape Race, Newfoundland.

[26]The poem "Old Ironsides" (1830), by Oliver Wendell Holmes, Sr. (1809–94), measured contemporary affection for the frigate; when it was ordered dismantled, popular protest prevented its being "cut up."

[27]Oliver Hazard Perry (1785–1819) became a hero with his victory over the more experienced British forces during the Battle of Lake Erie, which not only ensured American domination of the lake but effectively ousted the British from Detroit.

[28]These words were uttered by Captain James Lawrence just before his death, and Perry commemorated thus his friendship with the fallen hero.

[29]James Alexander Perry (1801–?), one of five Perry brothers, all naval officers.

[30]Perry dated his letter "United States Brig Niagara. Off the Western Sisters. Sept. 10, 1813, 4 P.M."

[31]Legend credits Dorothy ("Dolley") Madison (1768–1849) with saving not only the spoons but other silver, the presidential china, a copy of the Declaration of Independence, and a portrait of Washington by Gilbert Stuart (1755–1828).

[32]On 11 September 1814, Thomas Macdonough (1783–1825) defeated his British opponents, forcing them to retreat to Canada.

[33]Key (1779–1843), a Maryland attorney, originally published in broadside *The Bombardment of Fort McHenry* and saw it reprinted in the Baltimore *Patriot* as "Defence of Fort M'Henry." The song did not become the national anthem until 1931.

[34]Andrew Jackson (1767–1845), later President of the United States (1829–37).

[35]Edward Michael Pakenham (1778–1815)—misspelled "Packenham" in the source text—had served in the Peninsular Wars where his maneuvers at the battle of Salamanca on 22 July 1812 contributed significantly to British victory.

[36]Perry's letter was dated 26 July 1813. The reply by Isaac Chauncey (1772–1840), commander of naval forces on Lake Erie and Lake Ontario, was dated 30 July 1813.

[37]On 7 November 1864, Jefferson Davis (1808–89) requested that slaves be purchased to work in the Confederate army, though not as enlisted soldiers. The Confederate House of Representatives authorized the use of slaves as soldiers on 29 February 1865, the Senate giving similar approval on 8 March 1865, by one vote. Two days later Robert E. Lee (1807–70) advised Davis to administer the new bill; it was signed by Davis on 13 March 1865.

[38]More recent figures suggest that about 179,000 African-American troops fought for the Union armies during the Civil War. The Fifty-fourth Massachusetts Regiment, with 650 African Americans, suffered nearly 250 casualties in leading the assault of Fort Wagner in South Carolina on 18 July 1863; Edward Ward Hinks (1830–94) commanded an all-Negro division of the XVIII Corps at the Battle of Petersburg on 15 June 1864, while Edward Ferrero (1831–99) led a similar unit, the 4th Division, IX Corps, Army of the Potomac, at the Petersburg Mine Assault on 30 July 1864.

[39]Emended here and below is "Niles's Register," the actual title to which Chesnutt—quoting from *The Black Phalanx*—did not have immediate access.

Race Ideals and Examples

Essay published in the *A.M.E. Review*, October 1913

When I rashly replied in the affirmative to your genial President's invitation to address the literary societies of your University,[1] my first thought was to avoid the beaten path of addresses to colored audiences by speaking to you simply as men and women, interested, in the same way, in the same things in which other people are interested. I have always thought that the matter of race is too much emphasized in this country; so much emphasized, that the far greater theme of humanity is often lost sight of.

But, upon second thought, I reflected that the matter of race will be a very vital thing in your lives. You will have all the problems of life with which others have to contend, and this in addition, and you will find all your other problems more or less colored by it. You are going out into the world, those of you who have finished your school career, and the rest of you when you have finished it, not only to fight your own individual battles, but the battles of your race.

Struggle is the law of life.[2] The progress of humanity is a history of struggle—man against nature always, man against man too often, and your race cannot escape the common lot. Only your struggle, let us hope, will be not with deadly weapons, but with heart and hand and brain. And for this struggle you must have a clear conception of what you are seeking—your ultimate ideal. Then you must have a plan of action, an ideal of life, by which you will approach this end. Then you must consider your personal equipment for the struggle; you must adopt your own personal ideals of character and conduct. You may not have all these important things clearly and sharply defined when you begin, but, if you have them even vaguely outlined, you can go forward with a certain degree of self-confidence, without which you are as likely to go to pieces as a ship without a rudder in a stormy sea.

Now, the object of education is to equip you with these ideals, these standards. What you accomplish, for yourselves, for your race, for humanity, will depend upon the kind of men and women you are, and the kind of men and women you are will depend largely upon yourselves—not entirely so, for if God has made a man wise and strong and gifted, he will rise above circumstances, and if he is a born fool or a weakling, circumstances will not greatly modify his character. But, fortunately, perhaps, for the world, most of us are of malleable clay, which may be molded by education and culture and by the force of our own will. Perhaps the most valuable attribute of a liberal education is the opportunity which it gives one to compare himself with others, to measure himself by accepted standards, and thus to ascertain what are his strong points, that he may best utilize them, and what are his weaknesses, that he may strive to correct them. There is no more valuable equipment of the struggle of life.

Now, I have no doubt that, in this temple of learning, conducted under the auspices of a great church,[3] and with a distinguished Greek scholar at its head, you have been trained in all the virtues, ancient and modern. The cardinal virtues of the ancients were justice, prudence, temperance and fortitude. You will need them all. Certainly you will value justice and seek to promote it, for you and your people have suffered and will suffer severely from injustice. Prudence you will need, perhaps more than any other people, in the struggle against odds—one of the most interesting traits of successful colored men is the fine diplomacy with which they steer their way along difficult channels; and this is doubly interesting and indeed admirable when it is accomplished without the sacrifice of self-respect. Temperance you will need in all things, all the more so because the Negro is by temperament so filled with the sheer joy of living that he is constantly tempted and too often yields to the temptation to get all the pleasure possible out of it—the list of our successful men contains too many instances of shipwreck due to overindulgence in pleasure. The fourth pagan virtue was fortitude—the capacity to endure hardship. Some of you, in your efforts to secure an education, have doubtless had special training in this virtue. You will all undoubtedly have opportunities to exercise it. No man's life is one of unbroken happiness. If you are uniformly fortunate in your affairs, as few men are, you will suffer in your emotions, and the philosophy which a liberal education has inculcated will enable you to endure bravely the "whips and stings" of fortune.[4] And courage, the ability to dare, to go forward, is the active form of that virtue of which fortitude is the negative.

In this Christian university you have doubtless had the moral virtues thoroughly inculcated into your minds. You have been taught the Ten Commandments,[5] not merely to know them, but to live them—they are the elementary ideals of civilized society. On them, in your education, have been superimposed the Christian virtues—faith, hope and charity—the greatest of which is charity, or, to put it philosophically, altruism, the love of humanity, the willingness to serve and to share with others.

There is another Christian virtue in which the race has been severely trained—that of meekness and humility. It is a fine trait of character, if not carried to the point of servility, or beyond the point of self-respect. There is a danger of going too far in that direction, or, in seeking a proper attitude toward the world, of going too far the other way. The happy medium, the attitude of respect for the rights and feelings of others, and of demanding with firmness and courtesy the respect of others for your own rights and feelings, is the most desirable one. You have no doubt been taught to cultivate race pride. I think what your teachers meant was race self-respect, for you and your forbears have suffered so severely from race pride as to make it doubtful whether that particular quality is a virtue. No man derives any merit from his birth; it is only what he does that counts; and while it is pleasant and valuable as a spur to effort to contemplate a long record of achievement in one's ancestors, it is no ground for demanding respect or consideration from others. True scholarship, as Dr. Jackson suggested Sunday in his able and eloquent address,[6] begets in the scholar a profound intellectual humility—one perceives, after he has learned only a little, that the field of learning is so wide that no one mind can hope to span it, the well of knowledge so deep that no one mind can hope to fathom it, and thus, by comparison, the scholar appreciates the littleness of man compared with the infinite, and is correspondingly humble.

To these fundamental and eternal ideals of conduct, advancing civilization has added new standards. For instance, one hundred years ago it was the custom, at dinner, for gentlemen to drink themselves under the table—indeed, it was almost requisite, if one would maintain his standing as a gentleman, that he get drunk at least once in twenty-four hours. How times have changed! Now we have our Presidents and Secretaries of State banishing wine from their tables and setting the example of total abstinence, while our fiery ex-President brings a libel suit against an editor who dared to charge him with intoxication![7] Profanity in those days was a large element of speech; today it is rarely heard among men of culture and refinement, and the coarseness of conversation which was reflected in eighteenth and early nineteenth century literature has almost entirely disappeared. Other more intimate personal standards have changed. A hundred years ago, before the invention of modern plumbing, a bathtub was a rarity. Those of you who have seen or read the witty and cynical play of Bernard Shaw, *Arms and the Man*,[8] the scene of which is located in Bulgaria, about 1865, will recall the scene in which the heroine, Raina, says to her Chocolate Cream Soldier, Captain Bluntchli, that in her country well-bred ladies wash their hands *almost* every day. And the scene between Petkoff and his wife in which he tells her that her sore throat comes from washing her neck every day, and says: "I don't believe in going too far with these modern customs. All this washing can't be good for the health; it's not natural. Look at my father; he never had a bath in his life, and he lived to be 98, the oldest man in Bulgaria." We will agree that the ideal of personal cleanliness is a distinct advance over the standards of medieval times, when to bathe was considered a pampering of the flesh and therefore unpleasing in the sight of God; and that the modern requirement of good breeding that the presence of a lady or gentleman in a room should not be obvious to any other senses than those of sight and hearing, is in every respect preferable.

It was once customary to eat with the knife, and drink from the saucer; but times have changed, and we must not only eat with the fork, but hold it a certain way. In fact, table etiquette has been refined to a point where, to simple minds, it sometimes may seem burdensome, but the rules are those of good breeding, and I need not say that good manners are no small part of one's equipment for life. It is only for this reason that I mention subjects that might otherwise seem trivial or in poor taste from the platform.

In your school life you have, of course, acquired a certain amount of learning. You have, or ought to have, secured, in addition to something of mathematics and geography and foreign tongues, a fair command of your own language, the ability to read and understand it and to express yourselves clearly and succinctly in well-chosen words. And your education will have been a failure if it has not taught you to think, to reason logically, from cause to effect, from premise to conclusion. For, after all, it is reason which distinguishes us from the beasts of the field, and a trained mind is your most valuable weapon for the battle of life.

Now, when you find yourselves, on leaving school, well taught, well bred, ardent, eager for the fray for yourselves, for your race and for humanity, what avenues are open to you, what obstacles will you have to overcome?

One of the formidable lions in your path, against which your life will be one of constant struggle, will be the deep-seated prejudice against your race. You will, unless you are very fortunate, find it rise to confront you at almost every turn. You all know what form it takes, or will know sooner or later. And when, in your bewilderment, your sense of wrong and injustice, you ask why these things should be, you will be told that you are inferior to other races. If you follow your first instinct, and deny the statement, you will be confronted by what seem like irrefutable proofs. You will be constrained to admit that your people, as a class, in the mass, are the poorest, the lowest in the social scale, the most illiterate, the least advanced in social organization and efficiency, of any single class of our polyglot population. If you reply that these things are explained by slavery and its consequences,[9] you will be told that that is not a sufficient explanation, and that the inferiority antedated slavery and is physical and mental, and more or less independent of circumstances; if you quote scientists to prove that fundamentally the Negro's mind is equally capable of development with the white man's, you will be told that, no matter if that be so, it is not equally developed, and that no number of laboratory experiments or psychological studies, demonstrating the physical and mental equality of races, will convince any one against the verdict of history, which shows one race always forging ahead in the race of civilization and another always lagging behind, in the rear.

Now, you will perhaps be able to convince yourselves that there is, or at least may be, something wrong in this argument. You will point to the common origin of mankind; you will explain the Negro's relatively low stage of development by unfavorable ancestral surroundings, by means of which the Negro in his native Africa was hampered by the fervid heat of the tropics, by the miasma of the jungle, by the constant struggle against wild beasts and venomous reptiles and insects, by great deserts and lack of harbors, which cut him off from contact with civilized centers, and, on our own continent, as I have said, by the numbing influence of slavery and the prejudice which was its outgrowth. And you will point to other so-called inferior races which have in our own time pushed rapidly forward toward the highest development.

But when all is said and done, you will never convince any one of the essential equality of the races except by the practical argument of achievement. When a sufficient number of colored men and women have accomplished worthy things in the various fields of human endeavor; when they have attained not only a fair average, but enough of them have risen to the top to make the rest of the world sit up and take notice, then prejudice will have lost its chief prop and will have to rest its existence on lower foundations which will not be able to withstand the forces of justice and fair dealing. And it is your privilege and your opportunity to help forward this work which is to lift the American Negro to the plane of acknowledged equality.

You have, as I have shown, been well equipped for the struggle. Your environment, with all its limitations, is infinitely superior to that of your less fortunate ancestors. Practically every door of opportunity is open to you—some of them not open very wide, to be sure, but perhaps none of them entirely closed. If, after the excellent fundamental training which this institution has afforded, you have the means, or the energy, the ambition and ability to acquire the means to qualify for the practice of a profession, or one of the useful mechanical arts, there are excellent schools all over the North, and some in the South, where you may study medicine, or law, or engineering, or the trades; and I think it is safe to say that, once qualified, you will be able to find, somewhere—it may require a little patience—an opportunity to practice whatever calling you may prepare yourselves for. The principal trouble, in the matter of development for colored people, is not the trained man, but the untrained man, the common man—and the vast majority of colored people are common men—some of them, I think we will have to admit, very common indeed. The trained man, the educated man, the capable man, of whatever race, seems to be able to take care of himself, in whatever place.

Now, there is a danger among our particular people, a danger which would exist perhaps in any other people similarly placed—the temptation to follow the line of least resistance. This is all right up to a certain point—the open road is a quicker way to success than the forest of difficulties. But the temptation is to do the easiest thing. If the easiest thing is the best practicable thing, as it often is, it is the thing to do, but if one does it simply because it is the easiest, the result is likely to be fatal to true progress. The ideal pursuit for every man or woman should be the most worthy pursuit within reach of which he or she is capable.

And here comes in the wisdom of the first choice. For society is very conservative. You start life in some career for which you are not especially fitted, for which perhaps you are temperamentally and intellectually unfitted. Before you know it, you have married perhaps, and have a family to support. You cannot change your pursuit without diminishing your income, and so you jog along in the old harness. The world is full of these square pegs in round holes. We have all known singers without voices, music teachers without a spark of musical talent, preachers without religion, doctors who knew little of anatomy or medicine, lawyers who knew little law, statesmen whose chief qualifications were a loud voice and the itch for office. You don't want to belong to this class. So be careful and try to find out what your aptitudes are before you select a career. But if you develop unknown aptitudes later on, and are sure of them, don't hesitate to make a temporary sacrifice for a permanent gain. Make it your ideal, as I have said, to do the most worthy thing of which you are capable.

Now, the achievements of a race are of a twofold nature—those of the mass and those of the individual. The social efficiency of a people, their ability to work together for the common welfare, is a fundamental requirement of racial efficiency. It finds its finest flower in government. As we look back through history and study the great nations of the past and of today, we see what the combined social effort of a race may accomplish. But this sort of social achievement is, for our day and for our people, practically closed. There will not be, for any of you, an opportunity to contribute to the foundation or growth of any great black nation or civilization. If Hayti and Liberia survive the pressure which stronger nations are bringing to bear upon them, they will do well.[10] Perhaps at some distant day great black empires may grow up in Africa, but certainly not in your day or mine. You will not have an opportunity in this country to demonstrate what the pure Negro race in the mass is capable of. You may be able, by individual examples, to prove from what black men can do alone, to argue what they might do together; but you will never be able, without drawing a color line in your own ranks, if that were possible, to get together enough men of pure Negro blood to prove anything in a large way. The most you can anticipate is that you will, by the race prejudice of others, be sufficiently segregated from the general social activities of the community, to force you to show what the negroid or mixed element of the American people are capable of along lines where they are permitted or compelled to act *en masse*, and your principal incentive to do so, next to the instinct of self-preservation, will be that you may thereby refute the slander of your essential inferiority and prove your fitness for equal participation in all community activities. I am not interested in American Negroes primarily as a race; I am interested in them as men. I should like to see their race lost sight of, except academically, perhaps, and only their humanity and their citizenship borne in mind. In our own land the most that any optimist could hope or ask for is that we have the opportunity, in proportion to our numbers and our powers, to contribute to the government of the nation of which we constitute so considerable a part.

Among your own people you can demonstrate your social efficiency by the conduct of successful co-operative business enterprises. You have already done much in the way of churches and benefit organizations and educational institutions. This very university is an evidence of racial capacity. True, it is neither entirely supported nor entirely conducted by colored men, but they have done most of it, and what they have done has been well done.

In fine, it seems to me that the most open field in which to labor to demonstrate racial quality and racial equality is the field of individual achievement. And in the last analysis, races are judged by their great men. It may be said that great nations produce great men, but, with equal truth, great men make great nations. Glance through the pages of history. The history of any nation is embodied in the history of its great men. Every great movement, in government, in law, in literature, in art, in religion, had its inception in some one man's mind, and its fruition in others whom he inspired. Every great invention which has contributed to the comfort and happiness of mankind has owed its origin to a germ of thought in some one man's mind. Therefore, however cramped the field of community enterprise may seem to colored people, whatever one man can do, that some one Negro or man of Negro blood, can do, if it be in him, provided, of course, that he have a fair opportunity. And great men, to a large extent, make their own opportunities. To design a great invention, one needs, besides an idea, perhaps a laboratory or a machine shop. To write a great book, a pen and ink, or a typewriter and a quire of paper. To paint a great picture, a palette and a square of canvas. And, therefore, to my mind, it is in the field of individual, personal, intellectual effort that the greatest opportunity of the Negro for the immediate future lies. Of course, environment is a powerful factor of development, and while the environment of the Negro in the United States is not ideal, it is better than it has been; it has not prevented the rise of notable examples of intellectual and esthetic development; and it is destined to grow better as the years go by.

Now, I do not know how many of you, if any of you, are material for great authors, or painters, or physicians, or merchants, or inventors, but if there are any of you, it will be an encouragement to you in your upward struggle to whatever level—and I am going to assume that you will all rise in life, which you must do to prove yourselves worthy of your opportunities here—to have before you some examples of men of similar origin who have demonstrated of what the Negro, or at least men of Negro blood, are capable.

The history of our land and our own times shows a long list of colored men who have attained honorable distinction in the higher walks of life. You know of most of them—some of them have been and are connected with your own institution, and in Dr. Washington's history of the American Negro[11] and other similar works you will find them all mentioned, with a résumé of what they have accomplished.

But I am going to conclude my remarks by going somewhat into detail in the case of a colored family which for three generations shed the luster of intellect and achievement upon its own members, upon their nation and the two races from which their blood was drawn, one of which was the Negro race. It is true that they, and the one or two others that I shall mention in passing, lived their lives and won their fame in a country where race prejudice is at a minimum. The example of our men at home shows what the Negro is capable of under adverse circumstances; the lives of these others will show what the Negro can do in a fair field, with no favor, and what may be expected of him in this country when such a condition shall prevail.

If any of you should have the good fortune to visit at some time during your lives the beautiful city of Paris—many of you, I know, have already done so—I can suggest to you a little pilgrimage which will be a source of satisfaction. Perhaps your first visit, after looking the city over, will be to the Louvre Museum. There, in one of the larger rooms, you will find two great paintings, great in size, design and execution, from the brush of Guillaume Guillon Lethière. Lethière was of mixed blood, a native of Guadeloupe, at that time and now one of the French West Indies. During the generation preceding 1850, Lethière was one of the great historic painters of France. For some years he was President of the Académie des Beaux Arts of Rome, a society at Rome for French painters, and later he was for a number of years President of the Académie des Beaux Arts in Paris. He painted many canvases, which are in various collections throughout France. The two to which I have above referred, "The Death of Virginia" and "Lucius Junius Brutus Condemning His Sons to Death," depicting two well-known events with which those of you who are students of Roman history are no doubt familiar, are among the most striking and beautifully colored pictures in the Museum.[12]

Then, pursuing your study of art, you will cross the Seine to the Luxembourg Museum, and there, in the gallery of foreign modern painters, cheek by jowl with Whistler, Sargent and the other great contemporary painters of lands other than France, you will find a striking canvas by Mr. Henry Ossawa Tanner, the American painter with whose history and achievements you are all doubtless familiar,—his father is a bishop of your own church—and who received, it is but just to say, his early artistic training and encouragement in his native country.[13] In Paris, where, other things being equal, there is little prejudice against color, even among Americans sojourning there, Mr. Tanner has enjoyed the distinction of being secretary of the Society of American Artists, in that great center of art and literature.

Some fine morning, if you will take a cab, and, leaving the Place de la Concorde, drive out the Champs Elysées to the Arc de Triomphe, and then, turning to your right, follow one of the beautiful avenues which radiate from the Round Point like the spokes of a wheel, you will come in a few minutes to a beautiful square in one of the choice residence quarters of the city. The city of Paris has some characteristics which are more or less peculiar to itself. For instance, they honor their great men by naming streets and avenues and public squares after them. The same is true, of course, with other nations, but particularly so in France, and in Paris. If you will take any guide book or atlas of Paris you will find, for instance, such streets as the Avenue Montaigne, Molière Passage, Jules Sandeau Boulevard, Boulevard Haussmann, Rue Jean Jacques Rousseau, Rue

Balzac, Rue Molière. Some great men have two streets named after them; for instance, last summer my daughter and I were trying to find in Paris the residence of a friend of ours, an American residing in that city. We were looking for a street named Rue Henri Martin. By mistake we paid our first visit to the Avenue Henri Martin, and after some considerable difficulty got ourselves properly oriented, Henri Martin being one of the great French painters who was thus doubly honored. There is also a Victor Hugo Avenue and a Victor Hugo Place.[14]

This public square at which you have arrived as your first stopping place was formerly known as Place Malsherbes. When I was in Paris upon a former visit some years ago[15] this square contained a handsome bronze monument on a granite base, designed by Gustave Doré, a famous French artist,[16] in honor of Alexander Dumas, *père*, the elder Dumas, so called. On the summit of the monument is a seated figure of the great romancer, and on the front and back of the base are two marble sculptures in bas-relief, one representing the figure of a musketeer, suggesting Dumas' famous novel, *The Three Musketeers*, and the other a group composed of a young girl reading one of Dumas' romances to two workingmen.[17]

Upon a more recent visit to Paris[18] I found that to this monument had been added, at the other end of the square, a beautiful marble memorial of Alexander Dumas, *fils*, son of Alexander the great. It represented a life-size figure of Dumas the younger under a marble canopy. On either of the four sides of the monument was a list of the author's principal plays and writings.

On another side of this beautiful little square, which is adorned with trees and flowers, is the pedestal for a monument to a third member of this illustrious family, General Thomas Alexander Dumas, the first of the line.[19] The money has been raised and the monument is in course of construction and will undoubtedly rest upon the pedestal at an early date.

Recently the name of this square has been changed from the Place Malsherbes to that of the Place des Trois Dumas—the Square of the Three Dumas. It is unique in that it is the only public square in Paris named in honor of three distinguished members of one family in three different generations, as this family itself was unique in more ways than one.

Continuing this little pilgrimage, and pursuing your course a few more blocks to the right, you will find yourself in the beautiful Cemetery of Montmartre, situated at the top of a sunny hill in the northern part of the city. Here, beneath a beautiful monument representing a recumbent figure of the great playwright, by the sculptor St. Marceaux, lies all that is mortal of Dumas the younger,[20] surrounded by the tombs of many illustrious Frenchmen, among them the painters Paul Delaroche, Horace Vernet, Ary Scheffer, Greuze and Troyon; Heinrich Heine, the poet; Ludovic Halévy, Henry Murger and Théophile Gautier, novelists; Jules Simon, philosopher and statesman; Ernst Renan, author and critic; Hector Berlioz, composer; Emile Zola, novelist—a fit resting place and fit company for the remains of a great man.[21] The elder Dumas and his father, General Dumas, are buried at Villers-Cotterêts, the birthplace of Alexander the elder.

And now since I am on the subject, and since this is by all odds the most conspicuous family of colored men in the world's history, perhaps I might profitably spend a few minutes in reciting some of the achievements which entitle these gentlemen, in the judgment of their contemporaries and successors, to the signal honors thus bestowed upon them, and through them, by inference, upon the race with which, as you will see, they were by blood and temperament so strongly allied. These facts, in much the same words as I give them, are gathered from authorities that may be found in any good library.

In the year 1760, a certain French nobleman, a Count or Marquis Davy de la Pailleterie, went to reside on estates which he owned in Hayti, then a French colony. While there, there was born to him by a black mother, a full-blooded Haytian Negress,[22] a son who was given the name of Thomas Alexander. The elder Dumas claimed that his grandfather and grandmother were married, but the fact is doubtful and rather unlikely. At any rate, the Marquis, returning to France eighteen years later, took with him his colored son. When the Revolution broke out the young Dumas, fired with patriotic zeal, enlisted as a private under his mother's name, Dumas, feeling that his father would not like his aristocratic name borne by a soldier in the ranks. But promotion was rapid in those days of liberty, equality and fraternity, and three years later the young mulatto found himself General Dumas, in command of an army, under the Directory,[23] with Napoleon as General-in-Chief.

In personal appearance he was tall, broad-shouldered, very dark for a mulatto, with a fine, manly face and bearing; very strong, an expert in all physical exercises. He was ardent and generous in character, quick to resent an insult or injury and equally quick to forgive; a patriot, sincerely devoted to the Revolution, but detesting its cruelties. Indeed, his tender heart subjected him to danger at the hands of the bloody triumvirate, with Robespierre[24] at its head, who were slaughtering the French nobility and directing the destinies of France. But he was able to redeem himself in their eyes by many military exploits, the capture of Mont Cenis, for instance, and his heroic defense of the bridge of Clausen against the Austrians, by which he won the sobriquet, in accordance with the classical nomenclature of the day, of "The Horatius Cocles of the Tyrol."[25] But General Dumas was not in sympathy with Bonaparte's ambitions, and fell into disfavor with him, with the result that, after distinguishing himself in the campaign in Egypt, he quarreled with Bonaparte and resigned from the army. On his way home he was taken prisoner at Naples, and remained in captivity for two years, emerging fatally injured in health. He returned home to live with his wife on a modest retiring pension of eight hundred dollars a year. The couple had already had one child, a daughter, and about a year after the General's return, a son was born, Alexander Dumas the second. The General died in 1806, at the age of forty-four. He was the first, and essentially the most admirable in character, of the three men who have borne the name of Alexander Dumas, a simple, heroic figure, whose fortune was unequal to his merit, a man of single purpose and brave deeds.[26]

The son of this distinguished soldier and patriot, and the most famous of the line, was Alexander Dumas, the great romancer, who was born in 1802 and died in 1870. His mother, the General's wife, was a white woman, the daughter of a tavernkeeper and small landowner, which made the great Dumas technically, therefore, a quadroon, or three-fourths white and one-fourth Negro. He was born and reared at Villers-Cotterêts, his mother's home, a small town some forty or fifty miles from Paris. The General, who had been put on half pay by Napoleon, died when his son was four years old; and as the Emperor continued to behave as meanly to his widow and children, the first years of a most prodigal life were years of decent poverty and thrift. Dumas, though afterward an omnivorous reader, was not a model schoolboy, and the local teachers could make nothing of him; but he had the run of the great forest about his native hamlet, he became an expert woodman, he developed a magnificent constitution and a turn for letters, and when, at twenty or so, he went to Paris to seek his fortune, he was physically as fit for the struggle for existence as any of the strong and ardent generation to which he belonged. It may be interesting to note that at one time he was intended for the church, but, fortunately for literature, the plan was abandoned.

He secured employment, through the influence of one of his father's military friends, as a clerk in the bureau of the Duc d'Orléans (afterward King Louis-Philippe);[27] but his mind still ran on literature, and he spent some years in reading in trying to learn to write. He had only published a volume of short stories and collaborated in a couple of farces, when at seven-and-twenty he forced the door of the Théâtre Français, the classical State theater, with his first five-act play, *Henri III et Sa Cour* (1829), and at one stroke operated a revolution in the theory and practice of historical drama. In 1831 he did the same for domestic tragedy with *Antony*, perhaps the boldest, adroitest and completest achievement in plan, construction and effect in the literature of the modern theater; then after a failure with *Charles VII et Ses Grands Vassaux*, an excellent play in verse, he scored a tremendous success with *Richard Darlington*;[28] and in 1832 produced perhaps his greatest play, *La Tour de Nesle*. "He was, indeed," says one critic,

> the very genius of the stage. He broke ground with the ease, the assurance, the insight into essentials, and the technical accomplishment of a master, and he retained those qualities until his final breakdown, a year before his death. His dialogue is bright, appropriate, vivid, eminently constructive and explanatory; he never eludes or tampers with his situation, but faces his problem boldly, and wrings his interest from the clash of character and the presentation of emotion in action; his plots are

made and conducted with admirable adroitness and lucidity; his expositions are models of clarity; his effects are brought off with surprising certainty and vigor. "All I needed," he said of himself, "was"—not scenery, nor choruses of monks, nor Hernani's horn,[29] nor any merely decorative stuff of that sort—but "four trestles, four boards, two actors, and a passion"; and the vaunt was absolutely justified. Dumas is the soundest influence in drama of the century, and to his example is owing not a little of the best of the French dramatists who have followed him.[30]

In 1832, however, he fell ill of cholera, went to Switzerland to recuperate, and wrote for the *Revue des Deux Mondes* the first of his famous and delightful *Impressions de Voyage.*[31] He was fond of adventure and change; his capacity of producing agreeable and brilliant "copy" was amazing, and these traveler's notes of his—in which a good deal of history and romance is worked in with abounding vivacity and wit—were among the best liked of his many benefactions to the public. He kept them going almost to the end. A prodigious worker (he would write for weeks on end at the rate of sixteen or eighteen hours a day), he was wont, after months of production, to renew himself with a round of hundreds, or thousands, of miles, and he never failed to put the experience into print. From 1832 to 1865, during the whole of his wonderful career, his romances and plays were interspersed with books of travel.

But it was as a story-teller pure and simple that Dumas was destined to gain the better and larger part of his abounding and enduring success. And this is as good a place as any to say that many of his novels and plays were written in collaboration with others, for which he was at times criticised by jealous contemporaries. But it is none the less a fact that apart from him his assistants were mostly unreadable, while in conjunction with him they were Alexander Dumas—that is to say, perhaps the most popular among modern novelists, and assuredly one of the greatest masters of the art of narrative in all literature.

He has told us that from the first it was a purpose of his life to put the history of France into novels, and his earliest essay was in the field of historical romance, the *Isabelle de Bavière* of 1835. It was followed by several other novels along different lines until the historical vein cropped up anew in his *Le Chevalier d'Harmenthal*, published in 1842. During this period appeared the D'Artagnan series, beginning with the *Three Musketeers,*[32] whose principal characters, D'Artagnan, Athos, Porthos and Aramis, are household words among all lovers of romance. Dumas carried this interesting and attractive group through a long series of novels, of which the first, as is always true in such cases, was the best, but all of which were good. During this period also appeared *The Count of Monte-Cristo*, next to the *Three Musketeers* the most universally popular of Dumas' novels, with its long lists of sequels.[33] Also the Valois cycle, or the series of novels dealing with the Court of Francis II; his wife, Catherine de Médicis; the four Henris, Marguerite de Valois, afterward Queen of Navarre and of France.[34] It is safe to say that Dumas' conceptions of the character of the leading figures in the gay and corrupt court life of that period, honeycombed with political and religious and amorous intrigue, have become, in the popular mind, the historical conceptions.

Most of these novels were cut into plays, of which *Monte-Cristo* alone furnished four. The play of that name, produced in our own day by Mr. James O'Neill, is one of the most popular dramas on the stage, and well worth witnessing.[35] He wrote, in all, sixty-seven plays, thirty-eight of them in collaboration, besides collaborating in many others published under the names of other authors. In the Lévy collection at Paris there are published ninety-two novels, in one hundred and seventy-five volumes, from his pen, and there are several others not published by that house; of these twenty-seven were collaborated.[36] He published eighteen books of travel, and fourteen miscellaneous works. And a bibliography which I have examined notes one hundred and twenty-five books written in whole or in part about him, ten of which are well considered biographies, the others mainly critical of his works. No one man, unaided, could have done all the rough work of such an output, before the invention of phonography[37] and the typewriter, and the world ought to thank Dumas for employing secretaries to assist him in producing what might otherwise have been a much smaller contribution to the instruction and entertainment of mankind.

Nor was the enormous fund of energy possessed by this remarkable man exhausted in literary production. He took an active part in the days of July.[38] In 1837 he received the red ribbon of the Legion of Honor. He even found time to get married to an actress, Mlle. Ida Ferrier, from whom he promptly separated, for his was not a nature to be bound by ties of any sort. He spent two years in exile at Brussels, partly because of his political opinions, partly because of his debts, for, although he made large sums of money, he spent it even more freely; he could resist a dun, but could never refuse a borrower.[39] He was in Italy four years, during which he helped Garibaldi in the struggle for Italian liberty, and wrote a life of that Italian patriot. In 1868 he founded a magazine and produced the last but one of his plays.[40]

But by this time the end was near. He had lived freely, had produced prodigiously, and at the end of sixty-eight years he retired to his son's villa at Dieppe, where, after a few months of painless physical and mental decline, he simply faded away.

It is regrettable that the personal conduct of this great writer cannot be held up as an example to the young. In life he was much of a scapegrace and a madcap and even more of a prodigal. He earned and spent, says one of his biographers, three fortunes, and it is certain that his revenue from his works was greater than that of any author of his day. But it was the old story, too common among men of genius, of easy come, easy go. He knew it, and joked about it—it is to be hoped that he regretted it.

The story is told of him that at Dieppe, in his last days, he said one day to his son Alexander, while jingling two napoleons in his hand, "They claim, Alexander, that I am a spendthrift. I can prove the contrary. I started in life in Paris with two napoleons, and I still have them."

His morals were loose. His son Alexander was an illegitimate child, as was also a daughter who won some small repute in the literary world.[41] He was vain, which some of his critics ascribed to his color, as they did also his moral laxity, and I may say in passing that it is for the new generation of colored people to disprove this slander, or if there were truth in it, to demonstrate that vanity and prodigality are not persistent race traits. But, numerous as were his faults, his virtues were equally conspicuous. His humanity was boundless in degree and incorruptible in quality. He was generous to a fault—in fact, his prodigality was mostly misdirected generosity—and he was never known to strike a foul blow.[42] "I love and admire you," said his friend Michelet, "for you are a force of nature." "Fundamentally good," was George Sand's verdict, "but too often drunk with power."[43] The fact is that he was a prodigy of temperament and power and the capacity of life and invention and achievement. His principal happiness was in work; he could work sixteen or eighteen hours a day, and be fresh for the start next morning. He talked still better than he wrote; and he wrote without any affectations of style, and with an ease, a gusto, a sincerity of mind, a completeness of method that are irresistible. And the lesson of his greater books—of the Valois cycle, for instance, and the long sequence of the *Mousquetaires*—is one by which the world may well have profited. Love, honor, friendship, loyalty, valor, the old chivalric virtues—these were his darling themes; and he treated them with a combination of energy and insight, of good sense and good feeling, of manliness of mind and beauty of heart, that has ranked him with the great benefactors of humanity.[44] And we can easily afford to forgive him his weakness for the sake of what he accomplished and for the glory which his achievements reflect upon the race from which a part of his blood was drawn.

Alexander Dumas (born 1824), son of the preceding, was born in Paris when his father was but twenty-one years old. He was of illegitimate birth, but was soon legitimized, and at sixteen, after a thorough course of training in first-class educational institutions, he left school for the world of letters and the society to which his father, then almost at his apogee, belonged, the lively and loose theatrical world of Paris. He was essentially respectable, however, and having sown a certain quantity of wild oats, and made a few experiments in literature, he settled down to earnest work, and began to take life seriously. He started in fiction, and succeeded; he went on to drama, religion, even, and succeeded. He was made a member of the Institute in 1874, and was at the date of his death in 1895,[45] the acknowledged best playwright, and one of the greatest artists in words in latter-day France, the country of the world which is easily first in dramatic literature and historic art.

His novels—from *La Dame aux Camelias* (1848) to *L'Affaire Clémenceau* (1866)[46]—are all readable, and more often than not are worth reading. His essays, letters, speeches, prefaces and occasional writings generally are brilliant and admirable in form, and in matter daring, paradoxical, suggestive in a very high degree. Of his sixteen plays, there is scarce one that is not literature, while five or six of them are masterpieces of construction, characterization and writing. He also collaborated in other famous dramas. He was not so prolific a writer as his father, but he was more of a stylist, and his product is of perhaps a more uniform standard of excellence as writing than that of the elder Dumas. His method is logical to a fault, he builds as for all time, he is an artificer even in theory, and his paradoxes are developed with scientific exactness and precision. A bitter and dazzling wit; an intelligence of uncommon energy, daring and intensity; a morality that is so genuine as to be sometimes offensive; an incorruptible honesty; a style hard, polished, chaste, flexible as a perfect sword blade, and a dramatic gift as real as his father's—these are his qualities, and they have made him not only remarkable but distinguished.

Now, my young friends, I have selected this particular family to speak about for several reasons—primarily because of their blood, and the just pride which you may for that reason feel in their achievements. Their education, their surroundings, the influences which molded their lives, were those of another country and another generation or generations—they were a French soldier, a French novelist, a French dramatist, and while their work belongs to the flower of the literature of the most intellectual nation in the world, there is about it, especially that of the great Alexander, a verve, a fire, an animation, a swing, a naturalness which are so peculiarly characteristic as to be ascribable to the African strain,[47] which was thereby shown to be valuable to the world of intellect, and which gives those who share their blood the right to be proud of them, and to look forward to and struggle toward a time when this great nation, with its large strain of Negro blood, shall produce many great men of color, in literature, in art, in the drama, in all the walks of life, whose names shall be worthy to be enrolled with those of Pushkin and Lethière, and the three Dumas, and whose achievements shall reflect glory not only upon their race, but upon a nation which shall be as proud of them as France is of this famous family. And it will be your opportunity, with the privileges which you have enjoyed here, and your duty to contribute by the formation of right ideals for yourselves and their realization in your own individual lives to their realization for your race.

↜

SOURCE: "Race Ideals and Examples," *A.M.E. Review*, 30 (October 1913), 101–15, edited in light of an incomplete typed text for an "Annual Address Delivered before the Literary Societies at Wilberforce University." Although the program for this occasion identified Chesnutt's title as "Ideals and Their Realization," both the typescript for the speech delivered on 16 June 1913 and the published essay were entitled "Race Ideals and Examples." The only noteworthy difference between the essay and what remains of the speech will be seen in n. 9. At the close of the essay appeared this explanatory note: "This address was delivered before the literary societies of Wilberforce University, commencement week, June, 1913. As a writer of fiction, Mr. Chesnutt stands at the head of American colored men of letters. We take pleasure in giving to our readers his views and ideals for Negro Youth.—Editor." Not noted was the fact that Chesnutt was awarded an honorary LL.D. degree.

[1]William Sanders Scarborough (1852–1926), a classical languages and literature scholar and essayist on the "Negro Problem" whose publications Chesnutt was familiar with by 1890, became the President of Wilberforce University in 1908.

[2]Here and below Chesnutt sounds the "survival of the fittest" note more emphatically than in his earlier nonfiction writings. See "Competition." See also "Alexander Dumas," wherein Chesnutt employs the 1859 Darwinian equivalent of Spencer's term "survival of the fittest": the "struggle for existence."

[3]The African Methodist Episcopal (A.M.E.) Church.

[4]Hamlet, 3.1.70.

[5]1 Corinthians 13:13.

[6]Thomas H. Jackson (1844–1925) was, in 1870, a member of the first class to graduate at Wilberforce University, and his performance as a student in the Theology Department resulted in his appointment as an instructor. An A.M.E. minister, he served at numerous churches throughout the United States, was an administrator at Shorter University in Little Rock, Ark., and in 1912 became a faculty member of Wilberforce's Payne Theological Seminary.

[7]In 1913, the President was Presbyterian Woodrow Wilson; his Secretary of State was William Jennings Bryan, a biblical fundamentalist. The ex-President referred to is Theodore Roosevelt. In October 1912, editor George A. Newett of Ishpeming, Mich., stated editorially that Theodore Roosevelt was a habitual drinker given to blasphemy. In May 1913, Roosevelt successfully brought a libel suit against him.

[8]George Bernard Shaw (1856–1950), *Arms and the Man* (1907).

[9]The following eleven words, present in Chesnutt's speech typescript, did not appear in the published article, the unfortunate consequence being that the Wilberforce graduate imagined here concedes the inferiority of African Americans.

[10]By 1913, the political instability in Haiti was legendary because of repeated revolutions, and its national debt was extraordinarily large. France and Germany, to which countries Haiti was most indebted, exercised considerable influence there; the United States, although its investment was not so great, seemed on the verge of intruding into Haiti's internal affairs in 1913 and would do so with the landing of troops in 1915. Liberia as well had a history of corruption and financial mismanagement. Unable to manage its debt, it appealed to the United States for assistance, and President Taft appointed a commission to investigate the situation in 1909. It proposed that the United States provide funds and that it control Liberian finances to ensure that the situation was righted. Instead, an international receivership including France, Germany, and England was established.

[11]Chesnutt is referring to *The Story of the Negro*, 2 volumes (1909).

[12]Guillaume Guillon Lethière (1760–1832). The two paintings are dated 1812 and 1828, respectively.

[13]Tanner was an expatriate who initially received his training in drawing and painting in Philadelphia; his father was Bishop Benjamin Tucker Tanner. While Tanner was, indeed, a successful artist, James McNeill Whistler (1834–1903) and John Singer Sargent (1856–1925) were more prominent American painters, and thus Chesnutt's high estimate of his accomplishment.

[14]Michel de Montaigne (1533–92), philosopher and moralistic essayist; Molière, pseudonym of Jean-Baptiste Poquelin (1622–73), playwright; Jules Sandeau (1811–83), novelist; Georges Haussmann (1809–91), prefect of Paris who redesigned and modernized that city's infrastructure; Honoré de Balzac (1799–1850), novelist; Henri Martin (1810–83), painter; Victor-Marie Hugo (1802–85), novelist, playwright, and poet.

[15]Chesnutt first visited Europe during the summer of 1896.

[16]Paul Gustave Doré (1833–83), history painter, illustrator, and sculptor.

[17]The Doré monument features the musketeer d'Artagnan, one of the primary figures in *The Three Musketeers*, or *Les Trois Mousquetaires* (1844).

[18]Accompanied by his daughter Helen, Chesnutt vacationed in Europe in July–August 1912.

[19]Thomas Alexandre Dumas (1762–1806) was the father of Alexandre Dumas *père*, whose son was Alexandre Dumas *fils* (1824–95).

[20]Charles René de Saint-Marceaux (1845–1915); the "younger" is Alexandre Dumas *fils*.

[21]Hippolyte Paul Delaroche (1797–1856), history and portrait painter; Horace Vernet (1789–1863), history and genre painter; Ary Scheffer (1795–1858), history and portrait painter; Jean Baptiste Greuze (1725–1805), genre and portrait painter; Constant Troyon (1813–65), landscape and animal painter; Heinrich Heine (1797–1856); Ludovic Halévy (1834–1908); Louis-Henri Murger (1822–61); Théophile Gautier (1811–72); Jules Simon (1814–96); Joseph Ernst Renan (1823–90), author of philosophical works and historical studies of religion; Hector Berlioz (1803–69); Émile Zola (1840–1902).

[22]Antoine-Alexandre Davy (c. 1714–86); Louise-Cessette Dumas (?–1772).

[23]The Directory was made up of five executives who controlled the French government in 1795–99.

[24]Isidore Maximilien de Robespierre (1758–94) was a leader of the French Revolution and a promoter of the Reign of Terror whose veritable dictatorship ended with his overthrow and execution in July 1794.

[25]A hero of legendary proportions in Roman history because he singlehandedly repelled an invasion at a bridge leading into Rome, Publius Horatius Cocles was a favorite subject for historical painters and operatic composers; Chesnutt may have been familiar with the poetic treatment of his story by Macaulay in *Lays of Ancient Rome* (1842).

[26]Here and elsewhere in this text, and more extensively in the later speech entitled "Alexander Dumas," Chesnutt is relying upon Arthur F. Davidson, *Alexandre Dumas (père): His Life and Works* (1902).

[27]"Citizen King" Louis-Philippe (1773–1850) was the monarch from 1830 to 1848.

[28]Both *Charles VII* and *Richard Darlington* were produced in 1831.

[29]In Victor Hugo's tragic drama *Hernani* (1830), Count Hernani, about to marry the woman he loves, hears a horn sounded by his enemy, Don Ruy Gomez. He has sworn to take his own life when he hears that sound; and he honors his pledge by doing so.

[30]The critic quoted is William E. Henley (1849–1903), poet and essayist. A portion of Henley's eulogium appears in his collection of essays *Views and Reviews* (1890). The publication in which the whole appeared, however, has not been located. A biographer whom Chesnutt may have consulted, H. A. Spurr (?–1906), partially quotes the same text in *Life and Writings of Alexandre Dumas* (1902) and identifies the now-elusive source: an essay on Dumas written by Henley in 1868 for *Chambers' Encyclopædia*.

[31]*Impressions de Voyage: En Suisse* (volume 1, 1834; volume 2, 1835; volumes 3–5, 1837).

[32]D'Artagnan also appears in *Vingt Ans Après* (1845) and *Le Vicomte de Bragelonne* (1848–50).

[33]*Le Comte de Monte-Cristo* (1844–45). Dumas himself was not the author of sequels to this work.

[34]The Valois series includes *La Reine Margot* (1845), *La Dame de Monsoreau*

(1846), and *Les Quarante-Cinq* (1848). Catherine de Médicis (1519–89) and her husband, Henry II (1519–59), were the parents of ten children, including three kings of France—Francis II (1544–60), Charles IX (1550–74), and Henry III (1551–89)—and one queen, Marguerite de Valois (1553–1615). Marguerite married Henry of Navarre (1553–1610), later Henry IV of France, who was treated by Dumas in *Les Brands Hommes en Robe de Chambre* (1856); her affair with Henry of Lorraine (1550–88), Duc de Guise—a prominent leader of the Catholic party during France's internal religious conflicts of this time—accounted for her relationship with each of the "four Henris."

[35]In the early 1880's actor James O'Neill (1846–1920) adapted the 1868 dramatic treatment of *Monte-Cristo* produced by Charles Fechter (1824–79). Through the rest of his career he starred in this spectacularly successful play.

[36]By the turn of the century, a "complete edition" of Dumas' works had been developed under the imprints of Michel Lévy frères, C. Lévy, and Calmann-Lévy.

[37]That is, stenography.

[38]That is, Dumas participated in the Revolution of 1830, which resulted in the overthrow of the Bourbons by the Orléanists.

[39]Dumas married Ida Ferrier (?–1859) on 5 February 1840; on 15 October 1844, they separated; and in February 1848, she obtained a legal separation. Declared bankrupt in 1850, Dumas exiled himself to Belgium in 1851.

[40]Dumas began his stay in Italy in 1860; his collaboration with Giuseppe Garibaldi (1807–82), *Mémoires de Garibaldi*, was published the same year. Between February and July 1868, Dumas published a newspaper, *d'Artagnan*. The play produced was a dramatization of his novel *Madame de Chamblay (Ainsi soit-il!)* (1857–58).

[41]Marie-Alexandrine Dumas (1831–?) was the author of *Au Lit de Mort* (1867).

[42]Chesnutt again relies on William E. Henley's *Chambers' Encyclopædia* essay (see n. 30). Wrote Henley, "His morals were loose, he was vain as only a man of colour can be, . . . he could commit astonishing offenses in taste; but his humanity was boundless in degree and incorruptible in quality, he was generous to a fault, he is not known to have dealt a single foul blow."

[43]Jules Michelet (1798–1874), French historian; George Sand was the *nom de plume* of novelist Amadine Aurore Lucie Dupin (1804–76).

[44]Chesnutt quotes Henley regarding the lesson of Dumas' greater books, from a passage in *Views and Reviews* and possibly the *Chambers' Encyclopædia* essay on Dumas (see n. 30). Henley, however, described Dumas as one of the "benefactors of the race," and Chesnutt altered this to "of humanity."

[45]Emended is Chesnutt's citation of 1898 as the year of his death.

[46]Emended is Chesnutt's citation of 1867 as the year of publication.

[47]While Chesnutt earlier dismisses the notion, popular during his lifetime, that African Americans are characteristically vain, he here embraces another racist truism: that those with Negro racial traits are more imaginative, more emotional and emotive, and consequently more sensitive than Caucasians. Albion W. Tourgée, a white champion of the African American, reflected this assumption in an 8 December 1889 letter to Chesnutt: "I incline to think that the climacteric of American literature will be negroloid in character,—I do not mean in form—the dialect is a mere fleeting incident, but in style of thought, intensity of color, fervency of passion and grandeur of aspiration. Literature rather than politics, science or government, is the [medium] in which the American negro—not the African for there is really but little of the African left—will win his earliest perhaps his brightest laurels." Chesnutt, in his reply, characterized himself as the kind of imaginative artist described by Tourgée. See *Letters*, ed. McElrath and Leitz, 46.

Abraham Lincoln: An Appreciation

Speech to the Bethel Literary and Historical Association,
District of Columbia, 7 October 1913

Among the figures which stand out preeminently in American History, perhaps the first is that of Abraham Lincoln. George Washington carved his name in imperishable letters on the roll of fame, and in his own day and until the advent of Lincoln, was truly "First in war, first in peace, and first in the hearts of his countrymen," as Henry Lee[1] said in one of his famous orations. But today all loyal Americans, who love liberty and who love their country and its institutions, while giving to Washington priority in the matter of time, and while in no way underestimating his services to his country and to humanity, perhaps give, in their heart of hearts, a warmer place to Lincoln.

And this for many reasons, in part political, in part personal. From the standpoint of immediate results accomplished, Lincoln's was the larger enterprise, and its success had a wider bearing upon the course of future events. Washington was instrumental in securing political liberty for thirteen colonies, aggregating a population of about two million[2] white people. He rescued them from what they called tyranny, taxation without representation, and certain economic restrictions. A colony other than English would have considered itself well and benevolently governed under the English colonial rule. Their real basis for complaint was not active misrule, but the seemingly resistless desire on the part of men of the Teutonic type to manage their own affairs, and so far as possible the affairs of other people. The colony fought a foreign enemy, three thousand miles, equal today to ten times the distance, from their base of supply. Lincoln held together a union of thirty-six states, aggregating a population of thirty million[3] free white people, and by his wisdom and humanity increased that free population by three million. He sounded the death-knell of human slavery the world over. It was doomed perhaps anyway, in the natural forward movement of society, but it might have dragged its slimy length along for another generation or two, to the immeasurable loss of liberty, decency and self-respect on the part of the American nation.

Lincoln was not a military chieftain. He had served a few months as captain of a volunteer company in the Black Hawk war,[4] but had never been in a battle.[5] But as commander-in-chief of the American army and navy, he displayed a judgment, a skill, a knowledge of men and motives, a comprehension of strategical situations which put many of his generals to the blush. The selection of generals, the disposition of commands, the movements of armies, the distribution of rewards and punishments, in this, the most important field of military leadership, Lincoln was supreme.

A prominent characteristic of Mr. Lincoln was his courage. Washington had led a revolution with substantially the mass of the populace behind him. Of course

there was a Tory element consisting of a relatively small number of landed proprietors and office-holders and creatures of privilege, who stood by the established
order, as there is always in any revolution. But the great force of public opinion
was behind the movement. Lincoln, on the other hand, went into the contest with
substantially half of the nation in arms against him and, with the other half divided in opinion. He was cautious; he had to be, and it required a vast amount of
courage even to feel his way through the forest of difficulties which surrounded
him. Nor was it a war in which all the emotions were enlisted on one side. Patriotism is a facile emotion in a conflict with a foreign foe—"My country, right or
wrong,"[6] is too often the slogan for unrighteous conflict. Washington fought a
war with people from across the ocean. The Civil War was fought between people
of the same nation, of the same blood, often between people of the same families.
It required a high degree of moral courage to declare war against the rebellious
states, with a hundred Northern newspapers clamouring for peace at any price.
Great men, eminent leaders in thought and in government, were advising Mr. Lincoln on every hand to placate the South. But with the wisdom which saw his duty,
and the courage which nothing could dismay, he went forward and did his duty as
he saw it, to the ineffable glory of his name and of his nation.

The greatest achievement of Lincoln was the abolition of slavery. In the modern era of harmony and good feeling,[7] as the result of which no painting of a Civil
War battle is allowed in the National Capitol, this service of Lincoln for humanity
has been minimized and sometimes slurred. It was pitiable how little was said, in
the late Lincoln Centennial celebration, about Lincoln the Emancipator. Perhaps
this was inevitable, because to give emancipation its proper importance it would
be necessary to properly characterize slavery, and to do this would be, by implication, to criticize the slave-holder, and in our time this is not considered good taste.
So warm has become the *rapprochement* between North and South, that slavery is
almost regarded in some quarters as a beneficent patriarchal institution, which
Uncle Tom's Cabin grossly slandered,[8] and which, but for its influence on free labor, it might have been well to perpetuate indefinitely. It is conceivable that the
people of the United States might have been well governed if divided into two nations. An equal expanse of territory in Europe, with a proportional aggregate of
population, is divided into many nations and governments. The New England
abolitionists advocated, academically, the reformation of the North & South.
They preferred to live in a free country, if one only half as large; just as the seces-
sionists preferred a wholly slave country to one which was partly free. The white
people of the Confederacy, had it succeeded in establishing itself, would doubtless
have been governed to their own liking, which is always the best form of government, or at least the most satisfactory to the governed, and the slaves would have
been at least no worse off than they were before. But by suppressing the rebellion
Lincoln not only preserved the Union for all its white inhabitants, but admitted its
black inhabitants to the blessings of freedom and citizenship.

It is a common thing to hear it said that Lincoln freed the slaves purely as a war measure, to embarrass and cripple the enemy. And there were not wanting ardent abolitionists, Seward and Sumner and others, who found the President unduly cautious and fearful. But Lincoln was working toward a tremendous goal. We all know his feelings toward this twin relic of barbarism; how he himself related that having witnessed on one occasion a slave auction in New Orleans, he made up his mind that God helping him, if he ever had an opportunity he would scotch that snake.[9] We know how, in his earlier professional days he had defended runaway slaves and unfortunate Negroes who had got into difficulties from one cause or another. But he was president of the entire nation. He had sworn to support the Constitution and laws of the United States. The Constitution and laws of the United States recognized and had fostered slavery. Slavery and slavocracy had dominated the politics and statesmanship of the Union for a generation. The United States might almost be said to have rested on slavery, which Robert Toombs declares to be the cornerstone of the Confederacy.[10] Many of the slave-holders in the border states were loyal men who had supported and fought for the Union. Lincoln wanted to destroy slavery, he welcomed the military necessity which made it possible for him to do so; but he wanted to do it lawfully, and in a manner which would respect the rights of the loyal slave-holders and disarm criticism among the fair minded. Hence his preliminary proclamation, warning the seceding states of what they must expect unless they laid down their arms. But when the crucial moment came, Lincoln affixed his signature to the Emancipation Proclamation, the world held its breath for a moment, and then liberty-loving people all over the globe raised their voices in acclamation, while the Southern Confederacy, with its foundation stone removed, toppled to its fall. This demanded a high order of courage. For Charles Sumner or William H. Seward to have abolished slavery would have been by no means so great an act. Sumner was a New Englander, trained in traditions of liberty and human equality. Negroes had always been citizens in Massachusetts, had always had the right to vote, when properly qualified. Seward was also of Northern abolition blood and training. But Lincoln, it must be remembered was of Southern birth, born in Kentucky, reared in Southern Illinois, which was settled by Southerners and within the sweep of Southern sentiment and Southern prejudice. It is something like a Northern and a Southern white man eating at the same table with a Negro. To one it is a simple matter, other things being equal he would have no objection to dining at the same board with any man, if he were clean, well dressed and well behaved. To the other it is a tremendous thing, almost like a convulsion of nature, so tremendous an event that when a president of the United States invited a distinguished mulatto to lunch with him, it seemed as though it might almost precipitate a second rebellion.[11] Not that Lincoln shared this feeling, but if he had at any time, he undoubtedly felt that freedom carried with it certain privileges, for, after the emancipation, as Frederick Douglass relates in his *Life and Times*, Lincoln invited that distinguished orator to dinner on one occasion, and Mr. Douglass, as he also said, never ceased to regret that he permitted a previous speaking engagement to deprive him of that pleasure and that wonderful opportunity.[12] But for a man of Lincoln's antecedents, the Emancipation Proclamation was a tremendous achievement.

But apart from what he accomplished for the nation and for humanity, I think the world loves Lincoln best for his personality. Not that he was particularly pleasing to look at; he was tall, ungainly, homely in his appearance, especially in the hideous garb which gentlemen wore in the sixties. But in the lines of his rugged countenance may be read the index of a great soul, a soul attuned to the love of humanity in whatever form.

He loved the poor man, for he himself had been born and brought up for many years as that despised creature, in the Southern states a poor white man. His family was quite obscure, and his enemies even claimed that his birth was irregular, but this is historically disproved . . . .

⁓

SOURCE: Incomplete typed text at the Fisk University Library. Chesnutt delivered this speech on 7 October 1913 at the Bethel Literary and Historical Association in Washington, D.C.

[1]Colonel Henry Lee (1756–1818), father of Robert E. Lee, said in his eulogy on Washington, 26 December 1799, "To the memory of the Man, first in war, first in peace, first in the hearts of his countrymen." In the typescript Chesnutt did not supply Lee's name; instead, he left a blank space between "as" and "said."

[2]Chesnutt left a blank space between "about" and "million."

[3]Chesnutt left a blank space between "of" and "million."

[4]During this 1831–32 conflict with the Sauk and Fox tribes in Illinois and Wisconsin, Lincoln was elected captain of a volunteer company organized at Richland, Ill., and attached to the Fourth Illinois Mounted Volunteer regiment. His tenure as captain lasted only a month, from 21 April through 27 May 1832; he was then enlisted as a private in the Independent Spy Battalion and served until 16 June 1832.

[5]Chesnutt does not allude to the outcome of the military action: the massacre of the famished warriors, as well as the women and children with them, in the summer of 1832.

[6]Chesnutt is modifying a toast made by Steven Decatur (1779–1820) at a dinner in his honor in Norfolk, Va., April 1816.

[7]Chesnutt thus recalls the earlier "Era of Good Feeling" that began in 1817 with the manifestation of a spirit of cooperation among the rival political parties and lasted through the mid-1820's.

[8]Published in book form in 1852.

[9]The incident referred to here is described in volume 1 of *Abraham Lincoln: A History* (1886) by John T. Nicolay and John Hay (1838–1905).

[10]Robert A. Toombs (1810–85), a Georgia-born member of the U.S. House of Representatives and the Senate, plantation owner, and Secretary of State for the Confederacy, was an ardent secessionist and, after the Civil War, an opponent of the enfranchisement of African Americans.

[11]Reference to Booker T. Washington's visit to the White House in 1901.

[12]Frederick Douglass, in chapter 12 of his *Life and Times of Frederick Douglass* (1881), relates that he had to decline the invitation "to take tea with him at the Soldiers' Home" in the District of Columbia.

Alexander Dumas

Speech to the Rowfant Club, Cleveland, O., 11 April 1914

One of the most conspicuous and famous names in France during the last century (preceding the death of the last male of the family in 1895), was that of Dumas—I might say the name of Alexander Dumas, for the same name was borne by three successive generations. If you have ever noted, on the shelves of a well stocked library, the long rows of French novels and plays signed by the name "Alexandre Dumas"; if, when a young man, you have sat up all night to finish *The Count of Monte-Cristo*; if you have followed the prodigious adventures of D'Artagnan and his three friends, Athos, Porthos, and Aramis, and have read your *Three Musketeers* every two or three years since. If you have laughed with Chicot the Jester; if you have followed with breathless interest the machinations of Catherine de Medici, and shuddered at the horrors of St. Bartholomew's Eve; if you have ever wiped away a furtive tear over the woes of Camille as interpreted by Sarah Bernhardt; then perhaps, when you visit Paris, you may like to learn in what esteem the memory of the gifted men who created these characters, is held in the city where they lived and wrote and died, and how their life and work is commemorated.[1] And if with this object in view, on some fine summer morning, you will take a taxi, or better, a *fiacre* or horse-cab, which gives you time to look about as you ride, and, leaving the Place de la Concorde, drive out the Champs Elysées to the Arc de Triomphe, and then, turning to your right, follow one of the beautiful avenues which radiate from the Round Point like the spokes of a wheel, you will come, in a few minutes, to a beautiful square in one of the choice residence quarters of the city. This square, which was formerly known as the Place Malsherbes, contains at one end a handsome bronze monument, on a granite base, designed by Gustave Doré, the famous French artist, in honor of Alexander Dumas, *père*, the elder Dumas. It represents the sturdy figure of the great romancer, seated at the summit of the monument, and on the front and back respectively of the base are two bronze groups, one representing a musketeer, suggesting Dumas' famous novel *The Three Musketeers*, and the other a young girl reading one of Dumas' romances to two working-men.

At the other end of the square stands a beautiful marble memorial of Alexander Dumas, *fils*, the son of Alexander the Great, as his friends liked to call him. It represents a life-size figure of Dumas the younger under a marble canopy. On each of the four sides of the monument is a list of the author's principal plays and writings.

On another side of this beautiful little square, which is adorned with trees and flower-beds, when I saw it some years ago, was the pedestal for a monument to a third member of this illustrious family, General Thomas Alexander Dumas, the first of the line. The money had been raised and the statue was in course of construction and would undoubtedly rest upon the pedestal at an early date.

Recently the name of this square has been changed from the Place Malsherbes to that of the Place des Trois Dumas—the Square of the Three Dumas. It is the only public square in Paris named in honor of three generations of one family— indeed it is rarely that three generations of any one family anywhere are deemed worthy of public honors.

Continuing this little journey, and pursuing your course a few more blocks to the right, you will find yourself in the beautiful cemetery of Montmartre, situated at the top of a sunny hill in the northern part of the city. Here beneath a beautiful monument, by the sculptor St. Marceaux, representing a recumbent figure (under a canopy) of the great playwright, lies all that was mortal of Alexander Dumas the younger, the third and last of the name, surrounded by the tombs of many illustrious Frenchmen (among them the painters Paul Delaroche, Horace Vernet, Ary Scheffer, Greuze and Troyon; Heinrich Heine, the poet; Jacques François Halévy, the composer; Henri Murger, Théophile Gautier and Emile Zola, novelists; Jules Simon, philosopher and statesman; Ernst Renan, author and critic who has been honored by the Rowfant Club in the incorporation of his Caliban into our magnum opus;[2] Hector Berlioz, composer—a fit resting-place and fit company for the remains of a great man. The elder Dumas and his father General Dumas are buried at Villers-Cotterêts, the birthplace of Alexander the elder.

If some day you visit the Théâtre Français, the temple of classic French drama, and ascend to the foyer, the Hall of Fame of French dramatists, over which sits enthroned the marble effigy of Voltaire, surrounded by those of Racine, Molière, Corneille,[3] and the others, a glorious galaxy, you will find among the moderns, on the newel-post at the foot of the staircase ascending to the foyer, the bust of Alexander Dumas *père*, and at the turn of the stair on the way up, the bust of his only less famous son. And there are numerous busts and portraits of the two Alexanders in the portrait and sculpture galleries of Paris.

In the Hugo Museum, in the Place des Vosges, which is in the quarter called the Marais, the scene of many of Dumas' novels, there are many mementoes of Dumas—numerous portraits, and "the pen," he says, in an inscription to Hugo, "with which my last fifteen or twenty works were written"—a characteristic note, reminding one of a reply made by our esteemed fellow townsman, who resides in New York, when asked, in a congressional investigation some years ago, how much he had paid for a certain railroad. He replied, "Well, really, I don't remember whether it was five million dollars or ten million."[4]

If the traveler is not informed and should have any curiosity to know what manner of men these were, and what were their achievements which were held, in this greatest literary and artistic capital of the world, to entitle them to these honors, and will look up the record of their lives, for which there is material in abundance, he will find the facts about as follows:

In the year 1760 a certain French nobleman, a Count or Marquis Davy de la

Pailleterie, went to reside on estates which he owned in Hayti, then a French colony. While there, there was born to him by a black mother, a full-blood Haytian
Negress, Louise-Cessette Dumas, a son, who was given the name of Thomas Alexander. Dumas *père* claimed that his grandfather and grandmother were married, but the fact is doubtful and rather unlikely. She died in 1772. In 1780 the
Marquis returned to France, and took with him his colored son, then eighteen
years of age. The young man was recognized as the son of the family, and lived for
several years the life of a young gentleman about town. At the age of sixty-four the
old Marquis, whose tastes in matrimony seem to have been somewhat bizarre,
married his housekeeper. The son did not approve of this step and quarreled with
his father, and enlisted in the 6th regiment of the army, the Queen's Dragoons,
and, to sever all ties with his father, he enlisted under his mother's name of Dumas,
which, however, he would not have been likely to do had he been legally entitled
to the title of Marquis. When the revolution broke out, we find the young Dumas,
fired with patriotic zeal, in the Republican ranks. But he was a good soldier, with
brains and ambition. Promotion was rapid in those first days of liberty, equality
and fraternity. He distinguished himself by his gallantry and good sense, and three
years later the young mulatto found himself General Dumas, in command of a division under the Directory, with Napoleon as General-in-Chief.

In personal appearance he was tall, broad-shouldered, very dark for a mulatto,
with a fine, manly face and bearing. He was very strong, and expert in all physical
exercises. His son Alexander devotes a large part of the first of the eight volumes of
Mes Mémoires[5] to his father, and relates many anecdotes concerning him. Among
other things, he says that at the riding school his father could throw his arms over
an overhanging beam, clasp his long legs—he was over six feet—beneath his
horse's belly, and lift the animal from the ground. Another story, which seems
even more improbable, is that he could stick a musket on each of four fingers, and
hold the whole four out horizontally.

He was ardent and generous in character, quick to resent an insult or injury,
and equally quick to forgive. It is said that on one occasion he was a guest in the
box of a certain fine lady at the theater. A gentleman came in, spoke to her, ignoring Dumas' presence, to which the lady called his attention. "Pardon, madame,"
he said, "I did not know he was a friend of yours, I took him for your lackey."
Whereupon Dumas seized this insolent individual by his collar and his belt, and
threw him over the railing into the parquet. He was an ardent patriot, sincerely
devoted to the Revolution, but detesting its cruelties. Indeed his tender heart subjected him to danger at the hands of the bloody triumvirate, with Robespierre at its
head, who were slaughtering the French nobility and directing the destinies of
France. But he was able to redeem himself in their eyes, by many brilliant military
exploits, the capture of Mont Cenis for instance, and his heroic defense of the
bridge of Clausen against the Austrians, by which he won the sobriquet, in accordance with the classical nomenclature of the day, of "The Horatius Cocles of the
Tyrol." But General Dumas, a sincere Republican, and no time-server, was not in

sympathy with Bonaparte's ambitions, told him one day what he thought of him, and fell into disfavor with him, with the result that after distinguishing himself in the campaign in Egypt, he quarreled with Bonaparte and resigned from the army. On his way home he was taken prisoner by the Bourbon government at Naples, and remained in captivity for two years, emerging fatally injured in health. He returned home to live with his wife on a modest retiring pension of eight hundred dollars a year. The couple had already had one child, a daughter, and about a year after the General's return a son was born, Alexander Dumas, the second, and greatest of the name. The General died in 1806, at the age of forty-four. He was the first, and essentially the most admirable in character of the three men who have borne the name of Alexander Dumas, a simple, heroic figure, whose fortune was unequal to his merit, a man of single purpose and brave deeds.

The son of this distinguished soldier and patriot, and the most famous of the line, was Alexander Dumas, *père*, the great romancer, who was born in 1802. The decade was prolific of great men. Victor Hugo was born in the same year. In 1809 came Tennyson and Gladstone;[6] in 1811 Thackeray and in 1812 Browning and Dickens. Dumas' mother, the General's wife, was Marie-Louise-Elizabeth Labouret, the daughter of a tavern-keeper and a small landowner.[7] She was a white woman, which made the great Dumas technically, therefore, a quadroon, or one-fourth Negro and three-fourths white. Rossetti called him "the immortal quadroon."[8] He was born and reared at Villers-Cotterêts, his mother's home, a small town some forty or fifty miles from Paris. The General, who had been put on half-pay by Napoleon, died when his son was four years old, leaving a very small estate; and as the Emperor continued to behave as meanly to his widow and children as he had to the father, the first years of a most prodigal life were years of decent poverty and thrift. Dumas, though afterwards an omnivorous reader, was not a model schoolboy, and the local teachers could make nothing of him; but he had the run of the great forest about his native hamlet, he became an expert woodman, he developed a magnificent constitution, and a turn for letters, and when, at twenty or so, he went to Paris to seek his fortune, he was physically as fit for the struggle for existence as any of the strong and ardent generation to which he belonged. It may be interesting to note that at one time he was intended for the church, but fortunately for literature and for the Church, the plan was abandoned. It would strain the mind to think of Alexander Dumas in a cassock. Instead, he entered a notary's office, where he studied law and acted as clerk for a while. But feeling the call of Paris, he left the office during the temporary absence of his employer, and flew off, with a companion, to Paris, where he visited the theater, saw Talma play, and was taken behind the scenes to meet him.[9] Upon his return he found that his master had anticipated his return. He took his clerk mildly to task, but Dumas, elated perhaps by his visit, chose to take offense, resigned his position and betook himself to Paris to seek his fortune. He called on various friends of his father, to solicit their interest in his search for employment. Some received him coldly, others were indifferent. Last of all he visited General Foy, an old comrade-at-arms of his father.[10] The general received him cordially, expressed his willingness to help him, and asked what he could do. It was the old story of the untrained man, and the interview reached the hopeless stage where the general asked him to leave his name and address, and if anything should turn up he would let him know. Fortunately the general overlooked Dumas as he wrote his name, and observed that he wrote a beautiful hand. He immediately recommended him for a clerkship in the bureau of the Duc d'Orléans, afterwards King Louis-Philippe. Here he earned his $250.00 a year. His mother came to Paris, and with such means as she possessed, they were able to conduct a modest menage in a modest quarter. But his mind ran on literature, and he spent some years in reading and in trying to learn to write. He read Shakespeare and cultivated the acquaintance of actors and playwrights. He tells, in his *Mémoires*, how he first met Charles Nodier, whom this Club has honored by the publication of his "The Bibliomaniac" in Mr. Ginn's excellent translation.[11] During the few days which elapsed between the receipt of his appointment and the beginning of his duties, Dumas, to pass the time, went one evening to the Porte Saint Martin Theatre, which was then performing a drama called *The Vampire*.[12] After some trouble in securing a seat, he found himself in the parquet, seated beside a middle-aged gentleman of benign aspect, engrossed in the study of a dainty little volume, which upon inspection proved to be an Elzevir, *Le Patissier François*.[13] Attracted by the title and its suggestion of delicate cooking, Dumas, who among his other accomplishments in later years boasted of his cooking, and was a gourmet of the first water—he said he could make sixty-seven sauces—ten varieties more than Heinz[14]—ventured to put a question. A conversation followed, beginning with eggs and the various methods of serving them, diverging into Elzevirs, bibliomaniacs, and vampires. The play was a melodrama of a pronounced type, full of mystery and horrors, a veritable thriller, which Dumas, with the catholic taste of a young man, thought very fine. His neighbor, however, indulged in strong expressions of disapproval, and in the third act left his seat, declaring that he could endure it no longer. A little later in the play a loud hiss came from behind the curtain of a private box, and Dumas, standing up with others to see who the disturber was, perceived his former companion, who had sought a new vantage ground from which to make his criticism more effective. The offender was promptly ejected from the theater. The newspapers next day, reporting the incident, mentioned that the ejected person was the well-known Charles Nodier, himself believed to be one of the anonymous authors of the piece, who had selected this unique method of criticising either his own work or that of his collaborators, more likely his own, for Nodier was as eccentric as he was erudite. He was the earliest pioneer of romanticism, of which Dumas was soon to become the chief exponent, and this community of taste no doubt formed the basis of the warm friendship which grew out of this chance meeting. A few years later, when Dumas had finished his *Christine*,[15] he applied to Nodier for assistance in securing a reading before the Committee of the Théâtre Français, recalling his attention to their meeting at the theater, and secured the reading, after much trouble. The play was accepted, but not produced until after the success of *Henri III et sa Cour*. A little later he became an intimate of Nodier's house, and at the "Arsenal," over the library of which Nodier was custodian, spent many pleasant evenings,[16] where he met the group of brilliant men whose friendship he enjoyed in varying degree—Lamartine, Hugo, the high priest of the Romantic movement, De Vigny, the author of *Cinq-Mars*, De Musset, Sainte-Beuve, author of *Causeries du Lundi*, Alphonse Karr, Theophile Gautier,[17] and other well known men of the day, some since well-nigh forgotten.

Dumas made several literary ventures, but he had only published a small volume of short stories, of which he assumed part of the expense, and of which he says four copies were sold; and he had collaborated in a couple of farces, when at seven-and-twenty he forced the door of the Théâtre Français, the classical State theater, with his first five-act play, *Henri Trois et sa Cour* (1829), and at one stroke operated a revolution in the theory and practice of historical drama.[18] In 1831 he did the same for domestic tragedy with *Antony*, perhaps the boldest, most adroit and completest achievement in plan, construction and effect in the literature of the modern theater.

Antony was performed for the first time at the Porte Saint Martin theatre in 1831. From start to finish everything went with a rush; the spectators literally had no time to collect their thoughts, for before the effect of one sensational curtain had worn off the next act was begun, and the growing excitement culminated in a kind of frenzy at the celebrated denouement when Adele's husband breaks in the door and, seeing his wife dead (she slays herself), turns to Antony, standing there with his bloody poniard in his hand, and demands an explanation, who says, coldly and firmly, "*Elle me résistait, je l'ai assassinée!*"[19]

The success of the play was greater than he or any of his friends (except De Vigny) had anticipated. It ran for 130 nights during a time of political disturbance which damaged the interests of all the theaters.

There are many anecdotes about *Antony*. On one occasion the stage manager rang the curtain down on the stab which killed Adele, before Antony had made his famous speech. Since the speech was the milk in the cocoanut, the audience, feeling itself defrauded, demanded that the curtain go up, and it did. But Bocage, who played Antony, was angry, and refused to go on. The clamor increased, and it looked as though there might be a riot, like those Mr. Vickery[20] told us about when Shakespeare was presented for the first time at the same theater some years earlier, when finally Mme. Dorval, who was playing Adele, had a happy inspiration.[21] Rising from her corpse-like posture, she advanced to the footlights and amid complete silence said, "Gentlemen, I resisted him, he assassinated me!" This happy variant delighted the audience, which dispersed in high good humor. We are accustomed to seeing the dead come before the curtain—I have seen Little Eva in a Tour show do a clog-dance between the acts after having gone to heaven in a golden chariot[22]—but to have the same thing happen in the play was a novelty which pleased the fickle Parisians. There is no record, however, that this rendering was ever repeated.

The denouement of *Antony* has been coveted by all actors who have had a chance of playing the part. One actor, however, a certain first young man of the provinces, thought he could improve upon it. This Don Juan of the footlights, proud of his fascinations, could not lose himself in the part and bring himself to pretend that a woman had resisted him; and he contended that the statement was untrue, because Adele had not resisted Antony. In vain did his friends point out to him that in speaking the words he was merely satisfying the requirements of the author and the drama. He was not to be convinced, and when it is borne in mind that Antony killed Adele to save her reputation the feelings of the audience may be imagined when the long expected speech was delivered with this remarkable emendation: "*Elle me résistait—cette-fois—et je l'ai assassinée!*"[23]

The play gave rise to an immense amount of discussion as to its moral and social significance. And while the universal verdict was that it was a masterpiece of construction, its moral influence was not considered healthy, and the troubles of Adele, her despair, dishonor, death, prefigure the invasion of the woman element in the flood of problem plays which have followed it, where the problem is the same old problem—how to eat your cake and have it at the same time.[24] There was this difference between *Antony* and *Henry III*: Dumas did not follow up the passionate adultery motive in his novels, while *Henry III* sounds the note which runs through the entire Valois cycle of his romances.[25]

Following *Antony*, after a failure with *Charles VII Chez Ses Grands Vassaux*—an excellent play in verse—he scored a tremendous success with *Richard Darlington*, and in 1832 produced his greatest play, *La Tour de Nesle*. "He was indeed," says a critic,

> the very genius of the stage. He broke ground with the ease, the assurance, the insight into essentials, and the technical accomplishment of a master, and he retained these qualities until his final breakdown a year before his death. His dialogue is bright, appropriate, vivid, eminently constructive and explanatory; he never eludes or tampers with his situation, but faces his problem boldly, and wrings his interest from the clash of character and the presentation of emotion in action; his plots are made and conducted with admirable adroitness and lucidity; his expositions are models of clarity; his effects are brought off with surprising certainty and vigor. "All I needed," he said of himself, "was—not scenery, nor choruses of monks, nor Hernani's horn, nor any merely decorative stuff of that sort—but four trestles, four boards, two actors, and a passion"; and the vaunt was absolutely justified. Dumas is the soundest influence in the drama of the century, and to his example is owing not a little of the best of the French dramatists who have followed him.

In 1832, however, he fell ill of cholera, went to Switzerland to recuperate, and wrote for the *Revue des Deux Mondes* the first of his famous and delightful *Impressions de Voyage*. He was fond of adventure and change; his capacity of producing agreeable and brilliant "copy" was amazing; and these traveller's notes of his—in which a good deal of history and romance is worked in with abounding vivacity and wit—were among the best liked of his many benefactions to the public. He kept them going almost to the end. A prodigious worker (he would write for weeks on end, at the rate of sixteen or eighteen hours a day), he was wont, after months of production, to renew himself with a round of hundreds, or thousands, of miles of travel; and he never failed to put the experience into print. From 1832 to 1865, during the whole of his wonderful career, his romances and plays were interspersed with books of travel.

But it was as a story-teller pure and simple that Dumas was destined to gain the better and larger part of his abounding and enduring success. And this is as good a place as any to say that many of his novels and plays were written in collaboration with others, for which he was at times harshly, even venomously criticised by jealous contemporaries. But it is none the less a fact that apart from him his assistants were mostly unreadable, while in conjunction with him they were Alexander Dumas—that is to say, perhaps the most popular among modern novelists, and assuredly one of the greatest masters of the art of narrative in all literature. Like Shakespeare, Dumas took whatever he would from whomsoever he could get it. The thing being carefully devised in consultation, the collaborator of the period was told to prepare a first draft; and then Dumas rewrote the result—minting it in his own die, and informing it with his own immense and radiant personality. In this respect he was, in literature, the counterpart of Peter Paul Rubens in painting, whose miles of canvases scattered through the galleries of Europe, were in large part executed by his pupils, being first laid out and afterwards retouched by the master, the result being none the less Rubens.[26] Dumas employed, from time to time, a number of these collaborators, one of the best of whom was Maquet, who assisted him with the D'Artagnan series and the Valois cycle, and Paul Meurice, who died not many years ago at an advanced age.[27] They were undoubtedly of great service to Dumas in working up the vast mass of historical and other detail employed in his novels. They were well paid, and any claims made for them in derogation to Dumas were made by others. Of course every successful man is apt to have his detractors, and Dumas was vulnerable at many points. Doubtless the following story, though a good one, had its inception in malice. Meurice, according to the story, was the author of *Les Deux Dianes*, one of Dumas' most amusing novels.[28] Dumas when traveling found this novel in a hotel, and opened it to pass away the time. He began reading it seriously, got interested in it, and was amused. Presently some one came to his room and found him with *Les Deux Dianes* in his hand.

"I am reading," said Dumas, in response to a question, "a novel of my own which I did not know, and which pleases me vastly."

Another story of the same sort, of which there are many, relates a conversation between Dumas and his son Alexander. They met one morning, and Dumas *père* said, "Good Morning, Alexander, have you read my latest novel?" "No, father." "Well, neither have I," replied the father.

He has told us that from the first it was a purpose of his life to put the history of France into novels; and his earliest essay was in the field of historical romance, the *Isabelle de Bavière* of 1836. It was followed by several other novels along different lines until the historical vein cropped up anew in *Le Chevalier d'Harmental* published in 1843, one of the very best of his novels. During this period appeared the D'Artagnan series, beginning with *The Three Musketeers*, whose principal characters, the shrewd and resourceful Gascon, D'Artagnan, the melancholy Athos, the subtle dandy Aramis, and the boastful and simple Porthos, are household words among all lovers of romance. No less well known are their four lackeys— Planchet, Mousketon, Grimaud and Bazin, whose characteristics are in each instance perfectly adapted to those of their respective masters. The same is true of their women—the terrible Milady, the wife of Athos, upon whom in the end, the fearful punishment of her crimes is extra-judicially inflicted; the mysterious duchess of Aramis, of whom we see for a long time only a handkerchief or perhaps a scented note; Porthos's mistress, the notary's wife, who buys his outfit as a musketeer; the gentle Madame Bonancieux, who inspires D'Artagnan to his first great adventure, the return of the Queen's diamond studs.

Dumas carried this interesting and attractive group through a long series of novels, of which the first, as is always true in such cases, was the best, but all of which were good. During this period also appeared *The Count of Monte-Cristo*, next to *The Three Musketeers* the most universally popular of Dumas' novels, with its long list of less popular sequels. Also the series of novels dealing with the Court of Francis II., his wife Catherine de Medici, the four Henris, Marguerite de Valois, afterwards Queen of Navarre and of France, and the lively author of that lively work the *Heptameron*.[29] It is safe to say that Dumas' conceptions of the leading figures in the gay and corrupt court life of that period, honeycombed with political and religious intrigue, have become, in the popular mind, the historical conceptions, and in the main, he seems to have followed history.

Most of these novels were cut into plays, of which *Monte-Cristo* alone furnished four. The version produced in our own day by Mr. James O'Neill, is one of the most popular dramas on the stage, and well worth witnessing. He wrote, in all, sixty-seven plays, thirty-eight of them in collaboration, besides collaborating in many others published under the names of other authors. In the Lévy collection at Paris there are published ninety-two novels from his pen, in one hundred and seventy-five volumes,—they appeared originally in many more volumes—and there are several others not published by that house. Of these twenty-seven were collaborated. He published eighteen books of travel, and fourteen miscellaneous works. And a bibliography which I have examined notes one hundred and twenty-five books written in whole or in part about him, ten of which are well considered biographies, the others mainly critical of his works. (No particularly good one in English.) His own *Mémoires* were published in eight volumes. No one man, unaided, could have done all the rough work of such an output, before the invention of phonography and the typewriter, and the world ought to thank Dumas for em-

ploying collaborators and secretaries to assist him in producing what might otherwise have been a much smaller contribution to the instruction and entertainment of mankind.

Nor was the enormous fund of energy possessed by this remarkable man ex-
hausted in literary production. He took an active part in the Days of July, in the
Revolution of 1830, which resulted in the overthrow of the government of Charles
X.[30] and the establishment of that of his cousin, the Duc d'Orleans, as King Louis
Philippe. On one occasion, after a certain street disturbance attending the funeral
of General Lamarque, where Dumas, as a lieutenant of the National Guard, was
in charge of the cavalry escort, a Legitimist newspaper announced—Dumas was a
Republican—that "M. Alexandre Dumas had been taken in the street fighting,
tried by court martial, and shot at 3 A.M.[31] We deeply deplore the untimely death
of a young and talented author." On which Dumas says: "The details were so circumstantial that I doubted my own existence, and I felt myself to see if I were
really there. I was convinced that the editor believed in my death, as it was the first
time his paper had found anything good to say of me. So I forwarded him my card
with best thanks."

This report brought a characteristic note from his friend Charles Nodier:—

Dear Alexandre,—I read in the paper that you were shot on June 6th. Be good
enough to let me know if this will prevent you from dining here tomorrow with our
usual friends. P.S. I shall be delighted to have the opportunity of asking you for
news of the other world.

Dumas' comment on this report recalls Mark Twain's famous telegram upon a
similar occasion: "Report of my death greatly exaggerated."[32]

In 1837 Dumas received the red ribbon of the Legion of Honor. He never
made the Academy. He was several times a candidate, and while his genius and
services to literature were recognized as qualifying him, his improvidence and unsettled life were too much for the conservatism of the Academy. His son, who as
we shall see, was of a very different temperament, easily succeeded here where his
more famous father had failed. The great Dumas even found time to get married to
an actress, Mlle. Ida Ferrier, from whom he promptly separated, for his was not a
nature to be bound by ties of any sort. He spent two years in exile at Brussels,
partly because of his political opinions, partly because of his debts, for, although
he made large sums of money, he spent it even more freely; he could resist a dun,
but could never refuse a borrower. Any hard luck story was successful with Dumas. He was in Italy four years, during which he helped Garibaldi in the struggle
for Italian liberty, and wrote a life of that Italian patriot. In 1868 he founded a
magazine and produced the last but one of his plays. Like Scott and Dickens, he
built himself a house, in the environs of Paris, which he called Monte-Cristo,
where he kept open house for actors and actresses and artists and people of letters
and stray dogs.

But by this time the end was near. He had lived freely, had produced prodigiously, and at the end of sixty-eight years he retired to his son's villa at Dieppe, where, after a few months of painless physical and mental decline, he simply faded away.

In life Dumas was much of a scapegrace and a madcap and even more of a prodigal. He earned and spent, says one of his biographers,[33] three fortunes, and it is certain that his revenue from his works was greater than that of any author of his day. But it was the old story, too common among men of genius, of easy come, easy go. He knew it, and joked about it—it is to be hoped that he regretted it. And the story is told of him that at Dieppe, in his last days, he said one day to his son Alexander, while jingling two Napoleons in his hand, "They claim, Alexander, that I am a spendthrift. I can prove the contrary. I started life in Paris with two Napoleons, and I still have them." His morals were loose, and did not improve with the passing years. His son Alexander was illegitimate, as was also a daughter, who won some small repute in the literary world.

He said, jokingly, one day, that he must have five hundred children scattered throughout Europe.[34] It seems more likely that the fervid imagination which created so many wonderful characters doubtless created several hundred of these children. He lived in the loose bohemian theatrical world of Paris, where marriage was in the main a mere form of words, and more often than not dispensed with. He was generous to his mistresses, and while very much in love and in earnest while the flame burned, there is no record of emotional tragedy to mar the easy flow of his amatory experiences. We can forgive his lapses for the sake of his achievements. Had he been different in any way from what he was, he might not have been the Dumas that we read and love. It is no pleasure to dwell on his faults. As the Jesuit Le Moyne said of Charles V.: "What need that future ages should be made acquainted with the fact that so religious an emperor was not always chaste?"[35]

In spite of his life, his novels are clean novels. He was, as George Sand said of him, "*foncièrement bon*," fundamentally good, and his faults were on the surface.

He himself wrote, in 1852, "I had, thank God, a natural sentiment of delicacy, and thus out of my 600 volumes there are not four which the most scrupulous mother may not give to her daughter." And in 1864, when the *Censeur* threatened one of his plays, he wrote to the emperor: "Of my 1200 volumes"—I might remark in passing, that Dumas novels were published as many volumes to the novel—"there is not one which a girl in our most modest quarter, the Faubourg Saint-Germain, may not be allowed to read." This may be a broad claim, for there are passages here and there, and certainly there are situations, which are not a moral example to youth. His heroes and heroines made love without the bounds of marriage, which is the standard theme of French romance, and, in fact, in every literature, seems to be the only theme capable of sustaining a novel of passion. But love at the hands of Dumas was treated as a simple, natural thing, like hunger or thirst or sleep, and adultery was merely an incident, not of the essential. Nowhere does he stop to philosophize about it, or glaze it over or even discuss it. His heroes and heroines make love according to their station, from king to groom, from queen to kitchen maid, with small regard for the marriage tie, but always with regard to the proprieties. A guardsman might kiss an innkeeper's daughter, or, perchance, to gain a point, a pretty lady's maid. But while a princess or a duchess may love a simple guardsman, he must be of gentle birth—she never stoops to a lackey. And while this laxity can not appeal to the stern moralist, of our day, nor did perhaps to those of that day, if there were any, there is generally some excuse which makes the reader sympathize with the sinner, while good morals (*bonos mores*) would demand that he condemn the sin. The mistress is either the wife of a notary—why is it that French novelists rap the legal profession so hard?—or a tradesman of some kind, generally a haberdasher—and as a rule he must be old and cold and bald and miserly; while the lover, of course, must be young and handsome and dashing and ardent—a model of manly grace and charm.

Dumas was no stylist. There is about even his best books a breadth of treatment which suggests the scene painter or the fresco artist. His characters are Homeric in their conception and treatment. One reads him solely for the story. His motives were elemental. He wastes little time on the meaner vices or the little virtues. To analyze, like Balzac, the narrow motives and spiritual writhings of the sordid, greedy bourgeois, to dissect, like Zola, the body and soul of a prostitute, or a dipsomaniac, was not his notion of literature.[36]

His strength and much of his charm lie in his simplicity and directness. Action is the word, and his invention was kaleidoscopic in its variety and spontaneity. His heroes are men of blood and iron, who know what they want and proceed to take it, by artifice at times but preferably by the strong hand. To take offense at a wink or a look or a careless word, to seek immediate satisfaction at the point of the sword, to eat and drink like Gargantua,[37] to seek dangerous adventure, to perform prodigies of valor, to kill often and to be killed many times, was the life of the swashbuckling guardsmen who supply the material for many of his best stories.

Dumas *père* is frequently compared with Scott. Both found their field of literary expression in historical romance. Each laid the scenes of his stories in the most romantic epoch of the history of their respective countries, Scott covering a wider field, and not confining himself to England. The fact that they wrote historical romance may account, in some degree, for the quantity of their output. To take a background of historical incident, to fill it in the main with historical personages whose characters and lives are matter of record, and to fit these to—or fit to these—the adventures of one or two imaginary characters, as Quentin Durward,[38] for instance, or D'Artagnan and his friends, is—one would imagine—less laborious than to make the entire story out of whole cloth.

"It is acknowledged," says Andrew Lang,[39] "that in such a character as Henri

III, Dumas made history live, as magically as Scott revived the past in his Louis XI or Balfour of Burley[40] .... He may fall short of the humor, the noble philosophy and kindly knowledge of the heart which are Scott's; while he has not that supernatural touch, that tragic grandeur which Scott inherits from Homer and from Shakespeare, yet in another Homeric quality, 'in the delight of battle' and the spirit of the fray, Scott and Dumas are alike masters. Their fights, and the fights in the Icelandic Sagas, are the best that have ever been drawn by mortal man; and Dumas is far more swift, more witty and more diverting than Scott. In all he does, at his best, he has movement, kindness, courage and gaiety."

Dumas' books reflect the better side, the fundamental side of his character.

Numerous as were his faults, his virtues were equally conspicuous. He was cheerful, industrious, loyal and open-hearted. His humanity was boundless in degree and incorruptible in quality. He was generous to a fault—in fact, his prodigality was mostly misdirected generosity—and he was never known to strike a foul blow. "I love and admire you," said his friend Michelet, "for you are a force of nature." "Fundamentally good," was George Sand's verdict, "but too often drunk with power." The fact is that he was a prodigy of temperament and power and the capacity of life and invention and achievement. His principal happiness was in work; he could work sixteen or eighteen hours a day and be fresh for the start next morning. He talked still better than he wrote; and he wrote without any affectations of style, and with an ease, a gusto, a sincerity of mind, a completeness of method that are irresistible. And the lesson of his greater books—of the Valois cycle, for instance, and the long sequence of the *Mousquetaires*—is one by which the world may well have profited. Love, honor, friendship, loyalty, valour, the chivalric virtues—these were his darling themes; and he treated them with a combination of energy and insight, of good sense and good feeling, of manliness of mind and beauty of heart, that has ranked him with the great benefactors of humanity.

Alexander Dumas (born 1824), son of the preceding, was born in Paris when his father was but twenty-one years old. He was of illegitimate birth (his mother being a Jewess), but was soon legitimised, and at sixteen, after a thorough course of training in first class educational institutions, he left school for the world of letters and the society to which his father, then almost at his apogee, belonged, the lively and loose theatrical world of Paris. He was essentially respectable, however, and having sown a certain quantity of wild oats, and made a few experiments in literature, he settled down to serious work, and began to take life in earnest. He started in fiction, and succeeded; he went on to drama, religion even, and succeeded. He was made a member of the Institute in 1874, and was at the date of his death in 1895, the acknowledged best playwright and one of the greatest artists in words in latter-day France, the country of the world which is easily first in dramatic literature and historic art.

His novels—from *La Dame aux Camélias* (1848) to *L'Affaire Clémenceau* (1866)—are all readable, and more often than not are worth reading. His essays, letters, speeches, prefaces, and occasional writings generally are brilliant and admirable in form, and in matter daring, paradoxical, suggestive in a very high degree. Of his plays, there is scarce one that is not literature, while five or six of them are masterpieces of construction, characterization and writing. He also collaborated in other famous dramas. He was not so prolific a writer as his father, but he was more of a stylist, and his product is of perhaps a more uniform standard of excellence as writing than that of the elder Dumas. His method is logical to a fault, he builds as for all time, he is an artificer even in theory, and his paradoxes are developed with scientific exactness and precision. A bitter and dazzling wit; an intelligence of uncommon energy, daring and intensity; a morality that is so genuine as to be sometimes offensive; an incorruptible honesty; a style hard, polished, chaste, flexible as a perfect sword-blade; and a dramatic gift as real as his father's—these are his qualities, and they have made him not only remarkable but distinguished.

Less prolific, he was more precocious than his father. He wrote his first play at twenty-one, his first long novel in six volumes, at twenty-two, his famous *La Dame aux Camélias*, better known as *Camille*, at twenty-two, was author of nineteen other novels, of which, next to *La Dame aux Camélias*, *L'Affaire Clémenceau* is perhaps best known to American readers. He is much better known as playwright than as novelist, and really stood at the head of the dramatic profession during his life.

He was the author of twenty-five successful plays, six of which were written in collaboration, the best known and most popular of which in America is *Camille*.[41] He also wrote sixteen works on philosophical and miscellaneous subjects. In these he discussed divorce, illegitimacy under the title of *La Recherche de la Paternité*.[42] His genius was more or less colored by the consciousness of his illegitimacy, and in the preface to his play *The Natural Son*,[43] and elsewhere, the psychology of that status is freely discussed.

Scattered through the writings of Dumas *fils* are many brilliant and cynical passages dealing with love, and woman and marriage, and the life here and hereafter. A few of these are eminently characteristic with apologies for the translation, which is my own:[44]

> When one sees life as God has made it, one can but thank him for having made death.

> At bottom, what is there serious in a life which one enters without demanding it and leaves without wishing it?

> One of my friends, a very lazy man, said: "It is useless to learn anything during life, since one will know it all after death."

> Life is the last habit which one should lose, since it is the first which one has formed.

> Among ten thousand men, there are seven or eight thousand who love women, five or six hundred who love woman, one who loves one woman.

> Woman is, according to the Bible, the last thing that God made. He must have made her Saturday evening. It is evident that he was tired.

It is often the same woman who inspires us to great things and prevents us from accomplishing them.

Men have sometimes the right to speak evil of women, never of *a* woman.

Marriage is the greatest of stupidities—and I very much hope that my daughters will be guilty of it.

Absolutely beautiful women have only just enough modesty to make their beauty valued.

The chain of marriage is so heavy that it takes two to bear it—sometimes three.

He wrote a good deal of advice to young people, among other things a very beautiful "Letter to a Child," which is too long to translate, but which is somewhat along the line of a morsel which runs as follows, with apologies for the translation:

Walk two hours every day, sleep seven hours every night; go to bed alone, as soon as you are sleepy; get up when you wake; go to work as soon as you have risen. Eat only when you are hungry, drink only when you are thirsty, and always slowly.

Some more didactic passages:

Speak only when necessary and say only half of what you think; write only what you can sign, do only what you can speak of. Never forget that others rely upon you, and that you cannot rely upon them. Value money neither more nor less than it is worth: it is a good servant and a bad master.

Avoid women until you are twenty, keep away from them after forty; never create anything without knowing what you are about, and destroy the least possible. Pardon everybody in advance, for greater security; do not despise men, nor hate them, nor laugh at them beyond measure; pity them.

Think of death every morning when you see the light again, and every evening when you reenter the shadows. When you suffer much, look your grief in the face, it will itself console you, and will teach you something. Force yourself to be simple, to become useful, to remain free, and wait to deny God until it has been well proved to you that He does not exist.

What influence his strain of tropical blood had upon the elder Dumas' character and genius is purely a matter of conjecture. He was vain, and vanity is supposed to be a Negro trait. But Charles Dickens was vain, in much the same way—he revelled in fine clothes and loud waistcoats and cravats and a profusion of jewelry, while Napoleon the Great was a monument of vanity; had old General Dumas flattered instead of criticising him, he might have ended his days in a far different manner. Nor was this strain of blood needed to account for his sexual laxity, as any casual survey of the lives of his literary contemporaries will make clear.[45] There was however about him a certain naïveté, an abounding good-nature, and a verve or swing which is almost as well punctuated as ragtime; and these, as well as his robust physical vigor, his brown complexion and his curly hair, may perhaps be safely attributed to his dark blood. He was not ashamed of it, often mentioned it with not the least self-consciousness—it was of no social or business disadvantage to him in France, where talent has always been recognized and rewarded in absolute disregard of race or color—and he wrote one novel, *Georges, the Planter of the Isle of France*, of which the race problem in one of its aspects formed the motive.[46]

The mother of his son Alexander was, as we have said, a Jewess, and in him there was still further complication of strains, which does not seem to have affected his genius for the worse; he was thrifty where his father had been prodigal, which trait some might attribute to this last addition, an obvious improvement.[47] It would be a problem for the Mendels and Wassermans[48] and the eugenists, why, in view of the widely proclaimed but scientifically unproved theory that the mixture of dissimilar races inevitably results in degeneracy, three successive generations of mixed blood should have produced so much ability. One might be inclined to think, since no pure white man of the family had especially distinguished himself, that possibly, at least in this instance, the result was due to the mixture, which had improved the original strain.

The famous men of this honored name are dead. Dumas *fils*, tho' twice married, left no son. His two daughters are married, one to a Paris banker, and the other to an officer in the French army.[49] Whether their children will inherit the talents of their ancestors is one of the riddles of life and heredity. It is not common for two generations to possess marked literary or artistic talent—another would be perhaps too much to hope for. But though there be none to bear it, the name of Dumas will be affectionately known as long as *The Three Musketeers* is read, and Dumas *père* will retain his place in history as one of the greatest of the literary giants of the gifted generation in which he lived and worked.[50]

↬

SOURCE: Typed text at the Fisk University Library. This speech was given before Cleveland's Rowfant Club on 11 April 1914. The records of the Club cite the title as "Life and Work of Alexandre Dumas," but that of the source text is here retained. Because this speech repeats much of the description of the Dumas family and the accomplishments thereof in "Race Ideals and Examples," the annotations of the same matters in that essay should be consulted. Only Chesnutt's expansions of his earlier account are glossed below.

[1]Described first are two works by Alexandre Dumas, *père*. Chicot is the jester and confidante of Henry III in the historical romance *Les Quarante-Cinq*. Catherine de Médicis, in *La Reine Margot*, plots with her Catholic son, Charles IX, against the Protestant prince Henri de Navarre; and the 1572 St. Bartholomew's Day massacre of the Huguenots by the Catholics figures in her story. Alexandre Dumas, *fils*, was the creator of Camille, the pitiable leading character in his novel *La Dame aux Camélias* (1848). She was portrayed in the stage version by the French actress Sarah Bernhardt (1844–1923).

[2]The "magnum opus" published in 1911 by the Rowfant Club was *The Tempest: A Comedy*, edited by Willis Vickery (see n. 20). Included with Shakespeare's play was Renan's continuation of *The Tempest*, the philosophical drama *Caliban* (1878).

[3]Voltaire (1694–1778), or François Marie Arouet, philosophical and political author best known for his satirical novel *Candide* (1759); Jean Baptiste Racine (1639–99), playwright; Pierre Corneille (1606–84), playwright.

[4]In 1867, Henry M. Flagler (1830–1913) became associated with John D. Rocke-

feller (1839–1937) and played an especially active role in the development of the Standard Oil trust until 1881. At that time he moved from Cleveland to New York City, and he focused on Florida railway and real estate development.

[5]*Mes Mémoires* (1852–55) is a primary information source for both Chesnutt and the biographical works he consulted.

[6]William Ewart Gladstone (1809–98), English prime minister and classicist.

[7](1769–1838); her father was, in fact, the proprietor of the Hôtel de l'Ecu and Commandant of the National Guard of Villers-Cotterêts; she married General Thomas Alexandre Dumas on 28 November 1792.

[8]Dante Gabriel Rossetti (1828–82), English poet.

[9]François Joseph Talma (1763–1826).

[10]Maximilien Sébastien Foy (1775–1825) was a general in Napoleon's army in Spain and a member of the Chamber of Deputies (1819–25).

[11]Charles Nodier (1780–1844) was a novelist and playwright. His "L'Amateur de Livres" (1841) was translated by Frank Hadley Ginn (1868–1938) of Cleveland and published by the Rowfant Club in 1900 as *A Translation of Charles Nodier's Story of the Bibliomaniac*.

[12]*Le Vampire* (1820) was written by Alexandre Piccinni (1779–1880), Nodier, and Achille Jouffroy (1785–1868).

[13]Chesnutt's bibliophile audience would have understood this to be a special volume. Elzevir was a Dutch publishing firm flourishing from the mid-sixteenthth century through the early eighteenth; its fine printing was long prized by book collectors. The work in question was first published in the seventeenth century.

[14]The H. J. Heinz Company of Pittsburgh, Pa., a maker of condiments, claimed to have fifty-seven varieties of sauces, pickles, and relishes.

[15]*Christine* (1830).

[16]"The Arsenal," a building fronting the Seine constructed during the reign of Francis I (1494–1547), had been transformed into a library; Nodier was its director. He lived there with his family, and on Sunday nights he invited many artistic celebrities to gather for conversation, food, and drink.

[17]Alphonse de Lamartine (1790–1869), statesman and Romantic poet; Alfred Victor, Comte de Vigny (1797–1863), Romantic poet and novelist whose *Cinq-Mars* was published in 1826; Alfred de Musset (1810–57), Romantic poet, novelist, and dramatist; Charles Augustin Sainte-Beuve (1804–69), literary critic who wrote favorable reviews of the works of French Romantic writers, often in his *Causeries du Lundi* (15 volumes, 1851–62)—a compilation of his weekly column of the same name which appeared in the magazine *Le Constitutionnel*; Alphonse Karr (1808–90), novelist and journalist.

[18]*Henri III et sa Cour* was hailed by the critics for its originality, or freedom from foreign influence, in its treatment of an episode in French history. The play was presented at the Théâtre Français more than 150 times between 1829 and 1894.

[19]"She was resisting me, I murdered her!" Chesnutt's greater reliance on Davidson's biography than in "Race Ideals and Examples" is seen especially in this paragraph: nearly the whole is a verbatim transcription. The explanation of the "verdict" on the qualities of *Antony* two paragraphs below is also derived from Davidson.

[20]Chesnutt left blank a space for a name here. Judge Willis Vickery (1857–1932) spoke on Shakespeare to the Rowfant Club members on 28 February 1914.

[21]Bocage was the stage name of Pierre Martinien Tousez (1797–1863); Marie Dorval (1798–1849).

[22]Little Eva is the angelic white child in Harriet Beecher Stowe's *Uncle Tom's Cabin*. The novel was first adapted for the stage by George Aiken (1830–76) in 1852: at the close of Act 3 in Aiken's adaptation, Eva dies but the script does not specify an ascen-

sion into heaven in a golden chariot. In the final scene, however, Eva appears on stage robed in white, on the back of a white dove, her arms extended in benediction over her father and Uncle Tom.

[23]"She was resisting me—this one time—and I murdered her!" That this was an unusual development is implied.

[24]John Heywood, *Proverbs*.

[25]Chesnutt describes this "note" below: these works feature "conceptions of the character of the leading figures in the gay and corrupt court life of that period, honeycombed with political and religious and amorous intrigue."

[26]Peter Paul Rubens (1577–1640) was a Flemish painter of landscapes, portraits, and historical and sacred subjects.

[27]By Dumas' own count, he collaborated with Auguste Maquet (1813–88) on forty-two volumes, including *Les Trois Mousquetaires*. François Paul Meurice (1820–1905), a dramatist, collaborated with Dumas on translations of *Romeo and Juliet* (unpublished) and *Hamlet* (1848).

[28]The story regarding the authorship was not maliciously fabricated. In an 1865 letter, Dumas acknowledged that this historical romance was written entirely by Meurice. Meurice had asked him for a loan; Dumas accommodated by allowing him to identify *Les Deux Dianes* (1861) as written by the better-known author so that the book's sale would generate the requested amount.

[29]*The Heptameron*, a collection of stories examining the nature of love, was written by Marguerite of Angoulême and Navarre (1492–1549)—not Marguerite de Valois.

[30]Charles X (1757–1836) was King of France from 1824 to 1830. Emended is the miscitation of the "Days of July" as occurring in 1831.

[31]The funeral of Maximilien Lamarque (1770–1832) took place on 5–6 June 1832; it was the occasion for a Republican insurrection in Paris.

[32]Mark Twain was the pen-name of Samuel Langhorne Clemens (1835–1910). This anecdote appears in Albert Bigelow Paine's *Mark Twain: A Biography* (1912).

[33]William E. Henley; see "Race Ideals," n. 30.

[34]The original source of this anecdote is Mathilde Shaw, *Illustres et Inconnus: Souvenirs de Ma Vie* (1906).

[35]Pierre Le Moyne (1602–71); Charles V (1500–1558). Chesnutt here, and below where he acknowledges him, relies upon Andrew Lang (1844–1912), Scottish poet and critic. In *Essays in Little* (1891), Lang refers to but does not identify a "recent work" in which this statement appeared.

[36]Honoré de Balzac offended nineteenth-century readers preferring "ideal" portrayals of human nature rather than his novelistic studies of aberrant personalities. For decades, Emile Zola too had been notorious for his frank fictional studies of human behavior and its motivations, including "animalistic" drives and the influence of sordid environments. Chesnutt articulates the genteel, Victorian reaction to both writers.

[37]Gargantua, a fictional character in *La Vie Très Horrificque du Grand Gargantua* (1534) by François Rabelais (1494?–1593), is a giant given to various excessive behaviors.

[38]The chivalric hero of Scott's *Quentin Durward* (1823).

[39]See n. 35.

[40]Louis XI (1428–83) and John Balfour of Burleigh (?–1688) appear in Scott's *Quentin Durward* and *Old Mortality* (1816), respectively.

[41]*Camille* was translated and performed in the United States as early as 1857. Chesnutt originally listed the six other works: "*Diane des Lys* [sic], *Le Demi-Monde*—indeed, Alexander Dumas invented the word demi-monde and first introduced it into the French Language—*Le Fils Naturel, L'Ami des Femmes, Denise* and *Francillon* [sic]." *Denise* and *Francillon* are actually separate works.

[42]Published in 1883.

[43]*Le Fils Naturel* (1858).

[44]Although Chesnutt twice draws attention to his having translated these reflections, whether he did so from an undiscovered source in which they were assembled or directly from the author's publications is not known. But nowhere else does he reveal the command of the canon of Dumas *fils* that is seemingly displayed here. Books by neither author are present in his personal library preserved at Fisk University.

[45]Chesnutt apparently noted that this paragraph was ambivalent in its first three sentences, referring to both Dumas *père* and his father, the General, with regard to "tropical blood" and a possibly inherited trait of vanity. He first added "pere's" to "Dumas'" in the first sentence; then, again in pencil, he canceled that and positioned "the elder" before "Dumas'"—focusing instead on the General. He did not, however, revise to make it clear in the third sentence that "his sexual laxity" refers not to the General's but to that of Dumas *père*. The rest of the paragraph remains focused on Dumas *père*.

[46]Published in 1843.

[47]Thriftiness is viewed by Chesnutt as a distinctively Jewish trait that is genetically transmitted to their progeny. Catherine Labay was the mother of Dumas *fils*.

[48]Gregor Mendel (1822–84) was an Austrian botanist whose experiments focused upon the effects of the genetic transmission of traits. August von Wasserman (1866–1925), a German bacteriologist, was more concerned with the mechanism of transmission.

[49]Dumas *fils* was first married to Nadeja Knorring in 1864; their first daughter was Marie-Alexandrine-Henriette (known as "Colette"), who was born in 1860 and acknowledged as theirs in 1864; their second, Jeannine, was born in 1867. In 1895, less than three months after the death of Nadeja, he married Henriette Regnier, with whom he had conducted a lengthy adulterous affair.

[50]Chesnutt here added in pencil two paragraphs possibly outlining extemporaneous remarks to follow his formal presentation. The first reads: "I should like had I time, to speak at length of Alexander Pushkin, the Russian poet &c." The second reads: "Not primarily Negroes. They were Frenchmen who happened to hv Negro blood. Consequently they wrote as Frenchmen, not as N's. In our country we of mixed blood are regarded as Negroes who happen to hv white blood, & we write primarily as Negroes. Develop—"

The Ideal Nurse

Speech delivered at the Provident Hospital graduation
ceremony for nurses, Chicago, Ill., 4 May 1914

Mr. Chairman, Ladies and Gentlemen:—

I am going to speak to the graduating classes of the Provident Hospital Training School for nurses, about their profession, and I have called the subject of my address "The Ideal Nurse." Of course anything that I shall say about nurses and nursing is purely from the layman's point of view, my information being derived solely from observation and reading, reinforced by several weeks of practical experience in a hospital and under the care of a nurse, and any mistakes that I may make must be ascribed to ignorance or lack of opportunity for more thorough examination, and I am sure you will pardon me for them in advance, for which I thank you.

Now, I have no means of knowing the motives which actuated each one of you young ladies in taking up the profession of nursing. It may have been merely the desire to occupy yourself, with some useful and congenial employment, the desire for a career, or, quite as likely, if not more so, it may have been the pressure of economic necessity—the need to earn a living. Women work for various reasons. They are no longer content to sit at home and do nothing, or occupy themselves in social or domestic pursuits, to "help mama" as the phrase goes, until marriage terminates their single state. For while marriage and motherhood will always remain the highest career for womankind, it is no longer regarded as the only one. Men no longer marry so young as they once did; more of them than formerly, for various reasons, do not marry at all, and, somehow or other, there do not seem to be men enough to go around. And the demands of modern life make it a great deal more expensive to support an idle woman; a hat now costs as much as a whole suit used to, and the amount necessary to dress a fashionable woman for the season would buy a small farm. So the women have gone to work, partly from necessity, partly because their own self-respect will not permit them to be mere barnacles and parasites on society. And the scope of their employment has steadily widened, until there is hardly an industry or an occupation into which they have not made their way. They man the shops and factories—we need a new verb there—they woman the shops and factories, as saleswomen and operatives, they fill the offices as stenographers and bookkeepers, they rub elbows with the men in the professions. There are a few industries, which they haven't yet broken into. I have never seen a woman structural iron worker, or able seaman, or railroad brakeman, though I have read of women who sewed through campaigns as soldiers and got on the pension list. This, of course, they could only get through guile and misrepresentation—otherwise trousers and a man's name—so it really doesn't matter much except to demonstrate to what woman is capable of. (Teachers.) And one profession the women almost monopolize—the profession for which you have prepared yourselves—I say prepared yourselves, for, while you have been trained by others, it is you who have done the work, it is your zeal and industry which have qualified you for graduation. Some of you, too, in the mixture of motives which impelled you to prepare for a career of productive effort, have no doubt been inspired by the wish to do something for humanity, something good and fine and noble to justify your existence. And let me say that, whatever your motive, you could not have chosen a pursuit which offers greater opportunities for usefulness, for honor, for the exercise of all the womanly talents and virtues or which offers greater rewards in the realization of results accomplished. Now, there are nurses and nurses. You will recall, no doubt, Mrs. Sairey Gamp, the nurse whom Charles Dickens has immortalized in his *Martin Chuzzlewit*.[1] Immortality doesn't always imply virtue, Judas Iscariot and Benedict Arnold are examples, and Mrs. Gamp is immortalized not for her talents, but for her shortcomings, not for her virtues, but for her vices. She resided, says her creator at a bird fancier's next door to the celebrated mutton-pie shop and directly opposite to the original cat's meat warehouse. She was a fat old woman with a husky voice and a moist eye, which she had a remarkable power of turning up and only showing the white of it. Having very little neck it gave her some trouble to look over herself, if one may say so, at those to whom she talked. She wore a very rusty black gown, rather the worse for snuff, and a shawl and bonnet to correspond. The face of Mrs. Gamp, her nose in particular, was somewhat red and swollen, and it was difficult to enjoy her society without becoming conscious of the smell of spirits. Like most persons who have attained to great eminence in their profession, she took to hers very kindly, in so much that, setting aside her predilections as a woman, she went to a lying-in or a laying-out with equal zest and relish. She was very fond of quoting a purely imaginary friend whom she called Mrs. 'Arris. Mrs. Gamp was the old style nurse,—let us hope the style has gone out entirely, who, when sitting up with the patient, slept most of the time and only woke up now and then to take a nip of gin from the bottle at her elbow; and who, if she were taking care of a sick child, and the child cried, either slapped it or gave it a dose of soothing syrup or some other opium-laden nostrum.

Then there is the nurse in *Romeo and Juliet*. She was hardly a sick nurse, but she had nursed Juliet in her infancy and still remained about her in the capacity of a duenna. It was customary in that age and in Juliet's country to watch young women closely until they were grown up and safely married. Indeed it is rare today to meet a respectably brought up young woman on the streets of an Italian City unchaperoned, unless of course she happened to be an American or English tourist. And the fact that Juliet's nurse was false to her trust was in part responsible for Juliet's woes and their tragic outcome.

The beautiful and efficient nurse is also no stranger to the pages of modern fiction, as many an interesting novel will demonstrate. The rich and impressionable young, or, old, patient whom she nurses through a dangerous illness and the resulting convalescence, discovers her talents and her virtues, wishes to have a monopoly of them, and is willing to pay the price, which, in every proper novel, is marriage.

(Or the wealthy lady adopts etc.)

Or the discriminating surgeon appreciates the quality of his fair assistant, and takes her into a life partnership. Miss Louisa M. Alcott, wrote a charming little volume of *Hospital Sketches*, based on her experience as a hospital nurse during the Civil War, and in Mr. Howells' very pleasing story *The Imperative Duty*, the quadroon or octoroon nurse's care restores the Yankee colonel to health; he marries her, and thereby creates for their daughter a problem which might have become a tragedy, had it not been happily settled by the loyalty and good sense of her lover.[2] Doubtless you, being so much more interested in the subject, could name me many other such stories, fiction perhaps, but all of which might well be true, for experience teaches that there is no situation, good nor evil, which the mind can conceive, which may not be paralleled in real life.

In history—history is largely a record of wars—in history the nurse has played a large part. In our own Civil War the military hospital nurses displayed great heroism. Inspired by patriotic zeal, they left their comfortable homes, exposed themselves to the dangers of the seat of war, endured the physical and emotional strain of constant contact with disease and blood and pain and death, and contributed in no small degree to the success of the Union arms with all the glorious results of that struggle. And on the rebel side, though their cause was wrong and justly lost, the women of the South made even greater sacrifices.

Perhaps the brightest ornament of the nursing profession in the history of the world was Florence Nightingale.[3] You doubtless have her books in your library and ought to be familiar with her life. Florence Nightingale, the daughter of William Edward Nightingale of Embley Park, Hampshire, and Lea Hurst, Derbyshire, was born at Florence, Italy, in May 1829, and very obviously was named after her birthplace. She was taught mathematics, the classics, and modern languages under the guidance of her father, a cultured and scholarly English gentleman, and thus highly educated and brilliantly accomplished she early exhibited an intense devotion to the alleviation of suffering, which led her in 1844, at the age of 15, to give attention to the condition of hospitals. She visited and inspected civil and military hospitals all over Europe; and in 1851, at the age of 22, went into training as a nurse in the institution of Protestant Deaconesses at Kaiserswerth on the Rhine, and studied with the Sisters of St. Vincent de Paul in Paris the system of nursing and management carried out in the hospitals of that city, which for a long time were the best in the world. On her return to England she put into thorough working order the Sanatorium for Governesses in Harley Street. Ten years was the term of apprenticeship thus served in preparation for the work of her life. In the spring of 1854 war was declared with Russia;[4] Alma was fought on the 20th of September and the wounded from the battle were sent down to the hospitals on the Bosporus, which were soon crowded with sick and wounded, their unhealthy condition becoming apparent in a rate of mortality to which the casualties of the fiercest battle were as nothing. In this crisis Miss Nightingale wrote on the 15th of October and offered to go out and organize a nursing department at Scutari. Lord Herbert,[5] who had already written a letter requesting her to go, which crossed that containing Miss Nightingale's offer, gladly accepted, and on the 21st of October she departed with thirty-four nurses. She arrived at Constantinople on the 4th of November, the eve of Inkermann—the beginning of the terrible winter campaign—in time to receive the wounded from that second battle into wards already filled with 2300 patients. Her devotion to the sufferers can never be forgotten. She would stand twenty hours at a stretch, in order to see them provided with accommodation and all the requisites of their condition, and a few months after her arrival she had 10,000 sick men under her care. But she saw clearly in the bad sanitary arrangements of the hospitals the causes of their frightful mortality, and her incessant labour was devoted to the removal of these causes, as well as to the mitigation of their effect. You may remember too, that at that time anesthetics were not used, and a large percentage of the wounded who were operated died from the shock; antiseptic dressing was unknown, and even in hospitals many died from gangrene & blood poisoning, thus rendering the labor & responsibility of the nurse more arduous and exacting. In the spring of 1855, while in the Crimea organizing the nursing departments of the camp-hospitals, Nurse Nightingale was prostrated with fever, the result of the unintermitting toil and anxiety; yet she refused to leave her post, and on her recovery remained at Scutari till Turkey was evacuated by the British, July 28, 1856. She, to whom many a soldier owed life and health, had expended her own health in the physical and mental strain to which she had subjected herself. In 1857 she furnished the "commissioners appointed to inquire into the regulations affecting the sanitary conditions of the British army" with a paper of written evidence,[6] in which she impressed forcibly and clearly the great lesson of the Crimean war, which she characterized as a sanitary experiment on a colossal scale. At the close of the Crimean war a fund of £50,000 was subscribed for the purposes of enabling her to form an institution for the training of nurses; this she spent in training a superior order of nurses in connection with St. Thomas's (the Nightingale home) and at King's College Hospital. From the Queen she received an autograph letter of thanks, and a cross set with diamonds, as also a bracelet set with brilliants from the Sultan of Turkey.

Her experience in the Crimea turned the attention of Miss Nightingale to the general question of army sanitary reform, and first to that of army hospitals. She published many books and magazine articles on nursing and hospitals, sanitation and social science, and in the year 1863 edited and annotated for the British Government the Report of the Commission on the Sanitary Condition of the Army in India.[7] From America and from different European governments her advice has been sought as to army sanitation: she assisted in founding the Red Cross Society.[8]

You may have read, and if not you will read, Longfellow's poem, "Santa Filomena." It was published in the first number of the *Atlantic Monthly*, in 1857, just after the Crimean War.[9] The poet begins by observing that noble thoughts and noble deeds lift our hearts to higher levels, and then says:

> Thus thought I, as by night I read
> Of the great army of the dead,
>   The trenches cold and damp
>   The starved and frozen camp,—
>
> The wounded from the battle-plain,
> In dreary hospitals of pain,
>   The cheerless corridors,
>   The cold and stony floors.

Lo! in that house of misery
A lady with a lamp I see
    Pass through the glimmering gloom,
    And flit from room to room.

And slow, as in a dream of bliss,
The speechless sufferer turns to kiss
    Her shadow, as it falls
    Upon the darkening walls.

As if a door in heaven should be
Opened and then closed suddenly,
    The vision came and went
    The light shone and was spent.

On England's annals, through the long
Hereafter of her speech and song,
    That light with rays shall cast
    From portals of the past.

A Lady with a Lamp shall stand
In the great history of the land,
    A noble type of good,
    Heroic womanhood.

Thus in this case of this brilliant and accomplished woman we have an illustration of the wealth of opportunity, which the profession of nursing offers for the exercise of all the powers of body, mind and heart. With every inducement to devote herself to a life of ease and luxury, in the highest sphere to which she was born and which she might have adorned with every intellectual and social grace; she chose instead to devote her life to the welfare of the sick and the suffering, and in her chosen career she found occupation for her well trained mind and for her great heart, and she reaped the reward of the love and appreciation, not only of those to whom she personally ministered, not only of those to whom her labors brought amelioration of their lot, not only of the sovereigns of the nations which had profited most by her labors, but of all the great mass of those who read and think and know what is going on in the world. Her name shines out as one of the brightest gems in the galaxy of noble womanhood which occupies so large a place in history, and is destined, in the age now at our very doors, when woman is to be emancipated from the trammels which have hampered her progress, to share still more largely and directly in the direction of the destinies of mankind. We may laugh at the vagaries of modern feminism, at the militant suffragette, at the lady policeman, but the sex which had produced such women as Florence Nightingale, Alice Freeman Palmer and Jane Addams,[10] is worthy of a more direct share in ruling the world than merely rocking the cradle, especially when for lack of the cradle they cannot influence the course of future events in that particular way. And the State of Illinois has given them an opportunity to prove their equality.

Of course not every nurse can be a Florence Nightingale. Very few women have either her talents or her opportunity. But as one star differeth from another star in glory,[11] yet each helps to enlighten the night, whatever its stellar magnitude; so each of you, in however humble a rank in your profession you may start, may yet feel that you are contributing to the great work of humanity, the great work of social uplift. For after all, society is composed of individuals, and the more individuals are nursed back from illness or injury to health and soundness, the better will be the general tone of the community, the better the principal and moral health of the next generation. It is often the wail of the pessimist that by our modern humanitarian methods we coddle the unfit, and, by interfering with the natural law of the survival of the fittest injure the race; that instead of allowing the weak and inefficient to be weeded out by disease and starvation, we nurse them and pamper them and turn them loose upon the world to perpetuate their kind. From a coldly scientific point of view there is an argument in this statement; yet who would return to the old Spartan custom of throwing the halt, the lame and the blind children into the water to drown like superfluous puppies, or to the old Chinese custom of casting unwelcome girl babies into the river; or to the old Norse custom of leading superannuated parents or relatives out into the woods and tenderly and tearfully smashing in their heads with a club? Is not any weakening of type which results from humanitarianism more than counterbalanced by the greater care which is taken to conserve the health of the strong and the efficient, as illustrated by the removal of adenoids and the care of the eyes and the teeth of school children, to say nothing of the moral gain due to the cultivation of sympathy and compassion and love for others?

But while war will always provide a spectacular theater for the demonstration of the nurse's usefulness and devotion, it is not after all, the principal field of her efforts. For every one man who dies in battle several hundred die in their beds; and it is in caring for these, in the hospital or in the home, that the trained nurse finds her chief opportunity.

Because of its facilities for the treatment of the sick and the injured, facilities which cannot be provided in the home without great expense, but which in the hospital are within the reach of all, the hospital has become more and more popular as a health resort, so to speak (using the term health resort as a place where sick people go in search of health). Not only those who must undergo operations, but the nervous or the unstrung seek the peaceful shelter of the hospital or sanitarium as a temporary refuge from the storms and stresses of life. To these the soft-footed, soft-handed, soft-voiced nurse is the best of medicines, while in certain diseases, the cure is almost entirely a matter of nursing. In increasing number women, even those whose home surroundings might seem all that could be wished, come to the hospital to perform the supreme function of their sex, without which the race would perish from the face of the earth; while the sick and wounded poor, victims of misfortune, vice or crime, whether their own or that of others, find in the hospital the haven of rest and recuperation which is denied them in the sordid environment of their own homes. And the nurse, the trained nurse, is the chief instrumentality through whom these benefits are conferred, the conduit through which flow the stream of benevolence which founded and sustains the hospital, the skill of the surgeon who operates, or the physician who prescribes. While in the home the trained nurse smooths the pillow and soothes the spirit of the sick patient and either leads the sick body and mind back in to the road to health or cheers and sustains them in the last and losing battle.

Now what must be the equipment of the Ideal Nurse? Given the right initial motive—the desire to help others, or, in default of high altruistic purpose,—for we are not all stamped with the same die—the earnest desire to succeed by qualifying one's self for the best type of service; given the requisite degree of education and intelligence, of which the passage of your entrance examinations is presumptive evidence; the first and prime necessity for the Ideal Nurse is training; and the first step in that training is the acquisition of those kinds of special knowledge which your profession demands of those who pursue it. You have to learn something about a great many things which to the average lay mind are incomprehensible without a dictionary. I doubt not that you in your Training Class have lectures, on at least certain aspects of all the various ailments which I find set out in the Annual Report of the Hospital. You must learn the meaning of such mysterious terms as Otitis Media, Splenomyelogenous, Cryptorchidism, Pyloric Stenosis, Chronic Parenchymatous—I can get along very well with Meningitis, Marasmus, Arteria Sclerosis, Carcinoma, Mumps, Measles and every-day affairs like that, but some of these complicated designations are beyond my comprehension. And before you can apply this particular kind of knowledge intelligently you must learn more of anatomy than Galen or Hippocrates knew,[12] more of physiology than the most learned physicians in Europe knew not many years ago: for the most important process of the body, namely the circulation of the blood, with all that involves—the heart as the central pumping station, the arterial and venous systems as the distributing lines, the lungs as the aerating, filtering plant, the kidneys as the purifier—was unknown until discovered by Harvey in the middle of the 17th Century.[13] Of course, the profession knew the anatomy of the body, the location of all these organs; they knew in an empirical way some of the functions performed by them; they knew that certain pathological conditions induced certain unhealthy results, and that the application of certain remedies brought relief; but of the marvellously complicated and yet wonderfully simple way in which these organs and their functions were all related to one another to form a perfect whole, the nurse in the freshman class today knows more than the wisest physician knew 250 years ago. While as to anesthetics and antisepsis, which are a modern development of the treatment of disease, she has an entire field of knowledge open to her of which the learned men of these former generations were entirely ignorant.

Then, given this preliminary instruction, or coincident with it, in the school of experience, she is trained to be punctual, accurate, methodical; she learns the value of little things—that the life of a patient may often turn on an accurate record of the pulse or temperature, or upon the punctual administration of the prescribed remedy. She must acquire, if she does not possess by native temperament, the virtue of patience, for the sick are often irritable and unreasonable. I have no doubt they sometimes swear at nurses. She must have all the Christian virtues. She must have faith that her labors will not be in vain, and that her efforts may not lag; she must have hope in order to cheer the patient, for cheerfulness is the best of medicines, and mental suggestion, as the success of a certain so-called religious cult has demonstrated, has powerful therapeutic value.

> Joy and comfort and repose,

says Longfellow again,

> Slam the door on the doctor's nose.[14]

She must have charity for human weakness, for nowhere is it more apparent than when the body is weak or diseased. The morbid body makes the morbid mind; just as the sound body goes with the sound mind. And what an opportunity the nurse has to study human nature! She sees the man or woman mentally and morally unveiled. What curious things she must learn when the patient, for instance, is in delirium! and how discreet she must be, thus unwittingly surprising the secrets of life and character! What unhappiness she might cause, if she were malicious or mercenary! And even in full consciousness the real nature of the patient becomes obvious. If he is greedy, or avaricious, or sensual, or vain, or profane, or selfish, his weakness is apt to stand out, because he has not the strength to conceal it. One can imagine that at times it may be difficult for the doctor or the nurse to retain any respect for humanity; but, fortunately for poor humanity, respect is not in all cases absolutely essential to love, and so the doctor and the nurse, conscious of their own humanity, can sympathize with human weakness and serve with no less of zeal and devotion. Now to secure this training which is necessary for the Ideal Nurse, the prime necessity is the hospital, if possible, the Ideal Hospital.

So far as my limited acquaintance with hospitals goes—I have had some, personally as well as indirectly—and so far as a necessarily cursory examination of Provident Hospital and a rather careful study of your 1913 catalogue has enabled me to discover, it seems to me that you have here well nigh the ideal training school and hospital. There are doubtless larger institutions, more liberally endowed. But you have here a commodious building adapted in plan and construction to the purpose for which it was intended, equipped with all the scientific appliances necessary for the treatment of wounds and disease. Its business management is in the hands of capable business men. It has an efficient superintendent, head nurse, a consultation staff which numbers in it the leading specialists of the City, and a large attending and dispensary staff of qualified practitioners. It is located in a large city, where there is abundant material for clinics, and the hospital cannot accommodate all the inside patients who apply. So it would seem that you have everything here that is essential or desirable in a hospital, for the training of nurses, both in theory and practice.

Now, having pursued your ideal in this ideal hospital, you are ready to go out into the world and practice your profession. You are in much better position than the ordinary college graduate, because your training has been technical, and you are prepared for immediate service. What shall you do? Where shall you go? What opportunities are open to you?

Your first thought, your preference perhaps, would be to be a hospital nurse. For in the hospital you have full scope for all your powers and attainments, you are not apt to forget anything and are sure to learn a great deal more than you know. It is more than likely that, because of your race, or rather because of the mean and unworthy prejudice against your color, the field of employment in most hospitals will be closed to you. But there are, in the United States, according to the *Negro Year Book* of 1913, sixty-three hospitals conducted for and mostly by colored people, which must give employment to several hundred nurses. Many of them have training schools for nurses connected with them. These training schools must have superintendents and teachers, and I see from your catalogue that Provident Hospital Training School has furnished the superintendents, head nurses and matrons for many of them. And there is a great field for the capable, executive young woman in fostering and promoting the establishment of other such institutions, as did Florence Nightingale.

The tremendous interest in and growth of social welfare work in our day has opened another wide field for nurses, including the colored nurse. The visiting nurses employed by the municipality or by private charitable organizations, are a valuable agency in the conservation of health, especially among the young. The visiting nurse comes like a celestial visitant into the squalid unsanitary homes of the poor, bringing with her the light of health and hope. The colored poor have been more or less neglected—generally more—in our American cities, but the public conscience is gradually awakening, and before very long there will be a much larger demand for colored visiting nurses.

Then there is the great field of the private nurse, employment in which, I imagine, must come largely thro the recommendation of the physician. It must be a great incentive to the undergraduate nurse, during her hospital training, to do her work well, when she realizes that in leaving school a large part of her professional success must depend upon the friendship and confidence and good will of her former preceptor. It is undoubtedly a powerful factor for discipline. There are many forms of illness which do not demand hospital treatment, but in which the attendance of a trained nurse is essential or desirable; as it is in convalescence after hospital treatment. I shall always remember with pleasure the soft-voiced, gentle-handed little nurse who washed me and dressed me and fed me and read to me as though I were a child; for several weeks of such a convalescence following several other weeks in a hospital.[15] She was paid for her services, the usual price, but for her warmhearted sympathy and devotion I could only repay her with grateful appreciation.

In this sphere there ought to be ample employment for the colored nurse. It would seem a refinement of race prejudice for a family which would employ a colored cook or butler or maid, to object to the presence in the household of a colored nurse. True, the position is not the same, the highly trained nurse represents a vastly higher type of personal service, as the physician a still higher type; and one would think that in the Southern States, where white people are accustomed to having colored people wait upon them, colored nurses would be in demand. Indeed, I believe they are; and one is inclined to wonder at the mental make up of the South Carolina statesman who recently introduced a bill, which among others was aimed to prohibit colored nurses from attending white patients. By a curious coincidence the same newspaper which announced the passage of this measure recorded the case of a little white child who was suddenly stricken with croup or diphtheria. The case demanded immediate attention. The only nurse available was a colored nurse. The child's mother at first objected to placing her darling under the care of a colored person, but yielded to the inevitable—how often the poor Negro must owe his chance to the fact that no one else can be got! The case was a critical one, but by unremitting and sleepless devotion to the little stranger who had been brought to her, this nurse, knowing as she did the mother's antipathy, rescued the little patient almost by force from the jaws of death and restored it to the arms of its anxious mother, who was duly grateful and appreciative. Thus this noble woman was able not only to perform a service for humanity, but in a larger sense, to render a valuable service to her race; for every forward step taken, every obstacle overcome, every new field of endeavor successfully invaded, lifts the race that much higher in the economic and social scale. It's an awful struggle, is n't it, this race problem? I have heard our genial and optimistic friend Dr. Washington say that if he could, after leaving this earthly sphere, be privileged to return again, and were permitted to choose his own reincarnation, he thought he would wish to be born an American Negro; that the joy of life lay in effort and struggle and that "to be a Negro in a day like this" as Mr. James Carrothers phrases it,[16] offered such an opportunity for effort and for struggle as to make life extremely pleasurable. Well, maybe so, tho I have a sneaking suspicion that a great many people are Negroes because they have to be and not because they want to be, and most of our effort and struggle is to attain to the point where that particular effort and struggle will no longer be necessary. Dr. Washington has made a great success out of being a Negro, but not many of us are thus highly favored. What you can do, however, in your chosen profession, is to prove the capacity of your race for all the multifarious things which the trained nurse most know and do. And while you will doubtless meet now and then with rebuffs and disappointments, you should not be discouraged; you should look on the bright side, and think rather of the things you have than of those you have not. Think of your great grandmother, who when she had a pain in the stomach thought she was conjured; who could not gain in a month as much as you can earn in a week, and probably did not get what she earned. Compare your condition with hers and cheer up! And perhaps, if you are faithful to your trust and to your race and to yourself, you may help to clear the pathway of your race for still further advancement. For the race is not altogether to the swift, the battle not entirely to the strong,[17] but in a large measure to him that holdeth out to the end.

I wish you all success in your profession. With proper effort you cannot fail. You owe it to yourselves to succeed. It would not be dealing with justice to yourself to fail, to have wasted three years of your life. You owe it to those who perhaps have exercised some self-denial and self-sacrifice to give you these opportunities. It would not be just to your instructors, who have given you of their time and of their effort. Nor would it be just to this noble institution, which has afforded you this golden opportunity to fit yourself for usefulness, and which stands out in this community & in this great country as an example of what the colored race can accomplish along lofty lines. You ought to so carry yourselves that when asked where you received your training, you will not only be proud to say at Provident Hospital, but so that Provident Hospital will be glad to have you say so, and that you thus, by reflecting credit upon your *alma mater*—which some of you in your strenuous training have sometimes looked upon as a *dura mater*—I am saying this solely for the sake of the pun[18]—and thus by increasing its prestige reciprocate in some degree the service it has rendered you.

And you owe it to your race, your struggling race, etc. . . .

⌐

SOURCE: Untitled and undated typed text at the Fisk University Library. On the evening of 4 May 1914, Chesnutt delivered this speech in Chicago at the graduation exercises of the Provident Hospital training school for nurses. The venue was the Y.M.C.A. at Wabash Avenue and 38th Street.

[1]*Life and Adventures of Martin Chuzzlewit* (1844).

[2]Louisa May Alcott (1832–88), *Hospital Sketches* (1863); William Dean Howells (1837–1920), *An Imperative Duty* (1892).

[3]Florence Nightingale (1820–1910), an English nurse and hospital reformer, was known as "the Lady with the Lamp."

[4]The Crimean War was fought from 1853 to 1856; England entered the war in 1854.

[5]Lord Sidney Herbert (1810–61) was England's Secretary of State for War.

[6]Her paper was privately printed in 1858 as *Notes on Matters Affecting the Health, Efficiency, and Hospital Administration of the British Army.*

[7]*Observations on the Evidence Contained in the Stational Reports Submitted to the Royal Commission on the Sanitary State of the Army in India.*

[8]The International Red Cross was founded in 1872 by Jean Henri Dunant (1828–1910), a Swiss banker inspired by Nightingale's work.

[9]*Atlantic Monthly*, 1 (November 1857), 22–23.

[10]Alice Freeman Palmer (1855–1902) was the progressive president (1882–88) and trustee (1888–1902) of Wellesley College and dean of women at the University of Chicago (1892–95); Jane Addams (1860–1935), a settlement worker and peace activist, was the Nobel Prize–winning organizer and resident head of Hull House social settlement in Chicago (1889–1935).

[11]1 Corinthians 15:41.

[12]Galen (130?–201?) was a second century Greek physician; Hippocrates (460?–377? B.C.) was also a Greek physician and is known as the "Father of Medicine."

[13]William Harvey (1578–1657), author of the *Essay on the Motion of the Heart and*

the Blood (1628), was the English physician who first expounded the theory of the circulation of the blood.

¹⁴"Poetic Aphorisms from the *Sinngedichte* of Friedrich von Logau," the section entitled "'The Best Medicines,'" translated by Longfellow in 1845 and included in Chesnutt's personal copy of *The Poetical Works of Henry Wadsworth Longfellow* (1888)—now at the Fisk University Library.

¹⁵Chesnutt suffered a stroke and was hospitalized in June 1910.

¹⁶James D. Corrothers (1869–1917) was a minister in various Protestant denominations. He had begun writing dialect poetry under the influence of his friend Paul Laurence Dunbar, some of which he collected in *The Black Cat Club: Negro Humor and Folklore* (1902); numerous later works appeared in various issues of *Century* magazine, and 1907 saw the publication of his *Selected Poems*. Quoted here is the opening line of "At the Closed Gate of Justice."

¹⁷Ecclesiastes 9:11.

¹⁸That one's "loving mother" may have proved a "hard," or demanding, "mother" is the witticism offered. The pun plays upon two meanings of the "hard mother" term since the dura mater is the tough, fibrous membrane that lies over the arachnoid and the pia mater, covering the brain and the spinal cord.

Women's Rights

Essay published in *The Crisis*, August 1915

I believe that all persons of full age and sound mind should have a voice in the making of the laws by which they are governed, or in the selection of those who make those laws. As long as the family was the social unit, it was perhaps well enough for the householder, representing the family, to monopolize the vote. But with the broadening of woman's sphere the situation has changed, and many women have interests which are not concerned with the family.

Experience has shown that the rights and interests of no class are safe so long as they are entirely in the hands of another class—the rights and interests of the poor in the hands of the rich, of the rich in the hands of the poor, of one race in the hands of another. And while there is no such line of cleavage in other social classes, yet so far as women constitute a class as differentiated from men, neither can their rights be left with entire safety solely in the hands of men. In the gradual extension of statutory rights, women are in many countries, the equals of men before the law. They have always been subject to the burdens of citizenship. The burden of taxation, generally speaking, falls more heavily upon them, perhaps because they are more honest in returning their personal property for taxation, or less cunning in concealing it. They are subject, equally with men, to the criminal laws, though there, I suspect, for sentimental reasons, the burden has not fallen so heavily upon them. Their rights need protection, and they should be guarded against oppression, and the ballot is the most effective weapon by which these things can be accomplished.

I am not in favor of woman suffrage because I expect any great improvement in legislation to result from it. The contrary, from woman's lack of experience in government, might not unreasonably be expected. Women are certainly no wiser or more logical than men. But they enjoy equal opportunities for education, and large numbers of them are successfully engaged in business and in the professions and have the requisite experience and knowledge to judge intelligently of proposed legislation. Even should their judgment be at fault—as men's judgment too often is—they have fine intuitions, which are many times a safe guide to action; and their sympathies are apt to be in support of those things which are clean and honest and which ought to make them a valuable factor in government.

⌒

SOURCE: "Women's Rights," *The Crisis*, 10 (August 1915), 182–83. Chesnutt's essay appeared in a symposium entitled "Votes for Women."

A Solution for the Race Problem

Speech delivered c. 1916

Several evenings ago a young man called at my house to talk over the Race Question; an intelligent, earnest, eager young man, filled with zeal for social service and the uplift of humanity. With the impatience of youth, he wanted to find an immediate solution for this vexed problem. We discussed various suggested remedies—education, property, the ballot, assimilation, segregation, expatriation—in fact every "'ation" except annihilation, which, historically, has settled some race problems. When he left, about eleven o'clock, I was glad to see him go, and the Race Problem was no nearer solution, except by about three hours time, than it was when we began. I don't know that we will be any further along with it when I shall have finished, except perhaps by another hour.

And yet, in spite of the difficulties which surround it, this problem is not insoluble, and indeed has been entirely solved as to some of its aspects, and is in rapid process of solution as to all of them, in several countries not far from our own shores, inhabited by mixed populations of the same kind as inhabit our own country, and under conditions, past and present, very similar to those which obtain in our own land. And I want, for a little while, to call your attention to some of these countries, and to consider how those conditions were brought about, as suggesting a way, and indeed the only conceivable way in which different races can live together harmoniously in the same country. For that is the only phase of the Race Problem with which we need practically concern ourselves at present.

The part of the world to which I refer, commonly designated as Latin-America, is that portion of the American continent lying to the south of us, which was settled by Spain, France and Portugal, who belong to the so-called Latin races of Europe, i.e., those whose languages are derived directly from the Latin tongue. The countries they settled extend from the southern boundary of the United States southward, embracing the West Indies, Central America and the whole of South America.

There are in Latin-America about fifteen million black and colored people, using the word "colored" as it is used in those countries, as meaning Negroid or of mixed blood. Of these, at least ten millions are partly white. The two countries containing the largest number are Brazil, with about 8,300,000 and Hayti with 2,900,000. The other four millions are distributed as I shall indicate in the various countries as I take them up.

First let us start nearest home. There are some Negroes in the Mexican coast cities, but they are negligible in number, and their status, as all through Spanish America, is governed by their class, which is not fixed by their race. Cuba, the Pearl of the Antilles, has a native population, by the census of 1907–8, of about 2,049,000, of which 609,000, or a little less than one third, are colored, 242,000 being unmixed Negroes, very dark, the rest of the 609,000 mulattoes of varying tints. Their white blood is Spanish, their language Spanish, their religion Roman Catholic. They all possess equal rights before the law, and these rights are respected. They vote, and exert political influence in proportion to their numbers and their intelligence.

Socially there is a color line—the island is only a few miles from the U.S.—but it is not closely drawn. Octoroons and people with only a slight trace of Negro ancestry, may be classed officially as whites, and it is not considered good taste to inquire too closely into a Creole's pedigree. Many Cuban Negroes are wealthy citizens, living in accordance with their means. Negroes or dark mulattoes are to be found in all the professions and nearly every branch of government service, notably in the police, army, post office and other public works. For a time it seemed as though the American occupation of Cuba following the war with Spain, might stir up race animosities, but the Cuban Negroes resented and resisted that influence, and the danger seems to be happily averted.[1] Travelers speak of the industry, sobriety and prosperity of the colored people of Cuba, and are especially struck by the good taste and quality of their dress. They have acquired, from association, the pride of bearing, the good taste in dress and demeanor of the Castilian, to which is added the native dignity of certain types of Africans. The Spanish mulatto is generally considered a fine physical and mental type of humanity, and produced, for instance, Antonio Maceo, who distinguished himself in the Cuban Revolution. Martinez Campos, the best Spanish governor of Cuba, was the son of an octoroon mother, tho born in Spain and therefore technically a Spaniard and not a Cuban.[2]

The republics of Hayti and San Domingo have no race problems, their populations being almost entirely colored, in Hayti the blacks predominating, there being only 250 white people out of a population of two and three-quarter millions, there obviously thus being no strain out of which to replenish the stock of mulattoes. The people of San Domingo, which, as distinguished from Hayti has been called the Mulatto Republic, are mostly of mixed Spanish and Negro blood. The political history of this island,[3] naturally one of the richest and most fertile spots on earth, has been most unfortunate, and has not reflected creditably upon the capacity of the Negro for government.[4] And the construction of the Panama canal, and certain naval and military exigencies resulting therefrom and from the generally disturbed condition of the world, has led the U.S., on one pretext or another, to intervene, very recently, in Hayti and practically take over the government.[5] This is regrettable, but seems to have been inevitable, tho I have no doubt the island, tho less free, will be more peaceful and prosperous under American rule.

Porto Rico, until the late war with Spain a colony, or rather a province of Spain, now an American dependency, is about one-half the size of Cuba, and about six times as densely populated.

The population is mixed, but the whites outnumber the combined black and colored people. Out of a total population of 809,000, 480,000 are white, 248,000 colored, and 78,000 black. Before the American occupation, 97,000 of them could read and write, 14,000 could only read, and 695,000 were illiterate. Schools multiplied under the U.S. and the percentage of illiteracy has been greatly reduced. Under the Spaniards, racial conditions were similar to those in Cuba, and I have not been able to ascertain that they have changed since the American occupation.

The French islands, Martinique and Guadaloupe, are two beautiful islands. "Not less interesting," says an American traveler, speaking of Martinique, than the natural features are the "inhabitants of this island, distinguished by beauty, thrift and a remarkable and peculiar individuality."[6] In 1895 they numbered nearly 500 to the square mile, aggregating 187,692, all of whom except 1,307, were either blacks or members of that remarkable mixed race which distinguishes this island. The mixed population shows every variety of color and type, but they are generally healthy and thriving. "Both men and women are so perfect anatomically," says this enthusiastic admirer, "that an artist wishing to create a 'Mercury' or 'Venus' need only take a cast of such a body, without making one modification from neck to heel."

"The people have an air of thrift and self-respect, which finds expression in the cleanliness and the taste displayed in their dress, streets, houses, customs and agricultural possessions."

They are such a type of people, I imagine, as might have grown up in Hayti had the whites not been driven out so soon,[7] or in Louisiana, had the Anglo-Saxon not superseded the colonial French. They have a colonial form of government, with considerable powers of self-government, except in fiscal matters. Each island has a Governor and a Privy Council and an elective assembly of 36 members, elected on a universal male suffrage, without distinction of race or color. Each island also sends two deputies and one senator to represent it in the French Parliament, and these are often colored men. There are so few white people in these islands, and these mainly the merchants and owners of large estates, that there is hardly room for a race problem. The closest and most friendly relations prevail between the colonies and the mother country, and colored men from the French islands have won distinction in France. General Alfred Dodds, some years before the present war the ranking general of the French army, is a colored native of one of these islands, as was Guillaume Guillon Lethière, a very famous French historical painter, who flourished in the middle of the last century, and whose canvases are found in the State Museums of the French capital and other cities.

There are other islands which I might mention, but I shall refer to only two, the English islands of Jamaica and Barbados, the white people of which are of the same ethnic strain as those of the U.S., and which in respect to slavery and its resulting conditions more closely resemble the U.S.

The population of Barbados comprises 180,000 black and colored people. Perfect equality of civil rights prevails; in fact, color distinctions in politics among free people ceased to exist in 1832, and all the people became free in 1835. It has a governor appointed by the Crown, a House of Assembly of 24 members, seven of whom are colored, elected on popular suffrage, a Legislative Council nominated by the Crown, an executive committee, one of whose members is a Negro. Education is not compulsory, but 75 per cent. of the Negroes and colored people born since 1860 are able to read and write. There is an excellent school system. In Codrington College, the oldest University in the West Indies, Negro or colored students were first received in 1840, and now form the large majority. Most of the people of all races belong to the Church of England. Sexual morality is perhaps better than in the rest of the West Indian Islands. Serious crime is rare among the natives. All through the West Indies it is the universal testimony that such a thing as assault by a Negro upon a white woman is unknown. 315 Negro and white constables are sufficient to maintain order. The products of the island are sugar and cotton. The greater part of the land belongs to white planters, resident and absentee, and as a rule the colored inhabitants work for fair wages on the white planter's land.

As to the door of opportunity in this little island of about 166 square miles, a poor mulatto boy of Barbadian birth rose to be Sir Conrad Reeves, Chief Justice of Barbados, winning in that capacity the universal regard of black, white and colored. President Barclay of Liberia, a statesmanlike and highly educated administrator, was a native Barbadian.[8] Another colored man of ability is now Solicitor General of the colony and is held to be in line for higher appointment.

* * *

In describing conditions in the British West Indies, Mr. Olivier says,[9] "The people of Jamaica are mostly Negroes with but little admixture of white blood. The predominant status is that of peasant proprietors, the majority of whom own land in small holdings, although in some districts considerable numbers still live and work for wages.

> Next in number to the nearly pure Negro peasant class comes the considerable class of mixed descent, which largely supplies the artisans and tradesmen. Very many of this class are landowners and planters, many are overseers and bookkeepers on estates, many commercial clerks, and some are engaged in the professions of law and medicine. Many clergy of all the Protestant denominations are black or colored; so are all the elementary schoolmasters and schoolmistresses and some of the teachers in the few second grade schools. There are not more than 15,000 persons in the island, about 1 in 43 (including Jews), who claim to be of unmixed white race. These whites predominate in the governing and employing class, and as merchants or planters direct and lead the industrial life of the island.
>
> Now what are the social relations in this mixed community? There is no artificial or conventional disqualification whatever to bar any Jamaican of Negro or mixed race from occupying any position for which he is intellectually qualified in any department of the social life of the island, including the public service. Many colored men are magistrates of Petty Sessions, more than one holds the office of chief magistrate of their parishes. These positions they fill with credit. According to their professional position they associate with the white residents on precisely the same terms as persons of pure European extraction.

In leaving the West Indies and proceeding to South America, Brazil is the largest country in Latin-America, both in extent of territory and number of inhabitants, also the country containing the largest number of Negroes and Negroids. This vast, rich in natural resources and only partially developed country, has the enormous area of 3,293,000 square miles, about the size of the continental United States, exclusive of Alaska, or about eight times the size of France, and a total population of approximately 20,000,000, about 6 to the square mile, of whom about 8,000,000 are white, 5,582,000 mulattoes and other mixed breeds, 2,000,000 Indians and 2,718,000 pure Negroes—8,300,000 or more, of more or less Negro blood.

Brazil was settled by the Portuguese and remained a dependency of Portugal until it became an independent empire under Dom Pedro, whose deposition is within the recollection of many of us, since which it has been a Republic.[10] The Portuguese discovered Brazil in 1499. They had been slave-traders, bringing Negroes from the Moorish coast and Senegal River to Portugal and Spain in the middle of the fifteenth century. As slavery in the United States was stimulated by the discovery of the cotton gin, so slavery in Brazil received a great impetus from the discovery of diamonds in the 18th Century and the eagerness to work the gold mines in Southeastern Brazil. The majority of the population at the beginning of the nineteenth century were Negroes, and the race is still almost predominant in certain parts of the country, and some of the east coast cities are almost solidly black.

The Negro and Negroid enter all careers, serve in all trades, professions and employments in Brazil, from scavenger to priest, college professorships, party leadership. And it is said that more than one of the presidents of Brazil has had a dash of Ethiopia in his veins.

Negroes constitute a large proportion of the standing army, of the police and of the navy. They furnish the bulk of the recruits for military bands and civilian orchestras. Some of the best music in Brazil is produced by mulattoes or pure-blooded Negroes. The white element controls most of the wealth of the country, and the small foreign white population, about 150,000 Germans and four or five thousand British wield an influence quite out of proportion to their numbers. The German influence has become less since the outbreak of the present war.[11]

"Yet the colored man," says Sir Harry Johnston, "administers, even if he does not rule, especially since the commencement of the Republic. At the present moment there is scarcely a lowly or a highly placed Federal or Provincial official, at the head of or within any of the great departments of State, that has not more or less Negro or American Indian blood in his veins."

The Honorable James Bryce, in a recent work on South America,[12] says, "In the *Indian* countries, the Mestizos [mixed white and Indian] and Whites are, for political and social purposes, practically one class and that the ruling class. In Brazil it is the Whites who rule, but many of them are tinged with Negro, fewer with Indian, blood.

> To understand the social relations of the white and colored races one must begin by remembering that there is in Spanish and Portuguese countries no such sharp color line as exists where men of Teutonic stock are settled in countries outside Europe. As this is true of the negro, it is even more true of the Indian. He may be despised as a weakling, he may be ignored as a citizen, he may be, as he was at one time, abominably oppressed and ill treated, but he excites no personal repulsion. It is not his race that is against him, but his debased condition. Whatever he suffers, is suffered because he is ignorant or timid or helpless, not because he is of a different blood and colour. Accordingly the Spanish Americans do not strive to keep off and keep down the Indian in such wise as the North Americans and the Dutch and the English—I do not mean the governments, but the individuals—treat their black subjects. There is not even such aversion to him as is shown in California and in Australia to the Chinese, Japanese, and Hindus. The distinction between the races is in Spanish America a distinction of rank or class rather than of color. Against intermarriage there is, therefore, no more feeling than that which exists against any union palpably below a man's or woman's own rank in life. Whereas in the United States the man of colour is discriminated against for social purposes, irrespective of his wealth, education, or personal qualities, in Spanish countries race counts for so little that when he emerges out of the poverty and ignorance which mark the Indian, his equality with the white man is admitted. . . .

> Brazil is distinguished from the other republics by the fact that in addition to her small mestizo population and her pure Indian population, most of it wild, she has a great mass of negroes and a still larger mass of mulattoes and quadroons. It is hardly too much to say that along the coast from Rio to Bahia and Pernambuco, as well as in parts of the interior behind these two cities, the black population predominates. In character and habits it somewhat resembles the negroes of the British West Indies and Santo Domingo, being superior to the Haytians, but inferior in

education and enterprise to the colored people of the southern states of North America.

We thank the distinguished Englishman for the compliment.

It is well treated—slavery was seldom harsh among the kindly natured, easy-going Portuguese—and bears no ill-will to its former masters. Neither do they feel towards it that repulsion which marks the attitude of the whites to the negroes in North America and South Africa. The Brazilian lower class intermarries freely with the black people; the Brazilian middle class intermarries with mulattoes and quadroons. Brazil is the one country in the world, besides the Portuguese colonies on the east and west coasts of Africa, in which a fusion of the European and African races is proceeding unchecked by law or custom. The doctrines of human equality and human solidarity have here their perfect work. The result is so far satisfactory that there is little or no class friction. The white man does not lynch or maltreat the negro. The negro is not accused of insolence and does not seem to develop any more criminality than naturally belongs to any ignorant population with loose notions of morality and property.

Theodore Roosevelt, in his book published shortly after his recent tour of South America,[13] verifies these conditions, saying, among other things, speaking of the racial makeup of the Brazilian population,

The great majority of the men and women of high social position in Rio are of as unmixed white blood as the corresponding class in Paris or Madrid or Rome. The great majority of the political leaders are pure whites, with an occasional dash of Indian blood. But any Negro or mulatto who shows himself fit is without question given the place to which his abilities entitle him.

And then he instances several whom he had met occupying places of importance in the professions and in political life, against whom he had seen no slightest evidence of discrimination on account of their color. "The working classes are divided between the whites and the blacks, but the white working men draw no line against the Negro, and in the lower ranks intermarriages are frequent, especially between Negroes and the most numerous of the immigrant classes from Europe"—by which I assume he means the Italians.

In the middle class these marriages are rare, and in the higher class almost unknown so far as concerns men and women in whom the black strain is at all evident. But even in the higher ranks there is apparently no prejudice whatever against marrying a man or a girl who is, say, seven-eighths white, the remaining quantity of black blood being treated as a negligible element.

Now, having outlined briefly a section of the world in which there are many millions of black and colored people, and no race problem, let us inquire for a moment how this came about. Antecedent conditions in these countries were in many essential respects similar to those in our own Southern States. Slavery existed there, in most places a crueler and severer slavery than that in the United States. The Spaniards were cruel slaveholders; the severity of the French planters drove Hayti to revolt, and all through the island the lot of the slave was hard. The

Portuguese as we have just seen, had less race feeling than any other colonizing Europeans, and under their code a slave who became free was immediately raised to the status of a freeman endowed with all civil and political rights, and the same was largely true in Barbados and some others of the English islands. Slavery was abolished by England in her colonies in 1835, in Hayti and San Domingo at the time of the Revolution in the first years of the 19th Century, in the Spanish islands in 1873, and in Brazil not entirely until 1889, though a process of gradual emancipation had been in force for some years.

In all these countries, as in the United States, the abolition of slavery was attended with more or less trouble growing out of so radical an economic change. In the United States, with war and the troubles of reconstruction, in Hayti, with the massacre and expulsion of the white race; in Jamaica, after emancipation, there were serious difficulties, similar to those which led to reconstruction in the South, growing out of the effort of the planters to devise a system of indentured service which should preserve to them most of the advantages of slavery and deny to the Negroes most of the advantages of freedom. In Brazil the sudden abolition of slavery led to the revolution in which Dom Pedro lost his throne and by which the Republic was established.

In all these lands there were left, as in our South, after the fall of slavery, vast numbers of ignorant Negroes, side by side, in some cases with a majority, in others with a minority of white people, excepting perhaps Hayti, but with the whites dominating government and industry, by virtue of their superior ability and training and their ownership of the soil and the productive machinery of industry. As in the South, the freed slaves owned nothing but their bodies, had no commodity to trade with but their labor. They were just as black, just as ignorant, just as unreliable laborers, in all respects similar to their cousins in the United States. Their former masters did not like emancipation any better than did the slaveholders of the United States. That they did not fight to retain slavery was probably due more to their lack of strength to resist emancipation than to any moral or political consideration.

And yet these diverse races, as we have seen, have ironed out their difficulties and are living peacefully side by side, respecting one another's rights, associating with each other on terms of theoretical equality and refusing to accept race as a ground for denying practical equality. The Negroes respect the white people, accept their leadership, look up to them as employers and leaders. The white people encourage the Negroes to advance in the world and accept them on whatever level they may advance to.

Now, how has this halcyon state of affairs been brought about? I will let Mr. Olivier tell you:—

> So far as a wholesome and hopeful equilibrium has been attained in these mixed communities, it has been brought into being by the steadfast exclusion of all theory of race discrimination. Race discrimination—not distinction of human capacity. . . . The civilization and morality of the Jamaica negro are not high, but he is on a

markedly different level from his grandfather, the African savage. The negro in Jamaica has been so far raised, so much freedom of civic mixture between the races has been made tolerable, by the continuous application to the race of the theory of humanity and equality: equality, that is, in the essential sense of endowment in the Infinite, a share, however obscure and undeveloped, in the inheritance of what we call the Soul. Evangelical Christianity, most democratic of doctrines, and educational effort, inspired and sustained by a personal conviction and recognition that, whatever the superficial distinctions, there was a fundamental community and an equal claim in the Black with the White to share, according to personal capacity and development, in all the inheritance of humanity—these chiefly have created the conditions that have done what has been done for the negro in the lands of his exile. Emancipation, Education, identical justice, perfect equality in the Law Courts and of the Constitution whatever it might be, these take away the sting of race difference, and if there is race inferiority, it is not burdened with an artificial handicap. Negroes are now indisputably the equals of the white men in categories in which one hundred years ago their masters would have confidently argued that they were naturally incapable of attaining equality. All such positive and materialised progress has been made by ignoring the obvious; by refusing to accept as conclusive the differences and the disabilities; by believing in the identities, the flashes of response and promise; by willing that there should be light where there seemed to be no light; by the methods of the visionary whose kingdom is not of this world, but who is insensately bent on assimilating this world to that kingdom;—*in part even by less than this*, by the mere resolute maintenance in the State of principles of common justice. The vast transplantation of slavery, the intercourse of white and black, have, in fact, brought advance in humanity to the colored people. This has been done, and further advance towards health in a mixed community can only be looked for by adherence to the attitude, nay, indeed, by the personal recognition and consciousness of equality. Whatever mob prejudices may dictate, statesmen and educated observers at least cannot fail to recognise this, and must recognize that to set up the opposite principle, the allegation of inequality, of insuperable race differences and degradation, and to take this as a guide for internal policy, is a sin against light that is certain to aggravate the disorders of any mixed community as it is today demoralising the Southern States of the Union.

The color line is not a rational line, the logic neither of words nor facts will uphold it. If adopted it infallibly aggravates the virus of the color problem. The more it is ignored, the more is that virus attenuated. It is quite possible to justify a political generalization—not as a truth, but as a working formula—that where the majority of the population are negro peasants, it is advisable to restrict the franchise. It is not possible, either as a working political formula, or as an anthropological theorem, to justify a generalisation that there is any political or human function for which colored persons are by their African blood disqualified. In various categories of human activity one may maintain that, as a rule, black and colored folk are not up to the normal standard of white, and are difficult and disheartening to deal with. But in other categories they are more liberally endowed than the average white man, not only with sympathetic and valuable human qualities, but with talent and executive ability for their expression.

The late Professor Josiah Royce, Professor of Philosophy at Harvard University, in discussing this question in a magazine article,[14] after commenting upon conditions in Jamaica, as I have described them, and referring to some of the moral and economic difficulties which trouble its overcrowded population, says: "Whatever the problems of Jamaica, whatever its defects, our present southern race problem in the forms in which we know it best, simply does not exist. There is no public controversy about social race equality or superiority." And then, after giving the Negro a good character, he goes on:

> There is no doubt whatever that English white men are the essential controllers of the destiny of the country. But these English whites, few as they are, control the country at present with extraordinary little friction, and wholly without those painful emotions, those insistent complaints and anxieties, which at present are so prominent in the minds of many of our own Southern brethren. Life in Jamaica is not ideal. The economical aspect of the island is in many ways unsatisfactory. But the negro race-question, in our present American sense of that term, seems to be substantially solved. How has it been solved?
>
> I answer, by the simplest means in the world—the simplest that is, for Englishmen—*viz.*: by English administration, and by English reticence. When first the sad period of emancipation and of subsequent occasional disorder was passed, the Englishman did in Jamaica what he had so often and so well done elsewhere. He organized his colony; he established good local courts, which gained by square treatment the confidence of the blacks. The English ruler also appointed a good country constabulary, in which native blacks also found service, and in which they could exercise authority over other blacks. Black men in other words, were trained, under English management of course, to police black men. A sound civil service was also organized; and in that educated negroes found in due time their place. Hence he is accustomed to the law, he sees its ministers often, and often, too, as men of his own race; and in the main, he is fond of order, and to be respectful towards the established ways of society. . . .
>
> Administration has given the negroes, in many cases, the true self-respect of those who themselves officially co-operate in the work of the law, and it has done this without any such result as our Southern friends nowadays conceive when they think of what is called "Negro domination."
>
> Yes, the work has been done by administration,—and by reticence. You well know that in dealing, as an individual, with other individuals, trouble is seldom made by the fact that you are actually the superior of another man in any respect. The trouble comes when you tell the other man too stridently that you are his superior. Be my superior quietly, simply showing your superiority in your deeds, and very likely I shall love you for the very fact of your superiority. For we all love our leaders. But tell me that I am your inferior, and then perhaps I may grow boyish, and may throw stones. So with races. Grant that yours is the superior race, then you can afford to say little about that subject in your public dealings with the backward race. Superiority is best shown by good deeds and by few boasts. . . .
>
> My study and comparison of conditions in the United States and in the West Indies, has brought me to the conviction that no solution of the American color difficulties will be found except by resolutely turning the back to the color-line and race-differentiation theory.
>
> In any case, the Southern race problem will never be relieved by speeches or by practices such as increase irritation. It will be relieved when administration grows sufficiently effective, and when the Negroes themselves get an increasingly respon-

sible part in this administration so far as it relates to their own race. This may seem a wild scheme. But I insist: It is the English way. Look at Jamaica and learn how to settle your race problem.

As to Brazil, Mr. Roosevelt, visiting only a year or two ago, refers the conditions he has described in that country to the different fundamental attitude of Brazilians toward the Negro.[15] "The difference between the U.S. and Brazil," he says, "is the tendency of Brazil to absorb the Negro.

My observation leads me to believe that in "absorb" I have used exactly the right expression to describe this process. It is the Negro who is being absorbed and not the Negro who is absorbing the white man. . . . This does not mean that Brazilians are or will become the "mongrel" people that they have been asserted to be by certain writers. . . . The great majority of the men and women I met, the leaders in the world of political and social effort, showed little if any more trace of Negro blood than would be shown by the like number of similar men in a European capital. Yet not only is there in some classes a considerable infiltration of Negro blood, with a corresponding tendency of the pure Negro type to disappear, but this process is regarded with hearty approval by the most thoughtful statesmen of the country, one of whom, himself of pure white blood, expressed their view to me substantially as follows:

"Of course the presence of the Negro is the real problem, and a very serious problem, both in your country, the United States, and in mine, Brazil. Slavery was an intolerable method of solving the problem, and had to be abolished. But the problem itself remained, in the presence of the Negro. It was not the slave-owner who inherited his slaves who was responsible for the problem. The slave-trader who brought the slaves into the country was the man who inflicted the ghastly wrong, not only upon the blacks but upon the whites. We, like you, have merely inherited the problem.

"Now comes the necessity to devise some method of dealing with it. You of the United States are keeping the blacks as an entirely separate element, and you are not treating them in a way that fosters their self-respect. They will remain a menacing element in your civilization, permanent, and perhaps even after a while a growing element. With us the question tends to disappear, because the blacks themselves tend to disappear and become absorbed. You speak of Brazil as having a large Negro population. Well, in a century there will not be any Negroes in Brazil, whereas you will have twenty or thirty millions of them. Then for you there will be a real and very uncomfortable problem, while for us the problem in its most menacing phase will have disappeared. You say that this result will be accomplished only by an adulteration, and therefore a weakening, of the pure white blood. I grant that this will have happened as regards a portion, perhaps a third, of our population. I regret this, but it is the least objectionable of the alternatives. We treat the Negro with entire respect, and he responds to the treatment. If a Negro shows capacity and integrity, he receives the same reward that a white man would receive. He has therefore every incentive to rise. In the upper ranks of society there is no intermarriage with the Negro of pure or nearly pure blood; but such intermarriage is frequent in the lower ranks, especially between the Negro and many classes of immigrants.

"The pure Negro is constantly growing less and less in numbers, and after two or more crosses of the white blood the Negro blood tends to disappear, so far as any different physical, mental, and moral traits of the race are concerned. When he has disappeared his blood will remain as an appreciable, but in no way a dominant, element in perhaps a third of our people, while the remaining two-thirds will be pure whites. Granted that this strain will represent a slight weakening in one-third of our population, the result will be that in our country two-thirds of the population will have kept its full strength, with one-third slightly weakened, while the Negro problem will have entirely disappeared. In your country all the white population will have been kept in its original race strength, but the Negro will remain in increased numbers and with an increased and bitter sense of isolation, so that the problem of his presence will be more menacing than at present. I do not say that ours is a perfect solution, but I regard it as a better solution than yours. We and you have to face two alternatives, neither of them without drawbacks. I believe that the one we Brazilians have chosen will in the long run, from the national standpoint, prove less disadvantageous and dangerous than the one you of the United States have chosen."

Thus we see a country in which the white people, the large majority of the population, are quite as white as those of our own land, who receive the Negro on terms of equality without that shrinking sensitive fear of contamination by his blood which stands in the way of his advancement in this country, and who have already absorbed a considerable element of dark blood with no results which they consider either deteriorating or shameful; a country in which it is the well-defined and settled public policy to so mix the three constituent races of the population, the white, Indian and Negro, with the resultant of a race at least so homogeneous that there will be no race feeling or friction or animosity.

* * *

I have now made plain to you, I hope, that there lie to the south of us several countries inhabited chiefly by people of our own kind or kinds. In all of them you can enjoy perfect equality not only in theory, but in fact, before the law; in some of them perfect social equality, in some of them social and political supremacy.

We have seen the peoples of Europe, when they suffer from caste or race or religious opposition, or economic pressure, when they find themselves deprived of political and social rights, find their way across the seas to distant lands, where they make for themselves home and country. Before the Great War began they poured into the United States at the rate of a million a year. The peoples of southern Europe, Spaniards and Italians, were flocking to Southern Brazil and Argentina. There is land enough in Brazil to furnish homes for all the Negroes of the United States, and they would no doubt be made welcome. It is one of the most productive countries, in the world, one of the richest in undeveloped resources, and the population is only six to the square mile. If it were peopled as thickly as Barbados it would hold 6,000 million people, four times the population of the whole world. Clearly there is room enough there for ten million Negroes, without crowding anybody, and in the predominantly black parts of the country industrial conditions are good.

Why, then, do colored people not emigrate from the United States to these happy regions?

Well, there are several reasons. Negroes are not, for one thing, an adventurous

race. They do not welcome a present hardship for the sake of a hypothetical benefit. Their one great migration to the West was involuntary, and seems to have inspired them with a distaste for emigration. Only a relatively small number of
them, though many lived within walking distance of the free states, escaped from
slavery. They are restless enough at home, but their restlessness does not extend
beyond our borders.

"As a rule," says a keen observer,[16]

> Negroes become attached to the people and customs of the first Caucasian lands of
> their adoption. Negroes from the United States, who go to Haiti, differing from the
> Haitians in speech, religion and usages, generally keep aloof and cannot attach
> themselves to the French language and entirely different habits of the Haitian
> blacks.

The same would be true of the Spanish and Portuguese countries. And again, there
are no steamship lines promoting Negro emigration for purposes of revenue. The
ground has not been broken. There is no little North American Negro colony in
Brazil, for instance, to bring out their brothers and sisters and write home to their
friends and relatives how well they are doing.

But another reason is that men can not live on rights alone. Rights are beautiful
things to fight for, to die for if need be, but they are not enough to live on. The
United States, taking it all in all, is the best country in the world. It is one of the
most extensive in territory, with plenty of room for ten times its present population. The West Indies are crowded to capacity. The United States is perhaps the
richest country in the world. Higher wages are paid in the United States than anywhere else in the world. There are greater opportunities for advancement here
than in any other country. This wealth and these opportunities are not equitably
distributed, and the Negro gets the short end of the short side; but even at that he
can earn more here, on the average, than anywhere else in the world. You all know
what colored people can earn in the U.S. today. In Jamaica, which has been called
the black man's paradise, manual labor commands about a shilling or 24 cents a
day.

In most parts of the United States, some education is within the reach of all. In
Hayti less than one in ten can read or write, and in Brazil the standard of literacy is
low. Scorned, flouted, discriminated against as is the Negro, elbowed aside politically and socially and industrially in the United States, the cold fact of the matter is
that in so rich and progressive a country the crumbs that fall from the national table are richer than the roast and fowl of these other lands. Our complaint is not
that we get so little, but that we do not have the opportunity to get as much as others do, that we are denied the equal chance.

And again, the colored people love their country, or at least are willing to love
it. They feel that they have earned the right to live in it and share its prosperity.
They prefer, as Dr. Washington advised them, "to cast down their buckets where
they are," but they want the equal chance, in order that their buckets may not
come up empty.[17]

The colored people want the friendship of the white people. They are bound to the white people, many of them by ties of blood, all of them by ties of custom, many of them by ties of friendship. Cement the union by the ties of justice and equal law, and they will be the first to acknowledge that the white people are the finest people in the world and to lick anybody who denies it.

Now, how can this devoutly to be wished for consummation be brought about? One thing is clear, that the race problem cannot be settled by the present methods. Education and wealth might ultimately solve it, though so far they have seemed at times to accentuate it, by presenting new surfaces for race friction. There is but one way to settle the race problem; that is to give the Negro equal rights. It is not difficult; given the will to do so on the part of the white people, it is the simplest thing in the world. What reasons are adduced against it? An instinctive physical repugnance? It surely is not physical repugnance which lives in daily and intimate personal intercourse with Negro servants, and yet will not sit beside them in theatres or street cars. Is it jealousy of the Negro, or fear of his possible supremacy? White people surely cannot believe in their boasted superiority, if it cannot assert itself in fair and friendly competition with numbers and every other advantage on their side. The white people seem to have very little respect for their own blood, anyway, when they permit fifteen-sixteenths of it in a person's veins to be despised and degraded by one-sixteenth of the blood of another race. Is it the fear of intermarriage? Certainly, the Negroes cannot marry the white people without their consent, and when enough of the white people want to, they will marry the Negroes with or without their consent, or else belie their record in history for taking what they want. They need have no fears upon this head.[18] Jamaica is overwhelmingly black, and yet the few whites have no difficulty in preserving their race purity and prestige while granting perfect civil and social equality to the darker race. And Mr. Olivier says:

> On the whole, however, it does not appear to me that admission to social and professional equality, when resulting from compatibility of temperament and interests, does, in fact, conduce necessarily or strongly to likelihood of intermarriage; at any rate, of frequent and habitual and unhesitating intermarriage.

And says Mr. Hill of the U.S. Geodetic Survey, speaking of Cuba: "Miscegenation has produced many mulattoes, but race admixture is no more common than in this country. The current expressions of fear concerning the future relations of this race in Cuba seem inexplicable."

The conditions in Brazil we have seen. They have no fear there but that the great majority of the people will continue to be white.

But suppose equality did encourage race admixture, and that there was some of it? Would it necessarily mean degeneration? Ask again our authorities.

Says Sir Sidney Olivier again:

> Notwithstanding all that it may be possible to adduce in justification of that prejudice against the mixed race, of which I have spoken, and which I have shared; I am convinced that this class as it at present exists, is a valuable and indispensable

part of any West Indian community, and that a colony of black, colored and whites has far more organic efficiency and far more promise in it than a colony of blacks and whites alone. A community of black and white alone is in far greater danger of remaining, so far as the unofficial classes are concerned, a community of employers and serfs, concessionaires and tributaries, with, at best, a bureaucracy to keep the peace between them. The graded mixed class in Jamaica . . . .

* * *

I quote Mr. Bryce on race admixture in Brazil, who says, conservatively:

What ultimate effect the intermixture of blood will have on the European element in Brazil, I will not venture to predict. If one may judge from a few remarkable cases, it will not necessarily reduce the intellectual standard. One of the ablest and most refined Brazilians I have known, had some color; and other such cases have been mentioned to me. Assumptions and preconceptions must be eschewed, however plausible they may seem.

The fusion of two parent stocks, one more advanced, the other more backward, does not necessarily result in producing a race inferior to the stronger parent or superior to the weaker. Conquest and control by a race of greater strength have, upon some races, a depressing and almost ruinous effect.

It has not had this effect on the Negro, who has profited, up to a certain point, by the contact with another race of greater strength, though with no particular credit to the oppressor, who conquered and controlled him for his own ends.

Again, the ease with which the Spaniards have intermingled by marriage with the Indian tribes—and the Portuguese have done the like, not only with the Indians, but with the more physically dissimilar Negroes—shows that race repugnance is no such constant and permanent factor in human affairs as members of the Teutonic peoples are apt to assume. Instead of being, as we Teutons suppose, the rule in this matter, we are rather the exception, for in the ancient world there seems to have been little race repulsion; there is very little today among Mohammedans; there is none among Chinese. This seems to suggest that since the phenomenon is not of the essence of human nature, it may not be always as strong among the Teutonic peoples as it is today.

And Mr. Bryce says in another place:

Blood is only one factor, and not the most important factor, in making of men. Environment and the influence of the reigning intellectual type count for more.

It may seem natural to assume that such mixed nations will, in respect of their aboriginal blood, be inferior to their European relatives. But this is a mere assumption. No one has yet investigated scientifically the results of race fusion. History throws little light on the subject, because wherever there has been a mixture of races there have been also concomitant circumstances influencing the people who are the product of the mixture which have made it hard to determine whether their deterioration (or improvement) is due to this or to some other cause.

And the Negro must do his part. He must prove himself so worthy of equality that the white people of this country will be ashamed to longer withhold it from him; ashamed of the hypocrisy which race prejudice makes of their religion;

ashamed of the hollow sham which race hatred makes of their democracy; ashamed of the lie it makes of their Constitution; ashamed of the laws which they have made the instrument of oppression and of the Courts which have upheld them; ashamed of the cowardly subserviency which permits a minority of the nation to override the most obvious dictates of justice and fair play. "If," as Kipling says—

> If you can keep your head when all about you
> Are losing theirs and blaming it on you;
> If you can trust yourself when all men doubt you,
> But make allowance for their doubting, too;
> If you can wait and not be tired by waiting,
> Or, being lied about, don't deal in lies,
> Or, being hated, don't give way to hating,
> And yet don't look too good or talk too wise;
>
> If you can dream—and not make dreams your master,
> If you can think, and not make thought your aim,
> If you can meet with triumph and disaster,
> And treat those two importers just the same;
> If you can bear to hear the truth you've spoken
> Twisted by knaves to make a trap for fools,
> Or watch the things you gave your life to broken,
> And stoop to build 'em up with wornout tools;
>
> If you can make one heap of all your winnings
> And risk it on one turn of pitch and toss,
> And lose, and start again at your beginnings,
> And never breathe a word about your loss;
> If you can force your heart and nerve and sinew
> To serve your turn long after they are gone,
> And so hold on when there is nothing in you,
> Except the will which says to them, "Hold on";
>
> If you can talk with crows and keep your virtue,
> Or walk with kings—nor lose the common touch,
> If neither foes nor loving friends can hurt you;
> If all men count with you, but none too much;
> If you can fill the unforgiving minute
> With sixty seconds' worth of distance run
> Yours is the earth, and everything that's in it,
> And—which is more—you'll be a man! my son.[19]

Now, I have no doubt that all of us here are in perfect accord in all that I have said, and that if it were left to us the color line would disappear tomorrow. But it will not be left to us, and legislative enactment is not alone sufficient to accomplish it, as experience with constitutions and civil rights laws has demonstrated. For in spite of these, I think it is true, that, if there is any American public policy on the subject, it is to preserve the color line, and this most certainly, if the South is to direct the public policy. The National Government, under the present administration,[20] has segregated the Negro in the public service to a large extent, and in the army the traditional policy is carried to such an extent that just at present the War Department hardly seems to know just what to do with the colored soldiers, except to keep them off by themselves.[21]

So the settlement of the Race question by the Brazilian method of absorbing the Negro is academic rather than practical, and will have to be left to the future. And we are relegated to other methods of getting together with the white people so as to live harmoniously and happily with them. Many of them, in fact I think most of them, are good people, and anxious to do the right thing as they see it. All we can do is to try to make them see it as we do, to maintain the principle of equal rights and equal opportunities to all men, with equal rewards according to their deserts, and to so conduct ourselves and so develop and use the power, intellectual, political, industrial and spiritual, that is latent in ten millions of people that it will be impossible to longer deny them these equal rights and opportunities. This can only be done by making the best use of every educational, industrial and professional opportunity and by the cultivation of a sound morality. There is no royal road to freedom and to opportunity; they must be fought for with every available weapon. With freedom and opportunity once secured, I venture that equality, in the broadest sense of the word, equality of capacity and of achievement will become less of a theory and more of an established fact. And if, in the course of time, the colored people do not prove themselves worthy of equal rights and opportunities, the blame will have to be placed upon the Creator who made them, and they will have to admit, as gracefully as they may, that they are fundamentally inferior. But I have no fear of any such outcome. The progress of the last fifty years makes the future brilliant with promise.

⌒

SOURCE: Incomplete and undated typed text at the Fisk University Library. When and where Chesnutt first delivered this speech are not known, though the reference to the very recent invasion of Haiti by the United States indicates that the passage containing it, at least, was written no earlier than late July 1915. That Chesnutt refers to World War I but not American involvement in it suggests that he composed his text prior to 6 April 1917 when Congress declared war on Germany. Chesnutt's handwritten notes at the top of the first page outline his opening remarks: "Have been in yr city before | No orator, but [canceled: "one subject &c"] if I can give | you someting [sic] to think about &c" appears above the title; and "Hav [sic] been in yr beau city before; &c &c Mrs. Ern, personally" is canceled below the title. These notes indicate that the speech was given outside Cleveland and possibly twice. If that was the case, Chesnutt may have been referring to a second delivery of "A Solution," or another version of it, when he wrote in a 24 December 1917 letter now at the Fisk University Library to the Reverend Archibald J. Carey (1868–1920?) of the Institutional Church in Chicago. He expressed his willingness to appear before its youth organization and indicated that he preferred 25 January 1918 (a Friday) or "a Sunday afternoon or evening." Wrote Chesnutt, "I have a very interesting lecture on the Negro in Latin America, which I think the society would find interesting." Related to "A Solution" is another incomplete and untitled manuscript, filed as "[The Negro Question]" at the Fisk University Library. It is viewed by the editors as leaves from an earlier draft or drafts.

[1]Cuba was under American military rule from 1898 to 1902. In 1906–9 and 1917–23, the United States again intervened in its affairs because of political instability.

[2]Robert T. Hill identifies Maceo (1845–96) in *Cuba and Porto Rico with the Other Islands of the West Indies* as representative of a "superior class of free mulattos . . . unlike any people in [the United States] with which they can be compared"; and he celebrates him for initiating the Cuban Revolution in 1895. Chesnutt also echoes Hill's impression of Arsenio Martinez de Campos (1831–1900), who brought the Ten Years War against Spanish rule to an end in 1878 and who stood in marked contrast with his successor Captain-General Valeriano Weyler y Nicolau (1838–1930). Hill ranks Campos as the most humane and least corrupt of the Spanish governors of Cuba.

[3]Both countries occupy the same island.

[4]Between the founding of the Haitian Republic in 1806 and the American intervention in its affairs in 1915, seventeen of twenty-four presidents were overthrown by revolution; eleven served for less than one year. Further, by 1915 Haiti's foreign debt amounted to over $21,000,000, this straining government finances since over 80 percent of its revenues went to debt service. In 1931, Arthur C. Millspaugh (1883–1955)—the 1927–29 Financial Adviser-General Receiver of Haiti—expressed in *Haiti Under American Control, 1915–1930* (1931) the popular conception of this country's economic instability: "Incompetence, demoralization and corruption in finance had brought the Government to virtual bankruptcy." The Dominican Republic had a similar history of indebtedness to European nations. The United States took over the collection of its customs, using the funds from 1905 to 1941 for debt payments. Violent political rivalries prompted the United States to put the country under the rule of its Marines from 1916 to 1924.

[5]American soldiers landed at Port-au-Prince on 28 July 1915 and were not withdrawn until 1934. A primary reason for the intervention in Haiti's affairs was strategic: viewed as necessary was the maintenance of American hegemony in the Caribbean and, more particularly, easy access to both Cuba and the Panama Canal. U.S. investment in Haiti—though not so sizeable as that in Cuba—was also a compelling consideration. The Woodrow Wilson administration was determined not to allow so unstable a country, whose debts to France and Germany were large, to fall under French or, more important in 1915, German control.

[6]Robert T. Hill is the traveler quoted. Hill attributes the statement below on the anatomical perfection of the Haitians to J. J. J. Cornilliac (1824–?).

[7]The insurrection led by Toussaint l'Ouverture resulted in the death of numerous slaveowners and the flight of other white inhabitants. Haiti achieved its independence in 1804, and its government was conducted by blacks.

[8]Chesnutt here, and below where he acknowledges his source, is deriving information from Harry H. Johnston (1858–1927), *The Negro in the New World* (1910).

[9]What followed the close of the previous paragraph is not known since a page of Chesnutt's typescript (p. 11) has not been located. P. 12 begins with a cancelation of the beginning of the present paragraph ("In describing . . . Olivier says,"). Presumably Chesnutt identified Olivier and began quoting him on the missing page. The canceled introduction is here restored to approximate the transition from the discussion of Barbados to the subject of Jamaica that Chesnutt most likely provided. Sydney H. Olivier was the author of the work quoted here and below, *White Capital and Coloured Labour*.

[10]Dom Pedro II (1825–91) ruled as emperor until forced to abdicate in 1889.

[11]World War I (1914–18).

[12]James Bryce, *South America: Observations and Impressions* (1912).

[13]Chesnutt wrongly assumed that Roosevelt's public reflections on race relations

were included in his book *Through the Brazilian Wilderness* (1914). Chesnutt quotes not that book but one of Roosevelt's 1913–14 articles on his South American travels that appeared in *Outlook*: "Brazil and the Negro," 106 (21 February 1914), 409–11.

[14]Josiah Royce (1855–1916) read "Race Questions and Prejudices" before the Chicago Ethical Society in 1905. It was published in April 1906 in the *International Journal of Ethics* and included in *Race Questions, Provincialism and Other American Problems* (1908). In *White Capital and Coloured Labour*, Olivier presented the same quotation of Royce that Chesnutt uses below.

[15]See n. 13.

[16]Chesnutt again quotes and paraphrases *Cuba and Porto Rico*.

[17]In his 1895 Cotton States Exposition Speech, included in *Up From Slavery*, Booker T. Washington described a ship at the mouth of a river and in need of fresh water. A message was sent to it, indicating that the water on which it rode was fresh and that the crew should cast down their buckets for it. Washington's point in this parable was that Southern white capitalists in need of a labor force for the economic development of the "New South" should not look to European immigrants but to the black population about them.

[18]Chesnutt canceled the derisive portion of this paragraph, beginning with "Is it jealousy" and ending here; then he wrote "stet." in the left margin, indicating that it should be retained.

[19]"If," *Rewards and Fairies* (1910).

[20]That of Democrat Woodrow Wilson, 1913–21.

[21]The War Department was a part of the executive branch of the government from 1789 to 1947. That is, the reference to African-American soldiers does not necessarily indicate that Chesnutt completed this passage after war against Germany was declared. In 1915 and in light of the possibility of U.S. involvement in the World War, summer camps for military training were established; and, in June 1916, war-preparedness was more dramatically improved when Congress increased the size of the Army.

George Meredith

Speech to the Rowfant Club, Cleveland, O., 11 March 1916

A paper on George Meredith, English novelist and poet, must depend, for its interest, almost entirely upon his writings. He committed no crime, was never in prison, though one may gather from certain references that at times the bailiffs were very near his heels for debt; he had no fantastic vices, was neither tramp nor opium-eater; he did not beat his own wife nor run away with his neighbor's—at least there is no record of any of these things, though most of us know that one can get away with a good many of them, provided he first establish a good reputation. Or, as was suggested by a clever young woman who was reading the rough draft of this paper, perhaps he has n't been dead long enough for them to leak out. This, however, is improbable, and Meredith's reputation will probably have to stand on his virtues, with no aid or hindrance from any vices.

Nor has Meredith any of the other adventitious aids to fame. Though he numbered many brilliant and some illustrious friends among the authors and statesmen of his day, he was not the bright particular star of any brilliant constellation which circled round him and sang his praises in verse and prose. Of a philosophic turn of mind, he founded no new philosophy. A social reformer, he led no reform, and the one spectacular theory which he put forth late in life, that of trial marriage, was impractical, not to say chimerical, and was received with protest and ridicule. He had his friends and admirers, but with all except his intimate friends, it was Meredith the writer rather than Meredith the man, who won their respect and admiration.

One reason why Meredith is a suitable subject for the consideration of the Rowfant Club, is that his works, especially the earlier ones, were all printed in limited editions—limited, not by intention, but by the demand for them—and that many first editions of Meredith were rare and valuable, as early as ten years before his death.

The only information which Meredith vouchsafed to inquirers about his birth and childhood was that he was born in Hampshire on the 12th of February, 1828. He did not recount his memories, nor did he ever discuss his intellectual development. This reticence on his part was responsible for much curiosity and some little calumny. Autobiographical details were sought to be traced in *The Adventures of Henry Richmond*, and gossip in London clubs secretly whispered strange stories of the sources of *Evan Harrington*.[1] He never took his friends into his confidence, and if they tried to sound him by trick or artifice, it was without success, so they could not well have defended him. If there were any undeserved aspersions cast upon his origin, he had himself to thank for their existence. His friends never drew from him more than this:

> My mother was of Irish origin, handsome, refined and witty. I think there must have been some Saxon strain in the ancestry to account for a virility of temperament which corrected the Celtic in me. . . . My father, who lived to be seventy-five, was a muddler and a fool.[2]

His father was almost as mysterious and obscure as François Villon's.[3] After Meredith's death the English journals discovered him in Augustus Meredith, who kept a tailor's shop in Cape Town, S. A.[4] The trade was hereditary, since Meredith's grandfather, Melchisedec Meredith,[5] was also a tailor, or, to speak politely, a naval outfitter, and quite a man of the world, who not only supplied naval officers with their clothes, but entertained them at his table and maintained cordial relations with them. "Old Mel," as he was called, is referred to in Maryatt's *Peter Simple*.[6]

George Meredith was born above the ancestral shop and baptized April 9th, 1828, in the Church of St. Thomas.

It seems quite likely that Meredith's reticence about his family may have been due to the fact that his father and grandfather were tailors, not an origin of which a gentleman in England would boast, although in *Evan Harrington*, the hero's confession of his humble trade is made a test of his manhood, and in the biographical note prefixed to Meredith's *Letters*, the tailoring ancestry of Meredith is set out by his son in full, and the portraits of "the Great Mel" and his wife are described as "family portraits" and the only family portraits in the novel.[7] Mrs. Mel's name was Anne, but her descendants are ignorant of her family, which, however, is said to have belonged to the professional class.[8]

That the family history was drawn on still further for the material of *Evan Harrington* appears from the statement in the *Letters* that one of Melchisedec's daughters—all beautiful girls—married a banker, another a brewer, another a lieutenant in the Royal Reserves, who later became a general and a K.C.B.,[9] and still another a Consul-General for the Azores, later a Knight of a Portuguese order.

Meredith's father took no active part in his education, and they never entered into direct relations with one another. Meredith's education began at St. Paul's School, Southsea.[10] His mother at her death left him a small inheritance, which sufficed for his education, his chief remembrance of school being three dreary services on Sunday, during which he invented tales of the St. George and the Dragon type. He was very fond of the *Arabian Nights*, and the result was seen in *The Shaving of Shagpat*,[11] his first published novel, which was written with duns at the door. Although on principle Meredith scorned the mercenary motive in writing, yet it is curious to note that in fiction, as elsewhere, necessity is the mother of invention, and how the spur of hunger can hasten the flight of Pegasus.[12]

His education was continued at Neuwied, Germany, at the school of the Moravian Brothers,[13] where there prevailed a spirit of liberalism, a peace, a sweetness of manners, that left their impress on the young Englishman's character. He remained in Germany until he was sixteen. (Familiarity with Germany in his novels.)

In 1845, he was articled to a lawyer,[14] who, says Meredith, had neither business nor morals, and he soon turned to journalism. His income was very small, his trustee having mismanaged his estate, and he needed money. He wrote leaders for the *Ipswich Journal*, social and literary articles for the *Daily News* and other papers.[15] Although as I have said, he was not the central luminary, he was one of the leading spirits of a group in London of young philosophical and positivistic radicals, among whom were John Morley, Frederick Harrison, Cotter Morison and Admiral Maxse, all of whom remained his life-long friends and correspondents.[16] He acted as correspondent for the *Morning Post* during the Austro-Italian War of 1866, staying for some time in Venice, doubtless acquiring during this experience the material for *Sandra Belloni* and *Vittoria*.[17] In 1867, he took charge of the *Fortnightly Review* during the temporary absence of the editor, his friend John Morley, in America.[18]

Meantime in his leisure hours, he read the poets, ancient and modern, English,

French and German—he was very fond of the French people, and thoroughly familiar with their literature. He was for many years reader and literary adviser to
Chapman and Hall, London publishers, and in that capacity is said to have discovered *The Story of an African Farm* and its author, and to have been a great assistance to George Gissing and Thomas Hardy, both of whom made grateful acknowledgment of their debt.[19]

He was twice married. His first marriage occurred when he was hardly twenty-
one years old. The lady was nine years his senior, and unlike the similar case of Dr.
Johnson, the marriage was not a success. They became estranged, separated, and
she died twelve years later.[20] They had one child, a son, Arthur, who died at the age
of thirty-seven.[21] Of the details of their married life little is known; but the lady was
clever, lively, cultivated and attractive, and Meredith never spoke of her but with
respect and admiration. It seems to have been a case of incompatibility. They were
too much alike. Says Meredith's son by his second marriage, in a note to the *Letters*: "Two highly strung temperaments—man and wife—each imaginative, emotional, quick to anger, cuttingly satirical in dispute, each an incomparable wielder
of the rapier of ridicule, could not find domestic comfort within the narrow
bounds of poverty and lodgings." This deplorable misunderstanding bore fruit in
the fifty sonnets entitled *Modern Love*, which is the story in poetic form of an unhappy marriage wrecked by a misunderstanding growing out of incompatibility.[22]
His first wife's father was Thomas Love Peacock, an essayist and novelist of merit,
who belonged to the brilliant coterie in which were numbered Coleridge and De
Quincy.[23] Meredith and he were intimate friends and Meredith's first verses were
dedicated to "Thomas Love Peacock, with the profound admiration and affectionate respect of his son-in-law."[24]

He was married, twelve years later, after her death, to Miss Vulliamy, by
whom he had a son and a daughter. Meredith lived at different places, but shortly
after his second marriage settled at Flint Cottage near Dorking, where he remained during the rest of his life.[25]

Meredith's literary output is of a volume worthy of a great author. Quality is
what counts, but given a certain quality, the greater the quantity the more important the service rendered to letters and to humanity. His first book was a small
volume of *Poems* (1851), now and for a long time a rare collector's item. He published nothing more with the exception of several magazine poems, for five years.[26]
His first serious contribution to fiction was *The Shaving of Shagpat*, published in
1856. Although I refer to it as serious, it was in fact a *tour de force*, a burlesque
which suggests that other great writers have made their first attempts along this
line. Thackeray's *Barry Lyndon* and the *Yellowplush Papers* are obviously in the
same category, and *Pickwick Papers* is little more.[27] *The Shaving of Shagpat: An
Arabian Entertainment*, was a reflection of Meredith's earlier reading of the *Arabian Nights' Entertainment* and his imaginings thereon in his boyhood. It is composed in a characteristic vein of the mock-heroic, with touches of passion and romance and exuberant humor. George Eliot, who was among the first to recognize

Meredith's budding genius, hailed it, in one of her reviews, "as an apple tree among the trees of the wood,"[28] and once the reader became accustomed to its puzzling qualities, its wit and genius prevailed with the discriminating public, although a second edition was not called for until 1865, nine years later, the publisher having sold his rights very shortly after the first publication, thus stamping the book as a failure from the standpoint of the general public and the publisher.[29]

On an occasion of this kind it would be impossible to sketch in more than the briefest form the plot of any one story; and it would be more or less a work of supererogation, since all of you are doubtless familiar with all of them. In the *Shaving of Shagpat*, Noorna bin Noorka, a waif found beside her dead mother in the desert, is rescued and reared by a certain chief. In her twelfth year an old beggar, to whom she had done a favor gives her a red book of Magic, which she studies, in her attempt to discover her father, and becomes adept in sorcery. She promises the Genie Karaz, in return for his aid in disenchanting her father, that she will give herself to the possessor of the Identical, or hair of fortune, which was on the genie's head. Noorna happens by accident to gain possession of the magic ring of the Princess Goorelka, another accomplished sorceress, which makes its possessor "mistress of the marvelous hair," which is a magnet to the homage of men so that they crowd and crush and hunger to adore it, even the "Identical." She disenchants her father, and then, anxious to evade her promise to Karaz, follows the example of Delilah in a similar episode,[30] tears the hair from his head, and drops it incidentally on that of an innocent clothier called Shagpat, who as the possessor of the Identical, in turn claims Noorna in marriage; but she likes him no better than Karaz, and the story recounts the exploits of her champion, the youth Shibli Bagarag of Shiraz, "nephew to the renowned Baba Mustapha, chief barber to the court of Persia," who, her spells inform her, is to free her from her servitude to the Identical. The story goes on to recount the adventures of Shibli in his long drawn out enterprise of shaving Shagpat, which seems to be about as difficult as all the labors of Hercules combined. There is only one blade in existence keen enough to reap the magic hair, which defies all mortal razors, and to find each of these is an Odyssey in itself. Shibli is more or less hampered by his own conceit, which has to be chastened before he becomes the perfect instrument for the great event, but the enterprise is finally successful, the flashing blade in Shibli's hand shaves Shagpat clean, to the consternation of the populace; the Identical is shorn off, and "day was on the baldness of Shagpat," and Shibli marries Noorna.

Various critics have attempted to read an allegory into this story, but Meredith humorously disclaimed any such intention. The thoughtful reader may gather whatever moral there is in the story from the verses on the third page:

> Thou that dreamest an Event,
> While circumstance is but a waste of sand,
> Arise, take up thy fortunes in thy hand
> And daily forward pitch thy tent.

And at the end:

Ye that nourish hopes of fame!
Ye who would be known in song!
Ponder old history, and duly frame
Your souls to meek acceptance of the throng.

Lo! Of hundreds who aspire
Eighties perish—nineties tire!
They who bear up, in spite of wrecks and wracks,
Were seasoned by celestial hail of thwacks.

Fortune in this mortal race
Builds on thwacking for its base,
Thus the All-Wise doth make a flail a staff,
And separates his heavenly corn from chaff.

Meredith's next book, *Farina: A Legend of Cologne*, published in 1857, is also a burlesque, although the subject is mediaeval, not Oriental. The story is a subtly ironical sketch of superstition and chivalry,—*Don Quixote*[31] in a different vein—and reflects the author's German education and one or two of his characteristic ideas. The young men of Cologne have formed a White Rose Club, sworn to uphold against all comers, the beauty of Margarita, a rich merchant's daughter. Only one youth, the slender, fair Farina, refuses to join this league of tender and quarrelsome fanatics. Farina is poor; as a student of chemistry he is also suspected of tampering with the black art; but, also after the manner of her sex, Margarita's heart is tender towards him, and he is in love with her. Without following the story, it terminates with a combat on the Drachenfels between Satan and a mysterious monk, who carries off Farina from prison to witness the ghostly combat. Satan is vanquished, and takes refuge underground in Cologne. The monk, who, by his conquest of the enemy of mankind, has become a spiritual hero, finds his hour of triumph to have passed into degradation. Kaiser Heinrich with his army is approaching the city, after a successful campaign, and the loyal populace are prepared to give him such a reception as is given to royal personages in the effete monarchies of Europe and to popular murderers in our own city, but Satan's overpowering stench, as he went underground, keeps the Kaiser at a distance from the city, and the blame of this pestilential odor is naturally laid by the citizens upon the luckless ecclesiastic. Farina however, solved the problem by furnishing the Kaiser with a bottle of his new essence, *Eau de Cologne*, thus making it possible for the king and his army to enter the city, and Farina's reward is the hand of Margarita. Thus the origin of this popular toilet preparation is accounted for.

The Ordeal of Richard Feverel, Meredith's first serious novel, published in 1859, established his reputation as a writer of original and brilliant parts. In the opinion of many, this story of a son sacrificed to the abstract system of a father who had lost his faith in human nature, is one of the profoundest tragedies in modern fiction. It is also a story of singular beauty of imagination and charm of description. The scene on the island when Richard first sees Lucy is perhaps the most beautiful prose idyl of love in English literature—an enchanting idealization of youth and romance.[32] The wisdom of the book, its penetrating observation, its immense cleverness, are the work of one of the most alert and acute of modern intellects, but this description in its lyrical beauty and deep feeling, could come only from a poet.

The novel has an unnecessarily tragic ending, which has been much criticized. It would seem to the reader that Richard and Lucy had suffered enough without the final blow.[33] In this novel the epigrams are produced, from what is called the "Pilgrim's Scrip," a volume of aphorisms of which Sir Austin is the author, as set forth in the first page of the story. This, in common with the Comic Spirit, was one of Meredith's devices for interlarding his stories with philosophical reflections.

In a later edition of *Richard Feverel*, the author cut out part of the story, not thereby improving it, in the estimation of his friends, and copies of the first edition are rare and valuable. I have seen it quoted at $225.00, which would now be probably a low figure.

Meredith's next novel, *Evan Harrington*, appeared serially in *Once a Week*, during 1860, under the title "He Would Be a Gentleman."[34] This is one of the two novels in which Meredith students attempted to read some of the biographical information of which he was so chary, and which his son acknowledges is in part true. It is the story of a tailor, Melchisedec Harrington, in private called "the great Mel, who had been at once the sad dog of Lymport and the pride of the town. He was a tailor and he kept horses; he was a tailor, and he had gallant adventures; he was a tailor and he shook hands with his customers." He had four children, his great aim and pleasure was to move in county society, where he was welcomed for his gay wit and manner. His social ambition was successful in seeing all his daughters make good matches; one married a major, another a wealthy London brewer, the third a Portuguese diplomatist. One of the husbands knew the father-in-law's trade, another came in time to suspect it, but the third was kept in ignorance. The ladies were ashamed of it, and agreed to keep away from the neighborhood of Lymport and to rescue their brother Evan from the bondage of tailordom.

The story relates how Evan determined in spite of them, to be a tailor in order to pay his father's debts, and proves that a tailor can be a gentleman. In spite of some caste prejudice on account of his trade, or his father's trade, which creates a situation very similar to that of Alvan and Clotilde in the *Tragic Comedians*,[35] Evan demonstrates his gentility, marries wealth and social standing, escapes from tailordom in spite of himself and when the book ends is attaché of the Naples legation. The book is notable for its extremely clever character studies, the best of which is Evan's sister, the Countess Louisa, with her aspirations for society, her vulgarity and her unscrupulous scheming.

For three years after publishing *Evan Harrington*, Meredith wrote nothing but poetry, his most important work being his fifty sonnets entitled *Modern Love*, and then published three novels in three years, the first one being *Sandra Belloni*, first published under the name of *Emilia in England*, followed by *Rhoda Fleming*,[36] which in turn was followed by the second Emilia book, *Vittoria*, a sequel to *Sandra Belloni*. The Emilia books are written along the theme of the Italian struggle for liberty, in the late forties of the last century, and *Sandra Belloni* has been characterized as an analysis of sentimentality. In *Rhoda Fleming* Meredith handles the sex question with unusual frankness, and essays the delicate and difficult task of describing the innate purity of a woman after a moral lapse. In this novel, as in most of Meredith's, in all perhaps except *Lord Ormont and His Aminta*,[37] the erring woman, Rhoda's sister Dahlia, pays the price, and as to her the end is tragedy.

One of Meredith's best and most remarkable novels is *The Adventures of Harry Richmond*.[38] It is perhaps his nearest approach to the novel of incident. Had all Meredith's novels been written with the vigor and swift action of *Harry Richmond*, there would have been no question of his popularity. Although the book takes its name from Harry, he is in reality one of the lesser characters, the principal one of which is Harry's preposterous father, Roy Richmond, who calls himself Augustus Fitzgeorge Frederick William Richmond Guelph Roy, portrayed as an unselfish, chivalrous warm-hearted man with great powers of fascination, voluble, volatile, more than half a charlatan, incorrigibly dramatic, a spendthrift of the first water and an impostor on the grand scale, with a plausible, radiant gayety about him which overpowers even his son's judgment till nearly the end of the tale, and which prevails with most women of his acquaintance. With all these charms and graces, added to an unusually handsome and striking person, he is without a single moral principle, having either lost them all or never had any. He is the son of an actress, Anastasia Dewsberry, but he firmly believed his father had been one of the royal family, and he therefore determined to claim royal honors for his son. He had been a music-master and had eloped with one of the two daughters of Squire Beltham. He squandered her fortune and drove her crazy.

The story deals with Roy's attempt to push a suit for recognition of his claims to royalty, and to make a match for Harry with a little German princess, in the course of which he wastes two separate fortunes which came to Harry, and a large part of the estate of Harry's aunt, Dorothy Beltham. All Roy's schemes are futile, and Harry, still a commoner, marries where his grandfather wished, while his spectacular father comes to a spectacular end. The interview in which the Squire denounces Roy is a tremendous piece of invective.[39] He has just crushed and humiliated Richmond, by disclosing the source of a mysterious gift of a large sum of money which Roy had supposed to be from a Royal source and therefore a secret acknowledgment of his claims, and he now proceeds to polish him off as follows:—

> You pensioner of a silly country spinster! Your son is willing to be tied to the stake beside you. Disown him, and I'll pay you money and thank you. I'll thank my God for anything short of your foul blood in the family. You married the boy's mother to craze and kill her, and guttle her property. You waited for the boy to come of age to swallow what was settled on him. You wait for me to lie in my coffin to pounce on the strong-box you think me the fool to toss to a young donkey ready to ruin all his belongings for you! For nine-and-twenty years you've sucked the veins of my family, and struck through my house like a rotting-disease. Nine-and-twenty years

ago you gave a singing-lesson in my house: the pest has been in it ever since! You breed vermin in the brain, to think of you! Your wife, your son, your dupes, every soul that touches you, mildews from a blight! You were born of ropery, and you go at it straight, like a webfoot to water. What's your boast?—your mother's disgrace! You shame your mother. Your whole life's a ballad o'bastardy. You cry up the woman's infamy to hook at a father. You swell and strut on her pickings. You're a cock forced from the smoke of a dunghill! You shame your mother, damned adventurer! You train your boy for a swindler after your own pattern; you twirl him in your curst harlequinade to a damnation as sure as your own. The day you crossed my threshold the devils danced on their flooring. I've never seen the sun shine fair on me after it. With your guitar under the windows, of moonlight nights! your Spanish fopperies and trickeries! your French phrases and toeings! I was touched by a leper. You set your traps for both my girls: you caught the brown one first, did you, and flung her second for t' other, and drove a tandem of 'em to live the spangled hog you are; and down went the mother of the boy to the place she liked better, and my other girl here—the one you cheated for her salvation—you tried to cajole her from home and me, to send her the same way down. She stuck to decency. Good Lord! you threatened to hang yourself, guitar and all. But her purse served your turn. For why? You're a leech. I speak before ladies, or I'd rip your town-life to shreds. Your cause! your romantic history! your fine figure! every inch of you's notched with villainy! You fasten on every moneyed woman that comes in your way. You've outdone Herod in murdering the innocents,[40] for he did n't feed on 'em, and they've made you fat. One thing I'll say of you: you look the beastly thing you set yourself up for. The kindest blow to you's to call you impostor.

One could wish that there had been no ladies present. It would be interesting to see what the old squire could have done if he let himself go.

Meredith's next novel, *Beauchamp's Career*, usually described by its author as his favorite, published in book form in 1868, having first appeared serially in the *Fortnightly Review*, was the outcome of an electioneering experience with his friend Captain (afterwards Admiral) Frederick Maxse, of the Royal Navy, who was standing as Radical candidate for Southampton after a brilliant phase of service in the Crimea.[41] The author frankly confesses it is a political novel, dealing with the live questions of the hour, but it is neither polemical nor dull. Nevil Beauchamp is a young naval officer of the best type, full of spirit, keen on his profession, chivalrous and tenacious of his purpose. He falls in love. The girl marries the other man. The marriage is unhappy, but she keeps a string on Beauchamp, flies to him when her husband becomes unbearable, and seeks his protection. But like Alvan in *The Tragic Comedians*, he wishes prudently to safeguard her position instead of impetuously carrying her off. She leaves him, having been saved against her will, and, when, later, after she has been freed from her husband, Beauchamp goes to propose to her on his own account, he finds that she has married another man. He becomes ill, and on recovering from his illness marries his nurse. A year later he is drowned in the Otley, when rescuing a little boy, a mere episode—another tragic ending not at all called for by the action of the story, and vehemently condemned by the ladies. Many a good novel is injured as a work of art by the popular demand for a happy ending, but there is little excuse for gratuitous tragedy. It seems to be due to a certain perversity of the author, he not only does not seek popularity, but seems sometimes to seek deliberately to evade it.

"But it is thankless to dwell on any such clause of construction," says a critic, "when the novel offers a wealth of pregnant insight and romance which is unrivaled in the entire series of the Meredith stories. . . . It is an ennobling and inspiriting book, and a large part of its attractiveness lies in the delineation of human nature in contact with the surge and spray of deep elemental forces in the modern world."

The Egoist, which appeared in 1879, was hailed as the greatest work from the hand of this master of paradox, brilliant observation and acute comment. In it Meredith revealed both his strength and his weakness. It was so full of the peculiar Meredith quality, that it at once captivated the lovers of Meredith, while his general force and interest attracted those whose attitude toward the writer had been distinctly critical. It is a novel in which the dramatic unities are well observed, since the real action covers only a few weeks, but the chief interest lies in the extremely clever analysis of motives.

The hero—protagonist is a better word, for Sir Willoughby is a poor hero—is a wealthy young aristocrat brought up in an atmosphere of feminine adulation. He is fundamentally selfish and entirely without a sense of humor. He thoroughly disgusts two successive fiancées by his stupendous egotism, and in terror at the prospect of being jilted a third time, and becoming an object of ridicule in the country society, he finally marries a third, whom he has been playing with all through the story, who began by loving him when he was beyond her reach, has learned to despise him like the rest, and only marries him, in a way, to get rid of him, and to escape his importunities.

The book contains some of Meredith's best characters, notably Clara Middleton and Vernon Whitford, the latter of whom Meredith drew from his friend Leslie Stephen, as he says in one of his letters.[42] One who can read Meredith and hasn't read *The Egoist*, will find it a very well of delight.

The Egoist has some examples of Meredith's worst atrocities of style in the brilliant prelude to this novel, and here and there in the later chapters. But the dialogue clashes with crisp repartee and brilliant epigram. Meredith here, even more than elsewhere, says James Thomson, "delights in elaborate analysis of abstruse problems, whose solutions when reached are scarcely less difficult to ordinary apprehension than are the problems themselves; discriminating countless shades where the common eye sees but one gloom or glare; pursuing countless distinct movements where the common eye sees only a whirling perplexity."[43] In this novel, the Comic Spirit, which, in Meredith's philosophy as applied to his novels, presides over life, is often referred to and made responsible for the events which transpire. One of Meredith's best known essays, by the way, was delivered to a London audience upon the Comic Spirit, or the Spirit of Comedy, and may be found among his collected writings.[44]

Meredith's next novel, *The Tragic Comedians*, is a close study in the well known story of the final love affair, one of a long series, in the life of Ferdinand Lassalle, a brilliant young Jewish Hungarian, the leader of the German Republican Socialists, who died, after a meteoric career, during which he clashed wits and wills with Bismarck,[45] on August 31, 1864, from the effects of a duel, adding another to a brilliant series of lives which have been cut short by this relic of barbarism, including those of Alexander Pushkin and Alexander Hamilton. The story follows very closely the facts as they occurred in real life, and were written by Frau Racowitza, the real lady in the story.[46] Chlotilde, a young German beauty, falls in love with Alvan, a clever Jew, and a notorious demagogue, who by birth and position is utterly antagonistic to all her inherited instincts. It is a study in race and caste problems, and along Meredith's favorite topic, the power of social convention in the lives of women, who rarely possess sufficient courage to be true to their own instincts where they come in contact with social rules. The hero resembles Sir Willoughby Patterne in wishing to master for his own purposes his sweetheart's mind, and in his fear of being jilted, which means ridicule, and Chlotilde has some of the traits of Clara Middleton and Diana Merion[47]—they will and they won't, to use the vernacular, are of one mind today and another tomorrow, and the golden moment passes, never to return.

Diana of the Crossways, issued in book form in 1885, was more immediately successful than any other of Meredith's romances, passing through three editions in the year of publication. One reason for this was that it was published in a time of political excitement, and like *Beauchamp's Career*, had a political motive. It handled with some daring the problems of modern marriage, but its chief recommendation was its reputation as a *roman à clef*—a novel with a key. It was supposed to be founded upon a contemporary story, which Meredith in the preface to *Diana* says was a calumny, of the radiant and witty Caroline Norton, Sheridan's granddaughter's communication to the *Times* of Sir Robert Peel's conversion to free trade.[48] Meredith was in love with Diana, whose character he discusses in one of the most interesting of his letters, and the result was a masterpiece which has had far more than an ephemeral or fictitious success.

Diana Merion is a clever and beautiful young Irish orphan, to whom men instinctively pay court. To secure a home and protection she marries a man she does not love, forms a friendship with the Tory premier, Lord Dannisburgh, whose Egeria she becomes, arouses her husband's jealousy, who sues her for divorce. She wins the suit, to her secret regret, since while her good name has been vindicated, she is still bound by hateful ties. She begins to write fiction, establishes a salon in London, lives beyond her means and gets heavily in debt, attracts the attention and eventually wins the love of a rising young politician, Percy Dacier, high in the councils of his party, and a nephew of her friend Lord Dannisburgh. Warwick threatens to sue for restitution of his conjugal rights, and Diana in despair agrees to elope with Dacier, but through accident this is prevented, and Dacier retires, but returns later and resumes his friendship with Diana. They are skating on thin ice, but Diana, though shaky at the knees, manages to keep her footing. Their final breach comes about through Diana's betrayal, to the *Times*, for a large sum of money, of a political secret which her lover had in a fatuous moment confided to her. He is implacable, and marries another woman. It is Diana's first and greatest love, but though Warwick dies soon after, it is too late.

Diana was Meredith's favorite character, as she is with most Meredithians. Erratic, unbalanced, adventurous, taking desperate chances, all too careless of her reputation, yielding to the pressure of material needs, a good sport, yet sound at the core, and hating intrigue, we sympathize with her in her loss of Dacier, and our contentment over her marriage with the faithful Redworth is something like her own seems to be, a sort of humdrum affair—a mild, milk-and-water heaven after a very lively lobster and champagne picnic on the edge of hell. We prefer her as a good woman, but we can't help thinking what a success she would have made as a bad one!

Meredith's next novel, *One of Our Conquerors*, the story of a merchant prince, published in book form in 1891, is the least popular of all the novels. This is due to two principal causes, the subject, the union of a man and woman who defy the conventional marriage laws, and to its style and construction. Mr. William Watson, in his famous article in the *National Review*,[49] had asserted, referring to *The Egoist*, that no milder word than detestable should be applied to Meredith's style. Nothing but the blunt phrase of "intellectual coxcombry" could adequately describe the airs of superiority, the affectation of originality, the sham profundities, the counterfeit subtleties, the pseudo-oracularisms of this book, but the invective applies more truly to *One of Our Conquerors*.

The story is that of a man who had married at twenty-one a middle aged widow for her money, who elopes with his wife's companion. They live together as husband and wife, Mr. Radnor amasses a large fortune in the city, has social and political aspirations and a daughter. His real wife, however, instead of suing for a divorce, against which she has religious scruples, prefers the subtler revenge of retaining her legal position as Radnor's wife, and thereby preventing him from marrying Natalie. She eventually relents, and dies, just a little too late. The story has a tragic ending. The Comic Spirit laughs, and Mr. Darwin, who maintained that every novel should have a pleasant ending, is again challenged.[50] Victor and Natalie had defied convention, and as in all of Meredith's novels, they must pay the price.

Lord Ormont and His Aminta, published in book form in 1894, is short and easy to read, and deals with a much similar situation as *One of Our Conquerors*, namely, a marriage from other motives than love, a subsequent romantic love affair with the husband's secretary, and the elopement of the wife with her lover. Unlike any other of Meredith's novels, the sin is not severely punished. The husband is not vindictive, he retains no rancor in his heart against the lover, and he magnanimously believes in the purity and justice of Aminta. He has the good taste to die in time to make it possible for the pair to marry one another and live happily for a long time afterwards.

Meredith's last novel, *The Amazing Marriage*,[51] forms a curious contrast to *Lord Ormont and His Aminta*. In both stories the heroine's character is developed through ill treatment of her husband's hands; but instead of driving her to vice, or, as in the case of Aminta, to elope with a worthy lover, the discipline of injustice matures the heroine of this story within her legal position. She refuses to live with her husband, but she will not take another man. Her husband makes several efforts to regain her, but due to certain flaws in his own character these are unavailing. He finally becomes a Roman Catholic monk, and after his death she marries a faithful lover, who like Redworth in *Diana*, has been patiently waiting in the background. The novel is the study of a weak man and a strong woman, and is said to be one of Meredith's best.

Meredith was never a popular writer. Indeed during the period when he was producing his finest novels he was practically unknown to the public. *The Shaving of Shagpat* was published in 1856, and *Diana of the Crossways*, published 39 years later, in 1885, was the first of his novels to find a place in Mudie's Circulating library.[52] A poor self-advertiser, he never courted popularity, and he spoke somewhat disparagingly of those who did. He said once to a visitor, when he was old and bedridden:

> With regard to journalists, men who are as influential as they are susceptible, a young author has a choice of two courses; either to have nothing to do with them, or to make use of them. For my own part, they make my flesh creep; I have never been able to tolerate them. Robert Browning certainly did not neglect them in his old age. Dickens and Thackeray petted them as a horseman pets his mount before putting it at an obstacle. As for Lord Tennyson, he was a past-master in the art of provoking panegyrics and dithyrambs.
>
> Here you have a real business man! He has made literature pay; he has even made a fortune out of it. Like an ingenious husbandman he has changed the barren field into a gold mine. "He bleeds me!" groaned his publisher piteously, but paid him all the same. It was useless for publishers to deprecate Tennyson's so-called eagerness for gain. They yielded to his demands, and the world would have its beloved poet at any price.

Perhaps his attitude toward the press was a result of the press's attitude toward him, or they reacted one upon the other.

What would an author, however thick-skinned, feel upon reading something like this, which appeared in a so-called literary journal, apropos of *The Ordeal of Richard Feverel*:

> It would even be unjust to compare such writings [*sic*] with the scavengers and dust collectors of ordinary life. The latter are necessary to the cleanliness and health of the community, while the literary refuse and rubbish, etc. . . . a long series of paltry dialogue, of a surprisingly fervent nature . . . . When the author moralises, he does not halt for words, but chucks them in anyhow, dragging along with him a string of vapid nonsense.[53]

No wonder he said, in one of his few interviews which he ever gave out:

The press has often treated me as a clown or a harlequin—yes, really! And with such little respect that my fellow-citizens can scarcely put up with me. [Do not cry out!] Certainly, at this late hour they accord me a little glory; my name is celebrated, but no one reads my books. As for Englishmen, I put them to flight because I bore them. With regard to foreigners, I am but an illustrious unknown. No one has bought my books—my novels or my poems. And now, book collectors snatch up my first editions, which are sold for twenty or twenty-five guineas. Formerly they would have wished me silent. I was exceedingly poor, and I needed, even as a negro does, to earn my bread. What articles, what patched-up criticisms have I written for magazines and provincial journals! At last, much later, a small inheritance allowed me to live in my own way; very modestly as you see, in this peaceful cottage. If I continue to write, despite the prevailing indifference to my work, it is because certain magazines, notably *Scribner's Magazine* in America, pay me liberally for my contributions. My contemporaries here know nothing of it.

Nor was his conception of light literature one likely to win popularity. He puts into the mouth of Alvan, in *The Tragic Comedians*, in a peculiarly Meredithian love-scene, the following language: "The vulgar demand to have their pleasures in their own likeness—and let them swamp their troughs! They shall not degrade the fame of noble fiction. We are the choice public, which will have good writing for light reading."[54]

Meredith's style was his greatest hindrance to popularity. Its most valuable characteristic is distinction, and distinction of style is always associated with learning and thought, neither of which are popular. Meredith's writing abounds in classical and historical allusion, is rich, often overcrowded with metaphors and similes, each of which demands a mental effort to follow, and the more recondite of them a severe mental effort, diverting the reader, however slightly, from the main thread of the story. For a cultured reader who enjoys thoughtful writing, Meredith is not hard reading, and some of his novels, *Harry Richmond* for instance, have a decided dash and vigor which a simple mind could follow, as a rule with but slight effort of the imagination. But one never sees the shop girl or factory girl, who got through the eighth grade, and who simply devours even *Jane Eyre*,[55] reading Meredith in the street-cars, and one can hardly imagine him writing tales for children. His fairy tale of Shagpat is as far beyond their mental grasp as the moon beyond their physical.

Those who study and admire Meredith most agree that to appreciate either his poetry or his prose the reader must become *en rapport* with the artist's mind, which in his case, owing to his originality of temperament and the peculiarities of his mental equipment must be the result, except in rare instances, of thought and study. One must either be born a Meredithian, or acquire that state by hard work. But those who pay the price are always satisfied with their bargain. His style is said to owe something to Carlyle, whom he admired, to Jean Paul Richter,[56] and there are some echoes of Bulwer Lytton. But after all, his style was his own, and obstinately so—he would write only as he wished to write. His philosophy, broadly speaking, was a belief in the wholesomeness of nature, and this note runs all through his prose writings and is the distinguishing feature of his poetry.

Meredith as Poet.

Until 1896, nearly fifty years after his first poem appeared, Meredith's poems were published at his own expense. He never clearly defined in his writings the border line between prose and poetry. He says in one of his letters: "I am astonished that Mr. X [an author who had published something on Meredith's poems], has separated my poetry from my prose. My thought unites itself spontaneously to prose and poetry, even as my flesh to my brain and my soul." It has been said of Meredith's poetry that in it he provided nuts but neglected to furnish a nut cracker.

He could not, he confessed, make the English language sing, and song is the essential element of poetry, which, like music, painting and sculpture, is practically one of the fine arts and makes its primary appeal to the emotions through the senses. The appeal must be direct and immediate, and not the result of analysis. It is impossible, in poetry, to separate the form from the content.

One test of the popularity of poetry is its quotability. A great part of Tennyson, much of Browning, for instance, (less of Shelley, and nearly all of Alexander Pope) is quotable and quoted. Though hailed by the best critics of his time as a great poet, and though his novels redound in aphorisms which appeal to the intellect, Bartlett's *Familiar Quotations* contains not one line from Meredith's pen; one couplet which is eminently quotable, seems to have missed deserved recognition:

> Lo, of hundreds who aspire,
> Eighties perish, nineties tire.[57]

Had this couplet been combined with twenty others as simple, into a story or a parable, like Longfellow's "Excelsior,"[58] instead of in the rather complex and not very musical verses which I have elsewhere read, it might have proved popular enough to furnish another fit subject for the distinguished parodist of this club.

His first book, the *Poems* of 1851, was highly praised by Tennyson for the individual flavor of its verses. Charles Kingsley in *Frazer's Magazine* commended the volume for "a certain quaintness of tone that suggested Herrick, for completeness and coherence in each separate poem, and for the sweetness and health that animated the general atmosphere."[59] Not all of this praise can be applied to all of Meredith's poetry, for most of it is characterized by the faults which Kingsley pointed out in these earlier verses, *viz.*, "laxity of rhythm, occasional lack of polish, and a tendency to overload the description with objective details to the confusion of the principal effect"—the latter being, as I have said elsewhere more simply in my own language, a fault common as well to Meredith's prose as to his poetry.

That he *could* sometimes make the English language sing, in spite of his own disclaimer, the following verses will reveal:—[60]

Love in the Valley.

Under yonder beech-tree standing on the green sward,
    Couch'd with her arms behind her little head,
Her knees folded up, and her tresses on her bosom,
    Lies my young love sleeping in the shade.
Had I the heart to slide one arm beneath her!
    Press her dreaming lips as her waist I folded slow,
Waking on the instant she could not embrace me—
    Ah! Would she hold me, and never let me go?

Shy as the squirrel, and wayward as the swallow;
    Swift as the swallow when athwart the western flood
Circleting the surface he meets his mirror'd winglets,—
    Is that dear one in her maiden bud.
Shy as the squirrel whose nest is in the pine tops;
    Gentle—ah! that she were jealous—as the dove!
Full of all the wildness of the woodland creatures,
    Happy in herself is the maiden that I love!

When her mother tends her before the laughing mirror,
    Tying up her laces, looping up her hair,
Often she thinks—were this wild thing wedded,
    I should have more love, and much less care.
When her mother tends her before the bashful mirror,
    Loosening her laces, combing down her curls,
Often she thinks—were this wild thing wedded,
    I should lose but one for so many boys and girls.

If this is not poetry, and lyric poetry at that, then there is no such thing. But Meredith's poetry is a subject in itself, and I will not take up more of your time with it.

Meredith's Letters.

George Meredith's *Letters*, edited by his son and published by Constable, in London, in 1912, in two volumes, is a most interesting and readable work. Had Meredith written his novels with equal freedom, they would probably have attained wider popularity. They cover the period from 1844 to 1899, many of the letters in the first volume are long and of little more than personal interest. The second volume is richer in quality, since it reflects a more mature outlook on life and literature, politics and philosophy. His letters are mostly addressed to his family and friends, showing him a devoted husband and father, and an affectionate and loyal friend. Some of his principal correspondents were Admiral Maxse, elsewhere referred to, Leslie Stephen, John Morley, his political leader, Sir William Hardman, Lady Hardman, Frederick Greenwood. Among others were Grant Allen, Mr. Balfour, J. M. Barrie, Algernon Swinburne, Alphonse Daudet, Holman Hunt, Edmund Gosse, Clement Shorter, G. M. Trevelyan, Theodore Watts-Dunton, and others.[61] Several of the letters are in French, and now and then there are bits of verse, some almost lyric in their quality, some mere doggerel, but suggesting how, had the author desired, he might have lightened somewhat the rather heavy product of his Muse. The letters reveal an appreciation of the work of his contemporaries which rejoices in their success, criticises kindly, if at all, and bears no mark of envy. The only utterance of Meredith's I have found which seemed a bit unkind was the reference to Tennyson, elsewhere quoted, though of course the letters were edited by a loving hand. Several hours might be pleasantly occupied here in reading extracts from the letters, if one had time.

Watts offers to paint his portrait as a gift to the nation, and he cannot consent to absorb any of the painter's precious time for such a purpose. But the portrait is afterwards painted. He writes to the newspapers, pleading for mercy to the defeated Boers.[62] Like every well known writer, the ladies would write him *their* views or ask him *his* views on his own characters, to which he replies, if at all, with generally a humorous and evasive frankness, and sometimes, in the case of a near friend, at considerable length.

The only reference in the letters to Meredith's ill-fated theory of trial marriage, suggested in an article in the *Morning Post*, in 1904, if I remember correctly,[63] and which was I believe that a contract union of ten years might be dissolved at the end of the term or else made permanent, is, I imagine, contained in the following letter to a Mrs. Simons, dated November 17, 1904:[64]

> Dear Madam,—The condition of the union of men and women is so delicate a subject that a mere touch on it, in the form of a suggestion, rouses an outcry from the whole army of Mrs. Grundy.[65] Yet that powerful person might reflect on the number of divorces, and consider that when distaste is between the couples, it is worse for the offspring. Happily there is a majority of marriages where the two jog on contentedly—with, however, too great an indifference to the minority. So we have a figure that presents a tolerably fair front to the world, and is conscious of spots on an irritated skin. All I have suggested is for the matter to be discussed.

His letters on woman's social, political and economic condition are in keeping with his advanced position on the subject of woman's rights. He believed that woman's development had been hampered by her too close confinement to the domestic and material sphere, and her too complete subordination to the will of man, and that the larger freedom which this modern struggle seeks will be for her benefit and that of the race.

Of *Richard Feverel*, a copy of which he had no doubt sent to her, he writes to Miss Vulliamy, whom he afterwards married:

> On consideration I thought that *The Ordeal* could not do you harm; I can only trust that it will not offend. It deals with certain problems of life, and is therefore not of a milky quality. I am afraid that it requires stout reading. If you weather it, unshocked, you will find my other works less trying.

He writes to a friend, when he is quite old and in poor health, that for several days he has been reading French novels, which are "impishly slimy." He was a great admirer of the French people and wrote a poem on Napoleon.[66]

Mr. Paul Lemperly, the well known bibliophile and a member of this club,[67] has a very complete Meredith collection, which it has been my privilege to examine. It comprises all the first editions of Meredith except the English first edition of *Evan Harrington*, although Mr. Lemperly has a copy of the first American edition, which was published before the first English edition, so that it is really *the* first edition.[68] His library contains also the memorial edition of Meredith, published by Constable and Company, and a number of privately printed poems, and one of Mr. Lemperly's own book plates signed by Meredith. His copy of the poems of 1851 contains Errata marked by the poet's own hand. The memorial edition of Meredith has a complete bibliography, and a list of the various cuts or elisions which were made in Meredith's novels in successive editions from time to time. I wish I might have been able to persuade Mr. Lemperly to bring or send his collection to this meeting, but it was a little too much to ask, in view of the size and value of it, and therefore, not being able to show you the best, I have nothing in the way of books or other Meredithiana to exhibit after the usual fashion of those who address this club.

It has seemed strange to many that the man who in his old age was recognized by the discriminating[69] as the greatest living English writer, should[70] have been passed over in the distribution of the Jubilee honors, while writers of inferior quality, such as Walter Besant and Conan Doyle,[71] were thus distinguished, or that[72] he was not buried in Westminster Abbey. As to the Knighthood, these honors would seem to be bestowed not primarily for merit, but for merit tested by popularity. England is very democratic and the government is merely the mouthpiece of the people, so that royal favor is perhaps in these matters only another term for popular acclaim.

As to his sepulcher, the matter was determined by the Dean of Westminster, who voted against[73] the deposit of Meredith's ashes—literally his ashes, because his remains were cremated—in the historic Abbey, for some unexplained reason, perhaps, said *The Academy*, due to his views on marriage expressed by him in an interview with a hapenny reporter and not in his books.[74] He shared this destruction with Swinburne, who died a month before him. Meredith was buried at Dorking, and was followed to the tomb by his neighbors, and the intimate friends of a lifetime, and only a few from the outside world.[75]

The following paragraph, which I believe was cut from a recent issue from the London *Athenaeum*,[76] will be of interest in this connection:

> It is with peculiar pleasure we note in one of the supplements of *The London Gazette* of last month the name of the grandson of George Meredith, Second-Lieut. George William Lewin Meredith, 18th Hussars, who has been awarded the Military Cross for service in the field in Flanders. We offer our heartiest congratulations to the young soldier and to his father, Mr. William Maxse Meredith, of Messrs. Constable and Company.[77] The pen and the sword have very often been interchangeable since the days of Aeschylus,[78] Dante, and Cervantes. Many a passage in Meredith's writings seems to proclaim the soldier who now happily bears his name in Flanders.

◡

SOURCE: Typed text at the Fisk University Library. Chesnutt wrote below the title, "A Paper read by Charles Waddell Chesnutt, before the Rowfant Club, March 11, 1916." The principal information and quotation sources for this speech were: Constanin Photiadès, *George Meredith: Life, Genius and Teaching*, trans. Arthur Price (1913); *The Letters of George Meredith*, 2 volumes, ed. William Maxse Meredith (1865–1913), published in 1912; and James Moffatt (1870–1914), *George Meredith: Introduction to His Novels* (1909).

[1]Meredith (1828–1909) was born at 73 High Street, Portsmouth. *The Adventures of Harry Richmond* was published in 1871; the title character in *Evan Harrington* (1861) is, like Meredith, the son of a tailor.

[2]His mother, Jane Eliza Macnamara Meredith (1802?–1833), was the daughter of a prosperous innkeeper; she died when her son was five years old. His father was Augustus Urmston Meredith (1797–1876). Meredith did circulate another, invented datum concerning his origins: that he was of high-born but illegitimate birth.

[3]François Villon (1431–62?), a Paris-born French poet, was originally named François de Montcobier or François des Loges after, respectively, the village where his father was born or the probable name of his father's farm. He was reared by Guillaume de Villon, the chaplain of Saint-Benôit-le-Bétourné. Chesnutt read a no-longer-extant paper on Villon before the Rowfant Club on 20 March 1915.

[4]Augustus Meredith, after opening his tailor establishment in London in 1841, emigrated to Capetown, South Africa, in 1849.

[5](1762–1814).

[6]Frederick Marryat (1792–1848), *Peter Simple* (1834).

[7]"The Great Mel" in *Evan Harrington* is an exuberant gentleman tailor.

[8]Anne Mitchell (1753–1828) was the daughter of a Portsmouth lawyer.

[9]Knight Commander of the Order of the Bath.

[10]Meredith began attending St. Paul's day school at Southsea, where the affluent boys were educated, in 1837.

[11]*The Shaving of Shagpat: An Arabian Entertainment* (1856), a novel in form and style akin to Richard Burton's translation of *Arabian Nights*.

[12]A mythological figure, a winged horse associated here with flights of imagination.

[13] Meredith was sent to the Moravian School at Neuwied on the Rhine, near Cologne, in 1842. He studied there for two years before returning to his father's shop in London.

[14]Meredith was bound to service by written contract as clerk to a solicitor named W. R. S. Charnock, a cultured man who belonged to the Arundel Club (in which Charles Dickens also held membership). Charnock released Meredith from his articles when the latter decided to give up law for a literary career.

[15]In 1860 Meredith began his career in journalism by working for *The Ipswich Journal*, writing columns of news notes and a leading article or two each week. At this time he also wrote for such London papers as the *Morning Post* and the *Daily News*.

[16]Philosophical positivism is a post-metaphysical mode of thought stressing the necessity of an empirical orientation to the determination of truth. John Morley (1838–1923) was a statesman and man of letters; Frederic Harrison (1831–1923) was a writer and founder of the *Positivist Review* (1893); James Augustus Cotter Morison (1832–88) was a biographer and philosopher; and Admiral Frederick Augustus Maxse (1833–1900) was a naval officer and novelist.

[17]Though Meredith was sent to northern Italy to cover the war for the *Morning Post*, he never reached the front lines during battle. *Sandra Belloni* (1886) was origi-

nally published as *Emilia in England* (1864); *Vittoria* (1867) was the sequel to *Sandra Belloni*. The novels sympathetically narrate the experiences of Emilia Belloni, daughter of an Italian revolutionary, in England and Italy during Italy's struggle for independence.

[18]Morley edited the *Fortnightly Review* from 1867–82.

[19]Meredith began his association with Chapman and Hall in 1859 when that publishing house brought out his first novel, *The Ordeal of Richard Feverel*. He wrote poems for the publisher's magazine *Once a Week* and read manuscripts for them for most of the rest of his life. *The Story of an African Farm* (1924) was written by Olive E. Schreiner (1855–1920), whose *nom de plume* was Ralph Iron; George Robert Gissing (1857–1903) and Thomas Hardy (1840–1928) were prominent English novelists.

[20]Meredith married the widow Mary Ellen Peacock Nicolls (1821–61) in 1849; she left him in 1858.

[21]Arthur Gryffydh Meredith (1853–90) was the only surviving child of several born to Meredith during his first marriage.

[22]Published in 1862.

[23]Peacock (1785–1866), now known principally as a poet; Samuel Taylor Coleridge (1772–1834), poet and essayist.

[24]Though he dedicated *Poems* (1851) to Peacock, the mercurial Meredith later accumulated and destroyed three hundred copies of it to conceal this dedication.

[25]Meredith married Marie Vulliamy (1840–95) in 1864; in 1867 they moved to Flint Cottage, near Box Hill, Surrey. Their children were William Maxse and Marie Eveleen (1871–?).

[26]He contributed poems to such magazines as *Fraser's*, *Chambers's Edinburgh Journal*, and *Household Words*.

[27]These works were initially given periodical publication in 1844, 1837–38, and 1836–37, respectively. Charles Dickens was the author of *Pickwick Papers*.

[28]Mary Ann Evans (1819–80), whose *nom de plume* was George Eliot, reviewed *Shagpat* in *The Leader*, 7 (5 January 1856), 15–17.

[29]*Shagpat* was originally published by Chapman and Hall, which also produced the second edition in 1865.

[30]Judges 16:19.

[31]Miguel de Cervantes' *Don Quixote de la Mancha* is a satirical treatment of the absurdities endemic to medieval romances celebrating the exploits of heroic knights who right wrongs, usually against impossible odds.

[32]Chapter 23.

[33]Richard dies in a duel; Lucy consequently loses her mind and dies.

[34]Serialized from 11 February to 13 October 1860.

[35]Published in 1880.   [36]Published in 1865.

[37]Published in 1894.   [38]Published in 1871.

[39]Chapter 52.   [40]Matthew 2:16.

[41]Serialized in the *Fortnightly Review*, August 1874–December 1875, and published in book form in 1876. Maxse, a political idealist like his fictional counterpart Nevil Beauchamp, twice failed to become a member of Parliament—at Southampton in 1868 and at Tower Hamlets in 1874.

[42]Leslie Stephen (1832–1904) was an English man of letters, known principally as a biographer and editor. In his letter of 8 April 1882 to André Raffalovich (1864–1934), Meredith wrote: "If you remember Vernon Whitford of the *Egoist*, it is a sketch of L. Stephen, but merely a sketch, not doing him full justice, though the strokes within and without are correct."

[43]James Thomson (1834–82), "Note George Meredith," *The Secularist*, 3 June 1879, 364–67. Chesnutt appropriates Thomson's description of *Beauchamp's Career*.

[44]Published as "An Essay on Comedy and the Uses of the Comic Spirit" in *New Quarterly Magazine* in 1877 and as a monograph with the same title in 1897.

[45]Ferdinand Lassalle (1825–64), a Breslau-born disciple of Karl Marx and a founder of the German Social Democratic Party, was killed in a duel over a love affair. Prince Otto von Bismarck (1815–98), a Prussian statesman nicknamed the "Iron Chancellor" of the German Empire, was a foe of the Marxists.

[46]Princess Racowitza, born Helene von Dönniges (1845–1911), wrote a memoir of her relationship entitled *Meine Beziehungen zu Ferdinand Lassalle* (1883).

[47]Heroine of the next summarized novel.

[48]Caroline Elizabeth Sara Norton (1808–77), granddaughter of dramatist Richard Brinsley Sheridan, was reputed to have had a love affair in the mid-1840's with Cabinet minister Sidney Herbert (1810–67). When the Cabinet's secret decision to repeal the Corn Laws was published in the *Times* in December 1845, causing Sir Robert Peel (1788–1850) to resign as Prime Minister, the common belief was that Herbert had told Caroline and she leaked the information to the editor of the newspaper.

[49]Poet and critic Sir John William Watson (1858–1935), "Fiction—Plethoric and Anaemic," *National Review*, 14 (October 1889), 167–83.

[50]Darwin's appreciation of prose fiction of the kind is disclosed in *Life and Letters of Charles Darwin, Including an Autobiographical Chapter*, ed. Sir Francis Darwin (1848–1925), published in 1887.

[51]Published in 1895.

[52]Mudie's Lending Library was founded in 1842 by English publisher Charles Edward Mudie (1818–90).

[53]"George Meredith's New Work," *Cope's Tobacco Plant*, 2 (January 1880), 430–31. It was signed "Sigvat," pseudonym of James Thomson.

[54]Chapter 6.

[55]Charlotte Brontë (1816–55); *Jane Eyre* was published in 1847.

[56]Jean Paul Richter (1763–1825), German Romantic novelist.

[57]John Bartlett (1820–1905), *Familiar Quotations* (1875). These lines, as Chesnutt notes earlier in this speech, appear in the final chapter of *The Shaving of Shagpat*.

[58]"Excelsior" was included in his *Ballads and Other Poems* (1842).

[59]Tennyson, as poet-laureate, routinely received complimentary copies of books of poetry published by English writers. In July 1851 he wrote Meredith a kind letter of encouragement and appreciation for his poems. Charles Kingsley (1819–75), an English novelist and poet, reviewed *Poems* in "This Year's Song-Crop," *Fraser's Magazine*, 44 (December 1851), 618–32.

[60]Chesnutt quotes from the expanded, 1878 version of "Love in the Valley," rather than the original that appeared in 1851.

[61]William Hardman (1828–90), an English politician and public servant, and his wife Mary Ann Hardman; Frederick Greenwood (1830–1909), editor of *Cornhill Magazine* (1862–68), and editor and founder of both *Pall Mall Gazette* (1865–80) and *St. James Gazette* (1880–88); Charles Grant Allen (1848–99), author and college professor; Arthur James Balfour (1848–1930), author and statesman; James M. Barrie (1860–1937), Scottish novelist and dramatist; Algernon Charles Swinburne (1837–1909), poet; Alphonse Daudet (1840–97), French novelist; William Holman Hunt (1827–1910), painter; Edmund W. Gosse (1849–1928), poet and man of letters; Clement K. Shorter (1857–1926), journalist and literary critic; George M. Trevelyan (1876–1962), history professor and literary critic; Theodore Watts-Dunton (1832–1914), journalist, poet, and novelist.

[62]George F. Watts (1877–1904) was a painter and sculptor. The Boer War began in 1899 and ended in 1902.

[63]Meredith's article on marriage appeared in "The Marriage Handicap," *Daily Mail*, 24 September 1904, 5. He also published his thoughts on marriage in "Paris Topics: Meredithian Marriages," *Daily News*, 12 October 1904, 2, and in an interview in the *Tatler*, "Marriage and Divorce," 26 October 1904, 123.

[64]The letter is dated 28 October 1863.

[65]A character in the 1798 play *Speed the Plough*, by Thomas Morton (1764?–1838); she came to symbolize the upper-class British concern for maintaining proprieties.

[66]"Napoléon" (1898).

[67]Paul Lemperly (1858–1939) lived in Lakewood, O., and engaged in publishing on an occasional basis. He was a nationally significant book and manuscript collector.

[68]*Evan Harrington* was published in New York by Harper & Bros. in 1860. The first English edition was published by Bradbury & Evans in London in 1861.

[69]Possibly a reference to a letter of congratulation presented to Meredith on his seventieth birthday, signed by thirty prominent men, including Edmund Gosse, Thomas Hardy, John Morley, Algernon Swinburne, and Leslie Stephen. They commended him for having "attained the first rank in literature."

[70]Editorially excised is the preceding word "who."

[71]Arthur Conan Doyle (1859–1930), Scottish physician and novelist best known for his "Sherlock Holmes" stories; Walter Besant (1836–1901), novelist, biographer, and critic. Queen Victoria's Golden Jubilee was celebrated on 21 June 1887; her Diamond Jubilee was celebrated on 20 June 1897.

[72]Emended to "that" is "why."

[73]Emended is "voted the."

[74]"Life and Letters," *Academy*, 76 (22 May 1909), 124.

[75]A memorial service for Meredith was conducted at Westminster Abbey. Like Swinburne, however, this agnostic had long since distanced himself from the Anglican church.

[76]"Notes and News," *Athenaeum*, no. 4602 (February 1916), 59.

[77]George William Lewin Meredith (1897–?). In 1895 William Maxse Meredith abandoned his career as an electrical engineer to become his father's business representative; at this time he also took a position with Constable & Company, which became Meredith's publisher after he left Chapman & Hall.

[78]Aeschylus (525–456 B.C.) was an Athenian playwright.

Social Discrimination

Speech delivered at the Amenia Conference, Amenia, N.Y., 25 August 1916

The topic assigned for discussion this evening is "Social Discrimination." This is the last citadel to be assailed in the fight for equality, and the most difficult and delicate subject on the program.

Of course in its wider sense, our whole fight is against social discrimination.

Society in its widest meaning embraces the whole social aggregate and involves all questions concerned with the living of *men and women* together. But I assume that our topic this evening is meant to have a narrower meaning, that is, to apply to the more intimate, personal association of human beings which we refer to as social intercourse.

The term, or what it stands for, has different meanings, or may be given different definitions. To the gentlemen who make the laws and set the social standards of the Southern States, social intercourse exists wherever people sit down together—on a railroad train, in a street-car, a hotel, a theater, a church, a public park, a public library, a public eating or drinking place, a public gambling hell, and so on down the social ladder, even to asylums, reformatories, jails, penitentiaries, and I have even read of an argument on the question of precedence where a white and a black man were to be hanged on the same scaffold and on the same day. All of these matters, and others which time will not permit me to mention, and which are involved, in the Bourbon Southern mind, in what they call "Social Equality," have been pretty well covered under different topics, and, as I say, I assume our discussion to relate now to what is commonly known as social intercourse—not admission to society in the narrow ultra-exclusive circle which is maintained by the snobbish and the wealthy, and which includes very few people of any race, but the privilege, or the right, if you choose to call it so, of friendly, familiar intercourse in home or club or social gathering, with people of kindred interests or occupations or standards of thought and feeling.

The subject is simple enough in the abstract, and is based on the theory that whatever is good in organized society should be open to the attainment of any member thereof, under the same conditions. Anything else, of course, is discrimination. But in practice, it is a thing that goes by favor. One cannot demand that another man invite him to dinner, or admit him to his club, or send him cards to parties or dances. Yet it is perfectly true that these things have very decided practical value. Many a valuable business or professional acquaintance is made around the social board or in the club room. In the larger cities the clubs are used as meeting places to discuss business matters and public questions. Men get an opportunity to meet one another in mental deshabille, so to speak, and thereby learn to know one another better, and to know themselves better. Many a colored man does not know how good a man he is, and many another overrates his own ability, because they have not had a fair opportunity for comparison of themselves with others. It is fatally easy to make prejudice an excuse for inefficiency. And, besides this opportunity for self-appraisement, there are the inspiring friendships, the mental and spiritual stimulus which comes from meeting, as I say, others of kindred standards of thought and feeling—something of the same benefit which we are all deriving from this gathering here at the beautiful home of our honored host.

As to the social position of colored people in the United States, so far as white people are concerned, generally speaking, as Mr. Pickens said about higher education, they have no social recognition or standing.[1] As a very distinguished writer and critic once wrote, in reviewing some of my own stories about people on the edge of the color line, "We no more expect to meet them in our parlors than we would the lower animals." There are a few sporadic exceptions in some of the great cities and perhaps in some of the smaller towns, where, within certain limits, social courtesies and club privileges are extended to certain individuals, doubtless everyone here, but broadly speaking the Negro and all his kin are social outcasts. I don't know if outcast is quite the right word; in its radical meaning it signifies one who is cast out; the Negro has never been in.

The reason for this condition is twofold. First and foremost, and sufficient of itself, is the traditional prejudice—not of the individual but of society as a whole. Many white persons will tell you that they personally have no prejudice against color, generally coupling the statement with the additional information that their fathers were active in the work of the underground railway, or an interesting story about some excellent colored servant they have or have had. But it would proba-bly never occur to some of these good people that a colored family living on the same street, living perhaps as well as they or better, would appreciate a social call or an invitation to dine.

Another reason, and perhaps the fundamental one, is the fact that the society of colored people is not considered worth cultivating. The American people are a race of climbers. I say it in no sense of disparagement; the desire to get on and up in the world is their ruling motive and the secret of their wonderful progress. In a country where theoretically all men are equal, the individual sedulously conserves and tries to use for his advancement every possible element of superiority which he possesses. To be white is a tremendous advantage in the United States, and if to as-sociate with colored people would harm a man or woman socially, or would not advance him or her, the chances are that they would not do it.

The only way therefore, it seems to me, to overcome this social prejudice, is for the people of color to make their society desirable. This involves of course, our whole propaganda. A people who are political and civil nonentities, who are de-spised and flouted in public, are never likely to be looked upon as desirable associ-ates in private. When the time comes that your white neighbor thinks of you as his equal in other respects, and feels that it will be of value to him, financially, intellec-tually or socially, to court the acquaintance of his colored neighbor, he will go af-ter it like he does everything else he wants. When a Negro shall own or control a bank or a railroad or a great business enterprise, I have not the slightest doubt that the board of directors will be willing to extend social courtesies to him. A promi-nent colored writer once said that one wholesale dry goods house or one great de-partment store on Broadway would do more to combat race prejudice than all the race problem meetings that could be held in a year.

As the colored people, collectively, shall cease to be despised, and as individu-ally they shall prove themselves, because of their intellect, character, talent or so-cial charm, not only tolerable but desirable socially, the discrimination of which we speak will disappear. What we can justly ask of the white Americans is not only that they cease to practice social discrimination *against* colored people, but that they begin to practice social discrimination *among* colored people—they do so already to a limited extent—that they first give to colored people an opportunity to demonstrate their social value, and then recognize it as it appears. If they will do the first, the second will follow as the day the night.[2]

The question is one that can only be solved by the operation of social forces, which sometimes operate slowly, but, like the mills of God, always grind their grist.[3] The most the humanitarian or the altruist or the reformer can do is to prepare the material, watch the process and keep the machinery cleaned and oiled so that the grinding may be not unduly prolonged.

⌒

SOURCE: Undated typed text at the Fisk University Library. On the evening of 25 August 1916 Chesnutt delivered this brief paper at the 24–26 August 1916 Amenia Conference on the race problem, which was organized by poet, literary critic, and civil rights activist Joel Spingarn (1875–1939). Spingarn, who hosted the conference on his Duchess County, N.Y., estate, wrote to Chesnutt on 16 August (Fisk University), inviting him to serve as the chairman of the session devoted to the subject of social discrimination against African Americans, requesting that he speak no longer than fifteen minutes by way of initiating discussion. Above the title of the typescript of this speech appears, in Chesnutt's hand, "Such" canceled and then "So thoroughly outclassed"—this apparently serving as a note for Chesnutt's remarks preliminary to reading his paper.

[1]The Amenia Conference featured a session on education. The previous speaker and leader of that discussion group was educator, orator, and author William Pickens (1881–1954), who earned a degree in classics at Yale University (1904). He taught Greek, Latin, and German at Talladega College (1904–14) and classics and sociology at Wiley College (1914–15); and he became the first African-American dean at Morgan College (1915–20). In 1920 he initiated his long association with the N.A.A.C.P.

[2]*Hamlet* 1.3.79.

[3]"Though the mills of God grind slowly, yet they grind exceedingly small; / Though with patience he [*sic*] stands waiting, with exactness grinds he [*sic*] all," Henry Wadsworth Longfellow's "Poetic Aphorisms from the Sinngedichte of Friedrich von Logau," the section entitled "Retribution" (1845).

The Negro in Books

Speech delivered in behalf of "The National Buy-a-Book Campaign in the
Interest of Negro Literature," Philadelphia, Pa., 5 December 1916

Mr. Chairman,[1] ladies and gentlemen: With potatoes at two dollars and a half a bushel, eggs at 68 cents a doz., butter at more than 50 cents a lb., bacon at forty-two cents a pound, and soup-bones at twenty-five cents apiece, without the marrow, I should be false to the interests of my publishers, my fellow authors and myself, had I not accepted Prof. Wright's invitation to come here and speak on behalf of his "Buy-a-Book Movement,"—a very worthy object, not only from the standpoint of the author and publisher, but for broader and deeper and higher reasons. If books meet a real need, as I shall endeavor to show you they do, it follows without saying that authors should be encouraged to write them, and the only effective encouragement for the production of books, is their purchase. No amount of praise, no volume of good words, will be of any benefit to a writer, unless attended by royalties, which are not only the most effective and most highly valued expression of appreciation, but are absolutely essential to promote further publication; for, even though an author might be willing to write for love of a cause, or for the pleasure of self-expression, publishers are hard-headed, cold-blooded people, who must have the wherewithal to pay for typesetting and paper and binding and advertising, and a profit besides. A publisher might take a chance once, but no publisher wants a second book from the pen of the author of an unsuccessful first book. And so, if the world wants books, it must be willing to pay for them.

Perhaps some of us have never thought of, and therefore never quite realized, the part that books play in our lives. Wise men have said that speech, the spoken word, is the most important faculty which distinguishes men from the lower animals; it gives man the power to communicate and therefore to compare, to reason, to work together for the common good. It may be said with equal truth that the book, the written word, is what has developed the civilized man from the savage. It makes it possible to record the experience of the race, instead of relying merely upon memory, thus enabling men in different places and in different ages to pool their knowledge and experience, and gain the benefit of the accumulation. To the daily newspaper, which on Sundays assumes in its size almost the proportions, and in its contents almost the variety of an encyclopedia, we look for information about current events. From the weekly and monthly journals we gather current opinion. The riper thoughts of the best writers and thinkers we get in the form of the bound books which are placed in our libraries. Our education is based on books. They are the sources of our knowledge of history, of the sciences; and as we learn other things by experience or experiment, we put them in books for the enlightenment of others. Our philosophy we learn from books. Our religion is founded on a Book. We find much of our mental relaxation and recreation and amusement in books. We form our conceptions of the lives and characters of others from what we read about them in books. This is true even of those who seldom read a book; they learn what little they know by association with those who have read and studied books. Thro the medium of books each one of us may become the heir of all the wisdom of all the ages, to the extent that we have time and the capacity to acquire it.

Now, this being so, how important it is that books should be good books; that those which gather and dispense current information should gather carefully and record accurately; that the opinions which books disseminate should be based upon carefully ascertained facts, and reasoned out logically and with freedom from prejudice; that the philosophy taught by books should be predicated upon sound reasoning; that, in the lighter forms of literature, the poem, the novel and the play, the sentiment should be clean and wholesome. There have been a few vile books, some of them extremely well written, from a literary viewpoint, which have left a trail of slime behind them for generations. There have been other books, clean enough so far as language is concerned, which have disseminated falsehood and error to the warping of the reader's mind and the injury of those against whom they were directed. And there have been good books, besides the Book of Books, which have been the joy and delight and inspiration of mankind.

Of the books of only one nation, and that a small one, books written many centuries ago, Lord Macaulay said, in tracing their influence upon mankind in after ages:

> If we consider merely the subtlety of disquisition, the force of imagination, the perfect energy and elegance of expression, which characterize the great works of Athenian genius, we must pronounce them intrinsically most valuable; but what shall we say when we reflect that from thence have sprung, directly or redirectly, all the noblest creations of the human intellect; that from hence were the vast accomplishments and brilliant fancy of Cicero,[2] the withering fire of Dante; the humor of Cervantes, the comprehension of Bacon; the wit of Butler; the supreme and universal excellence of Shakespeare? All the triumphs of truth and genius over prejudice and power in every country and in every age, have been the triumphs of Athens

wrought through the medium of those immortal books of which Macaulay speaks.[3]

Now, many books, especially in these our modern days, have dealt with the Negro, in large or in small part. And it is the purpose of my talk tonight to recall to your memory something of the way in which the Negro has been dealt with in books.

In the heated debate on slavery which ran through the generation preceding the Civil War, there were many books in defense of that institution, books which branded the Negro as brother to the beast, even denying him a soul, or ordinary intelligence. You can find one of them on the shelves of a large library, and students of history dig them out and wonder at them. There were, even at that day, some books written on the other side, but not so many. For instance, Whittier's *Voices of Freedom*,[4] which are found in his collected poems, were a strong protest against the wrong of slavery and a strong appeal for human brotherhood. The collected speeches and lectures of Wendell Phillips were masterpieces of forensic eloquence. The several autobiographies of Frederick Douglass furnished their contribution to antislavery literature. Lowell's *Biglow Papers* gave some hard raps to the peculiar institutions, and there were others.[5]

All these books dealt with the Negroes as slaves, the only status which, with few exceptions, they had, up to that time occupied in the United States. The abolition of slavery, the enfranchisement of the colored people, their efforts to advance along the avenues thus opened up to them, the efforts of the white South to prevent their upward progress, opened up a wide field of discussion and argument and gave rise to a flood of books dealing with the "Race Question," or the "Southern Question" or the "Negro Problem," as it is variously called, some of them in the form of serious or didactic books, others in the form of fiction; most of them written by white people with a rather low estimate of the Negro's mind and character, some by white men or women who were friendly to the Negro and wished to help him in his uphill struggle; some few, gradually increasing in number, by colored men and women, of which but one, so far as I am advised, has decried and slandered his own race. I refer to the book by W. H. Thomas, published by Macmillans several years ago. I expressed my opinion of it at the time in one of the literary reviews.[6] Some of the best of the books by colored men on this theme have been those of Dr. Sinclair,[7] Dr. Du Bois, Professor Kelly Miller[8] and Dr. Washington. George W. Williams wrote a very comprehensive *History of the Negro*. A recently published volume by Dr. C. V. Roman, of Meharry Medical College, entitled, *American Civilization and the Negro*, is an unusually well written and comprehensive study of all phases of the question.[9] Some of the more recent books which discuss the race problem incidentally to or as a part of larger themes are Rhodes' *History of the United States*, Professor Josiah Royce's *Race Questions and Other American Problems*, Greeley's *American Conflict*, Dr. Albert Bushnell Hart's *The American Nation*, and Lord Bryce's recent book on South America.[10] Of course there are many others, but you know them as well as I do. Sir Sidney Olivier's *White Capital and Black Labor in the West Indies* is an illuminating study of racial conditions, and how they have been satisfactorily worked out in the British West Indies.[11]

Sir Harry Johnston, the English traveler and publicist, has studied the Negro all over the world, and has written two almost monumental books, one on *The Negro in Africa*,[12] and another on *The Negro in the New World* ($10.00 apiece—libraries). He approaches the subject without prejudice, with an open mind, states what he has seen with perfect fairness, and draws the conclusion that the Negro or Negroid peoples, especially in the countries to the south of us, where they have been admitted to *real* equality with the whites, have demonstrated their fitness for all the duties and responsibilities of citizenship in the very highly specialized and complicated civilization of our time. Lord Bryce reaches the same conclusion, after extended travels through South America. Both Johnston and Bryce dispute the claim that the mixture of races tends to deterioration or degeneracy. Mr. Roosevelt's letters during his travels in Brazil last year bear out these conclusions.[13]

But what I am going to speak to you about more particularly tonight is the Negro in creative or imaginative literature, or *belles lettres*, as the French call it, as embodied in fiction and to some extent in poetry. This literature, in its best sense, is the expression of the life of a people. There was a time when imaginative literature was almost wholly founded upon idealism. The author imagined a perfect type of man or woman, a hero or heroine, of transcendent manliness or beauty, all of whose thoughts and deeds were noble; or an abandoned type of villain, all of whose deeds were base and unworthy. In more modern times, in art and literature, men and women are studied as we see them around us, no one perfect, no one hopelessly bad, all swayed by mixed motives, few entirely free from the taint of selfishness, none quite deaf to good impulses.

Now, it is obvious that in depicting character in literature—to draw any true picture of the life of a race or class of men, or of types of any race or class, it is necessary to know the race or class or type thoroughly, its manner of living, of thinking, of feeling; its outlook upon life, its aspirations, its ambitions, its aptitudes, its achievements—all the thousand and one things which go to make up its life.

The Negro, as one of the great divisions of the human family, whom fate has placed and kept in close contact with the white race for centuries, has naturally furnished material for a great deal of imaginative literature. I am going to refer briefly to some of it, and point out how in these writings the Negro has been used, then leave it to you whether or not there has been such a portrayal of his life and character as I have said true realism, and therefore true art, should give; and if, as I suspect, you shall find there has in large measure not been such a portrayal, I shall ask you to consider the sources from which such a portrayal might reasonably be expected to emanate, and suggest how you can encourage its production.

The literature of a country or of an age, as I have said, is considered, and as a rule is, a fair reflection of the social conditions of that age or country. But conventions, in literature, as in religion, in politics and in social usage, sometimes persist long past the point where they correctly mirror the time. This is particularly true where they are confused by prejudice. An amusing minor instance of this is the sort of dialect that many writers put into the mouths of their colored characters. I solemnly declare that during a long life, some fifteen years of which was spent in the South, just after the Civil War, I have no recollection of ever hearing a Negro say, "It am." Another classic solecism is that which puts into the mouths of colored servants, at the North, in our own day, the word "Massa." I think it safe to say that no colored servant at the North, and few anywhere, unless it be some old relic of antebellum days, ever uses the word "Massa," in any such way as it is employed by a certain school of novelists. It is a concrete personal suggestion of slavery, which even the most stupid Negroes are willing to forget, except as a historical fact, so far as the white people will let them. An imported English butler may refer to his employer as his master, but rarely, if ever, your American Negro. The Negro of a certain type is likely to apply to a white man in some relation of authority over him, or from whom he seeks or has received a favor, some title, such as "boss" or "colonel," or something of the kind, which implies authority without suggesting servility.

Another convention that dies hard and is indeed very much alive, is a contempt for mixed blood, so profound that in almost any novel or story, where such a character appears, whether the scene be located in our own country, in India, in China, in the Pacific Islands, or on any African or American or Asiatic coast, the half-caste, or the man with a touch of the tar-brush, is almost sure to be the villain.

The old theory, so pleasant to the superior race, that a mixture of blood simply results in combining the worst qualities of the parent strains, still persists, in spite of the obvious fact that in every country where racial admixture exists there are many people of that class who will average up in intellect, in manners, in morals and other social virtues, with any element of the population which has had no better opportunities, and the equally obvious fact that in every country, in our own conspicuously so, colored men have attained distinction in many walks of life. To meet a noble, or even a decent colored character in current American or English fiction is so rare as to create surprise. One evening not long ago, I sat in a moving picture theatre, where the film being exhibited was an admirable production of Flaubert's famous novel, *Salammbô*. When the picture of Mathô's lieutenant and companion, Spendius, for the role of which a full-blood Negro was cast, was first thrown upon the screen, a white woman seated beside me, a well dressed and seemingly refined person, remarked audibly, "Well, look at the coon! He's a spy and a traitor, no doubt," whereas, as the story developed, he was a model of loyalty and devotion to his leader, and in reality, though not in terms, the hero of the piece.[14]

Another persistent convention, which is retained either through superstition or because of its dramatic value, is the theory that a man with a remote strain of dark blood may beget, or a woman similarly dowered, may bear by the other parent,— a pure white person,—a black child. The latest literary crime of this kind was perpetrated by Wallace Irwin in a recent number of *McClure's Magazine*, followed by a deservedly short-lived play built upon it, called *Pride of Race*, in which a popular actor took the part of the near-white hero. It is only fair to say that both the author and the actor made the hero a very fine gentleman, wealthy, cultured, with all the social graces, loved and admired by all his friends, but all in vain to counteract the drop of dark blood, one in thirty-two, which resulted in a Negro baby of the full blood by a white mother. The author had the decency to say that such an instance would not be likely to happen more than once in a million times.[15] Modern eugenic science declares such a thing impossible. The Mendelian Law, applied to human beings, would not bear out any such theory; there is no scientific data on which to base it; and a course of observation extending over more years than I like to think of, justifies me in saying that I never saw the offspring of a mixed union, where one of the parents was of pure white blood, where the child was darker than the dark parent. Accidents may happen, of course, in the best regulated families, but not that particular kind of accident.

The situation is different in cases where both parents are of mixed blood; we all know that the chances for divergence are much larger in such cases, for scientific reasons which are foreign to my subject, and which it would require too much time to go into.

The Negro plays a small part in the literature of England. In Othello, the master of English drama created a fine and noble character, a brave and gallant soldier, whose charms of person and of character were sufficient to win the love of the beautiful lady whom he espoused. His weakness was that of an ardent temperament, which was played upon, with tragic outcome, by a cunning and unscrupulous subordinate. Thackeray occasionally brings in a colored character, as Miss Schwartz, in *Vanity Fair*,[16] the colored daughter of a sugar planter of the West Indies, whose swarthy complexion and crinkly hair are compensated by her millions and her amiable and generous disposition. It is said that Lady Nelson, the wife of Lord Nelson, the hero of Trafalgar, was a woman of this type, whom Nelson married for her money and neglected for the beautiful Emma Hamilton.[17] In Walter Besant and James Rice's novel, *My Little Girl*, the principal character is a mulatto, who, as is usual in fiction, despises his mother and hates his father.[18] He is an army officer, also of West Indian extraction, who thinks more about his color than any one else does, and lets it prey on his mind so as to spoil his life. Grant Allen, in his novel *Black and White*, a West Indian story, has a wide range of colored characters, and shows a keen insight into the psychology of race, both of the pure and mixed types.[19] The story of the "near white" lawyer and his English wife ends happily, while the story of the brown doctor and his hopeless passion for the aristocratic lady of the island, has a tragic outcome. Joseph Conrad, in *The Nigger of the Narcissus*, has drawn a striking but unpleasant character in the malingering black sailor.[20]

A familiar type of English story, which some American writers have adapted, and which, like the black baby myth, is maintained because of its dramatic value is the reversion to type motive. The black baby myth is a form of this motive—the physical reversion to type. The other form, of which I am now speaking, is the mental and moral reversion. A native is educated in England, preferably at Oxford or Cambridge. He distinguishes himself in scholarship or athletics and is well received socially. He returns to his native land, either as a missionary or in some subordinate administrative capacity. But the lure of the jungle is stronger than the superficial veneer of culture, and he relapses into barbarism and goes back to his bottle of trade-gin, his loin-cloth, his beads and his tomtom. I do not recall any instance where he has reverted to cannibalism. The same motive is used with the Indian in America.

In one of Mr. Louis Tracy's numerous novels, *The Flower of the Gorse*, two of the characters, one a rich American, the other his cousin, a London society man, have a remote Negroid strain, and in conformity with literary tradition, one of them runs away with his friend's wife and the other seduces a young French girl and is murdered by her fiancé, who declares, with the reader's entire concurrence, that he has rid the world of a viper.[21]

Henry Seton Merriman's *With Edged Tools* has an awful example of the mixed-blood villain.[22] The action is laid on the west coast of Africa.

But it is of course in America, where the Negro has played so large a part, though mainly a passive one in the history of the country, that the Negro is most frequently met with in fiction, dating from the abolition propaganda. *Uncle Tom's Cabin* is the example that comes first to every one's mind. In that much praised and much maligned but immortal work are embraced all types of colored people. Uncle Tom, the protagonist of the story, a model of fidelity and self-sacrifice; the inimitable Topsy, the unfortunate Cassie, the unworthy Sambo and Quimbo, George Harris and Eliza, who were so fair as to be able to "pass for white"—every type has its place, and they are all well drawn and true to nature. No criticism of this immortal work, the success of which is due to its appeal to elemental justice, has ever questioned the correctness of its delineation of Negro character.

Mrs. Stowe wrote other books in like vein, but she had used up most of her material in the one, and the others are but a pale reflection.[23]

Since the days of Mrs. Stowe almost every American writer of promise has recognized the dramatic value of the color motive and has attempted to utilize it, within certain narrow limits to which I shall revert later. One of the most successful of these was Judge Albion W. Tourgée, whose political novel, the *Fool's Errand*, dealing with Reconstruction and the rise and fall of the Ku Klux Klan, met with a popular success, which, for a time, was comparable with that of *Uncle Tom's Cabin*, and his *Bricks Without Straw* was only less successful. One of his earlier stories along the color line, *Toinette*, first published serially in the *Independent* and afterwards brought out in book form under the title of *A Royal Gentleman*, was on the beautiful octoroon theme, of which I shall speak further. Some of you will remember his *Pactolus Prime*, with its philosophic and rich bootblack, who gives all his wealth to his near-white daughter, who solves her problem by going into a convent.[24]

(Ignatius Donnelly.)[25]

Mr. George W. Cable was the next American author of distinction to attack the race problem in fiction. His *Old Creole Days* is a charmingly graceful and sympathetic portrayal of the trials and tribulations of the interesting mixed bloods of New Orleans in the olden days, and the no less interesting white creoles among whom they lived, and from whom they had their being.[26] The stories of Madame Delphine and Tite Poulette are perfect gems in miniature, and had the author written nothing else, would entitle him to his conceded place in the front rank of American story tellers. His *Grandissimes* was a further development of the same theme on a larger canvas, but equally well done. The story of "Bras Coupé" is a masterpiece; the character of the Negro who defied the lash, defied his master, and who preferred death to slavery, is a refreshing departure from the popular literary convention of the cringing, fawning menial who would lick the hand that struck him. Mr. Cable's later conception of the reconstructed Negro in the character of Cornelius Leggett, the grafting mulatto politician, in his *John March, Southerner*, is less happy and less convincing.[27]

Mr. Howells has tried his hand on the race question, in his very pretty novel, *An Imperative Duty*, as has Professor Bliss Perry in one of his few novels, *The Plated City*.[28] Mrs. Margaret Deland in one of her later novels, has resurrected the reversion to type motive, in the person of a colored Harvard College graduate.[29]

Walt Whitman[30] in many of his poems showed a profound sympathy with the sufferings of the slave.

Paul Dunbar, though best known as a poet, wrote some short stories of his people in *Old Plantation Days* and *The Strength of Gideon*,[31] and Dr. Du Bois has contributed to the subject recently a well written novel called *The Quest of the Silver Fleece*.[32] And there have been many stories by obscure or little known writers, many of them colored, founded mainly upon the wrongs of the Negro and mostly without literary value or recognition, but worthy of study as sociological documents and as showing the upward reaching of untried but aspiring minds.

In spite of the magnitude of the subject, it has, however, been seemingly impossible to approach it in fiction from but a few angles. Fundamentally it involves the most dramatic and popular of situations, that of strong contrast in social condition, the same theme as that of Miss Johnson's admirable *Prisoners of Hope* and of numerous novels and folk-lore stories of all lands, where King Cophetua marries the beggar maid or the highborn lady stoops to the lowborn nature's nobleman;[33] or where the hero, of humble beginnings rises to high social standing or political place. It is impossible, in a country where in many states intermarriage between the races is forbidden, and where for marriageable purposes one-sixteenth of Negro blood makes one colored, and where such marriages, if solemnized without legal sanction, which is denied, constitute "an infamous crime," it is impossible that romantic love, in anything but the beautiful octoroon motive, could be a successful theme for American fiction. The subject is considered sordid and low—even the social evil and its resultant diseases are in better taste. W. Pett Ridge, an English writer, has produced a volume of *Tales of Mean Streets*.[34] Possibly some student of humanity in the raw might sometime write some "Tales of Low People," under which titles stories of this kind might be acceptable. For white and black and brown and yellow people do intermarry, sometimes happily, but always with a possibility of tragedy for themselves or their offspring; and if ever race prejudice becomes so modified that the subject can be freely discussed, doubtless its latent possibilities may appeal to aspiring writers, casting about for novel themes.

The faithful servant motive—generally an old Negro uncle or mammy who loves the white folks better than his or her own black offspring,—is one of the commonest types of Negro in fiction. Uncle Tom is the prototype. Thomas Nelson Page, in "Marse Chan" and elsewhere has apotheosized this type.[35]

Joel Chandler Harris, in Uncle Remus, has delineated a delightful old Negro. There is not much opportunity for characterization in the role played by the old story teller, but what there is is of a pleasing and kindly character. Indeed the use of old Negro men and women in this capacity, as the medium for weird tales and shrewd philosophy, is a common expedient among short story writers. I have used it myself in my *Conjure Woman*.[36] Miss Lucy Pratt's Ebenezer stories, of which a little black school boy is the hero, are pleasing delineations of character.[37]

In the Rab and Dab stories, which first appeared in the *Atlantic Monthly*, Mrs.

Patience Pennington, in her *A Woman Rice Planter*, has given a delightful study of two little black imps and her efforts to civilize them.[38] Miss Jean Kenyon Mackenzie has also published in the *Atlantic* under the title of *Black Sheep*, some of her experiences as a Presbyterian missionary in the German colony of Kamerun, on the West Coast of Africa, where she has studied, with friendly Christian sympathy, the Negro in his native forests.[39]

While many writers have pleaded the Negro's cause in a more or less open way in fiction, he has been written down far more often. But it was left to the present generation to develop a writer who, prostituting a noble instrument to an unworthy end, has made the defamation of the Negro his principal theme and the foundation of his literary reputation and his very considerable financial success, in the person of Thomas Dixon, Jr. The popular success of this mediocre melodrama posing as historical literature is sufficient evidence that at least one type of Negro can be made popular in fiction or rather, made the subject of popular fiction.

Now, having seen the kind of books that are written about colored people, let us ask what kind of books we would like to have written about them?

First, in historical and sociological works, we want the facts in regard to them stated, not deductions drawn from preconceived ideas or lingering traditions. When the Negro as a soldier is referred to, we want the facts as to his numbers, his courage, his loyalty and his services, and he need not be afraid to stand by his record on those facts. When he is referred to as a politician, we want the record given as it is. Reconstruction politics were not a brilliant success, but they at least gave education and civil rights to the Negro, and the colored politicians were by no means responsible for all the mistakes of that epoch. We want books which, in recording the history of that period, will state the facts truthfully, take all the circumstances into consideration, and will not make from the record of those days, the deduction that the Negro is unfit to exercise the right to vote or to hold office.

When the Negro as a man and a social unit is referred to, we do not want him referred to *en masse* as lazy, shiftless and inefficient. Many Negroes are, but many more are not. We do not want it assumed that because he is of humble origin, that he is necessarily a low person—for, as I heard it wittily put the other day, it does not necessarily follow that because a man was born in a stable he is therefore a horse. It is amusing to read the Southern newspapers, since the beginning of the recent migration of colored laborers from the South to the North, and note their great alarm at and their eagerness to prevent, the loss of this shiftless and inefficient class of labor. It leads the thoughtful and uninformed reader to wonder whether these stories of the Negro's worthlessness are true, and it makes those who know the facts chortle with glee.

When, in imaginative literature, the man of color is referred to as a servant, we would prefer to have him presented now and then, as a self-respecting individual, faithful to his duties, of course, respectful to his superiors, but not the servile, groveling menial or the absurd buffoon depicted in so many stories. There are too many of the latter type, it is true, but they are fast ceasing to be the rule, if they ever were. We would like to see colored men in books in some other characters than those of servants and criminals. We would be much pleased to see them depicted now and then as successful business or professional men, our women as clerks, teachers or stenographers.

When the race admixture motive is employed in fiction, we would like, now and then, to find a broad-minded, noble-hearted white man, who, having perchance fallen in love with the beautiful octoroon, would not let the shadow of the black baby stand between his happiness and hers. There are several such books. Mr. Howells's *Imperative Duty*, to which I have referred, and Professor Perry's *The Plated City*, are instances in point. We would like to meet in American fiction, some of the liberal-minded white people who do not scorn dark blood, in however slight a degree, and some of those still more broad-minded, who do not scorn it in any degree. We know there are such white people, and we would like to meet them in books. A pleasing instance of this kind is found in Sir Conan Doyle's "The Yellow Face" in the *Adventures of Sherlock Holmes*, where etc.[40]

We would like to read a novel in which the man of mixed blood is not always a traitor and a sneak, a degenerate or a pervert. We would like to read about a colored politician who is not a grafter, willing to sell his vote, himself and his people for a very meager mess of pottage;[41] we would like to read about a colored preacher or social worker who would freely give his life for the uplift of his people; of the colored soldier who dies bravely for his country and his flag. We read of such people in the newspapers, and race magazines; we should like to meet them as in books.

Of course we could not expect to have all the colored characters in novels be people of these better types. Unfortunately, among colored people as among other racial types, there are plenty of the others, but what we can reasonably ask for is fairness, that the worst types be not used almost entirely, to the exclusion of the better.

And indeed, from the standpoint of the Negro himself, a little idealism, a little romanticism, would not be at all out of place. An occasional black or brown hero, a little braver, a little wiser, a little richer perchance, a little more self-sacrificing than one could reasonably expect to meet often in real life; an occasional black or brown heroine—aside from the octoroon, who is always beautiful in books—who is beautiful and loyal and charming, would be something by way of example or inspiration. Dr. Du Bois in his *Quest of the Silver Fleece*, has taken as hero and heroine, two black cornfield hands—from the standpoint of the average American reader what material could be more unromantic!—and has woven around them an idyllic love story with a happy ending.

Again, we would like to read a book, now and then, in which it is not such an awful tragedy to be colored. It is bad enough, of course; there are many hardships, many handicaps, much of scorn and contumely to contend with, but there are many colored people who, in spite of these things, manage to have a fairly good time and to maintain a reasonable measure of self-respect. Some of them, indeed, can give back quite a bit of scorn for scorning. And the life of the average American colored man is by no means one of undiluted tragedy. And the beautiful octoroon, rejected by the white lover who discovers her origin, doesn't always die, as she does in my *House Behind the Cedars*, or go into a convent, as she does in many other books. She sometimes marries a good dark man, who treats her well, and lives happily ever after.

In other words, the Negroes we want in books are natural Negroes—all sorts and types, without any color of prejudice to make them unduly bad, and no flavor of friendship to make them unnaturally good.

Now, how are we going to get such books, or such Negroes in books? There is but one way, and that is to encourage writers to write such books and create such characters, by building up a reading public among ourselves who will buy such books. There are some of them already, but up to date, at least, they have not been very popular. Several years ago an author published a novel serially in one of the 15-cent magazines, in which he made a mulatto character, a very decent fellow, by the way, eat his meals in the kitchen of the boarding-house where he roomed. A colored editor or newspaper writer took the matter up with the author and protested that a self-respecting colored man would n't do such a thing, that he would either eat at the table with the other boarders, or change his boarding-house. The author replied that it was essential to the development of his plot that this excellent mulatto stop at that particular boarding-house, and that with the friendliest feeling in the world toward the colored race, he had to consider his white readers, who bought his books, and that he had already been criticized for having him at the boarding-house at all!

Mr. Reginald Wright Kauffman, an author who lives at Columbia, in your own State, has recently published a novel, entitled *The Mark of the Beast*,[42] in which one of the principal characters is a degenerate white man of good family, who ravishes a young lady, a relative of his own, whom he had vainly sought in marriage, and then remains silent and permits an innocent, amiable and harmless mulatto to be lynched for his own crime. The author sent me a copy of his book. I complimented him on his courage. The other day I read in the Boston *Transcript* a letter from Mr. Kauffman, in which, among other things, he says:[43]

> My story, "The Mark of the Beast," takes a New Englander to the South and revolves about the lynching of a negro for a crime of which a white man was guilty—and the South doesn't like it. Southern papers refuse advertisements; they shout condemnation; not on moral grounds or on literary; they simply say that I have "indicted the South" and "don't understand the negro problem." What is not an indictment isn't likely to sound like one—to the innocent; but that is enough of my special case. What I want to protest against is a habit of the South, from the vicarious effects of which I am one of many sufferers; the habit forbidding any Northerner to write of the "negro problem."
>
> Charles W. Chesnutt, for whose "A Conjure Woman" readers will long be indebted, recently put the case to me thus: "The South is really so much the spoiled brat of the American family that if ever a writer sees fit to write about it in anything but an adulatory manner, he is apt to come in for a very sharp scolding." What has

spoiled the South? Why, so far as it is concerned, may anybody discuss graft or the absurdly so-called "White Slavery" and nobody child-labor or lynching? No New Yorker, so far as I can recall, scolded me for my exposure of certain New York conditions in "The House of Bondage." Why all this mystery on the part of Southerners, and especially Southern writers, about the "Negro Problem?" If there is a "Negro Problem," why do Southerners object to its mention? If there is a "Negro Problem" that Northern novelists are incapable of telling the truth about, why don't Southern novelists tell the truth about it? They tell nothing, yet the word "problem" implies something to be solved; novels may treat of any other problem, and no problem is to be solved by being let alone.

If we possessed among ourselves, a reading public large enough to buy as many books as Mr. Kauffman or any other friendly white author, or any colored author, would lose the sale of, because of Southern prejudice, many more such books would be written.

But whence can we reasonably expect such books to emanate? Who knows the Negro best, in his home, in his church, in school, in his work, in his play, in all the manifold phases of his life? Could any one but a Scotchman have written *Waverley*?[44] Could any one but an Englishman have written *Pickwick*? Could any one but a Frenchman have written *Les Misérables* or *The Three Guardsmen*?[45] Other things being equal, the life of a people is best recorded by those who know it and have lived it; in the case of the colored people by those who have shared their sorrows and sufferings and disappointments, their hopes, their successes, their joys, who know their aspirations, their social and spiritual strivings, their love and self-sacrifice for their children, their religious life, the gradual but perceptible growth of moral, ethical and social standards among them; the development among them of the cooperative spirit, in which lies the great social efficiency of the white races of Europe and America. It stands to reason that an author thus equipped, which could only be a colored author, given equal ability and skill to portray character, would portray it more truthfully than an equally competent man without his special advantages.

The conclusion of the whole matter is that you should encourage colored writers by buying their books, and you should encourage in the same way, other writers to write books which are friendly to your race. I am not advocating a school of fiction entirely for colored people—I should no more like to see literature segregated than anything else—and if colored writers write good literature, it will not fail of recognition at the bar of public opinion.

This "Buy-a-Book Movement," I imagine, was conceived with this idea, that colored people should show their appreciation of those of their own number and those of their outside friends who should take the chance of writing books which treat the Negro fairly. Cultivate the habit of buying such books. Buy them for Christmas presents. Ask for them at the Public Libraries. (Refer to printed list.)[46] Read the race magazines. Thus you will not only encourage the writing of good books about the Negro, but will promote the interest of the race and of humanity.

~

SOURCE: Undated typed text at the Fisk University Library. Chesnutt delivered this paper for "The National Buy-a-Book Campaign in the Interest of Negro Literature." He spoke at the Varick Temple, Philadelphia, Pa., on the evening of 5 December 1916.

[1]Richard R. Wright, Jr. (1878–1967), the Philadelphia clergyman who directed the "Buy-a-Book" campaign.

[2]By "fancy" Chesnutt means a vigorous imagination.

[3]Thomas Babington Macaulay, "On Mitford's History of Greece," *Knight's Quarterly Magazine*, 3 (November 1824), 285–304; Samuel Butler (1612–80), poet; William Mitford (1744–1827), historian.

[4]John Greenleaf Whittier (1807–92) published this volume of poems in 1846.

[5]James Russell Lowell (1819–91), began writing the poetical *Biglow Papers* in 1846, to express his opposition to the Mexican War and the territorial extension of slavery.

[6]See "A Defamer of His Race."

[7]William Albert Sinclair (1858–1926), a physician, was the author of *The Aftermath of Slavery* (1905).

[8]Miller (1863–1939), Professor of Sociology at Howard University, had explored social issues in *An Appeal to Reason on the Race Problem* (1906), *Race Adjustment* (1908), and *Out of the House of Bondage* (1914).

[9]Charles Victor Roman (1864–1934), teacher, historian, and physician, published this work in 1916.

[10]James Ford Rhodes (1848–1927)—misspelled "Rhoades" in the source text—was the author of the eight-volume *History of the United States from the Compromise of 1850* (1893–1906); Horace Greeley, *American Conflict* (1864); Albert Bushnell Hart (1854–1943), historian, *The American Nation* (1904); James Bryce, *South America: Observations and Impressions* (1912). The full title of Royce's book is *Race Questions, Provincialism, and Other American Problems*.

[11]The actual title is *White Capital and Coloured Labour*.

[12]Chesnutt appears to refer to *A History of the British Empire in Africa* (1910).

[13]See "A Solution for the Race Problem," n. 13.

[14]Gustave Flaubert (1821–80) describes Spendius as a former Greek, rather than black, slave in *Salammbô* (1862); a conniver, Spendius uses Mathô's unrequited love for Salammbô to promote his own career. The silent-film adaptation, *Calabria*, was released by Italia Film in 1914.

[15]"What Became of Deegan Folk?" by Wallace A. Irwin (1876–1959) appeared in *McClure's Magazine*, 44 (February 1915), 25–31, 164–82. Michael Lewis Landman (1883–?) adapted Irwin's short story for the stage as *The Pride of Race*. It premiered in Buffalo, N.Y., on 25 November 1915; and it ran for 79 performances after it opened in New York City on 11 January 1916. The popular actor referred to by Chesnutt was Robert C. Hilliard (1857–1927).

[16]Published in 1848.

[17]Lady Frances Nelson (1758–1831), whom Admiral Nelson met on the Caribbean island St. Nevis; Horatio Nelson (1758–1805), whose fleet defeated a combined French and Spanish fleet off the coast of Trafalgar, Spain, in 1805; Lady Emma Hamilton (1765–1815). Biographers of these figures do not support Chesnutt's claim of biracial ancestry for Lady Nelson; and her complexion is typically described as "English."

[18]Sir Walter Besant and James Rice (1843–82) collaborated on a dozen novels, including *My Little Girl* (1873).

[19]Allen published no novel with this title. Chesnutt was perhaps misremembering the title of another work by Allen, *In All Shades* (1886).

[20]Joseph Conrad (1857–1924) published this novel in 1897.

[21]Louis Tracy (1863–1928); the novel was published in 1916.

[22]Hugh Stowell Scott (1862–1903) wrote several works under the pseudonym of Henry Seton Merriman, including this novel published in 1894.

[23]Stowe continued her excoriation of slavery in *A Key to Uncle Tom's Cabin* (1853) and *Dred: A Tale of the Dismal Swamp* (1856).

[24]*Toinette*, pseudonymously signed "Henry Churton," appeared in 1874; Tourgée reworked the story as *A Royal Gentleman* (1881). Neither saw *Independent* serialization. *Pactolus Prime* was published in 1890.

[25]Donnelly (1831–1901) was a Minnesota social reformer, journalist, and politician who served as a Republican member of the U.S. House of Representatives (1863–69) and later participated in the formation of the Populist Party. A champion of the oppressed, he energetically expressed his views in his weekly, the *Anti-Monopolist*, from 1874 to 1879, as well as in his novel *Caesar's Column* (1891).

[26]Acts 17:28.

[27]The story of Bras Coupé appears in *The Grandissimes*. *John March, Southerner* (1894) reinforced popular images of the corrupt black politicians of the Reconstruction era.

[28]Bliss Perry (1860–1954), editor of the *Atlantic Monthly* in 1899–1907, published *The Plated City* in 1895.

[29]Margaret Deland (1857–1940) included "A Black Drop" in the collection of short stories *R. J.'s Mother and Some Other People* (1908).

[30](1819–92).

[31]Published in 1903 and 1900, respectively.

[32]Published in 1911.

[33]Mary Johnston (1870–1936), a Virginia-born historical novelist, published her first novel, *Prisoners of Hope, a Tale of Colonial Virginia*, in 1898. The story of the king is related by Horace E. Scudder (1838–1902) in *The Book of Legends Told over Again* (1902): the African King Cophetua wearies of the insincere females of his own social class; and, when he meets the daughter of a beggar, her ingenuousness is so beguiling that he asks her to marry him.

[34]Arthur Morrison (1863–1945), rather than William Pett Ridge (1857–1930), wrote *Tales of Mean Streets* (1894).

[35]"Marse Chan," the 1884 *Century* publication that brought fame to Page, first saw book publication in *In Ole Virginia, or Marse Chan and Other Stories* (1887).

[36]Uncle Julius McAdoo functions thus in all seven of the stories collected in *The Conjure Woman*.

[37]Lucy Pratt (1874–?). Chesnutt is apparently referring to short stories collected in *Ezekiel* (1909) and *Ezekiel Expands* (1914).

[38]Elizabeth Pringle (1845–1921) was a widowed rice planter and memoirist of coastal South Carolina. *A Woman Rice Planter* was published in 1913. Three "Rab and Dab" pieces appeared in the *Atlantic Monthly*: 114 (November 1914), 577–89; 114 (December 1914), 799–808; and 115 (January 1915), 90–98.

[39]Mackenzie (1874–1936) wrote a series of five "Black Sheep" installments for the *Atlantic Monthly*, the title of each including the appropriate roman numeral. They appeared in the following issues: 116 (October 1915), 431–44; 116 (November 1915), 656–66; 116 (December 1915), 785–95; 117 (January 1916), 66–74; and 117 (February 1916), 238–41. *Black Sheep: Adventures in West Africa* was published in 1916.

[40]"The Adventure of the Yellow Face" by Sir Arthur Conan Doyle appeared initially in the *Strand* in 1893 and was included in his second collection of Sherlock Holmes stories, *Memoirs of Sherlock Holmes* (1894).

[41]Genesis 25:29–34.

[42]Reginald Wright Kauffman (1877–1959), editor, war correspondent, and novelist, first gained prominence as a writer of juvenile books; after 1910, Kauffman gave up his work as a newspaper reporter to devote himself full-time to writing novels such as *The Mark of the Beast* (1916).

[43]A letter to the editor published in the *Boston Evening Transcript* has not been found. Chesnutt marked and attached a now-tattered clipping of the printed text (dated 11 November 1916) to the source text. Chesnutt directed himself to "Quote" it, and rendered here is the portion Chesnutt marked. Some of the words, at the end of the first paragraph and beginning of the second, are not available because of the condition of the clipping; what Kauffman wrote in these cases has been inferred from the context.

[44]Sir Walter Scott, *Waverley* (1814).

[45]Victor Hugo, *Les Misérables* (1862); Alexandre Dumas, *Les Trois Mousquetaires*.

[46]A reference to a "Buy-a-Book" brochure, listing publications of the kind, that was available to Chesnutt's audience.

Introduction to a Reading from an Unpublished Story

Speech to the Electrical League of Cleveland, Cleveland, O., 28 December 1916

As some of you know, I am more accustomed to attending meetings similar to this, in the capacity of reporter[1] than in that of speaker. On these occasions, as I have observed, the addresses are generally technical or instructive, and are devoted, in large measure, to the discussion of efficiency, which, as I gather, seems to consist in getting the most for the least—the most product from the least stock, the most work for the least wages, the most money for the least service. Now, I could n't tell you anything about efficiency; I have always paid too much for what I got, and got too little for what I did.

Of the technical side of electricity I only know that I know as much of what it is as any of you do, which is nothing at all. I know that a short circuit will cut off a current and that a current of sufficient voltage will kill. My practical experience with electricity has been chiefly with that now reformed gang of *train*-robbers, the street-car company,[2] that bunch of *light*-fingered gentry the illuminating Company,[3] and that organized band of *highwaymen* the Willard Storage Battery Company.[4]

Since I cannot instruct you, I shall hope to amuse you. If I fail, don't blame me, but blame Henry Davies—he is responsible for my presence here.[5]

Some years ago I published a book called *The Conjure Woman*, in which a Northern man had bought an old plantation in North Carolina, shortly after the Civil War, and had taken into his service as coachman an old mulatto who had been the slave of a former owner and who still lived on the place. The old man told a series of stories dealing with plantation happenings, of which the protagonist or principal character was an old conjure woman, a plantation witch, who possessed the power of conjuring or goophering people or things. The word "goopher," as it is used in the stories—it is probably a corruption of a West African word—means not only the charm, but the physical medium by which it is imposed, the mixture, or powder or what not, which produces the malefic result. The as yet unpublished story which I shall read you today is along the same line. It is one of a series, with an introduction and an epilogue or closing chapter. I shall read the introduction, one story and the epilog.

⌐

SOURCE: Undated and untitled typed text at the Fisk University Library. It served as an introduction to a reading of a short story before members of The Electrical League of Cleveland on 28 December 1916. Which story he read is unknown. His comments limit the known possibilities to two extant, then-unpublished pieces: "The Dumb Witness" and "The Marked Tree." But neither appears the one selected for presentation. Conjuring is not featured in the former; and, in the latter, no attention is given to what Chesnutt focuses upon in his introduction, the physical medium by which the marked tree is "goophered." Further, "The Marked Tree" is a particularly grim tale, an unlikely candidate for presentation at a businessmen's luncheon.

[1]That is, as a stenographer or court reporter.

[2]Reference to the Cleveland Electric Railway Company. The reform in question occurred in 1910 when negotiations with the city resulted in the Company retaining its ownership of the streetcars but agreeing to regulation of its operations for the common good.

[3]The Cleveland Electric Illuminating Company, founded in 1892.

[4]This firm built in 1915 a manufacturing plant encompassing fifteen acres on 131st Street. It dominated the U.S. market for automobile batteries. By 1918 it was producing 85 percent of those used in American vehicles.

[5]Henry J. Davies was the chairman of the Program Committee of The Electrical League of Cleveland, an organization formed in 1909 and made up mainly of electrical contractors and manufacturers. Davies, whom Chesnutt knew as a fellow member of the Cleveland Chamber of Commerce, had invited him to give a one-half hour reading at a noon luncheon at the Hotel Statler.

The Will of John Randolph

Speech to the Rowfant Club, Cleveland, O., 13 January 1917

John Randolph, of Roanoke, congressman and senator, was born at Cawsons, near the mouth of the Appomattox River, Virginia, June 2, 1773. He was seventh in descent from Pocahontas, daughter of the Indian chief Powhatan, by her marriage with John Rolfe.[1] His great-grandfather, William Randolph, came from England to Virginia in the 17th century.[2] His grandfather, Richard, divided among his heirs 40,000 acres of the choicest land on the James, Appomattox and Roanoke Rivers including Mattoax, two miles west of Petersburg, and Bizarre, a plantation ninety miles up. His father, John, youngest son of this Richard, married Frances Bland, daughter of a neighbor who lived at Cawsons.[3] The family connections were numerous and powerful. Cousin of Jefferson. His father died in 1775; in 1778 his mother married St. George Tucker of Bermuda.[4] On January 3, 1781, she was taken to Bizarre, before named, to escape from the British troops under Benedict Arnold, who was making a raid into that part of Virginia.[5] Here the boy grew up for years without much education, self-control or mental discipline, although he read, before his eleventh birthday, "*The Arabian Nights*, Shakespeare, Homer, *Don Quixote*, *Gil Blas*, Plutarch's *Lives*, *Robinson Crusoe*, *Gulliver* and *Tom Jones*."[6] It is, as has been said, most probable that to this list was added, "*Peregrine Pickle*, *The Newgate Calendar*, *Moll Flanders* and *Roderick Random*."[7] He is said, moreover, to have read, "Gibbon, Hume and Burke," to have known English history, and to have been at home in the English peerage. In the summer of 1781 he had a few months' schooling, and afterwards was again at school for about a year, at Williamsburg, Virginia, until the spring of 1784, when his parents took him on a visit to Bermuda, the home of his stepfather's family. In the autumn of 1787 he was sent to Princeton (N. J.) College,[8] for a few months; the next year he went for a short time to Columbia College in the City of New York.[9] It is not easy to say what he learned: "I am an ignorant man, sir," was his own statement in after years. The peculiarities of his nature early showed themselves. By the age of which we have written, he had read, "Voltaire, Rousseau, Hume and Gibbon"; and was as deistical in opinion as any of them. He had even imbibed a prejudice in favor of Mahometanism. In a letter to his father at this time,[10] sent from New York City, he forecast his love for politics when he said: "Be so good, my dear sir, when it is convenient, as to send me the debates of the convention in our state." He was too true a Virginian not to oppose the new Constitution of the United States which Patrick Henry and George Mason had so vehemently resisted.[11] It was at this time that he was often found at Federal Hall in New York City, where, as he said afterwards, in a speech to his constituents, "I saw Washington, but could not hear him take the oath to support the Federal constitution." The Constitution was in its chrysalis state: "I saw," said Randolph, "what Washington did not see, but two other men in Virginia saw it, George Mason and Patrick Henry, the secret sting which lurked beneath the gaudy pinions of the butterfly." The keenness of his scent for the centralization of power in the Federal government as against the states-rights doctrine of Virginia, was even then phenomenal. The first attorney-general of the United States government was Edmund Randolph of Virginia, his relative, and in 1790 John Randolph went to Philadelphia, Pennsylvania, to study law with him, which he did for four years, and then returned to Virginia to assume control of his property.[12] In 1796 he visited a friend in

Georgia, and stopping at Charleston, South Carolina, was thus photographed by a book-seller at whose shop he called:[13] "A tall, gawky-looking, flaxen-haired stripling, apparently of the age of sixteen to eighteen, with a complexion of a good parchment color, beardless chin, and as much assumed self-confidence as any two-footed animal I ever saw." The intensity and magnitude of this self-confidence is outlined in the toast he is said to have given at a dinner, pending the ratification of the John Jay treaty with England, in 1795, when he offered—"George Washington—may he be damned!" and as the company declined to drink it, he added—"if he sign Jay's treaty."[14] At the age of twenty-six he announced himself as a candidate for Congress, and spoke at Charlotte, Virginia, in the campaign against his opponent, the celebrated Patrick Henry, who had been summoned from the retirement of his old age by ex-President Washington, to support the Federal administration. It was the last public appearance of the veteran orator, who was indeed elected over Randolph, but did not live to take his seat.[15] In the course of, or after Randolph's speech in reply to his own, Mr. Henry remarked to a by-stander, "I have n't seen the little dog before, since he was at school; he was a great atheist then"; and after the speech, shaking hands with his opponent, he added, "Young man, you call me father; then, my son, I have something to say unto thee: 'Keep justice, keep truth,' and you will live to think differently." The seat to which Mr. Henry had been chosen was taken after his death by Randolph, who leaped at once into the arena of political debate as a full-blown Republican, or states-rights advocate, in opposition to the Federal party. His first notable effort was made January 9, 1800, on a motion to reduce the United States army. This army he spoke of as a collection of "mercenaries" and "hirelings," "loungers who live upon the public, who consume the fruits of honest industry under the pretence of protecting it from a foreign yoke"; he at last added, "The people put no confidence in the protection of a handful of ragamuffins." For this he was insulted and jostled that evening at the theater by two marine officers. Randolph at once wrote to the President of the United States (John Adams), a most astonishing note, which he closed by saying that the independence of the legislature had been attacked (in his person), and demanded "that a provision commensurate with the evil be made, which will be calculated to deter others from any future attempt to introduce the reign of terror into our country." The President vouchsafed no reply, but transmitted the note to the House of Representatives as relating to a matter of their privilege. Investigation was had by a House committee, and their report contained a sharp censure upon Randolph for deviating from the forms of decorum customary in official communications to the chief magistrate, and for demanding redress from the executive in a matter which respected the privileges of the House, thereby derogating from the rights of that body. With the autumn of 1800 came the presidential election,[16] the overthrow of the Federal, the rise of the Republican party, and the advent of Randolph to its leadership in the House of Representatives, where he became chairman of the committee of ways and means in 1801. His influence for a time was despotic, his audacity, titanic. This was always alike his eminent shining characteristic and weapon, and assuredly had behind it a basis of brilliant parts, but the lash of his tongue, pure and simple, in the inchoate condition of political parties, appears, throughout his early career especially, to have been his chief reliance for moving men. In carrying out the public policy which had given birth to the Republican party, Randolph was doubtless consistent, and almost without exception, to the end of his political career. But in doing so he found himself, not long after the inauguration of Mr. Jefferson, removed from the party leaders, headed by the President. Upon taking the reins of power they naturally occupied a somewhat different point of view from that which they had occupied when in opposition. For a time, however, Randolph's influence in the House was irresistible, his temper more and more domineering; in his congressional district he had no rival; in the House he overcame every resistance, and the session for 1803–1804 was a long series of party and personal triumphs. In the support he was constrained to give to the purchase of Louisiana under the Jefferson administration, he for once, at least, posed as a supporter of executive authority rather than as the champion of states-rights. In the unsuccessful movement to impeach Judge Chase of the United States Supreme Court (1804), instigated by President Jefferson, he was the ostensible prime mover, but he gained no prestige from his management of the prosecution.[17] In his resistance of the "Yazoo" claims, he precipitated the outward separation in sympathy and action between himself and the national administration, and became an antagonist of Mr. Jefferson and Mr. Madison.[18] He was thus, in politics, John Randolph of Roanoke, and nothing more. Going formally into opposition in the spring of 1806, he proclaimed himself no longer a Republican; he belonged, he said, to the third party—the quiddists or quids, that *tertium quid*, the third something which had no name.[19] But at the end of the congressional session he found himself a political wreck, and along with his decadence the true school of Virginia politics, says one of his biographers, was forever ruined.[20] In the canvass for the presidential election of 1808 he endeavored to bring forward James Monroe as the successor of Mr. Jefferson. But Randolph was a wretched intriguer and no office-seeker, and with few, if any of the other qualities which are needful to further a movement of that description. In 1811, when President Madison made Mr. Monroe United States Secretary of State, Randolph quarreled and broke with Monroe. His efforts to prevent the War of 1812 were futile,[21] and he was left out of Congress from 1813 to 1815. In a new movement towards the resuscitation of the old Republican party which next followed, he took an active part, but his political career, so far as party promotion and party influence were concerned, was ended. Continuing in the House of Representatives until 1817, although with repeated absences, he declined to serve from 1817 to 1819. In 1825 he was chosen to the United States Senate to fill a vacancy, but was defeated at the next election.[22] It was during his brief term in that body that he stigmatized Henry Clay, then United States Secretary of State, under President John Quincy Adams, in the famous words, "I was defeated, horse, foot and dragoons—cut up and clean broke down by the coalition of Blifil and Black George—by the combination, unheard of until then, of the Puritan with the blackleg,"[23] and he went on to call Mr. Clay's progenitors to account for bringing into the world "this being, so brilliant, yet so corrupt, which like a rotten mackerel by moonlight, shined and stunk." Mr. Clay forthwith challenged him to fight, and the duel took place April 8, 1826. Clay's second bullet pierced the folds of Randolph's white flannel wrapper. Randolph threw away his second fire, and thereupon offered his hand, which Clay could not refuse to accept. In 1829 he aided in the election of Andrew Jackson as President, and during the same year served in the Virginia constitutional convention. In June, 1830, he sailed upon a special government mission to Russia, stayed ten days at his post, and then spent nearly a year in England.[24] Returning to the United States, he next drew from the Federal treasury $21,407.00 for his services. In the South Carolina nullification troubles of 1832, Randolph broke with President Jackson, taking advanced Southern ground.[25] Preparing to return to England, he was seized by a last and fatal attack on his lungs, and died in Philadelphia, Pennsylvania, May 24, 1833. His remains were taken to Virginia and he was buried on his estate at Roanoke. By a will made in 1821, Mr. Randolph's slaves were emancipated—his will, executed in 1832, which contained no provision for emancipation, being set aside on the ground of the insanity of the testator.[26] Mr. Randolph's relation to the question of slavery may be dispatched in a few words. For years he professed the utmost aversion to the system, and by his will of 1821 freed his own slaves.[27] The allegation has been made that during the closing part of his public life he sought to perpetuate the doctrine of states-rights by using it to uphold the peculiar institution of his section, thus blocking out the path in which the great apostle of both slavery and states-rights afterwards walked[28]—following which path slavery in the United States came to grief, and the extreme states-rights doctrine forever lost hold upon the people. This allegation, however, calls for careful consideration from all to whom the subject matter is of concern. Mr. Randolph's life was written by Hugh A. Garland (New York, 1850, two volumes),[29] and by Henry Adams (Boston, 1882, "American Statesmen Series").

⌐⌐

SOURCE: Untitled, undated, and possibly incomplete typed text at the Fisk University Library. This is, presumably, the speech—or the sole surviving version thereof—entitled "The Will of John Randolph" that Chesnutt read before the Rowfant Club on 13 January 1917. That a final version that may have been delivered was of greater length is suggested by the minimal amount of attention that Randolph's will is given here. On the other hand, the title recorded by the Rowfant Club may describe a speech in which Chesnutt did not, in fact, write as he may have originally planned—opting instead for a more general biographical portrait. The principal information source consulted by Chesnutt was the work cited in the conclusion of his text, *John Randolph* (1882) by Henry Adams (1838–1918).

[1]Powhatan (1550?–1618); Pocahontas (1595?–1617); John Rolfe (1585–1622). In the margin Chesnutt wrote "1/128" and "1/256," indicating that he was attempting to calculate the fraction of Native American ancestry that was Randolph's. Randolph was Pocahontas's fourth great-grandson, actually sixth in descent from her. Thus he was at least 1/64 Native American.

[2]William Randolph (1649–1716) emigrated to Virginia about 1673 from Warwick-shire. Among other accomplishments, he served as speaker of Virginia's House of Burgesses, attorney-general, and trustee of the College of William and Mary, in addition to being a planter, ship-owner and -builder. His nine children married into most of Virginia's aristocratic families, which later accounted for John Randolph's "numerous and powerful" relatives to whom Chesnutt alludes.

[3]Richard Randolph (1690–1748); John Randolph (1742–75); Frances Bland Randolph (1752–88), mother.

[4]St. George Tucker (1752–1827) was a prominent jurist.

[5]Arnold led British raids against both Virginia and Connecticut.

[6]Alain René Le Sage (1668–1747), author of *Histoire de Gil Blas de Santillane* (1715–35); Plutarch (46–120), whose *Parallel Lives* describes twenty-three Greeks and three Romans of historical interest; Daniel Defoe (1661?–1731), *Robinson Crusoe* (1719); Jonathan Swift (1667–1745), *Gulliver's Travels* (1727); and Henry Fielding (1707–54), *Tom Jones* (1749).

[7]Tobias Smollet (1721–71), *Peregrine Pickle* (1751) and *Roderick Random* (1748); and Defoe's *Moll Flanders* (1722). *The Newgate Calendar* (1774) was a chronicle of post-1699 British crime.

[8]He went there in March.

[9]He began study there in May 1788.

[10]Dated 25 December 1788.

[11]Patrick Henry (1736–99), while a staunch member of the Federalist party, opposed the ratification of the Constitution on the grounds that it did not sufficiently guarantee the rights of states. George Mason refused to sign the Constitution because of the compromise on the issue of slavery that it contained and its assignment of too few controls on the powers of the federal government.

[12]Edmund Randolph (1727–1813) was Randolph's second cousin and son of John Randolph (1727–84). (The fame of the latter as a statesman led Randolph to style himself John Randolph of Roanoke in order to preclude confusion of the two of them.) Edmund refused to sign the Constitution but subsequently encouraged its ratification by Virginia. He was appointed Attorney-General of the United States in 1789 and Secretary of State in 1794.

[13]The friend in Georgia was Joseph Bryan (1773–1812), who later served in the U.S. House of Representatives (1803–6). By February 1796, Randolph had come to Charleston, visiting another friend, Henry Middleton Rutledge (1775–1844). The book-seller was Ebenezer Smith Thomas (1775–1845).

[14]John Jay (1745–1829), later the first Chief Justice of the U.S. Supreme Court (1789–95), successfully negotiated the "Jay Treaty" with England in 1794. Many Americans initially disparaged it because they felt it gave England too many rights in the Mississippi Valley and West Indies; even so, the treaty was ratified in 1795.

[15]In the source text Chesnutt wrote in the margin "first speech in ans. to P.H.'s last." Their debate occurred on 17 March 1799 at the Charlotte Court House. Randolph was still twenty-five when he debated Henry; Chesnutt's information source, the biography by Henry Adams, described him as twenty-six.

[16]Chesnutt's "Jefferson" in the margin of the source text prompted him to remind his audience who won the election in which Federalist John Adams was pitted against Republican Thomas Jefferson.

[17]On 5 January 1804, Randolph asked the House to inquire into the conduct of Samuel Chase (1747–1811), then Associate Justice of the Supreme Court. The House appointed a committee of inquiry that Randolph headed. Nearly three months later, on 23 March 1804, the committee's report listed seven articles of impeachment against

Chase, and the House formally charged him with sedition and treason. Ultimately, the Senate acquitted Chase, thereby establishing the principle that federal judges can be removed only for specific criminal acts.

[18]Randolph had first heard of the "Yazoo" scandal during his trip through South Carolina and Georgia in 1796. A newly elected Georgia legislature repudiated the previous one's sale of territory extending into Mississippi and Alabama. Litigation resulted; the Congress appointed an investigative committee; and Georgia attempted to resolve its problem by ceding its western lands to the federal government. The issue was ultimately brought before the U.S. Supreme Court; and in 1810 the original act of the 1795 legislature was ruled upheld.

[19]The "Quiddists," never formally organized, failed in their bid for control of the Republican party, primarily because of Jefferson's influence.

[20]Henry Adams.

[21]In a speech delivered in November 1811, Randolph argued passionately against a report which recommended that the United States increase its standing army by ten thousand in preparation for war.

[22]The vacancy was created when James Barbour (1780–1848) was appointed Secretary of War; Randolph won the seat in a special election, held 17 December 1825, on the fourth ballot and then only when his half-brother, Henry St. George Tucker (1780–1848), who had garnered the most votes on each previous ballot, withdrew his name; seeking re-election, Randolph was defeated by John Tyler (1790–1862) on 15 January 1827.

[23]Randolph thus demonstrates not only his extensive reading but his extraordinary oratorical talent by contemptuously linking, on the one hand, Blifil, the disingenuously pious son of Bridget Allworthy in Fielding's *Tom Jones*, with John Quincy Adams (1767–1848), a "Puritan" because of his ancestry. On the other, he associates Black George—the amoral gamekeeper and father of Tom's first beloved, Molly—with Henry Clay (1777–1852), a "blackleg" (or card-sharp, one who knows "how to play his cards"). In Randolph's mind, the canny Clay won appointment as Secretary of State for having swung the presidential election in Adams's favor. Randolph's disgust with Clay was apparent in 1811 when, coining the term "War Hawks" to characterize supporters of war with England, he denounced Clay and his allies in the House.

[24]Andrew Jackson appointed Randolph Envoy Extraordinary and Minister Plenipotentiary to Russia in gratitude for his services.

[25]Chief proponent of Nullification, John C. Calhoun (1782–1850) embodied the pro-states' rights that Randolph had espoused for years.

[26]Upon Randolph's death, his executors discovered three separate wills, written in 1819, 1821, and 1832; additionally, the second of these contained four codicils dated 5 December 1821, 31 January 1826, 6 May 1828, and 26 August 1831. While each of these documents contained specific and often conflicting instructions concerning the disposition of his estate, a common theme running through all but the last was his determination to free his slaves.

[27]Chesnutt wrote "Jeff Wash. Emanc." in the margin of the source text, possibly indicating his plan to extemporize on their attitudes toward manumission.

[28]John C. Calhoun.

[29]Garland (1805–54), *The Life of John Randolph of Roanoke*.

Address to Colored Soldiers
at Grays Armory

Speech delivered in Cleveland, O., 1917

You young men have a great opportunity. You have really been selected for a superior sort of service. In the early ages of history the warrior, the fighting man, was the great man of the community to whom all others deferred. The field of battle was the pathway to glory. The great epic poems, of the world's literature, consist mainly of the recital of the warlike deeds of their heroes, and in modern times successful generals have been rewarded in aristocratic countries with titles and estates, in our country and the countries south of ours by election to the presidency; and the common soldiers by pensions and medals and the grateful acclaims of their fellow citizens.

Once upon a time men fought for the sake of fighting—for I think we shall have to admit that man is a fighting animal. There are some human sheep, but the average man, I am sure we all believe, likes a scrap now and then; or, if he has been civilized to the point where he does n't care to participate, he likes to see a scrap. All the laws that have been passed do not seem able to suppress prize-fighting, and a whole neighborhood will run to see a dog fight.

Then again, men fight for selfish motives, for greed of gold or greed of territory. A careful study of the causes of this present war leaves no other conclusion but that Germany was guided by selfish motives from the first; that she was the aggressor, and wished to despoil France and Belgium of their colonies and their coal and coke fields so that she might extend her place in the sun. There have been many such wars. Our own Civil War was fought on the one side because the South wished to extend slavery politically over the whole country.

Then there are men and nations who fight for principle, from high and noble motives. No nation should go to war for any other reason. In this present war, France and Belgium are fighting for their altars and their fires, their hearths and their homes. Invaded by a ruthless enemy, it was either fight or perish. England's motives were high. She could not admit that a solemn treaty was a mere scrap of paper, or that her guarantee of the neutrality of Belgium was a hollow sham.[1] And she foresaw that France once conquered, England would be invaded; and the great governmental system which she had built up during the centuries, embracing one fourth of the most fertile and best governed land on the earth's surface, would become a mere appanage of Germany.

Other countries were drawn into the war by various motives, until came the time of the U.S. of America, as we call our country. We have gone into this war largely it would seem, for altruistic reasons. We believe in the principle of democracy. We have not, sad to say always lived up to it—far from it—but all our wars have been in support of it, and each one brings us nearer to its realization. The Revolutionary War resulted in the Constitution, which established the principle of free government for white men. They did not find it as free as it seemed on paper, and many old abuses, rooted in the customs and thoughts of the people, flourished for a long time after the Revolution, customs and laws which were not consistent with the doctrine of freedom and equality.

The cause of democracy was given a further impetus by the Civil War. It resulted in the war amendments which involved the abolition of slavery and the enfranchisement of the former slaves. Yet we all know that many of the old abuses still linger. Our Spanish-American War was an unselfish war for the most part, and it resulted in the emancipation of Cuba from the tyranny of Spain.

But no one of our wars was ever based upon a higher motive than this one. We might have kept out of it, by some sacrifice of war profits during the first two years of it, and some loss of self-respect and the respect of other nations. But we were confronted by a situation in which the freer and more democratic nations of Europe were in a death grip with an arrogant autocracy which was threatening to conquer and reduce them to vassalage. The very fundamental principle of democracy was at stake. At first it might not have seemed important that the German people should be willing to live under such a government, it was up to them to change if they did not like it. But when they attempted to force it on the whole world, with threats directed even to America, then it became apparent that the real future of democracy depended upon the destruction of autocracy everywhere. The Russian people rose and cast it out, and made it easy for the U.S. to say that not only the rest of the world, but Germany herself must be made safe for democracy.[2]

Now, young men, soldiers, you have been selected to take part in this noble work. You have a glorious opportunity to participate in a great adventure. In Europe, in the Middle Ages, the soldiers of the Cross[3] crossed Europe to free the Holy Sepulcher from the hands of the infidel. It is your privilege to cross the seas to help tear down the German eagle of autocracy and replace it with the banner of democracy. You will see new countries, hear other tongues, meet and fraternize with some of the finest people in the world. You risk your lives, of course, but we all have to die sooner or later, and reduced to percentages the risks of war are not so much greater than those of working on a railroad or driving a motor car. Your preliminary military training will give you erect figures, firm muscles, quick reactions, it will cultivate all the manly virtues, and when you return to civil life, as most of you will, you will be all the better for your excursion to Europe at the expense of Uncle Sam.

And when you do reach the scene of hostilities and find yourselves at the front, you will give a good account of yourselves. Any man who suggests a doubt as to the fighting qualities of the Negro brands himself as ignorant of history.

(Cite instances.)

The war records of the U.S. are filled with instances of the gallantry and devotion to duty of colored soldiers. The first man killed in the Revolutionary struggle was a mulatto, Crispus Attucks. He was buried from Faneuil Hall, his body was followed to the grave by a procession in columns six deep, with a long file of coaches belonging to the most distinguished citizens, and there is a monument to his memory on Boston Common.

The death of Major Pitcairn, of the English forces, at the hands of Peter Salem, a Negro soldier, ended the battle of Bunker Hill in favor of liberty.

The capture of Major-General Prescott, of the British Army, July 9, 1777, by Prince, a valiant Negro soldier, was an occasion of great joy throughout the country.

Negroes fought among the white soldiers in all the New England regiments, and some in separate battalions, and the military records of the day give them full credit for their gallantry.

The free colored men of Louisiana were organized into a regiment by General Andrew Jackson during the War of 1812, and three months later, after the battle of Mobile, General Jackson addressed the same troops as follows:

> Soldiers! The President of the U.S. shall be informed of your conduct on the present occasion, and the voice of the representatives of the American nation shall applaud your valor, as your general now praises your ardor.[4]

Negro soldiers and sailors rendered valiant service in the war of 1812, and constituted about one-fourth of the American forces engaged in the battle of Lake Erie.

Before colored troops were enrolled under the flag of the Union in the Civil War, there had been several instances of their bravery and daring upon the high seas. You remember the case of the schooner *S. J. Waring*, from New York, bound to South America. She was captured on the passage by a rebel privateer, and a prize crew put on board, and the vessel set sail for the port of Charleston. Three of the original crew were retained on board, among them a black man named William Tillman, the steward and cook of the schooner. One night, when the prize crew were asleep, Tillman, with a heavy club, put the captain and the mate out of commission, released a Yankee who was a prisoner in irons, and between them they overcame the crew, and Tillman as master, took the vessel to the port of New York.[5] The New York *Tribune* said of this event: "To this colored man was the nation indebted for the first vindication of its honor on the sea."[6] Another public journal spoke of that achievement alone as an offset to the defeat of the federal arms at Bull Run. The federal government awarded to Tillman the sum of $6,000.00 as prize money for the capture of the schooner; all loyal journals joined in praise of this heroic act, and even when the news reached England the Negro's bravery was applauded.

An instance with which we are more familiar was that of Captain Robert

Smalls, pilot on the rebel steamer *Planter* in Charleston harbor, who carried the steamer away from under the very guns of the enemy and delivered her to the blockading Union squadron.[7] A special bill was passed by both houses of Congress, by which the value of the steamer *Planter* was divided as prize money between Small and seven other Negroes who assisted him in this exploit.[8] He was afterwards commissioned a captain in the U.S. Army, and, after the war, continued to hold office under the federal government, while the Republican party was in power, until his death not long ago.[9]

Colored troops were first employed in the Civil War at New Orleans, then in possession of General Benjamin F. Butler,[10] and the first colored officer to be commissioned in that war was made a captain by Governor Moore, commander-in-chief of the state militia.[11] For several years after this war broke out, there was a great deal of discussion as to whether the Negroes would fight. Here you have an advantage over the colored men who fought in the Civil War. There was some suggestion from Southern sources a little while ago that Negro soldiers would not be wanted in this war; but these suggestions received no attention from the government, and you are going into the war at the very beginning.[12]

By 1863, colored regiments had been recruited in all the Northern states. The famous 54th regiment of Massachusetts was formed in the spring of 1863; beginning February 9th, by May 12th the regiment was recruited to full strength, all volunteers.[13] When the regiment left to go to the front, a public demonstration was held, four flags and banners were presented to the regiment, a presentation speech was made by Governor Andrew, which was responded to by the Colonel of the regiment, Robert G. Shaw, who led them through many battles, and fell among them at Fort Wagner.[14] The bravery and the gallantry of this famous regiment are commemorated by the beautiful monument to Col. Shaw by the sculptor St. Gaudens, on Boston Common, facing the State House. He is depicted in imperishable bronze, riding at the head of a group of his men, with fame in the form of an angel floating over him and extending a crown of bays to be placed upon his brow. When inquiry was made at Fort Wagner, under flag of truce, for the body of Col. Shaw, the answer was, "We have buried him with his niggers."[15] What loyal Americans thought of this noble soldier, is expressed in these lines:

> Buried with a band of brothers
>   Who for him would fain have died;
> Buried with the gallant fellows
>   Who fell fighting by his side;
>
> Buried with the men God gave him,
>   Those whom he was sent to save;
> Buried with the martyred heroes,
>   He has found an honored grave.

Buried where his dust so precious
    Makes the soil a hallowed spot;
Buried where, by Christian patriot,
    He shall never be forgot;

Buried in the ground accursed,
    Which man's fettered feet have trod;
Buried where his voice still speaketh,
    Appealing for the slave to God;

Fare thee well, thou noble warrior,
    Who in youthful beauty went
On a high and holy mission,
    By the God of battles sent.

Chosen of Him, "elect and precious,"
    Well didst thou fulfil thy part;
When thy country "counts her jewels,"
    She shall wear thee on her heart.[16]

The Colonels of your regiments, in this war, with some few exceptions, will, certainly at the beginning, be white men, largely because they have had the training and experience to qualify them for regimental command. Let us hope they will all be of the quality of Colonel Shaw, men under whose leadership it will be an honor to fight. All white officers who have led colored men praise their soldierly qualities, and seldom care to command any other kind of troops after having once had experience with them.

The battle of Fort Pillow was another engagement in which the Negro troops of the Union distinguished themselves by desperate daring. Fort Pillow is one of the blackest chapters in the history of the Civil War, but the atrocities which marked that sanguinary engagement were not those of the black Union soldiers, who, on the contrary, won the highest praise.[17] 300,000 colored troops fought under the Union banner in the Civil War, and thus by their own efforts helped to win the victory for the North and for freedom.

The valor of the colored troops in the Spanish-American war at San Juan Hill, and in the recent Mexican unpleasantness at Carrizal, are too fresh in your minds to need recalling.[18] Suffice it to say that their conduct added to the laurels already won by men of their race in our wars.

You are going into war again as colored troops. There are some of us who would like to see you fighting in the regiments with white men, side by side. It would be a better example of the democracy for which we are fighting. But, as I said before, manners and customs are slow to change, and the American army has been organized in accordance with the traditions of the past, by which the colored men are placed in different units. But there are some compensating advantages. Fighting as colored soldiers, any gallant deeds they may perform, will be credited to them as such. If they storm a difficult position, capture a redoubt, put a battalion of Huns[19] to flight, the credit for it will be given to them and can not be stolen by some white man. Any laurels that you may win in this war will thus be a gain, not only to yourselves and to your race, but to the cause of democracy, because it will prove, if proof were needed, the Negro's worth as a citizen and a patriot, and will bring that much nearer the day when the U.S. will be as safe for real democracy as it is trying to make the rest of the world.

You boys are in a much better position to fight in this war than many of your fellow citizens. A great many young men of German and Austrian descent have been selected to fight in the American army. I should not at all question their loyalty if they should feel somewhat sorry that duty requires them to fight the men of their Fatherland, the old country around which so many tender memories may cluster, the home of their parents, and perhaps of many of their close relations who may be arrayed against them in the armies of the central allies.[20] It is all the more to their credit that, in spite of these very natural feelings, they are willing to go and fight under the flag of their adopted country. But you are spared any such dilemma. No men of your race are enrolled under the banners of the central allies. Many of them, in the regiments from the French and British colonies have fought gallantly with the western allies, and have repeated the heroic record of American Negroes in battle. You will not be called upon to shoot down any man of color. It is a curious fact that black men, whose ancestors were brought across the ocean to this country in slave ships several generations ago to work for white men, are now being sent across the ocean in comfortable transports to kill white men. If any of you has any lurking grudge against the white race for its historic attitude toward the Negro, let him take it out on the Germans. They never did anything for you. The English in their colonies have treated black men fairly. They abolished slavery in their western possessions a generation before it ended in the United States, and have established in them a real democracy.[21] The French African colonies are administered in accordance with the French political doctrine of liberty, equality, fraternity, and their friendly attitude toward colored Frenchmen and travelers is traditional. The white men of the U.S. sacrificed half a million men for the freedom of the slave, which was only made possible by saving the Union. The Germans, on the other hand, are harsh in their Colonial administration, which is conducted with slight regard for the rights or feelings of the natives. Shortly after the war broke out, when the French and English were bringing black troops from Africa, the Germans criticized them for bringing black men to Europe to fight white men, as a reproach to civilization—this from men who torpedo peaceful merchant vessels and leave their crews to drown, men who have left Belgium like a sucked orange, who have bombed peaceful civilian populations, and slaughtered women and children, and who have preached and practiced the doctrine of ruthless frightfulness. We shall look to you to show the world that it is not because your faces are dark that they object to your fighting them, but because you are such good soldiers, such fearless fighters, that they are afraid to face you.

You are going from Cleveland to receive your military training in a section of the country where the climate is congenial, but where the social atmosphere, if not hostile, is at least not particularly friendly to colored soldiers. You will find some laws which you do not like, some customs which are not in accord with the more liberal customs of the North, and you will very naturally feel inclined to resent certain things. But you can not change the laws or social customs of the South during your brief stay there, and it will be necessary for you to exercise a certain amount of patience. This will not be a subject for reproach, but rather for praise; for a man who must expect to face the cold and hunger of the trenches, the shrapnel and cold steel of the enemy, poisonous gasses, and all the rigors of the battlefield, it ought to be a small matter to endure with dignified patience an occasional sneer or even a contemptuous word, and to consider the source, and value it no more than the unworthy motive behind it is worth. You will be in camps with Northern white soldiers, who will have a friendly disposition toward you. Your officers will do all they can to promote harmony and good feeling, not only for your sake and for the sake of the army, but for their own sake; for an officer who can not maintain order in his own regiment is not the ideal commander. Guard against any repetition of the unfortunate affair at Houston.[22]

Your friends at the North are on guard. They will see to it that your comfort and well being are looked after. The War Department under our fair-minded friend, Secretary Baker, is showing an increasing disposition to be fair to the colored soldiers.[23] Already over six hundred colored officers have been commissioned, and you will be led largely by men of your own race.[24] Generals and Colonels may plan the actions and dispose the forces, but the captains and lieutenants lead the real fighting, and you will have the opportunity to prove that men of your race can lead as well as they can fight, and thus nail another lie which seems to die hard. The civilian war agencies are not neglecting you, but, on the contrary, are showing every disposition to look after your welfare equally with that of the white troops. Only the other day, I heard, through another person, from Captain William Green, of the Cleveland company which recently went to Montgomery, that the colored troops had really the most desirable section of the cantonment;[25] that the people of the neighborhood had shown no evidence of hostility; that the Cleveland white officers had fraternized with the colored officers, and that there was every prospect of a pleasant sojourn in a genial climate during the somewhat arduous preparation for the fighting in Europe.

Young men, Cleveland looks to you to win praise for yourselves and your city. As I have said, you are setting out upon a great adventure, with a great shining goal before you. You will be doing your bit for humanity and for freedom, and we at home will be doing ours to aid you, to sustain you, with our resources, with our prayers, with our best wishes, confident that victory will rest upon your banners. Acquit yourselves like men, and when you return, covered with glory and honor, your fellow citizens will welcome you with open arms and open hearts. Good-bye and Good Luck!

⤳

SOURCE: Undated typed text at the Fisk University Library. When Chesnutt delivered this speech is unknown. He could not have given it until after 14 October 1917, when 639 African Americans received their commissions as infantry officers in the Army; the positive tone of the essay also suggests that he delivered it prior to 24 November 1917, when Chesnutt worriedly wrote to a friend in Montgomery, Ala., regarding the treatment of African-American troops stationed there (see nn. 24 and 25).

[1] By the terms of a conference held in London on 20 January 1831, ending the Belgian revolution, Belgium gained its independence from the Netherlands, and the so-called "great powers" agreed to guarantee its neutrality in any ensuing European conflicts; when, after declaring war on France on 1 August 1914, Germany invaded Belgium two days later with mobilized troops bound for France, England had no choice but to declare war on Germany the next day, 4 August.

[2] In his speech before a special joint session of Congress, convened on 2 April 1917, President Wilson used the famous sentence "The World must be made safe for democracy" as part of his appeal for a declaration of war against the Axis powers.

[3] The crusaders. When using the term he does, Chesnutt may have been alluding to the refrain of the traditional spiritual "We Am Clim'in Jacob's Ladder" or deliberately echoing "Stand Up, Stand Up for Jesus" (1858) by George Duffield (1794–1868).

[4] Chesnutt quotes more fully from this speech in "Perry Centennial." Much of the black military history treated here by Chesnutt was focused upon in that earlier address.

[5] The Confederate ship *Jeff Davis* captured the *Waring*, bound from New York to South America, on 7 July 1861. It was sailed to Charleston, S.C.; retained were three members of its original crew, including William Tillman (1834–?), William Stedding (the Yankee Chesnutt mentions), and Donald McLeod. Told he had become the property of the Confederate States of America, Tillman bided his time until he could organize the successful takeover of the ship just before midnight on 16 July 1861. The capture was more gruesome than Chesnutt implies: Tillman, armed with a hatchet rather than the "heavy club," killed the captain, Montague Amiel, and two mates, throwing the bodies overboard with Stedding's help.

[6] Chesnutt quotes from William Wells Brown's *The Negro in the American Rebellion* (1867).

[7] His surname misspelled "Small" in the source text, Robert Smalls (1839–1915), a dockside slave in Charleston, had been imprisoned by local Confederates to serve as part of the crew of the *Planter*. Early on the morning of 13 May 1862, Smalls, assisted by eight other conscripted slaves, piloted the *Planter* out of Charleston harbor, surrendering it to Union forces aboard the *Onward*, part of the blockade of the harbor.

[8] Congress acted less generously toward Smalls and his accomplices than Chesnutt states: half of the cash value of the ship was invested, and the earnings were assigned to them.

[9] The title of Captain constituted unofficial recognition of his naval success. He then served South Carolina in the U.S. House of Representatives continuously, except for two years, from 1874 to 1886. He was later a customs officer at the port of Beaufort, S.C.

[10] On 22 August 1862, Thomas Overton Moore (1803–76) authorized Major General Benjamin Franklin Butler (1818–93), commander of the Department of the Gulf, to

invite African Americans to enlist in the army. Reversed thus was Butler's previous policy of regarding captured slaves as "contraband of war" and refusing to arm them as soldiers. The resulting First Regiment Louisiana Native Guards, mustered in on 27 September 1862, was not, however, the first African-American group to be recruited by the Union. Beginning on 8 April 1862, blacks were enlisted in the First South Carolina Infantry, "Hunter's Regiment."

[11]While no official records verify that Butler indeed created African-American officers for his regiments, tradition supports Chesnutt's claim to that effect. The first such officer known to have served was William N. Reed (?–1864), who received a commission as lieutenant colonel on 1 June 1863 and as commanding officer of the First North Carolina Colored Volunteer Regiment (later the Thirty-fifth U.S. Colored Troops).

[12]Mississippi Senator James K. Vardaman sought congressional support to bar anyone of "Negro or colored" descent from enlisting or re-enlisting in America's armed forces after the passage of the National Defense Act in 1916, which authorized the peacetime expansion of the military in the United States. The alternative he offered African Americans desiring to enlist indicates his low opinion of them: "A negro may become an obedient effective piece of machinery, but he is devoid of initiative and therefore could not be relied upon in an emergency" (*Congressional Record*, volume 53, part 6, 64th Congress, 1st session, 1916, 5418 and 5571).

[13]Governor of Massachusetts John Albion Andrew (1818–67) received permission from Secretary of War Edwin McMasters Stanton (1814–69) to organize an African-American regiment on 26 January 1863.

[14]Robert Gould Shaw (1837–63) accepted for the regiment a national flag from Boston's young African-American women, a state flag given by the Colored Ladies' Relief Society, a white silk banner bearing the figure of the goddess of liberty, and the regimental colors. While the regiment indeed received the send-off from Boston on 28 May 1863 which Chesnutt describes, Shaw led it in only one battle, its first engagement, at Fort Wagner in Charleston harbor on 18 July 1863. Of some 650 African-American troops assaulting the fort, nearly 250 died.

[15]Chesnutt's probable source for this remark by a nameless Confederate was William Wells Brown's *The Negro in the American Rebellion*.

[16]Chesnutt quotes from Joseph T. Wilson's *The Black Phalanx*, wherein the author of the poem is not identified.

[17]The Union defeat at Fort Pillow, Tenn., occurred on 12 April 1864. After Union troops refused to surrender, General Nathan Bedford Forrest (1821–77) ordered an attack which completely overran the defenders—many of whom were nailed to buildings, burned to death, and buried alive. Among the soldiers defending the fort were 262 African Americans, 229 of whom died.

[18]The Twenty-fourth Infantry and the Ninth and Tenth Cavalry regiments, all organized following the Civil War and composed solely of African-American troops with white officers, participated in the assault of the San Juan Heights during the Spanish-American War, receiving much praise from their commanding officers; the conflict at Carrizal, on 21 June 1916, during the Mexican Punitive Expedition, involved a patrol from the Tenth Cavalry which unsuccessfully attempted to rout Mexican defenders of the small town.

[19]Racist epithet for Germans.

[20]Reference to the Central Powers (Germany, Austria-Hungary, Turkey, and Bulgaria) opposed by the Allied Powers (including the United States).

[21]In 1833, Parliament passed a law freeing colonial slaves.

[22]Racial tensions between whites and African-American soldiers in Houston resulted in violence on the night of 23 August 1917 because of an altercation involving a

white policeman, a black woman, and two black soldiers. In the riot that followed, both
blacks and whites died. Sixty-three members of the black Twenty-fourth United States
Infantry were subsequently court-martialed in November, with another fifty-five court-
martialed later in two separate trials respectively completed in January and March,
1918. Thus, 118 men were formally charged; of these, 110 were eventually found guilty
of crimes ranging from mutiny to murder; seven received acquittals; and one committed
suicide. Of those convicted, nineteen were hanged—thirteen on the morning of 11 December 1917, five on 16 September 1918, and one on 24 September 1918. Although the
rest received sentences of from two years to life imprisonment, all had been pardoned by
1938.

[23]Newton Diehl Baker became Secretary of War in 1916.

[24]Baker's authorization for the establishment of a camp for the training of African-
American officers at Fort Des Moines was officially announced on 23 May 1917. Of the
1,250 potential officers who arrived soon thereafter for training, 639 received commissions the following 14 October.

[25]Chesnutt probably refers here to Cleveland attorney William R. Green, a captain
who served initially with Company D of the 9th Battalion, organized in Cleveland in
the summer of 1917; it later became Company H of the 372nd Regiment and was slated
to be transported overseas for duty in 1918. Green's cheerful report of his company's
treatment at Camp Sheridan in Montgomery, Ala., was premature: a short while before
the company was to depart for Europe, white officers replaced Green and other African-
American officers in the regiment who had been declared physically unfit for battle—a
development unwittingly foreshadowed in a letter from Chesnutt to Green, dated 24
November 1917. In this letter included in Helen Chesnutt's *Charles Waddell Chesnutt*,
her father queried Green concerning reports of ominous treatment of African-American
troops of which he had read in newspapers.

Negro Authors

Speech to the Association of Colored Men, Cleveland, O., 1918

Mr. President, members of the Colored Men's Association,[1] ladies and gentlemen:—

I wish to assure you of my appreciation of the compliment implied in the invitation to address you today in a course of lectures and addresses by such
prominent citizens as those who have appeared upon your platform during this
season. I know you have not asked me to speak to you as an orator, for I am no
orator, as you all know very well from experience. I have been asked to speak
about Negro authors and playwrights. I almost wish I had been asked to speak
about Negro orators—I would like to get a crack at them. I say this in all good
nature, and without any special personal reference; they all do it, and I have said
to them all in private what I am going to say to you—from the great Doctor
Washington down—they talk to colored audiences as though they were talking

to children. Flattery is a pleasant thing, when skilfully administered, but your colored orator lays it on with a trowel. To imagine that a colored audience believes everything that the professional colored orator says, or that it believes that the orator himself believes it all, is really to insult their intelligence. If I were one of them, I should probably begin by telling you what a wonderful people you are, and how proud I am that I was born black, and how, if I could be born again and choose my sphere in life, I would choose that of an American Negro. You will notice that it is very apt to be a light mulatto who makes this statement, who can "get by" more or less and escape a good many of the disabilities and slights that the real Negro finds himself up against. And the statement about being born over again and choosing to be born black is a safe bet—your orator knows that his bluff will never be called—he would never have any more chance to choose how they would be born again than they had to choose how they would be born in the first place.

I am neither proud nor ashamed of the colored blood in my veins. If it has brought me any good, as I think it has—it gave me the impulse to write, the material for, and a hearing for the books to which I owe such little reputation as I have, and the invitation to address you today—I am duly thankful for it. If it has subjected me to any disabilities, as I am sure it has, as it has all of us who share it, I have tried to bear them with patience and to look upon the bright side of the shield.

There is a great deal of loose talk on this subject of race. Even our good friend Dr. Du Bois, whom we all love and admire, is not beyond criticism in this respect. In his autobiography published in a recent issue of the *Crisis*, on the anniversary of his fiftieth year, he thanks God, that while he has traces of good old Holland blood, some Indian and some French—in his makeup, he has none of Anglo-Saxon![2] Well, most of my blood is Anglo-Saxon, and I am not at all sore with God for giving me some of the blood of a race which produced Lincoln, Wendell Phillips, Garrison, Charles Sumner, John Brown, and whose blood flowed in the veins of Frederick Douglass and of Booker T. Washington. There are good Anglo-Saxons as well as bad, and we ought to distinguish between them. I am sure the time will come, sometime in the distant future when all the colored people of the U.S. will have Anglo-Saxon blood in their veins, for I am as firmly convinced as I ever was that there will be no permanent solution of the race problem in the U.S. until we are all one people. Do not let your orators deceive you when they tell you what a fine thing it is to be at the bottom, because you have so much higher to climb. Every one of them is trying to place his children higher in life than he is. If it is such a privilege to be so low down, why deprive our children of it? Would it not be more logical to push them down, so that they would have more of this privilege than we have? But you are not deceived. You all know that "to be a Negro in a day like this," as Mr. Corrothers has phrased it in a recent poem,[3] is a serious disability in the U.S., that it is no privilege to be despised and segregated and discriminated against, and that all our effort and struggle has been and is and must be for the future, to reach a level where we can seek the prizes of life on equal terms with other men. Those terms are hard enough without any special handicap.

And since I am no orator, and shall not flatter you, and since my subject gives me very few openings for funny stories to make you laugh, I shall address myself to my subject, and if I may, to your intelligence, and try to give you some facts, with which you may not be familiar, and perhaps some food for thought and some inspiration for effort.[4]

* * *

In history, biography and sociology and criticism the record is much better.

Brawley[5]—Poets
P. Wheatley
Dunbar
Braithwaite
Corrothers
Du Bois
J. W. Johnson
(C.W.C.)[6]

History:

Geo. W. Wms.
Du Bois
Washington
John H. Lynch[7]

Autobiography:

F. Douglass
Wm. Still
B.T.W. (*Up from Slavery*)

Biography:

Lives of Douglass,[8]
Lives of Washington[9]

Sociology:

Sinclair

〜

SOURCE: Untitled, undated, and incomplete typed text, with one page in holograph (the concluding list of names and titles), at the Fisk University Library. The speech was delivered before Cleveland's Association of Colored Men. Chesnutt's reference to W. E. B. Du Bois's autobiography as published in a recent issue of *The Crisis* indicates a late- or post-January 1918 composition date.

[1]The Cleveland Association of Colored Men conducted lecture series for its members. A decade earlier, Chesnutt had given two lectures in one such series, entitled the "Sunday Afternoon Lyceum," which ran from 4 October 1908 through 28 March

1909. "The Value of Fiction" was given on 22 November 1908, and "Negro Books and Playwriters" was presented 3 March 1909. The text of neither is extant.

[2]"The Shadow of Years," *The Crisis*, 15 (February 1918), 167–71.

[3]See "The Ideal Nurse," n. 16.

[4]The surviving typed portion of the source text ends here. Undetermined is how Chesnutt made the transition to the notes for extemporaneous remarks that follow.

[5]Benjamin G. Brawley (1882–1939) was a historian and literary critic who also published poetry, including *The Problem and Other Poems* (1904) and *The Dawn and Other Poems* (1911).

[6]Chesnutt himself.

[7]John Roy Lynch (1847–1939) was a member of the U.S. House of Representatives from Mississippi (1872–76; 1882) and the author of *The Facts of Reconstruction* (1913).

[8]Chesnutt's *Frederick Douglass* (1899) was one of several published by 1918, including those of Frederic May Holland (1836–1908), *Frederick Douglass: The Colored Orator* (1891); James Monroe Gregory (1849–?), *Frederick Douglass: The Orator* (1893); Laura Eliza Wilkins (1871–?), *The Story of Frederick Douglass* (1899); Booker T. Washington, *Frederick Douglass* (1900); and William Pickens, *Frederick Douglass and the Spirit of Freedom* (1912).

[9]Biographical volumes then available included those of Godfrey Holden Pike (1836–?), *From Slave to College President* (1902); John W. A. Shaw, *A Tangled Skein: A Vindication of Booker T. Washington and His Work* (1904); Frederick E. Drinker, *Booker T. Washington, the Master Mind of a Child of Slavery* (1915); Emmett Jay Scott (1873–1957), *Booker T. Washington: Builder of Civilization* (1916); Maude C. Giles, *A Man of Mark* (1916); J. W. Jackson, *To the Memory of Booker T. Washington* (1916); and Myles Rhynes, *The Prince of Ethiopia: Booker T. Washington* (1916).

The Mission of the Drama

Essay published in the *Cygnet*, January 1920

When Jupiter looked down from Olympus upon the race of men which he had called into being, he was impressed with a sense of failure. He had meant them to be happy, and to that end had provided that they should live calmly and peacefully and free from care. He saw peace and plenty and comfort and equality, but withal a deadly monotony. They lived and ate and drank and bred and died as a matter of course, with no more zeal or enthusiasm for anything they did than the beasts of the field. He had meant them to be different. So he sent the Comic Muse to cheer them up, to make them laugh, and thus, he hoped, to make them happy.

The result was not entirely satisfying. They became cheerful, indeed too cheerful. They laughed, and laughed and laughed, until their laughter became as monotonous and as empty and as little soul-satisfying as had been their equanimity, and it soon became apparent that too much mirth did not constitute happiness. So he recalled the Comic Muse, and sent the Tragic Muse to make them weep. If merriment would not make them happy, he would try what grief could accomplish.

And still they were not happy. The monotony of tears was no improvement on that of laughter. So he recalled the Tragic Muse and left them again for a while to their own devices. But, like a wise god, he did not like to confess failure. Neither did he care to scrap the race and wipe it out with fire or flood. While the gods knew nothing of political economy, or sociology, which are modern sciences, he realized, to use their terminology, that to destroy these imperfect creatures of his would be an economic waste and therefore indefensible and so, after further wise reflection, he sent them the Comic Muse and the Tragic Muse together.

This did not result in making men happy, in fact Jupiter was fast beginning to realize that it was beyond the power of the gods to make them happy, for happiness, like a beautiful dream, was always just beyond their reach. But the search for it and the hope of attaining it, encouraged by the team work of the Comic Muse and the Tragic Muse, made their lives worth living. Life was no longer monotonous, and they found, in the pursuit of happiness, the nearest point of approach to it of which the race was capable.

To drop the parable, this is the mission of the drama: To distract the mind from the dull, tiresome routine of daily life, and to project it into the realm of fancy. I met one summer a man of thirty who had been born and reared within six miles of Bar Harbor,[1] but had never visited the watering place; and we all know of the man who "never had seen Carcassonne."[2] The bookkeeper or bank teller who handles mechanically, for a pittance, the wealth of others all day long, may, as he looks at a popular play, learn how it feels to be an embezzler, or a burglar, or a malefactor of great wealth, and will return to his desk the better for his brief respite, and with no desire to emulate their exploits. The unwed or unsought maiden may experience, by proxy, for a few brief hours, all the emotions of courtship, of happy marriage, of widowhood, or of divorce. She can imagine herself a deserted wife, an alluring vampire, a great singer or a favorite movie actress, which seems to be the acme of feminine ambition these days, and then go back to her desk or her typewriter or her counter, or her kitchen, refreshed and stimulated by her excursion into a different world.

The appeal of the play is primarily to the emotions. If it reach the intellect, there is no harm done, but it must reach the emotions or it is no true example of dramatic art.

A play written to instruct, as, for instance, some of the pathological theses which have been presented to the public in recent years in the guise of plays, is foredoomed to ultimate failure. Curiosity may give them a certain vogue for a little while, but their day is brief. A play may point a moral, but if the moral be too pronounced, it is apt to kill the play. If it inspire to high endeavor, to patience under misfortune, to struggle against difficulties, to sympathy with suffering, to any good or noble thing, so much the better. Life is full of dramatic situations, with fine climaxes, in which virtue is rewarded and vice punished, and the good playwright, with an eye to his royalties and his fame, may well select these motives for his play. But the lesson must grow out of the play, and not the play out of the lesson.

But while the playwright is under no obligation to preach, he is, in view of the wide appeal of his art and its influence upon others, under an obligation not to corrupt. The bold, banal, indecent suggestion of much of the modern musical comedy and burlesque, restrained only by the limit set by the police authorities, is a disgrace to the stage and an insult to the intelligence of the public. Nudity on the stage is not art, however it may lend itself, when properly employed, to painting or to sculpture. Coarse or obscene suggestion is not wit on the stage, whatever it may pass for in a Pullman smoking compartment or a bar-room; and if the public would only demand of the stage at least some approximation to the same standards of decency that prevail in private life, and enforce their demand in the only effective way, by the withdrawal of their patronage from those who offend in this respect, the result would immediately become apparent.

The producers say, in reply to such criticism, that they give the public what it wants. But the growth of reform legislation along other lines proves that the public, when it speaks by its majority, wants, as a rule,[3] what is best, and the theatrical producers would find a much larger public for the better shows; for many of those who attend these objectionable pieces, attend them merely for lack of something better, and they, as well as others who now stay away, would support something which offered the same beauty of costume and stage setting with a little more real music and real acting and a little less vulgarity.

To cheer, to comfort, to stir, to amuse, in other words to entertain, is the real purpose and *raison d'être* of the drama. Its range is as wide as life itself, and any movement which seeks for it new and untried motives, capable of dramatic treatment, or new methods of presenting old themes, which at the same time can exert a refining or uplifting influence without sacrificing the fundamental part of the play to entertain by its appeal to the emotions, is worthy of popular support and encouragement. But, before all and after all,

The play's the thing.[4]

⮎

SOURCE: "The Mission of the Drama," *Cygnet*, 1 (January 1920), 11–12, emended in light of an incomplete typed text at the Fisk University Library.

[1]A picturesque resort town on the Maine coast.

[2]"I never saw Carcassonne," a medieval walled-city in southern France, is the complaint in the song "Carcassonne" written by Gustave Nadaud (1820–93). The lyric was included in his *Chansons Populaires* (1879).

[3]Not present in the source text is the qualification, "as a rule," which was added by hand in the typed text.

[4]*Hamlet*, 2.2.641.

Resolutions Concerning the Recent Election

Essay published in the *Cleveland Gazette*, 20 November 1920

WHEREAS, During the recent political campaign,[1] scurrilous and defamatory pamphlets, intended to stir up race prejudice and to excite public opinion against the colored people, and thereby to defeat the Republican State and National tickets and especially the colored candidates for the legislature, were printed and circulated throughout the State of Ohio;[2] and

WHEREAS, These pamphlets, while failing of their principal purpose, the defeat of the State and National tickets, were successful, by their base appeal to race prejudice, in defeating Messrs. William R. Green and Samuel E. Woods for election to the State Legislature;[3] and

WHEREAS, The statements contained in said pamphlets, when not lies, as many of them were, were so maliciously and brazenly distorted as to convey a false impression of the aims and hopes of the colored citizens in the recent election; and

WHEREAS, The pictures of Messrs. Green, Davis and Woods printed on the face of one of said circulars were procured by fraud and indirection and were reproduced in such a manner as to constitute gross libels both in their intention and their effect; and

WHEREAS, A certain renegade Negro lent his name and his likeness to the preparation of said circular, for the purpose of slandering and injuring his race;[4] and has since had the brazen effrontery to file a report with the Board of Elections stating that he had spent some seventy odd dollars for the benefit of William R. Green, Harry E. Davis and Samuel E. Woods, when in fact many thousands of the pamphlets signed by him were circulated, by mail, the postage alone on which would be many times said amount; and

WHEREAS, Said circulars imposed upon the ignorance or credulity of many voters, and by their vicious appeal to race prejudice and race hatred directly resulted in the defeat of two of the three candidates above referred to:[5]

NOW THEREFORE, BE IT RESOLVED:

That we hereby voice our sorrow and indignation that such campaign methods should have been employed in the State of Ohio against citizens who have always been loyal to the nation and to the public interest; that while we should not have been surprised at the employment of such methods in the South, where they are traditional and to be looked for, we did not expect them in our own State, where we have always received until now fair political treatment, and where we felt that our rights were secure; and that we regret that any party or any group of scheming politicians should have sunk so low as to resort to such desperate measures to bolster up a hopeless cause; that while we regret that the Republican electorate of Cuyahoga County should have so far failed in justice and generosity as to have defeated Messrs. Green and Woods[6] while electing all the other members of the Republican County ticket, yet at the same time we rejoice that the ulterior motives controlling the preparation and circulation of the circulars referred to, namely, the defeat of the State and National Republican tickets, were defeated; that we thank the many thousand white voters who supported the full ticket and were not misled by the false and insidious statements that were circulated; and that we hope and believe that many of those that were so misled will, upon fuller information and reflection, regret their action.

AND BE IT FURTHER RESOLVED, That we visit the weight of our displeasure and contempt upon Walter L. Brown, the putative author of the circular directed particularly against Messrs. Green, Davis and Woods, by branding him as a traitor to his race and to all the principles of decency and honor, and that we recommend to all good people that they ostracize him socially and personally, to the end that he and any others who may be tempted by offers of money or other reward, to engage in any such unworthy and despicable conduct, may know that they do so at the risk of social reprobation and punishment; and that a copy of this resolution be sent to every colored church, society, club and lodge, with the request that it be read in open meeting[7] and that a copy be sent to *The Gazette*.

BE IT FURTHER RESOLVED, That while fully recognizing that it cannot affect the outcome of the recent election, yet as a matter of self-respect and in furtherance of truth and justice, we issue a statement to the public setting forth the attitude of the colored voters in regard to this matter in the following language:

To The Public!

The circulars distributed in the late political campaign with the view of inciting race hatred and prejudice to the end of defeating thereby the National and State Republican tickets, failed of their real purpose but were successful in securing the defeat of two of the three colored candidates on the Republican county ticket,[8] by misleading the white[9] voters as to the personality and character of the candidates and the aims and objects of the colored people in their exercise of the franchise and the election to the legislature of men of their race and their friends.[10]

The circular bearing the alleged likenesses of Messrs. William R. Green, Harry E. Davis and Samuel E. Woods, purporting to have been written by a colored man who is so shameless as to sign his name thereto, was obviously concocted to convey the false[11] impression that it was issued in the interests or upon the authority of the three candidates named, whereas[12] in fact its purpose was to alienate from them the friendship and support of white people, especially of white women. The suggestion that the colored people want to or could "dominate" the city of Cleveland or the state of Ohio is absurd on the face of it, since they constitute, even with the so called "Southern influx," but a very small fraction of the state's population.

The Beaty Bill to which reference is made was not a campaign issue, nor was it sponsored or advocated by either of the three candidates named.[13] It[14] confers no larger rights than are already secured to all citizens by a civil rights law which has been on the statute books of Ohio[15] for many years and has been uniformly upheld by the courts and the majority opinion.[16] For the colored people or any other class of citizens to be satisfied with anything less than their lawful rights, would be to stultify themselves and make them unworthy the respect of decent people.

The appeal to race prejudice is dangerous to society and can be applied to the injury of any racial group or element of the population, and in the interest of democracy and good government, should be sternly discouraged. If politicians learn that such methods are likely to be successful in securing votes, the merits of candidates or issues will be ignored, elections will be debased, and no group in the community will be safe from such attacks.

We thank the many thousand white[17] voters who cast their ballots for Messrs. Green, Davis and Woods, including some broad-minded Democrats who did so to repudiate the methods employed to defeat them.

We regret that enough of the Republican electorate of Cuyahoga County should have so far failed of justice and generosity as to defeat Messrs. Green and Woods, while electing all the other members of the Republican County ticket.[18]

We regret that many of the white[19] women voters of the city and county permitted themselves to be induced by slander and falsehood to do a cruel and unjust thing in this their first exercise of the full elective franchise.[20]

We fully recognize that no action we may take can affect the outcome of the late election, and we issue this statement merely as a matter of self-respect and in furtherance of truth and justice.[21]

> Truth crushed to earth, shall rise again,
> The eternal years of God are hers![22]

Welcome T. Blue,
J. Walter Wills,
Harry C. Smith,
Committee on Resolutions[23]

⌒

SOURCE: "Sunday's Mass Meeting Puts Davis Over!" *Cleveland Gazette*, 20 November 1920, 1, emended in light of a typed text at the Fisk University Library. As with "Resolutions Concerning Southern Outrages," Chesnutt served as a collaborative author, producing a draft modified by the Committee on Resolutions of the Cleveland Association of Colored Men. The final version of the resolutions was approved at a meeting held on 14 November 1920, presided over by Chesnutt.

[1]The election occurred on Tuesday, 2 November 1920.

[2]On the Saturday preceding the election, 30 October 1920, the *Cleveland Gazette* published "Strong Appeal to Our Voters" on its front page. The article warned voters to beware of "the ridiculous and vicious southern Democratic race-hatred-breeding at-

tacks upon . . . our candidates" in the form of "circulars which now are being mailed to the voters of this county."

[3]William R. Green had become prominent in the Niagara Movement by 1907 and would later serve the local chapter of the N.A.A.C.P. as its president (1922–23). Harry E. Davis (1882–1955)—also named, erroneously, in the source text—was a Cleveland lawyer and civil rights activist; unlike Green and Wood, he was actually elected to the Ohio General Assembly, taking office in 1921 for the first of four consecutive terms and later serving as a state senator (see n. 5). He was the first African American to preside over the Ohio Senate. Samuel E. Woods (1871–?) was deputy sheriff in Cuyahoga County in 1908–11 and was active in local Republican politics.

[4]Chesnutt below identifies the author of the circular as Walter L. Brown, a prominent Democrat in Cleveland since 1901 and famous for having won a civil rights suit in 1909: he took to court the local African-American entrepreneur Samuel Clayton Green (1872–1915) for refusing to admit him to his ice-skating rink on a "whites only" night.

[5]The typed text does not include the words "two of," this portion of the draft having been produced when it appeared that none of the three black Republicans had been elected. In the draft this paragraph concludes: "thus leaving the large number of colored voters in Cuyahoga County with no direct representation in the State law-making body, to their great humiliation and disadvantage."

[6]The typed text included Davis's name after Green's.

[7]The remainder of this sentence does not appear in the typed text.

[8]At this point, the typed text initiates a new paragraph: "Representing as we do the group to which they belong, and having supported them, as we did, we of course regret their defeat, but, since defeat is a possibility which must be faced by every candidate in every election, we are less concerned with the result than with the methods by which it was brought about." Another new paragraph then begins in this manner: "These methods were directed to," at which point the reading in the source text—"by misleading"—follows.

[9]The word "white" appears only in the source text.

[10]Here the typed text includes the words, "and, by raising the race issue, of alienating from them the support and friendship of other voters."

[11]The word "false" appears only in the source text.

[12]In the typed text this sentence concludes: "the fact was exactly the contrary." Not present in the source text is the sentence that then followed: "The photographs from which the prints were made were secured by fraud and indirection, and so reproduced as to constitute a libel both in intent and in effect."

[13]"Beatty" has been emended to "Beaty." The text of the Beaty Bill (Bill No. 139) was originated by the N.A.A.C.P. and was intended to ensure more comprehensive civil rights for Ohioans. It was sponsored by the black state legislator A. Lee Beaty (1869–?) and defeated in the Ohio House of Representatives on 17 April 1919. It had been cited as proof of a desire to establish "Negro dominance."

[14]"Even had it been, it" initiates this sentence in the typed text.

[15]The phrase "of Ohio" appears only in the source text.

[16]In the typed text the word "public" instead precedes "opinion."

[17]The word "white" appears only in the source text.

[18]The typed text presents another sentence here: "The question of their fitness was not raised or discussed. They were defeated solely because of their color."

[19]The typed text does not include the word "white."

[20]The Nineteenth Amendment granted the franchise to women on 18 August 1920.

[21]The typed text concludes this paragraph with "and of political morality and fair play."

[22]This couplet from "The Battle-Field" (1837) by William Cullen Bryant does not

appear in the typed text, nor do the names of the Resolutions Committee members listed below.

[23]Welcome T. Blue co-founded the Journal Publishing Company in 1903 and was a real estate and insurance broker. J. Walter Wills (1874–1971) founded Ohio's then-largest African-American funeral home, the House of Wills. He was a significant contributor to the local chapter of the N.A.A.C.P., and he organized Cleveland's first African-American business organization, the Board of Trade. Harry C. Smith, who began editing the *Gazette* in 1883, had served three terms in the Ohio legislature, where he sponsored the Ohio Civil Rights Law of 1894.

The Autobiography of Edward, Baron Herbert of Cherbury

Speech to the Rowfant Club, Cleveland, O., 12 March 1921

One exceedingly readable autobiography has come down to us in the *Life* of Lord Edward Herbert of Cherbury.[1]

Editions. Cassell's. Ed. John Morley, Ed. by Wm. D. Howells.[2] The best I have had access to is the one edited by the present Sir Sidney Lee, published in 1886, when he was merely a B.A. of Balliol College, Oxford the text of which is taken from the first printed edition, issued from Horace Walpole's private press in 1764.[3] The manuscript was apparently not finished and presumably not intended for publication, and was in great danger of being lost to the world. It was discovered among the family papers about 1714, sixty-six years after the writer's death, in very bad condition.[4] A duplicate copy was found twenty-three years later, in 1737, and by collation with the original the book in its present form was edited.

Critics agree that the style of the book is remarkably good for that age, but differ in their estimates of its literary ranking, and of its author. Swinburne claims for it a place among the one hundred best books of the world.[5] Sir Sidney Lee says, in the preface to his edition: "Former editors have treated the work as a mere curiosity of literature. I have endeavored in my notes and elsewhere to prove that it deserves the serious attention of the student, not only of English literature but of English social history in the early seventeenth century."

Edward, Lord Herbert of Cherbury, was a Welshman. In his autobiography, he does not mention the date of his birth, but from certain events the dates of which are given, it is figured that he must have been born in 1581, and he was sixty-seven when he died. He was a writer, something of a poet, a diplomat, and on the whole a fine example of the upperclass Englishman of his day—I use the word Englishman generically. He was a brother of the poet George Herbert.[6]

Says John Morley in the introduction to his edition: "The story of duels and intended duels, illustrates in a whimsical way the hot-headed and punctilious Welshman."[7] "He is," as I saw somewhere said recently of Lloyd George, "He is Welsh of the Welsh; he has their faults—his emotionalism, his lack of continuity, his substitution of divination for logic, his intense pugnacity."[8]

His vanity is entirely obvious.

(Read from pages xi and xii of Lee's introduction, also pages xiii and xiv.)

Opinions differ as to his veracity. Horace Walpole judged him to be the incarnation of truthfulness. Lee, on the contrary, calls him a "liar, of course no common liar," he does n't call him a damned liar, but puts him, in effect, rather in the class of the expert witness when he says: "With plausible amiability he suppresses the truth, rather than commits deliberate perjury."[9]

He was sincerely religious, if not Orthodox. He was a dabbler in philosophy. As a soldier he won the esteem of the great captains of his day. He seems to have taken his knighthood as seriously as it was taken before Cervantes had laughed knight-errancy off the map of Europe. "Had he been ambitious," says Sir Horace Walpole, "the beauty of his person would have carried him as far as any gentle knight can aspire to go," and if we read his own story intelligently, it *did* carry him as far as any gentle knight ought to go. "As a public minister, he supported the dignity of his country, even when its Prince disgraced it." He was a poet of sorts, a historian of merit, and he added several reams to the incalculable mass of paper and tonnage of ink that have been wasted in religious discussion.[10]

I think this is a good point to take up what he has to say about himself, for it is his book which I am supposed to read from:

The author says, in the beginning of the book:

> I have thought fit to relate to my posterity those passages of my life which I conceive may best declare me and be most useful to them. In the delivery of which, I profess to write with all truth and sincerity, as scorning ever to deceive or speak false to any: and if this be one reason for taking my pen in hand at this time, so as my age has passed three score, it will be fit to recollect my former actions, and examine what has been done well or ill, to the intent I may both reform that which was amiss and so make my peace with God.

A most admirable sentiment, as well as a most convenient age for reform.

"Before yet I bring myself to this account, it will be necessary I say somewhat concerning my ancestors," which he proceeds to do at considerable length. He was of a fine old Welsh family, whose quality does not suffer from his description of it. (Genealogical Table in Lee's Edition.)[11]

"My grandfather's power," he says,

> was so great in the county that divers ancestors of the better families now in Montgomeryshire were his servants and raised by him. He[12] delighted also much in hospitality, as having a very long table, twice covered every meal with the best meats that could be gotten, and a very great family. . . .

My great-grandfather, Sir Richard Herbert of Colebrook,[13] was that incomparable hero who (in the History of Hall and Grafton[14] as it appears) twice passed
through a great army of Northern men alone, with his pole-axe in his hand, and returned without any mortal hurt, which is more than is famed of Amadis de Gaul, or
the Knight of the Sun.[15]

There are several other pages recounting more warlike exploits of this Sir
Richard Herbert, who was brother to the Earl of Pembroke.

Lee finds in these pages concerning his ancestors the most significant mis-
statements in Herbert's autobiography.

There he has not only his own but his forefathers' reputation to maintain, and he
sets his shoulder valiantly to the wheel. His glowing story of their noble deeds
passes with startling abruptness into an account of their tombs. He discreetly omits
to mention that his great-great-grandfather and his great-great-granduncle were
taken prisoners on the battlefield and *beheaded at Northampton.* Their death was
not disgraceful, but a well-developed sense of respectability apparently forbids the
mention of the ghastly detail.

Lord Herbert then takes up his nine brothers and sisters, "of all of whom,"
he says, "I will say a little before I begin a narration of my own life." His brothers were of course, and in fact all fine fellows, respectively distinguished scholars, soldiers, sailors, courtiers, his brother George Herbert being the poet of that
name. His three sisters made marriages such as would be expected of ladies of
their condition.

"I shall now" says the author, "come to myself:

I was born at Eyton, in Shropshire, between the hours of twelve and one of the clock
in the morning; my infancy was very sickly, my head continually purging itself very
much by the ears, whereupon also it was so long before I began to speak, that many
thought I should be ever dumb. The very furthest thing I remember is, that when I
understood what was said by others, I did yet forbear to speak, lest I should utter
something that were imperfect or impertinent.

A most remarkable and unusual instance of infantile prudence and self-control.

When I came to talk, one of the furthest inquiries I made was, how I came into
this world? I told my nurse, keeper, and others, I found myself here indeed, but from
what cause or beginning, or by what means, I could not imagine; but for this, as I
was laughed at by nurse and some other women that were then present, so I was
wondered at by others, who said they never heard a child but myself ask that question;

a philosopher in bud

upon which, when I came to riper years, I made this observation, which afterwards
a little comforted me, that as I found myself in possession of this life, without
knowing anything of the pangs and throes my mother suffered, when yet doubtless
they did not less press and afflict me than her, so I hope my soul shall pass to a better life than this without being sensible of the anguish and pains my body shall feel
in death.

For as I believe then I shall be transmitted to a more happy estate by God's great grace, I am confident I shall no more know how I came out of this world, than how I came into it; and because since that time I have made verses to this purpose, I have thought fit to insert them here as a place proper for them.

Then follow some three or four pages of Latin verse, the first poem being entitled "Vita," in which he takes up the life at its inception in the seminal fluid, follows it through the generative, gestative and parturitive processes and to the end of life, and a second poem entitled "De Vita Caelesti Conjectura." And, reasoning from the argument of these poems, he goes on to deduce the life hereafter.

> But to leave these discourses, and come to my childhood again; I remember this defluxion[16] at my ears above-mentioned continued in that violence, that my friends did not think fit to teach me so much as my alphabet, till I was seven years old, at which time my defluxion ceased, and left me free of the disease my ancestors were subject unto, being the epilepsy. My schoolmaster, in the house of my said lady grandmother, then began to teach me the alphabet, and afterwards grammar, and other books commonly read in schools, in which I profited so much, that upon this theme *Audaces fortuna juvat*,[17] I made an oration of a sheet of paper, and fifty or sixty verses in the space of one day.

This infant prodigy seems to have been as good as he was clever. He remembers that he was sometimes corrected for fighting with school fellows older than himself, but never for telling a lie or any other fault, "and I can affirm to all the world truly that from my first infancy to this hour I told not willingly anything that was false, my soul naturally having an antipathy to lying and deceit." (George Washington.)

Well, he studied Welsh, Latin, Greek and Logic under various masters, "Insomuch that at twelve years old my parents sent me to University College, Oxford, where I remember to have disputed at my first coming in logic, and to have made in Greek the exercises required in that college, oftener than in Latin." Another instance of youthful precocity, suggesting the parallel exploit of Jesus in the Temple at the same tender age.[18]

Shortly after his entrance into the University his father died, and his estate passed into the hands of a guardian. He returned to his studies at Oxford, where he had not been long when a match was arranged between him and the daughter and heir of Sir William Herbert of St. Gillian's whose father, had willed her a large estate upon condition that she married one of the surname of Herbert, otherwise the said lands to go to the heirs male, the object obviously being to keep the property in the family name. The lady continued unmarried until the age of twenty-one, none of the Herberts appearing in all that time who either in age or fortune was fit to match her. He was married at the age of 15,[19] and shortly afterwards went again to Oxford, "together," he says,

> with my wife and mother, who took a house and lived for some certain time there:
> And now, having a due remedy for that lasciviousness to which youth is natu-

rally inclined; I followed my book more closely than ever; in which course I continued till I attained about the age of eighteen, when my mother took a house in London, between which place and Montgomery Castle I passed my time till I came to the age of one-and-twenty, having in that space divers children. . . .

During this time of living in the University or at home, I did, without any master or teacher, attain the knowledge of the French, Italian and Spanish languages, by the help of some books in Latin or English, translated into those idioms, and the dictionaries of those several languages; I attained also to sing my part at first sight in music, and to play on the lute, with very little or almost no teaching. . . .

Being gotten thus far into my age, I shall give some observations concerning ordinary education, even from the first infancy till the departure from the University, being desirous to deliver such rules as I conceive may be useful to my posterity,

which he proceeds to do in great detail, and covering many pages, from which I can quote only briefly.

He maintains that the treatment of hereditary disease should begin by "giving the mother such medicines as may make her milk effectual for those purposes, for instance, for stone or gravel, posset drinks in which are boiled such things as are good to expel gravel and stone, and after to give unto the child such specific remedies as his age and constitution will bear." For gout, for instance, he commends "the bathing of children's legs and feet in the water wherein smiths quench their iron, as also alum water, the decoction of juniper berries and other remedies for different diseases."

He believes in the separation of teaching from discipline, and maintains that from the beginning of school life through the University, the boy should have a governor of manners as well as a schoolmaster, and that neither the master should correct him for faults of his manners, nor his governor for manners for the faults in his learning.

He gives advice as to what studies should be pursued and says that among other things it will become a gentleman to have some knowledge of both the diagnostic and the prognostic parts of medicine.

> This art will get a gentleman not only much knowledge, but much credit, since seeing any sick body, he will be able to tell in all human probability whether he shall recover, or if he shall die of the disease, to tell what signs shall go before, and what the conclusion will be. It will become him also to know not only the ingredients, but doses of certain cathartic or purging, emetic or vomitive medicines, specific or choleric, melancholic or phlegmatic constitutions, phlebotomy being only necessary for those who abound in blood.

He has very little confidence in apothecaries, and says that a gentleman should know how to prepare these medicines with his own hands, since "no man is sure to find with apothecaries medicines made with the true drugs when these are exotic or rare, or, when he has them, that they are not stale or rotten."

He instances several remarkable cures which he himself made of cases which had been given over by the physicians; which read like the advertisements of a quack medicine, but which I have n't time to read, and gives as a rule for curing all inward and outward hurts, such as ulcers, tumors, wounds, contusions and the like, that you must consult all pharmacopoeias or antidotaries of several countries, of which sort he has in his library the Pharmacopoeia Londinensis, Parisensis, Amstelodamensis, that of Queresetau, Bauderaui, Renedeus, Valerius Scordus, Pharmacopaeia Coloniensis, Augustana, Venetiana, Vononiensis, Florentina, Romana, Messanensis.[20]

"Having thus passed over all human literature, it will be fit to say something of moral virtues and theological learning," which he does at some length, remarking sagely in passing:

> Having thus recommended the learning of moral philosophy and practice of virtue as the most necessary knowledge and useful exercise of man's life, I shall observe that even in the employment of our virtues discretion is required; for every virtue is not promiscuously to be used, but such only as is proper for the present occasion,

a sentiment worthy of a Scotchman, not to say a Welshman.

Having finished with the education of the mind and the morals he takes up the physical training of a gentleman, and recommends to his posterity riding the great horse, fencing and dancing.[21] Speaking of the foils he says with much of self-appreciation: "And indeed, I think I shall not speak vaingloriously of myself, if I say that no man understood the use of his weapon better than I did, or hath more dexterously prevailed himself thereof on all occasions, since I found no man could be hurt but through some error in fencing."

He is fond of riding the great horse—, and gives rules in some detail for guiding him with the foot, with the rein and with the rod (riding crop), and how to make him prance or caracole for parade and triumph or fighting, gives rules for fighting a duel on horseback, and for training a charger for war. He says that a gentleman should learn to swim, but,

> I must confess that I cannot swim, for as I was once in danger of drowning by learning to swim, my mother upon her blessing charged me never to learn swimming, telling me farther that she had heard of more drowned than saved by it; which reason, though it did not prevail with me, yet her commandment did.

Lord Herbert added to his other virtues that of being a dutiful son. Presumably for that reason, lest it should seem indelicate, he does not mention that when she became a widow she married a young man just half her age.[22]

He does not approve of running horses because there is much cheating in that kind. Neither does he see why a brave man should delight in a creature whose chief use is to help him run away. He condemns dicing and carding, especially if the play is for any great sum of money, "or in dicing houses, where cheaters meet and cozen young gentlemen of all their money."

Meeting with Queen Elizabeth, 1600. (Lee 81.)[23] Eliz. 67 yrs. old, died in 1603; "ashes wanted fires."[24] Meets King James a little later and is made a Knight of the Bath.[25]

He is then made sheriff of Montgomeryshire.

Concerning which I will say no more but that I bestowed the place of under-sheriff as also other places in my gifts freely, without either taking gifts or reward; which custom also I have observed throughout the whole course of my life, insomuch that when I was Ambassador in France and might have had great presents, which former ambassadors accepted for doing lawful courtesies to merchants and others, yet no gratuity, upon what terms soever could ever be fastened upon me.

Which was saying a mouthful for an office-holder who lived in the age of Sir Francis Bacon and the Stuart Kings.[26]

About the year 1608 he had a difference of opinion with his wife about making provision out of their property for their two daughters,[27] and the lady held to her point of view, nor could she be moved.

"I told her then that I should make another motion to her, which was that in regard I was too young to go beyond sea before I married her, she now would give me leave for a while to see foreign countries; how be it; if she would" make the arrangement he had suggested concerning property, "I would never depart from her." She answered that he knew her mind, and though she would be sorry if he went nevertheless if he would go, she could not help it.

"This, whether a license taken or given, served my turn to prepare without delay for a journey beyond sea, so I might satisfy that curiosity I long since had to see foreign countries." So that he might leave his wife as little discontented as possible, he says, "I left her not only posterity to renew the family of the Herberts of St. Gillian's according to her father's desire, to inherit his lands," but the rents of all the lands she brought with her.

And still further to occupy her time he left her with child of a son, christened afterwards by the name of Edward.[28]

Accompanied by the proper suite of a wealthy nobleman on tour, he then proceeded to France, established the necessary social connections through the French Embassy and was invited to visit at the castle of Nimour, the seat of the Duke of Montmorency, Constable of France.[29] During this visit took place the first of the numerous duels to which the author refers, and that went no further than a challenge, the gentleman challenged seeing fit to go away rather than to fight. A gallant had carried away a young lady's hair-ribbon, and he refusing to return it, he regulated Lord Herbert to get it. The gentleman not giving it up, Lord Herbert challenged him, "Because," he says, "I thought myself obliged thereunto by the oath taken when I was made a Knight of the Bath." A note in the Walpole edition says that "this oath is one remnant of a superstitious and romantic age, and is no longer supposed to bind. It would be strange if every Knight like the true, conscientious Lord Herbert found himself bound to cut a man's throat every time a Miss lost her top-knot."

The Duke of Montmorency now moves to another country house, and lends Lord Herbert the castle at Merlou where he is already a guest, together with his forests and chases for hunting, his stable of fifty great horses, his ecuyer (equerry) or master of the horse and other servants, and orders that a table be kept for him. There he spent a very pleasant eight months hunting the stag and the boar, and he describes a very exciting boar hunt.

Returning to Paris, through the recommendation of the English Ambassador he was received at the house of the incomparable scholar, Isaac Casaubon.[30]

> Sometimes also I went to the court of the French King, Henry IV, who, upon information of me in the garden at the Tuileries, received me with all courtesy. . . . I went sometimes also to the court of Queen Margaret . . . and here I saw many balls or masks, in which all it pleased that Queen publicly to place me next to her chair, not without the wonder of some and the envy of another who was wont to have that favor.

(*Heptameron*.)[31]

At one of these balls he meets a certain M. Balgni, who seems somewhat ruder than became a very civil person, but of whom the ladies make a great deal.[32] Upon inquiry Lord Herbert was told that

> this gentleman was one of the gallantest men in the world, as having killed eight or nine men in single fight, and that for this reason the ladies made so much of him, it being the manner of all Frenchwomen to cherish gallant men as thinking they could not make so much of any else with the safety of their honor.

(A little cryptic.)[33]

At the end of the winter he takes his leave of the French Court, and returns to England.[34] He is commissioned by the Princess of Conti to carry a scarf to England and to present it to Queen Anne.[35] He takes ship from Dieppe in Normandy, suffers a shipwreck which he describes vividly, finally reaches London, goes to court, kisses the king's hand and gives him news of France. Sends the Princess of Conti's present to the Queen by one of her ladies in waiting rather than to presume to demand audience of her in person;

> but her Majesty, not satisfied herewith, commanded me to attend her, and demanded divers questions of me concerning that princess and the courts in France, saying that she would speak more at large with me at some other time; for which purpose she commanded me to wait on her often, wishing me to advise her what present she might return back again.

To have been a regular queen's pet.

Not many weeks later he returns to his wife and family and passes some time with them.

In 1610 he went to the low countries with Lord Chandos, and participated in the siege of the city of Juliers by the Prince of Orange.[36] During this siege he meets the M. de Balgni above referred to, who said to him in the presence of Sir Edward Cecil and divers English and French captains,[37]

> Monsieur, they say you are one of the bravest of your nation, and I am Balgni; let us see who will do best, whereupon leaping suddenly out of the trenches with his sword drawn, I did in the like manner as suddenly follow him, both in the meanwhile striving who should be formal, which being perceived by those of the bulwark

and cortine opposite to us, three or four hundred shot at least, great and small, were made against us. When M. Balgni finding such a storm of bullets said, Par dieu, il fait bien chaud it is very hot here, I answered briefly, You shall go first, or else I will never go. Hereupon he ran with somewhat speed and somewhat crouching, toward the trenches. I followed after him leisurely and upright and yet came within the trenches before they on the bulwark or cortine could charge again.

He then says modestly, "I could relate divers other things of note concerning myself, during this siege, but do forbear lest I should relish too much of vanity." He then slips up or falls down a trifle on his modesty and continues, "It shall suffice that my passing over the ditch onto the wall *first of all the nations there*, is set down by William Crofts, Master of Arts and Soldier, who had written and printed the History of the Low Countries."[38]

A little later, while staying in the French quarters to escape the interference of the English officers with a duel he was contemplating he met M. Balgni, again, and remembering his bravado,

told him I knew how brave a man he was, and that as he had put me to one trial of daring, when I was last with him in his trenches, I would put him to another; saying, I heard he had a fair mistress, and that the scarf he wore was her gift, and that I would maintain I had a worthier mistress than he, and that I would do as much for her sake as he or any else durst do for his. Balgni hereupon looking merrily upon me, said, "If we shall try who is the abler man to serve his mistress, let both of us get two wenches, and he that doth his business best, let him be the braver man"; and that for his part, he had no mind to fight on that quarrel. I looking hereupon somewhat disdainfully on him, said he spoke more like a *paillard*[39] than a cavalier; to which he answering nothing, I rode my ways.

Reverting at this point to England, he relates how a certain great person, whom he refrains from naming, but who was certainly Queen Anne, procured a copy of the picture of Lord Herbert which a painter by the name of Larkin[40] had made for him, and placed it in her cabinet, without his knowledge, giving occasion to those that saw it after her death of more discourse than he could have wished. And mentioning another instance of his picture having been taken by a friend without his knowledge, he says, with sad resignation, "and indeed I may truly say that taking of my picture was fatal to me, for more reasons than I shall think fit to deliver."

Then follows as I say, his affair with Sir John Ayres, the only real, honest-to-God duel, so far as I gather from his life, that he ever fought, but which was without serious consequences to either participant. It grew out of that same fatal beauty which was so attractive to queens and ladies of least degree. As to the incident upon which it is based, the reader is apt to feel a little skeptical of Lord Herbert's assurances, being inclined to suspect that he protests too much. (See page 128 Lee edition.)[41]

Sir John Ayres tries to accomplish his plot of assassination, and with a party of his friends waylays Lord Herbert, who puts up a gallant defense, and after a long and very active mix-up, Lord Herbert, with Sir John's dagger sticking in his side and his own sword broken a foot from the hilt, wounds Sir John in four places, almost cuts off his left hand, and at the close of the encounter remains master of the place and of his enemy's weapons. A surgeon having cured his wounds in ten days, he still thirsts for Sir John's blood and sends a message to him that he desires to see him in the field with his sword in his hand. Sir John answers that Lord Herbert had whored his wife and that he would kill him with a musket out of a window. The lords of the Privy Council send for Lord Herbert and Sir John Ayres to appear before them, but Lord Herbert absents himself on purpose and sends another challenge to Sir John, which he refuses to accept. The Privy Council orders them both apprehended. Lady Ayres writes a letter to her aunt, which is read in the Privy Council, in which she declares that her husband had lied in saying that Lord Herbert had ever seduced her, and especially in saying that she had confessed that fact, for she had never said any such thing. The Council, which exonerated Lord Herbert, praised him for his almost incredible achievements in the meeting with Sir John Ayres, and branded that gentleman as the most miserable man living. A month later Sir John attempts once more, unsuccessfully to assassinate Lord Herbert which seems to terminate the affair.

After several uneventful years in England, in 1614 he again joins the Prince of Orange, and has various adventures. A cavalier in the Spanish army sends a challenge to the Prince's army, challenging any cavalier to fight a single combat for the sake of his mistress. Sir Herbert feels bound to accept the challenge, but it is withdrawn before any harm is done or he had another opportunity to cover himself with glory.

Leaving the Prince's army, he visits the Spanish army, peace having been made,[42] visits Cologne, Heidelberg, Switzerland, Trent, Venice, where he is received by the English Ambassador.[43] Among other favors shown him he was brought to see a nun in Murrano, who being an admired beauty and singing extremely well was thought to be one of the rarities of the place and of the time. He is so impressed by the harmony both of her beauty and of her voice that he said to her, in her own language, "Die whensoever you will, you neither need to change voice nor face to be an angel." "These words it seemed were fatal [fateful], for going thence to Rome and returning shortly afterwards, I heard she was dead in the meantime."

He goes to Italy, and is invited by the duke, Charles Emanuel,[44] to serve him in the wars upon his own conditions, and stops while on a mission for the duke at the town of Burgoyne, partly to rest, but chiefly he frankly admits, because he had heard that the host's daughter there was the handsomest woman that his informant had ever seen.[45] He called at the inn, and the host's daughter not being within, told her father and mother that he merely wished to see their daughter, that divers persons had told him that she was the handsomest creature that ever they saw. They answered that she had gone to a marriage, that they would send for her, meanwhile giving him a bed which they saw he needed. Waking about two hours afterwards, he found her sitting beside him, waiting until he should open his eyes. He then describes her person and her dress in minute detail, and concludes, in characteristic vein:

> I am too long in describing an host's daughter, howbeit, I thought I might *better* speak of her than of divers other beauties held to be the best and fairest of the kind, whom I have often seen. In conclusion, after about an hour's stay, I departed thence without offering so much as the least incivility; and indeed after so much weariness it was enough that her sight alone did refresh me.

As to whether or not this commendable self restraint was due to his uneasiness is left to inference.

Well, he continues with the army of the low countries, but at the approach of winter military operations being suspended . . . .

↜

SOURCE: Incomplete, untitled, and undated typed text (plus one page in Chesnutt's hand) at the Fisk University Library. The *Year Book for 1922* of the Rowfant Club records Chesnutt having delivered on 12 March 1921 a paper with the title here given this speech. Sir Sidney Lee's introduction to his edition of Baron Herbert's autobiography (see n. 3) is Chesnutt's principal information source.

[1]Edward, First Lord Herbert of Cherbury (1582–1648).

[2]The Cassell's edition appeared in 1887. John Morley is not known to have edited Herbert's autobiography, though he was an influential editor, critic, and biographer who may have been involved in the production of an edition. William Dean Howells edited the *Lives of Lord Herbert of Cherbury and Thomas Ellwood* in 1877.

[3]Sir Sidney Lee (1859–1926) published *The Autobiography of Edward, Lord Herbert of Cherbury* in 1886; Sir Horace Walpole (1717–97) printed *The Life of Edward Lord Herbert of Cherbury, Written by Himself* at his estate, Strawberry Hill, in 1764.

[4]According to Walpole, the loss of the manuscript was detected in 1714.

[5]Lee's "Introduction" describes Swinburne's estimate of Herbert's *Life*.

[6](1593–1633).

[7]Chesnutt's source is the "Introduction" to the Cassell's edition of the *Life*, edited by "H.M." whom Chesnutt assumed to be Morley.

[8]Lloyd George (1863–1945) served as England's prime minister from 1916 to 1922. Chesnutt deleted a reference to "a recent editorial in the Manchester Guardian" as the source for his quotation concerning George.

[9]Lee refers to Walpole's judgment of Herbert, rather than to Herbert himself.

[10]Herbert was a prolific author of philosophical works and is principally known in this respect for *De Veritate* (1624). His rationalistic treatment of religious subjects earned him the sobriquet "Father of Deism."

[11]Appearing in Lee's "Appendix," this table begins with Herbert's third great-grandfather, Sir William Herbert of Raglan Castle, and continues to Herbert's fifth great-grandson, Edward James Herbert, then the third Earl of Powis.

[12]Edward Herbert (?–1593).

[13]Herbert's great-great-grandfather, Sir Richard Herbert of Colebrook (?–1469); his great-grandfather was known as Sir Richard Herbert of Montgomery.

[14]Edward Halle (?–1547), *The Unyonn of the Twoo Noble and Illustre Famelies of Lancastre and Yorke* (1548); Richard Grafton (?–1572), *A Chronicle at Large, to the First Yere of Q. Elizabeth* (1569).

[15]*Amadis of Gaul* (1508) was written by either Joao de Lobieira (?–1367) or Vasco de Loeira (?–1403).

[16]That is, discharges of fluid.

[17]Fortune favors the bold.

[18]Luke 2:42–50.

[19]He married Mary Herbert (1578–1634) on 28 February 1598.

[20]Lee identifies eleven of these works. See *The Life of Edward, First Lord Herbert of Cherbury Written by Himself* (1976), ed. J. M. Shuttleworth, which identifies all of them and corrects Lee's inaccuracies.

[21]A "great horse" was capable of supporting a rider wearing armor. Herbert thus suggests chivalric activities as exercise.

[22]Sir John Danvers (1588–1655), later notorious for having signed the death warrant of Charles I (1600–1649), married Herbert's mother in 1608.

[23]Chesnutt here cites a page number in Lee's edition for a description of Herbert's meeting with Elizabeth I (1533–1603).

[24]This abbreviated quotation from the "Elegy Written in a Country Churchyard" by Thomas Gray (1716–71) is a prompt to comment on the enduring reputation of Elizabeth I: "Ev'n in our ashes live their wonted fires."

[25]Herbert was made a Knight of the Bath on 24 July 1603 by James I (1566–1625).

[26]Despite his professed abhorrence of all forms of venality, Sir Francis Bacon was accused of and admitted to taking bribes in 1621.

[27]Beatrice (1604–?) and Florence (1605–?).

[28](1608–?).

[29]Henri, Duc de Montmorency (1534–1614).

[30]The English ambassador to France at the time was Sir George Carew (?–1612); Casaubon (1559–1614) lived in Paris for a decade, 1600–1610.

[31]Chesnutt apparently commented on the collection of tales entitled *The Heptameron*, assuming that the Margaret to whom he had just drawn attention was its author. It was not composed by Margaret or Marguerite of Valois but by her great-aunt Marguerite d'Angoulême.

[32]Damien de Montluc, Seigneur de Balgni (?–1612), had been a courtier of Henri IV since 1593.

[33]Chesnutt's comment is to the effect that Herbert's prose is sometimes difficult to decipher. "Balgni" is misspelled "Balgny" in the source text.

[34]January 1609.

[35]The Princess of Conti, Louise-Marguerite (1574–1631), the wife of Prince de Conti, François de Bourbon (1558–1614), was, like Marguerite de Valois, known for her illicit love affairs; Anne of Denmark (1574–1619) was the wife of James I.

[36]Grey Brydges, fifth Lord of Chandos (1579?–1621), served as commander of the English forces; "Chandos" is misspelled "Chandois" in the source text. Philip William (1554–1618), son of William the Silent (1533–84), was then Prince of Orange. Combined English and Dutch forces laid siege to Juliers on 17 July 1610; and the city surrendered on 22 August.

[37]Sir Edward Cecil (1572–1638) spent thirty-five years at war in the Low Countries.

[38]William Crosse published a continuation of Edward Grimeston's *Generall Historie of the Netherlands* (1608) in 1627.

[39]A lewd person.

[40]William Larkin (?–1619)

[41]Ayres's only claim to fame seems to have been his duel with Herbert. Chesnutt's page reference may indicate that he may have read to his audience more about the duel than is summarized below.

[42]Sir Henry Wotton (1568–1639) negotiated a cease-fire on 2 November 1614, which both sides ultimately failed to honor. The conflict resumed in 1615.

[43]Sir Dudley Carleton (1573–1632) was ambassador to Venice, Savoy, and Holland.

[44]Charles Emanuel I, Duke of Savoy (1562–1630), was then warring with his brother-in-law, Philip III (1578–1621) of Spain.

[45]The Duke had dispatched Herbert to Languedoc to lead four thousand Huguenot troops to the Piedmont in preparation for action in the Low Countries.

Remarks of Charles W. Chesnutt Before Cleveland Chamber of Commerce Committee on Negro Migration and Its Effects

Speech to the Cleveland Chamber of Commerce,
Cleveland, O., 4 February 1926

Mr. Chairman and Gentlemen of the Committee:

I am the only member of the Chamber,[1] to my knowledge, who is affiliated in the public mind with the group with which this report[2] is mainly concerned, and whenever any question arises touching their rights or interests, with which the Chamber does or might concern itself, they very naturally think of me as their representative in the Chamber, in default of any other, and assume that I might have an influence with the Chamber which I fear I have n't. I was approached the other day by one of them in connection with this report, and I immediately called up our able and affable secretary, and I imagine that at his suggestion this conference is being held.

So I appear here not only on the part of the colored people, to see that they get fair play, but as a member of the Chamber, an unappointed and unofficial and therefore volunteer and unrecognized member of the committee, so to speak, to see, if I can, that the Chamber does the fair thing, as I know it means to do. I should have been glad to serve on this committee or the sub-committee, but no one seems to have thought of it.

From a source which I am not at liberty to disclose, except that it was not from a member of the committee or a member of the Chamber, I have had the privilege of reading a document which purports to be a copy of what one or more members of the committee had in mind as to the manner in which the subject should be dealt with, perhaps the first tentative draft of the committee's report. As I have not been granted the privilege of seeing the report in its present form, and as I have been informed that it has been revised in some important respects, I may say some things which would not apply to the report in its present form. If I do you will pardon my ignorance, as I am shooting in the dark, or at least in the twilight, and if at a man of straw, because I have no better target, as it is obviously difficult for one to consider or discuss intelligently a thing which he has never seen.

With the statistics quoted in this survey I have very little fault to find. They were obviously carefully and honestly compiled from the best available sources, though one is inclined to wonder how some of them were arrived at, especially some of the health percentages given. Until quite recently vital statistics were not carefully or accurately kept even in so advanced a city as Cleveland, and I should not be at all convinced by statistics emanating from the far South, where they might very well ascribe the of late more occasional but still all too frequent lynchings and murders to heart failure or diseases of the respiratory organs.[3]

The criminal statistics are also open to argument.[4] Comparatively few of the major crimes which disfigure the front pages of our newspapers are committed by Negroes, certainly not more than their quota according to the population figures. Nineteen out of twenty of the holdups, payroll and bank robberies are committed by white men. The use of the mails to defraud is almost exclusively a white man's crime—with one conspicuous exception within a comparatively few years. The word "felony" is very comprehensive, ranging from "gun toting" to murder in the first degree. The poisoners, who have assumed prominence in the realm of crime here of late, are almost always white men or white women, with the honors in favor of the ladies. There are all too many colored bootleggers, but the big bootleggers are all white. The fact is that in any variety of crime which calls for a high degree of trained intelligence or business experience, the Negro is a mere piker compared with the white man. The leading newspaper in Columbia, South Carolina, lamented the other day, in an editorial, the fact that there are more white than Negro convicts in the South Carolina Penitentiary—this in a state with a colored majority of the population.[5]

As to the crimes or misdemeanors growing out of the Volstead law[6]—and I use that allocution advisedly—the Negroes are no more guilty than the whites. In fact, if the law should be as strictly construed as some violent prohibitionists maintain, I suspect that only a very small percentage of the members of this Chamber would escape guiltless. Some of the colored practicing lawyers here can tell you better than I how criminal statistics can be misleading; and there are colored doctors, one of whom at least is on the regular staff of Lakeside Hospital and the Western Reserve Medical School,[7] who could throw perhaps special light on questions of diseases and comparative mortality.

But of course the important part of such a report as this, assuming the correctness of its premises, is its argument, and especially its conclusions or recommendations. Such a report, emanating from a body like this, is intended to and does influence public opinion, despite the occasional sneer of some disgruntled individual. And it is important to all concerned and especially to the voiceless party, that its argument should be logical and its recommendations wise and just.

For instance, the argument that Negroes would be better off in the South from various standpoints, coupled with the suggestion that the immigration restrictions[8] be modified, is very illogical when considered in connection with the suggestion that the Negro be given equality of economic opportunity. The law restricting immigration,[9] coupled with the withdrawal of so many workers by the war, offered the Negroes of the United States their first opportunity to break into the great manufacturing industries, with a few exceptions, such as the coal mines and iron mills and the tobacco industry of the South. One would think that the citizens of a country should be given the first opportunity for the job at whatever they are capable of doing well. This I suspect was behind the labor union advocacy of the immigration law,[10] though their idea has always been that the jobs should go first to the white citizen, in which their employers have generally supported them, resorting to the Negro only when there was a shortage of white labor. The great economic opportunities lie in the North, and there has undoubtedly been as large or larger migration of whites from the South as of colored people—and, to the misfortune of the latter, they have brought all their prejudices and antipathies with them, as the Negroes, of course, have brought with them the characteristics they owe to nature, along with the weaknesses and limitations due to conditions over which they have had no control. The report concedes that Negro workers have given satisfaction when they have the opportunity.

The immigration law has good points. I don't object to the slogan, "America for Americans," provided it is applied to all Americans. As to the suggestion in the argument, for the reasons there cited, that the Negroes would be better off in the South,[11] I heard a story the other day bearing on that point. A certain colored man had migrated from southern Georgia to Boston. Another Georgia Negro, who maintained, like your committee, that the Negro would be better off in the South, visited his former friend in Boston. He looked around his friend's house and said, "Well, Joe, how you gittin' 'long up here in the great, free, rich No'th? I doan guess from the looks of things that you are doin' any too well, an' I s'pose you are about ready to go back to Georgia, where your real friends are?" "Well," said Joe, "I may not be doin' extra well in some ways, but I w'll never go back to Georgia. And mo'over I'm gonna write all my friends and relations in Georgia to leave there. And still fu'ther, as soon as I can raise the money, I'm going down there and dig up all my dead and brin' 'em away. Because while Boston is n't heaven, Southe'n Georgia suttenly is hell." So much for that.

That there have been and still are serious difficulties growing out of the northern migration is beyond question, but the suggestion of the committee seems to be that we get rid of the difficulties by getting rid of the Negroes. This, I fear, is an idle dream. They would not go in the first place, most of them, and since they have to live, or quite excusably think they have, you would have to support them either by giving them employment or through the charitable agencies or penal institutions. The white people of the North would have to scrap all their sacred principles of democracy and fair play before the Negroes would give up the far from equal chance they have here, for anything the South is likely to offer them in the near future.

The report is necessarily a contribution to the study of the American race problem, to which I have devoted considerable time and thought. The solution of that problem is still a mooted question. What it will ultimately be none of us know, though most social philosophers are agreed upon what must inevitably be in time, and it does not lie in segregation, either in residence, in schools, in industry, in sport, or in any place where human beings meet.

If the Negroes suffer some hardships in the process of adjustment to Northern conditions, it is no more than all pioneers have done, looking for compensation to the ultimate gain. Our Pilgrim fathers, as the Irish or Jewish orator often says, suffered hardships by sea and land—I will not go into detail—and look at the result, which they have generously shared with all the world!

As to the Negroes, your ancestors—if any of you here had American ancestors—I presume some of you did—though according to the population figures of Cleveland your quota would not be above 25 per cent. or thereabouts—your ancestors brought the Negroes from Africa by force and condemned them to personal slavery; emancipated them, partly as a military expedient, fundamentally for economic reasons, and, I still love to think, in some degree from humanitarian motives, and then abandoned them to peonage or praedial slavery, then you, even you to whom I am speaking, brought them or enticed them to the North and threw them into what the labor reformers call industrial slavery, though so much modified and under such conditions in spite of bad housing and a hostile climate, as to make them prefer it to anything they ever had before. They have been in your hands, and you have made them what they are after God got through with them, and some of them think at times in spite of their very religious propensity, that God is quite through with them—and it is no more than right that you should be fair and even generous towards them, if perhaps at occasional loss and inconvenience to yourselves.

The Constitution, though it has largely been nullified in modern times by judicial decision and executive encroachment, is still the fundamental basis of our liberties. The Declaration of Independence declared that all men were created free and equal. For a long time the North sought, with faltering footsteps, to follow these principles, while the South flagrantly and vociferously denied them. Of late years, or perhaps I might better say within a year or two, the South has been improving, and I fear the North has been slipping. North Carolina, for instance, has recently made very large appropriations for Negro schools, and without any provisions that the education of the pupils should be based upon the preconceived idea that they are unfitted for any human activity—and yet here is your committee indirectly making such a suggestion.

Only yesterday the State of Kentucky called out a thousand state troops, with machine guns and other equipment, to prevent the lynching of a self-confessed black murderer, the crime being a most atrocious one.[12] Compared with the action of the police in Northern cities, this is significant. In the Detroit residence segregation case, in which a murder, as the committee phrases it,[13] took place—I think a better word would be "homicide" or "killing"—since a jury of twelve white men and women with a prosecutor backed by the Ku Klux Klan and egged on by a fevered public opinion, did not find it to be murder. The record of the Detroit police in the case is nothing less than disgraceful. They were present, many of them, at the attack on Dr. Sweet's house, and made no effort whatever to protect his property or his family, but, on the contrary, the evidence showed that they were in perfect sympathy with the mob, and as Clarence Darrow, of counsel of the defense, said, they perjured themselves with a steadfast and perfect unanimity worthy of a better cause, with the exception of one or two "weak sisters," who, under a grilling cross-examination from the most skilful criminal lawyer of our day, admitted at least a part of the truth.[14]

As to segregation in the public schools, which your committee seems inclined to look upon with favor, it has been held more than once by the Supreme Court of Ohio to be unconstitutional.[15] It is easy to sit down and figure out advantages which the white people might derive from it, and to imagine some that would accrue to the colored people. I know that many white persons would like separate schools, and that a few short-sighted Negroes would not object to them, but the thinking colored people of the North abominate the suggestion, and will fight it vigorously, as they always have. It is far better for the colored children to suffer some temporary discomfort and humiliation, than to enjoy a factitious ease purchased at the cost of a sacred principle. Equality at the ballot box and in the schools are two things which the colored people have managed to retain in the North, and they mean to hold on to them like grim death, and I have no slightest doubt that they will find a sufficient number of fair minded white people to help them do it.

The suggestion that secondary education be directed to preparation for some particular kind of employment as one means of dealing with the problem of the Negro in the public schools, is almost superfluous, for it is already in successful operation in our high schools, and is one of the things of which the system is justly proud. The method is something like this. When the pupil presents himself or herself for enrollment the vocational adviser, who is one of the faculty of every high school, looks the pupil over, inquires as to the occupation of his or her parents, the pupil's cultural background, social standing and possible openings for employment or advancement, and then suggests courses of study. As a general rule it works out very well, although a noted educator in a recent address at a teachers' convention in this city, questioned the merit of the system, suggesting that no adolescent under eighteen is competent to select his pursuit in life, nor is any one else competent to choose it for him, and he cited many illustrious examples of men who did not discover the aptitudes which brought them success and fame until after they arrived at maturity.

Now, apply the formula to the colored pupil. He or she is quite likely to be unprepossessing in appearance and none too well dressed. His or her parents are probably working people, perhaps a laundress and a truck driver, with no social background. If they came from the far South there is, as in the case of many children of European peasant immigrants, little cultural background, their parents may not even know how to read and write. The pupil is colored, and has apparently little opportunity for finding a job as clerk or stenographer or saleswoman. The conscientious vocational adviser is likely to suggest domestic science for the girl, or dressmaking or millinery, and manual training of some sort for the boy. But the colored students who graduate from the Cleveland high schools are not too many to supply the demand among their own people for teachers and preachers and doctors and lawyers and dentists and clerks in various business enterprises, and to fill such public appointments as they can secure. They sometimes have to wait a while and are apt to become impatient and discouraged, but most of them in the long run find employment at whatever they have qualified themselves to do. One senior high school in Cleveland has graduated within ten years a colored student who is a musical comedy composer and producer. Several years ago one of his pieces ran at the Metropolitan Theater here for two or three weeks. At the performance I attended I sat beside an official of the Chamber who said it was his third visit—the first to see how he would like it, the next to bring his wife and daughter to share his pleasure, and this last time because he had n't had enough of it. Another boy from this high school is studying for the Catholic priesthood, which he could n't do without some knowledge of Latin. The third is a minor poet, who is commended by the best critics as a true poet, whose verses the best magazines publish and pay for, and for whom Boni and Liveright, the New York publishers, are just now bringing out a volume of poems.[16] Now, had these boys been scientifically directed by some entirely conscientious but narrow-visioned vocational adviser, they might have made indifferent or even good chauffeurs or cooks or automobile mechanics, but the world might have lost something infinitely more worth while. The same error of judgment might be made, of course in the case of a white pupil.

As to the question of residential segregation, which is an acute one all over the country, I confess I am up in the air. Under our laws a man has the right to buy and sell, land or anything else, and to speculate in it if he chooses, though I think it is poor taste and bad judgment, and I deplore any effort to capitalize race prejudice. But the white people have capitalized it against the Negro for so long for their own profit, that it is not surprising that an occasional temerarious member of the latter race should seek to even it up a little here and there.[17] But the problem is made by the white people when they seek to monopolize all the more desirable residence sections of the city. That the proximity in a neighborhood, or some neighborhoods, of a colored householder who may be as well educated and as well to do as his white neighbor, injures the latter's property, is undoubtedly true and deplorable, but it is largely due to a state of mind, and is so because the white people choose to think it so. They need have no more social contact with their colored neighbor than with their black garbage man, and they are very foolish to sacrifice their property for any such reason, and to act like spoiled children, and to hold mass meetings and throw bombs.

There are not many colored men who are able to live in choice neighborhoods, but if one of them can afford it there is no law to prevent it. There are recent decisions of the Supreme Court of the United States which forbid residence segregation by statute or municipal ordinance, and there is a case pending and as yet undetermined in the Supreme Court of the United States involving the right to establish segregation by private contract—in other words, to attempt to do an unconstitutional thing by indirection, and there is every reasonable probability that the court will deny that claimed right.[18] It could not consistently do otherwise. And in passing I am credibly informed that one of the most vociferous protestants on Wade Park Avenue has offered his home for sale to a colored man.[19] How he reconciles this with friendship or loyalty to his neighbors who still live there is one of the many mysteries which derive from this troublesome race problem.

I own a little property myself, and many of those who claim to be injured by this sort of thing are my business patrons and some of them my personal friends of long standing. I sympathize to a certain extent with any man whose property is injured, whether foolishly or not, but it is not the Negro's problem. His problem is and always has been to get a decent place to live in, which the white people, as this report admits, have not to any appreciable extent helped him to do.

The rest of what I have to say can be expressed in a few words. Of course the important part of a report like this, assuming the correctness of its premises, lies partly in its recommendations. In this report these seem to have been taken verbatim from a speech made by the late President Harding at Birmingham, Alabama, in October, 1921. This utterance of the President was not acceptable to the Southern whites, because it asked for the Negro more than the Southern whites were prepared to grant, nor to the colored people, since, while it demanded for them a great deal, it spoiled it by some very offensive suggestions which the Committee have had the good taste to omit from their recommendations.[20]

I am surprised that the committee or the man who had the intelligence to compile this in many respects admirable report, should have found it necessary to adopt for its recommendations, this poorly written quotation from President Harding, who however great and good a man he was, was generally recognized as a writer of notoriously bad English. And yet, after all, I am not so much surprised, for the wisest men have never done any better on this subject. If I am permitted I would like to make a few suggestions as to the recommendations as they appear in the document which I have examined.

"1. Full participation by the Negro in political rights of citizenship." If the words "and civil" were inserted before the word "rights," or, better still, if it were made to read "all the rights of citizenship," it would be beyond criticism.

"2. Equality of economic opportunity for the Negro, based upon the honest capacities and deserts of the individual."

This is about as obscure as anything President Harding ever wrote or said. If the committee understands it, they are smarter than I am. The word "honest" in that connection means nothing—one cannot imagine a dishonest capacity. What President Harding meant, if he knew himself what he meant, was perhaps "proved" or "demonstrated" capacity. Unless the committee desire to confine their recommendations entirely to President Harding's words,[21] I think this recommendation could be materially improved.[22]

"4. [In the draft which I have had, though its number has probably been changed, if it is still in the report, still quoting President Harding.] Natural segregation without narrowing any rights, such as are proceeding in both rural and urban communities in the Southern states."

This is bad grammar to start with, for the President uses a plural verb with a singular noun. That, however, is an immaterial detail—even Homer nods[23] occasionally. But there is no such animal. Natural segregation, whatever that may mean, has never had a chance to proceed in the South. Nothing has been left to nature. The whites have taken the job off nature's hands, and segregated the Negroes in every possible way—with some backdoor reservations—from the cradle to the grave.[24] "Without narrowing any rights" is a mere phrase. There can be no segregation without a narrowing of rights —that is what it is intended for. This paragraph is so obscure that I doubt if President Harding knew what he meant by it himself.

"5. Equal educational opportunities for both blacks and whites, care to be taken by the states and the nation to avoid educating people, whether white or black, into something they are not fitted to do."

I think this recommendation should be made positive instead of negative, and that it had better read something like this: "Equal opportunities for all children, regardless of race, color or religion. Care to be taken by state and nation that every child be given the opportunity to acquire a good general education and then be encouraged to develop any special aptitude which he may be found to have, which will better fit him for service to the community."

If I have made any constructive suggestions which commend themselves to the committee, I hope they will be accepted in the spirit in which they are offered, which is to help make this report worthy of the distinguished source from which it will emanate, and beyond any reasonable criticism.[25]

⌒

SOURCE: Typed text dated 16 February 1926, in the Rowfant Club Papers Collection, Western Reserve Historical Society Library. On 4 February Chesnutt, accompanied by Alexander H. Martin and Harry E. Davis, addressed the Cleveland Chamber of Commerce concerning a committee given the charge of reporting on the condition of African Americans in Cleveland (see "Race Report Due," *Cleveland News*, 5 February 1926, 9). On 16 February he submitted to the Chamber the text of his remarks. A clipping of an article describing the situation is at the Western Reserve Historical Society Library in the Chesnutt Collection. It appears to have been cut from a no longer extant issue of the weekly newspaper *Negro World*. It relates that Chesnutt's remarks were "recently published in *The World*" and quotes a more recent statement by him: "This report . . . had not been approved by the committee, or even considered by them, was made public without authority, and which the officials of the Chamber of Commerce afterwards repudiated [*sic*]. If the Cleveland Chamber of Commerce should ever issue a report of this committee or any other upon the subject of racial conditions in Cleveland I shall be very much surprised if it is not a fair and impartial one."

[1]Chesnutt became a member of the Cleveland Chamber of Commerce in March or April 1912.

[2]Chesnutt refers to a "Report on Negro Migration and Its Effects." He had obtained a copy now in the Chesnutt Papers Collection, Western Reserve Historical Society Library.

[3]The "Report" stated that throughout the country the death rate in 1920 was from 50 to 86 percent higher among African Americans. The death rate of black Clevelanders was cited as approximately twice as high as that of whites.

[4]The "Report" related that one-third of Clevelanders arrested in 1922–25 were African Americans, "seven times as great as the percentage of white arrests." Recently arrived Southern blacks, it was stated, were seen by local court officials as "worse" than Northern ones. The most common offenses were "stealing, bootlegging and illicit relations."

[5]That there were 37 more whites than blacks in the state penitentiary, once regarded as "practically an institution for the incarceration of black criminals," was observed in "Whites in Shameful Majority," Columbia, S.C., *State*, 6 January 1926, 4. Lamented by two state judges quoted was the rise in crime among the white citizens of South Carolina. A similar editorial entitled "What Are We Going to Do about It?" appeared the next day in the Charleston, S.C., *News and Courier*, 7 January 1926, 4.

[6]Named after Minnesotan Andrew J. Volstead (1860–1947), a member of the U.S. House of Representatives (1903–23), this act enforced the provisions of the Eighteenth Amendment, which prohibited the manufacture, sale, and transportation of alcoholic beverages. It took effect on 1 January 1920.

[7]Dr. Charles H. Garvin (1890–1968) joined the staff in 1919.

[8]The "Report" recommended the restriction of immigration by Southern African Americans to Cleveland.

[9]Chesnutt here refers to national restrictions on foreign immigration into the United States.

[10]That is, national law restricting foreign immigration, not immigration of Southern African Americans to the North.

[11]The point mainly implied by the "Report" is that the advantages of emigrating from the South are outweighed by the problems that have attended the "negro invasion of Cleveland." Blacks encounter severe difficulty in buying homes outside the "Negro Quarter"; they are charged disproportionately high rates for rented housing; health problems such as pneumonia and tuberculosis are rampant because of poor housing conditions and the severe weather to which Southern blacks are not well adapted; and educational programs do not meet the needs of the young who fare poorly in both segregated and integrated schools. The explicit statement to which Chesnutt alludes was made by an unnamed local physician. In the section of the "Report" dealing with "Health," he is quoted: "There is no question that the negro is unable to stand the climate in this section of the country (the north) and is far better off where he came from in the South."

[12]On 19 January 1926 an African American named Ed Harris murdered Clarence Bryant as well as his two children and "assaulted" Mrs. Bryant. On 3 February nearly one thousand armed soldiers protected the Lexington courthouse in which Harris

pleaded guilty and was sentenced to be hanged on 5 March ("Doom Negro Slayer in Sixteen Minutes," *New York Times*, 3 February 1926, 1, 8).

[13]The "Report" refers to white reactions to recent attempts to integrate "exclusive residential neighborhoods" in Cleveland and suburban Shaker Heights. It observes that the "desirability of preventing a recurrence of incidents of this nature is emphasized by recent events in Detroit where murder has been committed and strained race relations exist, as a result of similar efforts to establish residence in white districts." The author(s) of the "Report" undoubtedly had in mind Dr. E. A. Bailey, who had recently been forced to vacate a house in Shaker Heights, and Dr. Charles Garvin (see n. 19).

[14]Recent attempts by African Americans to live in a white neighborhood in Detroit had resulted in their being intimidated and their vacating their homes. When the house of Dr. Ossian H. Sweet was surrounded by a mob intent on forcing his removal, the consequence was the death of a white, Leon F. Breiner. The physician, his wife, and nine other African Americans were charged with responsibility for the crime, and they were defended by the nationally prominent attorney Clarence S. Darrow (1857–1938). After deliberating for forty-six hours on 27 November 1925, the jury could not reach a verdict. See "New Trial for Negroes," *New York Times*, 28 November 1925, 17, and "1,500 Hail Attack on Racial Isolation," *New York Times*, 4 January 1926, 7.

[15]The "Report" acknowledges that when Northern cities have experimented with enforced segregation, "the constitutionality" of doing so "has been challenged and the attempts subsequently abandoned." (For a recent Ohio decision against segregation in schools, see "Bars 'Jim Crow' Schools," Cleveland *Gazette*, 25 July 1925, 1; a history of such decisions is provided in "'Jim Crow' Schools Again Barred," Cleveland *Gazette*, 20 February 1926, 1.) Alluding to data indicating that students in black schools have fared better than those in "mixed" schools in that they have developed "pride in their own school and their accomplishments," the "Report" views positively the probable consequences of either encouraging voluntary segregation or redefining school districts according to race.

[16]The musical composer may be Noble Sissle (1889–1975), who also attended Central, where Chesnutt's daughter Helen was employed as a teacher. Working in collaboration with Eubie Blake (1883–1993), he had achieved international renown. *Shuffle Along* (1921), for example, enjoyed an 18-month run on Broadway, followed by a two-year tour. Langston Hughes (1902–67), too, was graduated from Central High School. His first book of poems, *The Weary Blues*, was published in 1926. The aspirant to the Roman Catholic priesthood, who was undoubtedly taught Latin by Helen, is unknown.

[17]The "Report" had pointed out that the exceptionally high rents being charged were exacted, not by whites, but by African-American property owners.

[18]Chesnutt's confidence may have been based upon the N.A.A.C.P.-backed planned assault on segregation in housing described in "1,500 Hail Attack on Racial Isolation" (see n. 14). Therein it was announced that attorneys Louis Marshall (1856–1927) and then-president of the N.A.A.C.P. Moorefield Storey (1845–1929) would argue the "Curtis or Washington" case before the U.S. Supreme Court. Helen Curtis had been prevented from completing the purchase of a house in the District of Columbia by a court injunction issued on the ground of an agreement among owners of property on the street that none would sell to a person of African descent within a period of twenty-one years. The appeal failed. The holding in Corrigan *et al.* v. Buckley, 271 U.S. 323 (1926), was that such covenants do not violate the Fifth, Thirteenth, and Fourteenth Amendments of the U.S. Constitution.

[19]The reference to bomb throwing at the end of the previous paragraph is intended to recall the bombing of African-American Charles Garvin's home on 31 January 1926. The presence of Dr. Garvin at 1114 Wade Park Avenue is the reason that the white man

alluded to here wanted to sell his house in the once all-white neighborhood near the eastern boundary of Cleveland.

[20]On 26 October 1921, Warren G. Harding (1865–1923) addressed a crowd of 100,000 blacks and whites in Birmingham. He advocated full economic and political rights for African Americans, insisting as well that equal educational opportunities should be available to all. What Chesnutt may have found offensive were his pronouncements to the effect that neither social equality nor racial amalgamation can be viewed as tolerable ("Harding Says Negro Must Have Equality in Political Life," *New York Times*, 27 October 1921, 1, 11). In light of Chesnutt's antagonistic attitude toward Black Nationalism (see "Race Prejudice: Its Causes and Its Cures"), it is noteworthy that Marcus Garvey (1887–1940) praised the speech, agreeing that neither social equality nor miscegenation is desired by African Americans ("Negroes Endorse Speech," *New York Times*, 27 October 1921, 11).

[21]The "Report" did not present the entire statement as a quotation of Harding. It read: "2. 'Equality of economic opportunity,' for the negro, based upon 'the honest capacities and deserts of the individual.'"

[22]Chesnutt turns here from the second to the fourth recommendation. The third read thus: "Uncompromising opposition to 'every suggestion of social equality, or amalgamation of the races'; Recognition of a 'fundamental, eternal, inescapable difference' between negroes and whites; and development of the negro as a distinct race along its own lines in accordance with its own peculiar traditions and aspirations."

[23]Alexander Pope, *Essay on Criticism* (1711).

[24]John Dyer (1699–1758), "Gronger Hill" (1726).

[25]Chesnutt closed the source text with a final paragraph, "Respectfully submitted in writing at the request of the committee," and, on the line below, his typed name.

The Negro in Art

How Shall He Be Portrayed?

A Symposium

Essay published in *The Crisis*, November 1926

We have asked the artists of the world these questions:

1. When the artist, black or white, portrays Negro characters is he under any obligations or limitations as to the sort of character he will portray?

2. Can any author be criticized for painting the worst or the best characters of a group?

3. Can publishers be criticized for refusing to handle novels that portray Negroes of education and accomplishment, on the ground that these characters are no different from white folk and therefore not interesting?

4. What are Negroes to do when they are continually painted at their worst and judged by the public as they are painted?

5. Does the situation of the educated Negro in America with its pathos, humiliation and tragedy call for artistic treatment at least as sincere and sympathetic as *Porgy* received?[1]

6. Is not the continual portrayal of the sordid, foolish and criminal among Negroes convincing the world that this and this alone is really and essentially Negroid, and preventing white artists from knowing any other types and preventing black artists from daring to paint them?

7. Is there not a real danger that young colored writers will be tempted to follow the popular trend in portraying Negro character in the underworld rather than seeking to paint the truth about themselves and their own social class?

Here are some answers. More will follow:

————

1. The realm of art is almost the only territory in which the mind is free, and of all the arts that of creative fiction is the freest. Painting, sculpture, music, poetry, the stage, are all more or less hampered by convention—even jazz has been tamed and harnessed, and there are rules for writing free verse. The man with the pen in the field of fiction is the only free lance, with the whole world to tilt at. Within the very wide limits of the present day conception of decency, he can write what he pleases. I see no possible reason why a colored writer should not have the same freedom. We want no color line in literature.

2. It depends on how and what he writes about them. A true picture of life would include the good, the bad and the indifferent. Most people, of whatever group, belong to the third class, and are therefore not interesting subjects of fiction.[2] A writer who made all Negroes bad and all white people good, or *vice versa*, would not be a true artist, and could justly be criticised.

3. To the publisher, the one indispensable requisite for a novel is that it should sell, and to sell, it must be interesting. No publisher wants to bring out and no reader cares to read a dull book. To be interesting, a character in a novel must have personality.[3] It is perhaps unfortunate that so few of the many Negro or Negroid characters in current novels are admirable types; but they are interesting, and it is the privilege and the opportunity of the colored writer to make characters of a different sort equally interesting. Education and accomplishment do not of themselves necessarily make people interesting—we all know dull people who are highly cultured. The difficulty of finding a publisher for books by Negro authors has largely disappeared—publishers are seeking such books. Whether the demand for them shall prove to be more than a mere passing fad will depend upon the quality of the product.

4. Well, what can they do except to protest, and to paint a better type of Negro?[4]

5. The Negro race and its mixtures are scattered over most of the earth's surface, and come in contact with men of other races in countless ways. All these con-

tacts, with their resultant reactions, are potential themes of fiction, and the writer
of genius ought to be able, with this wealth of material, to find or to create interesting types. If there are no super-Negroes, make some, as Mr. Cable did in his
Bras Coupé.[5] Some of the men and women who have had the greatest influence on
civilization have been purely creatures of the imagination. It might not be a bad
idea to create a few white men who not only think they are, but who really are entirely unprejudiced in their dealings with colored folk[6]—it is the highest privilege
of art to depict the ideal. There are plenty of Negro and Negroid types which a real
artist could make interesting to the general reader without making all the men
archangels, or scoundrels, or weaklings, or all the women unchaste. The writer, of
whatever color, with the eye to see, the heart to feel and the pen to record the real
romance, the worthy ambition, the broad humanity, which exist among colored
people of every class, in spite of their handicaps, will find a hearing and reap his
reward.

6. I do not think so. People who read books read the newspapers, and cannot
possibly conceive that crime is peculiarly Negroid. In fact, in the matter of serious
crime the Negro is a mere piker compared with the white man. In South Carolina,
where the Negroes out number the whites, the penitentiary has more white than
colored inmates.[7] Of course the propagandist, of whatever integumentary pig-
ment, will, of purpose or unconsciously, distort the facts.[8] My most popular novel
was distorted and mangled by a colored moving picture producer to make it appeal to Negro race prejudice.[9]

7. I think there is little danger of young colored writers writing too much
about Negro characters in the underworld, so long as they do it well. Some successful authors have specialized in crook stories, and some crooks are mighty interesting people. The colored writer of fiction should study life in all its aspects. He
should not worry about his social class. Indeed, it is doubtful whether the general
reading public can be interested today in a long serious novel based upon the social
struggles of colored people. Good work has been done along this line with the
short story, but colored society is still too inchoate to have developed the fine
shades and nuances of the more sophisticated society with which the ordinary
novel of manner deals. Pride of caste is hardly convincing in a people where the
same family, in the same generation, may produce a bishop and a butler,[10] a lawyer
and a lackey, not as an accident or a rarity but almost as a matter of course.[11] On
the other hand it can be argued that at the hand of a master these sharp contrasts
could be made highly dramatic. But there is no formula for these things, and the
discerning writer will make his own rules.[12]

The prevailing weakness of Negro writings, from the viewpoint of art, is that
they are too subjective.[13] The colored writer, generally speaking, has not yet passed
the point of thinking of himself first as a Negro, burdened with the responsibility
of defending and uplifting his race. Such a frame of mind, however praiseworthy
from a moral standpoint, is bad for art. Tell your story, and if it is on a vital subject, well told, with an outcome that commends itself to right-thinking people, it

will, if interesting, be an effective brief for whatever cause it incidentally may postulate.

Why let Octavus Roy Cohen or Hugh Wiley have a monopoly of the humorous side of Negro life?[14] White artists caricatured the Negro on the stage until Ernest Hogan and Bert Williams discovered that colored men could bring out the Negro's more amusing characteristics in a better and more interesting way.[15]

Why does not some colored writer build a story around a Negro oil millionaire, and the difficulty he or she has in keeping any of his or her money?[16] A Pullman porter who performs wonderful feats in the detection of crime has great possibilities.[17] The Negro visionary who would change the world over night and bridge the gap between races in a decade would make an effective character in fiction.[18] But the really epical race novel, in which love and hatred, high endeavor, success and failure,[19] sheer comedy and stark tragedy are mingled,[20] is yet to be written, and let us hope that a man of Negro blood may write it.

⌒

SOURCE: "The Negro in Art, How Shall He Be Portrayed?: A Symposium," *The Crisis*, 33 (November 1926), 28–29. The published essay is emended in light of three typed documents at the Fisk University Library: a draft revised by hand; the finished version derived from that draft; and an incomplete copy of the latter. The questions with which "The Negro in Art" begins were posed by *The Crisis* to the contributors to the issue-by-issue symposium it was conducting. Chesnutt's responses begin below the single rule; and they were followed by his full name. The editors wish to thank the Crisis Publishing Co., Inc., publishers of the magazine of the National Association for the Advancement of Colored People, for authorizing the use of "The Negro in Art."

[1]Edwin DuBose Heyward (1885–1940), novelist and playwright, sympathetically depicted the African Americans of Charleston's now-famous tourist attraction Catfish Row in his novel, *Porgy* (1925).

[2]The sentence, "Next to being free, art should be true to life," follows here in the typed text.

[3]Here, in the typed text, appears "Mere education and accomplishment are not enough. The writer must have a story. There are plenty of Negro or Negroid characters in current novels."

[4]In the typed text, Chesnutt combined his responses to questions four and five in a single answer numbered "4–5."

[5]Not present in the typed text is "as . . . *Coupé*." Chesnutt refers by name to the heroic slave in *The Grandissimes*.

[6]The beginning of a new sentence, "It might strain the reader's imagination, but," appears here in the typed text.

[7]"A real artist will not write about a type which he has not studied, and a real artist will feel free to dare anything" appears here in the typed text.

[8]In the typed text, this sentence ends with "for which there is no remedy but the truth."

[9]This sentence does not appear in the typed text. The Micheaux Film Corporation released a silent film version (black and white, 35 mm, 9 reels) of Chesnutt's *The House Behind the Cedars*; when Chesnutt viewed it is not known, but in a 29 January 1924 letter to Oscar Micheaux (at the Western Reserve Historical Society Library) Chesnutt referred to it as having been made and to its being shown "before very long." Unlike the novel, the film concludes happily with the marriage of Rena Walden and Frank Fowler.

[10]The source text substitutes "butler" for "bootblack."

[11]Appearing here in the typed text is "The King Cophetua and the beggar maid motive is hardly possible in such a society." See "The Negro in Books," n. 33.

[12]The final two sentences of this paragraph do not appear in the typed text.

[13]The words "too subjective" in the source text replaced "all conscious or unconscious propaganda."

[14]South Carolina novelist Octavus Roy Cohen (1891–1959) stereotypically treated African Americans in humorous tales featuring Florian Slappey, a detective from Alabama. See, for example, *Polished Ebony* (1919) and *Assorted Chocolates* (1920). Ohioan Hugh Wiley (1884–69) featured black characters in comical prose fictions.

[15]This paragraph is not present in the typed text.

[16]Here the typed text reads "an Oklahoma Negro oil millionaire, man or woman." The sentence was both revised and extended in the source text.

[17]The concluding words of this sentence, "has great possibilities," replace the phrase "would make a good character" in the typed text.

[18]The words "decade would make an effective character in fiction" replace the ending of the sentence in the typed text, "lifetime has been used in a small way."

[19]Not present in the typed text is "love and hatred, high endeavor, success and failure."

[20]The phrase "as in some of Shakespeare's plays" follows here in the typed text.

Address Before Ohio State Night School

Speech dated February 1928

When I was asked by our young friend Mr. Ghean to talk to you on the race problem I hesitated. It has been a long time since I last spoke in public, and I was never an eloquent speaker, but the subject is so vital to all of us, and there is so much ignorance and misinformation and wicked propaganda upon it that I decided that I might perhaps help some young person to get the right slant upon the subject. There is more than one race problem in the world—in Asia, Africa, in Europe, in other parts of America.

There is practically but one race problem in the United States. The Jews have a Jewish problem, in which race plays a distinct part, though superficially it is a matter of religion and any social segregation of Jews is a matter of their own choice or one of which the solution is in their own hands. There is some race friction in California and the Far West over the Mongolian question, and there is a recent curious recrudescence, as I shall indicate later, of the social side of the Indian question.

But the great race problem of the United States is the Negro Problem. In essence it is a very simple problem. By the inspired doctrine of the Rights of Man, developed by the French philosophers (Rousseau *et al.*) and promulgated by the Constitutional Assembly of 1789, which Thomas Jefferson wrote into the Declaration of Independence, all men are entitled to certain inalienable rights by virtue of their humanity.[1] By the Constitution equality of rights was vested in all citizens. Negroes were not citizens, and at that time there were many who scarcely conceded that they were men. I read in a newspaper not long since an Associated Press dispatch from Mississippi which suggested that this idea may still persist. It reported a railroad accident in that state in which, to quote the language of the item: "Three *men* and four Negroes" were killed.

* * *

mixed—most human conduct is dictated by mixed motives—but however much they may have galled the pride of the conquered rebels, however great the difficulty of their enforcement, you will find no colored man who does not regard them as just and wise and as the most important part of the Constitution.[2] They were intended, in principle, to give the Negro equality before the law, which in its essence means equality everywhere, because there is only one kind of equality and that is—equality. As soon as we begin to condition equality, to limit or confine it, it ceases to be equality.

The difficulty with the amendments lay and still lies in their enforcement. Those of you who have read McMasters' *History of the United States* will have learned that it was a long time before all the white people attained political equality.[3] The Bill of Rights abolished imprisonment for debt[4] but it persisted for a long time and is still practiced, and any lawyer will tell you. The difficulty of enforcing the amendments was comparable with the difficulty of enforcing the 18th Amendment,[5] with this difference; that after the election of Hayes as President the Republican party abandoned the Negro in the South,[6] while the time has not yet come when the Anti-Saloon League will abandon the Volstead law, the effort to enforce which has become more or less of an expensive and ghastly and sometimes almost obscene joke.

The Negro demands and must for his very existence demand equality. A great many white people, whose number seems to have been increasing, refuse to concede it to him. It is not a problem to be settled by compromise. The Negro could not safely yield any vital claim. The only possible settlement must be made by the white people. The Negro can do many things to make the solution easier, but in the end it is the white man's and not the Negro's problem.

Now, what is this equality that the colored people demand and cannot do without? Of course it does not imply and is not dependent upon parity of mental endowment, nor upon equal attainment. These things, other things being equal, cannot be conferred by law or by social custom. It means simply equality of opportunity—or as we phrase it, a white man's chance—in politics, in industry, in education, in the public service, in the social and professional activities of the community—in fact an equal opportunity everywhere, not in the dim and distant and uncertain future when the race has performed the impossible feat of lifting itself by its boot-straps to the highest level of the white race, but now, while they are living and can make some use of that freedom of opportunity. (Worth nothing to a dead man.)

Now, I am going to consider briefly some respects in which this denial of equality hampers the progress and poisons the life of the Negro. I use the word Negro purely in the popular sense. It is not, as I shall show later, a good term to describe ethnologically or biologically the mixed people so designated. The white people saddled it on them and most of them have accepted it and are striving earnestly to dignify, if not to glorify it, though there are many who resent it and prefer to be called colored people whenever it is necessary to refer to their racial origin.

By the denial of the ballot one-tenth of the population of the United States is deprived of any direct representation in the Congress of the United States, which makes our national laws and regulates our relations with foreign countries. Representation in the House of Representatives is based upon population. Before the adoption of the 14th Amendment the population of the slave states for this purpose was figured upon the entire white population, plus three-fifths of the colored population. Under the present Constitution the whole of the colored population is counted in the basis, thereby providing for many more congressmen from the Southern States. Any one who reads the newspapers knows that these congressmen are unfriendly to the Negro. At the present moment perhaps the two most conspicuous Democratic members in the House, Cole Blease of South Carolina and Mr. Heflin of Alabama,[7] direct a large part of their energies to fulminating and projecting legislation against the Negro. (Separate car law D.C.) Instead of representing their constituents, they misrepresent them. Instead of working in their interest, they are working decidedly against them.

Furthermore, there is not to my knowledge a single colored representative in any Southern legislature. So far as the daily life of the people is concerned, the legislature[8] is more important even than Congress. It regulates domestic relations, crime and punishment, the administration of estates, marriage and divorce, corporations and partnerships—in fact, all the more intimate relations existing between men and women. It is easy to see and the well known facts demonstrate that this lack of representation results in colored people being discriminated against all along the line. They are Jim Crow-ed from the cradle to the grave. They are segregated in all public places, in schools, in hotels, in railroad trains, restaurants, public parks, public libraries and everywhere else. They are taxed to pay for these things, they are subjected to the very thing which caused the revolt of the American colonies from Great Britain—taxation without representation.

Education

In the matter of education, the schools for white and colored are always separate and the colored schools and school houses are always inferior. There are large Southern cities in which there is no public school for colored children above the eighth grade, and in the smaller towns and rural districts the public school for colored children is more or less of a joke. The recent incident of which you have all read in the newspapers, which involves another race question, was that of Martha Lum, nine years old, the daughter of an American citizen of Chinese descent—I imagine he was naturalized before the present strict exclusion law was adopted[9]— who attended the Rosedale Consolidated School in Mississippi until it occurred to somebody that her Mongolian features stood in the way of her being classed as white, and that since the constitution of that state provides separate schools for "children of the white and colored races" Martha would have to go to a colored school. The case was appealed to the Supreme Court of the United States, which confirmed the right of the state to separate children in any way it may desire in its public schools, and denied that a separation made on racial lines is in conflict with the 14th Amendment.[10]

Now, let us see what this means to Martha and incidentally what it means to all the other colored children in Mississippi. By authentic figures, in Bolivar County where Martha's suit was brought, the per capita expenditure for public schools in 1925 was $44.33, for white children; for colored children, $2.26. In the city of Cleveland the per capita expenditure for the education of children runs from $75.00 in the grade schools to over a hundred in the high schools. Moreover there is not in the whole state of Mississippi a consolidated rural school for Negroes which Martha could attend. As things are, Martha has by court decision effectively been denied an education. In some Southern towns and counties there are no colored schools whatever, and in many of them the per capita expenditure is even less. It is true that of late certain states, North Carolina especially, has been seeking to correct this condition, and has at present a large and expensive program for Negro schools.

What effect has this denial of equality upon the Negro in industry? He is not popular in the labor unions, many of them will not admit him to membership, and the most powerful group of labor unions in the country, the four big railroad brotherhoods, by their constitutions deny him membership.[11] Next to the public service the railroad industry is the largest organized industry in the country. The railroads are semi-public organizations, and yet on the thousands of miles of railroads in the United States there is no Negro locomotive engineer, no Negro fireman—except perhaps on one or two small Southern railroads—no colored conductor—the only railroad employment, including the Pullman service, open to colored people, is that of car washers, section men, porters and maids on Pullman cars.

Now, what is the reason given by the Negrophobes for this denial of equality? The ancient Romans, when they conquered a people and sacked a city, always had a good moral reason for it. Their English and American successors in conquest, when they steal a country (specify) or exploit a weaker people, are always able to justify it to their own satisfaction.

The reason given not long ago for denying the Negro equality was the fear of Negro domination. This from a people vastly in the majority everywhere except in perhaps two Southern States.[12] The argument was that Negroes should n't vote, because the white vote might conceivably be equally divided and one Negro vote would determine the election, and that would be Negro domination.

We were told and are still told about the awful results of Reconstruction, how the white people suffered from Negro misrule. The Negroes never ruled the South. Their votes were exploited by the carpetbaggers,[13] who were white men, just as the white slaveholders had exploited their labor a short time before. Except perhaps some small change, so to speak, no colored man got rich out of Reconstruction. And the injury to the white people was largely to their feelings. They had no indemnities to pay. None of them were executed as traitors. They suffered less than any other rebels in history. We have regarded them as erring brothers and have almost apologized to them for having fought them.

But the excuse has now been changed. All these things are justified, it is solemnly declared, by the imperative necessity of preserving the purity of the white race. If the colored people are treated as equals, the result will be intermarriage or miscegenation, deterioration, degeneration, evidenced by vice, by crime, by feeblemindedness and a long train of such calamities. The broad proposition is thus laid down.

Laying aside for a moment the purity of the white race, let us consider this generally accepted statement. If miscegenation results in these things it ought to be perfectly apparent in the colored race. They are a mixed race. It would be impossible to preserve their purity even if they could convince themselves or the white people could convince them that it was a desirable thing, the mischief is already done. Whenever I go into a congregation of colored people my first impression is how black they are. And at the end of the meeting, supposing it lasts an hour or an hour an a half, I am thinking how white they are. You cannot always tell from a man's complexion whether he has any white blood, and by the same rule, as I shall show, it is not always certain that a man with a white face has no colored blood.

Criminality

One of the forms of degeneration with which the Negro and his cousins are charged is criminality. A casual study of the crime records of the United States for the last few years will demonstrate, I think, beyond the possibility of a doubt, that the Negro is a mere piker compared with the white men in the matter of crime. Crap shooting, petty larceny, drug addiction, cutting and occasionally shooting are his most frequent crimes. But the really serious offenses, such as fraud, the wholesale robbery of widows and orphans through fake mortgage companies, bank robberies, hold-ups, atrocious and sadistic murders, are mainly committed by white people. A Negro may kill his wife in a fit of jealous rage, but after he has killed her, he does not bash her head in with a hammer. One might occasionally violate a woman, but after he has committed the crime, he does not dismember or mutilate her body.

The Governor of South Carolina some months ago, wrote a letter to the Charleston *News and Courier* in which he complained because the state penitentiary had more white prisoners than colored. He said very truly that it was a disgrace to the white race. This was in a state, too, where until within a very few years, if not now, the colored population was largely in excess of the white. I imagine that no colored man will find any fault with the governor of South Carolina's statistics, they are quite willing that the white people should excel them in the matter of serious crimes.[14] In spite of all their disabilities, the colored people of the United States have made a great record since the emancipation of the slaves. President Coolidge[15] in his message to Congress the other day commented upon the fact that they had made greater progress than any other group of people in the same period. They have many thousands of graduates from good colleges, including Harvard and Yale, and there are many masters of arts from Columbia and Chicago Universities. (Phi Beta Kappa keys.) They are largely represented in the learned professions, by which I mean law and medicine. Neither among white people nor colored people is it essential that a man be learned in order to be a preacher.

They have made very promising beginnings in the matter of business, even big business. There have been three classed as millionaires, and there are several others on the way, and the aggregate of their joint possessions is represented by a very large figure. (Insurance Co's, Toilet preparations, real estate.)[16]

They have many teachers both in the colored schools and the mixed schools. A generation ago the Negro was silent, so to speak, he had not found his voice. There were not more than two or possibly three men among them who had any standing in literary circles. The Negro is no longer silent, in fact he is very vocal, vociferous indeed, and sometimes strident if not blatant. (Schuyler in *Mercury*.)[17] He has a large newspaper press. Articles written by colored men are not only published by the best magazines but are solicited. Publishers not only accept books written by Negroes, when they meet the standards, but solicit them, and offer prizes for them.

I might enumerate many other activities in which colored people have distinguished themselves—notably music and the stage.

Now, these are not signs of degeneration. And yet most of the outstanding figures in the colored race happen to be of mixed blood. I say *happen*, because there are many extremely capable black men. Perhaps in spite of the assumption that one drop of black blood makes the whole man black, the mulattoes have had better opportunities. Frederick Douglass, Booker T. Washington, Senator Blanche K. Bruce,[18] and other prominent colored men in the last generation were mulattoes pure and simple, they were the children of one white parent and one colored, and by the current superstition with regard to race admixture they ought to have been degenerates instead of very able and distinguished gentlemen.

These are not signs of degeneracy. The prevailing doctrine is that the child of mixed blood inherits the worst qualities of both parents and none of the good. Why may they not combine the best qualities of both?

Alexander Pushkin, the Russian Shakespeare, whose centenary was celebrated just before the Great War broke out, was a colored man. (Specify. Greatest Russian poet, was killed in a duel in his 30s like our own Alexander Hamilton who, by the way, it was suggested had Negro blood in his veins.)[19]

The famous Dumas family of France, three generations of distinguished men, were of white and Negro origin. (Specify.)

General Alfred Dodds was for many years, and until not long prior to the Great War, the ranking general of the French Army. He was of mixed blood, born in Guadeloupe, one of the French West Indies.

One of the editors of the London *Times* not long ago was a man of color.[20] I might stretch out this list indefinitely, if I had time to check it over.

If miscegenation always produced such results as this, it would be a splendid thing for the world. Of course it does n't, but there are enough of these instances to explode the lie that the mixture of races is necessarily fraught with disastrous results. (Lord Bryce.) Brazil. Barbadian Ch. J.[21]

And, by the way, who is responsible for this mixture of races? Not the colored people. They have been the passive factor. Ever since white men began to wander over the face of the earth in search of adventure and of wealth, they have industriously mixed their blood with that of darker races. Every treaty port, every city along the vast littoral of Asia, of Africa, of South America, and the islands of the sea is filled with mulattoes and half-castes—I use the term "filled" in the popular sense, meaning that there are a great many of them.

I read the other day that there is a special charity home in Manila, P.I. for American mestizos, i.e., the natural born children of American soldiers. And in Haiti, where the population is almost solidly black, the small remaining number of mulattoes has been greatly increased since the American occupation. (Our marines have to be amused.)

The white people of the South have of late been vastly exercised over this question and have passed drastic laws against racial intermarriage. In Virginia a law recently enacted forbids marriage between white people and persons of any colored blood whatever, excepting only those who can trace their descent to an admixture of Indian blood before the Revolutionary War.[22] (Disastrous result.)

Every winter in some one or more Northern States' legislature somebody introduces such a bill which so far, in spite of the KKK which always sponsors it they have all been defeated. But this it seems to me is merely locking the stable door after the horse is stolen. These frantic efforts to preserve the purity of the white race are a little late. The damage has to a large extent already been done. In every state of the South except Georgia, up to the time of the Civil War and until very recently, there were laws prescribing the degree of Negro blood which a white man might have and still be white, generally based upon the number of crosses. (Specify.) These laws would not have been passed had there not been a widespread mixture of the races.

Now, in the case of Virginia the proponents of this law stated that there were in that state already from fifteen to twenty thousand near-whites who were either passing or might easily pass for real whites. I made a slight calculation, based on the census population of Virginia, and found that by these figures already one in 100 of the white people of Virginia is admittedly of mixed blood. (Must be many more, given reason.)

In Louisiana in the old regime racial relations were very liberal. (Specify. Cable etc.)[23] When a few years ago there was an anti-intermarriage law passed, a certain sheriff in one of the parishes decided to look through the old marriage records and find out how many white people were colored. The story goes that shortly after this search was made the building was burned down and all the records with it.[24]

No, the Negroid people of the United States cannot, consistently with their self-respect, be satisfied with anything less than equality and all that the word implies, the kind of equality in which the French believe, and which is embodied in the motto carved on the front of every government building in France, "*Liberté, Egalité, Fraternité*"—Liberty, Equality Fraternity, these three, but the greatest of these is equality. As I have shown, liberty is impossible without equality. And certainly fraternity, brotherhood, friendship, is impossible without equality. How can I call a man friend or have any really friendly feeling toward him, who thinks himself too good to eat with me, to drink with me, to sit with me, to ride with me, to go to school with me, to worship God with me, or, exercise with me any activities of organized society?

I told my young friend that I would be willing to answer questions. I suspected that one of them would be, do I believe in the intermarriage of the races? I think the question is beside the subject. Personally I believe that marriages are happier and more successful where people marry their own type. But experience has demonstrated that the races will mix, and if they are to continue to mix I believe it ought to be in a lawful way. Though lawful in all but a few of the Northern States, there is very little intermarriage at present in the United States.[25] The social penalties are so great that none but the brave or the reckless would dare it. To pass laws preventing it, however, is to deny equality and to relieve from any legal responsibility the white participant in such an admixture. (Elaborate. Recent case in Ga., col. girl kills a white lover.)

In spite of their handicaps, as I say, the colored people are doing very well. They have proved their essential equality in the field of intellect, the scientists acknowledge it. They have by their own efforts largely supplied the things which law and custom have deprived them of. They have their own churches, their own societies of all kinds, and, given the start they have, the only thing which can keep them down is the prejudice of white men. If you young people have any belief in democracy, if you believe that caste, based on race or color or wealth is not a good thing for a free people, then you will cast your influence and lend your efforts toward a more liberal and tolerant policy on the part of the American people toward this important element of our population.

⌁

SOURCE: Incomplete typed text at the Fisk University Library. Chesnutt dated the source text February 1928, not specifying the day of the month. The first paragraph indicates that the topic of the speech is the race problem, but his description of his address on the first page is here employed as the title.

[1] On 26 August 1789, France's National Assembly adopted *The Declaration of the Rights of Man and of the Citizen*, which ultimately became the preamble to the French constitution, itself adopted on 3 September 1791. Though Chesnutt seems to contend here that Jefferson incorporated material from the *Declaration* into the Declaration of Independence in 1776—a patent impossibility—he more likely meant to imply that both Jefferson and France's legislature drew upon identical sources in formulating their respective statements.

[2] In the portion of the text now lacking, Chesnutt apparently described the Thirteenth, Fourteenth, and Fifteenth Amendments of the U.S. Constitution.

[3] John Bach McMaster (1852–1932), *A History of the People of the United States from the Revolution to the Civil War* (1883).

[4] The Seventh Amendment, ratified as part of the Bill of Rights on 15 December 1791.

[5] The prohibition amendment, which the Volstead Act (referred to below) was unsuccessfully designed to enforce.

[6] Hayes was elected in 1876 and held office as the reversal of Reconstruction era policy began.

[7] Coleman L. Blease (1868–1942) was not a member of the House but served a term as Senator (1925–31). James T. Heflin (1869–1951) was a representative from Alabama in the House (1904–20) and a Senator (1920–31).

[8] That is, state legislatures.

[9] In 1924, Congress passed the Johnson Act limiting immigration of the foreign-born to 2 percent of those of the same nationality already living in the United States and prohibiting entirely the immigration of Japanese.

[10] Though born in Bolivar County, Martha was told she could not attend a white school there. On 28 October 1924, her father filed suit against the trustees of the Rosedale Consolidated High School, contending that neither was she "colored" nor had the county provided a separate school for Chinese children. The Mississippi Circuit Court for the First Judicial District of Bolivar County decided on behalf of the plaintiff, but the state's Supreme Court sided with the defendant, holding: "It has been at all times the policy of the lawmakers of Mississippi to preserve the white schools for members of the Caucasian race alone" (Rice *et al.* v. Gong Lum *et al. Mississippi Reports*, 139 [1925], 763). Lum unsuccessfully appealed to the U.S. Supreme Court, in Gong Lum v. Rice, 275 US 78 (1927).

[11] See "Address to the Medina Coterie," n. 22.

[12] South Carolina and Mississippi.

[13] See "The Future of the Negro" for an earlier criticism of the kind.

[14] A letter of the kind addressed to this newspaper has not been located. See, however, "Remarks of Charles W. Chesnutt," n. 5.

[15] J. Calvin Coolidge (1872–1933) served as president of the United States in 1923–29.

[16] See "Advice for Businessmen," in which Chesnutt discusses the success of African Americans in these three areas of business.

[17] George S. Schuyler (1895–1977) was a correspondent for the *Pittsburgh Courier* who would later become business manager of *The Crisis* (1937–44). His "Our White Folks" had recently appeared in *American Mercury*, 121 (December 1927), 385–92.

[18] Blanche K. Bruce (1841–98) was a runaway slave who became a teacher, financially successful planter, adroit politician, and the second African-American Mississippian to serve in the U.S. Senate (1875–81). He won election as a Republican only a year

before Democrats assumed control of state politics, and was thus "swept" out of office as the effects of the Reconstruction were being effaced; but he subsequently enjoyed several federal appointments in the District of Columbia.

[19]The claim that Alexander Hamilton (1755–1804), like the Russian Pushkin, was of biracial origin cannot be substantiated. His father was the fourth son of a lesser Scottish landowner, while his mother was the child of French Huguenot parents who had moved to Nevis in the West Indies from France.

[20]Sir William Conrad Reeves. See "The Future American: A Stream of Dark Blood in the Veins of the Southern Whites," n. 7.

[21]Chesnutt refers to James Bryce and the subject of miscegenation in Brazil; Reeves (see n. 20) became a Chief Justice in Barbados. See "A Solution for the Race Problem," in which Chesnutt made the points he apparently intended to address again here.

[22]This law was passed in 1924.

[23]George Washington Cable described offspring of inter-racial unions in both his fictional and his nonfictional writings.

[24]This and the previous paragraph were rendered by Chesnutt from an incomplete and untitled holograph draft of a speech or essay on the difficulties faced by African Americans and the reasons they would want to pass for white if they could. It is filed under the title "[Crossing the Color Line]" at the Fisk University Library.

[25]At the time Chesnutt gave this speech, only nineteen states did not prohibit marriage between whites and African Americans.

Abraham Lincoln and Frederick Douglass

Speech to the John Harlan Law Club, Cleveland, O., 14 February 1928

Mr. President, members of the Harlan Club, ladies and gentlemen:

It is eminently fitting that this group should celebrate the memory of Abraham Lincoln, for without Abraham Lincoln, unless some other man with equal ability had performed his task, such a group as this would not have been possible.

The pulpits, the forums, the newspapers and the air have been full of eulogies of Lincoln for the past week. They have stressed his patience under harsh and unmerited criticism, his far-seeing statesmanship, his kindliness, his sense of humor, his services in saving the Union. He has grown with the passing of the years to heroic stature. But whatever he did and however he did it, the greatest thing that he did was to emancipate the slaves, and therefore I am going to speak of him as Lincoln the Emancipator. There are those who insist, and some of them are cynics of our own, that Lincoln issued the Emancipation Proclamation solely as a war measure, and with no particular regard for the humanitarian side of the question. That is no more true than that the Civil War was fought on the issue of States' Rights alone, as Southern historians would have the rising generation believe.

Horace Greeley characterized the Civil War correctly as the war to perpetuate slavery, from the Southern standpoint, and it might have been equally well described from the Northern standpoint as the war to abolish slavery. We are told that the question was purely an economic one, a battle between free and slave labor. I am quite sure that Wendell Phillips, William Lloyd Garrison, John Brown, Parker Pillsbury,[1] Frederick Douglass and the rest of the Abolitionists whose labors culminated in the Civil War, were vastly more concerned about the inhumanity of the institution than about the competition of free and slave labor. I am quite sure that Julia Ward Howe's famous "Battle Hymn of the Republic,"[2] the trumpet strains of which I never hear without emotion, was not inspired by any abstract economic principle. You recall those golden words of the closing stanza:

> In the beauty of the lilies Christ was born across the sea,
> In the glory of a vision that transfigured you and me,
> As he died to make men holy, let us die to make men free,
> Our God is marching on.

I first heard that hymn sung when it meant something, for I was born here in Cleveland, a hot bed of patriotic Unionism, just four years before the breaking out of the Civil War, and lived as a small child through that fearful conflict, in which my father participated.[3] And when the War came to its righteous end, thousands, nay, millions of good people thanked God as much for the abolition of slavery as for the preservation of the Union.

I think the briefest study of the life and utterances of Abraham Lincoln will demonstrate, that, as Professor Earle, of Ohio State University has stated and proved in a recent still unpublished book from which the newspapers have quoted, Lincoln believed in the equality of man, and, as to any man of such belief, that slavery was abhorrent to all his instincts. It is the text of his Gettysburg Address.[4] One of his most quoted statements was, quoting from the Scripture: "A house divided against itself cannot stand,"[5] to which he added that "this Republic cannot endure half slave and half free."

"Four score and seven years ago," he began his "Gettysburg Address," "our fathers brought forth upon this continent a new nation, conceived in liberty and dedicated to the proposition that all men are created equal." And before that, on July 7, 1863, he characterized the Southern revolt as "a gigantic rebellion, at the bottom of which is an effort to overthrow the principle that all men are created equal."[6]

In the series of debates between Lincoln and Stephen A. Douglas,[7] on the extension of slavery, he showed himself an orator of the first rank, and proved conclusively that he hated slavery.

When I was about eight years old I walked past the body of Lincoln as it lay exposed under a black catafalque in the southwest corner of the Public Square, in front of the old Forest City House, now the Cleveland Hotel. And had I been old enough to feel sufficiently deeply, and had I been able to express my feelings, they would probably have run along the line of those of the Good Gray poet, Walt

Whitman, where he sings:

> This dust was once the man, gentle, plain and resolute,
>   Under whose cautious hand
> Against the foulest crime in history known in any land or age
>   Was saved the union of these states.[8]

The opportunity to abolish slavery as a war measure was one which Lincoln welcomed. He wanted to save the Union, not solely as a Union, but as a free nation where the equality of man should prevail. Of course he was sworn to observe the Constitution and the laws of the United States, and that Constitution and those laws recognized slavery as an established institution, and it was necessary under those circumstances to resort to the device of a war measure in order to abolish it. But he did not have to abolish slavery. The abolition of slavery undoubtedly shortened the war, but I have no slightest doubt that the Union forces would have defeated the South without it. They had the men and the money; and "God," said Napoleon, "is always on the side of the strongest battalions."[9] Had the war been won without the abolition of slavery, it would have been difficult to abolish it. It would have become or would have continued to be the football of politics, as it had been for a generation. Lincoln saw the opportunity to rid the country of this incubus, and he seized it, and from us, of all men, his memory is entitled to gratitude and veneration.

Lincoln was an all-round man. He had a keen sense of humor. He loved a good story, and was not unduly particular about the theme of the story. I think he would have appreciated the story told by our friend Mr. Benjamin the other night at the dinner which our friend Mr. Walter Wills gave in his honor in this building.[10] (Can I tell the story?) I think he would have enjoyed the story of the lady school teacher who went home to her boarding house one evening for dinner and found beans on the table as the principal dish. She cited a passage from Scripture, Hebrews XIII, 8.[11] She would not quote the words, but some curious person at the table looked it up, and it read: "*Jesus Christ*! yesterday, today, and forever." Or he would have appreciated, I think, the story of the peddler who came into a busy office and asked the proprietor if he could n't sell him a nice motto for his walls, such as "Time is money," or "We have just fifteen minutes a day to devote to social visitors, and that time has already been used," or some of the many wise cracks or stale platitudes which feeble minds get up for the feeble-minded. The gentleman said, no, he did n't want any. "Well," said the salesman, "can I sell you a nice motto for your residence, for instance this beautiful sentiment, 'God bless our home'?" "Now you're getting warm," said the prospect. "I don't want that particular one, but if you've got one that reads 'God damn our boarding house,' I'll take half a dozen."

They had prohibitionists in those days; they did n't call them that, but they were just as persistent and just as meddlesome as the modern type. One of them, a very zealous lady, came to Mr. Lincoln one day and complained that General

Grant drank whiskey. Mr. Lincoln replied characteristically, "I wish I knew, madam, what brand he drinks. I would send a barrel of it to some of my other generals."

But whatever criticism might be directed to Lincoln's taste in stories, he lived a pure life. He had no Negro women to play with, like Washington and Jefferson and Hamilton and most of the founding fathers, as the phrase goes. No sexual scandal ever soiled his fame. No bastard daughter of his ever defamed her sire. His administration was not besmirched with graft and peculation of government funds. True, some army contractors became unduly rich, as they always do, but there were no Teapot Dome scandals.[12] He gathered around him a cabinet of the wisest and ablest and most liberal men of his generation.

And again we venerate his memory, not only as the Emancipator, but also as the Martyr, because his assassination was the direct sequel of the abolition of slavery. True, he fell at the hands of a fanatic, but every martyr is a victim of fanaticism, sometimes camouflaged as religion, sometimes as justice, sometimes as patriotism. You will recall Dr. Johnson's definition of patriotism in his famous dictionary: "Patriotism is the last refuge of a scoundrel."[13] There is no villainy, from predatory war to human slavery, that has not been excused or justified by patriotism or religion.

We love Lincoln, the honest, wholesome, lovable man of the common people—Honest Old Abe. We celebrate the birth of Lincoln, the great Emancipator, the exponent of human equality. We venerate the memory of Lincoln the Martyr, who died for humanity, just as did Savonarola or John Huss, or even the Master himself.[14]

Gentlemen, these are my sentiments, and frankly, I should not think much of any American colored man who did not share them.

FREDERICK DOUGLASS

I have spoken of Mr. Lincoln first, because of his commanding place in history. But there were many others who, in their own sphere and in their own way, contributed to the great result of the war, the emancipation of the slaves, and not the least of these was the lion-headed, lion-hearted Frederick Douglass, the worthy peer of Garrison and Phillips as an Abolition orator. He won first freedom and then fame for himself, and helped to win freedom and opportunity for his unhappy people. I quote from a little book which I wrote many years ago on the life of Frederick Douglass:[15]

> If it be no small task for a man of the most favored antecedents and the most fortunate surroundings to rise above mediocrity in a great nation, it is surely a more remarkable achievement for a man of the very humblest origin possible to humanity in any country in any age of the world, in the face of obstacles seemingly insurmountable, to win high honors and rewards, to retain for more than a generation the respect of good men in many lands, and to be deemed worthy of enrollment among his country's great men. Such a man was Frederick Douglass, and the exam-

ple of one who thus rose to eminence by sheer force of character and talents that neither slavery nor caste proscription could crush must ever remain a shining illustration of the essential superiority of manhood to environment.

His achievements are recorded in the pages of history and in the various lives of Douglass written by himself and others, and they are a thrilling saga of heroic struggles against almost insuperable obstacles. During the early years of the Civil War he urged in all his addresses the abolition of slavery and the arming of the Negroes as the most effective means of crushing the Rebellion. When Mr. Lincoln granted permission for the recruiting of colored recruits, Douglass exerted himself personally in procuring enlistments, his two sons, Charles and Lewis, being the first to enlist.[16] He was instrumental in persuading the government to put colored soldiers on an equal footing with white soldiers, both as to pay and protection. I have an idea that had Mr. Lincoln been president twelve years ago, Colonel Charles Young would have been made a general and would have participated in the World War, instead of being exiled to Africa to die of the black fever.[17]

In the course of these efforts Douglass was invited to visit the President, who welcomed him with outstretched hands, put him at his ease, and listened patiently to all he had to say. Later on he sent for him several times to discuss questions growing out of changed conditions among the freed slaves. And President Lincoln anticipated the Booker Washington-Roosevelt episode and demonstrated his belief in the equality of man by inviting Mr. Douglass to dinner. Unfortunately Mr. Douglass had a speaking engagement that night, and he had always made it a rule to keep his engagements.[18] He afterwards regretted that he had not made an exception of this occasion, and I am quite sure that his colored audience would have willingly, even joyfully excused him because of the honor which would have been reflected upon his race. For, next to the marriage relation, the dining table is the badge of social equality.

When slavery was abolished and the occupation of the abolitionists was gone, Douglass, in his representative capacity, was still of great service in helping to adapt the freed slaves to the new conditions of freedom. His proved ability made him available for political recognition. He never ran for an office, but he filled many appointive positions at the hands of the various administrations which succeeded that of Lincoln. Under President Grant he was a member of the legislative council or governing body of the District of Columbia. Under President Hayes he was marshal for the United States for the District of Columbia. Under President Garfield he was appointed Recorder of Deeds for the District, an office which he held during the terms of Garfield and Arthur, and nearly a year after President Cleveland's inauguration. In 1889 President Harrison appointed him Minister to the Republic of Haiti.

Mr. Douglass's work was done before I appeared on the active stage of life, but it was my privilege while a young man to hear him speak upon one occasion and to enjoy a very interesting conversation with him in which he spoke with enthusiasm of the substantial progress made by the Haitians in the arts of government and

civilization, and with indignation of what he considered slanders against the island due to ignorance or prejudice.[19] I wonder if he has not turned over in his grave
more than once within the last ten years.

So I think it meet and fitting that we should join at this time, with our tribute to
Abraham Lincoln, in a similar tribute to the first, and in view of his origin and his
environment, perhaps the greatest leader of our people. Greatness is always relative, but surely no one of his time could have done better what he did.

Since none of the New Negro poets, or old ones, so far as I know, have seen fit
to eulogize Mr. Douglass fittingly, I shall read, as I did here once before, if I remember correctly, the beautiful sonnet by Theodore Tilton, on this grand old
man. It is the estimate of a contemporary, himself a fervid lover of humanity.[20]

> I knew the noblest giants of my day,
>   And he was of them—strong amid the strong:
> But gentle, too: for though he suffered wrong,
>   Yet the wrong-doer never heard him say,
> "Thee also do I hate." . . .
>   A lover's lay—
> No dirge—no doleful requiem song—
>   Is what I owe him; for I loved him long;
> As dearly as a younger brother may.
>
> Proud is the happy grief with which I sing;
>   For, O my Country! In the paths of men
> There never walked a grander man than he!
>   He was a peer of princes—yea a king!
> Crowned in the shambles and the prison-pen!
>   The noblest Slave that ever God set free.

⌒

SOURCE: Untitled typed text at the Fisk University Library. This speech was delivered
to the John Harlan Law Club of Cleveland, an organization for black attorneys, on 14
February 1928.

[1]Parker Pillsbury (1809–98), like the others named here, was prominent in the anti-
slavery movement.

[2]Julia Ward Howe (1819–1910), a poet, abolitionist, and suffragette, was the author
of "The Battle Hymn of the Republic" (1862).

[3]Andrew Jackson Chesnutt.

[4]Delivered at the dedication of the national cemetery in Gettysburg, Pa., on 19 November 1863.

[5]Mark 3:25.

[6]"Response to a Serenade," delivered in Washington, D.C.

[7]During the series of seven debates in 1858 between Lincoln and his opponent in the
Illinois election for the U.S. Senate, Democrat Stephen A. Douglas (1813–61) alleged
that the Republican Party was promoting sectional warfare, advocating the abolition of
slavery, and promoting social equality of the races. Lincoln denied the charges and focused the debates on the question of whether Douglas considered slavery moral. Douglas was re-elected; Lincoln became president two years later.

[8]"Hush'd Be the Camps To-Day" (1871).

[9]Chesnutt's possible source was James A. Froude (1818–94). In the second volume of *Short Studies of Great Subjects* (1870), he wrote, "If Providence, as Napoleon scornfully said, is on the side of the strongest battalions, it provides also . . . that the strong battalions shall be found in defense of the cause which it intends shall conquer."

[10]Charles H. Benjamin (1856–1937) was a mechanical engineer who had served as a professor at the Case School of Applied Science (1889–1907) and as dean of its School of Engineering (1907–21).

[11]Emended is "viii,13."

[12]Chesnutt's reference to sexual scandal may also have been an allusion to Grover Cleveland, who fathered a child out of wedlock in 1876. The Teapot Dome scandal involved the illegal leasing of the naval oil reserves at Teapot Dome, Wy., and Elk Hills, Calif., in 1922 by Secretary of the Interior Albert B. Fall (1861–1944). In 1929 he was convicted of bribery, sentenced to imprisonment for one year, and fined $100,000.

[13]James Boswell, in his *Life of Samuel Johnson*, quotes Johnson thus. The definition does not appear in Johnson's *A Dictionary of the English Language*.

[14]Girolamo Savonarola (1452–98) and John Huss (1373?–1415) were Roman Catholic clerics condemned to death for expressing unorthodox beliefs. The "Master" is Jesus.

[15]*Frederick Douglass*, published 28 years previously.

[16]In 1863, Charles Remond Douglass (1844–?) and Lewis Henry Douglass (1840–?) enlisted in the Union army's Fifty-fourth Massachusetts Volunteers.

[17]Charles Young (1864–1922), the third black graduate of the U.S. Military Academy at West Point, received his commission as second lieutenant in 1889. He served on active duty in the Spanish-American War and commanded a cavalry squadron against Pancho Villa in Mexico in 1916. When the United States entered World War I, Lt. Col. Young was deemed physically unfit because of nephritis and hypertension. It was alleged that the actual cause was a desire to prevent him from rising to a higher rank. In 1917, however, he was promoted to colonel and retired from the regular army. In 1919, while on active duty with the Ohio National Guard, he was sent to Africa as advisor to the Liberian government. In 1922, while visiting Lagos, Nigeria, Young died from nephritis.

[18]See "Abraham Lincoln: An Appreciation," n. 12.

[19]In "Self-Made Men," Chesnutt relates that he heard Douglass give two speeches. He did not, however, mention that they had had a conversation. He is possibly referring here to another occasion on which their paths crossed.

[20]Chesnutt quotes the first of 19 numbered poems in *Sonnets to the Memory of Frederick Douglass* (1895) by Theodore Tilton.

Remarks of Charles Waddell Chesnutt, of Cleveland, in Accepting the Spingarn Medal at Los Angeles

Speech delivered at the annual national meeting of the National Association for the Advancement of Colored People, Los Angeles, Calif., 3 July 1928

Madam Chairman, Lieutenant Governor Fitts, Officers of the National Headquarters, Honored Delegates, Ladies and Gentlemen[1]—and any others, if any there be, who managed to slip by the doorkeepers or climb in the windows, and may therefore happen to be here:

I imagine that the proper response from a literary man upon an occasion of this kind would be an ornate and scholarly oration exemplifying the literary style and quality of his writings. But even if this be so, you have had so much eloquent and uplifting oratory during the week and during the evening that I am going to breach the custom, to use a legal expression, and put my sentiments into simple and almost colloquial form.

In expressing my sincere thanks for, and my profound appreciation of the signal honor which has been publicly conferred upon me here, I shall outline a few of the reasons why I value this medal and what it signifies. I shall state these reasons, not in the order of their importance, but as they occur to me.

First, the intrinsic value of the medal. It is made of gold, the king of metals, ever since the dawn of history the medium of exchange and the symbol of wealth and power and splendor, with which the perfervid imagination of the Hebrew sacred poets paved the streets of Heaven, and of which the Negro singers have made the slippers in which to walk those streets.[2] How comfortable golden slippers would be I don't know, but they would certainly look fine!

Again, I value this medal because it is an exquisitely beautiful work of art, worthy of a place in any collector's cabinet. On its shining face stands the serene and majestic figure of Justice, the scales in one hand, the sword in the other, and on the obverse side an appropriate inscription.

Another reason is that this medal originated in the great heart of its founder, Joel E. Spingarn, distinguished scholar, teacher, author, publisher, and friend and supporter of all good causes, who has done so much from its inception to make the National Association for the Advancement of Colored People the success it is to-day.[3]

Still another reason that I value this medal is the personnel of the Committee of Award,[4] all of them men of distinction and all but two of whom I have known personally for many years, and whose wisdom and good judgment, as evidenced by their selection of the winner of the medal from year to year, and especially this year, I am in no position to question. I should not have chosen myself, but I bow to their decision and feel honored by their confidence, which has added my name to the roll of able and distinguished men and women who have been selected to receive this reward of merit, which I value also because of the company in which it places me.[5]

Then, again, this medal is particularly valuable to me because the award is made, through the hands of your distinguished Lieutenant Governor, by the National Association for the Advancement of Colored People, the first successful and worthwhile organization for the protection of the rights and the promotion and advancement of all worthy interests of the Negroid group which we designate as the colored people or as the American Negro. For nineteen years, led by a band of noble and devoted men and women, it has conducted a vigorous and increasingly effective campaign against racial intolerance. The result you all know. It has been reported in detail throughout the week of this Conference. The Association is the spokesman of the race and its approval is the highest of honors. This medal is a service medal, given me by the people I have sought to serve, and honor from one's own people in one's own country is worth more than from all the rest of the world combined. It is an earnest[6] of the love and respect and confidence of a great group which is growing in numbers, in wisdom, and in social efficiency—in all the respects which make for good citizenship. I am proud to be numbered among them and to be found worthy of their esteem.

Another reason that I value this honor is that it has enabled me to spend a whole week with my good friends of the National Office of the Association and by this intimate daily intercourse to exchange views upon many weighty subjects and still further strengthen and cement the ties of friendship which bind us.

These might seem to be sufficient reasons for my appreciation of this honor, but there is one more, and that not the least important, though it is only a collateral reason, and that is that it gave one the opportunity to revisit your beautiful city. Some years ago, before the Great War and before the big boom which put Los Angeles on the map, I was here for a day or two.[7] I came to see the country and was n't particularly interested in the people. I had no acquaintance in the city, I stopped in a downtown hotel, and except for the colored servants and an occasional well dressed man or woman on the street, I would n't have known that there were any Negroes in the city.

When my distinguished friend Mr. Johnson, the National Secretary,[8] advised me of my selection as the recipient of the Spingarn medal for this year, he said in his letter that if it were not convenient for me to be present at Los Angeles the medal could be delivered to a proxy, and a subsequent ceremony take place in Ohio. Mrs. Chesnutt[9]—some of you have met her and others of you may have seen this quiet, unassuming little woman who leads me around and looks me up when I get lost—as I have been several times in this land of the wide open spaces—who tells me what to do, and when and how to do it—when she had opened and read my letter, she handed it to me and said, "Of course you are going to Los Angeles. It would be beneath our dignity to receive this medal by proxy." "Well," I replied, "I was never very strong on dignity; as Florian Slappey or Lawyer Evans Chew would say,[10] 'It's sump'n I've got eve'ything e'se but.' However, a second ceremony would be a little tame, like eating hash or getting married to the same woman the second time."

Then she went on and told me that another reason why I was going to Los Angeles—note the language, not why *I should go* but why *I was going*—was that she had never been to the Pacific Coast, and that it had been the dream of her life to go there, and that this was her golden opportunity. So, as a result of these various inducements, I found myself able, in due course of time, to say, like the American soldiers at Lafayette's tomb,[11] "Los Angeles, we are here. What have you?"

Well, I began immediately to find out what you have. I found your city grown to be the metropolis of Southern California, with a population which your citizens modestly claim is larger than that of Cleveland, though I suspect the census takers made a mistake or have a grudge against your city and have not given you proper credit for your numbers. Instead of a few Negroes, here and there, I have found a large and progressive body of colored people, with many outstanding representatives in the professions and in business. I am stopping at a hotel owned and managed by colored people, which for its size and cost is as beautiful and as well managed as any hotel I have ever seen. I have found your people well represented in the schools and in the public service. And your hospitality,—well, *superb* is none too strong a word for it.

One of your number, a young architect whose talent is almost genius, took my party and me for a little afternoon spin of 150 miles, in the course of which we visited several handsome homes which he had built. I have ridden over a thousand miles in automobiles and have only paid two or three small taxi fares.

Since I have been here I have gained much useful information and had some illusions shattered. On some of these drives I learned, among other things, that this is a land not only of wide open spaces but of wide open statements. If I asked my host about the size of a park for instance, or of an oil refinery, or the citrus fruit crop, and he did n't know the correct answer he would say so, but would add that it was the biggest in the world, and after I had checked up on a few of these statements, I reached the conclusion that they were probably true.

I came here with the preconceived notion that this was a dry country. I found it dry enough, in the present-day use of the word, to reasonably satisfy even Mr. Volstead, if that were possible, but my thought had been with reference to the aridity of the climate. But one of the gentlemen, if I remember correctly, informed me that it required thirty-five barrels of water for every pound of produce grown in Los Angeles County. When I recalled the mountains of vegetables and fruits and nuts I had seen in your great markets, and the thousands of acres of them I had seen growing, this seemed incredible, but my informant was a man whose name is a synonym of veracity,—it is generally admitted that he could no more tell a lie than the infant George Washington—and I was forced to revise my opinion about the dryness of the climate. If the statement were true—and I could not doubt it, in view of my friend's reputation for truthfulness—you must have almost as much water here as there is in the Pacific Ocean.

Since I have been here I have met many former friends and fellow townsmen, and some pupils of mine in the dim and distant past when I taught school, and they have all vied with one another to make our stay among you pleasant. One of them, an old friend of my young manhood, has devoted almost his entire time to our entertainment. So I thank the Spingarn Medal Award Committee and Mrs. Chesnutt for having induced me to come to Los Angeles.

It was suggested to me by Mr. Johnson that it is customary for the winners of the Spingarn medal to say something, in accepting it, about how they happened to do the things which entitled them to this reward, and what they had in mind when they did them, and since my writings are my chief title to recognition, I shall follow that custom.[12]

I was always an omnivorous reader. Indeed I cannot remember when I did not read. My maternal grandmother[13] once remarked in my hearing that had she not been present at my delivery she could have believed that I was born with a book in my hand. And I observed, as soon as I was capable of intelligent observation, that the Negro in fiction had become standardized, and that there were very few kinds of Negroes. There was the bad Negro, as most of them were, who either broke the laws or made himself obnoxious to the white people by demanding his rights or protesting against his wrongs; the good Negro who loved old "Massa" and preserved the same attitude toward his children as they had taken to him, that of a simple and childlike deference and respect—the good old Uncle and Mammy types; and the modern "white man's nigger," as we call him, who, as teacher or preacher or politician or whatever you will,

> "Crooks the pregnant hinges of the knee,
> Where thrift may follow fawning."[14]

Then there was the wastrel type, who squandered his substance in riotous living, and the minstrel type, who tried to keep the white folks in good humor by his capers and antics.

Now, I knew very well that while these types were true enough so far as they went, they were by no means all the types of Negroes. I knew there were among them many thrifty, progressive and serious-minded people, with a sincere respect for their own type, with high aspirations for themselves and their children, whose ideals of character and citizenship were of the best, with no more respect or deference for white people than their attitude toward the Negro entitled them to, and a keen resentment of race prejudice and social intolerance.

When I began to write serious books, after the usual apprenticeship aspiring authors must go through, I thought I saw the literary and artistic value of different types of Negroes than these, and I set out to depict them in my books. I did n't write my stories as Negro propaganda—propaganda is apt to be deadly to art—but I used the better types, confident that the truth would prove the most valuable propaganda; that it is infinitely more effective in a novel to have a character do a fine and noble deed, and thus let him speak for himself and his people, than merely to say he was a fine and noble fellow and a credit to his race.

While I was born in the North, my father, who had left the South and gone North in the late fifties of the last century and had served four years in the Union army, returned along with the carpet-baggers to North Carolina, where he was born, and where he had some ancestral property.[15] I was brought up in North Carolina as one of the colored people, and have ever since remained one of them, so that I knew whereof I spoke when I sought to depict their lives, their sufferings and disappointments, their hopes and fears, their successes and failures. I tried to write of them not primarily as a Negro writing about Negroes, but as a human being writing about other human beings, and whenever I let my feelings get the better of me and become dogmatic and argumentative in a book, I found that its artistic quality suffered, and its success accordingly. My physical makeup was such that I knew the psychology of people of mixed blood in so far as it differed from that of other people, and most of my writings ran along the color line, the vaguely defined line where the two major races of the country meet. It has more dramatic possibilities than life within clearly defined and widely differentiated groups. This was perfectly natural and I have no apologies to make for it, for we are all one people, and the suffering and triumphs, the failures and successes of one of us are those of all of us.

My books were written, from one point of view, a generation too soon. There was no such demand then as there is now for books by and about colored people. And I was writing against the trend of public opinion on the race question at that particular time. And I had to sell my books chiefly to white readers. There were few colored book buyers. At that time the Negro was inarticulate, I think I was the first man in the United States who shared his blood, to write serious fiction about the Negro. But in this later and happier, though yet far from perfect age, there are a number of colored men who write books, and a still larger number of white men and women who write books about the Negro, who, if they do not write the Negro up at least seek to tell the truth about the conditions in which he lives, and the truth is in the Negro's favor.

The great pioneer work of fiction about the Negro, *Uncle Tom's Cabin*, wasted no long pages in anti-slavery argument. It has been some time since I last read it, but I recall few, if any, diatribes against slavery. It was its description of the institution as affecting the lives of its victims, white, black and those of mixed blood, that stirred the heart and conscience of the nation and was perhaps the most powerful influence in the abolition of slavery.

My books had their day and I hope that, as my good friends, the Spingarn Medal Committee, have decided, they contributed somewhat to the advancement of colored people, as I meant them to do. I am writing another novel, dealing with present day conditions, and when it is published,[16] as I confidently expect it will be, those of you who, for whatever reason, have read none of my other books, will have an opportunity to get acquainted with my work, and those of you who survived reading my other writings will have the opportunity to renew our acquaintance.

Again I thank you, sir, and the committee and the Association, for this splendid testimonial. It will be a strong incentive to further effort along the same line and help me to prove still further that your confidence and esteem are not misplaced.

꒰

SOURCE: Typed text at the Fisk University Library. Chesnutt delivered this address on 3 July 1928.

[1]Mary White Ovington (1865–1951) was then Chairman of the Board of the N.A.A.C.P. Buron R. Fitts (1895–1973) was Lieutenant-Governor of California in 1927–31.

[2]Chesnutt alludes to Revelation 21:21. The musical reference is to "Oh Dem Golden Slippers" (1879) by James A. Bland (1854–1911).

[3]Spingarn, Chairman of the Department of Comparative Literature at Columbia University and one of the founders of the publishing house Harcourt, Brace & Co., was the N.A.A.C.P. Chairman of the Board (1913–19), Treasurer (1919–30), and President (1930–39). In 1914 he originated the award presented annually for "the highest or noblest achievement by an American Negro during the preceding year."

[4]The committee members were: Chairman John Hurst (1863–1930), clergyman; Theodore Roosevelt; John Hope (1868–1936), educator; Oswald Garrison Villard (1873–1949), publisher of the *New York Evening Post*; James H. Dillard (1856–1940), educator; and W. E. B. Du Bois.

[5]The thirteen previous recipients were: Ernest E. Just (1883–1948), medical researcher; Charles Young; Harry T. Burleigh (1866–1949), musical composer; William S. Braithwaite; Archibald H. Grimké (1849–1930), clergyman and civil rights advocate; W. E. B. Du Bois; Charles S. Gilpin (1878–1930), actor; Mary B. Talbert (1866–1923), educator; George Washington Carver (1864–1943), botanist and agricultural chemist; Roland Hayes (1887–1977), singer; James Weldon Johnson (1871–1938), poet, novelist, and editor; Carter G. Woodson (1875–1938), historian; and Anthony Overton (1865–1946), banker.

[6]That is, assurance—though the word normally implies a promise or token of something to come. Chesnutt perhaps intended "earnest expression."

[7]Chesnutt visited Los Angeles and San Diego in July 1915.

[8]James Weldon Johnson.

[9]Susan Perry Chesnutt (1862–1940).

[10]Characters in the prose fictions of Octavus Roy Cohen; see "The Negro in Art," n. 14.

[11]Colonel Charles E. Stanton, as he saluted the grave of the Marquis de Lafayette (1757–1834) in the Picpus Cemetery in Paris on 4 July 1917, declared: "Lafayette, we are here."

[12]Chesnutt received the award in recognition of his "pioneer work as a literary artist depicting the life and struggle of Americans of Negro descent, and for his long and useful career as scholar, worker and freeman of one of America's greatest cities."

[13]Chloe Sampson Harris (1806?–?).

[14]See "The Disfranchisement of the Negro," n. 12.

[15]In 1866.

[16]Chesnutt refers to his manuscript "The Quarry."

The Negro in Present Day Fiction

Speech delivered in Oberlin, O., c. 1929

Mr. (Miss) Chairman and members of the Dunbar Forum, I regard it as a high privilege to appear before a group of students of literature in this old and historic institution of learning with its glorious tradition of human equality and equal opportunity for all.[1] I was an infant in this town when the classic antislavery incident, the rescue of "Jerry" an escaped slave took place at Wellington.[2] My father was among those arrested and indicted for violation of the fugitive slave law. That was one law of which the sacredness was not recognized by the descendants of the stern New Englanders who had settled the Western Reserve.[3] Incidentally, the warrant against my father was nolled[4] because one of the "t's" in his name was put in the middle instead of with the other at the end, thus constituting what the judge, who was unfriendly to the law, construed as a misnomer. I have been mildly amused during my life at the different spellings of my name, but this was one instance where it saved my male progenitor from a sojourn in jail.

When I began to write books about life along the color line and amongst the colored people, there were not a great many such books. Mrs. Stowe had written the epoch-making *Uncle Tom's Cabin* and her other books along the same line. Judge Albion W. Tourgée had written *The Fool's Errand*—probably the first of what we call nowadays "best sellers,"—*Bricks Without Straw*, and several other novels about the freed slaves, Reconstruction and the old Ku Klux Klan.

Paul Laurence Dunbar was looming above the horizon as a poet—I think his one or two novels were written after I began to write.[5] The Rev. Thomas Dixon was spawning his libels on the Negro in the guise of fiction. But the modern novel, depicting the different types of colored people with their emotions, their aspirations, their love affairs, in fact, all the complications and involvements of modern life, was not in evidence, and for a very good reason—there were no modern Negroes. Most of them were absorbed in the struggle for bare existence, and the difficult effort to adjust themselves to new conditions.

The novel, even more than sculpture or painting, is the flower of culture. Poets are said to be born. The greatest of epic poets, Homer, was in a sense a primitive, at least he led the great procession of poets which has flowed down the stream of time. The *Iliad* was simple poetry. It was poetry of action. The poetic figures were not worked to death. Homer could turn a fine line without plagiarism. He did not have to scan a thesaurus or a library to ascertain whether or not some one else had used the same trope or simile in the same connection. Such a poet is born.

The sort of psychological poetry, which searches the heart for motives of action, Homer could not have written. His themes were simple, his motives direct. Love, with little sentiment, ambition, war, hate, revenge, avarice. Analytical poetry, like Browning's for instance, is, like fiction, the outgrowth of culture. So almost until our own day, there was very little worth-while literary output by American colored writers. In other countries several writers of color had distinguished themselves, but not as Negroes. The two Alexander Dumas were Frenchmen first, last and all the time, and only incidentally colored. The same was true of Alexander Pushkin, the Russian Shakespeare. In America there had been a few feeble sprouts of genuine poetry by colored writers, but the environment was not congenial, and they faded early. A few biographies, human documents, could be found on the bookshelves, but most of the Negro output was beneath criticism. The Negro stood mute, as the legal phrase goes, before the bar of literary judgment.

But in our own day—I may well say in *your* own day—mine is mostly behind me,—the Negro has become articulate, indeed, voluble, sometimes garrulous, and now and then even strident. The criticism so plaintively voiced almost yesterday by Dr. Du Bois and James Weldon Johnson, that colored writers could not find a hearing with publishers and editors, is no longer well founded.[6] The subjects which only yesterday were tabooed in the discussion of race contacts and relationships are open to any writer. Publishers vie with one another for books by colored writers or about Negro life. The Negro is the literary fashion of the day, and the interest in him seems to be not merely a fad but a genuine sociological development, likely to grow rather than to die away.

Southern white writers were among the first to discover the value of Negro life as literary material. The South had exploited the Negro's labor by slavery and peonage; it had exploited the Negro's uncast vote by counting it for the white congressional representation, and now they began to exploit him in literature.

To their credit, be it said, the modern Southern white novelist has not set out on purpose, generally speaking, to degrade the Negro. Indeed the present day attitude—"pose" would be perhaps an unkind word—is that of liberality—the tempered liberality of the more enlightened South—not equality, God save the mark!—but a recognition of the common humanity of darker people, of their cultural advancement, of their aspirations—mostly pathetically hopeless from the Southern viewpoint. They note their social aspirations, their improvement in dress and manners, and find them more or less amusing. Some ascribe them less to increasing self-respect than to a simian imitation of white people.

I want to comment on these present-day Negro novels—by which I mean the novels about the Negro, whether written by white or colored authors. I set out some time ago to collect them all, but they came along so fast I soon found that my restricted means would render this burdensome, so I had to fall back more or less on the public and lending libraries, and even then I have n't read them all. In fact, I got pretty well fed up on them, as the phrase goes, but I have read the outstanding ones, and enough of them to discuss them intelligently.

When Mr. Carl Van Vechten's *Nigger Heaven*[7] appeared I criticised it—the title was the most offensive feature—but in the book he spoke of me and my writings in so friendly and complimentary a fashion that my guns were spiked. It is difficult to call a writer a liar and a horse thief who declares that you are a great man and a wonderful writer. It was in a sense the pioneer of a flood of such books. Many of them are written with great literary skill. They deal with all phases of the Race Problem—amalgamation, both legal and illegal, "passing" for white; that perversion of the Mendelian theory, the mythical black baby that is born to a seemingly pure white mother or father; the struggle for equality and the heart-breaking incidents attending it. And on the still more tragic side, lynching, burning at the stake, disfranchisement and the whole list of wrongs and outrages, as lengthy as the catalogue of Homer's ships. Subjects which once were spoken of only in whispers are not only printed in capital letters, but exhibited upon the stage.

In fact, Negro books have multiplied with that mushroom fecundity which marks the growth of every new thing in this wonderful country, in this wonderful age—witness the radio, the airplane and the talking movie, to instance the three latest. And I regret to say, the moral equality of these books has not kept pace with their growth. In fact they seem to grow baser and baser. Compared with some of the more recent output, Mr. Van Vechten's *Nigger Heaven* is a Sunday School tract.

If the term "Negro Literature" is taken in the broad sense in which it is being used nowadays, as including books by colored writers and books about the Negro, and if by the word "literature" is meant merely books and other writings, there has been for a long time a very large body of Negro literature. Any comprehensive library has many examples. Before the Civil War, and even since, there were many books by Negrophobes maintaining the hopeless inferiority of the Negro, some of them even denying him a soul—which meant more then than it does in our own day, when some advanced thinkers and writers claim there is no such thing as an immortal soul. However, those old-time writers were quite sure that white people had souls. Of course the obvious and often the declared purpose of such a line of argument was to justify slavery. And, on the other hand books against slavery were very numerous.

Of course most of these books were written by white men. But there were occasional colored men and women who wrote. Phillis Wheatley was the first Negro poet in America. I saw a pageant the other day in which Phillis was represented by a very handsome light-colored girl, while in fact she was a pure-blood dark Negro, brought from Africa while a small child. Her mistress treated her as a human being, in fact more as companion than slave, and from instruction at her mistress's hands and by her own study and reading she acquired a fine command of cultivated English. Phillis's poetry was highly complimented by prominent people, though it is only just to say that others found no especial merit in it. However, it measures up fairly well with the average of the literary output of her day. She was a canny business woman as well as a popular poet, as evidenced by the fact that many of her poems are dedicated to the rich people of Boston who belonged to the social circle in which Mr. and Mrs. Wheatley moved. As Mr. Brawley puts it, she was the obituary poet of the Boston aristocracy.[8]

Then there were the various editions of Frederick Douglass's *Autobiography*, William Still's *The Underground Railroad*, J. Madison Bell's poems, George W. Williams's *History of the Negro as a Soldier*.[9] Then the poems and novels of your patron saint, Paul Laurence Dunbar, a real poet and a good fellow.[10] His fame rests principally upon his inimitable dialect pieces, but there is a chaste and dignified beauty in many of his poems in straight English. Also Booker T. Washington's *Up from Slavery* (a wonderful human document), a few collections of sermons, and numerous pamphlets and obscure books emanating from colored sources. A friend of mine, the late "Billy Bolivar" of Philadelphia, died leaving a library of two thousand such books.[11] Mr. Carter Woodson must have a great many, as also Mr. Schomburg of Brooklyn.[12] Mr. Arthur Spingarn of New York, staff attorney of the N.A.A.C.P., is an ardent collector of such books, and Dr. R. R. Moton's name is in the List of American Private Book Collectors as specializing in books about the Negro.[13]

All these books can be included in the broad meaning of the word "literature," but when we come to literature in the narrower sense, that is, to *belles lettres*, "beautiful writing," imaginative writing, such as poetry or fiction, essays like Hazlitt's or Macaulay's, solid though less brilliant works of history, like those of Lecky, Prescott and Motley,[14] nothing of this sort worth while, by any high standard, had, up to our own day emanated from colored American writers, and for the best of reasons. Literature, like the fine arts and the best music, is, as I have said, the fruit of culture. "You cannot gather grapes of thorns or figs of thistles."[15] It is true that Aesop was a slave, and Horace the son of a freedman, but they were able and brilliant men, enslaved by conquest, but having a background of freedom and culture.[16] The Negro in America had no such background. Some of our intellectuals are spending a lot of time trying to dig up a great and glorious past for the African Negro. They claim for him the greatness and power of the Pharaohs, and attribute to him the art and architecture of ancient Egypt.[17] But I fear this is one of the things that people believe because they like to believe them. Quite probably the ancient Egyptians, like the modern white Brazilians and Cubans, and for that matter Italians, Spaniards, Portuguese, and to a degree North Americans, had a Negroid strain. According to Dr. Boas there is no such thing as a pure race,[18] but even the most liberal classification could hardly credit the Negro with Egyptian civilization.

The term "Negro Renaissance" is a more or less inaccurate expression. "Renaissance" or "renascence" means, literally, new birth. It is applied chiefly to the revival of art and letters in Europe in the 15th and 16th centuries, after the long night of the Dark Ages. But Southern Europe had possessed, before the Dark Ages, a literature and an art even superior to that of the Renaissance. The *Iliad* and the *Aeneid* are still the greatest of epics and the art of Phidias has never been excelled.[19] I said once to Dr. Locke that I thought a better word to describe the modern American Negro would be the "New American."[20] In my opinion the American Negro, so called, or miscalled, is destined, if his ultimate absorption into the composite American race is long deferred, to develop a type which is very widely different from the West African type from which he has descended. There are, I will venture to say, very few Negroes whose American ancestry dates back even a hundred years, who have n't some white blood, and by the same token there are many white people who have some dark blood.

A corollary of this argument is, of course, that the very worthy achievements of the American Negro can by no means be attributed entirely to his dark blood. The white people rarely claim any credit for them, partly perhaps because to do so would be to acknowledge their blood relationship, which, though entirely obvious, they prefer to ignore, and partly because of the sense of fair play, sadly distorted at times it is true, after all a characteristic of the English people from whom the American Negro derives most of his white inheritance, which, perhaps unconsciously, inhibits the white man from claiming at one end what he disowns at the other. It is either that or a generosity we have never suspected which makes him concede to the Negro as Negro the very considerable contributions of people of mixed blood.

And now, having determined what we mean by Negro, and what we mean by literature, and put ourselves in a position to speak intelligently about Negro literature; having cleaned out the underbrush of the pre-Civil War period, and cut out the deadwood of the past generation, we can approach the very lively, the almost rank new growth of Negro books which has sprung up since the War-to-end war,[21] which it has n't, and to make the world safe for democracy— which it equally has n't—and discuss the good and the bad in them.

In the first place they approach the Negro from a new viewpoint. The old Uncle Tom type seems to have disappeared entirely. He was a likable old fellow, almost too good to be true, but we cherish a pleasant memory of him, and always read with interest any item identifying the original Uncle Tom, of which there would seem to be almost as many as there are pieces of the true cross[22] in Catholic countries. The story itself is immortal. Next to the Bible it has been the best seller in the history of book publishing. It has been translated into every tongue which has a written form and has been running on the stage steadily ever since it was dramatized. There is always a "Tom show" going somewhere, sometimes half a dozen at once, and now that the talking movie has arrived it has a new medium of expression.[23] It might pay the new school of Negro writers to analyze the reasons for its success. It grew out of a condition which, happily, no longer exists. A modern writer cannot repeat the incidents, unless he dates his story before the Civil

War. But *Uncle Tom's Cabin* registered because it dealt with deep-seated, fundamental realities, things which exist in all men, regardless of worldly station—the relations of husband and wife, parent and child, the right to the fruits of one's toil—the freedom of one's own person,—and indeed of one's own soul, for in spite of Uncle Tom's pronouncement it is exceedingly difficult for one to be the captain of his soul[24] and control his own spiritual development, when his body all his life is under the control of some one else.

The old "mammy" type is fading, although it still survives in the novels written by Southern white authors and is still going strong in "mammy songs" along with the "mother, home and heaven" doggerel which flourishes in vaudeville. One would gather from reading Southern stories and novels of the old school and from Southern oratory of the present day, that every white child born in the South had a colored "mammy," though statistics prove that not one white Southerner in ten was a slaveholder, and therefore there could n't have been mammies enough to go around. The Southerners not long ago proposed to erect a monument to her at Washington, but however touching the memory of the faithful slave may be to the children of the master, the relationship seems not to be one which the black mammy's own children held in especial honor, perhaps for the reason that the care and affection which she is assumed to have lavished upon her white nurslings were taken from her own children.[25]

The self-seeking colored person who fawns on the white folks and for selfish reasons tries to prove himself the type of Negro which he assumes that they like, has also more or less disappeared from fiction, though he still survives to a degree in real life in certain preachers and teachers who

> "Crook the pregnant hinges of the knee,
> That thrift may follow fawning."[26]

The beautiful octoroon, the product of the white man's sin for several successive generations, and the victim of his passions, has given way to the modern sophisticated "near white" or "high yellow" who has been to college, and takes advantage of her complexion either by "passing" for white or at least exercising in public the privileges of the "caste of Vere de Vere." Sometimes she puts it over quite far, and marries into the old Knickerbocker or Mayflower families. It is quite within the bounds of probability that the offspring of some such ambitious and enterprising lady may yet sit in the presidential chair. A man of Indian descent who does not deny his origin, is pretty close to it, and a man said to have been of Negro descent who did deny it has occupied the throne itself.[27]

The crude and stolid field hand has almost disappeared from fiction, although Dr. Du Bois made a brave but not entirely successful attempt to idealize him in his first novel, *The Silver Fleece*.[28] In place of him we have the migrant, the factory operative or mill hand. The squalid cabins of the plantation have given place to the sordid tenements of great cities. The overseer with his bullwhip has been replaced by the foreman with his time clock. The jolly carefree

buck-and-wing dances and hoe-downs have given place to the black bottom of
the hectic cabaret and night club, and the bang of the banjo, while still going
strong, to some extent, to the sob of the saxophone. The black face minstrel has
yielded place to the talented actor in the legitimate drama. Always excepting the
perennial Uncle Tom, colored actors now star in *The Emperor Jones*, *In Abraham's Bosom* and other plays which demand a high order of histrionic talent.[29]
Topsy has been replaced by the Florence Millses and Josephine Bakers,[30] and the
real talent of Bert Williams and Ernest Hogan by the finer artistry of Charles
Gilpin and Paul Robeson.

Then we have some entirely new types which derive entirely from modern
conditions. The colored doctor, for instance, unknown a generation ago, is the
most outstanding representative of the race, at least in numbers and in earning
power. He has been used quite freely and effectively in Negro fiction. The colored lawyer is not so popular a subject. Indeed the colored lawyer in the South is
largely conspicuous by his absence. By the way, the first one in the United
States, I believe, was John M. Langston, an alumnus of Oberlin, perhaps the
first colored graduate.[31] I read somewhere the other day that the first colored
lawyer in North Carolina had been recently admitted to the bar of that state.
This was a misstatement, because fifty years ago, when I was on the verge of
manhood, John M. Leary, a colored man and a brother of Sheridan Leary, a
former resident of Oberlin and one of John Brown's raiding party, was a practicing lawyer and an able one, in Fayetteville, North Carolina, where I lived at
the time.[32] The Negro preacher is almost virgin soil for the fictionist, but the
black Elmer Gantrys[33] and grafting bishops will surely come into their own, as
well as the devoted men who give their lives and their talents for the uplift of
their race for a meager recompense.

Colored readers have sometimes criticized the Negro characters of Mr. Octavus Roy Cohen, the Jewish writer of Alabama. I am free to say that I have
found some of his stories very amusing. The imaginary best "cullud society" of
"Bummingham" with its hodgepodge of lawyers, doctors, preachers, barbers,
hairdressers, gamblers and shrewd swindlers, if overdrawn and therefore libel-
ous, has some semblance of reality, though I can't imagine a lawyer being admitted to the bar even of Alabama, with as little learning, legal or otherwise, as
lawyer Evans Chew. Florian Slappey is a quite convincing type of the happy-go-
lucky hand-to-mouth type of social parasite who spends most of his time
scheming how to get something for nothing. One fault I have to find in that
connection is that our up-and-coming colored story writers have let this shrewd
white man preempt this financially rich vein of Negro literature. Cohen's only
real competitor is Hugh Wiley, another white man, with his vivid stories of the
Negro labor battalions in the Great War, of crap-shooters and "Lady Luck."
One thing I cannot forgive the Cohen output is the illustrations. The artist seems
to use the same tame gorilla as the model for every character, male or female—
black, brown and yellow. There are perhaps some Negroes as ugly as Cohen's

characters are depicted—there are homely people in all races—but we ought to be thankful to the Creator that He did n't load down the whole race with such a burden.

The grafting colored politician is another somewhat sinister development attending the progress of the colored people. Dr. Du Bois in his novel *The Dark Princess*[34] has depicted very vividly this type in Chicago, and I suspect has done the Chicago Negro no serious injustice.

There has been much criticism among colored readers and critics about the types portrayed in the current Negro novels. With much of this criticism I concur heartily. Looking back cursorily I find no outstanding noble male character in any of the Negro novels, written by white or colored writers. The male characters are either weaklings, like the principal male character in *Nigger Heaven* and in *Birthright*,[35] or addicted to degrading vices, such as gambling, lechery, drunkenness, the use of narcotics, or else somewhat unbalanced, like the hero of the *Dark Princess*. Porgy, with his goat and his wagon, is an interesting character, but no particular credit to his race, and the returned soldier in *Home to Harlem* is by no means an admirable character.[36]

The Southern white writers manifest, apparently, much fairness in dealing with their Negro characters. It is to be regretted that they do not choose finer types, but they would probably reply that they use the material at hand. Catfish Alley is doubtless an interesting place, and Mr. Heyward seems very familiar with it, but I am unable—it may be snobbishness on my part or a certain Victorian hangover—to get up much enthusiasm over the characters in *Porgy* or over the profane and crafty Aunt Mamba with her stolen second-hand false teeth, and her efforts to annex a white family.[37] The Charleston white people may admire that type of Negro, and there may be some of them, but I imagine most of the colored people of Charleston are quite satisfied not to "belong" to white families. Hagar was not much improvement, and Lissa, after all, plays a small part in the story—she is merely the lay figure on which to drape the other characters.

One noteworthy thing about most of these Southern white writers is that they tell the truth about their own people—how they rob and exploit and scorn and degrade their dark neighbors. Sometimes, as in *Mamba's Daughters*, the active villain, like the black overseer in the old days, is made a colored man. A curious corollary of this is Mr. Rudolph Fisher's colored character in *The Walls of Jericho*[38] who works the residence segregation racket for his own not at all high-minded purposes.

The heart of any romantic novel is the heroine—perhaps I should say the female protagonist in speaking of the present day Negro novel, for precious few of them are given any heroic attributes. With the exception of Mary in *Nigger Heaven*, or the heroine of Walter White's first novel,[39] and the women of Miss Fauset's novels,[40] they are all unchaste. When I wrote that sentence a week or two ago I had not read Miss Fauset's latest novel,[41] in which I regret to say the

heroine joins the scarlet, or at least the pink sisterhood. Of course I recognize
that female virtue has gone out of fashion in fiction—I hope not so much so in
real life—but I feel about the matter something like I do about the Octavus Roy
Cohen illustrations. I *know* that these characters are not the best types or even
average types of the womanhood of the race. Of course the female rebel is more
interesting or more easy to make interesting—vice has the edge on virtue in fiction—most of the interesting women in romance have sinned for love or for
profit—Beatrice Esmond, *Tess of the d'Urbervilles*, Maggie Tulliver in *The Mill
on the Floss*, *Anna Karenina*,[42] etc., but it remained for one of our most eminent
young colored writers to have his heroine sin for no apparent reason whatsoever. She did not love her paramour, she got nothing out of it, she was not responding to any resistless sex urge, nor even to curiosity, but her lover asked,
and she just consented, and did some other foolish things afterwards which contribute to the development of the story but which stamp the heroine with mental
as well as moral weakness.

One of the vilest of the colored women characters in present day fiction is
Black Sadie,[43] who so far as I could gather, had no morals. So far as she was decent at all, it was a matter of animal instinct—many animals are decenter than
many humans. Sadie was a constitutional thief and robbed even her benefactors
with perfect sangfroid. She would take jewels or any other portable property
which was not locked up or nailed down and could be easily turned into money,
without blinking an eyelash. The book is brilliantly written by, I am informed, a
white Baptist preacher of Richmond, Virginia, who displays an intimate and
circumstantial familiarity with the baser side of Negro life and character which
suggests not only careful study but personal experience.

Claude McKay's *Home to Harlem* is very well written, but I don't recall a
decent woman character in the book. Some of the male characters are steeped in
baseness, some of which is so vile as to be merely hinted at. But the very nadir of
vileness is reached in a novel by a colored writer, W. Thurman.[44] It is called *The
Blacker the Berry*, and by way of foreword the author quotes an alleged Negro
folk saying,

> The blacker the berry
> The sweeter the juice.

The novel is founded on the assumed scorn of light-colored people for dark
women—which in my opinion the author grossly exaggerates—and the gradual
degeneration of his heroine growing out of her sensitiveness to this discrimination. I can say frankly that he hasn't helped the dark girl a particle, if she needs
any help.

I read the other day an item which I cut out of a newspaper, which voices
some rather pertinent reflections on the prevalent type of these books. It is a
quotation from a recent number of the *Birmingham News*, based on an expression by Dana Skinner, dramatic editor of *The Commonweal*:[45]

"Those who have tried to keep tab," says the editor,

on what is being done in the way of productive literary art among Negroes cannot fail to recall the bold intermixture of animalism permeating that part of it about which most of the raving is done. It seems to be a swirling current into which much of the best talent is drawn and too much of the really proven literary talent is condoning and encouraging, either by complimentary mention or dubious silence, leaving it a right-of-way which causes it to boldly overshadow any literary art that might be really constructive.

The sad fact that it emanates from motives that appear, on the face, to be both mercenary and devoid of exalted idealism, adds a new danger to its popularity. We have never been able to see any masterly merit in either its conception or its portrayal.

It flits from one cesspool of vice to another, holding up the worst in Negro life to public gaze as though there were nothing worthier and better to show. Certainly, it sells to a thrill-hungry, unsuspecting public curiously agape for fads.

As far as we have been able to see, it starts low, remains low, maintains a sensual note and glories in a sensual imagery suggestive of its authorship and origin. Without venturing a criticism on any particular literary effort, one can select what is styled the successes and study them according to approved standards of art to find that they exploit the worst features and explode the best theories of Negro home and social life. A literature that is truly interpretative must be in some sense moralistic; it must exalt those of low degree as well as the mighty. It may deal with the sensual for moral purposes. It must glorify the humble and degrade the haughty. It must do it—a course of events common to everyday life and everyday people. Its filth must have a moral purpose as well as an informative portrayal.

Men's vices are not to be depicted for the sake of proving them vile, only to no purpose beneficial to them or to others.

There are dark spots in Negro life—so in the life of all peoples. There is no merit in selling it to the public at the price of transient popularity or paltry coin. The literature that lives is not built that way and the authors who have courted fame by that route are known only by chance even though they may have reaped a harvest of temporary fame and ill-gotten gain.

In the columns of a previous issue attention has been called to a type of Negro literature written by Negroes fairly degrading to Negro womanhood, and this is true not because Negro womanhood is worse than the womanhood of any other race, but because Negro authors are not better nor more discriminating.

We know of no author who has risen to fame on the carcasses of the womanhood of his race.

Mr. Skinner's criticism is a just rebuke both to those who produce this mercenary slush and also those able, discriminating literary Negroes who condone it either by their complimentary mention or their silence. There is heroism worthy of the pen, there is tragedy and comedy worthy of the footlights in Negro life. Also there is vice and animalism outside of New York's Black Belt and the price of its glory is a poor compensation for its bland portrayal.

But what as to the future of Negro literature? I am not concerned about the white writers about the Negro, but what about the colored writers? They have learned to write, and to write well. Their contributions to the best magazines are not only acceptable but solicited. They write with a verve and a swing like their

actors and singers put into their work. Naturally a somewhat indolent people—
Miss Fauset has said the Negro's capacity for rest is one of his most valuable
characteristics,—it keeps the white people from working him to death and gives
him time to live, with strength enough left to enjoy life—when they are doing
something they enjoy doing, they develop a surprising industry. Some of you
may have seen the screen picture *Hearts in Dixie*, a picture of low life, but not
base life,—among the Negroes along the Mississippi River.[46] If so, you will remember "Stepin' Fetchit" who has a "mizry" in his feet whenever he is asked to
chop wood or fetch water, but who is a marvel of terpsichorean agility when the
banjo or the fiddle starts a dance.

This *élan*, this verve, is reflected in the verse as well as in the prose of our colored writers. The work of our best poets glows with the divine fire. The colored
writer has a great subject—the life of ten or twelve million people, becoming every
day more diversified, more complicated—with the fundamental emotions and interests common to all humanity, colored or differentiated by those interests and
feelings which grow out of their own peculiar position. Out of these distinguishing
traits, building on the great fundamentals and imponderables, they can evolve a
body of writing sufficiently distinctive to be classed as Negro literature and at the
same time heartily and cordially welcomed as American literature.

Doubtless some of you have literary aspirations or have written things. In
addition to the poets widely recognized whose poems appear in the leading
monthlies and in the anthologies, there is a surprising quantity of promising
verse and short stories that appear in the colored magazines. The colored writer
has all the literary machinery. There are some excellent Negro critics. Mr.
Braithwaite and Benjamin Brawley perhaps first, Mr. George Schuyler is
one, a columnist, who writes *à la* Mencken[47] with a fine dash of wit. Eugene
Gordon, a discriminating critic who wields a hammer so heavy that, when he
has finished a critical article one must search the broken fragments which strew
his passage to see if there is any good thing left.[48] Mrs. Alice Dunbar-Nelson is
another discriminating reviewer.[49]

In addition to Mr. Braithwaite's Anthology there are anthologies of Negro
Poetry, *Colored Who's Who's*,[50] and the latest development, a Negro *Bookman*
magazine. So no literary gem of purest ray need remain in oblivion for lack of a
medium of publicity.

I shall probably not be here to see it, although I don't know, I came of a long-
lived family and events are moving very rapidly, but some day there will no
doubt be a Dickens, or a Balzac, or a Dostoievski[51] who will depict in lasting
colors the real life—not merely the hectic night life, of the American colored
people. May I hope that this writer may come from your ranks?

⌐

SOURCE: Undated typed text at the Fisk University Library. Chesnutt indicates on the
title page that this speech was delivered in Oberlin, O. Internal references suggest composition in 1929 see nn. 6 and 45.

[1]The Dunbar Forum was a student organization at Oberlin College. Oberlin was, in 1835, the first American college to admit African Americans.

[2]Chesnutt was born in Cleveland on 20 June 1858. In September, Jerry (or John) Price was arrested by a U.S. Marshal. The Chesnutt family returned to Cleveland shortly after the birth of a second son, Lewis, on 16 January 1860.

[3]The Western Reserve encompassed 3.3 million acres in what is now northeastern Ohio, extending 120 miles west of Pennsylvania and south beyond the present cities of Youngstown, Akron, and Willard.

[4]To "noll" is to cancel a legal proceeding against a party.

[5]All four of Dunbar's novels appeared after Chesnutt "began to write," but he formally became a novelist before Chesnutt when his *The Uncalled* was published in 1898.

[6]Du Bois agrees with Chesnutt regarding the greater degree of recognition being given black writers and artists. But he also complains about rejections of their works by white publishers and the readerships they control in his essay "Criteria of Negro Art," *The Crisis*, 32 (October 1926), 290–97. Johnson was more positive than Chesnutt indicates. He acknowledges the complaints of "some younger Negro writers" in "Negro Authors and White Publishers," *The Crisis*, 36 (July 1929), 228–29; but then he virtually dismisses the alleged problem: "I believe that Negro writers who have something worthwhile to say and the power and skill to say it have as fair a chance today of being published as any other writer."

[7]This 1926 work by Van Vechten (1880–1964) includes the character Byron Kasson who views Chesnutt as a masterful stylist and one who has pictured accurately and with insight the wide variety of different types of African Americans. Another character, Mary Love, also lauds Chesnutt's literary achievement. Chesnutt is not known to have reviewed the novel.

[8]Brawley critically analyzed Wheatley's writings in *The Negro in Art and Literature in the United States* (1913), offering commentary as well in *A Social History of the American Negro* (1921) and *A Short History of the American Negro* (1927). In none of these does he relate that Wheatley had a penchant for penning eulogies to the great and near-great in Boston.

[9]James Madison Bell (1826–1902), *The Poetical Works of James Madison Bell* (1901); George Washington Williams, *History of the Negro Troops in the War of the Rebellion, 1861–1865* (1872).

[10]In addition to four novels, Dunbar—an Ohioan—published nine collections of poems during his lifetime.

[11]William Carl "Billy" Bolivar (1849–1914), driven by an early and steady interest in book collecting, founded the Afro-American Historical Society in 1897 with his own collection of over three thousand items.

[12]Known as the father of black history, Woodson—an ardent book-collector—helped found the Association for the Study of Negro Life and History in 1915, and established the *Journal of Negro History* the following year. Arthur A. Schomburg (1874–1938) helped establish the Negro Society for Historical Research, was elected president of the American Negro Academy in 1922, and collected over ten thousand books, manuscripts, and pamphlets related to African-American culture which the New York Public Library acquired in 1926.

[13]Arthur B. Spingarn (1878–1971) gave his collection of African-American literature to Howard University. His brother Joel E. Spingarn was the originator of the N.A.A.C.P. Spingarn Medal awarded to Chesnutt in 1928; and Arthur's commitment to that organization resulted in his serving as president from 1940 to 1966. Robert R. Moton (1867–1940), a noted bibliophile, discusses his literary values in his autobiog-

raphy, *Finding a Way Out* (1920); he succeeded Booker T. Washington as principal of Tuskegee Institute in 1915, where he served for twenty years.

[14]William Hazlitt (1778–1830), *The Round Table* (1817); Macaulay, *Essays Critical and Miscellaneous* (1843); William E. H. Lecky, *A History of England in the Eighteenth Century* (1883); William H. Prescott (1796–1859), *History of the Conquest of Mexico* (1843) and *History of the Conquest of Peru* (1847); John Lothrop Motley (1814–77), *The Rise of the Dutch Republic* (1856).

[15]Sir John William Watson (1858–1935), *Epigrams of Art, Life and Nature* (1884).

[16]Though the life of Aesop (620?–564? B.C.) is shrouded in legend, a major source for material about him is Herodotus (484?–420? B.C.), who preserved the tradition that Aesop had been a slave. Horace (Quintus Horatius Flaccus, 65–8 B.C.) observed in his *Satires* that, while his father's family had been servants, his father was a small landowner who gained his freedom from slavery before Horace's birth.

[17]Chesnutt appears to have in mind Edward Wilmot Blyden (1832–1912), author of numerous works advancing this argument. See, for example, *Christianity, Islam and the Negro Race* (1887) and *From West Africa to Palestine* (1912).

[18]Franz Boas, *Anthropology and Modern Life* (1928).

[19]Phidias (c. 500–c. 432 B.C.) was considered the greatest sculptor in ancient Greece.

[20]Alain L. Locke had recently published *The New Negro: An Interpretation* (1925).

[21]In 1914, H. G. Wells published *The War That Will End War*.

[22]That is, the cross on which Jesus died.

[23]Post–Civil War touring companies mounted truncated versions of *Uncle Tom's Cabin* generically referred to as "Tom Shows." No less than eight silent-film adaptations of the novel had been produced by 1929. An American version with sound was not available until 1987.

[24]William E. Henley, "Invictus," *Echoes* (1888).

[25]Julia Peterkin (1880–1961), who fashioned sympathetic portraits of South Carolina African Americans in novels such as *Black April* (1927), observed that African Americans should be gratified by a proposal before Congress to honor the black mammy with an appropriate monument ("The Negro in Art," *The Crisis*, 31 [September 1926], 238–39). Prompted by a suggestion from Mississippi's U.S. Senator John Sharp Williams (1854–1932), Congress had passed a resolution in 1923 to erect a monument in honor of black mammies.

[26]See "The Disfranchisement of the Negro," n. 12.

[27]Charles Curtis (1860–1936) born on what was then land belonging to the Kansa (Kaw) tribe in northeastern Kansas, was one-eighth Kansa on his maternal side; a lawyer, Curtis rose through the ranks of local and national Republican politics, initially opposing the presidential nomination of Herbert C. Hoover (1874–1964) in 1928 but later serving as vice-president in his administration. The president "said to have been of Negro descent" is Warren G. Harding.

[28]*The Quest of the Silver Fleece* (1911).

[29]Paul Green (1894–1981), *In Abraham's Bosom* (1926), starring Jules Bledsoe (1898–1943); Eugene O'Neill (1888–1953), *The Emperor Jones* (1920), starring Charles S. Gilpin and then Paul Robeson (1898–1976), who was also a distinguished singer.

[30]Florence Mills (1895–1927) was a torch-singer who starred in several Broadway productions including *Shuffle Along*. Josephine Baker (1906–75), turned down for *Shuffle Along* because, at fifteen, she could not legally work on Broadway, became a celebrated dancer in Paris in the 1920's.

[31]Langston (1829–97) was, in 1854, the first African American admitted to the bar. He founded the Law School at Howard University in 1868.

[32]John S. Leary (1845–1904) was not the first but the second African American admitted to the North Carolina bar, practicing law in Fayetteville before becoming the dean of the Law School at Shaw University. Lewis Sheridan Leary (1836–59) was one of five blacks who participated in John Brown's 16 October 1859 raid on Harper's Ferry, where he died the following day.

[33]*Elmer Gantry* (1927) by Sinclair Lewis (1885–1951) critically describes a corrupt white revivalist.

[34]Published in 1928.

[35]Thomas S. Stribling (1881–1965), *Birthright* (1922).

[36]Claude McKay (1890–1948), *Home to Harlem* (1928).

[37]Like Hagar and Lissa who are discussed below, Aunt Mamba is a character in *Mamba's Daughters* (1929).

[38]Rudolph Fisher (1897–1934), *The Walls of Jericho* (1928).

[39]Walter F. White (1893–1955), *The Fire in the Flint* (1924).

[40]Jessie Redmon Fauset (1882–1961).

[41]*Plum Bun: A Novel Without a Moral* (1929).

[42]Beatrix Esmond is a character in Thackeray's *Henry Esmond* (1852); *Tess of the d'Urbervilles* (1891); Maggie Tulliver is the heroine of George Eliot's *The Mill on the Floss* (1860); Leo Tolstoy, *Anna Karenina* (1877).

[43]Thomas Bowyer Campbell (1887–?), *Black Sadie* (1928).

[44]Wallace Thurman (1902–34), *The Blacker the Berry* (1929).

[45]Richard Dana Skinner (1893–1941) reviewed *Harlem*, a play by Thurman and William Jourdan Rapp (1895–1942), in "The Play," *Commonweal*, 9 (6 March 1929), 514. Skinner's comments provided the occasion for the editor from which Chesnutt quotes: "Are Negro Writers Exploiting Their People?" Birmingham *News–Age-Herald*, 10 March 1929, 10.

[46]*Hearts in Dixie* was released in 1929. It starred Stepin' Fetchit (1892–1985), born Lincoln Theodore Monroe Andrew Perry.

[47]Henry L. Mencken (1880–1956) was a journalist and essayist distinguished by his iconoclasm, acerbic sense of humor, and Olympian perspective on the human condition.

[48]Eugene Gordon (1890–?) wrote for the Boston *Post* and contributed short stories to *Opportunity*.

[49]The widow of Paul Laurence Dunbar, Alice Dunbar-Nelson (1875–1935) was a teacher, editor, book-reviewer, and short story writer.

[50]Braithwaite edited the annual volumes of *Anthology of Magazine Verse* from 1913 through 1929. *Who's Who in Colored America*, edited by Joseph J. Boris, first appeared in 1927.

[51]Fyodor Mikhailovich Dostoevsky (1821–81).

Advice for Businessmen

Speech delivered in Cleveland, O., 1930

When our good friend Mr. Meade[1] asked me the other day to speak to you on some aspect of business, I forgot a number of things for a moment and said yes. I overlooked the fact that my health is so poor that I have begun to retire from my own business, which is a very hard thing to do as long as one can crawl around. I overlooked the fact that, like Will Rogers, I know nothing about business except what I have read in the newspapers.[2] As to the particular lines of effort with which you are occupied, I am sure the least informed of you knows more than I do. Such excursions as I have made outside my own line have n't been particularly profitable, but quite the contrary. If I put up a building it was likely to be in the wrong place or at the wrong time. If I bought a stock, I paid too much for it and did n't know when to sell it. So any one who followed my example closely would find himself directly headed toward bankruptcy.

However, there are certain basic principles which ought to be borne in mind by all business men. They may not insure success, but they may guard against failure. Chance, or luck, as we call it, is the source of many successes. But with a proper foundation one is more apt to be in position to take a chance. If you plan a building venture your knowledge of the real estate market and the trend of values will save you much subsequent worry and possible loss. If you put up a store building across the street from a baseball park, or any other kind of park, or in any neighborhood which is not built up with residences, business is likely to be dull there and you will find it difficult to rent or sell your building. So, speaking from sad experience, I should say, don't build until you know something about the situation. Don't depend too much on the advice of interested people. If you are making a building loan, don't rely entirely on your banker. His business is lending money, and he will lend it to you on almost any proposition that is perfectly safe for him. He will appraise your property, at a low figure and charge you for the appraisal. He will lend you a certain percentage on the value of the property, from 40 to 60 per cent., at the market rate of interest, and an annual payment of a certain percentage on the principal. You think at the time that his terms are harsh; that he is unduly cautious. But he does the thing I am advising you to do—he looks back, at the history of the neighborhood, he looks forward to its future. And yet with all his wisdom and experience he often slips up. The battle-fields of finance are thickly strewn with the wreckage of mortgage companies, so much so that it is difficult to get second mortgage loans, and in the past few years many first mortgages have been foreclosed at a loss to the owners. And bankers and money lenders don't always guess right. They are like every one else, at the mercy of the unforeseen. Property in Cleveland between East 65th Street and 105th Street, between Cedar Avenue and Wade Park, was not so long ago regarded as choice residence property. Along come the enterprising Van Sweringen brothers, build a rapid transit railroad and following that open up practically all of Cuyahoga County to the east for choice residence sections.[3] As a result, all the new people, the climbers, the would bes, the people who make neighborhoods, move out of the old district, and can by paying anywhere from $25.00 to $2,500.00 down, buy a modern home on some one of the Heights.[4] Fine homes in the old district are turned into lodging houses, and club houses or eating houses, and no new single or two-family houses are built. The neighborhood I mention has become almost entirely apartment house property. And that kind of property moves slowly, and in the present state of the real estate market, moves downward and many a man who has been holding property as a mainstay for his old age, can dimly discern through thickening financial fog, the portals of the poorhouse looming up before him.

But of course you gentlemen, especially those of you connected with the building trades know these things as well as I, and are making your real estate deals in the outlying territory, so far as race prejudice will permit you. It has a better prospect of increase in value than the older and more stagnant neighborhoods. You are not likely to be able to sell a house for much more than it costs. You members of the building trades see to that, though the land will probably appreciate. But you will need to buy with caution. Some of the super-realtors, high pressure salesmen, in opening up new allotments, discount the future increase for five or ten years. For example, the Beach Cliff allotment at Rocky River was unloaded on the public nine or ten years ago at prices which have n't been reached yet.[5]

Most business, in the way of bargain and sale is done on credit, or on borrowed money. There are very few men or companies so rich that they have in hand the cash to stock a big drygoods store or other similar enterprise. A man or group of men conceive such an idea. They get together what cash they can, and start the business. As soon as it becomes a going concern, they buy on credit, 30, 60 or 90 days. Then they establish a line of credit at a good bank, with their stock of goods as security, one hand thus washing the other, until they get a good start. Then perhaps they put out a bond issue, which is only another way of borrowing money, or turn their business into a corporation and borrow the money by selling stock. There are chances for a slip-up all along the line, and the man of poor judgment is apt to be riding for a fall any time. Many years ago when there was a saturnalia of interurban railroad building, Henry Everett and his associates borrowed enough money on the proposed Cleveland-Painesville and Eastern Railroad, to build the road, and the stock that represented the value of the completed railroad was pure "gravy" so to speak. But times changed. The road no longer pays.[6]

The reason suburban railroads don't pay is, of course, the automobile, either in personally owned cars or in busses. The story is told of how the pioneer and still the principal cheap car manufacturer, Mr. Henry Ford,[7] went to New York City to probably the first automobile show, and carried with him a working model of the first Ford car. He demonstrated it at the show, and let it be known that he would take orders for it at $500.00 each, to be delivered some months later. He took orders for 100 cars, came back to Detroit, took his contracts to a bank or banks, with a cost sheet showing the expense of manufacture, and borrowed the money needed to fill the orders, and thus laid the foundation of one of the greatest fortunes of modern times.

Van Sweringens built up their vast business on credit. They foresaw certain developments, gained the confidence of the great bankers and borrowed the money to build, etc.

One of the greatest of the problems which colored people meet is how to get into business. They have n't inherited the aptitude, like the Jews; nor have they had, nor can they get, like white people, the preliminary experience acquired by contacts as clerks, or salesmen. With a population of ten or twelve million they have not, in the United States, one really big drygoods or department store, or one wholesale store of any description—I should say to my knowledge, and I don't know everything. One of my children said to me the other day that when they were little I told them that I was a mahatma,[8] and that a mahatma knew everything, but that as time went on they discovered their mistake and learned that to be sure about anything they had to go beyond me. A colored man who died only the other day, a man of my own generation, T. Thomas Fortune, a former editor of what is now the *New York Age*, once said that one big whole-sale or department store on Broadway, New York, would do more to settle the race question than floods of talk or rivers of ink.[9] That same great city, with several hundred thousand colored people, has n't even one really good hotel.[10] Summer before last, my wife and I spent several weeks at Los Angeles, California,[11] and stopped at a beautiful little new hotel, equipped with all modern conveniences, admirably managed, and charging a very reasonable rate for rooms and meals. Some months later, after our return home, we learned that the colored men who ran the hotel had been unable to make ends meet and had turned the property over to the real owners, the white men, I believe they were Jews, who had financed it. At which news I sighed regretfully, because I had regarded and quoted the hotel as a brilliant demonstration of how colored men could succeed in the hotel business.

(Wormleys in Washington.)[12]

Another line of business which colored people used to dominate is the barbering industry. Carelessness on their part or the superior energy or ability of white competitors caused the colored barbers to lose out. The last outstanding example of success in this line in Cleveland was our friend Mr. George Myers,[13] who died suddenly the other day. More than a popular and useful citizen, an institution, a sort of liaison officer, between the white and colored people. (School board, City Hall, replaced by Mrs. Martin and the three city councilmen.)[14] I welcome the opportunity to pay a deserved tribute to his memory. Mr. Myers' only real rival, again so far as I know, was Mr. Alonzo Herndon, of Atlanta, Georgia, who died a year or two ago, and left an estate estimated at a million dollars.[15]

But to offset the loss of this profitable business, colored people have discovered and developed the toilet and beautifying end of the business, and in the lessons of Madame Walker, Anthony Overton and Mrs. Malone of Poro College fame, have built up substantial fortunes in catering to the wants of colored people in this direction, having first convinced them by skilful advertising that these wants really existed.[16]

Other fields of industry and business have done well but not quite so well. There have been many colored banks but not many successful ones,—I can mention three which seem to be riding safely—the Bingo and Overton banks in Chicago and the Dunbar Bank in New York. (Really not a colored bank, financed and protected by a rich white man.)

Another line of industry in which colored men, following the line of least resistance have in a measure succeeded, is the life and benefit insurance business. In spite of some hard luck, there is at least one large company which is making money.

In insurance, as in banking, success is measured by two things—first, the ability to get money, which is comparatively easy, second, the ability to use it safely and profitably, which is rather difficult. I have mentioned already the attitude of banks toward real estate and building loans. I don't imagine colored banks could safely do otherwise.

It is rather unfortunate that just about the time that colored people might have been able to compete with others in small businesses, the methods of doing business changed radically. A small grocery cannot compete successfully with the great chain stores which control millions and therefore can buy in large quantities at much better prices. A small furnishing store cannot compete with a great department store, or the great mail order houses which sell everything from toothpicks to ready made houses. Of course, if colored capital could be got together in banks or local companies, it would be possible to swing large loans, that time does n't seem to have arrived yet.

Now, gentlemen, I guess I have proved what I started off by saying, that I don't know anything about business. I shall not insult your intelligence with trite advice, to be thorough in your work, to carry out your contracts to the letter, to take care of your money, to look out for favorable opportunities to invest it, and in general, to do the things which honest and prudent men do, without which no man can succeed in business or deserve to succeed. Colored people are forging ahead rapidly, and I am sure we all hope they may gradually work their way up to the top of successful business.

⌣

SOURCE: Undated and untitled typed text at the Western Reserve Historical Society Library. Chesnutt's reference to the death "the other day" of George A. Myers suggests that this speech was delivered shortly after 17 January 1930. The identity of the group addressed is not known.

[1]Possibly Frank B. Meade (1867–1957), who was a locally distinguished architect. In partnership with James M. Hamilton (1876–1941), he strongly influenced the style of residential structures erected in the Cleveland suburbs.

[2]William P. Rogers (1879–1935), a humorist who enjoyed a successful stage career, became internationally famous through his books and newspaper writings as the "cowboy philosopher." Chesnutt here appropriates Rogers's signature catch-line when commenting upon current events: he assured those whom he entertained, "All I know is what I see in the papers."

[3]Mantis J. (1881–1935) and Oris P. (1879–1936) Van Sweringen purchased in 1916 the Nickel Plate Railroad, which afforded most of the right-of-way they needed to establish rail service in 1920 between Cleveland and their suburban Shaker Heights residential development.

[4]The "Heights" lie to the east of Cleveland, and the area was developed in the 1920's as residential communities. Only fifteen African-American families lived in Shaker, Garfield, and Cleveland Heights; Chesnutt explains in "The Negro in Cleveland" that they were able to buy homes because they were "not obviously Negroid."

[5]Rocky River, incorporated as a city in 1930, is on the shore of Lake Erie nine miles west of Cleveland.

[6]Henry A. Everett (1856–1917) controlled the Cleveland Electric Railway. He and others established the Cleveland-Painesville & Eastern Railroad in 1895, and thus owned almost all of the northern Ohio interurbans. The syndicate of which he was a member extended its lines yet farther by absorbing two other railways; but the passenger traffic it hoped for never materialized.

[7]Ford (1863–1947) was the founder and president of the Ford Motor Company in Detroit (1903–19).

[8]One who is venerated for his great knowledge and spirituality.

[9]Fortune did not actually die the "other day" but on 2 June 1928, at least a year and a half earlier; George A. Myers's recent death, referred to below, occurred on 17 January 1930.

[10]That is, one good hotel at which African Americans may lodge.

[11]Late June through early July 1928. See "Remarks of Charles Waddell Chesnutt."

[12]James Wormley (1819–84) opened his hotel at the corner of H and 15th Streets in 1871, establishing a reputation for its decor and the quality of food served. Frequented by congressmen, it was operated after Wormley's death and until 1893 by his eldest son. As was the case with the Los Angeles hotel previously cited, Wormley rented the building.

[13]George A. Myers (1859–1930), after working at Benson's Barber Shop in Cleveland's Weddell House, established his own successful business in another hotel, the Hollenden, employing numerous barbers. Myers interacted well with the politicians who frequented his establishment; and by the early 1890's he was very much involved in Republican politics, particularly in organizing the African-American vote in cooperation with Mark Hanna and William McKinley. While he was not interested in a political career per se, he remained active in state and local affairs until his death.

[14]Mary B. Martin (1877–1930) was, in 1930, the first African American elected to the Cleveland Board of Education, and served two terms. In 1930, three councilmen were African Americans.

[15]Alonzo F. Herndon (1858? 1868?–1927) was a rural Georgian who began cutting hair in Senoia, opened his own shop in Jonesboro, and moved in 1882 to Atlanta where he eventually owned three shops employing seventy-five people. In 1905 he became involved in the sale of insurance, establishing an agency whose profits dwarfed those possible for barber shop operators such as Myers.

[16]Sarah Breedlove McWilliams (1867–1919) founded the C. J. Walker Manufacturing Company. "Madame C. J. Walker" produced haircare products for African-American women which were vended by door-to-door salespeople. As financially successful was her competitor whose name Chesnutt did not recall, writing "Mrs. Mc_____." Mrs. Annie T. Malone (1869–1957) marketed Poro Products for haircare. Poro College in St. Louis, founded in 1917, was the first school dedicated to teaching African-American cosmetology. Anthony Overton was President of the Douglass National Bank in Chicago and catered to a black clientele.

The Negro in Cleveland

Essay published in the *Clevelander*, November 1930

There are in Cleveland, according to the best available information, about 75,000 persons of African descent, classed as Negroes, though they vary in blood from one thirty-second to full Negro, and in color from ivory or pale pink to ebony.

They reside, for the most part, in the district lying between 14th Street on the west and 105th Street on the east, and between Cedar and Woodland Avenues, with some extension to the south, from Woodland, and to the east from 105th, and quite a number out Kinsman way, in what is known as Mt. Pleasant. In these districts they can purchase or rent and occupy property without objection, and many of them own their own homes. Other residential districts are resistant to their advent, sometimes by intimidation or violence, but there are quite a few scattered in the district between Superior Avenue and the lake, in the vicinity of East 105th Street.

FORBIDDEN GROUND

The whole Heights development is practically closed to them, though a few families not obviously Negroid have secured a foothold. It is about as difficult for a Negro to buy property on the Heights, except in one village, as it is for the traditional camel to pass through the eye of the traditional needle.[1] This exclusiveness is maintained by care in sales, and by restrictive clauses in deeds, the legality of which is doubtful and has never been thoroughly tested. The objection to their proximity does not include servants, so that Negroes in fact live all over the city.

Negroes as a class live on a low economic plane. Most of them are poor, some of them very poor; many of their children go to school undernourished and insufficiently clad. They have no rich men, measuring wealth by a very low standard, although their aggregate possessions would reach a very respectable figure. Of the upper tenth, a few own handsome, well-furnished homes with many evidences of taste and culture. The majority live in drab, middle or low class houses, none too well kept up, or in the moderate priced apartment houses which are found in their neighborhoods; while the poor live in dilapidated rack-rented shacks, sometimes a whole family in one or two rooms, as a rule paying higher rents than white tenants for the same space.

The first and fundamental concern of all men is the supply of their physical needs—food, clothing and shelter. To meet these simplest wants on the lowest plane demands money, and to get money one has to find work. Much of the Negro labor is common labor. The restriction of immigration, by lessening competition has helped the Negro in this field, though the multiplication of machines has been a strong counter-agent. Odd jobs are the least dependable form of employment, and many colored people have no other source of income. Domestic service, skilled or unskilled, supports many others.

When such numbers of them came North during and after the war,[2] many were employed in the mills and factories at high wages, but the return of the white soldiers and, later, the financial slump, reduced this employment materially. There are many colored men in the building trades, especially in the rougher and harder work. They are received in most of the building trades unions, the notable exceptions being the electrical workers, the plumbers and the structural iron workers. But in the distribution of work through the unions, they are generally the last to be considered.

In spite of liberal resolutions passed from time to time by the American Federation of Labor, many unions, including most of the railroad unions, exclude Negroes from membership.

The waiters', waitresses' and cooks' unions do not admit colored members.

Due to the disappearance of the old-time system of apprenticeship, it is hard for a colored youth to learn a trade, and the trade schools conducted by the Board of Education are so tied up by rules and regulations, largely dictated by the labor unions, that it is difficult for a Negro boy to acquire a trade in them. He cannot study unless he secures in advance the promise of a job where he can do practical work on part time during his studies, or where he will be permanently employed at the end of his course. The difficulty in placing them has caused the officials to discourage the attendance of Negro students. A colored youth can take elementary training in the East Technical High School, but practical training in many trades can only be acquired in factories which discourage or limit the number of apprentices and especially Negro apprentices. The advantage of labor unions to the Negro lies chiefly in the advance in wages secured by the unions, which is reflected in the wages paid for common and non-union labor.

GAINING A FOOTHOLD

The thousands of places as clerks and salesmen in the great department and chain stores are closed to them with very few exceptions. Recently one of the chain store companies has had a store in a colored neighborhood with an entire Negro personnel.

There are no Negro conductors or motormen on the Cleveland Street Railway. In Detroit, where the street railways are city owned and operated, there are about one hundred. The East Ohio Gas Company, the Ohio Bell Telephone Company, indeed none of the great public utilities, employ colored people in anything but the humblest positions. In many of the industrial plants they are employed for the harder kinds of labor but have suffered disproportionately by the recent industrial decline, being generally the first to be let out when the force is reduced.

The development of business among Negroes in Cleveland has been backward, for obvious reasons—the lack of capital, experience and inherited business aptitude. Nevertheless, there are many kinds of businesses owned and operated by them. There are ten undertaking establishments, many small groceries, drug stores, restaurants, barber shops and pressing shops, and at least two small factories which manufacture brass specialties and metal grinding materials. There are few partnerships and no commercial corporations. They operate a number of gasoline service stations, including a chain of seven. There are colored photographers, caterers, music and furniture dealers; they conduct several hotels and various other business enterprises.

The number of Negro newspapers varies from time to time. At present there are two.[3] They publish news of special interest to their group, including in every issue a list of lynchings and other outrages, as well as a chronicle of successes.

The Negroes of Cleveland are well represented numerically in the learned professions. There are about thirty-five colored lawyers practicing in the courts of the city and county, mostly in the Municipal and Police Courts. They have little commercial business, because most of their clients are of their own people, who have no large commercial or manufacturing business, for which reason a Negro lawyer is never appointed receiver or referee in an important case, though they are often appointed by the judges to defend criminals, the county paying their fees. Several of them have been recommended and others declared qualified by the Citizens' League and the Bar Associations when they run for office, and are well spoken of by the white lawyers and judges.

In the medical profession the Negro fares even better. There are fifty Negro doctors practicing in Cleveland. Six are attached to the staff of Lakeside Hospital, the main teaching unit of Western Reserve University, which has been very generous toward the Negro physician. One of them, who has been in the Department of Pediatrics for nine years, was sent to Harvard last year by the Department of Surgery for special study under a famous specialist. There is one in the Ophthalmological Department and one in the Department of Neurology.

Charity Hospital, a Catholic institution, has a Negro physician in the roentgenological department. The Salvation Army maternity home and hospital for colored women has an all-Negro staff, with the exception of a white chief-of-staff, and for years there has been a colored physician on the courtesy staff of Charity Hospital in minor surgery and medicine.

A LUXURY

There are several dentists, but dentistry is one of the decorative arts and does not thrive among poor people in hard times, although in the boom years following the war the amount of gold used by Negro dentists must have seriously depleted the gold reserve of the nation.

There is a widely varying attitude toward the Negro in the social service agencies, embracing in the term those supported in whole or in part by the Community Fund.

The Y.M.C.A. and the Y.W.C.A. do not admit colored members, though colored students are received in the Y School of Technology and the Y.M.C.A. branch at Cedar Avenue and 77th Street is open to all young people without discrimination. The executive secretary in charge of the branch was captain in a colored regiment of the A.E.F.[4] The Phillis Wheatley Association for colored working girls,[5] probably the most widely known of the Negro welfare agencies, occupies a large and commodious building, erected by popular subscription, at 40th Street and Cedar Avenue, where it furnishes rooms for young women and conducts an employment agency and a restaurant which is open to the public. It conducts training classes in domestic service and home economics, presents pageants and plays, and has an auditorium which can be rented for meetings. It also has a branch on East 105th Street.

The Neighborhood Settlement, on 38th Street, long known as the "Play House," serves colored and white children on equal terms, and has long been doing a great cultural service for the Negro. Its very capable dramatic club, the Gilpin Players, has a small theater on Central Avenue, and it has also presented plays in the Little Theater at Public Hall.[6]

FOR THE RACE

The Negro Welfare Association[7] is performing a very useful service in opening up new fields of employment for Negroes, in probation and Big Brother work and other welfare activities. The local branch of the National Association for the Advancement of Colored People concerns itself with racial discrimination of all sorts.

No colored children are received at any Cleveland Orphan Asylum, though

Negro orphans are looked after very thoroughly by the Cleveland Humane Society. None of the "old folks' homes," male or female, are open to Negroes, except the Cleveland Home for Aged Colored Persons on Cedar Avenue, near 40th Street. This institution was founded and is managed by colored people and has places for sixteen inmates, all of which are taken.

The Salvation Army conducts a rescue home for colored women on Kinsman Avenue. Its other ministrations seem to be extended to the colored poor impartially, though it does not furnish lodging to the Negro "down-and-out."

The place where colored people get the best break is the public service. The reason is obvious—in Cleveland they vote, and they are learning, under an increasingly efficient leadership, to use their vote effectively. In certain districts the Negro vote is controlling, due to residence segregation, whether voluntary or forced. There are a colored Representative in the State Legislature, three members of the City Council, a member of the City Civil Service Commission and an Examiner in its office, and a member of the City Planning Commission. The Garbage Collection Department is entirely manned by Negroes, including the superintendency.

There are colored patrolmen and detectives, but no Negro firemen—perhaps for social reasons, since the firemen live in the stations. They are called for jury duty just as other citizens, though not accepted on juries quite as often. They have at least one clerk or deputy in each of the county offices, and have put forward candidates for the office of judge, so far without success. The supply of judgeships is so small and the demand and salaries so large that a colored lawyer has a small chance of election to one of them. There are several colored probation officers in the Juvenile and Municipal Courts.

In the Federal Post Office, where places are under the Civil Service, they hold many of the low salaried positions, as office clerks, postal clerks and mail carriers. Several of them are or have been employed as government meat inspectors in stockyards and abattoirs.

There has never been racial segregation in the public schools. A colored woman is a member of the Board of Education,[8] elected thereto by popular vote, the majority of which was white. The office pays no salary and there is little opportunity for graft.

There are nearly a hundred colored teachers in the public high and grade schools, and colored teachers are trained in the Normal School. They sometimes claim they are discriminated against in admission to the Normal School, but perhaps they are unduly sensitive. The requirements for registration are very rigid, as to education, health and "personality," and many of the white applicants do not qualify.

The Quincy Avenue branch of the Cleveland Public Library employs one colored young woman, and the Sterling Branch Library has two, one being a library school attendant and working in the library on part time. Another, a college graduate, is working full time and attending Cleveland College. The library has five colored pages. The total number of professional librarians in the whole system is between three hundred and fifty and four hundred, besides others who work part time, so that the Negro is not over-represented.

There is a Negro underworld and there are many Negro criminals. But crime, under the 18th Amendment and the Volstead Law, has become a major industry, and Negroes do not conduct major industries.

ONLY PETTY CRIME

There are small bootleggers and drug peddlers among them, a great deal of policy and "numbers" gambling, an occasional gas-station or grocery holdup, with perhaps an incidental murder, but colored men as a whole have neither the money nor the organization to carry on big bootlegging and racketeering enterprises, nor the reckless daring which marks the bank burglaries and payroll hold-ups which fill so much space in our police records. They have small opportunity for embezzlement or official graft. The most conspicuous instance of alleged criminality in Cleveland along this line among Cleveland Negroes involved only two hundred dollars. Other racial groups have taken precedence over the Negro in the field of crime, in which he might cheerfully admit his inferiority.

Socially, in the narrow sense of the word, colored people in Cleveland are strictly segregated. There are a few, close to the color line, who exchange social visits with a few white people. I do not know more than one place down town where I could take for luncheon a dark-colored man.[9] A few years ago the Chamber of Commerce had for its speaking guest a very prominent and very dark Negro. It secured accommodation for him at a leading hotel, after another hotel had refused to entertain the Chamber's guest except upon condition that his meals be served in his room.

With the exception of the City Club,[10] which has several colored members, I know of only three clubs in Cleveland with club houses which have any colored members, and they have only two in the aggregate, both members of the same family and superficially white. I do not refer, of course, to colored clubs, of which there are two that own their own club houses, but they do not conduct restaurants.

There is a civil service law which forbids discrimination in public places, but it is difficult and expensive to enforce. One does not care to have to bring a lawsuit or swear out a warrant every time one wants a sandwich or a cup of coffee. A dark face may occasionally be seen at a hotel dining table, at some dinner given by a professional or civic organization of which he is a member, but almost never otherwise.

The church, in modern times, has become largely a social institution. There are a few colored members of white churches,[11] but most of the Negroes belong to their own churches, of which there are more than they need, or can properly support. Some of them have pastors with a high sense of civic duty who are capable and earnest leaders.

The reaction to the barrier of segregation which confronts the Negro almost everywhere has resulted, in Cleveland as elsewhere, in the effort to supply among his own people many of the opportunities which he is denied. A few days ago an insurance agent called on me to solicit automobile insurance. He stated proudly, as what he considered a fine selling point, that his company wrote no insurance for colored people or for anyone living between Cedar and Woodland Avenues.

INSURANCE AND BANKING

To meet such discrimination, which is general all over the country, Negroes have organized their own insurance companies, of which nine have agencies or branch offices in Cleveland, all of which carry substantial amounts of insurance. They have no banks with checking accounts, but have three mortgage and loan companies, of which one expects shortly to meet all the requirements of the State Banking Department necessary to make it a regular bank. These institutions furnish employment for a number of young colored men and women, giving them the opportunity to learn by experience, sometimes, as elsewhere, at the expense of their stockholders, how to conduct financial operations safely and profitably. Several of the large banks in Cleveland have more capital, deposits and surplus than all the Negro banks in the United States. The Negro financial enterprises are small things, but as an index are not to be despised, and so far they have had no such catastrophes as have ingloriously terminated the career of so many of the much larger mortgage and loan companies of Cleveland.[12] Fortunately, they have no stockbrokers.

The Negro has almost lost several of his ancestral occupations. The Italians and Greeks, perhaps because they are better business men, have almost entirely taken over the shoeshining parlors, though Negroes are generally employed to do the work.

The jobs as hotel help had practically vanished until the recent walkout of the union workers resulted in the employment of several hundred Negro cooks and waiters who had formerly been crowded out by the unions.

The increase of white barber shops has almost put the Negro barber out of business, so far as white patronage is concerned, and the Barbers' Union, in which no Negro is admitted to membership, has been trying to complete their ruin by proposing a state barber's licensing law requiring examination and acceptance by a committee dominated by the union.

The denial to the Negro of membership in beneficial and fraternal societies has resulted in the formation among their own group of a similar organization for practically every such order, often with the same name, to the amusement of the social cynic, and often to the exasperation of the white orders. There have always been Negro Masons, but now there are Negro Elks, Moose, Knights of

Pythias, Odd Fellows, Eagles, etc., *ad infinitum*. Why, asks the white Moose, indignantly or plaintively, do they not originate something of their own? They answer that what is good enough for the white people is good enough for them, and, moreover, that the white orders have used up all the worthy names in the fauna and flora, leaving only the skunk, the snake, the buzzard and the jimson weed for the Negro to choose from.

There is a Negro lawyers' club,[13] though colored lawyers are freely admitted to the two other local bar associations, and there is a Negro Medical Association, though there are several colored members of the local Academy of Medicine.

There is a race problem in Cleveland, but it is not acute. From the Negroes' side it is mainly concerned with a fair living, a decent place to live, making his way in the world on equal terms with others, and living at peace with his neighbors. With these things, or any of them, denied to any material extent, that the problem might become acute is evidenced by the race riots which a few years ago convulsed Chicago, Detroit and St. Louis. With fair play, the Negro makes a very good citizen. He vastly enjoys his small successes and considers himself a regular fellow. Abuse him and he becomes in his own eyes a martyr, and the martyr complex is not conducive to good citizenship. It might, conceivably, make the colored people a fertile soil for socialist or communist propaganda; for whatever the weakness of communism, it teaches human equality, which makes an irresistible appeal to those who are denied it.

The greatest handicap which the Negro in Cleveland, as elsewhere, has to meet is his color, which he cannot change, and the consequences of which he cannot escape. Plausibly good reasons are given for any discrimination of which the Negro is a victim, but on analysis it all fines down to his color, which makes generalization in his case easy and exposes him to all the inherited prejudgments which have grown up about him. A white man can live down the lowest origin. The Negro's color is always with him.

The better class of white people in Cleveland are in some ways very generous toward the Negro, and can generally be relied upon to respond liberally, financially, to any call on their part for money for any worthy purpose. But they could render them a better service by cultivating fraternal or, if that be too much, at least friendly relations with them, not so much by way of condescension, as from man to man, thereby making their advancement easier along all lines. For they still have a long and hard road to travel to reach that democratic equality upon the theory of which our government and our social system are founded, not to desire and seek which would make them unworthy of contempt.

↬

SOURCE: "The Negro in Cleveland," *Clevelander*, 5 (November 1930), 3–4, 24, 26–27. Following his signature, Chesnutt was identified as "Attorney, Court Reporter, and Author."
    [1]Matthew 19:24.

[2]World War I.

[3]In 1930, there was only one, the *Cleveland Gazette*. The *Cleveland Advocate* failed in 1924, and its successor, the *Cleveland Herald*, ceased publication in 1927; and their publisher, Ormond A. Forte (1887–1959), did not initiate another, the *Cleveland Eagle*, until 1935. The *Cleveland Journal* was published from 1903 to 1912.

[4]The Cleveland city directory identifies Charles E. Frye as secretary, then manager, and then executive secretary of the Cedar Avenue Branch. The A.E.F. (American Expeditionary Forces) landed in France under the direction of General John J. Pershing (1860–1948) in 1917 and took part in thirteen major operations during World War I. Troop A, comprised of African Americans, served as a field artillery unit.

[5]Established in 1911.

[6]The Neighborhood Association was founded in 1915 and was soon known as the Playhouse Settlement because of its dramatic productions. In 1920 the association formed its Dumas Dramatic Club, renaming it the Gilpin Players in 1922. Karamu— "place of joyful meeting" in Swahili—was the name of the theater acquired in 1927.

[7]Founded in 1917.

[8]Mary B. Martin.

[9]A photograph of Chesnutt appeared with this essay, making it clear that he appeared neither "dark" nor even "colored" and that he himself was able to dine where he chose.

[10]Incorporated in 1912 to facilitate discussion of civic concerns.

[11]The Chesnutts were among them at two Episcopal churches: St. Mary's and then Emmanuel.

[12]Reference to the effects of the Great Depression following the 1929 stock market crash.

[13]The John Harlan Law Club.

Post-Bellum—Pre-Harlem

Essay published in *The Colophon*, February 1931

My first book, *The Conjure Woman*, was published by the Houghton Mifflin Company in 1899. It was not, strictly speaking, a novel, though it has been so called, but a collection of short stories in Negro dialect, put in the mouth of an old Negro gardener, and related by him in each instance to the same audience, which consisted of the Northern lady and gentleman who employed him. They are naive and simple stories, dealing with alleged incidents of chattel slavery, as the old man had known it and as I had heard of it, and centering around the professional activities of old Aunt Peggy, the plantation conjure woman, and others of that ilk.

In every instance Julius had an axe to grind, for himself or his church, or some member of his family, or a white friend. The introductions to the stories, which were written in the best English I could command, developed the characters of Julius's employers and his own, and the wind-up of each story reveals the old man's ulterior purpose, which, as a general thing, is accomplished.

Most of the stories in *The Conjure Woman* had appeared in the *Atlantic Monthly* from time to time, the first story, "The Goophered Grapevine," in the issue of August, 1887, and one of them, "The Conjurer's Revenge," in the *Overland Monthly*.[1] Two of them were first printed in the bound volume.

After the book had been accepted for publication, a friend of mine, the late Judge Madison W. Beacom, of Cleveland, a charter member of the Rowfant Club, suggested to the publishers a limited edition, which appeared in advance of the trade edition in an issue of one hundred and fifty numbered copies and was subscribed for almost entirely by members of the Rowfant Club and of the Cleveland bar. It was printed by the Riverside Press on large hand-made linen paper, bound in yellow buckram, with the name on the back in black letters on a white label, a very handsome and dignified volume.[2] The trade edition was bound in brown cloth and on the front was a picture of a white-haired old Negro, flanked on either side by a long-eared rabbit. The dust-jacket bore the same illustration.

The name of the story teller, "Uncle" Julius, and the locale of the stories, as well as the cover design, were suggestive of Mr. Harris's Uncle Remus,[3] but the tales are entirely different. They are sometimes referred to as folk tales, but while they employ much of the universal machinery of wonder stories, especially the metamorphosis, with one exception, that of the first story, "The Goophered Grapevine," of which the norm was a folk tale, the stories are the fruit of my own imagination, in which respect they differ from the Uncle Remus stories which are avowedly folk tales.

Several subsequent editions of *The Conjure Woman* were brought out; just how many copies were sold altogether I have never informed myself, but not enough for the royalties to make me unduly rich, and in 1929, just thirty years after the first appearance of the book, a new edition was issued by Houghton Mifflin Company. It was printed from the original plates, with the very handsome title page of the limited edition, an attractive new cover in black and red, and a very flattering foreword by Colonel Joel Spingarn.

Most of my books are out of print, but I have been told that it is quite unusual for a volume of short stories which is not one of the accepted modern classics to remain on sale for so long a time.[4]

At the time when I first broke into print seriously, no American colored writer had ever secured critical recognition except Paul Laurence Dunbar, who had won his laurels as a poet. Phillis Wheatley, a Colonial poet, had gained recognition largely because she was a slave and born in Africa, but the short story, or the novel of life and manners, had not been attempted by any one of that group.

There had been many novels dealing with slavery and the Negro. Harriet Beecher Stowe, especially in *Uncle Tom's Cabin*, had covered practically the whole subject of slavery and race admixture. George W. Cable had dwelt upon the romantic and some of the tragic features of racial contacts in Louisiana, and Judge Albion W. Tourgée, in what was one of the best sellers of his day, *A Fool's Errand*, and in his *Bricks Without Straw*, had dealt with the problems of reconstruction.

Thomas Dixon was writing the Negro down industriously and with marked popular success. Thomas Nelson Page was disguising the harshness of slavery under the mask of sentiment. The trend of public sentiment at the moment was distinctly away from the Negro. He had not developed any real political or business standing; socially he was outcast. His musical and stage successes were still for the most part unmade, and on the whole he was a small frog in a large pond, and there was a feeling of pessimism in regard to his future.

Publishers are human, and of course influenced by the opinions of their public. The firm of Houghton Mifflin, however, was unique in some respects. One of the active members of the firm was Francis J. Garrison, son of William Lloyd Garrison, from whom he had inherited his father's hatred of slavery and friendliness to the Negro. His partner, George H. Mifflin, was a liberal and generous gentleman trained in the best New England tradition. They were both friendly to my literary aspirations and became my personal friends.[5]

But the member of their staff who was of most assistance to me in publishing my first book was Walter Hines Page, later ambassador to England under President Wilson, and at that time editor of the *Atlantic Monthly*, as well as literary adviser for the publishing house, himself a liberalized Southerner, who derived from the same part of the South where the stories in *The Conjure Woman* are located, and where I passed my adolescent years. He was a graduate of Macon College, a fellow of Johns Hopkins University, had been attached to the staff of the *Forum* and the *New York Evening Post*, and was as broad-minded a Southerner as it was ever my good fortune to meet.[6]

Three of the *Atlantic* editors wrote novels dealing with race problems— William Dean Howells in *An Imperative Duty*, Bliss Perry in *The Plated City*, and Mr. Page in *The Autobiography of Nicholas Worth*.[7]

The first of my conjure stories had been accepted for the *Atlantic* by Thomas Bailey Aldrich, the genial auburn-haired poet who at that time presided over the editorial desk.[8] My relations with him, for the short time they lasted, were most cordial and friendly.

Later on I submitted to Mr. Page several stories of post-war life among the colored people which the *Atlantic* published, and still later the manuscript of a novel. The novel was rejected, and was subsequently rewritten and published by Houghton Mifflin under the tile of *The House Behind the Cedars*. Mr. Page, who had read the manuscript, softened its rejection by the suggestion that perhaps a collection of the conjure stories might be undertaken by the firm with a better prospect of success. I was in the hands of my friends, and submitted the collection. After some omissions and additions, all at the advice of Mr. Page, the book was accepted and announced as *The Conjure Woman*, in 1899, and I enjoyed all the delights of proof-reading and the other pleasant emotions attending the publication of a first book. Mr. Page, Mr. Garrison and Mr. Mifflin vied with each other in helping to make our joint venture a literary and financial success.

The book was favorably reviewed by literary critics. If I may be pardoned one quotation, William Dean Howells, always the friend of the aspiring author, in an article published in the *Atlantic Monthly* for May, 1900, wrote:

> The stories of *The Conjure Woman* have a wild, indigenous poetry, the creation of sincere and original imagination, which is imparted with a tender humorousness and a very artistic reticence. As far as his race is concerned, or his sixteenth part of a race, it does not greatly matter whether Mr. Chesnutt invented their motives, or found them, as he feigns, among his distant cousins of the Southern cabins. In either case the wonder of their beauty is the same, and whatever is primitive and sylvan or campestral in the reader's heart is touched by the spells thrown on the simple black lives in these enchanting tales. Character, the most precious thing in fiction, is faithfully portrayed.[9]

Imagine the thrill with which a new author would read such an encomium from such a source!

From the publisher's standpoint, the book proved a modest success. This was by no means a foregone conclusion, even assuming its literary merit and the publisher's imprint, for reasons which I shall try to make clear.

I have been referred to as the "first Negro novelist," meaning, of course, in the United States; Pushkin in Russia and the two Dumas in France had produced a large body of popular fiction. At that time a literary work by an American of acknowledged color was a doubtful experiment, both for the writer and for the publisher, entirely apart from its intrinsic merit. Indeed, my race was never mentioned by the publishers in announcing or advertising the book. From my own viewpoint it was a personal matter. It never occurred to me to claim any merit because of it, and I have always resented the denial of anything on account of it. My colored friends, however, with a very natural and laudable zeal for the race, with which I found no fault, saw to it that the fact was not overlooked, and I have before me a copy of a letter written by one of them to the editor of the *Atlanta Constitution*, which had published a favorable review of the book, accompanied by my portrait, chiding him because the reviewer had not referred to my color.[10]

A woman critic of Jackson, Mississippi, questioning what she called the rumor as to my race, added, "Some people claim that Alexander Dumas, author of *The Count of Monte Cristo* and *The Three Musketeers*, was a colored man. This is obviously untrue, because no Negro could possibly have written these books"—a pontifical announcement which would seem to settle the question definitely, despite the historical evidence to the contrary.

While *The Conjure Woman* was in the press, the *Atlantic* published a short story of mine called "The Wife of His Youth" which attracted wide attention. James MacArthur, at that time connected with the *Critic*, later with *Harper's*, in talking one day with Mr. Page, learned of my race and requested leave to mention it as a matter of interest to the literary public. Mr. Page demurred at first on the ground that such an announcement might be harmful to the success of my forthcoming book, but finally consented, and Mr. MacArthur mentioned the fact in the *Critic*, referring to me as a "mulatto."[11]

As a matter of fact, substantially all of my writings, with the exception of *The Conjure Woman*, have dealt with the problems of people of mixed blood, which, while in the main the same as those of the true Negro, are in some instances and in some respects much more complex and difficult of treatment, in fiction as in life.

I have lived to see, after twenty years or more, a marked change in the attitude of publishers and the reading public in regard to the Negro in fiction. The development of Harlem, with its large colored population in all shades, from ivory to ebony, of all degrees of culture, from doctors of philosophy to the lowest grade of illiteracy; its various origins, North American, South American, West Indian and African; its morals ranging from the highest to the most debased; with the vivid life of its cabarets, dance halls, and theatres; with its ambitious business and professional men, its actors, singers, novelists and poets, its aspirations and demands for equality—without which any people would merit only contempt—presented a new field for literary exploration which of recent years has been cultivated assiduously.

One of the first of the New York writers to appreciate the possibilities of Harlem for literary purposes was Carl Van Vechten, whose novel *Nigger Heaven* was rather severely criticized by some of the colored intellectuals as a libel on the race, while others of them praised it highly. I was prejudiced in its favor for reasons which those who have read the book will understand. I found it a vivid and interesting story which presented some new and better types of Negroes and treated them sympathetically.

The Negro novel, whether written by white or colored authors, has gone so much farther now in the respects in which it was criticized that *Nigger Heaven*, in comparison with some of these later productions, would be almost as mild as a Sunday School tract compared to *The Adventures of Fanny Hill*.[12] Several of these novels, by white and colored authors alike, reveal such an intimate and meticulous familiarity with the baser aspects of Negro life, North and South, that one is inclined to wonder how and from what social sub-sewers they gathered their information. With the exception of one or two of the earlier ones, the heroine of the novel is never chaste, though for the matter of that few post-Victorian heroines are, and most of the male characters are likewise weaklings or worse.

I have in mind a recent novel, brilliantly written by a gifted black author, in which, to my memory, there is not a single decent character, male or female.[13]

These books are written primarily for white readers, as it is extremely doubtful whether a novel, however good, could succeed financially on its sales to colored readers alone. But it seems to me that a body of twelve million people, struggling upward slowly but surely from a lowly estate, must present all along the line of its advancement many situations full of dramatic interest, ranging from farce to tragedy, with many admirable types worthy of delineation.

Caste, a principal motive of fiction from Richardson down through the Victorian epoch, has pretty well vanished among white Americans. Between the whites and the Negroes it is acute, and is bound to develop an increasingly difficult complexity, while among the colored people themselves it is just beginning to appear.

Negro writers no longer have any difficulty in finding publishers. Their race is no longer a detriment but a good selling point, and publishers are seeking their books, sometimes, I am inclined to think, with less regard for quality than in the case of white writers. To date, colored writers have felt restricted for subjects to their own particular group, but there is every reason to hope that in the future, with proper encouragement, they will make an increasingly valuable contribution to literature, and perhaps produce chronicles of life comparable to those of Dostoievsky, Dumas, Dickens or Balzac.

⌒

SOURCE: *The Colophon* 2, Part 5 (February 1931), n.p.

[1]Seeing previous periodical publication were four of the short stories. Three, rather than two, featuring Uncle Julius McAdoo appeared in print for the first time in the collection. Almost three decades later, Chesnutt also misremembered Aunt Peggy's more limited role; she is not present in all of the tales.

[2]Madison W. Beacom (1854–1927). Chesnutt refers to the "Large-Paper Edition," which was the second 1899 printing of the first edition. Sheets for 160 copies were produced.

[3]The image of an "Uncle" between two rabbits was, rather, a transparent exploitation by Houghton, Mifflin & Co. of the highly successful Remus tales.

[4]By "editions" Chesnutt means printings. The first edition plates were used for five printings in 1899–1900. That Chesnutt was not made "unduly rich" is reflected in the small press runs for the following number of copies: 1,528, 160, 518, 500, and 514. Additional sheets (number unknown) were not produced until the sixth printing in 1928, rather than 1929. The papers of Houghton, Mifflin at the Houghton Library, Harvard University, also provide the sales figures: 1899, 1,536 (trade printing) and 146 ("Large-Paper" printing); 1900, 239; 1901, 82; 1902, 10; 1903, 26; 1904, 14; 1905, 35; 1906, 65; 1907, 31; 1908, 25; 1909, 43; 1910, 18; 1911, 17; 1912, 19; 1913, 25; 1914, 16; 1915, 19; 1916, 30; 1917, 18; 1918, 16; 1919, 22; 1920, 12; 1921, 16; 1922, 28; and 1923, 8.

[5]Chesnutt's relationship with Houghton, Mifflin began in 1897. Francis Jackson Garrison (1848–1916) had been employed by the firm since 1871. He was an ardent admirer of Booker T. Washington; and, while typically curt in his correspondence previous to 1901, he became particularly supportive of Chesnutt when he read the manuscript of *The Marrow of Tradition*. When that novel failed to realize Houghton, Mifflin's sales expectations, Chesnutt's relationship with him ended. George H. Mifflin (1845–1921) became a partner of the firm succeeding Hurd & Houghton in 1872 and

was president from 1908 to 1921. Their correspondence, too, was not maintained after the manuscript of *The Colonel's Dream*, published by Doubleday, Page & Co. in 1905, was declined by Garrison.

[6]Walter Hines Page (1855–1918) was a North Carolinian whose journalistic and editorial work earned him the editorship of *Atlantic Monthly* in 1895. Also a member of the Houghton, Mifflin staff through early August 1899, he became Chesnutt's principal advocate, collaborating with him on the conceptualization of *The Conjure Woman* and advising him on how to reshape the "Rena Walden" manuscript into *The House Behind the Cedars*. When Houghton, Mifflin rejected *The Colonel's Dream*, Page suggested how he might revise the manuscript and then accepted it for publication by his own firm, Doubleday, Page & Co.

[7]Perry succeeded Page as the *Atlantic Monthly* editor; *The Plated City* deals with the offspring of inter-racial marriages. Page's *Autobiography of Nicholas Worth* (1909) indicts, among other regional shortcomings, racism in the South.

[8]Aldrich (1836–1907) was editor of the *Atlantic Monthly* from 1881 to 1890.

[9]"Mr. Charles W. Chesnutt's Stories," *Atlantic Monthly*, 85 (May 1900), 699–701.

[10]*The Conjure Woman* was reviewed by Lucian L. Knight in "The Literary World," *Atlanta Constitution*, 9 April 1899, Magazine Supplement, 9. A photograph of Chesnutt did not appear in this issue.

[11]MacArthur (1866–1909) was co-editor of *The Bookman* (1894–1900). This revelation occurred not in *The Critic* but in "Chronicle and Comment," *Bookman*, 7 (August 1898), 452. Chesnutt was described as a "coloured man of very light complexion."

[12]John Cleland (1709–89), *Fanny Hill, Memoirs of a Woman of Pleasure* (1748–49).

[13]Possibly Wallace Thurman's *The Blacker the Berry*. See "The Negro in Present Day Fiction," wherein several works of the kind are criticized in this manner.

UNDATED ESSAYS AND SPEECHES

The Writing of a Novel

Speech written after 1899

Given the traditional pen, ink and paper which represent the financial outlay required to enter the field of letters; given furthermore some facility of expression in English or one's mother tongue; given experience or imagination; or somewhat of both; given the creative impulse, the would-be author faces his task. And in order that we may not, with him, waste a great deal of time in deciding what form his effort shall take, let us assume that he has concluded to write a novel. If he has in any way qualified himself to attempt such a task, he will realize, ere he puts his pen to paper, that there are certain fundamental elements which enter into the construction of any work of the imagination which can be properly called a novel.

The first of these, I think, which will suggest itself, is the purpose which the writer has in view. A man may write a novel to amuse, to instruct, to inspire, to promote a cause. I refer of course to the objective purpose: primarily most men who write, write much as the spider spins his web, or the bee gathers honey, or the snake secretes venom—for the creative impulse, alas, is not always guided by high and noble instinct. It will be observed, however, that well-nigh every great work of fiction was inspired by some worthy motive, and that those to which no purely altruistic end can be imputed, have served some purpose beneficial to mankind. The Hebrew Scriptures, Greek Orators and Poets. Caesar.[1] The Roman Classics. Voltaire. Shakespeare. Scott. Dickens. Dumas. Balzac. Mrs. Stowe. Novels of evil purpose not wanting, but usually short-lived. "The good men do lives after them";[2] the evil decays and perishes.

Having decided what end he has in view, the author must next select a theme for his story. This will perhaps ordinarily suggest itself in connection with his purpose. One seldom has a strong purpose without having first thought deeply upon some phase of human life, and the purpose-novel, to be effective, must deal with subjects upon which the author is informed, and has convictions. In an age like ours there is no lack of subjects. The Marriage Relation. Religion. (*Robt Elsmere.*) Patriotism. (Floods.) Slavery. Race Questions. *Uncle* & more. Dickens. Balzac. (*Cousin Bette, Cousin Pons. La Lys dans la Vallée.*) Maeterlinck. Dissection. Ibsen. (Social Misfits.) Turgenieff. Tolstoy. Tyranny.[3]

Of novels to amuse or entertain, there are many themes. Love and Adventure. Happy Love. Unhappy Love. Hatred. Revenge. Fidelity. And the crop of French novels of adultery.

Next your novel must have a plot. The plotless novel is in reality no more than a character sketch. Unless written with exceptional charm of expression or upon some theme of immediate and compelling importance a novel must have such a dramatic movement, such an unfolding of events, such a play of characters, and such uncertainty of outcome as to hold the reader's attention through four hundred solid pages of reading matter. Mark Twain I believe has said, that there are only forty-seven plots in all literature, and that the whole body of books is the mere rearrangement of these elements.[4] Lest the aspiring novelist should think that by finding these forty-seven plots he would find it easy to write a novel, it may be suggested that there are as many different combinations, or nearly so, as are possible with a pack of fifty-two playing cards, and most of us know how rarely in the course of a year or even of a lifetime, one gets the cards to take thirteen tricks in a game of whist. Amazing fertility of invention of great romancers. Scott. Victor Hugo. Alexander Dumas. Ingenuity of lesser lights. Wilkie Collins.[5] Conan Doyle. Geo. Meredith. Some novels memorable for their plots. In detective stories, for instance, the plot is the *raison d'être* of the book. The same rule applies in lesser measure to the novel of adventure.

Robinson Crusoe. Take us out of ourselves, beyond the dull trammelled life of convention, out into the freedom of Arcadia.[6] Salt sea breeze. Desert Isle. Republicans like to read about princes. Recent Experience.

Having conceived more or less clearly his plot, the novelist must now create the characters with which to carry on the action of his story, and this is perhaps the most important element in a work of creative imagination. For as man is the crown and flower of creation, so a good character is the highest product of the creative imagination. As the Greek sculptors of the age of Pericles could produce a statue representing a perfection more ideal than could be found in any one human being,[7] as the great masters of the art of painting can by combining the excellences of many models, infuse them with the fire of genius and make them live upon the canvas, the joy and the despair of those less gifted, so the master minds of fiction have created characters more real, more convincing than those of even the men and women whom we see around us. Nowhere is the kinship of humanity to divinity more apparent than in its power to create out of thin air, creatures who live and breathe and love and hate and do and die,[8]—and yet live on forever. There are characters in fiction which are more immortal than the names of those who wrote them. Many a legend has been handed down for centuries, and has become a part of the literature of mankind, of which the name of the author is lost in oblivion. As a great portrait painter may so idealize the living face as to bring out all the good and leave out all the bad, so the great master of fiction may take a historical character and make of him or her a person much more vital than the real man or woman could ever, in our human experience, have been.

Great characters of fiction.
Henry Esmond
Becky Sharp
Rebecca in *Ivanhoe*
Shylock
Falstaff
D'artagnan and Companions
Sherlock Holmes
David Copperfield
Micawber
Uriah Heep
Jean Valjean[9]
&c.

I had forgotten to say, what may perhaps be just as well said here, that a novel should have a background. This is perhaps a subject which will take care of itself. A novel of warlike adventure must perforce be located at some place and in some period where a war was in progress. A novel which dealt with the proscription of the Jewish race in modern times could not be better located than in Russia. If one take for his theme slavery or its tragic consequences, our own

South would be his natural field. Most desert Island stories are located in the tropics, but one of the most charming of recent appearance had for its scene of action an uninhabited island in the mouth of the St. Lawrence River. He who[10] would write a convincing story of realistic life, which depends for its interest upon the human heart and its emotions, upon the love of woman, upon the lust of power will write best if he confine himself to the scenes with which he is familiar. *The Helmet of Navarre. Robert Tournay.*[11] No atmosphere. The Inevitable Russian Princess or Mediatized German Grand Duke.

Picture to yourself a woman young, beautiful, of noble form and faultless contour. Give her if you wish a fine mind and a great soul, and then turn her into a parlor filled with well-dressed people, in a gown which does not fit, and you have the novel without style, in company with the great books which make up the world's literature. As a fine mind and a great soul may command recognition and respect in spite of a gown which does not fit, so doubtless a great book may win a place in literature in spite of crudities of form. And yet in the long run, when books like the deeds of men are sifted through the sieve of time, those live longest which have most claims upon human interest. A character I have said may outlive its creator. So a book may for the beauty of its form long outlive the purpose which gave it birth. Indeed it is so with most great books. And by style I do not mean fine writing, at least not necessarily fine writing—good writing of course, but that is best which best subserves its end. Style may be simple and direct. It may be florid, ornate. It may content itself with direct statement; it may deal with figures of speech and flowers of Rhetoric. All have their place. And were I writing a technical guide to authorship, I should say to the literary aspirant, adapt your speech to your thought and your thought to the situation. I read the other day in either an old novel, written when novel writing was in its evolutionary . . . .

〜

SOURCE: Undated and incomplete typed text at the Fisk University Library. This speech could not have been given prior to 1900 when the novel by Bertha Runkle to which Chesnutt refers, *The Helmet of Navarre*, was published.

[1]Chesnutt refers to Julius Caesar's *Commentarii*, a history of the first seven years of the Gallic Wars and part of the Roman Civil War.

[2]Inversion of " 'The evil that men do lives after them,' " Shakespeare's *Julius Caesar*, 3.3.75.

[3]Mrs. Humphrey Ward (1851–1920), *Robert Elsmere* (1888), a novel which explores faith and doubt; *Uncle Tom's Cabin*; Balzac's *La Cousine Bette* (1846), *Le Cousin Pons* (1847), and *Le Lys dans la Vallée* (1836); Maurice Maeterlinck (1862–1949), playwright and essayist; Henrik Ibsen (1828–1906), playwright; Ivan S. Turgenev (1818–83), novelist.

[4]Twain is not known to have stated this.

[5]Wilkie Collins (1824–89), novelist.

[6]A locale in ancient Greece that has for centuries epitomized pastoral simplicity.

[7]Pericles (c. 490–429 B.C.) was the ruler of Athens during Greece's "Golden Age"— also referred to as the Age of Pericles.

[8]Chesnutt conflates Acts 17:28 and the commonplace "do or die," the first recorded use of which appears in *The Island Princess* (1621) by John Fletcher (1579–1625).

[9]Henry Esmond is the hero of Thackeray's novel of the same name, and Becky Sharp appears in his *Vanity Fair*; Rebecca appears in Sir Walter Scott's *Ivanhoe* (1820); Shylock is a character in Shakespeare's *The Merchant of Venice*; Sir John Falstaff appears in three Shakespeare plays, *The Merry Wives of Windsor*, *Henry IV, Part One*, and *Henry IV, Part Two*, while a character named Sir John Falstaff appears in *Henry VI, Part One*; D'Artagnan and his companions are characters in Dumas' *The Three Musketeers*; Sherlock Holmes is Arthur Conan Doyle's detective-hero in numerous works; David Copperfield is the title character of Dickens's novel (1850), in which Mr. Wilkins Micawber and Uriah Heep also appear; Jean Valjean is the protagonist of Hugo's *Les Misérables*.

[10]"He would" is the source text's reading.

[11]Bertha Runkle (1879–1958), *The Helmet of Navarre*; William Sage (1864–?), *Robert Tournay* (1900).

Why Do We Live?

This is an old question—the unsolved problem of the ages; a large question, which involves the whole human race for all time. We find ourselves here; we accept the situation. That we should live is part of the universal plan, with which few of us have either the temerity or the desire to interfere. The more intimate, personal inquiry, which each individual can answer for himself, would be, "Is life worth living?"

I should answer unhesitatingly, Yes. The pleasures of sense, the physical and social activities of life, are worth the having. The obstacles we encounter in their pursuit, give us the joy of the conflict and oftentimes the glory of the victory. To the cultivated mind the study of nature in its manifold forms, including man, its flower and crown, is a source of never-ending wonder and delight. I think life would be well worth living if it lasted but ten or twenty or fifty or seventy years, and that were all. But when one reflects that through the medium of recorded thought one can live back in mental retrospect, over six thousand years of history, and in imagination can project himself indefinitely into the future; and when to this is added the blessed hope of immortality, he would be ungrateful indeed who did not accept the boon of conscious existence and be thankful to the Creator who has taken him from the cold and senseless earth and made of him living spirit,[1] able to perceive, however vaguely, something of the wonder and the glory of the universe.[2]

↬

SOURCE: Undated typed text at the Fisk University Library. The single page of text is of such "finished" quality that one suspects it to be the beginning of a now-incomplete essay or speech of much greater length. An alternative identification is that of a complete reply to a query posed by a magazine or newspaper editor intending to collect responses from a variety of public figures. But a publication of this kind by Chesnutt is not known.

[1]Genesis 2:7.

[2]The concluding phrase appears in chapter 6 of Charles Darwin's *The Descent of Man* (1871).

Joseph C. Price, Orator and Educator

An Appreciation

Essay written after 2 August 1923

Joseph C. Price made his appearance on the scene of human activity at a very opportune time. The freedmen of the South had just emerged from the night of slavery into what was as yet only the twilight of freedom. They were, as a rule, the rawest kind of common labor, without class consciousness, organization or leadership. Had their former masters chosen to accept the new conditions gracefully, they might have led the ex-slaves where they chose. The whites were accustomed to lead and the Negroes to follow. But it was perhaps too much to expect of poor human nature that the former masters should not resent the enforced equality before the law of their former slaves, and hence there was for a time and still is, for that matter, a feeling on the part of the whites that they must keep the Negroes down politically and socially, and a conviction on the part of many Negroes that they cannot safely trust their Constitutional rights in the hands of the white South.

There was a sort of leadership of the colored people after the Civil War. The Freedmen's Bureau, with its schools and other activities, did valiant service. While the post-bellum military occupation continued, the Negroes' rights were enforced in a measure by military force. With the advent of Reconstruction and the enfranchisement of the ex-slaves came the carpet-baggers, who, with the aid of some educated colored men, undertook to lead the freedmen politically. Their record is spread upon the pages of history. The carpet-baggers were not all scalawags and scoundrels, nor were their activities confined to spoliation of the State. They established the free school system and made other constitutional changes in the way of liberalizing the former systems of State government. Certainly during their sway and while the Negroes exercised the suffrage freely, colored people had a larger measure of liberty than they have ever enjoyed since, were represented in State and County governments, and sent some of their own men to Congress, where, both in House of Representatives and Senate, their records were such that a candid student of history is led to suspect that, had they been white, they would have ranked very well as legislators.

What the colored people needed most of all was wise and unselfish leadership, not only politically but in every walk of life—in education, in religion and in industry. They had developed some of these leaders, but their need was still obvious and most acute when Joseph C. Price grew to manhood.

When Price came on the scene, oratory had not yet become one of the lost arts. Its golden age in America had been the period shortly preceding the Civil War. Webster, Hayne,[1] Lincoln, Stephen A. Douglas, Wendell Phillips, Frederick Douglass—nearly all of that brilliant galaxy of pro-slavery and anti-slavery orators were dead or superannuated—slavery was abolished and their occupation gone. But oratory as a means of advocacy still survived. Politics had not yet developed into a commercial card-index business affair, run mainly for the benefit of big business. There were still burning issues growing out of the old conflict, and new issues were developing. The "Boy Orator of the Platte" had not yet thrown his free silver glove into the ring, but there were many good public speakers.[2]

The modern methods of propaganda have done for oratory what the railroad did to the stage coach. It is no longer possible for one man even in a lifetime, to face and speak to all the people of the nation. They can be reached better through the press, with its continents of paper and oceans of ink, aided by cheap postage, the franking privilege and the rapid distribution of mail matter. The whole country can read tomorrow morning what Mr. Coolidge or Senator Reed, or Mr. Borah said today,[3] transmitted while it was being said, by multiple telegraph wires and hot off the press almost before the speaker had said, "Gentlemen, I thank you."

Radio receiving sets are not distributed as widely as the newspapers, but those who are fortunate enough to possess them of sufficient range, can tune in on almost any broadcasting station and listen to a speaker, but the "kick" is not quite the same as when one caught the flash of the orator's eye, and the eloquence of his gesture, nor is the orator thrilled and inspired to greater heights by the enthusiasm and applause of his auditors. Canned oratory is no better than canned music,—at best it is only a passable substitute.

But orators, though they are born, like great painters and musicians, are not born equipped for effective service. Their talents demand training. Frederick Douglass had taken his degree in the school of slavery, of which he could speak compellingly from the beginning. But the abolition of slavery, as difficult and bloody and expensive as it had proved to be, was simple compared with the preparation of the freed people for the responsibilities of freedom. The one, when the time was ripe, was accomplished by the stroke of a pen. The other was obviously a matter of a long time, perhaps of generations, and its leaders required the learning of the schools to fit them for effective service. In this field, in which Dr. Price distinguished himself as orator and advocate, he had to depend directly upon his personality for any effect he might produce. It was as a public speaker that he won distinction and was able to find the means to carry on constructive work along other lines.

It was not my privilege to know Dr. Price intimately. He was about ten years my senior and I left the South, where I knew him, when I was twenty-five years old.[4] But he was often in Fayetteville, North Carolina, where I lived, and he was often there in conference with Bishop J. W. Hood, I believe at that time senior bishop of the African Methodist Episcopal Zion Church, who lived at Fayetteville. I was brought up in that church, at the old Evans' Chapel, since replaced by a more modern church edifice. When Dr. Price spoke in Fayetteville I heard him, and, like every one else present, was impressed by his eloquence, his earnestness in the cause of religion, his church and his people.[5]

I cannot resist the temptation at this point to pay a tribute to the memory of that sincere Christian, and real spiritual leader of his people, Bishop James W. Hood. A man of unimpeachable character, a wise administrator, with a clear vision of the weaknesses as well as the underlying strength of an as yet undeveloped people, he had just that practical outlook upon life which made him a safe guide. He had no conspicuous gift of oratory, but was a good preacher. He was also a ready writer and contributed articles to the religious press concerning conditions among the colored people. All who knew him loved him, and when, in the fullness of years, he laid down his burdens, those whom he had served and among whom he had lived, mourned him most sincerely. Not the least important thing he did was to encourage the young orator, Joseph C. Price.

Oratory has never been an art that is practiced primarily for its own sake. Aside from the orator's personal reward of satisfaction, it has always been associated with some cause—good or bad, according to the viewpoint. In ancient Greece and Rome Demosthenes and Cicero spoke in the interests of the State. Pitt and Canning in England sponsored great issues in the British Parliament. In our own country Daniel Webster defended the Constitution. Wendell Phillips, Frederick Douglass and the rest of the abolition orators attacked slavery and John C. Calhoun defended it. John B. Gough was a fiery antagonist of strong drink.[6]

Joseph C. Price was born on February 10, 1848,[7] at Elizabeth City, North Carolina. His parents were both slaves. Until after the Civil War there is no record of his having attended school. In 1863 his mother left Elizabeth City for Newbern, North Carolina, where her son went to the Freedmen's Bureau school established shortly after the war, and laid the foundations of what was to be a liberal education. He was a diligent student and his success in school was largely due, like his success in after life, to hard work. He was the outstanding pupil of his school and of his class, but though precocious, he was not a phenomenon.

His teachers in the freedmen's school advised him, when he had finished their course, to enter Shaw University, located at Raleigh, N.C., which he did in

1873. His engaging personality, his love of music, a fondness for athletics and a lively sense of humor made him very popular with his fellow students.

His talent for public speaking made him a leader in the school debates. A logical thinker, with firm convictions on any subject he had thought out, a clear exposition of his views in a magnetic voice made him a formidable opponent in the forum of argument. On one occasion, with some of his fellow students, he attended a public meeting at which Hon. James H. Harris, a colored political leader of the reconstruction period, was the principal speaker.[8] The large audience was thrilled by the eloquence of the speaker. He made during the course of his address some light and rather flippant remark about young men. Some of young Price's companions called upon him to follow the speaker. In a ten-minute speech, following the example of Fox[9] in his reply to Pitt in a famous parliamentary debate, young Price not only pleaded guilty to the charge of being young but gloried in his youth, because it gave him so much more time and vigor for his work. This speech was his introduction to the public and was the beginning of his recognition as an orator of unusual power.

It was while in Raleigh, at one of the University revivals, that Price underwent a religious experience that turned his thoughts from teaching or politics, to the Christian ministry—the third of the chief careers which at that time were open to educated men of color. He taught for a while, and became principal of the Wilson High School for colored pupils.

Recognizing the call to preach as imperative and desiring to qualify himself adequately for what he regarded as a noble and indeed sacred calling, he went to Lincoln University, in Pennsylvania, where he spent six years, completed the classical studies which he had begun at Shaw University, and in addition took a course in theology. To pay his expenses, always a problem with colored students, who had no wealthy parents to support them, he taught school during the summer vacations. Having finished his school studies, he was received into the ministry of the A.M.E. Zion Church.

Dr. Price had not been without temptations to draw him away from the ministry. Honorable John Hyman,[10] a colored congressman from the Eastern Congregational District of North Carolina, offered to secure him an appointment in one of the government departments at Washington with a salary of twelve hundred dollars a year, truly magnificent pay for a poor young man starting out in life at a period when the daily wage of a good mechanic was from one to two dollars.

But very wisely, as it turned out, he resisted the temptation, and from the date of his ordination as an elder started on his brilliant and successful career as a leader of his people.

For this career he was eminently fitted. In addition to his gift of eloquence, his personal qualifications for Negro leadership were of the best. He was tall and very dark, physically an ideal representative of his race. For whatever he accomplished the race could claim full credit. No one could say of him, as has been said of Senators Bruce and Revels, John M. Langston, Frederick Douglass and Booker T. Washington, that his ability was due to his white blood, for, like another brilliant Negro orator of the same period, Robert Brown Elliott,[11] he had no white blood,—to all appearances they were both Negroes of the full blood and gave the lie to those who decried the education of the Negro as a waste of time and of good material for manual labor. He had a soft, smooth skin, perfect teeth, a well rounded face and a robust constitution. He had one characteristic which is invaluable to a man in public life; he seldom forgot a name or a face or failed to recognize and greet cordially his acquaintances. In a private letter written to Hon. John C. Dancy after Dr. Price's death, President Rendall of Lincoln University said of him: "Dr. Price was richly endowed with many of the attributes of greatness, and he possessed them in a splendid combination."[12]

His principal achievement in the cause of education was in connection with Livingstone College, an A.M.E. Zion Church institution at Salisbury, N.C., which was a new and struggling enterprise. Like all colleges, from Harvard University down, it was always in need of money. It began with no endowment and was supported by the meager contributions of the churches and the small tuition fees paid by the students. The work of the teachers was largely a labor of love. They were not well paid—few teachers are, for teaching is and has always been an underpaid profession. They lived, but not very high. They found their chief reward in watching the expansion of the minds and the upbuilding of the characters of the young men who passed through their hands.

While Dr. Price was still a student, he was called upon to use his gift of oratory to assist in raising funds for this school.

Ordained Elder in 1880, on the same day he was appointed a delegate to the General Conference of the A.M.E. Zion Church, held at Montgomery, Alabama. He was ordained by Bishop Hood, at Charlotte, N.C., and accompanied him to the General Conference. Objections were made to his admission as a delegate so soon after his ordination, and before his graduation from the Theological Seminary, but these objections were all met and overcome by Bishop Hood. Price delivered a sermon on "Indestructible Kingdom," which was acclaimed as the best sermon preached at a gathering of experts in pulpit oratory. So moving was its eloquence, that old and venerable bishops rose from their seats, and the faces of strong men were bathed with tears of joy and gratitude to God for having raised up such a champion for their faith and their church. Later on in the conference, when a fraternal message was read from the other great colored Methodist body, the African Methodist Episcopal Church, Price was called upon to respond, and did so in an impromptu speech that confirmed and strengthened the impression made by his sermon, and from that time forward he was the foremost man in his church,—not officially, for he never became a bishop, indeed, never sought but rather avoided the office as one which would hamper and restrict him in the work to which he was to devote his life—but foremost in the public eye, its ambassador to the outside world.

In the following year, 1881, Price was graduated from the Theological Department of Lincoln University at the head of his class. Two years before, he had been graduated from the classical course, and had been the valedictorian of his class.

Far back in those days, before Mr. Bryan or Mr. Volstead[13] were heard of, the temperance movement, as it was then called, was very active and Price had been identified with it from his youth, having joined the Band of Hope in school and taken a temperance pledge, to which he remained consistently faithful, throughout his life.[14] One of the leaders of the nation-wide temperance movement was the well-known philanthropist, William E. Dodge, of New York,[15] a friend and benefactor of Dr. Price, who knew and admired him, was anxious that he should take part in the prohibition fight then being inaugurated in North Carolina, and, immediately after his graduating exercises, paid his expenses to the Prohibition State Convention at Raleigh. Here, in a new environment, to a different audience, he repeated the success he had made at the General Conference. There he had addressed a company of his own people. Here the gathering, the greatest ever assembled in the state, embraced the ablest and most distinguished men of North Carolina. Eloquent speakers, including such men as Governor Jarvis, Senator Merrimon, Judge Dick[16] and others of similar note, appeared upon the rostrum and stirred the hearts of their hearers.

The cause was one which appealed to all good people, and many prominent colored men were present to lend their influence and support. For the first time in history, the Southern white people were seeking the Negro vote. There was no political question involved, and for the time being anti-Negro feeling was at its lowest ebb. All over North Carolina white and colored people met on the platform and in the audience on a plane of civic equality.

During a lull in the proceedings some one called for "Price." As a tall, black young man rose and stepped forward, the vast audience, mostly white, but with a sprinkling of dark faces, was hushed for a moment, wondering what the idea was, but the first few words of his speech, by the silvery quality of his voice, arrested the attention of the whole audience, which listened to him for fifteen minutes with every manifestation of approval and delight. He became the lion of the hour. Speaking engagements were made for him all over the state, and he consistently maintained the standard set by his Raleigh speech. Everywhere he was heard by white and colored and cheered by all for his services in behalf of humanity and the home. Governor Jarvis of North Carolina, in a letter to Honorable John C. Dancy, declared that "Dr. Price was one of the most forceful and eloquent speakers he had ever listened to," and adds, that "in all his speeches he never heard him utter a word that was calculated to engender ill feeling between the two races," a tribute to Dr. Price's good sense and diplomacy as well as to his eloquence, for it requires good sense, diplomacy and some self-restraint for a colored man to discuss the race problem without saying some things which white people would not like, however true they might be. And yet Dr. Price was no truckling time-server. In 1893 when a "Jim Crow" car law was proposed in the North Carolina legislature, Dr. Price headed a committee of protest and it was defeated, though later on such a law was enacted and is still in force. He believed in the future of his race, and like Booker T. Washington, was a consistent optimist. It was his doctrine and teaching that nothing in his race's condition should keep it down. It was on the upgrade, today was better than yesterday, tomorrow would be better than today. It would be a long and hard fight, but the stars in their courses[17] were fighting the battle of right against wrong, of knowledge against ignorance, of justice and manhood against injustice and prejudice, and God was on their side. Such teachings, presented with burning eloquence and convincing earnestness could not but endear him to his own people.

Almost immediately after the close of the temperance campaign in which Dr. Price had thus distinguished himself, he was sent, at the instigation of Bishop Hood, as one of the Zion delegates to the Ecumenical Conference of all the Methodist churches of the world which assembled in London in 1881. One of the subjects up for discussion at this conference was "Methodism a Power in Purifying and Elevating Society." There was no set program and Dr. Price, during the proceedings, secured the floor. For five minutes he spoke, "his melodious voice" says Dr. Penman, an Englishman who was present, "penetrating every part of the large chapel, and captivating every hearer." Many rushed to the front and remained standing until he finished. "He had," said this gentleman, "the finish of Punshon and the force of Spurgeon," two great English preachers.[18] "From first to last we were charmed with his felicitous phrase-coining and his chaste and finished oratory. No pen can adequately describe the effects of this speech—certainly mine cannot,—on the English members of the conference, and still more on the English audience that crowded the gallery." Dr. Marshall, of Mississippi, a white Methodist delegate, responded to the noble sentiments enunciated by Dr. Price and they shook hands while the whole audience applauded. Judge Walter Clark, of the North Carolina Supreme Court, a lay member of the conference, wrote Mr. Dancy that as a speech he never heard one to excel it in point of matter and eloquence.[19]

It was on this trip that Dr. Price began what he regarded as the chief work of his life, upon which his fame will chiefly rest, the campaign for the building of Livingstone College at Salisbury, and at Bishop Hood's suggestion Dr. Price remained for a year in Great Britain and made a lecture and preaching tour during which he collected money for the establishment of this proposed educational institution. His lecture "From Bondage to Freedom," and his masterful sermons, characterized by an inspiring current of love and humanity, brought him a hearing. At the end of his stay, he had collected enough money to pay all of his expenses and had to the credit of the college more than $10,000.00. Shortly after his return home he married Miss Jennie Smallwood, who had spent her early years at the North but who had been trained at Scotia Seminary, Concord, N.C. By her he had five children. The site for the school was secured at Salisbury and the land paid for with the English contributions. The white citizens of Salisbury contributed largely to the erection of the buildings.

One of the disappointments of Dr. Price's life was the failure to bring together the A.M.E. and A.M.E. Zion churches, the two chief colored branches of Methodism, a project to which he devoted a great deal of time and consecrated effort. This union has often been mooted since, but is as yet unaccomplished.

In 1889, before a committee of the North Carolina legislature, Dr. Price urged the establishment of a State College for the higher education of the colored people of the state, but this project, when he had about won the committee over to his support, was defeated through the influence of some leading colored men, who protested against what they regarded as a premature effort in this direction.

In 1885, in Lincoln Hall, at Washington, D.C., he spoke with Isaiah C. Wears of Philadelphia—whom Dr. William Wells Brown declared to be the greatest Negro controversialist and debater[20]—and Frederick Douglass, the great colored orator. After Mr. Douglass and Mr. Wears had spoken, as Dr. Price was introduced, the audience began to leave, but when his resonant voice sounded out with its opening sentences, the crowd stopped and resumed their seats. He spoke for half an hour, with such eloquence that Mr. Douglass and Dr. Wears met him on his way to his seat and congratulated him, while the audience expressed by their tumultuous applause their appreciation and delight.

About this time Dr. Price set out to raise $25,000.00 for additional buildings to accommodate the increasing number of students at Livingstone College. Opening with three teachers and two students, at the end of the second year there were ten teachers and two hundred students. Dr. Price secured $5,000.00 from his friend Mr. William E. Dodge conditioned upon his raising $20,000.00 more.[21] He went to California and secured the interest of Reverend Alexander Walters, afterwards a bishop of the A.M.E. Zion Church, gained the attention of Senator Stanford, who gave him $5,000.00, of Mrs. Mark Hopkins, who gave $1,000.00 and of Mrs. Pleasant, who supplied the nucleus of the college library.[22] The $25,000.00 was collected, the buildings were erected, and Dr. Price had completed the monument to his memory. During all these years he was in great demand as a temperance lecturer and every winter spoke, in the North and in the South, under the auspices of the National Temperance Society. He was spoken of in the same sentence with John B. Gough and other noted temperance advocates. In Boston he spoke to cultured audiences in the People's Church and addressed noonday meetings of business men, at one of which he was introduced by the mayor of the city.[23] He was the first man of color to speak from Henry Ward Beecher's pulpit in Plymouth Church, in Brooklyn, New York.[24] In 1890 he delivered a notable address before the National Educational Association at Minneapolis, Minnesota, on "Education and the Race Problem," in which he stressed the education of head, heart and hand as necessary to the solution of the race problem. In the winter of 1893 he addressed by special invitation the Nineteenth Century Club, of New York, the first colored man to enjoy that honor.[25] Another speaker at the same meeting was President Winston, of the University of North Carolina, and both discussed the vexed "Race Problem."[26] The press of New York characterized the debate as an eloquent and logical disputation. He spoke often in the leading churches, both white and colored, both North and South, and, in that respect forecasting Dr. Washington, sought to harmonize the two races. He pleaded for justice and fair play. In politics he supported measures rather than men, and, for this reason President Cleveland offered him the Liberian mission, which he declined with thanks.[27] He was often urged to be a candidate for Congress in the Second North Carolina District, but never permitted his name to be used in that connection. He was devoted to the education of his race, and did not permit his interests to be drawn aside for any honor or opening that might be offered him, in other fields, yet he was always urging the recognition of men in his race for places of responsibility, when they were properly qualified. His effort was to conciliate the whites and win their friendship by appealing to their senses of justice and fair play, in a courteous and manly fashion, informed by culture, which could not fail of appreciation from those able to appreciate merit and tact. When he delivered an address at Wofford College, Spartanburg, South Carolina, a white institution conducted and patronized by the best blood of that state, the young men, as he was about leaving the next morning, presented him with a fine gold-headed cane inscribed with his name.

His later years were devoted to the study and discussion of the social, religious and material interests of his people. He advocated the self-evident proposition that a race, to count for anything in the world, must accumulate property of every kind, must acquire homes, must respect the laws of God and man, and learn how to cultivate the social graces. These doctrines are inculcated at Livingstone College, where the students are taught, along with the other elements of a liberal education, that the best and most loyal citizen is he who possesses an interest in the soil, and that to own land, to pay taxes and to contribute to the wealth of the state and the nation, is the best preparation for the full enjoyment of political and civil rights.

Dr. Price died at the early age of thirty-nine.[28] Any mistakes that he made have long since been forgotten, but the good he did lives after him[29] and will continue to live in the annals of his church and of his race, and in the work of the institution to which he devoted so much of the zeal and energy of his short but brilliant life.

‿

SOURCE: Undated typed text at the Western Reserve Historical Society Library. The reference to Mr. Coolidge—the appropriate title for the U.S. President—indicates that this essay was not completed before 2 August 1923 when his predecessor, Warren G. Harding, died in office.

[1]Robert Y. Hayne (1791–1839) was a U.S. senator (1823–32) when he became known as one of the principal defenders of the doctrine of states' rights. The South

Carolinian gained widespread fame when, in 1830, he debated Daniel Webster, arguing that the sovereignty of states is not subject to judicial review.

[2]William Jennings Bryan was the chief spokesman for the "Free Silver" movement. In 1896 and twice thereafter he was the Democrat nominee for the U.S. presidency.

[3]Republican J. Calvin Coolidge completed the term of Warren G. Harding and was himself elected to the presidency in 1924; James A. Reed (1861–1944), Democrat U.S. senator from Missouri (1910–28); William E. Borah (1865–1940), Republican U.S. senator from Idaho (1907–40) and chairman of the Senate Committee on Foreign Relations from 1924 to 1933.

[4]Price was born on 10 February 1854 and Chesnutt on 20 June 1858. Below Chesnutt incorrectly cites Price's year of birth as 1848, and thus the description of a ten-year difference in their ages.

[5]James W. Hood (1831–1918). When, at Fayetteville's Evans's Chapel, Hood delivered the 14 November 1880 eulogy for Chesnutt's late mentor at the State Colored Normal School, Principal Robert Harris, Chesnutt transcribed it for *The Star of Zion*, and it was subsequently published in a collection of Hood's sermons, *The Negro in the Christian Pulpit* (1884). Chesnutt's relationship with Hood was very likely professional as well as religious: his activities in Virginia and the Carolinas after 1863 included service as the assistant superintendent of public instruction in North Carolina. Chesnutt's misnaming of him as John, below, has been editorially emended.

[6]William Pitt (1708–78), English statesman and orator; George Canning (1770–1827), appointed English Foreign Secretary in 1822 and Prime Minister in 1827; John B. Gough (1817–86), a recovered alcoholic who, from 1845 until his death, drew immense crowds to his highly emotional temperance lectures.

[7]Price was born in 1854.

[8]James H. Harris (1832–91) left North Carolina for Oberlin, O., before the Civil War; was a recruiting officer in Indiana in 1863; and returned to the South after the war. He immediately became active in Republican politics at the state and national levels, and was a well-known champion of equal rights for African Americans. He declined President Johnson's offer of an appointment as U.S. Minister to Haiti, preferring to represent the freedmen at the state's constitutional convention in 1868–69; in 1872 he was elected to the North Carolina Senate.

[9]Charles J. Fox.

[10]John A. Hyman (1840–91) was the first of four African Americans to represent North Carolina's Second Congressional District in Washington, D.C.; he was elected in 1874 and served until March 1877.

[11]Hiram R. Revels (1822–1901) was an A.M.E. minister elected to the Mississippi State Senate in 1869; he was the first African American to become a U.S. senator when the Mississippi legislature chose him in 1870 to complete an unexpired term running to 3 March 1871. John M. Langston was active in Republican politics at the national level after the Civil War and was rewarded for his service by being appointed the U.S. Minister to Haiti (1877–85). He then became the president of the Virginia Normal and Collegiate Institute, holding that position until 1887. After successfully charging election fraud in a race for a seat in the U.S. House of Representatives, he served an abbreviated term (1890–91). Robert B. Elliott (1842–84) appears to have been born in England and, by the beginning of the Reconstruction, had settled in South Carolina where he was an editor of the *South Carolina Leader*. He was elected to that state's House of Representatives in 1868 and then to the U.S. House of Representatives (1870–74). Editorially emended is Chesnutt's misspelling, "Browne Elliot."

[12]Isaac N. Rendall (1825–1912)—misspelled "Randall" in Chesnutt's typescript—was the president of Pennyslvania's Lincoln University from 1865 to 1905. John C.

Dancy (1857–1920) studied at Howard University while enjoying an appointment to the Treasury Department arranged by Congressman John A. Hyman; but less than a year after his appointment to this desirable position, this idealist resigned in order to devote himself to teaching in his hometown, Tarboro, N.C. He soon became involved in politics, however; was elected Recorder of Deeds in Edgecombe County; and, because of his service to the Republican Party, was appointed the Recorder of Deeds in the District of Columbia. Traveling abroad in 1879, he returned to the United States to lecture on what he had seen, joining Joseph C. Price on a profitable tour. He not only knew Price personally but, from 1885 through the year of Price's death, 1893, he was familiar with the role Price played in the A.M.E. Zion church as educator, orator, and fundraiser; during these years Dancy was editor of its *Star of Zion* and then the *African Methodist Episcopal Zion Quarterly.*

[13]Like the sponsor of the Volstead Act, William Jennings Bryan was vehemently opposed to the sale and consumption of alcohol.

[14]A Band of Hope chapter was organized by Robert Harris at the State Colored Normal School, where Chesnutt succeeded him as principal.

[15]"Merchant Prince" William E. Dodge (1805–83) was a New York member of the U.S. House of Representatives in 1866–67, a long-term spokesman for the Evangelical Alliance, and President of the National Temperance Society from 1865 until his death. A statue of the well-known philanthropist was erected in New York City in 1885.

[16]Thomas J. Jarvis (1836–1915) was Governor of North Carolina in 1879–84. Augustus S. Merrimon (1830–92) was a U.S. senator from North Carolina from 1873 to 1879, an Associate Justice of the state's Supreme Court, and then the Chief Justice from 1889 until his death. Robert P. Dick (1823–98) was an Associate Justice of the North Carolina Supreme Court from 1868 to 1872 and then served as a federal district judge until his retirement in 1898.

[17]Judges 5:20.

[18]William M. Punshon (1824–81) was a Methodist minister renowned for his oratorical ability. Charles H. Spurgeon (1834–92) was a popular Baptist preacher whose Metropolitan Tabernacle in London regularly accommodated an audience of 6,000. Dr. Penman was neither identified nor listed as present in *Proceedings of the Ecumenical Methodist Conference* (1882).

[19]Charles Kimball Marshall (1811–91), popularly referred to as "the silver-tongued orator," was known after 1880 for his advocacy of the African-American cause in the South. Walter Clark (1846–1924) was a judge in the Superior Court of North Carolina (1885–89), Associate Justice of the state's Supreme Court (1889–1902), and its Chief Justice (1903–24).

[20]Isaiah C. Wears (1820–1900), misnamed Isaac by Chesnutt, was active in several literary societies in Philadelphia and was for many years the head of the Banneker Institute there. Although he never held political office, he participated as a speaker in many political campaigns. According to William Wells Brown's *Rising Son* (1874), "Fidelity to the freedom and elevation of his own race kept him always on the alert, watching for the enemy," for example, The Colonization Society.

[21]Although Chesnutt focuses on 1885 in the previous paragraph, his reference to "about this time" indicates the early 1880's since Dodge died in 1883. It is unlikely that he is referring to Dodge's son with the same name (1832–1903).

[22]Alexander Walters (1853 or 1858–1917) informed Bishop James W. Hood in St. Louis that he had never taken tobacco or whiskey, and he was immediately judged the right man for the ministry at the Zion Church in worldly San Francisco, where he served from 1883 to 1886. He was made Bishop in 1892. Leland Stanford (1824–93), was a railroad magnate, Republican governor of California (1861–63), and U.S. senator (1885–93);

despite his "rugged individualism" in business, he was a noteworthy philanthropist of his time. Mary Sherwood Hopkins (?–1891), after the death of her first husband, railroad magnate Mark Hopkins (1813–78), was widely described in the press as "America's Richest Widow." Mary Ellen "Mammy" Pleasant (1812?–1904) appears to have been the "Mrs. Pleasants" to whom Chesnutt refers in the source text. She emigrated at mid-century to California from Boston where she had been involved in abolitionist activities. Operating a boarding house and then serving as the housekeeper of a local banker, Thomas Bell (1819?–92), she proved a successful businesswoman who continued to support projects designed to ameliorate the conditions under which African Americans lived.

[23]The People's Church, whose cornerstone was laid in 1877, was a prominent Methodist congregation.

[24]Beecher, a Congregational minister, was ranked in the 1880's with William M. Punshon and Charles H. Spurgeon as one of the greatest preachers of his age. His 1847–87 sermons at the Plymouth Church regularly drew audiences of 2,500 people.

[25]The Nineteenth Century Club was an intellectual improvement organization with chapters in several American cities. Chesnutt appears to refer to the winter of 1892–93.

[26]George T. Winston (1852–1932), formerly a Professor of Latin and German, served as the president of the University of North Carolina in 1891–96.

[27]Emended here is "Siberian."

[28]Price died on 25 October 1893.

[29]*Julius Caesar*, 3.2.75.

The Term Negro

Essay written before 2 June 1928

Why should any class of American citizens receive a special designation unless there is some good purpose to be subserved thereby? Good citizenship would rather tend toward lessening than emphasizing differences between citizens of a common country.

But if such a designation be employed it should be a correct one; that is to say, sufficiently comprehensive to take in all those to whom it is applied. If it be not a correct designation; if for that reason or any other it give offense to any of those to whom it is applied, then it is not the best designation. Applying this test, in my opinion the word Negro is not correctly descriptive of the people of African descent in the United States. There is certainly no logical reason why a people with an infusion of white blood which ranges from a small fraction to a proportion which renders distinctions of race imperceptible, are not correctly designated by a term which describes a native of tropical Africa and perhaps his descendants of the full blood. The word Afro-American possesses a certain dignity, has a scientific basis, and is perhaps sufficiently comprehensive to take in all of the class referred to. But it is cumbrous.

The term "colored" as applied to people partly or entirely of Negro descent is used the world over, and in the United States its meaning is not surrounded by doubt or uncertainty. No one refers to Chinamen or Japanese or Indians as "colored." It has been used by people of refinement who were careful of the feelings of others, from the beginning of our national history.

One who is at all familiar with the newspapers and periodicals conducted by colored men is aware that a lively controversy has been waged for some years on the question of the title by which the colored people should be known, and opinions vary according to their source. Very able men of full Negro blood or who occupy representative positions in the great colored churches, whose membership is constituted mainly of very dark people, insist strenuously upon the word Negro. Men of mixed blood like editor T. Thomas Fortune, whose only sign of Negro ancestry is a little deeper tint than that of the ordinary white man, reject the term Negro as not properly descriptive of themselves and a very considerable part of the colored race. Women of refinement of all shades of color find the word "Negress," which has recently been employed extensively in the newspapers, exceedingly offensive.

Distinctions of color are unduly emphasized in the United States. As a matter of sociological interest, it is perhaps well enough to keep track, in a certain large sense, of the progress and development of this class of our citizens. But as between man and man the color of a person should be a purely personal and private matter. It has been suggested by Mr. Booker T. Washington, whose word carries great weight, that to retain the word Negro as descriptive of the colored people would "keep them from forgetting their origin and their traditions." They are not likely to forget, or to be permitted to forget either, for a long time to come, but a very casual reading of the newspapers will suggest that their happiness and their welfare might be considerably promoted if other people did not have the fact so constantly in mind, and if the newspapers would lay less emphasis upon questions of race.

↜

SOURCE: Undated and untitled typed text at the Fisk University Library. Chesnutt could have written this at any time prior to the death of T. Thomas Fortune on 2 June 1928 since he refers to him as though he is still alive. The reference to Booker T. Washington, who died in 1915, is ambivalent in this respect.

Index

Index

In this index an "f" after a number indicates a separate reference on the next page, and an "ff" indicates separate references on the next two pages. A continuous discussion over two or more pages is indicated by a span of page numbers, e.g., "57–59." *Passim* is used for a cluster of references in close but not consecutive sequence.

Library of Congress Cataloging-in-Publication Data

Chesnutt, Charles Waddell, 1858–1932
    [Selections]
    Charles W. Chesnutt : essays and speeches / edited by Joseph R.
McElrath, Jr., Robert C. Leitz III, Jesse S. Crisler.
        p.   cm.
    Includes index.
    ISBN 0-8047-3549-2 (alk. paper)
        1. Afro-Americans—Civil rights.   2. Afro-Americans—Social
conditions.   3. United States—Race relations.   4. American
literature—Afro-American authors—History and criticism.
I. McElrath, Joseph R.   II. Leitz, Robert C.   III. Crisler, Jesse S.
IV. Title

E185.61.C548   1999
814'.4—d21
                                                      98-30654
                                                          CIP

Printed on acid-free, recycled paper

Last figure below indicates year of this printing:
08   07   06   05   04   03   02   01   00   99